BOOKS BY LIVA BAKER

Miranda: Crime, Law and Politics   1983
*I'm Radcliffe! Fly Me! The Seven Sisters and
the Failure of Women's Education*   1976
Felix Frankfurter: A Biography   1969
World Faiths (JUVENILE)   1965

MIRANDA:
CRIME, LAW AND POLITICS

MIRANDA:
CRIME, LAW AND POLITICS

LIVA BAKER

New York   ATHENEUM   1985

LIBRARY OF CONGRESS CATALOGING IN PUBLICATION DATA

Baker, Liva.
Miranda: crime, law, and politics.

Bibliography: p.
Includes index.
1. Right to counsel—United States.   2. Confession
(Law)—United States.   3. Criminal procedure—United
States.   4. Police questioning—United States.
I. Title.
KF9625.B35   1983   345.73′056   81-69127
ISBN 0-689-11240-8   347.30556

Published simultaneously in Canada by Collier Macmillan Canada, Inc.
Composed by American-Stratford Graphic Services, Inc., Brattleboro, Vermont
Manufactured by Fairfield Graphics, Fairfield, Pennsylvania
Designed by Mary Cregan
FIRST ATHENEUM PAPERBACK EDITION

For David

ACKNOWLEDGMENTS

A great many people helped me with this book. Most I have acknowledged in the bibliography and source notes. To others I want to add a special thanks:

The staffs of the libraries from which I collected material, especially those at the Library of Congress—the law librarians and the men and women who administer the study facilities.

All those who trudged through the manuscript at earlier stages: David Baker, Ronald K. L. Collins, Molly Curry, John P. Frank, Sheila Gellman, Barbara Sachs, Victoria Schuck, Jane Ann Spellman.

My daughter, Sara Baker, keeper of the books and tape recorder during a trip to Phoenix to discover Miranda.

Thomas A. Stewart, editor in chief and vice-president of Atheneum, truly a writer's editor.

Ronald K. L. Collins, Stanton P. and Michelle Sender, Barry Silverman: They know what and they know why.

Leonard Baker. "Wherever I go . . . ."

CONTENTS

ERNEST MIRANDA'S BOOK

CHAPTER 1

Phoenix, Arizona. 11:15 P.M., March 2, 1963.

The final scenes of *The Longest Day* had faded from the screen, and the Saturday night theater crowd had vanished into the warm night. Eighteen-year-old Lois Ann Jameson,* who tended the refreshment stand at the Paramount Theater in downtown Phoenix, finished work and sat down in the lobby for a few minutes with a fellow employee, a young man who was taking the same bus as she was. At 11:30 they left the theater and walked two blocks to the bus stop at Seventh and Monroe streets, where they boarded a northbound bus at 11:45.

Lois Ann got off the bus at Seventh and Marlette, in northeast Phoenix, at 12:10 A.M. and turned east on Marlette, walking toward her home on nearby Citrus Way. A car pulled out of a driveway in front of her, so suddenly she had to jump back to avoid being struck, and also turned east. It stopped in front of a group of apartment houses down the block. A man got out and walked toward her. She often passed people on her late-night walk home, and she paid him little notice.

When he came abreast of her, he grabbed her with one hand and put the other over her mouth. "Don't scream," he warned her, "and I won't hurt you."

"Let me go, please let me go!" she cried, but the sounds were muffled behind his hand.

He dragged her to the parked car, tied her hands behind her, laid her

---

* Not her real name.

3

down in the back seat, her face toward the rear of the car, and tied her ankles together. He told her to lie still, reinforcing the command by holding a cold, sharp object—she never was sure what it was—at her neck.

He returned to the driver's seat, started the car, and drove off, continuing east on Marlette, turning south on Tenth, then east again on Rose Lane, his unwilling passenger all the while begging him to let her go, he repeating the warning to keep quiet and he wouldn't hurt her. They were now on streets unrecognizable to Lois Ann, and after driving for about twenty minutes, he stopped the car somewhere in the desert.

The desert surrounding Phoenix is a lunar landscape of surpassing beauty. From where she lay on the back seat, Lois Ann could see the silent red ash mountains, their rough edges outlined against the midnight sky, competing for the eye's attention with the prayerful arms of the giant saguaros.

Her abductor got into the back seat of the car, unbound Lois Ann's ankles, and ordered her to remove her clothing. She later offered different versions of what happened next:

> 1. She removed her jacket and panties, her captor removed her skirt, slip, and bra. When asked by police how she did it with her hands tied, she explained:
> 2. Her captor removed all her clothing, tearing the shoulder straps of her slip as she struggled.

Her captor then removed his jeans and undershorts but left his T-shirt on.

There were no preliminaries. There was no conversation except for one brief exchange.

"You can't tell me you have never done this before," the man said.

"No, I haven't," the girl replied.

The police report, cold and ungarnished, omitting Lois Ann's tears, described the next scene:

> The victim then informed the officers that the suspect forced himself upon her and made penetration and reached a climax. However, again in questioning the victim more extensively, she told officers conflicting stories regarding the number of times the suspect had made penetration and reached a climax. Finally she said that the suspect had attempted to make penetration and at first was unsuccessful. He then sat back on the seat and in a few minutes tried again and was successful.

Her captor then put his undershorts and jeans back on, climbed into the driver's seat again, and told Lois Ann to dress. While she was dressing, he asked her for money, and she gave him the four $1 bills in her purse. When she finished dressing, he ordered her to lie down. He covered her head with a jacket and drove to Twelfth Street and Rose Lane, about four blocks from her home, where he let her out.

4

Chapter 1

En route he had said, "Whether you tell your mother what has happened or not is none of my business, but pray for me."

Badly shaken and still frightened, Lois Ann started walking toward Citrus Way, where she lived with her mother, sister, and brother-in-law. She soon broke into a run. She did not think to note the license plate number of her abductor's car before it disappeared into the night.

"She came home," her sister said, "pounded on the door, her hair was all over like she had been in a fight, and her dress was brand new, a new suit, and it was a mess, and she was crying and carrying on, and I asked her what was the matter, and she would not tell me."

It was fifteen minutes before Lois Ann got herself under control. Finally, she told her sister that a strange man had picked her up when she got off the bus after work and had taken her out into the desert.

"Lois Ann," her sister said, "he didn't touch you, did he?"

"Yes," Lois Ann answered.

"All right," her sister said. She immediately telephoned the police.

At 2:08 A.M., March 3, an officer of the Phoenix Metropolitan Police Department was dispatched to Citrus Way to investigate a possible kidnapping. Lois Ann's sister answered the door. The young woman, she told the officer, had been raped.

The policeman's first interview with Lois Ann was brief. If the events of the recent hours had been deeply disturbing to her, they were becoming more and more commonplace to local police. Rising in solitary sun-washed splendor out of the desert, Phoenix had built its fame, fortune, and reputation as a winter watering place for lesser jet-setters and a safe, warm harbor for spending the golden years. An easterner, temporarily blinded by the glare, required some time to adjust to the light, to recognize the little pastel-colored adobe houses in the central city as kin to taller, darker tenements in Harlem and North Philadelphia and Southeast Washington, to realize that poverty and discrimination and crime resided here no less than elsewhere. Lois Ann Jameson was only one of 152 rape victims in Phoenix that year—29 more than the previous year, 43 more than in 1958. By the next year there would be 160; by 1970 the 1963 figure would nearly double, to 300. Street crimes—muggings, rapes, robberies—were increasingly frequent, and a victimized public was growing fearful. These developments were, later, to add a political dimension to Lois Ann's case. At the moment, however, her rape was an all-too-routine police problem.

She outlined the events of the night, and the policeman took her to Good Samaritan Hospital to be examined. The Phoenix Detective Bureau was notified, and two more officers met Lois Ann at the hospital.

Lois Ann related the recent events in fuller detail at the hospital and gave police a description of her abductor: "Mexican male, 27–28 years,

5

5"11", 175 pounds, slender build, medium complexion with black short cut curly hair, wearing Levi's, a white T-shirt, also dark rim glasses." He seemed to have the beginnings of a mustache and a heavy growth of whiskers. On further questioning, Lois Ann said the man had no accent, and she conceded that he could have been Italian or "of similar foreign extraction" as well as Mexican. Later she said she had not noticed any scars, tattoos, or other identifying marks. However, she declared with assurance, she would recognize him if she ever saw him again.

She was less certain about the car. She thought it was an old model, possibly a Chevrolet or a Ford, "light green with good paint and clean on the outside." Inside, its brown upholstery had grown shabby and smelled of paint or turpentine; a homemade device—a loop of rope attached to the back of the front seat—assisted rear-seat passengers in pulling themselves up.

On Sunday morning, Lois Ann went to police headquarters and viewed a five-man line-up but failed to identify her captor of the night before. Police interviewed her again, and she elaborated on her previous story. Discrepancies began to emerge.

Why, an officer asked, had she no bruises or abrasions on her body if, as she claimed, she had fought her attacker?

Lois Ann couldn't answer.

Was she a virgin prior to the events of Saturday night?

Yes.

Doctors at Good Samaritan Hospital had taken a vaginal swab and found mobile sperm. However, they had said, she was not a virgin.

Would she risk taking a polygraph examination? If she was not telling the truth, the officer told her, she could be charged with filing a false report with the police.

She would risk it.

As a police officer drove her home, she pointed to a '55 Chevrolet. Its design—particularly the body and taillights—was similar to the vehicle in which she had been kidnapped. But she couldn't be positive.

On Monday, March 4, Officer Carroll Cooley, a five-year veteran of the Phoenix Detective Bureau, Crime Against Persons Detail, went to Citrus Way to interview Lois Ann again. Lois Ann, however, had gone to work, and Cooley took advantage of the girl's absence to interview her sister, who appeared knowledgeable about the events of Saturday night.

"Lois Ann is a very shy and naïve girl," she told Cooley. If the girl had no marks or bruises or rope burns on her, it was because she had been taught at home not to resist an attacker, lest she be beaten or otherwise harmed. Lois Ann, her sister declared, was indeed a virgin, whatever the doctors at Good Samaritan Hospital said. Perhaps, she suggested, the doctors were mistaken, Lois Ann being a big girl.

Officer Cooley went from Citrus Way to the Paramount Theater. Lois

6

Chapter 1

Ann said she was too busy to talk with him but agreed to meet him the following day.

On Tuesday Cooley and another detective went to Citrus Way and brought Lois Ann to the detective bureau, where they talked to her at some length. They explained how she could possibly have been mistaken about what had happened, how she could have become involved with someone, then for reasons known only to her, made a police report. It was not an uncommon occurrence.

"Yes," she said in a low voice, nodding her agreement.

Would she tell the officers the true story?

Of course. And she reiterated her original statement. She did, however, add that she had exaggerated her struggle against her attacker in her original statement, and that was why she had no bruises or rope burns on her arms.

But there were some geographical inconsistencies in her original statement.

On the way home—that is, westbound on Rose Lane—had the automobile stopped at the intersection of Rose Lane and Sixteenth Street?

No.

But, the officer said, there was a stop sign at Rose Lane and Sixteenth Street.

Her abductor had run the stop sign.

Well, the officer continued, had the vehicle continued straight ahead on Rose Lane from Sixteenth Street, or had it turned on Sixteenth Street?

Straight ahead, to Twelfth Street, where she got out of the car.

Was she sure?

Yes.

Positive?

Yes.

The officer pointed out her mistake. Rose Lane westbound, he said, ended at Sixteenth Street and picked up again at Fifteenth Street. There was only a vacant field between Fifteenth and Sixteenth streets on Rose Lane, with a ditch running next to Sixteenth Street.

Lois Ann could not explain.

Next, the officer showed her the file of known local sex offenders—the Mexican and white male file—but she was unable to find her abductor among them.

Could she at least offer a better description of the man and his automobile?

She could add very little to what she had already told police.

On Thursday, March 7, Officer Cooley picked up Lois Ann at her home and drove her to police headquarters for a polygraph examination. The results were inconclusive; the police sergeant who administered the test said there was some question of whether or not Lois Ann had taken medication prior to the examination; there was also some indication that she had lied in answering some of the questions.

After driving Lois Ann home, during which time she pointed out the exact location on Marlette where she had been abducted, Officer Cooley went to the Paramount Theater to talk with the girl's co-worker who had taken the bus with her on Saturday night. The young man corroborated her description of the bus trip, but he had nothing substantial to add.

It was almost a week since the incident, and police had nothing to go on except Lois Ann's vague and inconsistent statements, plus a hospital laboratory report which indicated the presence of "mobile sperm"; doctors, however, had said she was not a virgin, and the lie detector test had been inconclusive.

Although the shame and defilement endured, often for long periods, by victims of rape make it the most feared and most heinous of crimes, the penalties for its commission more severe than those for other categories of assault, it is difficult to get a conviction for the offense. Not all accusations of rape are true, and police are often skeptical when they are approached with a report of rape. Prostitutes may cry "Rape!" when they haven't been paid. A rape charge has traditionally been a convenient and effective method of revenge. The mentally unbalanced as well as young children have been known to fabricate stories of rape. Even in cases of true rape, the gathering of evidence is difficult; the circumstances are highly emotional, and there are rarely witnesses. Juries, which often tend to make a woman's character the issue, are difficult to convince.

Police were almost ready to forget the incident, count it just one more false rape report. Then the case broke.

Lois Ann had been badly frightened by her experience, and her brother-in-law had been meeting her at the bus stop at Seventh and Marlette after work. On Saturday, March 9, a week after the incident, he noticed, as he walked to the bus stop about 11:45 P.M., an old-model Packard moving slowly along Marlette. A short time later he saw the same automobile on Seventh Street, then again on Marlette. He noted the license number: DFL-312.

He met Lois Ann when she got off the bus. As they walked together toward Citrus Way, they both saw the car, parked now at Ninth Place and Rose Lane. They walked toward it to get a better look, but the car sped away. Lois Ann said it resembled the automobile in which she had been driven into the desert the previous week.

Her brother-in-law contacted police, and on Monday, March 11, Officers Cooley and Wilfred Young went to Lois Ann's home for more information. Her brother-in-law described the car he had seen late Saturday night, and the two detectives took him to a nearby used car lot where they found a 1953 Packard. The taillights, he said, were exactly like those on the automobile he had seen cruising near the bus stop on Saturday night.

Cooley and Young returned with him to Citrus Way, where they talked with another brother-in-law. The latter was anxious to explain Lois Ann's behavior.

Her statements did appear inconsistent, he admitted, but, he said, the detectives should understand something about Lois Ann. She was a little slow, he explained; she had an IQ of a twelve- or thirteen-year-old, and she had left school after failing several years. She was also shy, so shy that in the eleven years he had known her, he would bet she hadn't spoken thirty words to him. The officers should consider these factors when they evaluated what she told them.

Cooley and Young next checked out all the automobile registrations with DLF in the number—999 registrations. Eventually they found not DFL-312 (which was registered to a late-model Oldsmobile) but DFL-317, which was registered to a four-door 1953 Packard. It belonged to Twila N. Hoffman of 210 North Labaron Street, Mesa, a Phoenix suburb.

On Tuesday morning Detectives Cooley and Young went to 210 North Labaron Street in Mesa, but the house was empty. Talking with neighbors, they learned that Twila Hoffman and the young man with whom she was living had moved out two days earlier. His name was Miranda. Ernest Miranda. Yes, he was Mexican. In his early twenties. He worked for United Produce in Phoenix. He and Twila had used a United Produce truck to move their belongings. He had a mustache.

Officials at United Produce confirmed that an Ernest Miranda was employed there. He was a night dockworker. He had not, however, worked the night of March 2–3. Officials could not give police his new address.

On the morning of Wednesday, March 13, the officers discovered through the post office that Ernest Miranda was now living at 2525 West Mariposa in Phoenix. Mesa police records revealed several previous criminal convictions. One was for assault with intent to commit rape.

When Detectives Cooley and Young arrived at 2525 West Mariposa, a 1953 Packard stood in the driveway. One of the detectives peered inside. A rope had been strung along the back of the front seat, just as Lois Ann had described it.

At twenty-three, Ernest Miranda, or Ernesto Arturo Miranda, as he was sometimes known, already had a police record and a history of sexual problems. He was born in Mesa in 1940, the fifth son of Manuel A. Miranda, a house painter who had come to Arizona from Sonora, Mexico, at the age of three. His mother had died in 1946, at the age of thirty-four. His father had remarried the following year, and for all practical purposes, the child Ernie's family life had ended. He and his father drifted apart, he did not get on well with his stepmother, and he never developed close relationships with his older brothers.

For the priests and nuns at the Queen of Peace Grammar School in

Mesa, he was not an ideal elementary school student either. He was absent more than he was present, and on the days he was present, his disciplinary problems overshadowed his academic achievements. He managed to finish the eighth grade in 1954, during which he was arrested for car theft—his first felony—and put on probation. Nearly a year later, in May 1955, he was arrested for burglary and sent to Arizona State Industrial School for Boys at Fort Grant. Disciplinary problems there were solved with the razor strop, and he returned to Mesa in December 1955 something less than either reformed or rehabilitated.

The following month—in late January 1956—fifteen-year-old Ernie was arrested for attempted rape and assault. His version of the incident: He was walking past a house where he glimpsed a naked woman lying in bed. He considered the scene at least provocation, if not invitation. He found the front door unlocked, entered, and slid into bed beside the woman, where he remained until her husband came home and called the police. Ernie was sent back to Fort Grant for a year.

Upon release from Fort Grant the second time, in January 1957, Miranda went to Los Angeles, but his freedom was short-lived. In May Los Angeles police picked him up for curfew violations, for demonstrating a lack of supervision, and for peeping Tom activities; he spent three days in the Los Angeles County Detention Home.

Following his release from custody—for the third time in less than three years, all before he was eighteen years old—he found a job as a carry-out boy at a Los Angeles supermarket. By September he had again been arrested, this time on suspicion of armed robbery. He was not convicted. Soon after, he was again arrested on suspicion of armed robbery and spent forty-five days in the custody of the California Youth Authority. He was then deported to Arizona.

While under the juvenile authority in Los Angeles, he had been referred to a psychiatrist, but no treatment had been instituted.

Six arrests and four imprisonments of one sort or another between the ages of fourteen and eighteen did not make much of a foundation on which to establish a responsible and rewarding adult life. Ernie made a new start. In April 1958, he joined the United States Army.

The setting had changed; the man had not. His service record closely resembled his civilian record. Six of the fifteen months in the army he spent at hard labor in the post stockade at Fort Campbell, Kentucky—he had gone AWOL and been caught again in a peeping Tom act. In July 1959, he received an undesirable discharge.

While in service, he had been referred to a psychiatrist, but he made only one visit.

For the next month or so he traveled: around Kentucky, a visit to his parents in Arizona; Nashville, Tennessee; and finally, in August, Pecos, Texas, where he spent two weeks in the county jail for vagrancy.

On December 6, 1959, a deputy sheriff in Nashville caught him driving

Chapter 1

a car which had been reported missing in Birmingham, Alabama (years later he admitted he had been supporting himself at the time by selling stolen cars). The court appointed a lawyer to defend him, but he had no real defense. The lawyer, believing it was his responsibility to get Miranda as light a sentence as possible, entered a plea of guilty. Miranda was sentenced to a year and a day in the federal penitentiary at Chillicothe, Ohio.

His lawyer had tried to counsel him, to advise the young man that as a youthful offender he could be paroled anytime and that upon his release from Chillicothe his parole officer would help him find a decent job. Some of these efforts, the attorney pointed out, had in fact been remarkably successful in similar cases. But Miranda's response, based, his lawyer thought, on a natural distaste for court-appointed lawyers from the local establishment, was one of cold and silent contempt.

It was an increasingly common pattern among American youth: trouble-maker to truant to trafficker in serious crimes. While some students read *Beowulf* and conjugated French verbs, others learned how to jimmy locks noiselessly and how to walk flat-footed and close to walls to keep wooden floors and stairs from creaking. Each mapped his own entry to the Pepsi generation. Crime was only a mirror image of the rags-to-riches story.

After two months at Chillicothe, Miranda applied for a transfer to the federal correction institution at Lompoc, California, saying he wanted to be nearer his family in Arizona. Sent there in May, he remained until January 4, 1961, when he was released. (The day before his release, the electric prison gate had slammed shut as he was waving good-bye to visitors and had sliced off the top third of his right index finger. Lois Ann Jameson had not noticed any identifying features about her kidnapper.)

For a little more than two years after his release from prison, Miranda's life assumed some semblance of normality. When he left Lompoc, he remained in California, where he met Twila Hoffman. He was twenty-one, she was twenty-nine, separated from her husband but unable to afford a divorce. In August he moved in with her, her eleven-year-old son, and her ten-year-old daughter. The following year he and Mrs. Hoffman had a daughter of their own. For the first time in his life, perhaps, Ernest Miranda enjoyed close family relationships.

Miranda and Mrs. Hoffman returned to Mesa, where she found a job in a local nursery school. Miranda's employment record—menial jobs in motels and restaurants—was no better than that of his previous record at first: A couple of weeks were about as long as he held a single job. Then, in August 1962, he went to work for United Produce in Phoenix. His employer liked him. "He was one of the best workers I've ever had," said the foreman of the warehouse where Miranda worked. "I wish I had a hundred more like him."

Good fortune, though, had little capacity for endurance in Ernest Miranda's life, and now policemen were standing at the front door of his new home.

He had returned earlier that morning, Wednesday, March 13, 1963, from United Produce, where he had worked from 8:00 P.M. until 8:00 A.M., and gone to bed. He had been asleep for only about an hour when Officers Cooley and Young knocked. Mrs. Hoffman answered the door. She called Miranda.

The officers asked him to come to the police station with them to discuss a case they were investigating. "We told him we didn't want to talk in front of his common-law wife . . ." Officer Cooley explained.

"I didn't know whether I had a choice," Miranda said later. "I got in the car and asked them what it was about. They said they couldn't tell me anything." The two policemen drove him downtown to headquarters.

There is a sameness about police headquarters, whether they are in Los Angeles, California; El Paso, Texas; or suburban Rockville, Maryland. Andrew Schiller, describing Chicago police headquarters in *Harper's Magazine*, once put it this way: "There are three kinds of people here . . . people with uniforms, people with brief cases, and people with trouble." Ernest Miranda was one of the people with trouble.

At the detective bureau the officers put together a line-up—three Mexicans from the city jail, all about the same height and build, to stand with Miranda. He was, however, the only one with tattoos wearing a short-sleeved T-shirt and eyeglasses. The officers then called in Lois Ann, who viewed the four men through a two-way mirror. She said she could not identify her abductor in the group, although she thought number one—Miranda—had similar build and features. If she could hear him speak, perhaps . . .

Detectives Cooley and Young took Miranda into interrogation room 2.

"How did I do?" Miranda asked.

"You flunked," one of the officers answered, inaccurately. The detective began to question him about the rape of Lois Ann Jameson.

In March 1963 the Constitution of the United States and the constitutions of most states, including Arizona's, were strangers to the interrogation rooms of America. The protections they guaranteed a defendant in the courtroom—the right to remain silent, the right to counsel, the right to confront witnesses, the right to cross-examine—in general* did not apply outside the door of the courthouse, the structure which the legal scholar Yale Kamisar has styled the "mansion" of American criminal procedure, as opposed to the police station, or "gatehouse of American criminal procedure," where "ideals are checked at the door, 'realities' faced, and the prestige of law enforcement vindicated." At Arizona's constitutional convention in 1910 a proposal to abolish the third degree had been defeated, a Maricopa County delegate asking, "Do you intend . . . to array yourselves on the side of criminals; do you

---

* One exception was the FBI. Its agents had begun as early as the 1940s to inform suspects of their right to remain silent as well as to consult legal counsel.

intend to put the State of Arizona on the line protecting criminals?" In 1934—and the principle still applied in 1963—the Arizona Supreme Court had written that although for police to warn a criminal suspect like Ernest Miranda that anything he said could be used against him later was "the better and safer course," such a warning was not legally required.

The interrogation room was the undisputed—and isolated—territory of the police, with no attorneys present, no witnesses, no tape recorders. When Detectives Cooley and Young ushered Ernest Miranda into interrogation room 2, they left constitutional protections outside. Miranda stood alone.

The detectives testified at Miranda's trial later in the year that neither threats nor promises had been made in exchange for his confession to the crime of rape, but simply, and without coercion of any kind, the officers had questioned the suspect, who, Cooley said later, "was not unknowledgeable about his rights. He was an ex-convict . . . and had been through the routine before."

Shortly, Cooley said, Miranda admitted not only "that he was the person that had raped this girl" but that he had attempted to rape another woman and to rob still another.

Miranda described the scene in interrogation room 2 differently:

> Once they get you in a little room and they start badgering you one way or the other, "you better tell us . . . or we're going to throw the book at you" . . . that is what was told to me. They would throw the book at me. They would try to give me all the time they could. They thought there was even the possibility that there was something wrong with me. They would try to help me, get me medical care if I needed it. . . . And I haven't had any sleep since the day before. I'm tired. I just got off work, and they have me and they are interrogating me. They mention first one crime, then another one, they are certain I am the person . . . knowing what a penitentiary is like, a person has to be frightened, scared. And not knowing if he'll be able to get back up and go home.

Miranda claimed that in the privacy of interrogation room 2 the officers did indeed promise him that if he confessed to robbery as well as rape, they would drop the robbery charge.

Whichever version is true, Ernest Miranda emerged from the interrogation room a confessed rapist. Unsure in her visual identification, Lois Ann had asked to hear his voice and had been summoned to the interrogation room. Miranda looked up when she entered.

"Is that the girl?" one of the officers asked.

"That's the girl," Miranda answered, believing, his defense lawyers said later, that she had already identified him in the line-up.

Detectives Cooley and Young reported that Miranda then told them essentially the same story Lois Ann Jameson had told them ten days earlier.

Would he put the story in writing? Cooley asked. Miranda said he would.

Following a signed typed statement that Ernest Miranda was confessing voluntarily, that he understood his rights—although what rights were not specified—that what he said could be used against him, that he was twenty-three years old and had completed the eighth grade in school, he wrote in a spidery cursive hand:

> ... Seen a girl walking up street stopped a little ahead of her got out of car walked towards her grabbed her by the arm and asked to get in the car. Got in car without force tied hands & ankles. Drove away for a few miles. Stopped asked to take clothes off. Did not, asked me to take her back home. I started to take clothes off her without any force, and with cooperation. Asked her to lay down and she did, could not get penis into vagina got about ½ (half) inch in. Told her to get clothes back on. Drove her home. I couldn't say I was sorry for what I had done. But asked her to say a prayer for me.

It was 1:30 P.M. The entire interrogation had taken less than two hours. It had been routine: no blatant brutality, no explicit duress. Apparently civilized as interrogations go.

Unknown to the participants, however, this brief moment in time was to become significant in constitutional history. Ernest Miranda the man was to be largely forgotten as his name became a code word and his case, celebrated, criticized, and exploited, roiled the surface of law and national politics, bringing out the best in some men and the worst in others. It symbolized all that was right with the administration of criminal justice and all that was wrong with it. It also dramatized the struggle of a society, dedicated from its birth to equal justice for all, to obey its own mandate, to uphold its ideals, and at the same time to preserve itself in time of crisis. Regarding this last, Ernest Miranda's story has neither beginning nor end.

In the literature of confessions, two factors emerge as dominant in determining a confession's reliability. It must, of course, be voluntary. Coercion, physical or psychological, is not conducive to truth telling. Even the bishop of Beauvais had insisted that the confession of Joan of Arc be not forced from her, and the framers of the American Constitution, not' many generations removed from the tortures of the English judges sitting in Star Chamber, had been careful to include in that document the provision that "No person ... shall be *compelled* in any criminal case to be a witness against himself." (Italics added.)

But what constituted compulsion was not easy to define with precision. By the early 1960s the more blatant—and savage—techniques—the rubber hose, hunger, exhaustion—had nearly disappeared from the station houses of America, although incidents still occurred. By March 1963 various people involved in the administration of criminal justice had begun to wonder about interrogations exactly like the one during which Ernest Miranda confessed to the rape of Lois Ann Jameson. Did the dominating presence of uniformed officers, all of whom wore badges of authority and many of whom wore guns, constitute compulsion of a sort? Was the questioning of a suspect by a policeman an inherently coercive situation which held the potential for producing an unreliable result? Not only might an innocent man be convicted, but equally important, might a guilty man go free to rob, to murder again?

The second consideration in evaluating confessions had to do with an imbalance in the legal situation: the fearful image of the state's marshaling its superior resources against an individual, particularly a poor or uneducated or otherwise disadvantaged individual. Did the poor lack the safeguards of the wealthy, who knew their rights, knew they did not have to confess, and often had easy access to legal counsel?

These were the considerations uppermost in recent discussions among lawyers and others involved in the administration of criminal justice. One of the methods discussed for reducing the inequalities between the powerful state and the powerless individual was providing the individual with a lawyer, putting someone familiar with the rights of defendants in a position to assert them between the two unequal participants in the interrogation.

In 1959 a special committee appointed jointly by the Association of the Bar of the City of New York and the National Legal Aid and Defender Association had published a survey disclosing that although no state yet specifically provided for defendants to be represented by counsel at the interrogation stage of criminal proceedings, the general direction of state legislation was to provide counsel at ever-earlier stages; the discrepancies between the quality of justice meted out inside the station house and the courtroom were beginning to diminish. Most states, including Arizona, provided for representation by counsel at the trial stage, and on March 18, 1963, less than a week after Ernest Miranda's arrest, the United States Supreme Court in the landmark case called *Gideon* v. *Wainwright* required *all* states to provide counsel to the indigent at that stage. Even in 1959 judges in many states, including Arizona, appointed counsel at the arraignment stage; some provided counsel at the preliminary hearing stage. In California the state authorized public defenders to enter a case "upon request of the defendant or upon order of the court," and these attorneys had been known to do so while defendants were still in police custody. The New York City bar association committee recommended: "If the rights of the defendant are to be fully protected, the defense of a criminal case should begin as soon after arrest as possible. There is a strong argument that the time a defendant needs counsel most is immediately after his arrest. . . ." Bold words in 1959, but the committee stopped short of naming a specific point at which counsel should be provided.

At his first press conference after taking office in 1961, Attorney General Robert F. Kennedy announced the appointment of a Committee on Poverty and the Administration of Criminal Justice—known as the Allen Committee for its chairman, Francis A. Allen of the University of Michigan Law

School—to evaluate the quality of justice being offered the poor in the courts. Although this committee concerned itself only with federal courts, its existence, its research, and its recommendations affected conditions of the poor in all courts, state as well as federal.

The Allen Committee had turned in its report on February 25, 1963, only weeks before Ernest Miranda's interrogation by Officers Cooley and Young at Phoenix police headquarters. Among its recommendations: "counsel be appointed early enough in the criminal proceedings to insure protection of defendant's legitimate interests"—that is, "no later than at first appearance before the United States Commissioner" or arraignment. Although the Allen Committee recognized that the United States Supreme Court had already indicated that in some specific instances an arrested person might have a constitutional right to counsel earlier in the proceedings and the committee acknowledged that this right might be expanded further, it decided *not* to recommend appointment of counsel any earlier. Such a recommendation would, the committee concluded, be "vigorously opposed" by "those who fear its consequences on law enforcement"; it would be self-defeating, it reasoned, to jeopardize the acceptance of an overall improvement in federal court procedures. On March 8, 1963, President John F. Kennedy had sent the proposal, which incorporated the committee's recommendations, to Congress. It later became part of the Criminal Justice Act of 1964.

A little more than a month later, on April 21, 1963, the Ford Foundation announced a grant of $215,000 to the prestigious American Law Institute, a national organization of prominent judges, lawyers, and law faculty members, for a study of the law governing criminal procedures from the time a suspect fell under suspicion until a formal charge of crime was lodged in the court—the law of arrest, search, detention, interrogation, discharge without formal charges, access to counsel, arraignment, bail—for design of a model code of pre-arraignment procedure which could be used as a guide in modernizing those procedures. The area had been, institute director Herbert Wechsler told members assembled in Washington for the annual meeting in May 1963, one "of greatest tension in our culture and in our legal system." There was also concern among the members, many of them state judges and prosecutors and others involved in law enforcement within the states, that unless the states found ways to protect suspects from officials who abused their power in the interrogation room, the U.S. Supreme Court would do it for them.

Police officers themselves were becoming aware that procedures of the interrogation room might in the near future be subjected to judicial supervision. Fred E. Inbau, law professor, pioneer in the teaching of American criminal procedure, outspoken warrior against crime as well as author, with John E. Reid, of one of the most popular police manuals—*Criminal Interrogations and Confessions*—had cautioned officers in the 1962 edition of the volume that although decisions of the United States Supreme Court as well as those of the highest courts in thirty states still did not require that police inform suspects of their constitutional rights not to be compelled to incriminate themselves, "it is problematical whether the present Court may eventually require the warning as an element of due process in state cases." It was entirely possible, Inbau warned his readers, that the conditions under which Ernest Miranda had been interrogated, particularly the failure of the officers to inform him of his constitutional rights *before* he confessed, might in the future be eliminated by judicial fiat.

While they had been alone in interrogation room 2, Officers Cooley and Young had also questioned Miranda about other recent unsolved local crimes. He had confessed to the robbery of another eighteen-year-old girl in a downtown parking lot on November 27, 1962, and the attempted rape of still another young woman, also in a downtown parking lot, on February 22, 1963. The robbery victim later identified Miranda in a line-up; police could not locate the attempted rape victim.

Miranda was booked into the city jail on charges of rape and failure to register as an ex-convict—the addition of the latter a not uncommon police technique for using a lesser charge to hold a defendant until the more serious charge could be more thoroughly investigated. On March 14 he was taken before a city magistrate on the lesser charge; he was summarily convicted and sentenced to ten days in jail. Later that day he was transferred to the county jail.

On March 15, 1963, at 9:05 A.M., police brought Miranda back to interrogation room 2, the same room in which he had made his confession earlier, and questioned him about a number of purse snatchings that had occurred in the vicinity of the November robbery to which he had confessed. At first he denied all of them, then said it was possible he might have committed them. He couldn't remember.

The same day he was arraigned before a justice of the peace. He was charged with the kidnapping and rape of Lois Ann Jameson on March 2–3, 1963, and the robbery of another woman on November 27, 1962, although he always maintained that police had promised he would not be prosecuted on the latter charge.

As early as 1901 the Arizona Territory provided for representation by counsel at the trial stage. Ernest Miranda was assigned an attorney to defend him at his trial in Maricopa County Superior Court, and the date was set for May 14.

Alvin Moore was seventy-three years old at the time of his appointment as Ernest Miranda's lawyer. He had grown up on a farm in the Oklahoma Territory, had taught school for nine years while he studied textbooks from the LaSalle University School of Law, a Chicago-based correspondence school, and been admitted to the Oklahoma bar in December 1922. He had served as a lieutenant colonel of infantry during World War II, moved to Phoenix in 1951, and built a comfortable civil practice over the decade following.

Moore was not atypical of the criminal defense bar in those days. The criminal law never has attracted either large numbers of lawyers or, except in rare instances, the top law school graduates. The Samuel Liebowitzes, the Clarence Darrows, the F. Lee Baileys are the exceptions, and Perry Mason is a figment of literary and media imagination. In capital cases, of course, *all* courts attempted to engage the best available counsel. But in the early 1960s the new activist attorneys in their beards and bell-bottoms, bred by the activist mood of the U.S. Supreme Court, had not yet appeared in American courtrooms; the government-financed public defender network had not yet reached a large number of communities; and most lawyers appointed by the courts to defend the poor in less than capital cases fell into three categories: young men just out of law school seeking experience, practicing on the poor; "uptown" lawyers squeezing time out from more lucrative corporate practices about which they were considerably more knowledgeable and in which they were considerably more interested; and courthouse "regulars"—that band of attorneys who lived off court appointments, many of them more skilled at plea bargaining than in cross-examination. The quality of the criminal defense bar generally—although there were exceptions—was not high. The responsibility must be divided among the courts, the law schools, and the American character.

If lawyers for poor criminal defendants were paid at all by the courts—and many were not—they received substantially less than prevailing legal fees, and they were allowed no funds for investigation of their cases.* Alvin Moore received $100 from Maricopa County for defending Ernest Miranda in Superior Court and $100 for the appeal to the Arizona Supreme Court. What fees criminal lawyers got depended on judicial approval—as did future appointments—and a good many judges were more interested in clearing dockets than in considering legally imaginative arguments in which some new concept of law might be invoked. Cases were assigned at the last minute, and lawyers too frequently went to trial ill-prepared.

The traditions of legal education in this nation generally have not improved the quality of the criminal defense bar. Since the late eighteenth century, when Judge Tapping Reeve in his little school in Litchfield, Connecti-

---

* Since passage of the Criminal Justice Act of 1964 and similar state legislation requiring courts to appoint and pay attorneys for indigent defendants, more money became available. In the 1970s pay for public defenders and court-appointed lawyers at least began to approach the level of that for prosecutors, and defense attorneys began to be allowed funds for investigations and related expenses—funds prosecutors always had. However, none of these attorneys could make as much as attorneys in, for example, full-time corporate practice.

cut, and George Wythe as professor of law and police at the college of William and Mary in Williamsburg, Virginia, established the first law schools in America, the curriculum planners have neglected the criminal law, including only enough for a graduate to pass the bar examination and stumble through whatever criminal cases a small-town general practice might require. In the 1960s, when the U.S. Supreme Court was taking a hard look at what had been followed as procedure and used as evidence in American courts for the past two centuries and thereby fomenting a revolution in the criminal law, Columbia University Law School, not atypical of American law schools generally, offered one required course and two electives in criminal law; the total number of courses in property law ranged from thirty-one to forty-four. The ambiance no doubt reflected the demands of the clientele, but it also reflected the attitudes of faculty members, administration, and trustees, all of whom had been trained in the same system, making it a triumph in self-perpetuation as well. Declared Supreme Court Justice William J. Brennan: "[I]t is hard to see how students can be blamed for coming away from law school with the feeling that perhaps the institution also shares the unfortunate tendency of the community to disapprove of lawyers who undertake the defense of people charged with crime."

Which is where the American character comes in. Americans have always been quick to defend what are considered the respectable freedoms: press, religion, assembly. But those accused of crime have had few defenders. Few men have rushed to uphold the constitutional prohibitions against unreasonable search and seizure or against compelled self-incrimination when it was a kilo of heroin that was seized or a confession forced from a father accused of bludgeoning his daughter to death.

Truman Capote, in his book *In Cold Blood,* recorded the sentiments of the two lawyers appointed by the court to defend Dick Hickok and Perry Smith, accused of brutally murdering the Herbert Clutter family on their farm near Holcomb, Kansas.

"I did not desire to serve," Arthur Fleming, former mayor of Garden City, Kansas, said. "But if the court sees fit to appoint me, then of course I have no choice."

"Someone has to do it. And I'll do my best," said Harrison Smith. "Though I doubt that'll make me too popular around here."

Alvin Moore was no more enthusiastic about defending Ernest Miranda than these Kansas lawyers were. He did not like trying criminal cases. His distaste for them stemmed less from the sparseness of economic reward or from the accompanying social stigma than from rancor in his soul. He had discovered early, he said, that "in close association with criminals, you begin to think like criminals," and in "self-protection," he added, "I gradually withdrew from the practice of criminal law." Only his sense of civic duty persuaded him to accept court appointments to try criminal cases—he had added his name to the Maricopa County Superior Court's list of available attorneys a month or so earlier because some of the younger lawyers were striking for higher fees and there was at the time a scarcity of lawyers to defend the city's poor—and he was to tell the jury at Ernest Miranda's trial later in the year that "as an attorney, and as a father, it is one of the cases I don't like to be involved with, but, however, under our legal procedures, regardless of the type of case it is, the defendant is entitled to the best defense he can have." Indicating the depth of his aversion to the case he was trying, Moore added: "You know, perhaps a doctor doesn't enjoy operating for locked bowels, but he has to. . . ."

For all his reluctance to practice criminal law at this time of his life, Alvin Moore was a cut above the average court-appointed lawyer. If he was no Samuel Liebowitz intellectually or professionally and if his skills were a little rusty—he had not actually tried a criminal case for several years—he was no stranger to the criminal courtroom. He had had a lively criminal practice as a young man in Oklahoma, where he had represented defendants in thirty-five rape cases, only one of whom had been convicted. Overall, Alvin Moore seemed a fortunate choice to try Ernest Miranda's case.

Miranda's record pointed to a possible defense of insanity, and on May 13, 1963, the day before he was to have gone on trial, Alvin Moore filed a notice with the court of his intention to prove insanity both at the time of the alleged rape and at the time of the trial. On May 14 the court appointed two psychiatrists to examine the defendant, and his trial was reset for June 19, 1963.

Leo Rubinow, M.D., examined Miranda at the county jail on May 22 and again on June 4. Reviewing his service record and his religious, family, employment, and marital histories, Dr. Rubinow declared Miranda "oriented in all spheres," but "immature, psychologically, and somewhat inadequate. There is, emotionally, instability, and inability to control. Impulse is lacking . . . he is unable to control his sexual impulses and drives.

"Insight is lacking, judgment and reasoning are somewhat impaired, but at neither interview was there any evidence of any psychotic manifestations noted or elicited, nor history of any psychotic episodes obtained."

Most devastating to Alvin Moore's case was this finding: "He is not insane nor mentally defective, he knows the difference between right and wrong, he knows the nature and consequences of his acts, and is able to understand the proceedings against him and to assist in his defense."

James M. Kilgore, Jr., M.D., examined Miranda at the county jail on May 26, 1963. He declared, after reviewing Miranda's past: "It is my diagnostic impression that Mr. Mirande [*sic*] has an emotional illness. I would classify him as a schizophrenic reaction, chronic, undifferentiated type. . . ."

Dr. Kilgore's conclusion, however, coincided with Dr. Rubinow's: "It is my opinion that Mr. Mirande is aware of the charges that have been brought against him and is able to cooperate with his attorney in his own defense. Although Mr. Mirande has an emotional illness, I feel that at the time the acts were committed that he was aware of the nature and quality of the acts and that he was further aware that what he did was wrong."

On June 18 the court held a hearing to determine Miranda's mental condition. On the basis of the two psychiatrists' reports, that court found the defendant "able to understand the nature of the proceedings and to assist in his defense." The lawyers were directed to proceed to trial.

The trial is civilization's mechanism for determining guilt or innocence rationally and bloodlessly. The courtroom is a hushed place, belying the raw human emotions ever ready to break out. The crime, however heinous, is recounted in an orderly fashion; evidence of it—a confession, a knife, a gun, a blood-stained shirt—is reduced to a lifeless exhibit. The trial ritual is the most sophisticated mechanism devised thus far—in a long series of mechanisms that include ordeal by fire or boiling water with God as judge—in the attempt to bring objectivity to the solution of problems involving the strongest and most fundamental of human emotions: the desire for vengeance.

Its nature is accusatorial; its parentage, English. It is the result of centuries of protest, of Englishmen against the secrecy, arbitrariness, and excesses of the crown and of Americans against the secrecy, arbitrariness, and excesses of Englishmen.

It is conducted according to rules of procedure and evidence developed piecemeal since biblical days. These rules were meant to equalize the inherently unequal contest between the individual and the state not out of some vulgar sentimentality toward criminals but in order to discover truth and dispense justice. They were meant to apply to rich and poor, accused and accuser, in time of crisis and in time of well-being. They include such items as the presumption of innocence until guilt is proved, the right of an accused to counsel, to confront his accusers, and to cross-examine witnesses, the right to be judged by a jury of one's peers, the right not to be compelled to incriminate oneself. They celebrate the dignity of the individual. They also celebrate the integrity of the state.

That's the ideology of the trial. It is often obscured by the reality of the prostitutes, pimps, wife beaters, murderers, and dope pushers who frequent the courtrooms, of the overworked and hastily prepared lawyers who plea-bargain away their clients' freedoms, of harried judges forced to dispense justice with the efficiency and compassion of a Xerox machine.

The trial of Ernest Miranda for kidnapping and rape began on the morning of June 20, 1963. (He had been convicted the previous day on the companion charge of robbery.) Like those of most trials, the proceedings were almost perfunctory. There were no melodramatics, no oratorical contests between the prosecution and defense attorneys, no surprise witnesses, no last-minute rescue of the defendant by discovery of some long-forgotten principle of law or some new piece of evidence. These are not generally the stuff of real life.

There was not even much emotion, except during Lois Ann Jameson's testimony. Sometimes her voice was so soft she had to be asked to speak louder. Once the proceedings had to be stopped, and the spectators sat silent while she tried to compose herself to complete her fearful recitation of the events of the night of March 2 and the early morning of March 3. Otherwise, it was only a routine and clinical examination of a crime, a victim, and a defendant.

The prosecutor, Deputy County Attorney Laurence Turoff, calmly and deftly led his four witnesses—Lois Ann, her sister, Officers Cooley and Young—through their testimony, trying to establish in the jury members' minds that Lois Ann Jameson had been kidnapped and raped by Ernest Miranda, that she "did not enter into this act of intercourse with him willfully, but in fact she was forced to, by his own force and violence, directed against her."

State's exhibit one—the only exhibit—was Ernest Miranda's written confession. Its details coinciding with Lois Ann's story, it was a convincing item.

Alvin Moore did not have much of a defense. He offered no evidence and called no witnesses. He had none. The testimony of the psychiatrists, on which he had hoped to rely, would not have helped Ernest Miranda's case. Fearing the effect on the jury if the defendant was questioned about his previous record, Moore decided against putting Miranda on the stand.

In questioning Lois Ann, he tried to plant doubt in the jury members' minds by maximizing the inconsistencies in the girl's narrative and minimizing the extent of her resistance to her captor. "You have in this case a sorrowful case," Moore admitted in summing up his arguments to the jury, "but you don't have the facts to require that you send a man to prison for rape of a woman who should have resisted and resisted and resisted, until her resistance was at least overcome by the force and violence of the defendant. . . ."

Questions regarding the use of Miranda's confession as evidence against him at his trial nagged at the lawyer. He was bothered, although it seemed more of an instinct than a well-thought-out argument, by the manner in which Officers Cooley and Young had questioned their suspect. He believed Miranda had not been informed effectively of his constitutional rights. Even back in World War II, as a provost marshal, Moore had instructed his MPs that when they stopped another soldier, they could ask his name, rank, and serial number, but for information beyond that, they *must* advise him "that he could stand silent or he could talk, but if he talked it might be used against him." The Phoenix police had not observed these proprieties, and doubts about their behavior in interrogation room 2 lingered. As soon as the prosecutor, during his questioning of Officer Cooley, introduced Miranda's confession into evidence, Alvin Moore struck:

Mr. Moore: Officer Cooley, in the taking of this statement, what did you say to the defendant to get him to make this statement?

A I asked the defendant if he would tell us, write the same story that he had just told me, and he said that he would.

Q Did you warn him of his rights?

A Yes, Sir, at the heading of the statement is a paragraph typed out, and I read this paragraph to him out loud. . . .

Q But did you ever, before or during your conversation or before taking this statement, did you ever advise the defendant he was entitled to the services of an attorney?

A When I read—

Q Before he made any statement?

A When I read the statement right there.

Q I don't see in the statement that it says where he is entitled to the advise [sic] of an attorney before he made it.

A No, Sir.

Q It is not in that statement?

A It doesn't say anything about an attorney. . . .

Q It is not your practice to advise people you arrest that they are entitled to the services of an attorney before they make a statement?

A No, Sir.

Mr. Moore: That is all.

Moore made formal objection to the use of the confession as evidence, but his objection was, at the time, inaccurate: "We object because the Supreme Court of the United States says a man is entitled to an attorney at the time of his arrest." Up to that time the Supreme Court of the United States had said nothing of the sort, at least not categorically, and the judge overruled Moore's objection.

Yale McFate was a veteran of six years on the Maricopa County Superior Court bench, and his instructions to the jury were given in the straightforward and dispassionate manner of an experienced judge. He explained, as he had many times before, that it was up to the men and women of the jury to decide, on the basis of what they had seen and heard that day, whether or not the witness could be believed, whether or not the evidence offered by the prosecutor proved the state's case. He explained the difference between "reasonable doubt" and "all doubt." He defined "rape" in terms of Arizona law and told the members of the jury that they would have to determine whether or not Lois Ann Jameson had "resisted to the utmost" her attacker.

McFate also painstakingly described Arizona law on the use of confessions. He reminded the members of the jury that he had allowed, over Alvin Moore's objection, the introduction of the written confession as evidence against Ernest Miranda. He added, however, that they need not be bound by his ruling and should determine for themselves whether or not the defendant's statement had been given voluntarily—a condition for its use. He then outlined the factors involved in coercion and voluntariness: Violence, threats, promises of immunity and the like did, of course, render a confession involuntary. Arizona law countenanced neither the truncheon nor the "things are bound to go better for you, Ernie, if you tell us everything" device popular among policemen. However, he added, coming to the point that was emerging as a significant issue within the law enforcement community at that moment, "the fact that a defendant was under arrest at the time he made a confession or that he was not at the time represented by counsel or that he was not told that any statement he might make could or would be used against him, in and of themselves, will not render such confession involuntary."

The jury of nine men and three women deliberated for five hours, but in the end they believed the prosecutor: Ernest Miranda was guilty of kidnapping and raping Lois Ann Jameson in the desert outside Phoenix in the early-morning hours of March 3, 1963. He was sentenced on June 27, 1963, to two concurrent terms in the Arizona State Prison at Florence—twenty to thirty years on the kidnapping charge and twenty to thirty years on the rape charge.

Appellate courts do not decide the guilt or innocence of the convicted. Reviewing the trial record, they consider only whether he or she had a fair trial, whether the required procedures were followed, whether all parties acted within the law. There is no jury, and lawyers present their arguments directly to the judges in briefs and oral arguments. The judges sit either in panels, usually of three, or, in more difficult and/or capital cases, *en banc*.

Alvin Moore believed that the Maricopa County Superior Court had not given his client Ernest Miranda a fair trial, and accordingly he decided to appeal to the Arizona Supreme Court, that state's highest judicial body.*

At the time Moore did not realize the significance of the issues surrounding Miranda's confession. Actually he believed his brief contained other examples of improper procedure of equal, if not more, importance. Yet some doubts regarding the propriety of procedures in the taking of Miranda's confession continued to nag, even though Arizona law as it stood at the time had not been violated. The young man had confessed orally, apparently with no warning that what he said could be used against him; the statement he had signed preceding his written confession did not specify which rights he was supposed to have been aware of, and his interrogators had not spelled them out.

"Was this statement made voluntarily?" Moore asked the judges of the Arizona Supreme Court in his brief, "and was appellant (a Mexican boy of limited education) afforded all the safeguards to his rights provided by the

* The Arizona State Court of Appeals, an intermediate judicial body between superior and supreme courts, did not exist in 1963. Its first judges were elected in 1964, to begin work on January 1, 1965.

Constitution of the United States and the laws and the rules of the Courts?"
Moore believed not, and he asked Arizona's highest court to reverse Ernest
Miranda's conviction because the young man's confession had been improperly obtained and should, therefore, not have been used as evidence against
him.

Moore filed his brief with the Arizona Supreme Court on December 10,
1963. That court would not decide Miranda's case for nearly a year and a
half. During that time the issues surrounding confessions which Alvin Moore
had attempted to confront, would become subjects of controversy nationwide, and the Phoenix lawyer and his client, adjusting to the routine of still
another prison, would not be the only ones awaiting the decision with some
eagerness.

CHAPTER 2

Washington, D.C. June 22, 1964. The final session of the United States Supreme Court's 1963 term.

What the black-robed justices decreed this day would have a good deal to do with whether or not the judges of the Arizona Supreme Court acceded to Alvin Moore's request and reversed the conviction of Ernest Miranda.

The gleaming white marble temple from which they ruled bespoke the nature of their power, although it had not always been so. Their present home had been completed only in 1935, a monument to the late Chief Justice William Howard Taft's persistence in prying funds from the Congress. Prior to that, the Court had met for seventy-five years in the old Senate chamber in the Capitol, across First Street, where the justices did not even have a dining room and simply retired behind a screen at the rear of the bench to eat lunch and listen to arguments at the same time. Whether it was hoped or only believed that the judiciary would be the weakest branch of government, the Court was not originally held in high esteem—Alexander Hamilton had called it the "least dangerous branch"—and it was relegated for the first half of the nineteenth century to whatever vacant rooms in the Capitol could be found, at one point meeting in a local tavern.

Settled into their own building for nearly three decades now, the justices had not only a large and impressive courtroom in which to hear arguments and from which to announce their rulings but spacious three-room office suites (a room for each justice, one for clerks, one for secretaries) with open fireplaces. They had a private dining room in which to lunch—not even guests could be invited—and a private parking garage from which a private elevator whisked them to their chambers. Heavy bronze gates sealed off the corridors that led to these private areas.

As the justices often did, they had saved the most controversial decisions until last, and on this final day of the term each of the nine men, leaning out of his high-backed leather chair and bending slightly forward on the raised bench, took his turn at reading an opinion or registering his dissent. There were twelve decisions handed down that day. The justices' voices droned on, flat and expressionless, rarely hinting that these nine men were dictating standards of behavior in the most powerful nation in the world.

The United States Supreme Court, known as the Warren Court for its chief justice, Earl Warren, at this moment in constitutional time did not stand at the zenith of its popularity. On the contrary. In the eleven years since Warren had become chief justice, the justices had become increasingly cantankerous, upsetting long-established customs and altering long-established procedures, all in the name of upholding the constitutional rights of the individual. They had interfered in the operation of the public schools of the nation, declaring racial segregation unconstitutional there. They had meddled in local politics, attacking malapportioned voting districts. They had tampered with the operations of government, interfering with the ways officials could deal with citizens who espoused unpopular ideas and with the way police could deal with the criminal defendants. As the 1960s approached the halfway mark, the U.S. Supreme Court was approaching the high point thus far in its support of civil liberties. Each decision had involved taking power from one group and redistributing it, usually to people previously disadvantaged politically, socially, or economically, thus altering traditional balances.

The public reaction was not surprising. There were proposals in Congress to limit the Court's jurisdiction, to limit the justices' terms of office, and to limit the effects of their decisions. So far none had become law, although some had come close. Later in 1964 the congressmen would inform the Court of their continuing pique by giving all federal judges *except* Supreme Court justices a $7,500 salary increase; the latter were given only $4,500.

"Impeach Earl Warren" signs cluttered the American landscape and criticism of the Court was heard from all segments of American life. Judge Learned Hand of the U.S. Court of Appeals for the Second Circuit, one of the nation's most respected judges sitting on one of the nation's most respected courts, second in power only to the U.S. Supreme Court itself; the Conference of Chief Justices, made up of the ranking judicial officers of the fifty states; the American Bar Association (whose criticism Chief Justice Warren had felt particularly keenly; he had resigned from the organization); the National Association of Attorneys General; the International Association of Chiefs of Police; the American Legion; and the Omaha Women's Club—all had gone on record, with varying degrees of credibility, as disapproving the role assumed in recent years by the U.S. Supreme Court.

Typically the justices gave no outward indication that they were even aware of these currents in public thought. This very term had been one of great significance for Court and country. The justices had ordered states to redraw certain of their election districts on the basis of population, invalidated a Washington State requirement that its employees swear they were not "subversives," and directed the public schools of Prince Edward County, Virginia, closed since 1959, to reopen and desegregate.

Chief Justice Warren, weary after six months as both chief justice and head of the Warren Commission—which only the previous week had finally finished taking testimony in its investigation of the November 1963 assassination of President John Kennedy—had opened this day's Court session by declaring that the state of Maryland could not be a party to a policy of racial segregation at a private amusement park in Glen Echo, a suburb of the nation's capital, a decision that effectively integrated that park. The Court reversed the convictions for trespass in three cases of Negroes who had sat in at segregation lunch counters and restaurants in the name of racial desegregation.

The loyalty-security program of the U.S. government had to absorb still another blow when the Court declared unconstitutional a section of the Subversive Activities Control Act of 1950 that regulated the use of American passports.

The conviction of Nico Jacobellis, manager of a motion picture theater in Cleveland Heights, Ohio, for showing an "obscene" film, *Les Amants,** was reversed on the ground that the conviction had violated the constitutional guarantee of freedom of the press.

It was not a decision day calculated to win allies for the Supreme Court, and the major decision handed down that day only exacerbated the situation. *Escobedo* v. *Illinois* it was called. It involved interrogation by police and confession by a suspect in questionable circumstances—exactly the kinds of circumstances for which bar groups like the American Law Institute were seeking remedies. It was the most controversial Court decision having to do with criminal justice to date. It was significant for what it said and what it did not say, what it promised and what it held back, and it would be a linchpin of the Arizona Supreme Court's decision in Ernest Miranda's case.

Danny Escobedo was a twenty-two-year-old Chicago laborer of Mexican heritage with no previous run-ins with the law. On the night of January 19, 1960, his brother-in-law, Manuel Valtierra, was fatally shot. At two-thirty the following morning, Escobedo was arrested at the home of a sister for whom he was baby-sitting, and taken to the Fillmore Avenue district police station, where he was questioned for fourteen or fifteen hours. He made no statement and was released at five that afternoon, when his lawyer, Warren Wolfson,

* This particular case owed its prominence in the literature of the law to Justice Potter Stewart's disinclination to define precisely what pornography was and his taking refuge in the explanation "But I know it when I see it."

whom Escobedo had retained previously in connection with a personal injury action against the Chicago Transit Authority, obtained a state court order.

Ten days later, on January 30, one of the other suspects in the case, Benedict DiGerlando, told police Escobedo had done the shooting. Police again arrested Escobedo, along with his sister Grace, widow of the late Manuel Valtierra, and a friend, Bobby Chan. On the way downtown to police headquarters, police told Escobedo he had been fingered as the assassin and might as well confess.

"We have you sewed up pretty tight," an officer said.

But Escobedo refused to admit anything. He had consulted Wolfson during the previous week, and following the lawyer's instructions, he told police: "I am sorry, but I would like to have advice from my lawyer." They arrived at headquarters, a plain brick building once described as smelling of "washing compound and misery" about a mile and a half south of Chicago's Loop, between eight and nine in the evening.

A fundamental rule of interrogation, police manuals say, is isolation of the subject. Escobedo continued to ask to talk to his lawyer, who was in the building; police consistently told him Wolfson did not want to see him. Wolfson repeatedly tried to talk with his client; although Illinois law at the time allowed an attorney to see a client in custody, police that night, from the desk sergeant to the lieutenant in charge, refused Wolfson's requests. At one point Escobedo and Wolfson glimpsed each other through an open door, but when they waved, police closed the door. After several unsuccessful attempts to see Escobedo over a period of three or four hours, Wolfson finally went home at about one the following morning. Police testimony at Escobedo's trial did not substantially dispute these points.

While Wolfson was trying to see his client, Escobedo was being questioned by police. Their tactics were routine, designed to entrap, according to the best police manuals of instruction. A police officer testified at Escobedo's trial: "I informed him of what DiGerlando told me and when I did, he told me that DiGerlando was [lying] and I said, 'would you care to tell DiGerlando that?' and he said, 'Yes, I will.' So I brought . . . Escobedo in and he confronted DiGerlando and he told him that he was lying and said, 'I didn't shoot Manuel, you did it.'"

It was the first time Escobedo had admitted any knowledge of the crime. The details differed, but the strategy was the same as that which Officers Cooley and Young had employed following Ernest Miranda's appearance in the line-up before Lois Ann Jameson. Lois Ann had asked to hear Miranda's voice and had been summoned to interrogation room 2.

"Is that the girl?" one of the officers had asked.

"That's the girl," Miranda had answered, having previously been told she had identified him in the line-up.

And the result was essentially the same. Miranda confessed; Danny

Escobedo made incriminating statements that further implicated him in the crime. He insisted through his trial that a friendly Spanish-speaking officer, who claimed to be a friend of his brother, had privately promised him he would not be prosecuted if he agreed to be a witness against DiGerlando, who Danny maintained was the real assassin; the officer denied this, just the way Phoenix police had denied promising Ernest Miranda immunity from prosecution on one of the charges if he admitted all the crimes. No one, however, told Escobedo he had a right to remain silent during the three or four hours police questioned him.

Shortly after midnight an assistant state's attorney was summoned, and a nervous, agitated, and exhausted Danny Escobedo dictated a statement. At his trial his "confession," like Miranda's, was state's exhibit number one. He was convicted of murder and sentenced to twenty years in the Illinois State Penitentiary.

From prison Escobedo filed a pauper's appeal to the Illinois Supreme Court. The Chicago public defender's office had no appellate lawyers in the early 1960s, nor were there yet Office of Economic Opportunity lawyers— these were to come later—and the lawyers who argued cases like Escobedo's came from a pool of volunteers insufficiently large to handle the caseload. The Illinois Supreme Court had attempted to solve the problem by assigning to every lawyer in the state a criminal appeal defense approximately two to three years after admission to the bar—a kind of social dues.

At the time Barry L. Kroll was a young associate in a Chicago law firm. Having recently completed his three-year army tour of duty and billed at the lowest rate in the office, he had the lightest workload of the firm. He was not without appellate experience—as a captain in the judge advocate general's office he had had two years' experience briefing and arguing cases in the United States Court of Military Appeals. But like Alvin Moore, he had, he said, "no taste for criminal law." Nevertheless, when an older member of the firm was assigned by the state supreme court to take Escobedo's appeal and Kroll was asked to help, he readily agreed.

On appeal, the Illinois Supreme Court could not make up its mind. In its original decision handed down on February 1, 1963, that court ruled Escobedo's "confession" inadmissible at his trial on the ground that he had given it in response to promises of immunity, and reversed his conviction. When the state asked for and was granted a rehearing, the court reversed itself on the ground that the police officer had denied making the promises and the trial judge had believed him; Escobedo's conviction was affirmed.

Escobedo asked Kroll's firm to take the case to the United States Supreme Court.

"I prevailed on one of the senior partners," Kroll said, "that since we had done all the research and written a lot of it, I could probably do it in a short period of time."

"Well," the senior partner replied, "so long as you don't use any office time, go right ahead."

Prior to the growth of public defender organizations which have assumed some of the caseload in recent years, it was largely lawyers like Kroll who took cases like Danny Escobedo's to the U.S. Supreme Court. They were described in a survey of their backgrounds at the time as the "casuals"—that is, they argued these cases apart from their regular practices or careers. Some came from law school faculties; others were engaged by institutions such as the American Civil Liberties Union or the National Association for the Advancement of Colored People; still others came from the private bar, often appointed by the Supreme Court itself, and generally considered to have been given a singular honor—in contrast with the stigma which was often felt to be attached to a court appointment at the trial level.

Utilizing the briefs and records he had prepared for the Illinois Supreme Court, Kroll drew up a request to the Supreme Court of the United States to hear Danny Escobedo's case—the form is called a petition for a writ of certiorari—and submitted it on July 1, 1963, eleven days after Ernest Miranda's trial in Maricopa County Superior Court. Kroll argued that the overall circumstances and conditions of Escobedo's interrogation by the Chicago police had denied him the due process of law guaranteed him by the Fourteenth Amendment to the United States Constitution. In particular, Kroll cited the admission at Escobedo's trial of the statement obtained from him "after his request to consult with his personal counsel, who was present at the police station demanding to consult with petitioner, was arbitrarily denied by the interrogating police." And he raised the question being asked by many people within and without the law enforcement community: that "of the permissible limits to which law enforcement officers may go before they transgress the inalienable rights to due process guaranteed to all accused." On November 12, 1963, the U.S. Supreme Court announced it would hear Danny Escobedo's case. Oral argument was scheduled for Wednesday, April 29, 1964.

Kroll's two years of appellate practice before the U.S. Court of Military Appeals had taught him, he said, "to bob and weave." However, he had never argued a case in the U.S. Supreme Court, and he was properly respectful of the challenge. He scheduled his vacation so that it spanned the time he was to argue Escobedo's case and drove to Washington, arriving on Sunday, April 26. Monday he spent in the lawyers' section of the courtroom familiarizing himself with the milieu while other lawyers argued their cases. When the Court adjourned at 3:00 P.M., he went upstairs to the Supreme Court library on the third floor to read, reread, and re-reread the record in Escobedo's case. On Tuesday he did exactly the same thing.

At argument on Wednesday he was prepared for the justices who questioned him closely regarding the case records and the specific requirements of Illinois criminal procedure as well as related cases that had been before the U.S. Supreme Court. To his answers he added:

> Now, [Danny Escobedo] convicted himself in that police station, under an accusatorial system. He convicted himself as a result of the interrogation that went on there. He convicted himself. And what did the attorney do thereafter? What could he do? The focus of the trial was now shifted. Instead of being one to determine his guilt or innocence, the whole focus of the trial was now shifted to determine whether this piece of evidence was now admissible or not.
> We feel that, in order to have the effective assistance of counsel, you've got to have the assistance at the time you need it.

James R. Thompson, assistant state's attorney for Cook County (and later governor of Illinois), argued the case for the state of Illinois. Like Kroll, he answered questions regarding the record in Escobedo's case, Illinois criminal procedures, and previous decisions made by the U.S. Supreme Court, following which he came to the core of his argument. Like all law enforcement officers, he was committed to the protection of society and to the presentation of society's case in court, a position that required, many of them believed, latitude for law officers to conduct their business effectively and that by definition precluded appeals to the soaring themes of individual liberties. Thompson countered Kroll's statement with warnings of dire consequences should the justices heed the latter's arguments:

> If this Court were to hold that Danny Escobedo had a constitutional right to consult with his counsel at the police station upon request, then that constitutional right is not only extended to Escobedo, who had money enough to retain counsel and who had retained counsel banging at the precinct doors; but that constitutional right, it seems to me, cannot but help be extended to a man who does not have money for counsel.

If, the state's attorney concluded, the U.S. Supreme Court were to hold that a defendant under arrest had the right to counsel during questioning in a police station, it logically followed that any confession taken in the absence of counsel could not be admitted as evidence in a trial; the obvious consequence was, he added, providing a surface off which echoes would reflect for some time, "essentially there will be no more confessions."

Now, nearly two months later, the U.S. Supreme Court was about to make public its decision in Danny Escobedo's case. The margin of the majority was five to four, a margin that was becoming increasingly frequent, especially in criminal cases.

Sitting at the far end of the bench, as was traditional for the Court's most recent appointee, owlish-looking in dark horn-rimmed glasses, Arthur J.

Goldberg was reading the opinion he had written for the Court. The son of poor Russian-Jewish immigrants, he had come to the Court not from a large corporate practice, as many justices in the past had, but from labor's side of the bargaining table. Having helped mobilize labor's vote for John F. Kennedy in the 1960 election, he had been appointed secretary of labor in the Kennedy administration and to the Supreme Court in 1962 on the resignation of Felix Frankfurter. It had surprised no one when he had joined those justices identified with the defense of individual rights: Chief Justice Warren, Hugo L. Black, William O. Douglas, and William J. Brennan, Jr., who made up the majority that day.

Confronting the dominant questions surrounding interrogations, the dependability of the statement, and the integrity of the government, Goldberg swept aside Thompson's warnings of disaster in law enforcement. "We have learned," the justice said, "the lesson of history, ancient and modern, that a system of criminal law enforcement which comes to depend on the 'confession' will, in the long run, be less reliable and more subject to abuse than a system which depends on extrinsic evidence independently secured through skillful investigation."

Goldberg added a paragraph in the nature of his own warning:

> We have also learned the companion lesson of history that no system of criminal justice can, or should, survive if it comes to depend for its continued effectiveness on the citizens' abdication through unawareness of their constitutional rights. No system worth preserving should have to *fear* that if an accused is permitted to consult with a lawyer, he will become aware of, and exercise, these rights. If the exercise of constitutional rights will thwart the effectiveness of a system of law enforcement, then there is something very wrong with that system.

Then he laid down the ruling of the United States Supreme Court:

> . . . Where, as here, the investigation is no longer a general inquiry into an unsolved crime but has begun to focus on a particular suspect, the suspect has been taken into police custody, the police carry out a process of interrogations that lends itself to eliciting incriminating statements, the suspect has requested and been denied an opportunity to consult with his lawyer, and police have not effectively warned him of his absolute constitutional right to remain silent, the accused has been denied "the Assistance of Counsel" in violation of the Sixth Amendment to the Constitution as "made obligatory upon the States by the Fourteenth Amendment," . . . and . . . no statement elicited by the police during the interrogation may be used against him at a criminal trial.

As Court opinions go, it seemed a long list of conditions, a rare instance then of the U.S. Supreme Court's speaking not in generalities but in specifics and dictating the operating procedures of police. As such, it was not popular

33

among law enforcement officers, who were beginning to resent the Court's interference in their treatment of criminal defendants.

The case was only the latest in a long line of criminal cases which had come before the Supreme Court by the first half of the 1960s and through which the rights of the individual defendant had been upheld over the claimed necessities of law enforcement. Police were beginning to complain that the Court was making their work unnecessarily difficult, grumbling in one of the most quoted analogies of the day, that the Court was requiring them to "fight by Marquis of Queensberry rules," while allowing criminal defendants "to butt, gouge, and bite." Prosecutors painted a dreary picture of law enforcement, citing decreases in the number of convictions because of Supreme Court decisions and predicting the worst.

"Someday, I guess, the Court will rule that we can't talk to a suspect without first giving him a lawyer," complained one official, his attitude of fatalism a prevalent one at the winter conference of the National Association of District Attorneys in Houston, Texas, later in 1965. "When that happens, believe me, the ball game is over. You're going to see a lot of killers and rapists walking out of police stations with thumb to nose." He added, catching a note that would become more significant in the following months: "We shall see how the public will like that."

The decision in Danny Escobedo's case generated confusion as well as resentment. What were law enforcement officers to do about an accused too ignorant to request counsel, too poor to engage counsel, too overawed by the power of the state to assert what rights he or she possessed? People like Ernest Miranda. At exactly what point did the question of a lawyer come into play? Were all rights to be formally recognized, and if so, how? These questions, although unarticulated, underlay the brief Alvin Moore had submitted in behalf of Ernest Miranda to the Arizona Supreme Court six months previously.

They were not abstract problems posed to an academic community that could solve them in abstract terms on paper over a long period of time. They were concrete questions with which the policeman on the beat, the district attorney, the defense lawyer, and the trial judge had to wrestle every working day, and the lack of guidance left their professional conduct in considerable doubt.

What had become plain, though, as the implications of *Escobedo* were clarified, was that the interrogation room door had opened a crack and the United States Constitution could not be so cavalierly left outside as it had been traditionally.*

---

* In its most practical application, the decision reversed Danny Escobedo's conviction for the murder of his brother-in-law. It did not, however, end his troubles with the law. According to Kroll, police picked him up nearly every time he was spotted. Twice he was arrested, tried, and acquitted on minor charges. The third time he was convicted of conspiracy to sell amphetamines and spent five years in jail. Since then he apparently has had no confrontations with the law. Barry Kroll, who practices civil law in Chicago, attended Escobedo's wedding in June 1978.

For the future of criminal justice as it was meted out in America during these times, perhaps the most significant effect of the Supreme Court's decision in Danny Escobedo's case was the response it elicited in the dissenters to it. Their phraseology differed from that of police and prosecutors, but their meaning did not. Nor did the degree of their passion.

Dissent "is an appeal to the brooding spirit of the law," Chief Justice Charles Evans Hughes had written in 1928, "to the intelligence of a future day, when a later decision may possibly correct the error into which the dissenting judge believes the court to have been betrayed." Taken together, the dissents in the case of Danny Escobedo gave momentum to the growing sentiment among Americans within and without the law enforcement community that courts had gone too far in their protection of the constitutional rights of criminal defendants. At the same time some forces were combining to advance Ernest Miranda's case, other forces were combining to erode it.

The senior justice among the Court's four dissenters, John Marshall Harlan, was known personally as the soul of courtesy and professionally as a quiet scholar of the Constitution, rarely given to intemperate outbursts. His judicial writings, particularly his dissents—and he seemed to be more often in dissent during these times—however, did not always reflect this mild manner. The majority opinion, he declared now in a seven-line dissent, the brevity of which belied its intensity, was "ill-conceived," a ruling which "unjustifiably fetters perfectly legitimate methods of criminal law enforcement."

Potter Stewart was, like Harlan, also to be found increasingly often among the dissenters on the Warren Court. That Court in *Escobedo* had in effect, Stewart declared, advanced the beginning of judicial proceedings from trial and its preliminaries to the arrest stage; in so doing, he charged, the Court "converts a routine police investigation of an unsolved murder into a distorted analogue of a judicial trial . . . and frustrates the vital interests of society in preserving the legitimate and proper functions of honest and purposeful police investigations. . . ."

The two ex-Justice Department officials on the Court, fearing for the future of law enforcement, joined in the third dissent. Byron R. White, former deputy attorney general and President Kennedy's first appointment to the Court, wrote it for himself and Tom C. Clark, President Harry S Truman's attorney general.

In these cases the Court traditionally divided into two blocs: the justices who claimed to assert a right already residing in the Constitution—the majority in *Escobedo*—and those who claimed a new right was being invented—the dissenters in *Escobedo*. Justice White was of the latter persuasion. It would be "naive," he declared, to think "the new constitutional right announced will depend upon whether the accused has retained his own counsel . . . or has asked to consult with counsel in the course of interrogation." It would be only a matter of time, he feared, before the Court would bar from evidence *all* admissions made by criminal suspects, regardless of their degree of voluntariness. The Court had gone too far.

White's accusation that *Escobedo* was just the beginning could be borne out only over time. It was inevitable, though, given the questions left unanswered, the confusions created, and the controversy within the Court itself, that *Escobedo* would have progeny. It was less apparent, as the last opinion was announced and the Chief Justice officially recessed the Court for the summer, ending the 1963 term, that the effects of what the U.S. Supreme Court had done to bring due process of law into the station house would not be limited to the individuals immediately concerned and not even to the law enforcement community but would extend much farther, all the way into the highest levels of national politics.

CHAPTER 3

===========

Following a small family party on January 9, 1965, to celebrate his fifty-second birthday, Richard Milhous Nixon retreated to the privacy of the study in his Manhattan apartment. It was a comfortable room, radiating snugness and warmth. The bookshelves were crammed. A mantel display of elephant figures in teak and ivory and stone dominated the décor. Old-fashioned easy chairs and sofas invited unwinding. A fire burned in the fireplace.

He settled into an easy chair and in the manner of the solitary man he was, began to compile his private accounting of the year just past and to assess his prospects for the future. He scribbled some New Year's resolutions on one of the long yellow legal pads which were to become so familiar a part of his equipment, resolving to:

—Set some goals
—Daily rest
—Brief vacations
—Knowledge of all weaknesses
—Better use of time
—Begin writing book
—Golf or some other daily exercise
—Articles or speeches on provocative new international
   or national issues

Then he turned out the light and stared into the fire.

He had been a member of the House of Representatives for two terms. Californians had elected him to the Senate in 1950. He had barely gotten to know his way around that side of Capitol Hill when he had been chosen by the Republican candidate for president in 1952, Dwight D. Eisenhower, to run for vice president. The vice presidency had taken him nearly to the top of the mountain, and the prospects that he could go to the summit were good. He was young, personable, and politically shrewd. If there was a tenseness about him, if he seemed overly serious at times, if an air of suspiciousness surfaced occasionally, or if his conduct of his political campaigns seemed a little ruthless, his supporters tended to shrug it off. His showings at the polls refuted whatever negative arguments that arose.

Then he had run for the presidency itself in 1960 and had lost to John Kennedy. Two years later he had run for the governorship of California against Edmund G. ("Pat") Brown and lost again. Of all the fames that are fleeting, that acquired in political struggle may be the most fleeting. The winner had suddenly become a loser, and he had, he thought, put politics behind him.

Now, in 1965, he was a New York lawyer in a downtown firm—Nixon, Mudge, Rose, Guthrie, Alexander & Mitchell, a national corporate shaker and mover. He was prosperous for the first time in his life. He had a solid practice and rode to the office in a chauffeur-driven Cadillac. He worked hard, often eating lunch at his desk in his office, which was on the twenty-fourth floor at 20 Broad Street and overlooked the East River.

He also had more leisure than ever before. He became a regular at theaters and concert halls, absorbing the culture he craved and for which he previously had little time; on the golf courses of the fashionable clubs to which he belonged; at Toots Shor's, where he talked sports, which he had always loved; and in the stands at Yankee Stadium. His daughter Tricia had been presented to society at the International Debutante Ball the previous December. Despite his election losses and despite his having embarked on a second career only two years before, at the age of fifty, he was one of the most successful men in the United States.

And he looked it. People who glimpsed him strolling on Fifth Avenue noticed he no longer wore his habitual frown and had put on weight, although the few pounds had not entirely obscured the jutting jaw and ski jump of a nose that in the recent past had given cartoonists so much pleasure. People who had known him in the old days now detected a new self-confidence and an unaccustomed relaxed air about him.

For all the surface serenity, Nixon was restless. He had come to the realization, he said, that "there was no other life for me but politics and public service. Even when my legal work was at its most interesting I never found it truly fulfilling . . . if all I had was my legal work, I would be mentally dead in two years and physically dead in four. . . ."

Even as he mused before the fire that January night, issues and men were emerging, and events conspiring, to interrupt his comfortable routine. Soon he would be seen less frequently at the theater and concert halls and more frequently in the armories and high school auditoriums and makeshift platforms on country airstrips in nearly all the states of the Union, as once more he resumed his old political life.

One issue had already appeared, had, in fact, been a staple of the recent presidential election campaign in which the Republican candidate, Barry Goldwater, had lost to the incumbent president, Lyndon B. Johnson, and, given that issue's potential for growth and exploitation, was not likely to disappear. "Crime in the streets" was a catchall phrase for random crimes, crimes like the rape for which Ernest Miranda had been convicted. They had in common chance encounters, arbitrary selection of victims, the use of knives and guns escalating the violence. They were the sorts of assault the public could not defend itself against.

Following a period of relative tranquility in the 1940s and 1950s, when the nation was preoccupied with World War II and its aftershocks, and paralleling the U.S. Supreme Court's expansion of the rights of criminal defendants, crime rates had suddenly and substantially increased. Each year the FBI published the ominous news in its *Uniform Crime Reports*: a 6 percent rise in serious crimes in 1962 over 1961, a 10 percent rise in 1963 over 1962, 13 percent in 1964 over 1963. Since 1958, the organization had reported in 1964, the incidence of crime had been growing six times faster than the American population.

These numbers, however, failed to convey the fears and frustrations that had assumed a disproportionate share of people's lives. Anyone who had not had a bicycle stolen knew neighbors who had. Children's lemonade stands were held up. Muggers roamed the more affluent sections of cities and suburbs; people who had not been mugged had listened to friends tell what it was like. Fear of rape limited the activities of women, not only young but elderly women. Locked automobiles disappeared from driveways. Houses on quiet streets were broken into and burglarized. Banks were robbed in broad daylight. Technologically and psychologically underequipped to deal with such violence, police seemed to have little effect on it.

The public reacted. Doors closed. Dead-bolt locks crammed the counters of hardware stores. Doberman pinschers became apartment dwellers. Guns found their way into night-table drawers. Private houses acquired burglar alarms, and iron grilles striped lower-story windows. Downtown streets emptied at dusk. Housewives bought tear-gas pens and enrolled in judo classes. Department store managers hired guards, and private security became big business. In Washington, the State Department set up a special guard system to protect women *inside* the building.

Crime had moved out of the newspaper headlines into people's lives, and the people, generally unacquainted with the complexities of the phenomenon, were ready to believe it when politicians, by some sleight of hand, made it seem the result of decisions handed down by the United States Supreme Court, including that in the case of Danny Escobedo.

Less than a month after that decision, Richard Nixon had been present when former President Eisenhower, in a political translation of the dissents to it, had set the tone for the decade in a speech to the 1964 Republican National Convention the night before Senator Goldwater was nominated for president of the United States. Declared the old political soldier: "Let us not be guilty of maudlin sympathy for the criminal who, roaming the street with switchblade knife and illegal firearms seeking a helpless prey, suddenly becomes upon apprehension a poor, underprivileged person who counts upon the compassion of our society and the laxness or weakness of too many courts to forgive his offense."

The delegates, a stomping, screaming crowd that itself had demonstrated an inclination to violence earlier when it had hooted and booed Governor Nelson A. Rockefeller of New York off the podium, had stomped and screamed their approval of the former president. Goldwater had responded immediately. At a press conference following his nomination he had promised that if elected, he would "do all I can to see that women can go out in the streets of this country without being scared stiff." That night, in his acceptance speech to the convention, he had introduced the phrase *violence in our streets*, which was to serve candidates for some years. He warned: "Security from domestic violence, no less than from foreign aggression, is the most elementary and fundamental purpose of any government, and a government that cannot fulfill this purpose is one that cannot long command the loyalty of its citizens."

A campaign aide, Richard G. Kleindienst, had suggested that Goldwater make what later became known as law and order the principal domestic issue of his campaign, and the candidate had flailed away with it, a truncheon thudding in a regular cadence against the soft spots on the body politic.

—[September 3, Prescott, Arizona] It is on our streets that we see the final, terrible proof of a sickness which not all the social theories of a thousand social experiments has even begun to touch. Crime grows faster than population, while those who break the law are accorded more consideration than those who try to enforce the law. Law enforcement agencies—the police, the sheriffs, the FBI—are attacked for doing their jobs. Law breakers are defended. Our wives, all women, feel unsafe in our streets.

—[September 11, the American Political Science Association, Chicago, Illinois] Today's Supreme Court is the least faithful to the constitutional traditions of limited government, and to the principle of legitimacy in the exercise of power.

—[September 15, St. Petersburg, Florida] [T]he Supreme Court ordered that a criminal conviction should be reversed, no matter how guilty the defendant, if it were shown that some technical violation of constitutional rights occurred anywhere in the course of investigation and trial. If there is any flaw in one confession, all confessions . . . must be thrown out. . . . Something must be done

... to swing away from this obsessive concern for the rights of the criminal defendant. . . .

—[September 16, Macon, Georgia] I would be very, very worried about who is the President for the next four or eight years thinking of one thing only—the make-up of the Supreme Court.

—[September 29, Chillicothe, Ohio] Do you want Lyndon's cronies appointed to support him? Or do you want seasoned, independent men who will support the Constitution?

Goldwater's opponent, the incumbent president, did not say much about "law and order," except to accuse the Republican candidate of talking in meaningless generalities. Lyndon Johnson was a supporter, even an admirer, of Chief Justice Warren as a judge and the Supreme Court as an institution; in fact, as Senate majority leader during the late 1950s he had rescued the Court from near destruction when its enemies in the Congress had attempted to emasculate it legislatively. Although there were available very little reliable data regarding the root causes of crime, Johnson tended to see, where Goldwater saw only thugs, the wasted youths of the ghetto, born into sunless flats, stealing food to stave off hunger and stealing gloves to keep out the cold, their only law the law of the streets. He saw the nation's police as professionally undertrained and technologically underequipped, frustrated in their inability to cope with the rapidly growing criminal population. He saw the courts, overloaded and approaching gridlock, as impotent, the corrections system, which failed to correct, as self-defeating. And within a matter of weeks, following his triumph over Goldwater, he initiated a dialogue with Congress in which he urged the legislators to remedy these conditions.

For the president was, of course, reelected. In the end Goldwater's law and order rhetoric, while it hit some sensitive nerves, did not cause the desired reflex action, and his foreign policy—what one commentator called "ultimatum diplomacy"—struck voters as impulsive and reckless. Throughout the campaign Lyndon Johnson dominated the news as he signed a housing act and a Medicare bill, coped with the various international crises—Nikita Khrushchev's fall from power, China's first nuclear explosion, a small war in Indochina in which the United States was becoming increasingly involved. Overall, the presidential campaign had amounted to the Republican's incessant attacks on government versus the Democrats' attempts to put government to work for people, particularly poor people, another political expression of a movement, which had begun at the turn of the century with Theodore Roosevelt's Square Deal, to bring the less favored into the mainstream of American life without revolution.

The dimensions of Republican defeat were large. On November 5, Lyndon Johnson carried forty-four states and the District of Columbia, a total of 486 electoral votes. Barry Goldwater carried five Deep South states plus his own state of Arizona—a total of 52 electoral votes. Republicans also lost 2 seats in the Senate, 38 in the House of Representatives, and 500 in state legislatures.

Barry Goldwater was through as a national candidate. The law and order issue he had exploited, however, was not. It was Richard Nixon's kind of issue. He had made his political reputation on a similar issue, communism, particularly domestic communism. Crime held much the same potential. It was an increasingly serious threat to internal security. Despite its complexities, it could be reduced to code words and simplistic solutions for political purposes, as Senator Goldwater had demonstrated. And it evoked deep fear.

"People react to fear, not love," Richard Nixon once told an aide. "They don't teach that in Sunday School, but it's true."

And perhaps as important as any of these factors, crime was somehow linked with another even more sensitive and troubling problem in American life: Race. The presidential campaign and election of 1964 had coincided with a period of vigorous civil rights activity—sit-ins, drives in the backwoods of the South to write the names of blacks onto the voting rolls—and of violence—race riots in New York City, Rochester, Jersey City, Philadelphia—all of which had led to the passage of the Civil Rights Act of 1964 legislating voting rights, prohibiting racial discrimination in public places and all tax-supported facilities, establishing methods of equal employment opportunity and public school desegregation. (Barry Goldwater had voted against the bill in the United States Senate.) Race and crime were often scrambled together in the public mind, their common denominator fear—fear of being mugged physically on a street corner and fear of being mugged economically by the newcomer in the labor market—and the United States Supreme Court, beginning with its 1954 order to desegregate the public schools of America, had been responsible for both "crimes." Goldwater's campaign had exploited what was known then as the white backlash, and he had sought a hospitable center of gravity for the Republican party in the South, which, when added to the old reliable Republican midwestern, Rocky Mountain, and northern New England states, would win him, he believed, the presidency.

Although Goldwater's southern electoral strategy had not worked in 1964—he had taken less than half of the Old Confederacy—aspects of it were not beyond salvage, and it had served to maneuver into position politically three men whose influence would grow during the next several years and who would, in fact, have a substantial impact on political and even judicial events for a decade: George Corley Wallace of Alabama, J. Strom Thurmond of South Carolina, and, of course, Richard Nixon himself.

The squirrellike face of Governor George Wallace of Alabama had become familiar nationwide by January 1965. Two years before, in June 1963, he had stood in the door of Foster Hall to challenge the national government in his resistance to racial desegregation at the University of Alabama, had won national prominence by his gesture, futile though it proved. He had discovered the political profit in the fusion of race and crime into one issue and in the United States Supreme Court as a convenient scapegoat for both. He had campaigned in 1964 as far afield as Wisconsin as an independent candidate for president, attracting surprisingly respectable numbers of voters at primaries in Wisconsin, Indiana, and Maryland. A southerner, Wallace had threatened also to siphon off Goldwater's southern votes and was ultimately persuaded by one of Goldwater's aides not to run as a third-party candidate in the November election. But Wallace was looking ahead, and he would not be so malleable in 1968.

J. Strom Thurmond, Democratic senator from South Carolina, former governor and unreconstructed Dixiecrat, had grown impatient with the politics and social programs of Democrats John Kennedy and Lyndon Johnson as well as with the Supreme Court decisions that meddled in the operation of his state's courts and ordered the desegregation of public schools. Where Thurmond came from, Edgefield, South Carolina, although blacks were a majority until the 1980 census, streets in white neighborhoods were paved, those in many black neighborhoods were not; white neighborhoods had sewage systems, most black neighborhoods did not; and at Strom Thurmond High School, desegregated under court order in 1970 and 65 percent black— many white students had transferred to a segregated academy up the road— "Dixie" was the school song, Confederate Rebel the school nickname, and the Confederate flag the school symbol at athletic events. A politician who showed a shrewd and strong instinct for survival, Thurmond was not unaware that the conservative Republican party just then beginning to emerge in the South was the wave of Dixie's future. In 1964 he had sensed that the time had come for him to abandon his Democratic party again—he had been the Dixiecrat presidential candidate in 1948—when his fellow conservative, states' rights advocate, good friend, and southern hero Barry Goldwater took control of the Republican convention. Thurmond had astonished the nation one day in September by announcing he had actually joined the Republican party, then by campaigning for Goldwater all that fall. Together, Thurmond and Goldwater had brought new respectability to Republicanism in the South, which had shown the depths of its contempt for the policies of Yankee Republican Abraham Lincoln and his post–Civil War followers by voting solidly Democratic for nearly an entire century. Thurmond's apostasy added considerable momentum to the revival of the two-party system in the South, where some Republicans swept into office in those states where Goldwater had won. Over the next four years Thurmond consolidated his position in the national party, his voice becoming influential as well as demanding. He had something Richard Nixon wanted—he could deliver a lot of southern votes—and he would exact a high price.

And then, of course, there was Richard Nixon himself. He had not been idle in 1964. It was the first national campaign in twelve years in which he had not been a candidate. Because he lacked a political base after his move from California to New York and lacked money and support after his defeats in 1960 and 1962, Nixon's only hope for 1964 had lain in a deadlock between the extreme liberal and extreme conservative candidates, Nelson Rockefeller and Barry Goldwater, during which the Republican leaders would remember his long service to the party and the narrowness of his 1960 defeat while blocking out, of course, his defeat for the California governorship. The deadlock had never come.

When Goldwater was nominated, Nixon was realist enough to recognize certain inevitabilities of the future. One was Goldwater's defeat, probably a spectacular one, in November. The other was the Republicans' need for a candidate for 1968 who was not an extremist of either liberal or conservative persuasion. Never one to let opportunity go begging, Nixon and some of his close political aides, shortly before the Republican convention of 1964, had gone out to Montauk Point on the southern fork of Long Island, a favorite retreat of Nixon's, and begun to plan for the next four years.

Outward signs of Nixon's 1968 candidacy had appeared at the 1964 convention. James Bassett, an old friend and former aide, had written in the *Los Angeles Times:*

> In certain quieter rooms of this . . . convention . . . an informal group of erstwhile GOP leaders is earnestly working to make Richard Nixon the party's nominee for President. Not this year, however, but in 1968. They are proceeding on the rather melancholy assumption that Arizona's Senator Barry Goldwater won't make it. "After November," they ask rhetorically, "who better than Nixon can rebuild the Republican Party? In fact, who'll be left?"
>
> . . . At 51, identified with the GOP center, Nixon would be the likeliest man to weld together the dissident elements of right and left. This he would accomplish by persuasion, by conferences, by speechmaking, by traveling, and by writing. . . .

Which is exactly what Nixon did. When Goldwater had invited Republican liberals not to campaign for him, it was Nixon who had tried to repair the damage to party unity. Although Nixon believed the presidential candidate "inept," when Goldwater had needed help in his campaign, it was Nixon who had made a thirty-three-day, thirty-six-state, 50,000-mile tour in the candidate's behalf—a tour which happened to offer Nixon also the opportunity to reestablish his credentials with local party leaders and earn a little gratitude from the new Goldwaterites who could prove a significant factor in the next presidential election. He had added another dimension to his political image: good old Dick Nixon, always available, ready to buck you up as well as congratulate you, to help when you need him. No job was too tough. Reliable, that's what he was. Plucky, too.

Two days after Goldwater's defeat, during which the Republican party had been left in an "extreme state of disarray," Nixon had held a press conference in which he had made a strong plea for Republicans to reunite. He had decided that he himself would assume responsibility for getting them together, a job he believed would confer on him "a significant advantage in the race for the 1968 presidential nomination."

He did not add that to his New Year's resolutions as he sat in front of the fire after dinner on that January night in 1965. It was much too early for that. But, he later said, that night "I started not only to think seriously about running for the presidency again but to think about where I would begin."

About two weeks later, on January 22, a grateful Barry Goldwater introduced Nixon at a Republican National Committee meeting in Chicago as the hardest-working member of the Republican team in 1964, then added his personal thanks.

"Dick," said Goldwater, "I will never forget it. I know that you did it in the interests of the Republican Party and not for any selfish reasons. But if there ever comes a time I can turn those into selfish reasons, I am going to do all I can to see that it comes about."

By spring 1965 Nixon was lunching regularly at The Recess, an exclusive club at 60 Broad Street, with political aides and Republican eastern establishment figures to discuss 1968. By summer 1965 voters polled by Gallup would choose him as the best Republican to run in 1968, with a lead of nearly two to one over his nearest rival. In mid-1965 Maurice Stans, who had directed the Bureau of the Budget under Eisenhower, began to remedy Nixon's financial handicaps.

Out of the presidential election of 1964 had emerged the participants in the next one. As they came into sharper focus over the next four years, it became clear that George Wallace, Strom Thurmond, and Richard Nixon, each in his own way, were to influence substantially the administration of criminal justice in America.

CHAPTER 4

The issues raised in Danny Escobedo's case did not die with the demise of Senator Barry Goldwater in presidential politics. They became, rather, a major subject for debate and discussion at judicial conferences and bar association meetings, in law reviews and the public press, and even within Washington officialdom, thus raising the temperature of the controversy considerably and emphasizing the urgency of the situation.

In August 1964, less than two months after the U.S. Supreme Court's decision in *Escobedo*, James Vorenberg of the Harvard Law School faculty and director of the American Law Institute's new project to devise a model code of pre-arraignment procedure, addressed the annual meeting of the Conference of Chief Justices in New York City. The group, particularly in recent years, had been vulnerable to—and critical of—review by the United States Supreme Court.

For Vorenberg, it was less a question of what was happening in the matter of taking confessions from criminal suspects than of "How soon?" and he would not be "shocked," he said, "if the Supreme Court should lay down a flat rule barring confessions obtained from suspects—indigent or not—who have not been furnished with an opportunity to talk to a lawyer. *Escobedo* certainly points in this direction." So did several decisions handed down in state court cases. It would be far better, he suggested, if the separate states developed "their own protective procedures" rather than wait on U.S. Supreme Court action.

In June 1965 the first draft of the American Law Institute's "Model Code of Pre-Arraignment Procedure" had been submitted for comment to a

Chapter 4

three-day meeting of an advisory committee made up of prominent legal scholars, judges, prosecutors, police, and lawyers. The draft, a preliminary note explained, represented an attempt to "strike a compromise between giving full scope to the demands of law enforcement and maximum protection to persons involved in investigation of a crime." It recommended "dragnet" arrests as well as leeway for police to question a suspect for up to twenty-four hours after his arrival at a police station. While the model code would have permitted a suspect to retain counsel during interrogation, it failed to provide counsel for those too poor to afford it or too ignorant, inexperienced, or frightened to request it.

On June 16 Chief Judge David L. Bazelon of the U.S. Court of Appeals for the District of Columbia Circuit wrote a long letter to Nicholas deBelleville Katzenbach, who had been appointed the previous February to succeed Robert Kennedy as attorney general of the United States and who as deputy attorney general had been vigorous in enforcing civil rights. In his letter the judge focused on that very aspect of the draft code, suggesting it would be applied inequitably, that the disadvantaged would suffer—people like Ernest Miranda, who had explained following his being taken to police headquarters, "I didn't know whether I had a choice. I got in the car . . ." and following his interrogation, ". . . knowing what a penitentiary is like, a person has to be frightened, scared. And not knowing if he'll be able to get back up and go home." Bazelon believed, he said, the new attorney general might "share my misgivings" about those sections of the model code draft. The judge wrote:

> These provisions would, in my experience, primarily affect the poor and, in particular, the poor Negro citizen. I doubt that the police would, for example, arrest and question the entire board of directors of a company suspected of criminal anti-trust violations. . . . I cannot understand why the crimes of the poor are so much more damaging to society as to warrant the current hue and cry—reflected in the proposed code—for enlarging police powers which primarily are directed against those crimes. . . .

Katzenbach's answer, on June 24, surprised a lot of people. The new attorney general indeed did *not* share the judge's "misgivings." On the contrary, Katzenbach replied:

> The underlying assumption of your approach appears to be some conception of equality. . . . It would be ridiculous to state that the overriding purpose of any criminal investigation is to insure equal treatment. Obviously criminal investigation is designed to discover those guilty of crime. . . . Your suggestion that police questioning will primarily affect the poor and, in particular, the poor Negro, strikes me as particularly irrelevant. The simple fact is that poverty is often a breeding ground for criminal conduct and that inevitably any code of procedure is likely to affect more poor people than rich people. I do not think the dissimilarities in outcome for the rich

47

and poor are so great as you suggest. The failure to arrest a Board of Directors for questioning about an anti-trust violation does not strike me as an example of unequal treatment. The investigations of anti-trust violations and of violent urban crime are simply not comparable, and the anonymity and mobility of modern urban life often do not permit postponement of arrest when crimes of violence are involved. . . .

The exchange of letters was circulated among legal scholars across the nation, and finally, the *Washington Star* obtained the two letters, which it published on August 4. Publication in other newspapers as well as national magazines followed. Becoming a national news story, the Bazelon-Katzenbach correspondence, because of the authors' stature, gave the controversy added dimension and put it within the public's reach.

As if to underline the urgency of the problem of interrogation and confessions, on January 27, 1965, New York City District Attorney Frank Hogan, head of the most respected prosecutor's office in the nation, had suddenly dropped murder charges against George Whitmore, Jr. An illiterate nineteen-year-old black, Whitmore had been convicted the previous year of the 1963 murders of two young women in their East Eighty-eighth Street apartment on the basis of a confession he had made to police officers after twenty-two hours of secret questioning. It had been a sensational case and a gruesome one, the girls having been slashed to death, and police were understandably nervous. After eight months of investigation they had finally arrested Whitmore as the murderer and, as was their custom—New York City police at the time relied on confessions for about 50 percent of their convictions in homicide cases—questioned the young man until he "confessed."

"We got the right guy," the chief of detectives said afterward, "no question about it."

Now, however, in the first month of 1965, thanks to the further investigations of a skeptical assistant district attorney, the sixty page, typewritten, meticulously detailed "confession" had been totally discredited. Another man had been arrested; he was later convicted.

However great the urgency, the problems surrounding the taking of confessions were not going to be solved without considerable judicial debate. As cases involving *Escobedo* issues made their way through the courts, both state and federal, the American judicial community polarized. At one pole stood those lower-court judges who interpreted *Escobedo* broadly—that is, to mean the assistance of counsel must be furnished an accused in the interrogation room unless he or she actually waived the requirement, even though counsel had not been requested. At the other pole stood those lower-court judges content to limit *Escobedo* to the facts and circumstances of that case—that is, counsel must be provided when the accused requested it upon being taken into custody, as Danny Escobedo had. The Arizona Supreme Court justices belonged to the latter group.

On April 22, 1965, the five justices of the Arizona Supreme Court, sitting *en banc*, as was customary in capital and other important cases, handed down their decision in the case of Ernest Miranda. The author of the opinion was Ernest W. McFarland, sixty-nine years old, a former U.S. senator and Democratic majority leader during the Truman administration as well as a former governor of Arizona. He was the court's newest member, having been elected to it only the previous November. The decision was unanimous. Ernest Miranda's conviction for kidnapping and rape was affirmed.

The heart of the opinion was McFarland's distinguishing the circumstances in Ernest Miranda's case from those in Danny Escobedo's. The justice listed the circumstances he believed *Escobedo* v. *Illinois* required before a suspect's constitutional rights could be said to have been denied:

(1) The general inquiry into an unsolved crime must have begun to focus on a particular suspect;

(2) The suspect must have been taken into police custody;

(3) The police in its interrogation must have elicited an incriminating statement;

(4) The suspect must have requested and been denied an opportunity to consult with his lawyer; and

(5) The police must not have effectively warned the suspect of his constitutional right to remain silent.

Ernest Miranda had met the first three criteria, but unlike Escobedo, Miranda had not, so far as is known, requested an attorney at that stage, and he had not been positively refused one. Whether or not he had been advised of his constitutional right to remain silent was a matter of dispute. McFarland resolved it this way:

Defendant had a record which indicated that he was not without courtroom experience . . . he was certainly not unfamiliar with legal proceedings and his rights in court. The police testified they had informed the defendant of his rights, and he stated in his written confession that he understood his rights (which would certainly include the right to counsel), and it is not for this court to dispute his statement that he did. His experience under previous cases would indicate that his statement that he understood his rights was true.

Finally, McFarland concluded, the facts of Ernest Miranda's case indicated that his confession to Officers Cooley and Young had been voluntary, that he had not been coerced in any way, that neither detective had made any threats or promises, and that Miranda had thoroughly understood his rights.

49

His constitutional rights had not been denied, his confession had been properly obtained, and his conviction was affirmed.*

But not without Justice McFarland's describing again the centuries-old controversy, at the core of the criminal law, that was to intensify and increasingly, over the next decade or more, to occupy the hearts and minds of presidents, legislators, lawyers, constitutional scholars, police, judges and the public: What price security?

> What is the purpose of the right to counsel? . . . [W]ithout question it is to protect the individual rights which we cherish, but there must be a balance between the competing interests of society and the rights of the individual. Society has the right of protection against those who roam the streets for the purpose of violating the law, but that protection must not be at the expense of the rights of the individual.

The decision of the Arizona Supreme Court brought temporary relief to prosecutors all over the state who had feared that courts might decide to require defense counsel at every police interrogation. But even the prosecutors knew the relief was only temporary, that judges and lawyers were looking for ways to open the station house, to reveal its secrets, and that sooner or later—probably sooner—they would find ways.

The uneasiness was nationwide. There was also uncertainty within law enforcement communities as courts continued to divide on how the unresolved issues in Danny Escobedo's case should be settled. The United States Court of Appeals for the Seventh Circuit (Wisconsin, Illinois, Indiana) and state courts in Maryland, Illinois, Virginia, Ohio, and Wisconsin had resolved them the way Justice McFarland had for the Arizona Surpeme Court, holding strictly to the facts and circumstances of *Escobedo*. The U.S. Court of appeals for the Second Circuit (Vermont, New York, Connecticut) and state courts in California, Oregon, Massachusetts, and Tennessee had extended *Escobedo* and insisted that counsel must be provided an accused even though it had not been requested. Ernest Miranda's conviction probably would have been reversed had his case been heard in a court in the latter group.

FBI Director J. Edgar Hoover and the assistant attorney general in charge of the Criminal Division of the Justice Department were hastily attempting to formulate uniform rules for FBI agents to follow during investigative interviews and for United States attorneys to follow regarding the use of evidence in the courts. Hoover feared that with the law "at present in a state of flux," a suspect's confession to an FBI agent in San Francisco might well be invalid in the District of Columbia if the case were prosecuted "be-

---

* On the same day the Arizona Supreme Court unanimously also affirmed Miranda's conviction on the companion robbery charge.

fore a judge whose view on the propriety of the interview is different from that prevailing in the Federal court in San Francisco."

If that state of judicial affairs did not present anomaly enough, courts in New Jersey and Pennsylvania had interpreted *Escobedo* to mean that counsel must be requested; on May 20, 1965, the U.S. Court of Appeals for the Third Circuit (Pennsylvania, New Jersey, Delaware, the Virgin Islands), for all practical purposes the ultimate authority for state trial courts operating within that circuit, concluded the opposite: that no request for counsel was necessary. A few weeks later, on June 9, tensions increased when the chief justice of the New Jersey Supreme Court directed all New Jersey state judges to ignore the federal ruling. The situation, said a justice of the Pennsylvania Supreme Court, in a classic example of judicial understatement, "creates a serious problem for this Court and jeopardizes the finality of our judgment. . . ."

There was also dissension within courts, although none perhaps so vocal—nor so significant for the future—as that within the United States Court of Appeals for the District of Columbia Circuit.

Although this court functioned as a standard federal appellate court no different from the courts in the other ten circuits, it also functioned at the time as a state supreme court in the sense that it was, until the entire District of Columbia court system was redesigned in 1971, the highest appellate court for citizens of the federal enclave. Life in the national capital, behind the marble monuments and the office buildings where policies affecting an entire nation were forged, went on much as in any other city. Of the 2 million people who lived in the metropolitan area—which included adjacent Maryland and Virginia suburbs—nearly 13 percent worked in the main local industry, government. Those of the rest who were not lawyers were dentists, plumbers, accountants, clerks, waiters, furniture salesmen, policemen, firemen, and undertakers. They watched television and followed the waning fortunes of the Washington Senators baseball team. They had automobile accidents, sued their neighbors, got divorces, and committed crimes. The rate at which they committed crimes exceeded that of most American cities.

The ninth largest city in the nation, Washington ranked fourth in total criminal offenses, second in murders, third in aggravated assault, fourth in robbery and burglary, fifth in auto theft, and seventh in forcible rape and larceny. The statistics took on more meaning when the wife of a State Department official, walking her dogs in Montrose Park on the edge of the fashionable Georgetown section of Washington, was raped by three teen-agers, a twenty-three-year-old embassy secretary was raped in her apartment, and seven children were stabbed in Lincoln Park in the northeast, largely black section of the city. Crime played no favorites; all parts of the city were vulnerable. It was cases like these that came to the U.S. Court of appeals for the District of Columbia Circuit, the highest local court with appellate jurisdiction in criminal matters at the time.

Two ideologically opposed blocs of judges, their public brawling a fact of Washington legal life since the mid-1950s, divided the local appeals court in 1964–65, their acrimony, which was rumored to have spilled over into personal relationships, apparent in the frequency of their dissents and passion of their opinions and, occasionally, in their extra-judicial writings and speeches. One bloc was led by Chief Judge David Lionel Bazelon, who had been appointed to the court in 1950 by Democratic President Harry Truman and who had recently written to Attorney General Katzenbach objecting strongly to the way the poor would be treated under the early draft of the American Law Institute's model code of pre-arraignment procedure. The other bloc was led by Warren Earl Burger, appointed to the court in 1956 by Republican Dwight Eisenhower, who, in his endorsement of 1964 Republican presidential candidate Barry Goldwater, had made public his distaste for society's "maudlin sympathy for the criminal who, roaming the street with switch-blade knife and illegal firearms seeking a helpless prey, suddenly becomes upon apprehension a poor, underprivileged person who counts upon the compassion of our society and the laxness or weakness of too many courts to forgive his offense"—a distaste his appointee shared.

Judges Burger and Bazelon both were midwesterners: Burger came from St. Paul, Minnesota; Bazelon had been born in Superior, Wisconsin, and spent his youth in Chicago. Both men came themselves from poor backgrounds: Burger was the son of a railroad cargo inspector who supplemented his income occasionally as a traveling salesman of candy, coffee, or patent medicine; Bazelon was the son of a storekeeper; both had worked hard for their law school tuition. Both judges had served as assistant attorneys general before they were appointed to the federal court. And because the court on which they sat, the home court for the federal government, was a national court deciding—in addition to local criminal cases—significant issues of public law (it was often called the "second most" important court), both men were highly visible. Two judges on this court already had been appointed to the U.S. Supreme Court: Wiley B. Rutledge and Fred M. Vinson, the latter as chief justice. It was common-change knowledge that when a Democrat was in the White House, David Bazelon at least had to be on the list of candidates when a vacancy occurred on the Supreme Court; in the future, if a Republican were elected, Warren Burger could not be ignored. Their positions were not unlike those of the governors of New York and California when presidential elections lay ahead.

The judicial positions of the two men and their followers had become so solidified that the outcome of a case involving *Escobedo* issues depended upon the make-up of the panel* of judges that heard it. Warren Burger's bloc closely matched the dissenters to *Escobedo* and allied itself judicially with law enforcement. This group would have decided Ernest Miranda's case the

---

* All but the most significant cases were heard and decided by three-judge panels.

way the Arizona Supreme Court had. In 1964–65 Burger himself had decided for the government against defendants in 77 percent of the criminal cases in which he was involved. David Bazelon's bloc supported and was supported by the judicial decisions of the Warren Court and in its opinions interpreted broadly the principles laid down by the majority in *Escobedo*. This bloc probably would have reversed Ernest Miranda's conviction. In the eighteen months following the U.S. Supreme Court's decision in *Escobedo*, eleven cases involving *Escobedo* issues, either tangentially or as the main issue, came before the U.S. Court of Appeals for the District of Columbia Circuit. The results were typical of that court. Of the eleven cases, convictions in six were affirmed, all but one—in which the *Escobedo* issue was peripheral—by panels on which Burger bloc judges were in the majority. In five of the eleven cases, convictions were reversed, all by panels on which Bazelon bloc judges were in the majority.

The rivalries, the controversies, the judicial splits which the writings of Burger and Bazelon publicized, what each stood for pointed up with particular clarity the issues that divided the nation's courts, setting federal and state judges, eastern and western judges, northern and southern judges against each other following *Escobedo*. Indeed, the divisions among the judges of the U.S. Court of Appeals for the District of Columbia Circuit, like the divisions within the Supreme Court itself, pointed up the major questions being asked during those turbulent times about the administration of criminal justice: How to balance, in Arizona Supreme Court Justice McFarland's phrase, "the competing interests of society and the rights of the individual"?

The "interests of society" were championed by Warren Burger. The "rights of the individual" were championed by David Bazelon.

Warren Burger was outspoken and insistent, his principles firmly established, his confidence in the rightness of his convictions imperturbable, at least publicly. His friends called his opinions "solid," "vigorous," "forceful." His enemies called them "belligerent," "contentious," "vinegary." Generally he took a functional analysis approach to the Constitution, with efficiency of administration and social considerations given more weight than individual rights—in which position he stood in direct opposition to the trends in the administration of criminal justice established by the Warren Court in the 1960s.

It was not that he would deny justice to the individual; he was no legal ingenue, and he was familiar with what went on in the station houses of America. Although his legal practice in St. Paul prior to his coming to Washington had been limited largely to the establishment of trusts and the settling of estates—not, of course, for the Ernest Mirandas and Danny Escobedos of the community—he had paid his social dues. As a founder of the St. Paul Human Relations Council, a civic organization dedicated to improving racial relations in the city, Burger had devoted a considerable amount of his considerable energy to the racial desegregation of his hometown, and St. Paulites long recalled his role in appealing the case of a black college student who, he believed, had been unjustly convicted of a crime.

But Burger believed that in the 1960s the price of justice had become intolerably inflated. In its heightened concern for protecting the constitutional rights of the criminal defendant, the United States Supreme Court under Earl Warren, through its tone as well as its decisions like *Escobedo*, was causing the overloading of the American criminal justice system until it barely worked at all. Defendants who in the past would have pleaded guilty early on glimpsed hope of freedom in the new rules and insisted on going to trial, dramatically increasing the number of trials. Courtroom procedures had become considerably more complicated, multiplying the amount of time required to dispose of each case. Appeals based on the new rulings also multiplied. As a result of these developments, court dockets had become congested beyond all judicial imagination, and the courts had come almost to a standstill. While one lawyer fought for justice for his client, fifty men and women were waiting for their turns at the same courtroom door. Justice delayed, Burger said many times, was indeed justice denied, and not all the procedural protections of the defendant devised by courts compensated for the justice denied by the hopelessly overburdened court dockets.

For Burger, *Escobedo* epitomized the difficulties the courts faced. Having generated a "rash of sweeping claims" by attorneys, particularly attorneys for the poor who felt duty-bound to adjust their clients' circumstances to every new court ruling, it was, Burger declared, being overrelied on as "the sovereign remedy to cure the ailments of every accused." The delays that resulted only defeated the purposes of the soaring phrases, and the ideals lost their meaning.

Underneath the rhetoric lay what appeared to be a judicial cosmology that assumed the benevolence of government, the view that law enforcement officers at this advanced stage of civilization were essentially decent, fair men, and reasonable overstepping of procedural bounds ought to be allowed as they went about their difficult task of collecting evidence against criminals (closer in time, perhaps, to the rack and the screw, the authors of the U.S. Constitution seemed to view government, particularly its law enforcement arm, as at least fallible and possibly malevolent). Burger and the other judges in that bloc on the court of appeals tended to trust police and prosecutors and to allow them considerable latitude, dismissing procedural irregularities as "technicalities" and trial errors as "harmless."

David Bazelon and his group of judges on the local federal appellate court held opposing judicial views. In 1954 Bazelon had written his court's most famous opinion, that deciding the case of Monte Durham, a convicted felon with a record of mental illness. It threw open the insanity defense to reexamination in the light of developments in psychology, psychiatry, and sociology and stimulated judicial interest in modernizing the old rules. A longtime student of the behavioral sciences, Bazelon tended to seek out the causes of criminal behavior in external forces. A core question was, he once wrote:

> Whether a free choice to do wrong can be found in the acts of a poverty-stricken and otherwise deprived black youth from the central city who kills a Marine who taunted him with a racial epithet, in the act of a "modern Jean Valjean" who steals to feed his family, in the act of a narcotics addict who buys drugs for his own use, or in the act of a superpatriot, steeped in cold war ideology who burglarizes in the name of "national security"?

His opinions were replete with similar questions, and more than his colleagues, he seemed to see the criminal as victim as well as victimizer. There could be no true criminal justice without social justice. Bazelon had become, by 1964, a respected, if controversial judicial figure—one critic called his views "welfare criminology"—and a leading authority on mental health and the law.

For Bazelon bloc judges, an accused was not guilty legally unless the entire criminal process conformed to the letter as well as to the spirit of the law. There could be no procedural irregularities, and errors were often considered harmful. Closely resembling that of the Warren Court majority, it was an approach that by definition elevated the *rights* of the individual and the *responsibilities* of police, prosecutors, and trial judges. These judges, out of suspicion of government, held law enforcement to the highest procedural standards. Their deepest commitment was to due process of law.

The facts in each criminal case were, of course, quite different, and of those that came to the federal appeals court during the period following the U.S. Supreme Court's decision in *Escobedo*, none presented exactly the same circumstances and conditions as had Danny Escobedo's. Warren Burger's bloc, while meticulously acknowledging that *Escobedo* was the law of the land and that its restraints must be enforced, had little trouble in distinguishing the facts and circumstances of the cases before it and those in Danny Escobedo's. The Bazelon bloc, on the other hand, had little trouble in finding close analogies between the cases before the local court and Danny Escobedo's.

There was also a fundamental difference in emphasis. For the *Escobedo* ruling to be applied, by Burger bloc standards, police must have taken positive action against a suspect, as they had against Danny Escobedo when they actually prevented him from conferring with his lawyer. The *Escobedo* ruling, Burger declared in a majority opinion in June 1965, a year after *Escobedo* had been decided by the U.S. Supreme Court, was "not to be read as rendering inadmissible all uncounseled utterances made by an accused person. . . ." It must, rather, be read narrowly, "in light of its facts and especially

55

of the purposeful exclusion of appellant's waiting lawyer from an opportunity to counsel his client while police pursued their interrogation."

Judges of the Bazelon bloc applied the *Escobedo* ruling not only when police took affirmative action against a suspect but also when they merely neglected certain procedures. Dissenting in the same case, George T. Washington, generally a member of the Bazelon group of judges, admitted that the suspect had been given the routine warnings and been informed of his right to retain counsel; however, he added, "the majority seems to focus on the fact that appellant had not requested a lawyer prior to his interview with police ... the right to counsel does not depend on a request by the defendant." Washington would have reversed the man's conviction.

Where one judge would punish only sins of commission, another would also punish sins of omission.

In a nutshell, that was the controversy in which the nation's judges were involved during the troubled period following *Escobedo*. It was as old as established government and as new as tomorrow's case. Even now, while the Warren Court was proceeding in one direction, another judicial era was in the making, and the judicial personality of Warren Burger was emerging as a force in it.

Warren Burger had a natural warmth and a genuine liking for people, and according to one who knew him in his earliest days on the court, the most difficult part of the transition from assistant attorney general to judge was not in the work but in the adaptation to the relative isolation of the United States courthouse after the bustle of the Justice Department and daily contact with high-echelon government officials. By the mid-1960s he had begun to emerge from his isolation.

At the same time that Burger was establishing his credentials as a conservative judge, he was also rising from obscurity in the reserved but real forum of judicial politics to earn a national reputation. Appointed for life, the members of the federal judiciary do not run for office, and the federal judge is often perceived as an apolitical creature. The image is deceptive. There are several channels for judicial ambition within the profession, and Warren Burger was involved in them.

One channel of ambition was the law school lecture, where judges established their intellectual credentials. To be invited to give the Oliver Wendell Holmes lectures at Harvard, the Carpentier lectures at Columbia, the James Madison lectures at New York University added to one's prestige and prominence. Other law schools sponsored less prestigious but not professionally unnoticed lectureships, and Warren Burger was invited to give the Fourth Annual Edwin A. Mooers Lecture at the Washington College of Law of the American University in the District of Columbia in April 1964. The previous week David Bazelon, in an address given as part of the Edward Douglass White lecture series at Georgetown University, had told his audience: "We are beginning to realize that the rising crime rate is not caused merely by weak law enforcement. Poverty in all its manifestations . . . is the chief factor producing antisocial behaviors. . . . A successful war on poverty would come close to solving the crime problem." In contrast, Burger spoke on the advantages of strengthening law enforcement, taking for his text the controversial exclusionary rule.

The device the U.S. Supreme Court had come up with in 1914 to answer the question of what was to be done about police misconduct in the apprehension of criminals was called the exclusionary rule, or, as Judge Burger generally referred to it, the Suppression Doctrine: evidence which had been obtained illegally—confessions obtained in the way Danny Escobedo's had been obtained, for example—could not be admitted as evidence in court but must be excluded, or suppressed.

The exclusionary rule was Warren Burger's particular evidentiary bugaboo. It had divided lawyers and judges, prosecutors and police for the half century since its establishment. Its application could free a murderer or an innocent man; the failure to apply it could result in the conviction of a murderer—or of an innocent man. In the public's mind, a judge's use of it, sparingly or extravagantly, often characterized him as either a hanging judge or a coddler of criminals.

Judge Burger subscribed to what Robert H. Jackson had written for the majority of the U.S. Supreme Court in 1954: "That the rule of exclusion and reversal results in the escape of guilty persons is more capable of demonstration than that it deters invasions of right by the police." In short, it didn't work.

It didn't work, Burger said later, because it rested on a false assumption: that "we can deter Peter by punishing Paul." He suggested to the local law school audience that day that society redirect its efforts and instead of relying on an unreliable rule to regulate police behavior, go to the root of the problem. One remedy he had thought of, he said—and it was his custom to offer proposals for future debate—was establishment by communities of independent (predominantly civilian) commissions to investigate complaints of unlawful behavior on the part of law enforcement officers, to hold hearings, and to recommend appropriate penalties: in effect, to deal with Peter directly.

He warned, in a judicial paraphrase of Barry Goldwater's campaign rhetoric a few months later—what Goldwater said from the gut, Burger said from the cerebrum—many people were "losing respect for the law and the administration of justice because they think that the Suppression Doctrine is *defeating* justice," and, he concluded, a frantic edge developing in the tone of his message, "the wrath of public opinion may descend alike on police and judges if we persist in the view that suppression is a solution. . . . We can well ponder whether any community is entitled to call itself an 'organized society' if it can find no way to solve this problem except by suppression of the truth in the search for truth."

Burger's was an important judicial white paper, although the significance for the future of criminal justice could hardly have been recognized at the time.

Another important outlet for judicial ambition was the bar association, where ability, interest, and a willingness to work traditionally have been recognized through committee appointments—David Bazelon for some years had been a member of ABA committees concerned with mental illness and the law. In August 1964, three months after *Escobedo*, Warren Burger had been appointed to a prestigious ABA subcommittee. At its annual meeting the American Bar Association had authorized a three-year $750,000 project for the study of American criminal justice. Like the American Law Institute's projected formulation of a model code of pre-arraignment procedure, the ABA study was expected to produce a set of guidelines on which officials involved in state and other local criminal justice systems could draw.

When ABA president Lewis F. Powell, Jr., who three years later as a dissenter to the report of a presidential crime commission indicated his disapproval of the U.S. Supreme Court's decision in *Escobedo*, and committee chairman J. Edward Lumbard, then chief judge of the U.S. Court of Appeals for the Second Circuit and inclined in his opinions for that court to interpret *Escobedo* narrowly, were looking for a chairman for the subcommittee which was to devise guidelines for defense and prosecution lawyers, Burger's name stood out. Burger had not been particularly active in ABA committee work in the past—he had served on only two (from 1950 to 1952 as Minnesota representative on the professional Ethics and Grievances Committee and in 1961 on the Judges' Advisory Committee to the Professional Ethics Committee) and never on any of the various committees involved in the administration of criminal justice. But Lumbard knew Burger as a "topnotch" judge. Becoming acquainted when Lumbard was U.S. attorney for the Southern District of New York and Burger an assistant attorney general, they had sat together as judges during one of Judge Burger's visits to the Second Circuit and had kept in touch. Lumbard was aware that Burger's eight years as a federal judge on a court with a criminal docket larger than those of many other federal courts had afforded him considerable experience in criminal matters. Burger was, Powell and Lumbard decided, a suitable appointment, and he was made chairman of the Advisory Committee on the Prosecution and Defense Functions.

Sitting on a court with national visibility and influence, Warren Burger was beginning to make himself known, within the judicial community at least, as a thoughtful commentator and craftsman of the law. He had not yet drawn particular attention outside the legal community. But he had personal charm, considerable energy, and strong opinions on the significant issues which were dividing the American public as well as all those involved in the administration of criminal justice since *Escobedo*. More important, perhaps, he had aligned himself philosophically with the Republican party and its

1964 candidate for president and had joined in the backlash to the Warren Court.

It was here, during these years on the U.S. Court of Appeals for the District of Columbia Circuit, that Warren Burger was coming to life and light judicially, that the road to the chief justiceship of the United States began.

CHAPTER 5

For the two years since his trial in June 1963, Ernest Miranda had been an inmate of the Arizona State Prison, a maximum-security institution with red-roofed Spanish-style buildings, nestled in the desert hills outside Florence, that obscured the tiers of metal-barred cells inside and belied its grim mission. Although he had no idea that his case was being swept into the current of legal history, Miranda sensed that he had not received full justice at the hands of the state, and like hundreds of similarly situated prisoners across the nation, he filed a request for his case to be reviewed by the U.S. Supreme Court following the decision against him in the Arizona Supreme Court.

Requests like Miranda's—the petitions for certiorari—came into the United States Supreme Court by the hundreds each term: more than 1,600 the year Miranda submitted his. They bore censors' stamps from Joliet, Illinois; Lewisburg, Pennsylvania; Lorton, Virginia; Raiford, Florida; Leavenworth, Kansas; Ossining, New York; and Florence, Arizona. Some were hand-written in pencil or crayon on dime-store paper; others were painstakingly typewritten. Many were in stiff, formal legalese, betraying the influence of the jailhouse lawyer.

Some had merit; most did not, and the Supreme Court usually dismissed 70 percent of them without discussion. All were pathetic. Partly for the quality of the materials with which they were written and partly for the quality of the arguments they presented, law clerks to the justices referred to them as flimsies.

Ernest Miranda was appealing in forma pauperis, "in the way of a pauper," which meant that because of his lack of means, he need not pay the

Chapter 5

$100 filing fee for docketing his case in the Supreme Court and need submit only one petition rather than the usually required forty copies. He *was* required, though, to attach an affidavit confirming his inability to pay and a copy of the final judgment of the Arizona Supreme Court, both of which he failed to attach. The clerk of the U.S. Supreme Court, on June 18, 1965, returned Miranda's petition for certiorari to him with the explanation that these last items were missing.

Meanwhile, Miranda's case had come to the attention of the Phoenix chapter of the American Civil Liberties Union (ACLU). Nationally, for nearly fifty years, the ACLU had provided volunteers to represent in both lower and appellate courts individuals of every political color and conviction whose constitutional rights were believed to have been violated. Clarence Darrow's famous defense in 1925 of John Thomas Scopes's right to teach the theory of evolution in the Dayton, Tennessee, public schools had been ACLU-sponsored. The organization had participated in the Sacco-Vanzetti proceedings and in the litigation involved in bringing James Joyce's *Ulysses* to the United States. It also had defended the Ku Klux Klan and the German American Bund. Before he was appointed to the U.S. Supreme Court, Felix Frankfurter had been a member of its board, and it counted some of the nation's most prominent lawyers among its volunteers: Morris Ernst, Arthur Garfield Hays, Osmond K. Fraenkel. By the 1970s it would be involved in more U.S. Supreme Court litigation than anyone except the solicitor general and would have established a drawing account of something in the neighborhood of $15 million worth of legal work with some of the most prestigious firms and law schools in America.

The Phoenix office in 1965 was run by Robert J. Corcoran, a volunteer, who had recently left the Maricopa County attorney's office and entered the private practice of law. His job was to engage attorneys for all those local people, many of whom had real and "substantial constitutional and legal claims for redress," who were not represented by counsel in the courts only because they could not pay the legal fees.

On June 15, 1965, in looking over the *Pacific Reporter* advance sheets—the unbound announcements of recent court decisions in the Pacific states—for current judicial developments, Corcoran had noticed the April 22 decision of the Arizona Supreme Court in Ernest Miranda's case. As a former deputy county attorney he was entirely familiar with Arizona law surrounding the taking of confessions and with the requirements of law enforcement officers in the apprehension of criminals. When he himself had been assigned to interrogate a major suspect in a criminal case, he had been fastidious about informing the suspect of the right to remain silent, the right to the assistance of an attorney, and the fact that anything said could be used against him or her. In all the time he was deputy county attorney, he never lost a confession to the Constitution, and he believed that the matter was ripe for consideration by the United States Supreme Court.

61

The same day Corcoran wrote Miranda's court-appointed lawyer, Alvin Moore, and told him so. Although the ACLU could not pay more than out-of-pocket expenses, he told Moore, the organization was interested in getting the case before the U.S. Supreme Court and would help Moore in its preparation. He explained that the California Supreme Court had already expanded on the U.S. Supreme Court's *Escobedo* ruling, holding that an accused "*must* be advised that he does have the right to counsel. . . ." However, he lamented, "Our supreme court is limiting *Escobedo* to its facts and will only apply it when Danny Escobedo comes to Arizona and kills his brother-in-law and all of the same circumstances ensue as had occurred in Illinois."

Detective Cooley had advanced the argument that because Miranda was an ex-convict, he already knew his rights. The Arizona Supreme Court had advanced the same argument in its decision in Miranda's case. If it were so that ex-convicts knew all about the law, Corcoran added in his letter to Moore, "I believe your experience confirms mine that . . . we would both have defended and I certainly would have prosecuted people who would have been entitled to receive an LL.D." The assumption by courts that "two prior felony convictions are equal to two years of law school" might also be reviewable in the U.S. Supreme Court, Corcoran suggested.

Alvin Moore declined to take Miranda's case to the U.S. Supreme Court, citing a lack of funds and a lack of physical stamina. But Corcoran had other resources. He was at about this same time in touch with Rex E. Lee, a young Phoenix attorney recently arrived from Washington, where he had been a law clerk to Justice Byron White of the U.S. Supreme Court. From time to time Corcoran had gone to Lee for advice on such matters as Supreme Court procedures, and he took Miranda's case to the ex-clerk.*

"You know, this is the next big one," Rex Lee told the ACLU attorney. Lee had clerked for White the year *Escobedo* was decided.

"Would you like to take it up?" Corcoran asked.

"Brother, would I ever!" Lee replied. "This is a reputation maker to end all reputation makers!"

But he could not. A Supreme Court rule prohibited its ex-clerks from practicing before it for two years.†

Corcoran next telephoned John J. Flynn, chief trial attorney at Lewis, Roca, Scoville, Beauchamps, & Linton, one of the city's largest and most reputable law firms—thirty lawyers and a Washington, D.C., office. Prestigious though it was, the firm devoted considerable time and effort to unpaid public

---

* Law clerks to the justices are recent law school graduates who spend a term or two as assistants to the justices, a custom begun by Justice Horace Gray. At the time Rex Lee was clerk to White, each justice had two clerks and the chief justice had three. Their duties varied, depending upon the needs of the individual justice they served. They should not be confused with the clerk of the Supreme Court, a permanent court office, established in 1790, to deal with the Court's paper work.

† In 1981 Lee, then dean of the Brigham Young University Law School, was appointed solicitor general of the United States by President Ronald Reagan.

service, and it was a matter of some comment in the community that one could commonly observe the elite of national and international society waiting side by side in the lobby on the ninth floor of the Phoenix Title and Trust Building with some of the city's most disreputable characters. Flynn himself, a specialist in criminal law, attracted a substantial number of clients other firms would normally disdain. The firm had a standing arrangement with the ACLU to handle two of its cases a year, and Corcoran asked Flynn to take Miranda's case as one of the two for that year. Flynn agreed.

Flynn in turn enlisted the aid of John P. Frank, a nationally respected authority on constitutional law and, in 1965, the principal appellate attorney for Lewis & Roca, as the firm name was abbreviated locally.

The firm would bear the costs; neither lawyer would be compensated for his time. Frank later estimated the cost of taking Miranda's case to the U.S. Supreme Court at $50,000 in office time alone, not counting travel time, printing of briefs, records, and other expenses.

When Robert Corcoran told Ernest Miranda that one of Arizona's leading criminal lawyers had agreed to take his case to the United States Supreme Court, Miranda wrote Corcoran from Arizona State Prison: "Your letter . . . has made me very happy. To know that someone has taken an interest in my case, has increased my moral [sic] enormously. . . . I would appreciate if you or either Mr. Flynn keep me informed of any and all results. I also want to thank you and Mr. Flynn for all that you are doing for me."

They were a well-matched pair, John Flynn and John Frank, perfectly complementary. Preparation of the case divided naturally: Flynn, the trial attorney, a man of great personal charm and mental quickness, was to argue it before the Supreme Court; Frank, the scholar, articulate and thoughtful, was to assume the major burden of preparing the brief. They were assisted by several of the firm's younger attorneys.

Forty years old in 1965, John Joseph Flynn had found his niche in the courtroom. A couple of inches short of six feet, trim, articulate out of breadth of knowledge, dramatic out of a fine sensitivity to his audience, he was a commanding presence in or out of court. It was said in Phoenix that when John Flynn was about to present his final argument in a case, lawyers and other students of criminal law took the day off to listen, and there was often standing room only when Flynn stood up to address the jury.

He had a toughness that all his Irish warmth and capacity for pranks and laughter failed to obscure, and he fought for his clients as if he were still a marine fighting in the South Pacific, where he had been twice wounded during World War II—he had, in fact, gone AWOL from the hospital one of those times to get back to the front.

He had stumbled into the field of criminal law, he said, "out of hunger." Concentrating on no special field at the University of Arizona Law School, he had been graduated in 1949 after telescoping undergraduate and law school into three and a half years. Because his grades had not recommended him to the large law firms in town, he had signed up to defend the poor, living on $50 and $100 cases; he had soon acquired a reputation for courtroom ability as well as for taking cases for nothing, both of which assured him of a large but not necessarily lucrative practice. He spent two years as a deputy county attorney, during which time he learned the art of prosecution from the inside, and it was later recalled that when idleness threatened the young law enforcement officer, he often strapped on a .45 and went out to make arrests himself. He was fast, shrewd, and unbending, a formidable courtroom opponent. A local county attorney once called him the "Muhammed Ali of Arizona. You can hit him and hit him, but he'll always bounce back. And if you let your guard down, he'll paste you."

He prepared each case with utter dedication. He was good for seventy-two hours at a stretch. When he took a case, nothing else mattered, and his demons drove him until the final verdict was in. It was also said of him later that "when he went in for a fight, he went in for a funeral."

His mastery of the facts and circumstances of a case was spectacular, but it was always the facts he was after. He was not a bookish man, and he didn't concern himself much with abstract notions of justice. It was immediate and concrete notions of justice and its opposite on which he had built his legal practice: an innocent man waiting on Death Row, a criminal suspect being pushed around a station house. His working in his shirt sleeves said something about the inner man. A tendency to switch to the present tense in telling a story betrayed his action-oriented being. Generalizing on the demands of criminal work, he would describe the case he was currently working on as if there were no other and would conclude:

> It gets to you. . . . The most difficult case . . . is the case in which you're satisfied your client is innocent, and indeed he is innocent. That's the case that really burns you up. Emotionally and otherwise . . . because there's the potential through your fault of an innocent man being convicted because you did not do something, or you did something you should not have done. You have to live with it.

He felt about Ernest Miranda the way he felt about most of his clients. He was a lawyer, a very good one, and his loyalty was to the law. It neither required nor encouraged making moral judgments on them. About Miranda's case he said: "I fought it on technicalities of the law, constitutional grounds, protected every right he possibly had. . . . That's what he's entitled to. And that's exactly what a person who's accused is entitled to, whether he's guilty or whether he's innocent. . . . That's what our whole system is structured around."

John Paul Frank had been born in Appleton, Wisconsin, earned BA, MA, and LLB degrees from the University of Wisconsin and a JSD from Yale Law School. He had been a clerk to Justice Hugo L. Black of the U.S. Supreme Court (October term 1942) and had taught American legal history,

Chapter 5

with an emphasis on the United States Supreme Court, at the University of
Indiana and Yale law schools before joining the firm of Lewis & Roca in
Phoenix, to which, a victim of chronic asthma, he had migrated to take ad-
vantage of the hot, dry climate.

A student of the Supreme Court all his adult life, he had written, as of
1965, a casebook on constitutional law; *Justice Daniel Dissents*, a biography
of Peter V. Daniel; *Lincoln as a Lawyer*; *The Marble Palace—The Supreme
Court in American Life*; *The Warren Court*; and a biographical work on Justice Black. He was also a member of the American Law Institute, a frequent
contributor to the nation's legal journals, and a participant in bar association
meetings and judicial conferences, his particular interest at that time the reform of civil procedures.

He was, however, no ivory tower scholar, the dichotomy in his nature—
as well as its general progressive tendencies—symbolized by identification of
his early heroes: progressive historian Charles A. Beard and John Peter Alt-
geld, reformer governor of Illinois in the late nineteenth century. As an associate professor at Yale he had been one of three authors of an amicus curiae
(friend of the court, a suggestion or statement of law offered to assist the
court) brief submitted to the U.S. Supreme Court by the Committee of Law
Teachers Against Segregation in Legal Education—187 law professors from
schools across the country—in the case of a black student who was appealing
his denial of admission to the University of Texas Law School on the basis of
race. Frank later also served as adviser to NAACP attorney Thurgood Marshall in preparing the arguments against racial segregation in the public
schools.

Frank was in 1965 an established appellate lawyer, a familiar figure in
courts within and without his own state of Arizona: tall, though not husky,
impeccably dressed, horn-rimmed glasses adding to the impression of intellect, urbane, articulate, deferential but not easy to sway, and undramatic in
the way of appellate courts.

Temperamentally he felt more comfortable in appellate work—the
"bookish end of the law"—where, he believed, his talent as well as his interests lay. Not the least of its attractions, he admitted, was not having to meet
the accused dope peddlers and murderers who were his clients—appeals
being based solely on facts already contained in the record, the client could
very rarely add anything of value.

He need not, however, stand face-to-face with a client for his passions to
become involved. He could, he said, "get mad about a matter of principle."
Indeed, he could. As a law clerk to Justice Black, he was fond of recalling, he
once wrote a note to the justice regarding a Court opinion in which Black was
joining—inadvisedly, or so Frank believed: "This is a damned Fascist outrage!"

The specific point about Miranda's case, Frank said some years later,
was that like another of his clients, a truck driver accused of murdering his

mistress, Miranda had confessed to the crimes of rape and kidnapping right away, without either thought or advice about alternatives or consequences.

> ... To this day I don't know whether Miranda was guilty of the crime of rape or not [Frank said]. He did something, but I don't know whether it was aggravated assault or rape. And in the case of my truck driver, following Miranda the case was reversed and sent back, and he got what I suspect he deserved, which was manslaughter. And in both cases, because these people confessed before they had counsel, and they confessed right away, they were twisted into confessions which took them to the top degree of the offense with which they were charged, instead of what I rather imagine would have been a more accurate disposition of their cases. . . .

Rule 22 (1) of the U.S. Supreme Court rules required petitions for writs of certiorari—or petitions for cert, as they were commonly abbreviated—to be filed within ninety days of the final lower-court judgment in a case. That allowed Flynn and Frank until July 20, 1965, or about a month after Robert Corcoran had engaged them: one month to review and analyze the background of confessions litigation since it had first become a significant issue on the dockets of the American courts, particularly the U.S. Supreme Court; one month to sort out the cases, find the combination of precedents that would dispose the justices to look favorably on Ernest Miranda's case.

The literature of constitutional law is written slowly, painstakingly, precedent building upon precedent. At every step, the authors sit back, look over the shoulders of the readers, answer questions and challenges as new cases make their way to the Supreme Court. They may erase a line, rework a paragraph, edit a page, tighten the logic. Finally, perhaps decades later, a new chapter emerges.

Coinciding with the natural egalitarian trend of the time, the constitutional revolution of which Ernest Miranda's case was about to become a chapter had begun about thirty years before. It was called by some people the due process revolution, because it was characterized largely by a change in the manner in which the due process of law clause contained in the Fourteenth Amendment to the Constitution was applied. This movement, slow, uneven, reluctant though it was, was not an insignificant development. Had it not occurred, substantially expanding the rights of the individual, Ernest Miranda's case probably would never have been taken to the United States Supreme Court.

The framers of the Constitution, in allocating some powers to the states and others to the federal government, had made Americans citizens of two separate jurisdictions. In the administration of criminal justice it was like living in two different countries. Violations of federal law—kidnapping, narcotics offenses, counterfeiting, illegal still operations, treason and such—were tried in federal courts, where the Bill of Rights, without dispute, protected an accused. Violations of state law, however—and most common ("street") crimes for which police tended to rely on confessions (murder, rape, housebreaking, armed robbery, auto theft, and such) were violations of state law—were tried in state courts, where the Bill of Rights did not protect the accused, at least not all of it all of the time. Generally criminal justice had long been the responsibility of the separate states, which had their own bills of rights and had devised their separate rules and procedures.

Left to themselves, however, many of these state systems of criminal justice were no better than they had to be. In 1931 the National Commission on Law Observance and Enforcement, or, as it was less formally known, the Wickersham Commission, revealed widespread violent and brutal police practices, some with racial overtones. Commission investigators had documented hundreds of examples of beatings, pistol whippings, strappings, lynching threats, solitary confinement in rat-infested jail cells, application of the "water cure"—holding a suspect's head under water for long periods—and protracted questioning, all in order to elicit confessions for offenses that ranged from murder to stealing a hog. Some convictions obtained by these methods had been reversed in appellate courts; others had not. Respectful of the healthy tension that necessarily exists between state and federal governments, however, the U.S. Supreme Court had been reluctant to invade the territory of the state courts, and only the direst of constitutional emergencies could provoke that body to action.

The first such emergency arose in 1932 with the case of the Scottsboro boys, nine young blacks convicted of the rape of two white girls in the open gondola of a freight train as it rumbled through rural Alabama one hot summer afternoon in 1931. Although it was a capital case, the appointment of counsel to defend the boys, all of whom were illiterate, had been less than casual—all the members of the county bar had been appointed, imposing no obligation or responsibility on any single member. The trial, punctuated by the obscenities of a mob that had gathered to demand vengeance on the perpetrators of the crime most despised and feared by southerners, was no more than a gesture toward dispensing justice. The boys, with little ado, were sentenced to death.

The U.S. Supreme Court reversed the convictions and ordered new trials. Justice George Sutherland spoke for the Court. He was seventy years old and six years short of retirement. He had been a Republican senator and a campaign aide to former President Warren G. Harding, who had appointed him to the Court in 1922. During his public life he had been identified with the cause of economic justice for the rich more often than with social justice for the poor, particularly the black poor. His opinion in the case of the Scottsboro boys, however, became his best-known judicial writing: "[I]n a capital case, where the defendant is unable to employ counsel, and is incapable adequately of making his own defense because of ignorance, feeble minded-ness, illiteracy, or the like it is the duty of the court, whether requested or not, to assign counsel for him as a necessary requisite of due process of law. . . ."

For the first time, the U.S. Supreme Court had overturned a state court criminal conviction because the defendants, a majority of the highest federal court believed, had not had a fair trial—had not been afforded "due process of law."* The movement toward Ernest Miranda's case had begun.

Four years later, in 1936, a second emergency arose, and the U.S. Su-preme Court for the first time reversed a conviction in a state court because a coerced confession had been used to obtain the conviction. The methods of coercion had been particularly cruel in this case, called *Brown* v. *Mississippi*. The accused were three poor, illiterate black men. One had been hung to the limb of a tree by a rope and whipped until he confessed; the others had been taken to the jail, forced to strip, then laid over chairs and beaten with a buckle-studded leather strap until they, too, confessed. They had appeared at their trial for murder with rope burns and wounds still evident. They had, nevertheless, been convicted and sentenced to death; the Mississippi Su-preme Court had upheld the verdict.

Said Chief Justice Hughes for the U.S. Supreme Court in reversing the convictions:†

> The State is free to regulate the procedure of its courts in accord-ance with its own conception of policy, unless in so doing it "of-fends some principle of justice so rooted in the traditions and con-science of our people as to be ranked as fundamental." . . . It would be difficult to conceive of methods more revolting to the sense of justice than those taken to procure the confessions of these peti-tioners, and the use of the confessions thus obtained as the basis for conviction and sentence was a clear denial of due process [of law].

* The late Samuel S. Liebowitz, at the time one of New York City's leading criminal law-yers and later a Kings County Court judge and New York State Supreme Court justice, made an international reputation when he defended the Scottsboro nine at their retrials. The case eventually went back to the U.S. Supreme Court in 1935 as *Norris* v. *Alabama*, and Chief Jus-tice Hughes, writing for the majority, ruled that the retrials, too, had been unconstitutional. Ul-timately the rape charges were dropped against some of the defendants; others were paroled; one escaped. Ruby Bates, one of the complainants, later recanted; there had been no rape at all, she said. Clarence Norris, who resurfaced at the age of sixty-four in 1976, when he applied for a pardon from Alabama for a 1946 parole violation, was believed to be the sole survivor of the nine. Governor George Wallace signed the pardon on October 25, 1976.

† Contrary to popular opinion, a conviction reversed by the U.S. Supreme Court does not immediately or necessarily open the prison gates. Brown's case was remanded to the local trial court, where he pleaded nolo contendere to a charge of manslaughter. He was sentenced to seven and a half years in prison with credit for two and a half years already served. His codefen-dants were sentenced to two-and-one-half- to three-year terms, also with credit for time already served.

Chapter 5

In both *Powell* v. *Alabama*, as the case of the Scottsboro boys is formally known, and *Brown* v. *Mississippi*, the rationale of reversal had been the same: The defendants had been denied the due process of law guaranteed by the Fourteenth Amendment to the Constitution. That rationale, however, was not to endure. In 1937, the year following the Court's decision in *Brown*, Franklin Roosevelt appointed the senior senator from Alabama, Hugo Lafayette Black, to the Court. Black, perhaps more than any other member of it, made the due process revolution possible.

Born in rural Alabama, Black retained a simplicity of speech that belied his political shrewdness and keen intellect. He was no country bumpkin. During his ten years in the Senate he had spent his leisure browsing in the stacks across the street at the Library of Congress, and he was widely read, particularly in Greek and Roman history and literature. He understood despotism on the highest intellectual level, and he spent the remaining years of his public life attacking what he considered contemporary judicial despotism, which he believed was encouraged by the Supreme Court's application of the phrase *due process of law*.

Like much of the Constitution, the phrase is necessarily vague, demanding from judges the most strenuous efforts of interpretation. It is necessarily spacious, limited only by judicial imagination. Black did not approve of it as a justification for reversing state court decisions. It conferred on judges, he believed, entirely too much power; he called it a "shoot the works clause." His own method of protecting individual liberties against infringement by government, either federal or state, was to apply to the states the Bill of Rights, which had been attached to the original Constitution for precisely that purpose in connection with the federal government. Had he been on the Court at the time, he would perhaps have suggested that the Scottsboro boys had been denied not due process of law but the right to counsel required by the Sixth Amendment and that Brown had been compelled to incriminate himself, a use of force prohibited by the Fifth Amendment. It was a controversial method, and Black's success did not come either easily or immediately.

About the Bill of Rights itself, there was less controversy. The first eight of these ten amendments read like a shopping list of abuses of power to which tyrants typically resort in their accumulation of power, their insurance of self-perpetuation. They guarantee to the individual the freedoms of religion, speech, press, and assembly and the rights of petition and to bear arms; abuses through quartering of troops are controlled; unreasonable searches and seizures are prohibited; trial for a capital or otherwise infamous crime must be on presentment or indictment of a grand jury, except in military cases; double jeopardy is forbidden; private property cannot be taken for public use without just compensation; protection to an accused in criminal prosecutions is provided not only by the right to counsel and the prohibition against compulsory self-incrimination but also by the requirement of speedy and public trial by an impartial jury in the place where the crime was committed;

69

accused persons can compel witnesses to appear in their behalf, and both excessive bail and cruel and unusual punishment are prohibited. If there was considerable debate and disagreement regarding the meaning of "cruel and unusual" punishment, "excessive" bail, and such, by the late 1930s there was little discussion of their applicability to the federal government.

The controversy swirled around the Fourteenth Amendment, ratified in 1868 in a spirit of vengeance against the South. It declared in Section 1: "No *State* shall make or enforce any law which shall abridge the privileges or immunities of citizens of the United States; nor shall any *State* deprive any person of life, liberty, or property, without due process of law; nor deny to any person within its jurisdiction the equal protection of the laws [italics added]."

Did that section make the Bill of Rights applicable to the states? The judges could not agree, and investigations to discover the intent of its authors and supporters in the post–Civil War Congress offered no conclusive answers.

Hugo Black's personal investigations of the purposes of the Joint Committee on Reconstruction and of the congressional debates, however, had persuaded *him* that the due process of law clause contained in the Fourteenth Amendment was intended to enforce adherence by the states to the Bill of Rights.

His principal antagonist on the Court was Felix Frankfurter, appointed in 1939, two years after Black. The two men shared the political and social goals of the Theodore Roosevelt–Woodrow Wilson–Robert M. LaFollette–Franklin Roosevelt progressive tradition, and Frankfurter, a Jew born in Vienna, where law was arbitrary, the caprice of whoever came to power, was no less cognizant than his brother Black of the excesses in which officers of the law sometimes indulged. But they held deeply entrenched and contrary judicial convictions. They could often be found on the same side when Supreme Court votes were taken in criminal cases, but they disagreed on methods.

Frankfurter believed the due process of law clause of the Fourteenth Amendment did not apply the Bill of Rights to the states but had to stand alone. If it merely incorporated specific provisions of the Constitution already set out, he reasoned, it was redundant and meaningless—the Fifth Amendment, in addition to its other provisions, already held a due process of law clause. Moreover, he said, "a construction which gives due process no independent function but makes it a summary of the specific provisions of the Bill of Rights would tear up by the roots much of the fabric of the law in the several states," which, as Hughes had said in *Brown*, were free to devise their own procedures so long as a fundamental fairness was preserved.

Due process of law, as Frankfurter defined it, embodied all the fundamental principles of the Anglo-American traditions of justice. In deciding whether a state conviction violated that Fourteenth Amendment guarantee, one could not pick out a specific act, such as a forced confession, and denounce it as depriving a man of due process of law. One must, instead, review the proceedings in a case to determine whether, as a whole, "they offend those canons of decency and fairness which express the notions of justice of English-speaking peoples" or, as Justice Holmes had once pithily and earthily put it, whether a state's administration of its criminal law "makes you vomit."

The difficulty in this approach, as Black saw it, was that it was too subjective. Although Black admitted that the Bill of Rights was not always crystal-clear—the prohibition on "unreasonable" search and seizure, for example, demanded a degree of subjectivity—it was clearer than "due process of law." And what offended Black or William O. Douglas, his most frequent ally on the Court for many years, did not necessarily offend the chief justice or George Sutherland. In the end, relying on a subjective due process standard encouraged, or at least held the potential for, judicial despotism.

In the early days of the U.S. Supreme Court's involvement in state criminal justice, the Frankfurter interpretation largely prevailed. But Black was nothing if not persistent. Writing an opinion for the Court, which was, as Felix Frankfurter always said, a symphony, not a solo, Black would uphold the due process of law concept, then inject his own view via a footnote. Occasionally he voted with the majority, then wrote a concurrence explaining his own route to the result. And he wrote dissents.

Although, Black said in 1968, "I have never been able at any one time to get a majority of the Court to agree to my belief that the Fourteenth Amendment incorporates *all* of the Bill of Rights' provisions and makes them applicable to the states," he gradually wore enough of the brethren down. Most of the provisions of the Bill of Rights, through a process called selective incorporation, were, in fact, made applicable to the states. The freedoms of the First Amendment, the Fourth Amendment's prohibition against unreasonable search and seizures, the Fifth Amendment's prohibition against compulsory self-incrimination, the Sixth Amendment's rights to confrontation of witnesses and to the assistance of counsel—all were parts of state administration of criminal justice in 1965, as John Flynn and John Frank were preparing to take Ernest Miranda's case to the U.S. Supreme Court.

Recalling much later his successful twenty-year struggle to convince the Court that the Sixth Amendment's guarantee of the right to the assistance of counsel ought to apply to state court trials as well as federal, Black said:

> . . . I dissented every time it came up. Sometimes I would get one of my colleagues that was with me to write the dissent. But we continued to dissent, and we just kept on dissenting. Well, the Court, instead of holding it and agreeing with it, would say that even if my rule were adopted, it would not apply to this case because of so and so.
>
> Well, they finally got to where there wasn't much of that argument left. . . .

If the due process revolution had made Ernest Miranda's request to be heard by the Supreme Court possible, it had also made it imperative that his lawyers base their case, a state case, on the Bill of Rights, not on the Fourteenth Amendment's due process of law clause. The question was: On which provision in the Bill of Rights should they build their argument? Flynn and Frank had barely begun work on the petition for cert when the debate began. Miranda's case involved a violation of either the Fifth or the Sixth Amendment, but which was it? Which of his rights had been denied? The right not to be compelled to be a witness against himself, guaranteed by the Fifth Amendment? Or the right to counsel, guaranteed by the Sixth Amendment? John Flynn, personally familiar with the interiors of station houses, with the people who inhabited them, with the tricks, the promises, the threats, believed it was the Fifth Amendment. John Frank, on speaking terms with justices and conversant with the fine points of constitutional law, believed it was the Sixth Amendment.

John Frank had noted in his own textbook *Cases on Constitutional Law* the course of development being followed by the U.S. Supreme Court regarding coerced confessions, pointing out that in *Brown* the physical abuse of the defendants had been blatant but that in the next significant case, *Chambers* v. *Florida*, decided four years later, in 1940, there was "sharp factual dispute" over whether there had been any actual physical abuse of the defendants.

In that case an elderly white man had been robbed and murdered in the small town of Pompano, Florida. The community was enraged, and the police responded accordingly. They rounded up some forty black men from their homes in and around Pompano, arrested them without warrants, held them incommunicado for five days with little sleep and less food, and questioned them day and night until some confessed. On the basis of these "confessions," four black tenant farmers—Izell Chambers, Jack Williamson, Charlie Davis, and Walter Woodward—were convicted of murder and sentenced to death.

Many of the confessions cases that came to the Supreme Court involved alleged murders, robberies, or rapes—especially rapes—of whites by blacks in southern states and the beating of blacks into confessing. Several cases, including *Chambers*, were brought by the NAACP through its Legal Defense Fund, created only the year before, in 1939, for that purpose. The organization operated on a shoestring; the NAACP lawyer who took *Chambers* through the lower Florida courts had received $177 collected in nickels and dimes from local churches. The lawyers were less interested in furthering justice in the abstract than in fighting racial discrimination in the police stations and courthouses of America.

Chambers was one of the early cases in which a big, burly, sallow-skinned black named Thurgood Marshall was involved. He helped write the brief for it, although a shortage of funds prevented him from going to Wash-

Chapter 5

ington to hear the case argued in the Supreme Court. Other briefs he himself was to write and argue—including the big one in 1954, *Brown* v. *Board of Education*, in which he successfully prevailed upon the Court to declare racial segregation in public schools unconstitutional. Later he was involved in Ernest Miranda's case, although in a way that perhaps no one could have foreseen.

The justices of the Supreme Court voted in conference to reverse the conviction of Izell Chambers and his codefendants. Hugo Black was assigned to write the opinion.

Black was not without experience in the matter of coerced confessions. Even before he had absorbed some lessons of tyranny on an intellectual level in his study of ancient history, he had learned some practical lessons in the same subject on the personal level.

Following graduation from the University of Alabama law school, Black had left rural Clay County, where he had been born, and sought his fortune in Birmingham. In 1914 he had been elected county solicitor—the title given the Jefferson County prosecutor. As he was working through an overloaded docket, he noticed that confessions were coming out of the city jail at Bessemer—a coal and steel town about ten miles south of Birmingham but still within his county jurisdiction—at about the same rate of speed that cast-iron piping was rolling off the local assembly lines. On investigation, he discovered the local version of one of the great ongoing horror stories of history: the third degree. He persuaded the local courts to conduct a grand jury investigation, and the report, written by Black himself, documenting some particularly brutal police practices on their prisoners who were largely blacks, was made public in September 1915:

> We find that a uniform practice has been made of taking helpless prisoners, in the late hours of the night, into a secluded room . . . and there beat them until they were red with their own blood, in the effort to obtain confessions. We find that this cowardly practice, in which four big officers[,] with pistols safely strapped on their bodies, would thus take advantage of ignorance and helplessness, has been continuously in operation for a long number of years. A leather strap with a buckle on one end, [*sic*] and a big flap on the other was invented for the purpose of assisting the officers. . . . In this room were none present but the officers and the helpless prisoner often innocent of the crime of which he was charged, arrested without warrant, on the vague suspicion of these instruments of law and order. . . .

Very little of consequence had occurred as a result of the investigation, although a citizens' committee had held public hearings. Black was able to get four officers indicted but was unable to get convictions. The *Birmingham Age-Herald* ultimately excused the officers' brutality as no worse than that of police in other cities—a comparison the Wickersham Commission confirmed fifteen years later with firsthand reports and statistics—and the *Birmingham Ledger* did not include the investigation in its list of Hugo Black's accomplishments as prosecutor when he resigned in 1917.

Having seen the victims limp into the hearing room, however, the young prosecutor remained an implacable enemy of all procedures that carried the odor of unfairness to the defendant. Between 1940, when he wrote the Court opinion in *Chambers*, and 1964, when Danny Escobedo's murder conviction was reversed, the U.S. Supreme Court decided thirty-six state cases involving confessions. In twenty-six, or nearly three-quarters, the Court decided in favor of the criminal defendant. Hugo Black either wrote the Court opinion, wrote a concurring opinion, or silently joined the majority in all twenty-six. In ten cases the Court decided against the criminal defendant; Hugo Black dissented in nine of them and did not participate in one. He did not once vote to deny an individual his constitutional rights in a confessions case.

On Lincoln's Birthday, 1940, appropriately enough, Black announced the U.S. Supreme Court's unanimous decision in *Chambers* v. *Florida*, reversing the convictions of the four men.* The decision was based, of course, on denial of the Fourteenth Amendment's guarantee of due process of law to criminal defendants in state courts—the due process revolution had barely begun in 1940—a foundation Black could not see go unnoticed, and he twitted his brethren a little in a footnote, complaining that "there has been a current of opinion—which this court has declined to adopt in many previous cases—that the Fourteenth Amendment was intended to make secure against invasion all the rights, privileges, and immunities protected from federal violation by the Bill of Rights. . . ." But grounds he did not agree with in no way diminished the poetry or the passion in the body of the opinion:

> The determination to preserve an accused's right to procedural due process sprang in large part from knowledge of the historical truth that the rights and liberties of people accused of crime could not be safely entrusted to secret inquisitorial processes. The testimony of centuries . . . stood as proof that physical and mental torture and coercion had brought about the tragically unjust sacrifices of some who were the noblest and most useful of their generations. The rack, the thumbscrew, the wheel, solitary confinement, protracted questioning and cross questioning, and other ingenious forms of entrapment of the helpless or unpopular had left their wake of mutilated bodies and shattered minds along the way to the cross, the guillotine, the stake and the hangman's noose. And they who have suffered most from secret and dictatorial proceedings have almost always been the poor, the ignorant, the numerically weak, the friendless, and the powerless.

* Prior to the Supreme Court's decision, Izell Chambers had been committed to the state hospital for the insane. Following the decision, the other three defendants were retried and finally acquitted on March 9, 1942.

The justices were "not impressed," he said,

> by the argument that law enforcement methods such as those
> under review are necessary to uphold our laws. The Constitution
> proscribes such lawless means irrespective of the end. . . . Today
> [1940], as in the ages past, we are not without tragic proof that the
> exalted power of some governments to punish manufactured crime
> dictatorially is the handmaid of tyranny. Under our constitutional
> system, courts stand against any winds that blow as havens of ref-
> uge for those who might otherwise suffer because they are helpless,
> weak, outnumbered, or because they are non-conforming victims of
> prejudice and public excitement. Due process of law, preserved for
> all by our Constitution, commands that no such practice as that
> disclosed by this record shall send any accused to death.

Hugo Black always considered the final lines of *Chambers* his best writing
and often read them to his law clerks.

These early attacks on state administration of criminal justice by the Supreme Court provoked virtually no criticism. Editorial comment on *Chambers* was largely congratulatory, as was Black's mail. Except for the insertion
of Black's full *Chambers* opinion in the *Congressional Record* by New York
Democratic Senator Robert F. Wagner, no congressional notice was taken. A
quarter century later reaction to the Supreme Court's decision in the case of
Danny Escobedo would consume many whole pages of the *Congressional
Record.* But in 1940 moral sentiment clearly favored the victim of police brutality.

Also, street crime was not then the concern it became later. Americans
were preoccupied that year with presidential politics and the war in Europe.
It would be another decade, according to the Gallup polls, which purported
to measure the desires and fears of the American people, before crime made
its way to the top ten of national concerns.

If *Chambers* provoked little comment, it also provoked little change.
State supreme court justices generally, although not all, ignored these early
federal incursions into state confessions cases and continued to allow forced
confessions as trial evidence. Just as persistently, although the justices seemed
to recognize that their direction was upstream, the U.S. Supreme Court continued to reverse convictions so obtained and in the process began to develop
a formula for use in determining which confessions ought to have been admitted as evidence, deciding at various times to consider the defendant's state
of mind, the presence of threats, physical deprivation, access to counsel or
friends, the length of time he or she had been detained and interrogated.
Gradually, as more and more confessions cases came to the Court, the degree
of coercion required for the justices to reverse a conviction lessened.

Paralleling this development, in approximately inverse proportions, the
sophistication of the methods of coercion increased. As beatings, starvation,

even protracted questioning began to disappear—although the cruder methods have never disappeared entirely—subtler methods replaced them. A former district attorney recalled the station house in the early 1960s:

> "We threatened and we promised and we beat and we had kids strip themselves," he said, and reenacted a station house drama in which police questioned a reluctant suspect:
> " 'Hey! Take off your clothes!'
> "The guy'd say, 'What?'
> " 'Take off your clothes.'
> "Big, brave guy, he'd take off his shirt, he'd take off the trousers . . . shoes, socks.
> " 'C'mon, let's go.'
> " 'What do you mean?'
> " 'C'mon, take off your underwear.'
> " 'What do you want to know?' "

The chief of police in a metropolitan area recalled his days on the homicide squad in the early 1960s: "You build up a rapport with a defendant, hopefully [*sic*] one that's likable. . . . An embrace of comfort, you're talking to someone and you just touch their hand; suddenly people will just open up to you. . . . I've held defendants, with my arm around them, like a comforting father. . . . Through my experience I knew that a friendly tone of voice, a touch of the hand, really set up communication. . . ."

To protect defendants in federal courts against such practices, the Supreme Court had ruled that detention of a suspect incommunicado was sufficient to invalidate a confession. In state cases, as John Frank had pointed out in his casebook, something more than incommunicado detention was required, the Supreme Court being less anxious to interfere, but even here a course of development was easily discerned.

In putting together the petition for cert in Ernest Miranda's case, however, John Frank bypassed the lesson of his own textbook and continued to insist it was not a self-incrimination but a right to counsel case. *Escobedo*, its immediate predecessor, had been exactly that.

Once again, Hugo Black's influence is evident. Black, for whom Frank had clerked, had an abiding passion regarding the right of a criminal defendant to the assistance of counsel, and he had written the Court opinions and dissents in the leading right to counsel cases. It was a passion that seemed to have been inherited by at least some of his law clerks, and out of six significant cases that had come before the U.S. Supreme Court just prior to 1963, a period in which the right to counsel was being expanded, four had been argued before that Court in behalf of the criminal defendants by former law clerks to the justice.

There was good reason grounded in precedents for basing Miranda's case on the Sixth Amendment. The right to counsel had, in fact, developed much like the right not to be compelled to incriminate oneself: a gradual expansion by the Supreme Court.

The first case, that of the Scottsboro boys, was limited in its application to capital cases. Then, in May 1938, less than a year after taking his seat on the Court, Black began his quest to secure the right to counsel for all criminal defendants. A 1790 law, implementing the Sixth Amendment's guarantee, required the assistance of counsel for persons tried in federal courts for capital crimes. In 1938 Black, writing for the Supreme Court majority, had secured this guarantee for *all* defendants in federal courts when he overturned the conviction of a U.S. marine who had been accused of spending counterfeit money, then tried, convicted, and sentenced, all without benefit of counsel.

Then, in 1942, the Court, having taken two steps forward, took a step backward. Smith Betts, a farm hand living in Carroll County, Maryland, was accused of robbery. At his trial he had requested, but had been refused, a lawyer for his defense. It was not, the judge had told him, the practice in Carroll County to appoint counsel for indigent defendants except in prosecutions for murder and rape. Betts was found guilty and sentenced to eight years in prison.

The U.S. Supreme Court affirmed Betts's conviction. Owen Roberts wrote the Court opinion. Roberts had been a Philadelphia corporation lawyer, a lifelong Republican, and a special prosecutor of the Teapot Dome scandals during the Harding administration, the combination of which had seemed to Herbert Hoover appropriate for a Supreme Court nominee in 1930. Roberts was known for his mechanistic interpretation of the Constitution, and his best-known quotation concisely summarized his judicial mind set: The Supreme Court had "only one duty—to lay the article of the Constitution which is involved beside the statute which is challenged and to decide whether the latter squares with the former."

Roberts was not one of those who, like Black, would impose the Bill of Rights on the states; at this time that view was shared only by Black's frequent judicial ally on the Court William O. Douglas. So there was no nonsense about applying the Sixth Amendment to trials in state courts. The Sixth Amendment, said Roberts, guaranteed counsel only in federal courts. He described the difference between the case of Smith Betts and that of the Scottsboro boys as one of degree of procedural unfairness and concluded that "while want of counsel in a particular case may result in a conviction lacking in such fundamental fairness, we cannot say that the [Fourteenth] Amendment embodies an inexorable command that no trial for any offense, or in any court, can be fairly conducted and justice accorded a defendant who is not represented by counsel."

Hugo Black dissented with some vehemence. A dissent is more of a solo than is a Court opinion on which a majority must agree. A dissent need not please anyone except the author. After letting the majority have the back of his hand for its refusal to invoke the Sixth Amendment's guarantee of counsel, Black concluded:

> Denial to the poor of the request for counsel in proceedings based on charges of serious crime has long been regarded as shocking to the "universal sense of justice." . . . And most of the other States [thirty-five of the forty-eight] have shown their agreement by constitutional provisions, statutes, or established practice judicially approved, which assure that no man shall be deprived of counsel merely because of his poverty. Any other practice seems to me to defeat the promise of our democratic society to provide equal justice under law.

Betts attracted little public attention and less criticism when it was handed down on June 1, 1942, a lack which disturbed two young government lawyers, Benjamin V. Cohen and Erwin N. Griswold, the latter a future dean of Harvard Law School and U.S. solicitor general, enough to complain in a letter to the *New York Times* that Owen Roberts's was too literal a way to approach constitutional interpretation, that surely 160 years under the U.S. Constitution justified "an expanding rather than contracting recognition of what the right to counsel means in a democracy in the 20th century." The decision in *Betts*, they added, echoing a thesis frequently put forward by Hugo Black in his opinions during these internationally troubled times, came "at a singularly inopportune time. Throughout the world men are fighting to be free from the fear of political trials and concentration camps. . . . At a critical period in world history, *Betts* v. *Brady* dangerously tilts the scales against the safeguarding of one of the most precious rights of men. . . ."

Betts nevertheless stood as a precedent for the next two decades. The Sixth Amendment to the Constitution did not guarantee a defendant counsel in a state court except in a capital case. If the U.S. Supreme Court reversed the conviction of a defendant who had been denied counsel, it was because the proceedings generally had offended the sense of decency abiding in a majority of the Court.

Then came *Gideon.*

Dissents become law as a result of two basic factors, often acting in tandem: The times change or the justices, products of new times, change. In the administration of criminal justice, both of these occurred. At the same time that the social and political egalitarianism following World War II was raising individual rights to new levels of importance, and the Court increasingly embraced civil libertarian concepts, deaths and resignations altered the make-up of the Court. By 1962, the year Clarence Earl Gideon's case came to the Court, the entire majority in *Betts* had been replaced.

Statistics of Supreme Court decisions in state criminal cases tell the story. Between 1940 and 1954 the Court rate of affirmance of convictions in right to counsel cases was 36 percent. Between 1954 and 1962 the rate of affirmance had dropped to 14 percent. No convictions in right to counsel cases were affirmed after 1958. The rationale for reversal, however, had not changed; it was still due process of law which had been violated, not the defendant's right to counsel under the Sixth Amendment. It would take Gideon, whose case was clearly in the current of judicial history, the next logical step in the evolution of criminal justice, to change that.

His petition for certiorari reached the U.S. Supreme Court on January 8, 1962. Nearly five months later, on June 1, when the justices decided to hear his case, they included in the order the unusual request that lawyers for both sides discuss in their briefs and arguments whether or not the Court's holding in *Betts* should be "reconsidered." At their conference on June 22 they chose Abe Fortas to argue Gideon's case.

Advocacy for the poor had come a long way since *Chambers*. Abe Fortas was a distinguished appellate lawyer, with specialties in corporate finance, antitrust law, taxation, and communications and a philosophical interest in criminal law. He was a partner in Arnold, Fortas & Porter, one of Washington's most prestigious law firms , the paying clientele of which included Lever Brothers, Western Union, the American Broadcasting Company, Braniff Airlines, and others equally affluent. The partners had decided at the beginning to take public service cases, too, and the firm's nonpaying clientele included more than 100 government employees accused of disloyalty during the McCarthy era and Monte Durham, in whose cause Fortas had argued in 1954 before the U.S. Supreme Court of Appeals for the District of Columbia Circuit for some liberalizing of the rules of the insanity defense. And now Clarence Earl Gideon.

Fortas was a member of a committee appointed by Chief Justice Warren to rewrite the Federal Rules of Criminal Procedure, and he had known for many years on a personal basis the justices before whom he was to argue Gideon's case.

He knew his way around Washington, he knew his way around the appellate courts, including the Supreme Court, and he knew his way around the history and abstractions of constitutional law.

Officially the state attorney general represented the state of Florida, but briefing and arguing the case against Gideon were actually assigned to a twenty-six-year-old assistant attorney general in the office, Bruce R. Jacob. The arrangement presented some nice ironies: all the resources of a brilliant lawyer from an influential law firm representing the poor, uneducated prisoner who had been denied an attorney at his trial; a young, inexperienced assistant attorney general representing the state of Florida, which had denied Gideon the counsel he had requested.

Gideon's case was argued before the Court on January 15, 1963. Fortas first described the crime—breaking and entering the Bay Harbor Poolroom in Panama City, Florida, and stealing some wine, possibly some cigarettes, and a small sum of money. (In choosing the case to challenge *Betts*, the justices had shrewdly passed over those which involved heinous crimes— a conviction for sodomy of a seven-year-old girl was one—and settled on a case unlikely to arouse the public's wrath.) He next described Gideon's trial, at which the defendant had told the court he had neither funds nor a lawyer and asked the judge to appoint one. The judge had refused; it was not the practice in Bay County, Florida, as it had not been in Carroll County, Maryland, two decades before, to appoint counsel to represent a defendant in a noncapital case. Fortas, in the brief he had submitted to the Court prior to argument, had listed some of the problems the defendant could not solve without legal advice: He could not, for example, "evaluate the lawfulness of his arrest, the validity of the indictment or information, whether preliminary motions should be filed, whether a search or seizure has been lawful, whether a 'confession' is admissible, etc." His logic was not unlike John Frank's regarding Miranda's situation. "He cannot," Fortas added, "determine whether he is responsible for the crime as charged or a lesser offense. He cannot discuss the possibilities of pleading to a lesser offense. He cannot evaluate the grand or petit jury. At the trial he cannot interpose objections to evidence or cross-examine witnesses, etc. He is at a loss in the sentencing procedure." The courtroom was a foreign country to most lay people, the jargon of legal proceedings, a foreign currency.

At argument, Fortas, in his soft but firm voice, gently chided the justices for their preoccupation with abstractions:

> I do believe that in some of this Court's decisions there has been a tendency from time to time, because of the pull of federalism, to forget, to forget the realities of what happens downstairs, of what happens to these poor, miserable, indigent people when they are arrested and they are brought into the jail and they are questioned and later on they are brought in these strange and awesome circumstances before a magistrate, and then later on they are brought before a court; and there, Clarence Earl Gideon, defend yourself.

If Clarence Darrow couldn't do it, Fortas added—and he couldn't; when Darrow was to be tried, the first thing he did was get a lawyer—Clarence Earl Gideon certainly could not.

Fortas reviewed those cases involving the right to counsel issue which had come before the Supreme Court following the case of the Scottsboro boys in 1932 and, in answer to a question from one of the justices, came to the heart of the argument, which coincided exactly with Hugo Black's judicial cosmology: where states' rights fit into a federal system: "I believe that Betts against Brady, laying down as it does the principle of case-by-case supervision by the Federal courts of State criminal proceedings, is antithetical to federalism. Federalism requires, in my judgment . . . that the Federal courts should refrain so far as possible from intervention in State criminal proceedings." The Fourteenth Amendment, not the Sixth, was the real thief of states' rights.

To the defendant's lawyer belongs the poetry of the law; to the attorney for the states is relegated the prose, what amounts to, in many cases, the mundane defense of the status quo. Assistant Attorney General Jacob spoke no soaring phrases but based his entire argument on the practical effects of a Court decision to reverse *Betts* and require counsel at trials in state courts; intrusion of the Court into areas historically reserved to the states; overloading the state treasury; the possible extension of such a rule to social services—psychiatrists, perhaps—and, of course, a prime concern of the law enforcement officer, the opening of the prison gates and the freeing, in Florida alone, of approximately 5,200 inmates who had been tried and convicted without counsel.

Fortas had been confident from the outset of a Supreme Court majority. He was, however, hoping for a unanimous decision, and he got it. The decision was handed down on March 18, 1963, along with six others involving federalization of criminal procedures and practices. Black Monday for states' rights, some commentators called it.

The chief justice, who assigns opinions when he is in the majority, had given Hugo Black the satisfaction of speaking for the Court that overruled *Betts* v. *Brady,* and there was understandable relish in Black's tone as he reviewed the cases which had led to Gideon's and concluded: "[A] provision of the Bill of Rights which is 'fundamental and essential to a fair trial' is made obligatory upon the States by the Fourteenth Amendment. We think the Court in *Betts* was wrong . . . in concluding that the Sixth Amendment's guarantee of counsel is not one of those fundamental rights." Gideon should have been furnished a lawyer at his trial. From now on, he and his kind would be.*

The U.S. Supreme Court's decision in Clarence Gideon's case did open the prison gates or at least set them ajar. In Florida, for example, over the next three years, between April 1, 1963, and April 1, 1966, 6,403 of the state's 8,000 prison inmates took advantage of the decision and filed for reconsideration of their cases; 2,506 were given new trials; 1,311 were released.

As Bruce Jacob had foreseen at oral argument, the imposition of a rule requiring counsel did limit state freedom. The rule was, however, generally

---

* Gideon's conviction was reversed, and his case sent back to the Panama City, Florida, court for a new trial. Represented by counsel at his second trial, he was acquitted. After that, his only known contact with the law occurred when he once picked a losing horse at the Kentucky Derby and somehow wound up in jail for vagrancy. When he told his story, the judge offered to hold him long enough for him to appeal for the right to counsel in trials for misdemeanors—an expansion of the rule laid down in his case which the U.S. Supreme Court did, in fact, make, although not until 1972. Gideon, however, preferred to plead guilty, obtain his release, and go on his way. Still a gambler and drifter, he died penniless in the Broward Medical Center, Fort Lauderdale, Florida, in 1972, at the age of sixty-one.

acceptable to the states. The way had been prepared through previous Court decisions and came as no surprise—indeed, in friend of the court briefs, it had been formally urged by twenty-three states and all but five of the fifty already made some provision for appointing counsel for indigents in felony cases.

In practical terms, the rule requiring counsel made judicial life easier for local courts in some ways; judges and prosecutors no longer had to make the difficult decision whether or not the circumstances of a case were special enough to require appointment of a lawyer, and they lost fewer cases on appeal through bad judgment. In addition, whatever states' rights issues were involved, and however the decision in Gideon's case overloaded the court dockets—and it did—talking against the obligation of a democratic society to provide a fair trial for a poor, uneducated fellow seemed immoral. Hardly anyone opposed the decision.

Three months after *Gideon* was handed down, reporters for the *New York Times* surveyed the fifty states and found that varying steps were being taken to implement the decision and provide lawyers for poor defendants, but steps *were* being taken. State legislatures were rewriting laws to conform to the *Gideon* rule and in some instances expanding it. They were appropriating money to pay court-appointed counsel—not grandly, but more respectably than before—and to open public defender offices. Local bar associations were preparing rosters of lawyers available for court appointments.

In August 1964 President Johnson signed the Criminal Justice Act of 1964 providing defense counsel to poor defendants in federal criminal courts at government expense.

Implicit in Gideon's case was the question of *when* an accused ought to be provided with a lawyer, the issue in Ernest Miranda's appeal. At oral argument Abe Fortas had talked of "what happens to these poor, miserable, indigent people when they are arrested and they are brought into the jail and they are questioned. . . ." However, when one of the justices had raised the very question and another had asked if the query was relevant to Gideon's case, Fortas had answered that it was not at issue in that case. He had added that in his private view, "there is a right to counsel as soon as practicable after arrest . . . just as I believe that a person who can retain counsel should have a recognized right to consult with counsel shortly after arrest." In retrospect, these comments of Fortas seem at least to look forward to Ernest Miranda's situation. That view is, however, retrospective, and Fortas later said that the "Miranda problem was certainly totally unfamiliar to me at the time . . . I had never encountered it or had any experience with it."

Gideon, of course, begat a whole generation of right to counsel cases and then, in 1964, the most important of all to that point, *Escobedo*. The right to counsel guaranteed by the Sixth Amendment to the Constitution was stretched until it reached from the trial court to the station house—but only under certain conditions.

Chapter 5

There was no doubt in John Frank's mind that Ernest Miranda's case fell into that category of cases. There was no doubt in his mind what he wanted to do and how he thought it ought to come out. He said later, in a clear echo of Barry Kroll's argument in behalf of Danny Escobedo:

> It seems to me that the right to counsel ought to mean the right to counsel in time to do yourself some good, that granting the right to counsel is an empty ceremony if a person is given that particular privilege, oh, let us say, the day after he's been executed. It is also an empty ceremony if he is given that privilege the day after it would do him any good. . . . The rich and the educated know that they're entitled to counsel, that they don't have to testify against themselves. The poor and the ignorant and the foreign-born don't know these things. I think that a legal system that is calibrated to take advantage of the ignorance of the ignorant is dreadful. . . .

John Flynn was ultimately persuaded, although he could never wholly quite stifle the thought that Miranda's case really involved incrimination of oneself without the proper protections against compulsion rather than the right to counsel. However, Flynn bowed to what he considered superior appellate wisdom and went along with Frank, who was also supported by two of their three assistants. The petition for cert was written wholly in the context of the Sixth Amendment and its guarantee of the "Assistance of Counsel" to the accused in criminal prosecutions.

The document John Flynn and John Frank produced during the early summer of 1965 was brief: nine pages, about 2,500 words, the length of a magazine article. Its brevity and the simple, straightforward presentation of the issues belied the concentrated effort that went into it, the research by several colleagues at Lewis & Roca, the detailed analysis of legal history, the careful selection of every word.

Into these nine pages they managed to cram descriptions of Miranda's interrogation by Officers Cooley and Young, the line-up identification, his confession, and his trial. They explained that the Arizona Supreme Court had given *Escobedo* "such a narrow construction that, for all practical purposes, the protections of the Sixth Amendment are not available to those persons so unaware of their rights or so intimidated that they do not request 'the guiding hand of counsel' at this crucial stage." They wanted to raise the question, they said, of whether counsel must indeed be requested, a condition they equated with giving "the knowledgeable suspect . . . a constitutional preference over those members of society most in need of assistance." And finally, they hoped to see ended the judicial confusion that followed *Escobedo*, and they asked the Court to hear their case "so that the current widely conflicting treatment of a basic constitutional right can be resolved and substantial and similar justice attained by all accused persons wherever they live." In conclusion, they paraphrased the credo of criminal lawyers, the loyalty to the law that had commanded Alvin Moore to defend Ernest Miranda at his trial, although the attorney had compared the task to a surgeon's operating for locked bowels, and was now commanding these two "uptown" lawyers to fight for the convicted rapist's constitutional rights in the United States Supreme Court. The Constitution was not selective; it applied to and was available to everyone: to the defendant in political crimes, to the defendant in white-collar crimes, and to the defendant in violent crimes. Only then were the ends of justice served. "There is little about the petitioner or the crime for which he stands charged that commends itself," the lawyers wrote. "But the cause of due process is ill-served when a disturbed, little-educated indigent is sentenced to lengthy prison terms largely on the basis of a confession which he gave without being first advised of his right to counsel. . . ." They attached a trial transcript for the justices to consult and, as required, Ernest Miranda's petition for permission to proceed in forma pauperis, along with his affidavit confirming his poverty, and sent the packet off to Washington. It was received in the clerk's office of the U.S. Supreme Court on July 16, 1965.

As was also required, the lawyers sent a copy of their petition to the opposition, in this case the state of Arizona, as represented by the Arizona attorney general, the chief law enforcement officer of the state. He in turn routed it to the Criminal Appeals Division, which at that time, before the enormous surge in criminal appeals, consisted of an assistant attorney general and a couple of law clerks.

Gary Kenneth Nelson was the assistant attorney general in charge of the division then. He was a young man, just past his thirtieth birthday on July 12, and only three years out of the University of Arizona Law School, where he had been on the dean's list as well as one of the top ten graduates in his class, and the moot court competition winner. There was something of the storybook character about him, even beyond his boyish good looks, and he had all the proper credentials for success in the legal profession. He had won scholastic honors in undergraduate school—Arizona State University, where he studied under a four-year scholarship. He had been a captain in Military Intelligence for two years after graduation in 1957, then continued on reserve duty while he attended law school from 1959 until 1962. He had placed fourth on the bar examination and served as a clerk to Justice Fred C. Struckmeyer, Jr., of the Arizona Supreme Court, following law school graduation. He had tried private practice briefly, then joined the attorney general's staff in 1964. Community-minded, he was active in his church as choir director, Sunday-school teacher, and lay minister. He was also active in the Boy Scouts, the local Lions Club, and the University of Arizona alumni association. He was a Republican in a largely Republican state, and not without political ambitions.

As is customary for the opposition when petitions for cert are filed in the U.S. Supreme Court, Nelson put together a response for the state.

Its official position was that the U.S. Supreme Court had in its decision in Danny Escobedo's case spent considerable time emphasizing that the defendant had repeatedly asked for and been denied counsel. Nelson, like the Arizona Supreme Court, would limit the decision to those particular circumstances. He had, however, no objection to the Court's granting certiorari. He agreed with Ernest Miranda's lawyers "wholeheartedly," he said, that "the confusion in this area must be dispelled in the interest of all concerned."

The statement was dispatched to Washington and received in the Supreme Court clerk's office on August 16, 1965.

CHAPTER 6

The United States Supreme Court was not in session in August 1965,* when Ernest Miranda's petition to be heard and the response of the state of Arizona arrived in the clerk's office. It had shut down for the summer, and the justices had scattered following the final Court session at the end of June. They did not, however, leave behind the Court's business. The search for justice recognized no seasonal differences, and cases came to the Court year-round, without letup. While most of the justices left town for varying periods of time each summer, they could be certain that mail sacks bursting with petitions for cert would be waiting at each destination, not excepting even remote Goose Prairie, Washington, at the foot of the Cascades, where Justice William O. Douglas spent most summers at his beloved, isolated Prairie House, six miles from the nearest telephone and in plain sight of a herd of elk feasting on his clover meadow. The summer of 1965 was typical. Roughly 700 cases, both criminal and noncriminal, came to the Court.

Several cases involving *Escobedo* issues had already made their way to the Court, but it had refused to hear them. The result, declared a justice of the Pennsylvania Supreme Court, was that "the law is in a state of serious confusion with no apparent hope of enlightenment from the Supreme Court of the United States, in view of its action in refusing certiorari in cases reaching conflicting results."

---

* The term traditionally ended in June each year and a new term opened the first Monday in October—hence the designation *October Term*, OT, which operated much like an academic year.

Chapter 6

Silence from the U.S. Supreme Court, however, should not be confused with somnolence. Because the nature of their work required some degree of secrecy, the justices tended to keep their professional deliberations within the marble walls, so that they often appeared impassive and unconcerned. But outward stolidity could be misleading.

The U.S. Constitution limited the Court to deciding "cases and controversies," and the justices were always meticulous—if not pious—in explaining how they had no control over what cases and issues came to the Court. True, as far as it went. While they could not control what cases came to them, they could decide which ones to hear. There was merit in the argument that decisions in cases like *Escobedo*, which left issues undecided, encouraged, deliberately or not, lawyers to follow up with the cases that would close the circle. Under the circumstances of *Escobedo*, it was less a question of waiting for cases to come than it was of waiting for the *right* case or cases.

It was also a matter of timing. Traditionally, after the Court had decided a case with broad ramifications for the administration of criminal justice, its members, before broadening or narrowing it, sat back and watched how it was received among the people it affected and how the lower courts responded. Sometimes such a process could consume years. The confessions issue, however, following the decision in *Escobedo*, required emergency attention.

Quantity quickly took care of itself. Immediately after *Escobedo*, in June 1964, lawyers, including John Flynn and John Frank, who filed two additional petitions for cert in cases peripherally involving confessions—"worming in on the party," Frank called it—began to look for some advantage out of it, and cases from every state in the Union came to the Court. Some involved only *Escobedo* issues; others involved those issues only south by southwest; still others were attempts to stretch the facts of *Escobedo* to fit their own. At the same time lawyers were conscientiously protecting their clients' interests, they were not immune to the attraction of being part of a prominent case which everyone in the legal community knew was going to be decided soon.

Quality was another matter. Questions had begun to swirl around the confessions issue in addition to the obvious one of whether an accused must request a lawyer or whether police had an obligation to furnish one in the interrogation room. Should it affect, for example, cases decided prior to Danny Escobedo's? Where should the cutoff point be? Should the ruling be extended, and, if so, how far? How much leeway should state courts be allowed to devise their own answers to the questions presented by *Escobedo*? What were the political effects—that is, how had *Escobedo* been received in the law enforcement community, and what would be the effects of either expanding or narrowing it?

So, while the people involved in the administration of criminal justice, from the accused to the appellate judge, tried to find their way out of the legal quagmire, the justices of the U.S. Supreme Court did what they could. Within about six months after *Escobedo*, by December 1964, they had quietly begun to collect and mark "Escobedo" or "hold for Escobedo" petitions for cert in cases that presented obvious *Escobedo* issues. By the end of the term, in June 1965, they had collected sixty-six. Over the summer Chief Justice Warren, whose office received the in forma pauperis petitions, put his law clerks to work identifying cases with *Escobedo* issues that came in while the Court was not in session.

The justices were not dismissing the problem in a cavalier fashion, as the Pennsylvania Supreme Court justice had implied. While the controversy continued outside the Court, its intensity increasing, they were aware that the business was far from finished, that they had a lion by the tail.

But they kept their thoughts to themselves. Chief Justice Warren and Justice William J. Brennan remained impassive when, as guests at the annual conference of the Third Judicial Circuit in late summer 1965—the circuit within which the dispute had been most intense—they listened to a panel discussion of the issues that had arisen since *Escobedo* had been decided. The participants were experts in their fields: New York City Police Commissioner Michael J. Murphy; Raymond J. Bradley, former director of the ACLU's Philadelphia branch and of the local Defenders Association; the police manual author and Northwestern University law professor Fred Inbau, who had been debating similar issues publicly for some time with University of Michigan legal scholar Yale Kamisar, also on the panel. Murphy and Kamisar belonged as well to the ALI's model code of pre-arraignment procedure advisory committee. The discussion gave the justices a rare opportunity to listen to the heartbeat of law enforcement at different pressure points. They remained, of course, noncommittal.

"It was a good discussion," Warren said, "it was a fair discussion; it was temperate; it was searching." Then he brought the house down with a typical homespun analogy: "After I had listened to both sides, I couldn't help thinking of the saying of the old hillbilly from Arkansas who said, 'you know, no matter how thin you make the pancake there are always two sides to it.' " He added a few lines that, freely translated, meant his Court was concerned and was watching to see how others defined the issues and devised ways of operating: "I have an idea that it is just such discussion that will bring about the right decision in all of these matters under discussion."

Commissioner Murphy and Professor Inbau, who had already accused the Supreme Court of handcuffing police, were only the latest in a series of similar critics that included no less than American Bar Association President Lewis F. Powell, Jr., who had said the previous January, while cautioning against Court criticism of the "unproductive and destructive sort," that "there is a growing body of opinion that the rights of law-abiding citizens are ·

being subordinated. The pendulum may have swung too far in affording rights which are abused and misused by criminals."

The preliminaries were nearly ended. It would shortly be incumbent upon the chief justice and his Court to break their long silence. The previous spring a young prosecutor at the conference of the National Association of District Attorneys in Houston had looked out over the room where his fellow prosecutors were popping champagne corks while they talked of George Whitmore and Danny Escobedo, and he made a comment the validity of which would outlive the conference: "Paris just before the Maginot Line collapsed must have been a little like this."

Congress, which prior to the installation of air conditioning in the Capitol in the 1930s was in the habit of adjourning before the July steam arrived, was still in session this summer of 1965, although women and children had been evacuated to Bar Harbor, Martha's Vineyard, and Bethany Beach, Delaware, decentralizing the social life temporarily, moving the drinks, the buffets, and the gossip to the various summering places. In season the city glittered socially, with overlapping political, diplomatic, and social circles, all heavily influenced by the style of whoever occupied the White House. About the most exciting social events in the summer of 1965, however, were a series of send-off parties for Patricia Roberts Harris, soon to leave for Luxembourg as U.S. ambassador.

In Congress the Senate was debating a constitutional amendment which would have allowed one of the two houses of a state legislature to be apportioned on the basis of something other than population—a direct and deliberate attack on the U.S. Supreme Court, which had ruled the previous year that both houses of state legislatures must be apportioned strictly on a population basis. On August 4 the bill was defeated.

The following day the Senate District Committee, which oversaw District of Columbia affairs and was under heavy public pressure to enact legislation to deal with rising crime rates, approved a new version of a bill that would allow police to interrogate suspects up to three hours before taking them before a magistrate to be formally charged.

And at the same time members of the Senate Judiciary Committee were pursuing the elusive judicial philosophy of the most recent nominee to the U.S. Supreme Court, Abe Fortas, prominent Washington attorney and Clarence Earl Gideon's courtroom champion, who had been named to succeed Arthur Goldberg, author of the Court's opinion in Danny Escobedo's case, on the latter's resignation. With Goldberg gone, the Court was evenly divided between the four justices who tended to uphold the rights of the individual and the responsibilities of the state and the four who tended to decide against the individual. Who succeeded Goldberg would be of critical importance when Ernest Miranda's case came before the Court, and it was not at all certain, as Fortas wriggled and squirmed—albeit without abandoning his customary urbanity—under the senators' questioning, toward which faction of the Court he would lean.

Fortas was one of the rare nominees to the Supreme Court who had come not out of politics or government—although he was not inexperienced in either field—but from the ranks of practicing lawyers. He might have remained there, able, sought-after, and prosperous, except for his friendship with a president of the United States. Fortas, in fact, had made such an important contribution to Lyndon B. Johnson that Johnson might not have been the president without the intervention of the private lawyer, and there was always a question about the two men: Would the superior talents of either have emerged without the help of the other?

As an assistant professor at Yale Law School, from which he had been graduated in 1933, first in his class, Phi Beta Kappa, and editor in chief of the *Yale Law Journal*, he had become a protégé of Professor William O. Douglas's, and when Douglas went to Washington to join the staff of the Securities and Exchange Commission, he took Fortas along. For the next decade or so Fortas moved confidently and aggressively through Washington's various concentric government circles, becoming eventually undersecretary of the interior. In 1946, he established, with Thurman Arnold, a former judge of the U.S. Court of Appeals for the District of Columbia Circuit, the law firm of Arnold & Fortas; when the two men were later joined by Paul Porter, a former chairman of the Federal Communications Commission, the firm became Arnold, Fortas & Porter.

It is not uncommon for government lawyers, particularly the more successful ones, to take their government-learned expertise into private practice, the better to serve clients who must deal with the myriad agencies and departments of the federal bureaucracy. The man who can find his way through that bureaucracy is a valued man indeed, and Abe Fortas and his high-powered partners, with their high-powered contacts as well as their expertise, over the years became some of the most valued.

The most valuable services Fortas ever performed, perhaps, he performed only two years after the founding of the firm. In 1948 he had known Lyndon Johnson for about ten years, mostly on a social basis, although, as Fortas said later, it was difficult sometimes to draw a line between social and official occasions in Washington. Johnson, then a congressman, was running for U.S. senator from Texas against an ultraconservative former governor of Texas, Coke Stevenson, and seven other candidates. Johnson, typically, had hired a helicopter, the *Johnson City Windmill*, and swooped down into farmyards and small towns all over the state of Texas in his fierce primary fight; he had come in second in the primary but had managed to win the runoff by exactly 87 votes out of more than 900,000 cast, a feat that earned him the nickname Landslide Lyndon. The winning votes, however, had come at a late date, and in a recount, from the Panhandle town of Alice, seat of Jim Wells County, which was run by an old-fashioned political operator named George Parr. Coke Stevenson immediately charged fraud and took his case to the federal courts; his lawyers persuaded a local federal district judge to issue an injunction to keep Johnson's name off the ballot in the November election pending an investigation of Stevenson's charges.

Abe Fortas was at the time in Dallas, taking depositions in an antitrust case. A mutual acquaintance summoned him to a lawyers' meeting in a Fort Worth hotel where Johnson's strategy was being mapped. Time was short; it was already nearing the end of September; Texas law required the candidates' names to be posted by October 3.

Fortas's strategy was to appeal the injunction to the U.S. Supreme Court as quickly as possible. This meant, because all the procedural niceties must be observed and all other avenues of appeal exhausted first, that the appeal had first to go to the U.S. Court of Appeals for the Fifth Circuit. Fortas quickly put together a brief, and another lawyer presented Johnson's case to Circuit Judge Joseph C. Hutcheson, Jr., because the appellate court was not in session. Hutcheson held that a single judge had no authority to stay the execution of the lower court's injunction; he would not convene a special panel; the appeal would have to await the opening of court in October.

But October was too late. There was nothing for it but to appeal directly to the U.S. Supreme Court. It was not in sesson either; however, the partners at Arnold, Fortas & Porter happened to know—and it was this sort of knowledge and resourcefulness for which their clients paid—that the senior associate justice in charge of Fifth Circuit matters, Hugo Black, was in town and, pleading that time was of the essence, persuaded him to hear their case.

Within twenty-four hours Black had gathered the lawyers for both Johnson and Stevenson in his chambers, called in the press, and listened to four hours of arguments, interrupted only by his questioning, which was sharp and knowledgeable. Fortas argued for Johnson; former Texas Governor Dan Moody, for Stevenson.

At the end Black announced his verdict: A federal district judge had no right to interfere in a state election that way; Black would grant the stay. The full Court, when it returned on October 5, refused to set aside Black's order, and Lyndon Johnson's name as Democratic candidate for senator remained on the ballot in November. That was, of course, tantamount to election in Texas.*

---

* Lyndon Johnson neither forgot his friends nor forgave his enemies. On Hugo Black's eightieth birthday, he gave a dinner party for the justice in the family quarters of the White House, to which he invited several of the participants in the election of 1948. After reminiscing about the turn of events, the president concluded: "That is not really the reason for this birthday party. But it sure as God is the reason I am giving it."

Lyndon Johnson and Abe Fortas remained close friends through the 1950s and early 1960s, so that it was not unnatural for Johnson, on assuming the presidency following the assassination of President Kennedy, to call in the man whom he could trust as well as whose legal skill and political acumen he admired, for advice on appointments, departmental problems, domestic programs, foreign policy, and the creation of the Warren Commission to investigate the assassination. Fortas served his friend and president well, and when the first U.S. Supreme Court vacancy was created by Arthur Goldberg's resignation in the summer of 1965—Goldberg had been appointed to succeed Adlai E. Stevenson as U.S. ambassador to the United Nations—Abe Fortas, so far as Johnson was concerned, was the only man to fill it. Fortas, however, was reluctant.

"God almighty, Mr. President," Fortas had thundered when Johnson had phoned him from *Air Force One* on the way back from Stevenson's funeral in Springfield, Illinois. "You can't do that. I've got to talk to you about it."

Talk they did. Fortas even refused the appointment in writing. But the greatest arm twister of them all rarely took no for an answer. On Wednesday, July 28, Johnson had telephoned Fortas again at his law office and invited him to a press conference, scheduled to begin within minutes.

"Look, you don't suppose he is going to lean on me some more about this," Fortas asked his law partner Paul Porter.

"Oh, I think you are off the hook from what I have heard," Porter replied.

Fortas, whose office was only a few blocks from the White House, hurried over. "I told him," Johnson later recalled in his memoirs, "that I was about to go over to the theater in the East Wing of the White House and to announce his appointment to the Supreme Court. I said that he could stay in my office or accompany me to the theater. He looked at me in silence for a moment. I waited. Then he said, 'I'll accompany you.' That was the only way I managed to get him on the Court." To the best of Fortas's knowledge, he never actually said yes.

Now, however, he was sitting in the witness chair in room 2228 of the New Senate Office Building as members of the Senate Judiciary Committee questioned him.

Senator James O. Eastland, the rotund, cigar-smoking Democrat from Sunflower County, Mississippi, who as chairman of the Judiciary Committee boasted he had special pockets put in his pants where he kept civil rights bills to prevent their emerging from his committee, opened the questioning of Fortas. Lyndon Johnson's is perhaps the most colorful characterization of Eastland's politics. "Jim Eastland," Johnson once said, "could be standing right in the middle of the worst Mississippi flood ever known, and he'd say the niggers caused it, helped by the Communists—but he'd say, we gotta have help from Washington."

Out of habit, perhaps, Eastland began with questions on his second favorite subject: Communists. Although Fortas and his law partners had defended a number of government employees who had been discharged for security reasons during the height of the McCarthy era, the subject held considerably less interest in 1965 than it would have a decade before, and the chairman's questioning was cursory.

Communism as a political issue had been superseded by crime in the streets, and it was not long before questioning of the nominee was taken over by the committee's crime fighter, former prosecutor John L. McClellan, Democrat of Arkansas. Judiciary committee hearings held in connection with Supreme Court appointments had become something of a ritual, the participants dancing around each other, their steps strictly prescribed. It all came down to the senators' trying to persuade the nominee to state positions he would espouse after he took his seat on the Court, the nominee's trying to answer with apparent candor but without making his positions known. It was one year after *Escobedo* had divided the nation's courts on questions regarding the appointment of counsel for criminal defendants in the interrogation room. It was one day after the Bazelon-Katzenbach correspondence regarding the American Law Institute's first draft of its model code of pre-arraignment procedure had been published in the *Washington Star*, and there was considerable interest among the senators in where the nominee stood on the issues that had emerged in each.

After his customary speech on the rise of lawlessness in America and the courts' negligence in putting a stop to it, McClellan got to the point. "I think," he said, "the Bazelon-Katzenbach letters present a markedly contrasting, if complete, philosophy and viewpoint with respect to law enforcement. . . . I would have some difficulty voting to confirm a nominee for a judicial position who expressed a viewpoint of only one of them." He added, as if either Fortas or anyone else present held any doubts: "You be the judge."

Fortas, suave, self-deprecating, and not easily aroused to anger, replied that he was indeed "distressed" by the language of the letters, which would, he believed, "precipitate controversy." However, he volunteered, the subject of the correspondence—the rights of the individual and the rights of police in the station house—"was one of the most difficult and one of the most important problems that we have in criminal jurisdiction and procedure."

He would not, of course, "break the rule" that prohibited Supreme Court nominees from speaking about matters that might come before the Court. He believed he could, however, "without any impropriety . . . repeat what I have said in the past. . . ." If any of the senators present thought they were about to be treated to a statement of his future judicial behavior on the matter of confessions, however, they were disappointed. He came down on both sides of the issue, offering not a clue:

> I believe that an adequate opportunity in the hands of the police to
> interrogate persons who are accused of crime or who are suspected

that they might have been involved is absolutely essential to law enforcement. At the same time I recognize that there comes a point at
which such persons should be brought before a judicial officer, such
as a magistrate, for the purpose of ascertaining whether there is
probable cause for their continued detention, and the great difficulty . . . which I confess I would not be able to suggest a solution
to . . . is where to draw that line.

"Would you say," asked McClellan, who could never forgive the Warren Court for its decisions on matters of racial desegregation, legislative apportionment, and, now, criminal justice, matters which, he said, in the euphemism of the day, should be handled by the legislative branch, "that
legislation might be appropriate in this field, that some legislation by the
Congress might be helpful in resolving it?" Another counterforce that would
not be without impact on the issues in Ernest Miranda's case had begun to
gather momentum.

Fortas thought the idea had potential, but he was not prepared to define, however hard the senator pressed, exactly "where the power of the Congress and the impact of the Constitution hit on this particular problem."

Senator Hugh Scott, a Republican and former assistant district attorney
from Pennsylvania, who agreed with the attorney general on this issue, took
the baton from McClellan. Scott was disturbed, he said, about Judge Bazelon's reasoning; it seemed to imply that the "person who is poor ought somehow because he is poor to have thrown into the balance of the judicial scales
something in his favor as against the State or the people so as to equalize this
unfortunate condition." If that kind of thinking entered into the decision
making of Supreme Court justices, Scott warned, there would be "considerable danger."

Fortas reassured him at once. Clarence Earl Gideon's defender believed,
of course, that "because a man is poor he should not be deprived of the representation of counsel and of the wherewithal, the facilities to make his defense
in our courts of law. But," he added, "I would utterly reject any suggestion
that the scales of justice should be weighted by one ounce or a fraction of an
ounce in his favor because he is poor."

He added wryly: "Justice is not like the progressive income tax."

Throughout the morning Fortas continued to answer the senators' questions without revealing anything of substance.

Five days later the committee unanimously approved his nomination to
the United States Supreme Court. The same day the committee approved the
nomination of Judge Thurgood Marshall of the U.S. Court of Appeals for the
Second Circuit, former special counsel to the NAACP, to be the first black
U.S. solicitor general, with Senators Eastland and McClellan voting against
him, as expected.

The following day, August 11, the full Senate approved both nominations, albeit not without a speech against the Fortas nomination by Senator Strom Thurmond of South Carolina. Like McClellan, the southern Republican had been consistently critical of the Warren Court, and he did not discern in Abe Fortas a man who would change its direction.

Some observers believed that Fortas's vigorous defense of government employees discharged on loyalty grounds in the 1950s and his arguments in behalf of Clarence Earl Gideon spoke volumes about his views on the Constitution and that when he took his seat in October, he would join the bloc of justices to which his predecessor, Arthur Goldberg, had belonged. Others believed his public indecisiveness on the subject of police interrogations during the Judiciary Committee hearings indicated not so much political necessity as unfamiliarity with the realities of station house life. He was, after all, an appellate lawyer whose major clients were not the Gideons but Braniff Airlines and Federated Department Stores, and his regular beat was the federal bureaucracy, not the local police precincts. So Abe Fortas on the eve of his elevation to the United States Supreme Court remained a question mark over Ernest Miranda's fate there.

Not so unpredictable was the public behavior of Richard Nixon. Nixon, who never seemed to vacation politically, appeared in the summer of 1965 at the suburban Maryland home of Louise Gore, Montgomery County delegate to the Maryland legislature, for a Republican fund raiser attended by senators and congressmen who made the county their home during the legislative sessions. Tanned after eighteen holes of golf at Burning Tree Country Club, Nixon gave a twenty-minute poolside pep talk aimed at increasing the number of Republicans in Congress.

His efforts, of which this was only one small sample, were directed ostensibly at bringing about a Republican revival following the 1964 disaster. Having made at least a tentative decision earlier in the year to begin again the long and arduous climb toward the presidency, the time he was spending at this and similar fund-raising events was serving also as a sounding time for Nixon, a time to listen to the mood of the crowds, to renew acquaintances with local Republican leaders, and to ingratiate himself with all those Republican candidates for governor, senator, congressman, and state legislator who might be useful three years hence.

In September a Gallup poll showed him running ahead of Lyndon Johnson in a southern straw vote—47 percent to 44 percent—and an appearance the same month in Des Moines, Iowa, during which he talked about foreign policy, having returned from a sixteen-day "private business trip" to Asia, gave off the unmistakable aroma of presidential politics. Some months later a writer in *Pravda*, the Communist party newspaper, commented that

Nixon's political friends appeared to be trying to put him into presidential orbit again.

"We shall see what happens," the Russian wrote. "But we feel that the launching will not be successful because the rocket itself is rather old-fashioned and the fuel is not popular."

CHAPTER 7

The United States Supreme Court opened its 1965 term on October 4 with a swearing-in. Abe Fortas, ninety-fifth justice in the Court's 174-year history, took his seat following two brief and solemn ceremonies traditional for appointees: The chief justice administered the constitutional oath in the Court conference room, with only the justices present, at 9:45 A.M., and at 10 the justices proceeded to the imposing marble-columned public courtroom where Fortas had distinguished himself as an advocate, and the clerk of the Court administered the judicial oath. Fortas's seat was known as the scholar's seat; it had been held by Oliver Wendell Holmes, Jr., Benjamin N. Cardozo, and Felix Frankfurter. Fortas looked more self-confident than he perhaps felt because a few months later he confided to Hugo Black, whom he had known for many years: "I'm still not convinced that I have the philosophical assurance which I think is needed for the Court. Perhaps it will come in time; perhaps not. . . ."

One of Fortas's closest friends and the man responsible for his appointment, the president of the United States, was unable to attend the swearing-in. Johnson had previously scheduled a meeting with Pope Paul VI in New York the morning of October 4 and was forced to break the tradition, begun with Truman, of the chief executive's attending the installation ceremonies of his Supreme Court appointees. The courtroom, however, was crowded with the new justice's family and friends, and following the oath taking, he and his wife held a brief reception in one of two public conference rooms to greet them. The justices then retired to their private conference room, where they

97

spent the rest of the working week discussing the 700 or so cases that had come in during the summer and deciding which ones to review.

By this time 126 cases involving *Escobedo* issues in some form had been set aside. Of these, 66 had come in before the Court had adjourned in June, 60 over the summer. One of those set aside was Ernest Miranda's.

On October 22 Justice Douglas and his third wife gave a party at the Court for the new justice and his wife. The guests, who included the new solicitor general, Thurgood Marshall, and Attorney General Katzenbach, as well as the many Fortas friends in the legal community, were preoccupied with the simultaneous appearance of two of Justice Douglas's wives—one of his ex-wives had married a friend of the Fortases. No one attached much significance at the time, although they would at a later date, to the presence of a financier named Louis E. Wolfson, who had retained Arnold, Fortas & Porter, now Arnold & Porter, the previous summer to represent him before the Securities and Exchange Commission, which was investigating one of his many companies. Prior to Fortas's nomination to the Supreme Court, Fortas and Wolfson had become friends, and Wolfson had invited Fortas to serve as a consultant to the Wolfson Family Foundation, a tax-free, charitable institution which the financier was establishing and with whose potential for good in student and race relations Fortas had been impressed. The day after the Court party, Saturday, October 23, Fortas and Wolfson met again at Fortas's Georgetown home and arranged that for $20,000 a year, Fortas would work with the foundation as a consultant. The agreement was part of the justice's private life. He was to discover later that his private and public lives could not be so easily separated.

The first critical stage in the process of taking a case to the U.S. Supreme Court is the conference at which the justices decide whether or not to consider it at all. The conference at which that decision in Ernest Miranda's case was made took place on November 22, 1965.

The proceedings of the conference were secret, not, the late Felix Frankfurter once explained, out of "love of secrecy or want of responsible regard for the claims of a democratic society to know how it is governed," but out of due regard for the effective functioning of the Court, which ought not to be "amenable to the forces of publicity to which the Executive and the Congress are subjected."

Justices Black and Douglas had at one time attempted to make the voting of individual justices public in cases where appeals were dismissed or certiorari denied, but they could never gather support for the scheme. The two justices began to write their own brief dissents in such instances if the cases were important ones, and Douglas eventually began to make his disagreements known in all cases.

The general outline of the conference, if not the specific discussions and voting records, was, however, known. On conference days—usually Friday, but occasionally on other days—at five minutes before the hour a buzzer sounded in each of the justices' chambers, the signal to gather in the private oak-paneled conference room adjacent to the chief justice's chambers for the daylong deliberations.

The chief justice slipped in from his office next door. Chief justices tend to look like chief justices, a case of the medium being the message, and the bearded, judge-like appearance of Charles Evans Hughes had once been compared to the appearance of "De Lawd Hisself." Earl Warren looked more as if he had walked out of some ancient Scandinavian saga rather than the Old Testament, but the overall effect was similar. He was big—six feet tall, more than 200 pounds—his blue eyes were as lively as ever, though his blond hair was turning white; his manner was as hearty as his voice implied, but there was also a streak of Viking toughness in him.

Down the hall came the rest:

Aristocratic-looking John Marshall Harlan, sauntering along, one hand on the big gold watch chain that had belonged to his grandfather, the first Justice John Marshall Harlan, the other holding a cigarette.

Hugo Black, his hands gnarled and his hair thinning at seventy-nine, but his body still wiry and his face tanned from hours spent on the tennis court.

Abe Fortas, the junior member: short, slight in build, his facial features soft, his hairline receding, but his air of urbanity undiminished.

Craggy-faced William O. Douglas, a familiar figure in Washington by 1965, in broad-brimmed western hat floppy with age, khaki pants and worn hiking boots, as annually he led fellow conservationists along the towpath of the century-old Chesapeake and Ohio Canal in an effort to save it from the highway builders and preserve it in its natural glory;* that day he looked as if his city clothes were making him itch.

Stocky, pug-nosed, still young-looking Potter Stewart.

Tall, slender Tom Clark, the inevitable bow tie out in front.

Little William J. Brennan with the face of a leprechaun and a grocery cart full of lawbooks and memorandums.

Byron White, the Whizzer, his scholarly mien belying his previous incarnation as All-American halfback for the University of Colorado in 1937 and a leading ground gainer for the Pittsburgh Steelers in 1938 and the Detroit Lions in 1940. Following his graduation magna cum laude from Yale Law School, as he prepared to leave for Washington to begin a clerkship with Chief Justice Fred M. Vinson, John Frank, who was a visiting professor at Yale that summer, had described him as "an unusually likeable fellow of great talent. He is doubtless almost as well known to the American public as the Chief Justice is!" At forty-eight, he was the youngest of the justices.

---

* The effort ultimately was successful. In 1971 the canal, towpath, and sections of the surrounding countryside were designated a national historic park. On May 17, 1977, the park was dedicated to the man most responsible for its preservation: William O. Douglas.

Upon entering the conference room, the justices shook hands with each other, a custom which had begun with Chief Justice Melville W. Fuller (1888–1910) and which Justice James F. Byrnes once compared to the referee's instructions to boxers: "Shake hands, go to your corners and come out fighting." It was intended, however, as a symbol of "mutual respect and courtesy" and a reminder that harmony of aims, if not of views, motivated the nine decision makers.

The conference room itself, with the portrait of John Marshall, the fourth chief justice and the man forever enshrined as the one who made the Supreme Court the powerful arm of government it had become, hanging above the black marble fireplace and the floor-to-ceiling shelves that held the decisions of all the federal courts, had little to distinguish it from the conference room of a large private law firm. In the middle stood a long, baize-covered table at which the justices sat for the daylong sessions, the chief justice at the head, the senior associate justice at the foot, the other seven ranged along the sides.

Each justice had a list of the cases to be considered that day. By this time each one was presumed to have done the necessary homework and had noted his tentative views on whether review should be granted or denied in each case. No petition was ever ignored, whether it came from a prestigious law firm or was scrawled in crayon and postmarked "San Quentin." But some petitions were more equal than others in the competition for the justices' attention.

Capital cases were, of course, always flagged; these were of paramount importance. The lower courts from which cases came could have significance, particularly when, as often happened, the circumstances and issues in a case were not clearly presented in the petitions for cert; then the lower-court opinions were looked to for guidance. The justices were familiar with the nation's courts and judges; they knew the difference between the California Supreme Court and the Florida Supreme Court; long experience had taught them that the opinions of Henry J. Friendly of the U.S. Court of Appeals for the Second Circuit, for example, were considerably more reliable than those of some hanging judge. And, of course, in important cases, the justices wanted to hear arguments by lawyers they knew were competent to deal with the issues; law clerks carefully noted on their memorandums that John Frank, known to the justices as experienced and sophisticated counsel, had submitted the petition for cert in behalf of Ernest Miranda.

For a case to be put on the agenda required only one justice's request. On the other hand, to keep the discussion within manageable limits, all the justices customarily indicated to the chief justice which of the cases they believed had no merit at all. Where agreement was unanimous, those cases were not even discussed.

When a case came from a state court, as Ernest Miranda's had, the Court had specific criteria for granting certiorari, although the potential for disagreement resided in each one. The mental process through which decisions evolved varied from justice to justice, and Simon E. Soboloff recalled that on becoming solicitor general of the United States, he had paid courtesy calls on each of the justices and discovered that "no two seemed to have exactly the same standards for certiorari; most of them said frankly that the standards defy formulation." Even John Harlan, a particularly rule-conscious justice, always said that whether or not a case was "certworthy" was "more a matter of 'feel' than of precisely ascertainable rules."

There were, however, some general rules. First, there must be a federal issue involved, one arising out of the Constitution, a federal treaty, or a federal law. Then the federal question must be a substantial one; it must have been raised properly in the state courts, thus affording the state court the opportunity to deal with it first; and the state court decision must not be able to be sustained on some independent ground of state law. The combination was not easily assembled in one case; the Court was not anxious to interfere in state matters. Ernest Miranda's case, however, qualified on all counts.

In Miranda's case, though, there were additional, nonjudicial considerations. Receptivity by the law enforcement community was perhaps the major one. Although the justices did not show their chagrin publicly, they were, in fact, acutely sensitive to the criticism by Congress and the state and federal judges as well as police and prosecutors that had accompanied their expansion of the criminal suspect's constitutional rights in recent years. They also recognized the potential for political mischief—the 1964 presidential election campaign had demonstrated it vividly—if they continued on that course. They had to choose carefully.

Many observers had expected the justices to wait for the American Law Institute's model code of pre-arraignment procedures to be completed before making their move on confessions, and some of the people involved in the project hoped for exactly that. Two months previously, in September 1965, James Vorenberg, executive director of the project, explained to an international legal conference at Ditchley Park, England, why: The model code when completed was to assist state legislatures in dealing with the problems of the taking of confessions; the judiciary, which could stop only what was wrong, was ill-equipped to set down what was right; detailed instructions to the law enforcement community was a legislative, not a judicial, function.

"It would be disheartening," federal Judge Henry Friendly, a member of the advisory committee of the ALI project, had told the state bar of California the same month, if the ALI project "should largely die aborning, if, instead of decision being made by Congress and the state legislatures, the most significant issues should already have been settled for all time by the casting vote of one or two respected men in a stately building in Washington—very likely in 'hard cases' where the full consequences of decision may have been clouded by understandable outrage over the facts at hand. . . ."

The Supreme Court, he warned, should not rush into writing codes of criminal procedure, "allowing no room whatsoever for reasonable difference of judgment or play in the joints."

The justices, however, were not inclined to wait. When the Court had resumed operations in late September, prior to the opening session on October 4, they had begun to winnow out some of the cases that had been marked "Escobedo" even while new petitions continued to arrive. In late October the chief justice's office had distributed to the other justices memos on each *Escobedo* case. The memos supplied the data relevant to a decision to grant or deny review: the vital statistics of the case; the character of the evidence; the circumstances under which it had been obtained; the use that had been made of it; the claims of *Escobedo* violations and whether or not they were substantiated; whether or not the violations had been properly raised in the lower courts; whether or not other procedural obstacles to review existed; and whether or not other than *Escobedo* issues were raised. Warren also had his law clerks submit to him a list of cases which they thought best raised a variety of facets of the confessions issue the Court wanted to hear argued; cases in which warnings of a defendant's rights had not been given; cases in which "arguably full warnings" had been given; cases in which the record was silent on whether or not warnings had been given; and cases involving questions of whether or not whatever decision was made should be made retroactive. Ernest Miranda's was the law clerks' first choice out of those cases in which warnings had not been given at all.

Discussion of the *Escobedo* cases had been scheduled originally for the regular conference on Friday, November 5; but there were too many, and a special conference was scheduled for Monday, November 22, the very day Judge Friendly's court had decided against a Buffalo man convicted on the basis of his confession of a narcotics offense, although following his arrest he had not been informed of his right to remain silent, his right to counsel, or that anything he said might be used against him in court. The respected chief judge of the circuit, J. Edward Lumbard, who was also a member of the advisory committee of the ALI project as well as Warren Burger's sponsor on the ABA criminal justice project, spoke for the court majority, which included Friendly:

> When an arrest is validly made without a warrant . . . it is particularly necessary that the police be permitted a questioning period of reasonable duration so that an informed decision to charge can be made. . . . [To] deny to the police or to federal agents such a routine method of screening the innumerable suspects who pass through their hands by prohibiting use of the fruits of questioning when they have reason to believe a crime has been committed, regarding which a suspect is likely to have some knowledge, would be an unrealistic obstruction that would tax the investigative resources of law enforcement agencies immeasurably and reduce the effi-

ciency of crime prevention and detection to a degree which would seriously endanger public safety. . . .

The agenda held 101 cases involving *Escobedo* issues. They had been culled from the approximately 150 *Escobedo* cases that had come in during the past eighteen months from twenty-five states as well as from the federal circuit courts of appeals.

The chief justice traditionally opened the discussion of each case. Every chief justice had his own style: Charles Evans Hughes was known for his efficiency; Harlan Fiske Stone, for his easygoing ways. Earl Warren's hallmark was his ability to translate abstruse legalisms into comprehensible language, an ability which he carried over into his opinion writing and which tended to lower his regard among some legal scholars to whom it implied gaps in his legal knowledge. It was, however, he said, "part of my idea of the Court as a people's court" to express "the concepts of the Constitution in common language."

Discussion then proceeded in order of seniority, from Hugo Black to Abe Fortas. Voting—should cert be granted or not?—proceeded in the opposite direction, from the most junior to the most senior, with the chief justice voting last. The unwritten but absolutely rigid rule was that four votes granted certiorari, and the case was then transferred to the arguments list.

A broad spectrum of views was aired in the conference room this November day, ranging from the senior associate justice's—Hugo Black's—urging on the brethren an expansionist interpretation of *Escobedo* to former Attorney General Tom Clark's urging of a narrow one. The most recent appointee, the question mark, Abe Fortas, despite his reputation as a defender of the legally disadvantaged in the courts, stood somewhere in the middle. He recently had instructed his law clerk to seek out a case that would move the law only a small step beyond *Escobedo*, and Justice Harlan, in his characterization of his brethren's comments during the discussion, noted that Fortas had been inclined to "make haste slowly."

The justices surprised everyone when the results of their conference were posted in the late afternoon of November 22. They had granted certiorari in not one but four cases involving five indigent prisoners who had been convicted on the basis of confessions. One of the four was Ernest Miranda's.

The cases chosen for review, the justices said later, in the decision on Miranda's case, shared "salient features." In none had the defendant been afforded a "full and effective warning of his rights" before police questioned him, although the statements that resulted from that questioning were admitted as evidence at each trial. In each case the defendant was "thrust into an unfamiliar atmosphere and run through menacing police interrogation procedures"; in Miranda's circumstances, for example, the "potentiality for compulsion is forcefully apparent"; an indigent Mexican defendant, "seriously disturbed . . . with pronounced sexual fantasies." In each case law enforcement officials had conducted interrogations ranging up to five days in duration, "despite the presence, through standard investigating practices of considerable evidence against each defendant"; eyewitnesses had identified three of the defendants, including Miranda; marked bills had been found in an accused bank robber's automobile; property stolen from his victim had been found in another defendant's home; in each case the need for a confession had been overstated.

What the justices failed to mention were the nonjudicial factors the choices illustrated. At the same time that the four cases selected shared significant features, they represented a broad spectrum of the state of confessions taking in the nation in 1965.

Carl Calvin Westover's was a federal case, one in which "arguably full warnings" had been given. He had been arrested in Kansas City, Missouri, about 9:45 P.M., on March 20, 1963, as a suspect in two local robberies. He was questioned by Kansas City police that night and again the following morning, but he denied any involvement in the crimes. He was then turned over to three FBI agents, who continued the questioning, this time regarding the robbery of a savings and loan association and a bank in Sacramento, California. The government agents had an advantage over the local police; Westover had been in custody for fourteen hours: questioned, pressured, sweet-talked, whatever police officers did in the privacy of the interrogation room short of physical brutality. Within a couple of hours, between 2:00 and 2:30 P.M., seventeen hours or so after Westover's arrest, the FBI agents emerged from the interrogation room with two signed confessions—one for each of the California robberies—which they had prepared during the questioning. At the head of each statement was a printed paragraph that Carl Calvin Westover had been advised of his rights. He was convicted on the basis of the confessions and sentenced to fifteen years' imprisonment. His conviction was affirmed by the U.S. Court of Appeals for the Ninth Circuit.

Like Ernest Miranda's, Michael Vignera's case came from a state, New York, which was at the time interpreting the Supreme Court's decision in *Escobedo* to mean that a criminal suspect must *request* counsel during police questioning. Like Miranda, Vignera had not been advised of his constitutional rights.

Vignera had been convicted in August 1961 of robbing a Brooklyn dress shop on the basis of a confession he had made after being hustled from one police station to another at least three times, questioned at each one, formally arrested at 3:00 P.M., then "detained" at the Seventieth Precinct in Brooklyn until 11:00 P.M., when an assistant district attorney took a formal statement. The "sole purpose" of that nocturnal interrogation, declared the petition for cert, was " 'to elicit a confession,' " according to the Court's own words in *Escobedo*, " 'to "get him" to confess his guilt despite his constitutional rights not to do so.' " Kings County Judge Samuel Liebowitz, defender of the

Scottsboro boys in the early 1930s, who had won a reputation as a harsh sentencing judge following his election to the bench, told the jury at Michael Vignera's trial: "Under our law, a police officer is not required to tell him 'you don't have to answer unless you wish and everything you say can be used against you.' The law does not require that that warning be given by the police officer in the State of New York. If it is not given, it does not because of the failure to give such advice invalidate the confession. . . ."

The fourth case the justices decided to hear that November 22 had been filed by lawyers for two men, Sylvester Johnson and Stanley Cassidy of Camden, New Jersey. They claimed their convictions for murder had been based on confessions obtained in violation of the Court's *Escobedo* ruling. However, their convictions had become final five years previously, in 1960, when the New Jersey Supreme Court affirmed them. The Court took this case, therefore, as a vehicle through which to deal with questions of retroactivity.

The justices did not at this conference select a case in which the record was silent about whether or not a defendant had been advised of his rights—a category that had been included on the chief justice's list—but two weeks later, at the urging of Justice Douglas, they added a fifth case to those which were to be argued and decided together, one involving exactly that issue. Roy Allen Stewart, a black man from Los Angeles with a sixth grade education, had confessed to robbery and first-degree murder after being held by police for five days, isolated with his interrogators, and questioned nine times during the period. There was no indication whether or not police had informed him of his constitutional rights to remain silent or to counsel during that time, and the California Supreme Court, which had previously applied the *Escobedo* ruling expansively—directly opposite the way the Arizona Supreme Court had applied it in Ernest Miranda's case—had gone a step farther and refused to presume, in the absence of some positive indication, that police had acted within the law as laid down in *Escobedo*. Stewart's conviction had been reversed, and the state was now appealing the reversal.

None of these cases involved physical brutality on the part of police—no rope burns scarred the necks of defendants; none had limped to his trial as a result of police violence. One case not chosen, for example, was that of a convicted burglar who had emerged from his interrogation with swollen hands and face. That kind of brutality the Court had already ruled against, beginning with *Brown* in 1936. And in no case was there much disagreement between prosecution and defense regarding the facts of the interrogation. Only the constitutional questions remained to be decided.

The crimes, if brutal, were not the most brutal ones among those the justices had to choose from. One that was passed over at this November 22, 1965, conference involved a man convicted for strangling, raping, and decapitating a woman, then trying to skin her. Another involved two defendants accused of attacking a couple in a car parked in a lovers' lane, beating up the boy and throwing him into a river, then raping and killing the girl. Word got around the Court that the chief justice was going to deny cert in those two cases no matter what happened on the rest.

The five confessions cases chosen for review held potential for dispassionate discussion.

As cases that are filed in the U.S. Supreme Court go, these were sharply focused—that is, there were not a lot of peripheral issues, such as search and seizure, which had to be considered. All were concentrated on admissibility of confessions as trial evidence.

And they did present a broad spectrum: two cases in which no advice on constitutional rights had been given, one in which "arguably full warnings" had been given, one in which the record was silent, and one that asked about retroactivity. The justices had taken a federal case, two cases from states which had interpreted *Escobedo* narrowly, one from a state which had interpreted it broadly. At oral argument they all would come together.

First, still another step in Supreme Court procedure had to be taken. Following a grant of certiorari by the United States Supreme Court, the next requirement for lawyers involved in a case was the filing of briefs. The petition for cert offered the reasons the Court should review the case; the brief was the written argument of the case itself. Lawyers submitted briefs, accompanied by the records of the lower courts, several weeks in advance of oral argument, in sufficient time for their courtroom opponents—called respondents—to submit replies and for the justices to read them, all prior to oral argument, scheduled in the confessions cases for the week of February 28, 1966.

The law firm of Lewis & Roca in Phoenix, Arizona, was a heady place to work following the U.S. Supreme Court's grant of certiorari in the case of Ernest Miranda. John Flynn and John Frank had gotten the firm involved in a major Supreme Court case, one posing substantial questions regarding controversial public policy. As they prepared the brief, pride mingled with a sense of history in the making drove not only the two principals but other members of the firm, too, to "almost frantic professional activity." People who were sharply divided on the merits of the case nevertheless were dedicated to its successful prosecution.

The brief for Ernest Miranda was submitted to the U.S. Supreme Court on January 19, 1966. It was a concise statement of the case. It reviewed Miranda's interrogation by Phoenix Police Officers Cooley and Young, his trial, and the decision of the Arizona Supreme Court. "Looking to where it is going by considering where it has been," Flynn and Frank described the growth of the law on right to counsel cases from its planting in *Powell* v. *Alabama* to the case of Danny Escobedo.

Having based their petition for cert on the Sixth Amendment (right to counsel) argument, they now based the brief on an elaboration of that argument, and they concluded:

> The day is here to recognize the full meaning of the Sixth Amendment. . . . As a matter of practicality in law enforcement, we cannot know the precise effects of giving counsel at the beginning as the law does at the end; but we can know that there is not the faintest sense in deliberately establishing an elaborate and costly system of counsel—to take effect just after it is too late to matter. . . . We invoke the basic principles of *Powell v. Alabama:* "He requires the guiding hand of counsel at every step in the proceedings against him." When Miranda stepped into Interrogation Room 2, he had only the guiding hand of Officers Cooley and Young.

Within two weeks after receiving the brief for Miranda, on February 9, 1966, Gary Nelson, assistant attorney general for the state of Arizona in charge of the Criminal Appeals Division, filed a brief in answer. Relying heavily on Justice McFarland's opinion for the Arizona Supreme Court, Nelson distinguished the facts and circumstances of Miranda's case from those of Danny Escobedo's: Chicago police had thwarted Danny Escobedo's efforts to talk with his lawyer, Phoenix police had not, since Miranda had not requested a lawyer; Escobedo had no police record and no previous experience with police routines, Miranda had a long record; Escobedo had been questioned not only by police officers but also by a skilled state's attorney, Miranda had undergone a routine police investigation; Chicago police had told Escobedo that another suspect had fingered him as the killer, Phoenix police had not used "chicanery" to trap Miranda; Escobedo had not been informed of his constitutional rights, Miranda had been so informed, although Nelson did not dispute his opponents' contention that Miranda had not been informed specifically of his right to counsel. So, Nelson concluded, the cases of Ernest Miranda and Danny Escobedo were "not equal and there is no Constitutional reason for this Court to equate them. . . ." He continued along a route popular among judges, including Warren Burger of the U.S. Court of Appeals for the District of Columbia Circuit, who were able to distinguish *Escobedo* from the cases that came to their courts:

> If a criminal has been clever in the commission of his crime, but is foolish or careless in his handling of the police interrogation of him concerning that crime, the evidence obtained as a result of the only honest investigative avenue left open to the law enforcement agency, [sic] should not be suppressed unless that evidence is determined not to be the product of the free and uncoerced will of the accused, or if it is obtained after the police have undertaken a course of conduct *calculated* to deny the accused his right to counsel. Certainly nothing less will be tolerated, but the United States Constitution requires no more.

Like Warren Burger, young Gary Nelson would not punish police for sins of omission.

Briefs for the participants in the other four confessions cases followed similar lines of argument. There were, in addition, the amicus curiae briefs submitted by interested groups which wanted to let the Court know their positions on particular issues. They were intended to add dimension to the arguments later in the context of experience or constitutional theory.

The American Civil Liberties Union, which had filed amicus briefs in the cases of Clarence Earl Gideon and Danny Escobedo, filed one. It had been put together largely by Anthony G. Amsterdam, a professor of law at the University of Pennsylvania at the time, a cooperating ACLU attorney, a member of the local ACLU Police Practices Committee, and a recent law clerk to the late Felix Frankfurter. He was just beginning to establish a reputation as a creative advocate in constitutional law; before the decade was out, he would convince the justices of the unconstitutionality of the death penalty. He had been assisted by Melvin L. Wulf, national ACLU legal director and three other ACLU lawyers. It was the only brief filed in these confessions cases which contemplated a "marriage of the Fifth Amendment [against self-incrimination] and the Sixth Amendment right to counsel," a union toward which, the authors said, the Supreme Court had been heading. It also was the only brief to document, with extensive quotes from leading writers on police interrogation techniques and police manuals, the inherent atmosphere of compulsion in the obtaining of confessions and statements from suspects by police. "Their basic attitude," the authors declared, "is one of getting the subject to confess despite himself—by trapping him into it, by deceiving him, or by more direct means of overbearing his will."

Duane R. Nedrud, executive director of the National District Attorneys Association, had spent the past year collecting statistical data from seventeen of the association's members in metropolitan areas relating to the use and effect of confessions in criminal cases. Although data were not complete in all seventeen, he believed they were the first significant data put together on the particular subject. They indicated that those areas where data were complete, the use of confessions in criminal convictions ranged from a low of 43.5 percent (Dade County, Florida, or Miami) to 82.9 percent (suburban Essex County, New Jersey), and he attached to his brief urging the Supreme Court not to expand *Escobedo* tables which he believed demonstrated that confessions did, in fact, play a substantial role in the conviction of criminals. This was the kind of practical information—which could not be extrapolated from the Constitution but only from day-to-day experiences of the law enforcement community—that the justices needed.

The third amicus brief, filed in the name of the New York attorney general and joined by the attorneys general of more than half the states, was of particular interest. On December 5, 1965, Louis J. Lefkowitz, attorney general of New York State, had told an interviewer that he was concerned by the "hamstringing" of law enforcement; he intended to study the briefs submitted by the lawyers in the confessions cases the Court had chosen to hear, after which he would decide whether or not to file an amicus brief for New York. Such filings, sometimes joined by other states, had become rather the fashion since twenty-three state attorneys general had submitted a common brief in support of Clarence Earl Gideon's case.

Lefkowitz did decide to file an amicus brief and engaged one of the nation's most prominent legal scholars and appellate lawyers to write it. He was Telford Taylor, a fifty-eight-year-old professor of law at Columbia University and appellate lawyer, former general counsel to the Federal Communications Commission, prosecutor of war criminals at Nuremberg, author of books on military and political subjects, and, in 1965, member of the advisory committee of the ALI project to devise a model code of pre-arraignment procedure.

Taylor persuaded the New York State attorney general's office to take an intermediate position, "not simply to go whole hog against the idea" of excluding uncounseled confessions as trial evidence, the idea that was generally being put forward for attorneys for the defendants, but to urge the Court to "go slow and make sure that this was not going to have repercussions that would be unfavorable."

On the grounds that "procedural developments in this area should take place in non-constitutional terms" the brief for the state of New York urged neither affirmance nor reversal of Miranda's and the other confessions cases. It asked, rather, that the U.S. Supreme Court stay out of the business of criminal lawmaking and allow the state legislatures and state courts to devise their own methods for protecting suspects from police strong-arm methods.

Lefkowitz's office circulated the brief to other state attorneys general in the hope of amassing support for New York's position. Twenty-six states* plus the commonwealth of Puerto Rico and the territory of the Virgin Islands joined. Alabama and Arkansas joined later. The states had made a U-turn since *Gideon.* Prior to the arguments in that case the Florida attorney general had urged his counterparts in the other states to submit amicus briefs asking the Court not to require them to provide counsel for indigent defendants in felony trials and to affirm Gideon's conviction. Only the attorneys general in Alabama and North Carolina had complied, while those in twenty-three states had signed an amicus brief asking the Court to require them to appoint counsel for indigent defendants at felony trials and to reverse Gideon's conviction. The states had been ready for *Gideon*; most of them already provided in some fashion for counsel, and Gideon's case was "vestigial." In early 1966, however, when the New York amicus brief was written, only three states (Cal-

---

* Arizona, Colorado, Delaware, Florida, Georgia, Idaho, Illinois, Kansas, Kentucky, Louisiana, Maine, Maryland, Missouri, Montana, Nebraska, North Carolina, North Dakota, Oregon, Pennsylvania, Rhode Island, South Carolina, Texas, Virginia, Washington, West Virginia, Wyoming.

ifornia, Oregon, Rhode Island) had rules excluding as evidence confessions given without prior warnings to a defendant of his full constitutional rights. Even these were of recent development, having been established only during the past year and then by judicial declamation rather than evolutionary development or statute. Gideon's was a case whose time had come. Miranda's was not.

Altogether the briefs in Miranda's and the other cases totaled more than 700 pages. Within them a justice could find almost anything he wanted to know concerning confessions. The abstractions, constitutional history, statutory history, practical application, statistics, precedents, issues currently in controversy, where the federal government stood, where the state governments stood—all were there. And they were presented not just by two sides, as was common, but from a wide spectrum of viewpoints: that of the law professor who weighed abstractions before he came to a conclusion, the appellate lawyer whose head held thirty years of precedents, the trial lawyer who looked at it from the defendant's side of the table in interrogation room 2, the prosecutor who looked at it from the police officer's chair in the same room.

The briefs were an instant success in the field of legal literature. To fill all the requests, John Frank ordered 500 copies of the brief for Ernest Miranda printed, paying personally for the 450 extra copies which the Court ordinarily would not have printed for official distribution.

There was, of course, widespread interest in these cases within the legal community. There was considerable speculation but no clear indication what the Court might do. If the past three decades of constitutional history were a guide, extending the ruling in *Escobedo* might appear the next natural step. However, moral sentiment and a good deal of legal sentiment, owing partially to the current crisis in law enforcement and the statistics of crime in the streets and partially to opposing conceptions of federalism, militated against it. The Court itself appeared evenly divided, with the most recent appointee, Abe Fortas, still a judicial question mark.

As John Flynn and John Frank prepared to leave for Washington to argue Ernest Miranda's case before the nation's highest court, they had not a clue.

EARL WARREN'S BOOK

CHAPTER 1

Bakersfield, California. Saturday evening, May 14, 1938.

Methias Warren, seventy-three, was sitting in his easy chair in the kitchen of his faded-yellow frame house on Niles Street, just off the town's main thoroughfare. He was alone—his wife had gone to Oakland for a series of eye operations—and he was alternately reading the newspaper and dozing. The evening was warm, and the windows and doors were open.

At about eight o'clock two tenants had come in to pay the $15 rent on one of the 100 or so small houses much like his own that Warren owned, chatted for a few minutes, and then left. They were the last to see Methias Warren alive. Later that night someone stole in, crushed his skull with a rusty piece of lead pipe, dragged him into the bedroom, emptied his wallet, and fled. The body was discovered by a handyman about nine-thirty Sunday morning.

Methias Warren's son, Alameda County District Attorney Earl Warren, had recently announced his candidacy for state attorney general. He was about to speak at a Masonic breakfast at the Claremont Hotel in Berkeley when he was handed a telegram. He read the message and stood stunned. For the first time his was the shock, his the disbelief followed by the hurt which he had seen so many times in the faces of others. The calm for which he was known, the warmth for which he was liked, the efficiency for which he was respected—all fell away like so many layers of outer clothing. Newspaper reporters watched the man who had sent 200 men to their deaths or to prison for murder sob. With visible effort, he finally pulled himself together, went home to his family in Oakland, then boarded a plane for Bakersfield.

Earl Warren himself did not participate in the investigation of his father's murder, explaining that in addition to his complete confidence in the Bakersfield police, "the judgment of a member of the family in such circumstances is not sufficiently objective to give proper leadership to such an investigation." Warren did, however, send members of his staff to Bakersfield to assist the local law enforcement officers.

They could only speculate on a motive. Robbery was the obvious one. Although he had chosen to live frugally, the elder Warren had prospered, less from what he had made as a mechanic for the Southern Pacific Railroad, from which he was retired, than from his local real estate investments. No one knew the true amount of his wealth. Most people in the area, however, were familiar with his habits. They knew that tenants in his little houses often brought the rent to him in cash and that he sometimes carried hundreds of dollars on his person. The murderer might also have been one of the Okies who, having dragged himself across Route 66 for half a continent from the Dust Bowl only to find Bakersfield something less than the El Dorado he had imagined, now lived in one of the tin shacks just outside town. An angry tenant of the elder Warren was another possibility, revenge for District Attorney Warren's crime busting, still another, although Earl Warren always dismissed that theory. He himself believed—and the Bakersfield chief of police agreed, at least in the essentials—"some itinerant came into our back yard for a personal reason, picked up the piece of pipe, entered by the kitchen door, smashed him on the head, took his wallet, pulled him into the darkened bedroom and fled. . . . It could well be that he went directly to the railroad and departed on a passing freight train."

Suspects were paraded through the Bakersfield police station for several months: an ex-convict, a painter who had lost his house for failing to make payments to the elder Warren, a local drunk, a business partner of Warren's, an itinerant refrigerator salesman, an unemployed neighbor who had left town suddenly, a former employee of Warren's—perhaps forty in all. Some were held for a short time and released; others were questioned and released immediately. The evidence was never enough, and the murder of Methias Warren was never solved.

Although Robert Powers, Bakersfield chief of police, took charge of the day-to-day operations, Earl Warren always seemed to hover in the background. His chief of detectives, Oscar Jahnsen, later recalled that "the boss told us all that we were investigating a murder and to act as we always had. There were rules to follow, rules he'd laid down a long time before. We were to go by those rules."

Among the suspects was a man who had been in Bakersfield—or could have been—at the time of the murder but who had since been convicted of another crime and sent to San Quentin. Chief Powers wanted to put an informer in the cell with him and wire the cell for sound with a Dictaphone.

Chapter 1

"I don't think it would work. I don't think Earl Warren would go for that," Jahnsen said.

"Well, why the hell not?" asked Powers. "What's wrong with that?"

"No, I don't think so," Jahnsen replied. "He doesn't like Dictaphones."

"Well, check with him," Powers said. "It's a possibility. It's his father."

Jahnsen checked. "I don't believe in Dictaphones," said Warren. The subject was closed.

Jahnsen himself at one point believed the murderer had been found. The detective questioned the suspect, then left to check out his story. When Jahnsen returned, he believed he had enough to get a confession. But

> When I got there [Jahnsen recalled years later] I found that they'd decided to question him themselves. They had been working on him for hours. No food. A light working on him. They hadn't touched him, of course. They knew better than that. But they'd been breaking him down, one after the other. By the time I got there, he was on the verge of collapse. I blew my top. I said to them that they'd blown the case. I told them that Earl Warren would never stand for a confession that was extorted from a suspect. . . . He loved his father and he wanted his murderer found, but he wouldn't break any of his rules or take advantage of his position even to convict the guilty man if he couldn't do it with solid evidence that was legally obtained.

When Jahnsen told Warren he had released the suspect, the "boss said I'd done the right thing," Jahnsen said.

In this early isolated incident, in which the degree of his emotion and personal involvement would never again be matched, Earl Warren had provided an answer to the question that would be asked him, first in one guise, then in another, many times over the years ahead: What price security? His refusal to eavesdrop on a prisoner's cell in San Quentin, to use a confession that had been extorted provided, at least in retrospect, a rare revealing glimpse of the future chief justice of the United States in whose hands Ernest Miranda's case now awaited action. This glimpse was, though, rare indeed. There was little else, even in retrospect, about Earl Warren's early public life that revealed the dimension of the future judge.

Earl Warren's story, which contains examples of social consciousness and social insensitivity, political courage and political opportunism, is one of change. Change is, perhaps, the most remarkable characteristic of his public life, and to this day people still try to discover the reasons for it.

His career had begun unremarkably enough. Following graduation in 1914 from Boalt Hall, the law school of the University of California at Berkeley, and military service during World War I, Warren had spent a short time as clerk to the Judiciary Committee of the California Assembly and as an aide to the Oakland city attorney. His public life had begun in earnest when he was appointed assistant district attorney of Alameda County in 1920. His boss resigned in 1925. Warren finished out the term, was elected district attorney in 1926, reelected in 1930 and 1934.

There was little about his official conduct during those eighteen years in the front lines of local law enforcement to suggest the scrupulousness with which later in his life he would defend the constitutional rights of the criminally accused. The most that could be said about him in those early years was that he was, perhaps, a little fairer than a lot of men in his position at the time.

It was not that he lacked opportunity, given the prevalence of crime in Alameda County. The county was the third largest in the state. It sprawled inland across the Bay from rich and cosmopolitan San Francisco. It was made up of nine cities and an almost equal area of farmland. It included two seaports, the western terminals of three transcontinental railroads, a fringe of industrial plants, genteel residential areas, filthy slums, ranches of 10,000 acres and up, cherry groves, a major branch of the state university, and a regular army of commuters to the glimmering, shimmering city across the Bay. It was a young and muscular county in a young and muscular state, but its very youth had deprived it of the traditions and civic sense of an older county on the eastern seaboard.

It had survived postwar depression and was enjoying the boom times of the twenties when Earl Warren became district attorney. Street crime—rape, mugging, and the like—was largely a phenomenon of the future, but organized crime was rampant. John Dillinger, Al Capone, Machine Gun Kelly, Bonnie and Clyde all were household names and had inspired smaller-time imitators. Alameda County, its docks and railroad yards lending it a quality of transience as well as providing a base for a booming industrial economy, attracted a substantial number of bootleggers, gamblers, narcotics pushers, loan sharks, prostitutes, and protection men, most of whom were entangled in local politics in a financial way.

Quietly, painstakingly—he was a plodder, not a quick study—Earl Warren began a cleanup campaign from his second-floor office in the old Oakland courthouse. He hired bright young attorneys just out of law school, conducted his investigations with thoroughness, and stated his cases with sober assurance in court. As a result, gangsters began to disappear from his jurisdiction.

Willard Shea, public defender for Alameda County at the time—an office Warren himself had been instrumental in having included in the 1927 county charter—said his opponent was "both vigorous and fair"—fair to the point of lending his own investigators to the public defender.

Warren was, however, no innovator then, and *fair* held some different implications in the twenties and early thirties from those it held in the fifties and sixties. In those days the U.S. Supreme Court had not yet extended the criminal sanctions of the Bill of Rights to the states—the case of the Scottsboro boys and *Brown* v. *Mississippi* were decided during the latter part of Warren's time as district attorney, and Izell Chambers's case was still in the future—due process of law held less interest for law enforcement than it would before the thirties were out; and judges asked prosecutors not "How did you get your evidence?" but only "What evidence have you got?" While the consensus was that the Alameda County district attorney's office was an unusually civilized operation under young Earl Warren—certainly more civilized than under his predecessor, when a deputy regularly carried a handful of signed search warrants in his pocket and simply filled in the names and dates as he needed them, a practice Warren had stopped immediately—there was no nonsense about constitutional rights or about a suspect's having a lawyer present when police questioned him. When a man was taken into custody in Alameda County, he was questioned by police; when they decided they had the right man, Warren's office was notified, a deputy and a stenographer were dispatched to the jail, and the interrogation was completed and recorded. There were also instances when men in the district attorney's office, with Warren's knowledge, actually hid suspects from their lawyers until the interrogations were over.

Willard Shea never heard Warren's office accused of using third-degree methods. The district attorney's men, however, said Shea, "question the defendants at great length and kind of wear them out, if you please. But I don't think his office was anything like as guilty of that as some of the police departments. But on occasion I thought they were a little bit rough."

Warren himself later confirmed Shea's judgment: "[I]n those days we *would* hold a fellow longer and the officers would try to be friendly, maybe. . . . [M]y officers might talk to him and might take a long time in getting an answer from him, but never by force.

". . . I'm sure that . . . some of our statements would not be accepted today [1971]. But I'm also reasonably sure that none of my people ever indulged in any force or coercion or any threats to get a man to confess."

Warren had, however, a somewhat broader conception of his office than the average district attorney that extended beyond its day-to-day operations and into the statewide administration of criminal justice. He believed strongly that state law enforcement officers were laboring under outmoded conditions, and he spent a good deal of time while he was still district attorney stumping the state legislature seeking support for laws to modernize the California criminal justice system.

Crime was not, of course, unique to Alameda County. It tormented the entire state, indeed the nation, as criminals made the most of the new technology. The Tuohy gang, using airplanes, had extended its bank-robbery operations over the whole of the Middle West. Machine Gun Kelly had adapted that modern instrument of death to his illegal pursuits. The kidnapping of Charles A. Lindbergh, Jr., in 1932 had terrorized the country, which was ill-equipped to deal with crime beyond its strictly local occurrence. In

California armed robbers twice heisted Columbia Steel Works payrolls from trains in the northern part of the state, then escaped by automobile, the escapes successful largely because pursuing police, from two different counties—Warren's own Alameda and Contra Costra—failed to cooperate with each other.

The same thing could have happened anywhere in the United States. There was little communication or cooperation among law enforcement units. County police had little contact with city police; Los Angeles police had practically nothing to do with San Diego or San Francisco police; state and local police knew little of each other's operations. The situation worked to the advantage of the criminal, and the result was a substantial increase in the freedom of underworld figures. Organized society, wrote Earl Warren in 1934, "is facing today . . . a war with organized crime."

The public outcry was predictable and typical. Anticrime groups formed, newspaper editorials screamed the war cry "Curb Crime," and the mood of repression set in.

If Earl Warren in those days was not in the vanguard of those who labored to advance the constitutional rights of the individual and was not above cutting a corner here and there, he was also not among those Californians who were calling for the remodeling of the entire state criminal justice system. There was nothing wrong, he believed, with California's criminal procedures that improved administration would not correct, and he set out to improve it. He had revitalized and become active in the various state law enforcement groups—District Attorneys Association, Peace Officers Association, State Bureau of Criminal Investigation—and in 1934, with their backing, he campaigned statewide for the passage in the November election of four constitutional amendments designed to streamline the state's delivery of criminal justice. All four were passed by overwhelming majorities.

One amendment was designed to improve the quality of judges, making state supreme court and other appellate appointments by the governor and a board subject to approval by the electorate—a procedure many states came to only decades later. Another was designed to save the time and money involved in dragging a defendant through a preliminary hearing before a magistrate, then into superior court perhaps two to three months later. The amendment allowed a defendant in any except a capital case, with the approval of the judge and prosecutor, to plead guilty before the magistrate.

A third amendment held considerable potential for cutting a corner off a constitutional right, although it was not perceived that way at the time. It provided that "in any criminal cases, whether the defendant testifies or not, his failure to explain or to deny by his testimony any evidence or facts in the case against him may be commented on by the court and by counsel, and may be considered by the jury." Thirty years later, in 1965, in the case of *Griffin* v. *California* the U.S. Supreme Court nullified the amendment when it reversed the murder conviction in a California court of a man who had refused to testify and whose refusal had been commented on to the jury by the prosecutor. Such a rule, declared William O. Douglas for the majority, violated the Fifth Amendment's prohibition against self-incrimination: "[C]omment on the refusal to testify is a remnant of the 'inquisitorial system of criminal justice,' " a penalty "imposed by courts for exercising a constitutional privilege. It cuts down on the privilege by making its assertion costly." (Chief Justice Warren took no part in consideration or decision in the case.) In 1981, the Court further expanded on the 1965 decision and ruled in the case of *Carter* v. *Kentucky* that a state trial judge, if requested, had a "constitutional obligation" actually to instruct the jury *not* to draw any conclusion from a defendant's refusal to testify. (The obligation had been imposed on the federal courts in 1939, in the case of *Bruno* v. *United States.*)

The fourth proposal for amending the California Constitution was the one on which Warren had spent most of his stumping time in the fall of 1934, talking it up not only within the state but at the American Bar Association meeting and the attorneys general's conference at which he had been invited to speak and writing it up in the *Tax Digest.* This amendment provided for the creation of a state department of criminal justice headed by a full-time attorney general—if the administration of criminal justice in America had progressed beyond the Neanderthalian, it had not progressed far beyond, and in California until this time the state attorney general had been allowed an outside practice and the office was nothing but a sinecure. Now, with the passage of the constitutional amendment, he was to be charged with the responsibility for coordinating the activities of law enforcement groups statewide, so that when necessary, Alameda and Contra Costa police, Los Angeles and San Diego police, state and local police could join together on common cases and common problems. It was an improvement in the administration of criminal justice that would give, Warren believed, "the representatives of the law at least an even break with the criminal."

The four constitutional amendments did not, of course, "Curb Crime," as the vigilantes had demanded. But they did give the state some wherewithal with which to deal with crime and, at the same time, at least in the context of the period, passed as somewhat enlightened measures where matters of individual rights were involved.

In terms of District Attorney Warren's future, the proposal for the creation of the state department of justice and the office of a full-time attorney general on which he himself had lavished his persuasive powers was perhaps the most significant. Earl Warren was plainly an ambitious man, and as soon as the office of attorney general accrued power and importance, he decided to run for it whenever the Republican incumbent was ready to retire.

The American prosecutor traditionally has been in a politically strategic position. The justice of his cause, the skill, determination, and courage with which he pursues it have proved both conspicuous and attractive to the electorate, and many men have risen to prominence and power from such beginnings. Indeed, at the time Earl Warren was prosecuting organized crime in California, Thomas E. Dewey was busting rackets in New York; if the latter's style was somewhat flashier than Warren's, the results were similar: Both men caught the public eye favorably.

In addition to this springboard, Warren also had a solid and broad base of support. He had been active in the California Republican party for nearly two decades, campaigning for local and national candidates. He had also quietly and shrewdly turned the Alameda district attorney's office into a base of operations and the law enforcement officers of the state into a loyal informal field operation. Old-timers among law enforcement officers long recalled him at meetings of the California Peace Officers Association, practically the only district attorney who came regularly, standing there between the dull speeches with a glass in his hand, sipping slowly while the others were getting drunk, giving them legal advice, discussing their problems, gossiping, "cultivating" them. "[E]very law officer in the state," one of them said later, "was for Warren."

So when the incumbent attorney general called Warren into his office before the election of 1938 and told the young man he intended to retire at the end of the year, Warren was ready. He ran and was elected.

He held the office for four years, during which he still seems in some respects a contradiction of his future public self. Professionally much of his support as attorney general had come from the conservatives in the state—conservative Republicans, conservative newspapers, the Allied Farmers—and he did little to alienate their affections. Although, like most attorney generals, he found a substantial portion of his work involved less conspicuous areas of the law—the rewriting and modernizing of old statutes, the drafting of new ones, the reform of policy—other parts of his work attracted headlines. He cast the deciding vote, as an ex officio member of the Judicial Qualifications Commission, against the appointment to the California Supreme Court of Max Radin, a University of California (Berkeley) professor and a supporter of the rights of organized labor and criminal defendants, among others. He opposed the pardoning of Tom Mooney, labor radical of World War I whose trial for the bombing of a San Francisco Preparedness Parade in 1916 had been a national cause célèbre because of the charge that Mooney's conviction had been obtained on the basis of his political views rather than on the evidence of his participation in the crime. Warren had refused to cooperate with a U.S. Senate committee which was investigating farm labor conditions and violations of civil liberties in California in 1939.

And he is most remembered, toward the end of his term, for his involvement in the forced evacuation of 110,000 Japanese, citizens and aliens alike, from the West Coast following the bombing of Pearl Harbor in 1941,* a case

* Warren was not the only high official involved in the evacuation. President Roosevelt issued the order for it. Tom Clark, at the time an assistant attorney general dispatched to Cali-

in which Warren himself responded to the fear that accompanies crisis and answered the question "What price security?" quite differently than the way he had after his father's murder.

The change in Warren's public character was first noticeable after his election as governor in 1942, when he began to demonstrate a serious interest in social programs in the state. In the early 1920s Warren had been a member of the right wing of the California Republican party and had campaigned for Calvin Coolidge for president in 1924. He had also supported Joseph R. Knowland, the politically conservative publisher of the *Oakland Tribune*, against Hiram Johnson, whose radical populism identified him as the people's representative in a feud that divided California Republicans for years; in turn, Knowland had supported Warren's several candidacies editorially. By 1948 the same Earl Warren had become a reliable member of the Republican liberal establishment—internationalist in foreign policy, progressive on domestic matters, opposed to the isolationist and laissez-faire right wing led by Senator Robert A. Taft of Ohio—and had been chosen by his party to run for vice president of the United States, on a ticket headed by fellow state governor, former public prosecutor, and eastern liberal establishment figure Thomas E. Dewey of New York. The Republicans lost—to incumbent President Truman and Senator Alben Barkley—and Warren returned to California to finish out his second term as governor; he was elected to a third term in 1950. During the nearly three terms he served as governor, he worked for such progressive social measures as prison reform, increased old-age pensions and unemployment benefits, improved health and welfare services, including compulsory health insurance (this last was unsuccessful), fair employment practices, better highways and schools—none of which was high on Calvin Coolidge's list of priorities.

In 1953 he was appointed chief justice of the United States, and the change became complete, so complete that his sponsor, Dwight Eisenhower, was said to have grumbled that Warren's appointment to the chief justiceship was "the biggest damn fool thing I ever did." The specific complaint may have been apocryphal. However, Eisenhower told his attorney general, Her-

---

fornia by the U.S. Department of Justice, helped the U.S. Army enforce it. U.S. Supreme Court Justice Hugo Black defended it in his Court opinions. A young undersecretary of the interior named Abe Fortas was one of the few in or out of government who protested it and worked assiduously to return the Japanese to their homes.

The nation has since recognized its shame. In July 1981 a federal commission, the Commission on Wartime Relocation and Internment of Civilians, began hearings to review the events leading to the incarcerations and to determine whether or not compensation ought to be offered survivors. Warren, in his *Memoirs*, published after his death, apologized for his own involvement. Tom Clark, in the introduction to *Executive Order 9066* by Maisie and Richart Conrat, apologized for the government's involvement.

Hugo Black did not apologize. On the contrary, "I would do precisely the same thing today, in any part of the country," he said many years later, believing the order had protected the Japanese from reprisals as well as protected the national security. "I would probably issue the same order were I President."

bert Brownell, Jr., that he would not again appoint to the U.S. Supreme Court anyone who had not served on a federal or state court. "[T]here would then be available to us," the president had reasoned, " a record of the decisions for which the prospective appointee had been responsible. These would provide an inkling of his philosophy."* He would not again buy a pig in a poke.

The considerations that go into a president's appointments to the Supreme Court are not always easy to sort out. It is the most important appointment a president can make—Senator Edward M. Kennedy of Massachusetts said in 1975 that the naming of a justice on occasion had "been the equivalent of a constitutional amendment." And like the constitutional amendment in whose simple statement all the exigencies must be provided for, so in one man must all the requirements reside: political, philosophical, intellectual, geographical, religious, age.

Like all presidents since John Adams in 1801 appointed John Marshall chief justice to maintain a Federalist fortress within the judiciary, insurance against the dangerous democratic schemes of his successor, Thomas Jefferson, Eisenhower considered only candidates who, he believed, would be coefficients of his own positions: John J. Parker of North Carolina and the U.S. Court of Appeals for the Fourth Circuit, who had been nominated to the Court once before, by Republican President Herbert Hoover, but rejected by the Senate; Arthur T. Vanderbilt, chief justice of the New Jersey Supreme Court; Orie L. Philips of the U.S. Court of Appeals for the Tenth Circuit; John W. Davis, one of the nation's outstanding constitutional lawyers and candidate for president on the Democratic ticket in 1924;† his own secretary of state, John Foster Dulles; and Earl Warren. The last-named candidate, having run for vice president in 1948, was identified with the eastern liberal wing of the Republican party of which the Eisenhower candidacy was the most successful product.

The president probably thought he knew Warren's philosophical inclinations. Earl Warren had been a Republican all his professional life, active in both state and national politics. His loyalty had been proved in a recent ordeal by sacrifice. At the Republican National Convention in midsummer 1952 in Chicago, Warren had been a competing candidate for president. But he had cast California's votes for an amendment to the convention rules which had to do with the seating of delegates and which gave the Eisenhower

* Eisenhower kept his promise in the rest of his Supreme Court appointments: federal Judges John M. Harlan, Potter Stewart, and Charles E. Whittaker (since resigned) and New Jersey Supreme Court Justice William J. Brennan, Jr.

† Eisenhower in his memoirs, *Mandate for Change*, included Davis in his list of candidates. It is hard to believe he was serious, however, not because Davis was a Democrat—he was, in fact, a political conservative—but because Davis was eighty-one years old at the time. His arguments in the public school desegregation cases in the early fifties—which he argued for the southern states against racial desegregation—were the last he ever argued in the U.S. Supreme Court.

faction a numerical advantage over the faction led by the candidate of the Republican conservatives, Senator Taft of Ohio. It had probably cost Warren his own candidacy, which had been based on a deadlock between the more powerful Eisenhower and Taft organizations, and Herbert Brownell, then Eisenhower's campaign manager, had reported the act of political courage to the boss. Warren had also given considerable assistance in California during the subsequent campaign. In 1953 he was nearly through his third term as governor of California and, like most people who had been in politics a long time, had made enough enemies to force him to think long and hard about a fourth term. Judgeships had been awarded for considerably less party service and loyalty, although the chief justiceship was something else again.

And there was the Nixon factor. There was talk then and long afterward that Eisenhower's young vice president, Richard Nixon, had wanted his rival who controlled the state Republican party machinery removed from California and national politics permanently. The two men, both ambitious, with overlapping territories, had been feuding since 1946, when Warren, running for reelection as governor, had refused to allow Harold Stassen, governor of Minnesota and a potentially strong Warren opponent in future presidential maneuvering, to make speeches in California for Nixon, who was running for Congress for the first time.

In 1948 Nixon had been neither a Dewey nor a Warren partisan at the national convention in Philadelphia, which he had attended as a nondelegate. He explained later in his memoirs that while he had "great respect" for Dewey, he thought the Republicans needed a "fresh face" in 1948—Dewey had run in 1944 and lost. He did not add that Dewey had spoken out against the sternly anti-Communist Mundt-Nixon bill, which was then a feather in Nixon's political cap, nor did he mention his irritation at Warren's behavior two years previously. Instead Nixon had lobbied for Harold Stassen, who had spoken out favorably on the Mundt-Nixon bill and who had wanted to campaign for him two years previously. When Stassen lost, Nixon campaigned for the Dewey-Warren ticket that fall, but there was no warmth between him and the vice presidential candidate. Where Nixon was bareknuckled, Warren was polite—to the point of blandness. Where Nixon was ardently partisan, Warren, a Republican survivor of a decade of politics in a state with a significantly higher Democratic registration, was as ardently nonpartisan. And Nixon, on his return home, grumbled to his administrative assistant, "Earl Warren might as well be sitting on his butt in Sacramento for all the help he's giving us."

In 1950 Nixon had conducted a successful, although particularly ugly and now famous, campaign for election to the U.S. Senate, all but accusing his opponent, Democratic Congresswoman and former actress Helen Gahagan Douglas, of treason; his governor and fellow Republican Earl Warren had withheld support until the last minute. Most recently, in the summer of 1952, Nixon, looking toward the vice presidency, was said to have boldly and baldly attempted to steal the California delegation from Warren and deliver it to Eisenhower even before the Republicans met in Chicago.

The Warren-Nixon dispute, however, whatever implications it held for the two principals, was irrelevant to national politics that year. Even before the convention Eisenhower was carrying in his billfold a list of vice presidential possibilities; Richard Nixon's was the first name. Herbert Brownell, Eisenhower's campaign manager and oldest adviser, labeled stories that Nixon had urged Warren's appointment to the Supreme Court in order to incapacitate the latter politically "the usual Potomac fever gossip."

Whatever Eisenhower's motivation, he informed Warren shortly after the 1952 election that the California governor would be considered for the first Supreme Court vacancy that occurred after the new president took office. Warren not only welcomed the offer, said Brownell, who believed appointment to the nation's highest court had been a "dream" of Warren's, but "thereafter made his plans with the thought in mind that the appointment would be made whenever the first vacancy on the Court occurred." Brownell, however, had been having difficulty finding a solicitor general, and in August 1953 Warren agreed to take the position until there was a place for him on the Supreme Court. On September 3 Warren announced he would not run for a fourth term as governor of California, and the following weekend he began to read Albert Beveridge's Pulitzer Prize–winning biography of John Marshall.

On September 8 Chief Justice Vinson died suddenly. After considerable discussion within the administration of whether or not Eisenhower's promise of a Supreme Court seat to Warren applied to a vacancy in the chief justiceship and of other possible nominees, the president authorized Brownell to offer the chief justiceship to Warren, who accepted eagerly. On September 30 Eisenhower announced to the newsmen assembled at a formal press conference in the Executive Office Building next door to the White House that he had appointed Earl Warren of California chief justice of the United States. Explained the president: "I certainly wanted a man whose reputation for integrity, honesty, middle-of-the-road philosophy, experience in Government, experience in the law, were all such as to convince the United States that here was a man who had no ends to serve except the United States, and nothing else."

Warren hastily closed his affairs in California, handed over the governor's office to the lieutenant governor, and took the oath as chief justice at the Supreme Court in Washington just past noon on October 5, 1953, the opening day of the 1953 term. Standing tall in his borrowed robes—his own had not been ready—he was sworn in by Senior Associate Justice Black before a courtroom crowded with 500 friends, family, and political notables, including the Eisenhowers and Nixons.

Statistics were abundant. Warren was the fourteenth man to hold the office, the first to be appointed by a Republican since Herbert Hoover appointed Charles Evans Hughes in 1930, the first to come from a background consisting solely of state offices, the fifth to have been governor of a state, the second to have been born west of the Mississippi River, the first to play a clarinet, the third to have seen military service.

He was the sixth to have had no judicial experience. Which did not mean that he could not be an effective chief justice. Roger B. Taney had had none either; John Marshall's had been minimal. Oliver Wendell Holmes, Jr., who had sat on the Supreme Judicial Court of Massachusetts for more than two decades prior to Theodore Roosevelt's appointing him to the U.S. Supreme Court, did not believe that experience had prepared him to do the work of the highest federal tribunal at all. Warren's lack of judicial experience did mean, however, that he had no record on which to base predictions of his judicial direction when he joined the U.S. Supreme Court.

Not a great deal was expected of him. John Gunther had written about him as governor in 1947: "Earl Warren is honest, likeable, and clean; he will never set the world on fire or even make it smoke. . . ." And at his appointment to the Supreme Court it was remarked that he had been hired as the bland manager of a team of all-stars.

He himself was not overly confident in his early Court days, and shortly after his arrival he complained to Robert Jackson that his legal experience—or lack of it—had not prepared him for the work; he was having difficulty, he said, in grasping the significance of many of the cases. Jackson had reassured him:

> Don't worry about that, Chief. We all go through the same experience. When I came to the Court, I thought I was pretty well prepared . . . I had been general counsel for federal agencies; then solicitor general . . . attorney general. Yet when I came to the Court I was plagued by some of the same thoughts you are expressing. I went to Chief Justice Hughes and told him of my doubts. He said, "Jackson, don't worry about that. When I came to the Supreme Court I had argued many cases before it, but it took me three years to know what my limitations were."

Both the self-confidence and the alteration in Warren's public posture began cautiously and almost imperceptibly. Initially, regarding the administration of criminal justice, he was inclined, as a former state law enforcement official, to allow the states substantial latitude in operating their law enforcement agencies and judicial institutions, and he seemed no less sanguine regarding the use of the exclusionary rule than would Warren Burger of the U.S. Court of Appeals for the District of Columbia Circuit; civil libertarians had groaned on February 8, 1954, when in the first case involving state criminal procedures decided since Warren had joined the court, the new chief justice had stood with the majority, which had refused both to invade the local territory and to invoke the exclusionary rule.

In this case police had had a locksmith make a key to the door of the defendant's home while he was out, installed a bugging device, and afterward gone in and out of the house with ease, collecting evidence of his illegal gambling activities. The question in the case was: Could evidence of a crime obtained as the result of an illegal entry be admitted at a trial in a state court? This time the majority said yes. The burden, said Robert Jackson for the majority, "of administering criminal justice rests upon state courts." Regarding the exclusionary rule, he wrote:

> Our cases evidence the fact that the federal rule of exclusion and our reversal of conviction for its violation are not sanctions which put an end to illegal search and seizure by federal officers. The rule was announced in 1914. . . . The extent to which the practice was curtailed, if at all, is doubtful. The lower federal courts, and even this Court, have repeatedly been constrained to enforce the rule after its violation. There is no reliable evidence known to us that inhabitants of those states which exclude the evidence suffer less from lawless searches and seizures than those of states that admit it. . . .

Civil libertarians need not have been so downcast, however, for Warren, inching out on his own, indicated that he was not completely satisfied with the Court's decision. The shadow of the young Warren who had insisted on holding law enforcement officers to high standards of behavior in their pursuit of his own father's murderer as well as, in retrospect, a hint of the chief justice's later positions can be discerned in this early case. If he was willing to allow the states to devise their own procedures, he was not as willing to condone blatant disregard of the law. He was not satisfied that the wrongdoers among the police go unpunished, and Robert Jackson added an unusual paragraph to the opinion, one to which only he and Warren subscribed, suggesting the officers' conduct in obtaining the evidence in question might constitute a federal crime for which they might be prosecuted under federal law (they were not).

Warren had always been a states' rights advocate. In the late forties, as governor, he had been conspicuous in the fight against federal encroachment on offshore oil, which he believed belonged to the states. On the Supreme Court he became a states' responsibilities advocate first. Faith in state action is a theme that persists through his early Court writings: "We are confident that the States will provide corrective rules to meet the problem which this case lays bare," or "where the Supreme Court of a state is vigilant in its protection of constitutional rights . . . few differences arise between it and the Supreme Court of the United States."

On discovering, however, the general lassitude of state officials, he in the end felt compelled to erase, in effect, long-cherished distinctions between state and federal authority and to bring the Bill of Rights into the operation of state criminal justice. Although he did not write the opinions in the most important criminal justice cases, he assigned the opinions when he was in the majority, presided over the Court at the time, and made his moral force a factor, joining in those opinions which raised the standards of due process of the criminal law in the states, and joining in the dissents from those that did not.

In 1961, when the Court decided that state courts could *not*, in fact, admit illegally obtained evidence into trials—*Mapp* v. *Ohio*—Warren was, of course, in the majority.

Earl Warren's changing was apparent, too, in other than criminal justice cases. He who had participated in the evacuation of Japanese from the California coast in 1941 had written the unanimous 1954 Supreme Court opinion which ordered the end of racial segregation in the public schools of America.

The change in his views on apportionment of state legislatures was only slightly less well known and dramatic, although its impact on the nation may have been greater. At least, Warren always thought so.

Beginning with the rapid industrialization stimulated by the Civil War and post–Civil War period, the nation had undergone a shift in population concentration; farmers had left the land and moved into cities to operate and profit from the burgeoning new industries. However, reapportionment of election districts had not kept pace with the shifts in population, and as a result, the taxpaying population had become concentrated in metropolitan areas while the political power had stayed on the farms.

In 1948 the Los Angeles area of California, with 5 million people, sent the same number of representatives to the state legislature as less populous areas with a tenth as many people, and there was a movement within the state to apportion the state senate on the basis of population. Governor Warren, also a vice presidential candidate that year, would have none of it. "Many California counties," he said, "are far more important in the life of the State than their population bears to the entire population of the State. It is for this reason that I have never been in favor of restricting the representation in the senate to a strictly population basis. . . ."

Sixteen years later, in 1964, the U.S. Supreme Court, which two years earlier, via *Baker* v. *Carr*, had become very much involved in the "political thicket" of election district apportionment, decided that *both* houses of a state legislature must be apportioned on the basis of population. Wrote Chief Justice Warren for the majority, directly contradicting Governor Warren: ". . . it would seem reasonable that a majority of the people of a state could elect a majority of the state's legislators. To conclude differently and to sanction minority control of state legislatures would appear to deny majority rights in a way that far surpasses any possible denial of minority rights that might otherwise be thought to result. . . ."

The Chief Justice considered it his most important Supreme Court opinion. It had, of course, achieved a new level in the functioning of political democracy, and it would not be without influence, as the voting maps of America were redrawn over the next decade and the politically disadvantaged, black and white, but particularly black, were drawn into the political system.

In Earl Warren resided the age-old riddles of the political man: Was he simply an opportunist who responded to whatever issue happened to be in vogue in order to advance himself? Or had he a large capacity for learning which led him from the Coolidge camp in 1924 to the Eisenhower camp by 1952 and on to the frontiers of civil libertarianism during the next decade? Did his horizons expand with his constituency, his moving from the Alameda County district attorney's office to the state governor's office in Sacramento to the office of chief justice of the United States in Washington? Or was his personal philosophy shaped at least in outline much earlier? Was the real Earl Warren not, perhaps, the tough law enforcement officer whose men sometimes were "a little bit rough" on their suspects and not above hiding them from their lawyers, but rather the grief-stricken son whose father had been murdered and who, however bereaved, steadfastly insisted on decent treatment for criminal suspects? Did he, then, only await the times, the egalitarianism that climaxed in the sixties, and the achievement of high office, the heady freedom of the chief justiceship, to give it opportunity for implementation? Or was he some complex combination of all these?

Generally students of the Supreme Court have attributed the changes to the total freedom offered by a lifetime appointment, a provision that the Constitution makers, only too familiar with royal meddling with judges in the quest for self-perpetuation, had shrewdly inserted and that since had bolstered many a federal judge's courage to defy political pressures and public passions. Warren himself attempted to answer the question in his *Memoirs*. His shift on the issue of legislative apportionment he attributed to a change in his perspective from parochial to national; in a few instances he admitted error. He may have furnished the most accurate explanation of the changes in his public behavior when in that simple down-to-earth way of his he told a *New York Times* reporter:

> It is always easier to obtain a conviction if you are permitted to use excesses that are prohibited by the Constitution. I'm no softer on crime than I was as a California prosecutor, but a lot of things change in 50 years. The third degree called for some restraints so that innocent people were not convicted, and all we did was to keep up with the times.

A lot of things had indeed changed in fifty years, not all of them in connection with the administration of criminal justice, although the parallels can hardly be ignored. And when all was said and done, Earl Warren was both the product and the expression of those fifty years.

When Warren was born in 1891 and during his formative years, the business of America had been perceived to be business. The justices of the Supreme Court had come then largely from the legal gentry—corporation lawyers, railroad attorneys, and the like—and the beneficiaries of their rulings, most of which had dealt with property rights, had been business and industry. The Court had struck down or interpreted narrowly acts of Congress that promoted the public welfare: income tax, antitrust, and labor laws including child labor laws. Between 1889 and 1932 the justices had struck down no fewer than thirty-eight such congressional acts. They had restricted the authority of federal regulatory agencies—Interstate Commerce Commission, Federal Trade Commission—created by Congress for the public's protection. They had struck down state laws—334 of them between 1891 and 1932—which regulated railroad rates, insurance company behavior, the working hours of bakers, even the safeness of stuffing materials used in bed comforters. All in the name of liberty of contract, more sacred in those times than liberty of person, particularly the poor person. The urgency in the voices of the farmer and the laboring man in those days was not heard within the marble palace, and Debs was a four-letter word among gentlemen.

But the disadvantaged had persisted in their demands, and gradually government had responded: Theodore Roosevelt's Square Deal, Woodrow Wilson's New Freedom, FDR's New Deal, Harry Truman's Fair Deal, and now Lyndon Johnson's Great Society, all attempts to do away with inequalities in American life. The Supreme Court had reflected this shift in political attention and concern, so that when Earl Warren came to the Court in 1953, it had been discovered that liberty of contract was not so sacred as had been believed during the 1920s, when he was starting out, and that the business of America was also the striving for the liberty and equality and justice that had been promised to all the people.

The discovery had been much assisted by the replacement on the United States Supreme Court itself of men of property and influence with men of humbler origins, whose fathers had not been prominent in public affairs or in authority but had been, like Earl Warren's, mechanics, and labor leaders, and farmers.*

The social consequences of world-wide depression as well as the rise of fascism abroad during the 1930s had taught Americans something about the ease with which tyranny becomes entrenched, about constitutional rights and justice, and they had applied their lessons to cases like those of the Scottsboro boys and Izell Chambers. World War II had heightened and accelerated the pace. It had been fought by farmers and bus drivers and factory workers and miners, by blacks as well as whites, poor as well as rich, and when they re-

---

* Fifty-six justices were appointed to the U.S. Supreme Court prior to the twentieth century. Of them, six, or just over 10 percent, had humble origins—born into the families of subsistence farmers, pioneers, and such—twenty-one, or just over 37 percent, came from the families of middle rank—professionals such as medical men, academics, middle-sized merchants—and 29, or slightly more than 50 percent, came from the ranks of the affluent—bankers, owners of large businesses, plantation owners, manufacturers, etc. Forty-five justices were appointed to the Court in the twentieth century (through the 1981 appointment of Sandra D. O'Connor). The share of the lower classes had increased to twelve, or 26.6 percent, up 16.6 percent; the share of the middle classes had risen to eighteen, or 40 percent, up 3 percent; the share of the upper classes had dropped to fifteen, or 33⅓ percent, down nearly 17 percent.

turned, they sought to create a world in which their concerns would be heeded as never before. Not since Jacksonian times, nearly a full century before, had there been such a step forward in any democratic society, an alteration in the quality of life for the many, an expansion of liberties, a redistribution of opportunities for the pursuit of happiness.

The United States Supreme Court had been in transition when Warren was sworn in as the 1953 term opened. Of the justices who would combine over nearly two decades to make a majority and confirm that expansion of liberties and redistribution of opportunities, only Hugo Black and William O. Douglas were on the Court. That it was responding to contemporary social currents, however, was evident in the fact that the most significant cases awaiting the action of the new chief justice were those asking for the racial desegregation of the nation's public schools.

These were the years Warren was talking about when he replied to the *New York Times* reporter, the years when he had advanced from office to office, shaped by events as much as he shaped them, maturing with his country, changing, changing, always changing. In 1966, as the Supreme Court prepared to hear arguments in behalf of Ernest Miranda and the other criminal defendants in the confessions cases, Earl Warren had become both the symbol and the cutting edge of egalitarianism.

CHAPTER 2

Earl Warren, chief justice of the United States, in the prime of his professional life, was sitting in his customary high-backed center chair the morning of Monday, February 28, 1966, the day Ernest Miranda's case was scheduled to be heard, and opened the proceedings, as was also customary, with the swearing-in of new members of the Supreme Court bar, including John Flynn of Phoenix, Arizona, whose appearance in behalf of Ernest Miranda would be his first in this court, and with the reading of opinions in antitrust, labor relations, and contempt of court cases.

Although in the confessions cases being argued that day Warren would display an unusual testiness, and his persistent question to counsel, particularly counsel for the prosecution, "But is it fair?" or some variation on it, would have a noticeably sharp edge, he was generally gentle with counsel, and his remarks, even when he was exposing their pretensions and sophisms, were permeated with a sense of concern and caring. Did he, perhaps, recall his own discomfiture as a young district attorney on his way to court and his ardent prayer that the streetcar on which he rode might meet with an accident before he arrived? Did he recall the dryness of his mouth when he rose to speak, the shaking of his knees, and the knot in the pit of his stomach?

It was an awesome thing to argue a case in the U.S. Supreme Court. The courtroom itself, as warm and intimate as the February day outside, set the tone. It was, first of all, large, larger than the local courtrooms in which most attorneys practiced. It was handsomely pillared in Siena marble, and its walls were paneled in rich oak. Curtains of red velour hung at the front, behind the bench, which was elevated from the floor, and it did nothing to undo the knots in an attorney's stomach to watch the audience rise as the crier smashed down his gavel and the justices filed through the curtains, all nine at once, it seemed, robed in black, and took their seats. The federal bureaucracy had spread uncontrolled—and it seemed at the time uncontrollable—but the United States Supreme Court was perhaps the last place in Washington where the elaborate equipment of government had not attached itself, and the advocate of a cause presented his arguments to the highest level of decision maker. Here, in this room alone, the laywer for Ernest Miranda could talk directly with the justices of the Supreme Court.

John Flynn, a giant in the courtrooms of Arizona, had been "scared to death" when he arrived here that morning. Ordinarily John Frank, as chief appellate attorney at Lewis & Roca, would have made the oral agruments to the justices, but in Ernest Miranda's case he had deferred to his partner's superior firsthand experience with police and knowledge of their ways.

"I think," Frank had said, "that what the Court really wants to hear more than anything are the practical aspects of what happens down in the police interrogation room from the fellow who is there handling it on a day-to-day basis. They don't want the esoteric treatise on the law; they know what the law is. . . . What they want to know is the practical application. So you argue the case." Frank had, however, accompanied Flynn to Washington and would sit at the defense counsel's table when Flynn addressed the Court.

Flynn was well prepared. He had stuffed his head with the contents of all the relevant Supreme Court decisions touching on the question of a person's right to counsel and had learned its history from earliest days to Danny Escobedo's case. He still had, however, an uneasy feeling that Ernest Miranda's case was really, in the end, a case involving compulsory self-incrimination, a Fifth Amendment case, with Sixth Amendment right to counsel implications.

It was establshed practice at Lewis & Roca to stage at least one moot court prior to any appellate argument, with members of the firm acting as judges and subjecting the lawyer assigned to argue the case to intense and wide-ranging interrogation. Before the arguments in Ernest Miranda's case the lawyers had held not one but several such sessions. The issues had been as hotly debated as they had been within the law enforcement community. One of the senior partners, in fact, believed what Flynn and Frank were urging in Miranda's case was "outrageous social policy," so Flynn had had the benefit of rehearsal against strong, well-developed arguments.

He had arrived at the Court early that morning not only to participate in the swearing-in ceremony but also to watch the justices in action before he had to face them. The case that preceded Miranda's on the schedule was the final appeal of Dr. Samuel H. Sheppard of Cleveland, Ohio, convicted of the murder of his wife in one of the previous decade's most sensational trials. His lawyer was F. Lee Bailey of Boston, and the courtroom was crowded.

Bailey was good that day, but he was no Francis Scott Key, no Henry

Clay, no Daniel Webster, who had packed the courtroom the century before, when the justices met across the street in the Capitol. Webster, they had said at the time, was a man "with a mouth like a mastiff, a brow like a mountain and eyes like burning anthracite," and when he stood up to speak, "stars and stripes came right out of the sky . . . when he argued a case, he could turn on the harps of the blessed and the shaking of the earth underground . . ."

The pace of the Court was more leisurely then. Arguments were measured not in minutes, or even hours, but in days, and there was time for oratory and drama. Court had been known to pause while Luther Martin, one of the Maryland bar's most eloquent but intemperate representatives, sobered up; it had been known to start over because a woman in the audience had missed the opening minutes. A chief justice would not in Daniel Webster's day have warned an attorney that he had three minutes left or that his time was up, as had become customary in this century when each side had been allowed one hour, then the time had been cut to a half hour—indeed, in this day of advanced electronic technology little signal lights glowed on the advocate's lectern: green for "go," yellow for "you have five minutes left," and red for "your time is up."

Although the oratory of yesterday's bar was discouraged, oral argument remained the heart of the appellate process. It was an opportunity for the justices, through a question-and-answer format, to test the hypotheses put forward in the lawyers' briefs and for the lawyers to correct any judicial misconceptions that might have arisen. It could be grueling for a lawyer. Prepared texts were frowned on—the justices had, after all, read the prepared texts, the briefs—and it was impossible to anticipate every question. Robert Jackson, solicitor general before he was appointed to the Court, used to say he made three arguments in every case he argued for the government: "First came the one that I planned—as I thought, logical, coherent, complete. Second was the one actually presented—interrupted, incoherent, disjointed, disappointing. The third was the utterly devastating argument that I thought of after going to bed that night."

F. Lee Bailey, in presenting the case for Dr. Sheppard, had reserved fifteen minutes of his allotted time for rebuttal following the state's presentation, a common practice among lawyers. Now he had completed his argument.

"Number 759," intoned the chief justice dispassionately. "Ernesto A. Miranda, Petitioner, versus Arizona. We'll wait just a few minutes until you get seated."

There was a pause and a rustling of papers as the justices turned to the briefs in Miranda's case, the lawyers in the *Sheppard* case collected their papers, and the lawyers for Miranda and the state of Arizona made their way to the main counsel tables that flanked the lectern.

"Mr. Flynn, you may proceed."

Standing at the rostrum, Flynn faced a formidable array of judges. To the immediate left of the chief justice at the center, as Flynn faced the bench, sat the senior associate justice, Hugo Black, eighty years and one day old on February 28, and no less contentious or skeptical than he had been at sixty. A "vigorous, restive, driving judge," the *Washington Post* had called him in its birthday feature the previous day. His quoting of the Constitution could be relied on absolutely; he carried a small Government Printing Office copy of that document in his coat pocket, the way most people carried a handkerchief, and when he looked sternly at counsel and asked, "Where does it say *that* in the Constitution?" counsel had better know precisely.

A restless man who sometimes appeared to wish he were elsewhere, the next man in seniority, William O. Douglas, sitting to the immediate right of the chief justice, was perhaps as well known for the books he had written about the remote areas of the world to which he had traveled as he was for his judicial opinions, the first drafts of which he often dashed off during oral arguments.

Tom Clark sat to the left of Black. His amiable ways and Texas drawl had survived nearly three decades in Washington, where he had begun his bureaucratic life as an obscure lawyer in the Justice Department and risen to attorney general before being appointed to the U.S. Supreme Court by his friend Harry Truman.

John Marshall Harlan sat to the right of Douglas. His eyes were deep-set, giving his head the kind of angles that attract sculptors; his expression was generally quizzical. He customarily refrained from questioning during argument of "notorious" cases, lest his questions "prompt unseemly newspaper speculations as to how he might vote."

William Brennan, his slight figure diminished even more by his big black leather chair, sat to the left of Clark. He, too, often sat quietly during oral arguments. Potter Stewart, known for the toughness of his questioning, sat to the right of Harlan; Byron White, who had acquired a reputation for needling attorneys, sat at the extreme left. And Abe Fortas, whose newness on the Court did not in the least inhibit his questioning of counsel, sat at the extreme right.

Perhaps in no other country could nine such men have sat together on a nation's highest tribunal. John Harlan had come out of old colonial stock, a genealogical aristocrat; Earl Warren's father had come from Sweden, William J. Brennan's from Ireland, Abe Fortas's from England: pure melting-pot America. They were Protestant, Catholic, and Jew. They represented every region of the country: the cities of the Northeast, the rural South, the still-developing but already muscular Southwest, the self-reliant and self-made Midwest, and the "manifest destiny," the West. They were Republicans and Democrats, and they owed their present positions to presidential patrons from both parties. They ranged in age from eighty to forty-nine; the oldest of them, Black, spanned nearly half the nation's history, his Court years the administrations of five presidents, Franklin Roosevelt to Lyndon Johnson. The youngest of them, White, was one of that new generation of Americans to whom the late President Kennedy at his inaugural in 1961 had passed the torch: "born in this century, tempered by war, disciplined by a hard and bitter peace, proud of our ancient heritage—and unwilling to witness or permit the slow undoing of those human rights to which this nation has always been committed. . . ."

The array of talent in advocacy assembled for these landmark arguments was not inconsiderable, although its range of experience was as uneven as it was broad. There was, of course, Thurgood Marshall, clad in the traditional striped pants and morning coat of the solicitor general—the first black man to be so clad. As counsel for the NAACP Legal Defense Fund he had argued before this same Court for three decades for the rights of black criminal defendants; now, as solicitor general, he found himself on the other side, that of the government. There was Telford Taylor, something of a celebrity within the legal community, having succeeded Robert Jackson as chief U.S. counsel at the Nuremberg trials of war criminals following World War II and now a professor of law at Columbia University and an appellate lawyer of some distinction. He was scheduled to argue in behalf of the state of New York and the 28 other states that had joined the brief against the Court's expanding the *Escobedo* ruling. He was well versed on the issues and had been named the previous year to the American Law Institute's committee charged with devising a model code of pre-arraignment procedure. There was also William Siegel, a veteran of twenty-six years of prosecuting criminal defendants in the legal rough-and-tumble of the Brooklyn, New York, criminal courts, here to argue for the state in the case of Michael Vignera, whose conviction for the robbery of a Brooklyn dress shop was being challenged.

And there were some inexperienced ones, too, like F. Conger Fawcett of San Francisco, who was representing convicted bank robber Carl Calvin Westover in the single federal case and was opposing no less a legal luminary than Solicitor General Marshall himself, who had argued thirty-two cases in this court. Only four years out of Harvard Law School and a specialist not in criminal law but in maritime regulation, Fawcett had signed on the indigent appellate panel of the U.S. Court of Appeals for the Ninth Circuit (Arizona, California, Nevada, Oregon, Washington, Idaho, Montana), and Westover's was his first criminal appeal. He had devoted large amounts of time to the case, however, hoping to compensate in dedication and scholarship for what he lacked in experience. And there was Gary Nelson, the young assistant attorney general for the state of Arizona whose appearance in Ernest Miranda's case was his first in the U.S. Supreme Court.

None of the counsel for the accused was paid. William A. Norris of Los Angeles, former clerk to Justice Douglas, was representing Roy Stewart, whose conviction for robbery and murder had been reversed by the California Supreme Court and was now being challenged by the state, by appointment of the U.S. Supreme Court itself. Conger Fawcett had been appointed by the U.S. Court of Appeals for the Ninth Circuit. Victor M. Earle III of New York, Michael Vignera's lawyer, had been engaged by the Legal Aid Society on terms similar to those on which the Phoenix ACLU had engaged John Flynn and John Frank: as a public service. Gene Haeberle of Camden, New Jersey, and Stanford Schmuckler of Philadelphia, lawyers for Sylvester Johnson and Stanley Cassidy, had also taken the case as a public service. There they were, seven successful lawyers facing the patricians of their profession and preparing to argue, amid the spreading climate of fear of crime, in behalf of one of society's most harangued-against segments: convicted criminals. They had spent hundreds of hours preparing their cases for the justices of the U.S. Supreme Court to hear, and now they were arguing for principle.

On the afternoon of February 28, John Flynn, a veteran of fifteen years in the criminal courtrooms of Arizona, opened the oral arguments in the five confessions cases with Ernest Miranda's—the Court had directed that Miranda's be heard first, making it the leading case, and thereby named it when the decision was handed down some months later. Arguments in the five cases, plus those of two of the three parties which had filed amicus briefs (the state of New York and the National District Attorneys Association, but not the ACLU), would consume nearly eight hours.

"May it please the Court," Flynn began in the traditional way. The U.S. Supreme Court was not his milieu. He was more at home in the hurly-burly of the station house, the jails, the county courthouses, with his clients. But as his law partner had said, his was exactly the sort of experience the justices wanted to hear. It is an easy step to sterility from the purity that the gleaming white marble pile that is the Supreme Court may have been intended to convey. The justices worked in an atmosphere far removed from the victims and the defendants upon whom they sat in ultimate judgment. They did not live in the communities where the crimes had been committed. They did not see the swollen faces of victims sitting outside the trial court, the strutting of a young defendant who knew he would get off with a wrist slapping—for the fourth time. They did not see the fear in the eyes of suspects facing police or the hopelessness in the faces of prisoners. They knew only what they read in the trial records, the lower court decisions, the briefs of the lawyers who stood before them. Only two of them, Warren and Black, had been professionally involved in station house life for any length of time, and that had been a long time ago. This absence of the quality of real life made it perhaps considerably easier to deal with issues, but it also had its drawbacks, and the justices intended to make up for it.

If Flynn was still nervous, his voice did not reveal it; it carried clearly and firmly out over the courtroom. His persistent belief that resolution of the confessions issues would depend upon the Fifth Amendment's prohibition against a person's being compelled to incriminate himself—not the Sixth Amendment's guarantee of the right to counsel, as he and his partner had stated in their brief for Ernest Miranda—proved well founded. He had barely finished describing Miranda's case when Justice Fortas interrupted. Oral argument had a well-defined structure: The challenger to the lower-court decision spoke first; its defender spoke second. But there were no restrictions on the justices' questions, and it was not uncommon for oral argument to become a free-for-all.

"You said that Miranda was not told that he might remain silent. Did you say that?" Justice Fortas asked.

And John Flynn, who had also said within the same sentence that Miranda had not been told of his right to counsel, answered, "That is correct," and thereafter adroitly, without missing a step, incorporated Fifth Amendment arguments with those of the Sixth.

It was Justice Stewart, only minutes later, who fulfilled John Frank's prophecy that it was experience, not abstractions, the justices wanted to hear. He had been concerned in *Escobedo* when the Court had declared that a suspect on whom a police investigation had focused had a constitutional right to consult with his attorney, and he had accused his brethren of converting "a routine police investigation of an unsolved murder into a distorted analogue of a judicial trial." The precise stage in the procedure at which constitutional guarantees should attach still concerned him.

"What do you think is the result," he asked Flynn, "of the adversary process coming into being when this focusing takes place? What follows from that? Is there then a right to a lawyer?" Stewart had wanted only to explore the logic of *Escobedo*, wondering what parts of the adversary system ought logically to be activated at this time? A jury, for example?

If John Flynn had not Daniel Webster's blaze or even Abe Fortas's former eloquence at argument before the Court, he was not, however, without resources, and he turned his answer into one of the core issues before the justices this day:

> I think that the man at that time has the right to exercise, if he knows, and under the present state of the law in Arizona, if he is rich enough and educated enough to assert his Fifth Amendment right, and if he recognizes that he has a Fifth Amendment right, to request counsel, I simply say that that stage of the proceeding, under the facts and circumstances in Miranda of a man of limited education, of a man who certainly is mentally abnormal, and who is, certainly, an indigent, that when that adversary process came into being, that the police at the very least had an obligation to extend to this man, not only his clear Fifth Amendment right, but to accord him the right of counsel . . . if he is barred from his rights, then there is no due process of law being afforded a man in Ernest Miranda's position.

It was Hugo Black's custom during oral argument to rock gently back and forth in his chair, his head cocked to one side as he listened, then to pounce at an appropriate moment. His soft voice and gentle Alabama accent sometimes belied the force of what he said. His questions and comments were often about absolutes. His first question that day was no exception:

> You have said several times . . . that in determining whether or not the witness in question shall be compelled to be a witness against himself, that it might depend to some extent on his literacy or lack of literacy, his wealth or lack of wealth, his standing or lack of standing—why does that have anything to do with it? Why does the amendment not protect the rich as well as the poor, the literate as well as the illiterate?

The Amendment—and by this point in the arguments the Fifth Amendment had become "the Amendment"; there was less and less discussion of the Sixth Amendment, except as a way of applying the Fifth—the Amendment, Flynn agreed, did indeed cover everyone. However, in application, "I would say that it certainly and most assuredly does protect . . . the rich, the educated and the strong, those rich enough to hire counsel, those who are educated enough to know what their rights are, those strong enough to withstand police interrogation and assert their rights. . . ."

His half hour was nearly up now. Just a few more questions regarding the meaning of "compulsion"—during which Mr. Justice Black declared it did not mean the accused "has to have a gun pointed at his head. . . . Control and custody. Why would that not tend to show some kind of compulsion?"—and John Flynn wound up the case for Ernest Miranda against the state of Arizona. Some of the briefs submitted to the Court had urged the justices to proceed slowly in this matter of confessions, to allow the states— the courts, the legislatures, the bar—to devise their own measures for protecting the rights of the accused in the station houses. To this, Flynn said:

> [T]he Constitution of the State of Arizona . . . has in statehood provided to the citizens of our state language precisely the same as the 4th Amendment to the Federal Constitution as it pertains to searches and seizures, yet, from 1914 until this Court's decision in Mapp versus Ohio, we simply did not enjoy . . . the 4th Amendment rights that were enjoyed by most of the other citizens of the other states of this union. . . . [Should solution of the confessions problem be left again to the states] it would be another 46 years before the 6th Amendment right in the scope that it was intended, I submit, by this court in *Escobedo* will reach the State of Arizona. . . .

He sat down, and Gary Nelson, assistant attorney general in charge of criminal appeals for the state of Arizona, took his place at the rostrum. Time was precious, and only seconds elapsed between Flynn's last words and Nelson's "May it please the Court." The justices had heard the case for the criminal defendant, the individual; now they were to hear the case for the state, for the society at large, for the Lois Ann Jamesons who walked home from work at midnight.

Sticking to his argument that the confessions issue was a Sixth Amendment issue, however much the justices talked Fifth Amendment, Nelson, it became clear early on, believed the Court was going to expand its *Escobedo* ruling in some way; it was only a matter of what it would do, how far it would go. When he was not under attack by Justice Fortas—who was gradually establishing himself as the constitutional logician in these cases, probing the structure of the adversary proceedings, exploring the rationale behind the various advantages afforded each side—Nelson was urging the justices not to expand *Escobedo* too far. If his presentation did not resound with soaring constitutional themes, it was at least partly because these belonged almost by definition to the lawyer for the criminal defendant for whom the Bill of Rights, the appeal to human freedom and the constraints on the behavior of the state, had been written, the ultimate protection against government power.

Gary Nelson did not believe the Constitution resided at the end of a nightstick. He held no brief for beating confessions out of suspects. But life in the station houses of Arizona looked relatively civilized to him, and he did not want to see the fruitful confessions avenue to conviction barricaded. He would prohibit, he told the court, "affirmative conduct" on the part of police or prosecutors "calculated . . . to deny the man the implementation" of his constitutional rights. However, he added, voicing the fears of law enforcement officers nationwide:

> I think if the extreme position is adopted that says he has to either have counsel at this stage or intelligently waive counsel, that a serious problem in the enforcement of our criminal law will occur. First of all, let us make one thing certain [he told the justices, speaking more slowly now, letting them absorb the full significance]. We need no empirical data as to one factor, what counsel, will do if he is actually introduced. . . . At least among lawyers there can be no doubt as to what counsel for the defendant is supposed to be doing. He is to represent him 100 percent, win, lose or draw, guilty or innocent. That is our system. When counsel is introduced at an interrogation, interrogation ceases immediately.

As he listened to the justices question John Flynn and Gary Nelson and to the attorneys' responses, it had become clear to Telford Taylor, scheduled to argue as amicus for the state of New York immediately following Ernest Miranda's case, that the justices were putting the confessions issues under the Fifth Amendment. This development had taken him by surprise, and he had quickly replanned parts of his argument. Now the chief justice addressed him, and he made his way to the rostrum.

Telford Taylor represented neither the Ernest Mirandas nor the Lois Ann Jamesons as he stood before the Supreme Court during its last hour the

139

afternoon of February 28. Tall, trim, looking as if he worked out regularly at the Harvard Club, he represented, rather, the states themselves as units of government within the structure of federalism—twenty-nine of them. He had no practical experiences to share, no intimate knowledge of station house procedures to impart. He only explained, in his undramatic way and cultured tones, that his clients, the chief law enforcement officers in more than half the states, would take a dim view of the Court's expanding its *Escobedo* ruling to require the presence of counsel during police interrogation. However wise such a ruling might be—and Taylor conceded its wisdom—it was not, he declared, a matter of constitutional dimension, and it would be better left to state legislatures and state courts.

He made his points in less than his allotted time, which in no way detracted from the importance of his argument. He reminded the Justices that when in 1961 the Court had decided, via *Mapp* v. *Ohio*, that illegally obtained evidence was not admissible in state courts, about half the states already applied exclusionary rules in their courts. State judges had been enthusiastic the following year when the Court had decided, via *Gideon* v. *Wainwright*, that the Sixth Amendment to the Constitution guaranteed the assistance of counsel in state as well as federal trials. Now, as the Justices prepared to decide a case of equal significance for the law enforcement community—however they decided—what the chief law enforcement officers thought about the matter, how the Court's decision would be received in the states was important.

Not all the justices had spoken this afternoon during the opening hours of argument in the confessions cases, and with the exception of Mr. Justice Stewart, who had reiterated his unwillingness to advance the stage of criminal proceedings at which constitutional rights came into play, the tenor of the questioning by those who did speak offered precious few clues. So there was no way of knowing, as the chief justice adjourned the Court promptly at 2:30, how the afternoon's arguments might have influenced them.

The following day, March 1, however, if one believed the tone of the justices' questions pointed with any certainty to their judicial inclinations, the clues came faster, beginning almost immediately following the opening of Court at 10:00 A.M. Duane R. Nedrud, executive director of the National District Attorneys Association, which had submitted an amicus brief and had been allotted time for oral argument, had barely gotten his presentation under way, his ministerial manner adding a touch of dramatics to the proceedings, when the chief justice bore down.

Not surprisingly for a spokesman for prosecutors, Nedrud had been trying to impress upon the Court the significance of the confession in the necessary task of apprehending criminals and the deleterious effect on confessions of the presence of counsel when Warren interrupted, beginning gently enough but becoming increasingly testy:

The Chief Justice: May I ask you this, please, Mr. Nedrud: If you agree on the facts that *Escobedo* should have been reversed, what would you say as to the man who did not have a lawyer, but who said he wanted a lawyer before he talked?

Mr. Nedrud: If he asked for a lawyer, and he does not waive his right to counsel, I think that he should have a lawyer. I think . . . I would go so far as to say that I think the state should appoint a lawyer if he asks for a lawyer. I do not think, however, that we should in effect encourage him to have a lawyer.

The Chief Justice: Why do you say we should not encourage him to have a lawyer? Are lawyers a menace?

Mr. Nedrud: Mr. Chief Justice, a lawyer must in our system of justice, *must* attempt to free the defendant. This is his job.

The Chief Justice: Because it is his professional duty to raise any defenses the man has?

Mr. Nedrud: Yes, sir.

The Chief Justice: Do you think in doing that he is a menace to our administration of Justice?

Mr. Nedrud: I think he is not a menace at the trial level. He is not a menace, *per se,* but he is, in doing his duty, going to prevent a confession from being obtained.

The Chief Justice: When does he cease being a menace?

Mr. Nedrud: Mr. Chief Justice, I did not say he was a menace. . . . I merely said he would prevent a confession from being obtained, and, if this is what we are looking for, we should appoint counsel even before the arrest stage, because the moment that a murder takes place, the Government is out looking for the criminal. . . . I am saying that . . . if you want to equalize, for example, the defendant's right against the policeman, naturally, he should have counsel, if this is what we are striving for.

The Chief Justice: Suppose we put it on the basis of not equalizing anything or balancing anything, but on protecting the Constitutional rights of the defendant, not to be compelled to convict himself on his own testimony.

Mr. Nedrud: Mr. Chief Justice, I, of course, do not interpret the Constitution. This is, of course, your prerogative, sir.

The Chief Justice: How do you interpret it?

Mr. Nedrud: I do not interpret that the defendant is entitled to a lawyer until the trial stage. . . .

The Chief Justice: Where do you get that authority?

Mr. Nedrud: As I read the Constitution, you asked me my opinion, and I said I have no authority to interpret the Constitution. I am saying this is the way I read the Constitution.

The Chief Justice: Has that been the way this Court has read the Constitution in days gone by?

Mr. Nedrud: I believe so.

Those who had been watching Hugo Black for signs of his inclinations were the next to be rewarded. "As a prosecutor," he told Nedrud, "I have found out over many years a very critical stage is when a person is taken to the police headquarters. There is nothing wrong with that. That is part of our government." However, he added, "a person is taken to police headquarters, under arrest, under detention. . . . Would you call that voluntary for him then for them to have him there in that situation and probe him about probable conviction of crime? Would you think of that as voluntary?" Black's tone, soft as it was, indicated that *he* did not think a confession given under such circumstances would necessarily be voluntary.

The brief for Michael Vignera had suggested a way to ease the pressure:

> When the proceeding has become accusatory, the police or prosecutor will be obliged to warn the accused of his absolute constitutional right to silence and of his right to consult with counsel *before* talking any further with police. . . . If the accused wishes to consult with the previously retained counsel, he will be permitted to do so and the interrogation will not continue while the police are awaiting the lawyer's arrival. If the accused does not already have counsel and is indigent, the police . . . may suggest the local public defender or Legal Aid Society and provide access to telephone communication . . . [or] if the police are unwilling or unable to recommend such counsel, they will simply terminate the interrogation at that point.

That morning the justices pursued the suggestion with some interest, attempting to determine first at what point the proceeding became accusatory and required warnings, then the make-up of the warnings themselves. Victor Earle gave them a formula:

> The Chief of Police in the District of Columbia last August promulgated a warning which . . . is now being given by all police officials in the District. It goes something like this: you have been placed under arrest. You are not required to say anything to us any time or to answer any questions. Anything you say may be used as evidence in court. You may call a lawyer or a relative or a friend. Your lawyer may be present here, and you may talk with him. If you cannot obtain a lawyer, one will be appointed for you when your case first goes to court.
> I might have a little quibble with that third point, because it suggests a little bit that you might not be able to get a lawyer now.

Later in the morning Abe Fortas, to whose questions and comments special attention was being paid because it was believed that if the Court divided, as it had in *Escobedo*, his would be the crucial vote, began to relate principles at issue in the confessions cases to principles laid down in Magna Carta; he was the only one of the justices to put the cases into a historical context. It happened during Kings County District Attorney William Siegel's argument in Michael Vignera's case, just after he had reminded the Court that confessions had traditionally been considered the "highest type of evidence" and that his office, which was in the business of prosecuting criminals, protecting the community from Ernest Miranda and Michael Vignera, did not "want to be deprived, we don't want to lose the opportunity to get that type of evidence. . . ." Fortas opened the exchange:

> Mr. Justice Fortas: Mr. Siegel, I suppose it is at least arguable that prior to Magna Carta and prior to the adoption of our own Bill of Rights most people who were convicted were guilty. Nevertheless, it has been the wisdom of the ages that some safeguards are necessary. Isn't that so?
> Mr. Siegel: I agree with that.
> Mr. Justice Fortas: I suppose that if one tries to look at this philosophically and morally in terms of the great human adventure toward some kind of truly civilized order, that these great provisions in the Magna Carta and in our own Bill of Rights were designed to do two things: one, to eliminate even the unusual case of an unjustified conviction, and, two, to lay out a standard for the relationship between the state, vis-à-vis the individual. Would you think that that observation is justified?
> Mr. Siegel: Undoubtedly, sir.
> Mr. Justice Fortas: That is to say . . . I think that perhaps one has to consider what we are dealing with here is not just the criminal in society, but it is the problem of the relationship of the state and the individual, in the large and total philosophical sense, viewed in the light of the history of mankind, part of that history being the Magna Carta and the Bill of Rights. . . .

The Magna Carta, forced on King John by a group of rebellious English barons in 1215, was no grand design for the establishment of constitutional government, no expansive expression of a new political philosophy. It was, rather, a conservative document put together haphazardly by the ruling class to protect its own interests, a written restatement of tacit understandings which had evolved over centuries between the king and his liege lords and an attempt to curb contemporary abuses of these understandings by the monarch. Most of its sixty-three provisions dealt with immediate problems of feudal relationships: dues, debts, dowries, inheritances, lands, rents, the rights and responsibilities of lords and vassals, and such routine matters as weights and measures to be used in the wine, ale, corn, and cloth trades. Even the famous Chapter 39 prohibiting the punishment of a man without application of "the law of the land"—from which the "due process of law" phrasing of the American Constitution had been derived—meant less in the thirteenth century than later.

The charter applied not to the Ernest Mirandas of the realm but only to "free men"—tenants, but not serfs, of the manor—and those in the classes above, or about 10 percent of the island's population. And the immediate effect was slight. Implementation of the original Great Charter lasted for about three months, although it was modified and reconfirmed some forty times by later medieval kings, according to the waxing and waning of the fortunes of liberty.

The significance of the document, however, lay not in its specific provisions but in its promise to the future. Now the king was bound by the law, a written law. Government was no longer the arbitrary master of the people but had started down the long road toward becoming the servant.

If Magna Carta was an important advance for civilization, a significant shift in the relationship between the individual and the state, a new premise on which government could be built, its finest expression was the American Constitution, with its eloquent afterthought, the Bill of Rights. The Constitution had been written by men who knew what excesses government could commit. They were educated men; they knew Roman history, the Caesars whose very name had come to symbolize those excesses; they knew English history and were familiar with the lengths to which government would go in the name of conformity and self-perpetuation—they were indeed part of *that* history. And they meant for it not to be repeated here.

It has often been said that the authors, in the vagueness of certain terms, were writing for the ages, for the quill pen and computer ages alike, the age of sail and the atomic age, as if they had been granted some extraordinary foresight. They did write for the ages, of course, but not in the way the thesis is usually presented. The SST, the assembly line, the arrival of the world's tired and poor on American shores, the cotton gin, the automobile, organized labor—none of these could have been predicted, and all were irrelevant. What underlay the discussions of the delegates to the Constitutional Convention in Philadelphia that summer of 1787, as they quibbled over procedures and bargained away sovereignty, was not how the nation of their children and grandchildren and great-grandchildren would change but rather how it would not. Their deliberations revolved around the unchanging character of humanity. The same greed and ambition that had motivated the Caesars and George III would motivate all governments to come, tyrants and reformers alike. And they dealt with it shrewdly.

They created in the Constitution not a code of laws but a structure for government, one in which a tension was required between its equal parts in order to keep them equal: between state and federal governments, among legislators, presidents and judges so that none could destroy the others. And when they were through, it was discovered that the people were not yet safe, and they added a Bill of Rights, ten amendments whereby they withheld some specific powers from the government, including the power to lynch a man judicially, thus creating another tension, this between the government and the governed. This intricate system of checks and balances, in which power was parceled out so that it could not be amassed in one person's hands, was the secret of their success. The structure they built was not for God, or for king, or for state; it was for people. It was the greatest shift of all in the relationship of man to his government, the one that made the cases of Izell Chambers, Clarence Earl Gideon, Danny Escobedo, and now Ernest Miranda not only possible but inevitable.

> Mr. Justice Fortas: . . . In other words, does this problem really affect the basic relationship of the individual and the state? It really goes beyond the administration of justice. . . . If one wanted to say that if the police get a 90 percent justifiable result, that ought to satisfy them, if you want to be pragmatic and practical about this. You can say, "Well, the police secured a conviction in 90 percent of the cases, it is all right." That is a very sensible attitude, from one point of view, but perhaps it is the point of view that has been rejected by history.

Solicitor General Thurgood Marshall, who had still been sitting on the U.S. Court of Appeals for the Second Circuit in April 1965, when Carl Calvin Westover's petition for cert was filed in the U.S. Supreme Court, had engaged in a lengthy colloquy with former Deputy Attorney General, now Mr. Justice White, regarding FBI practices in obtaining statements and confessions. The solicitor general, after much urging, had admitted that although the FBI warning to suspects included a phrase allowing consultation with an attorney, the federal government had no means of furnishing a lawyer to an indigent.

"We just *can't equalize* the whole thing," he explained finally.

The discussion took various circuitous routes to definition of who was allowed to consult a lawyer under what conditions, veering into federal rules for detaining suspects for questioning, returning to consideration of the counsel problem. Marshall was continuing undeterred in his argument that the government need not provide counsel to an indigent suspect when the chief justice interrupted with one of his "But is it fair?" questions.

> The Chief Justice: What would you do with this case? It happened in the District here just a few years ago. . . . There was a robbery from a restaurant and the robber not only took the money away from the woman cashier but beat her up in a brutal fashion. She gave a description to the police and the police went out to a certain area of the city and gathered up 90—not 9 but 90—people who might answer that description, got them out of bed, threw them into jail at night and didn't process them by morning. Some of them—a lot of them couldn't go to work because they were in jail for suspicion of robbery. . . . It happened that not one of these 90 was the guilty party. They found him later. . . .

Twenty-six years before, in 1940, the solicitor general, then counsel for the NAACP, had written in the brief for Izell Chambers, one of the twenty-five to forty black men rounded up by police in a similar fashion: "Equal protection and due process under the law are the pillars upon which our democracy rests. A denial of these to the humblest of our citizens is a threat to the liberties of all." He was the solicitor general now, though.

> Mr. Marshall: I have always been opposed to dragnet arrests of any kind but if I may say so, to really put that in proper focus, anybody that had a lawyer would have got his man out on a writ but you wouldn't have to get a lawyer to get a writ to get the other ones out. That is the way the law is now situated.
>
> The Chief Justice: I don't quite understand you. They were arrested in the middle of the night and if they could get on the phone . . . and get their lawyers and the lawyer says, "Don't talk to them . . ." and they would follow on that advice and the police could do nothing with them but with the rest of them who had no lawyers and perhaps were poor and couldn't afford at least at that time a lawyer, do you think that the police would have the right to retain them and question them ad lib?
>
> Mr. Marshall: As the law now stands I would say that the only redress they have would be that they were the subject of a dragnet arrest and had their rights denied by the dragnet arrest and anything that came as a result of it would go out. That is what I think the court should do in such a case. . . .
>
> The Chief Justice: You don't suggest that we overrule *Escobedo*?
>
> Mr. Marshall: No sir . . . [but] I don't want to give support to any theory that we believe *Escobedo* requires that a lawyer be appointed to an individual at the police precinct or at the arrest. . . .

The drama of the situation was understated; but the chief justice's sentiments were not, and what *he* thought was fair was becoming increasingly clear as the afternoon wore on.

Before the Court adjourned promptly at its accustomed hour of 2:30, Mr. Justice Black, who had been one of the most persistent questioners during these arguments, addressed Stanford Schmuckler, lawyer for the petitioners in *Johnson* v. *New Jersey*.

> Mr. Justice Black: Would it be revolutionary—I don't say this is a point— . . . if the Court were to say that [if] a man is held simply to interrogate him against his will by officers at a place where he does not want to be . . . that is compulsion which will invalidate the admission of the confession?
>
> Mr. Schmuckler: I would consider that to be an evolution.
>
> Mr. Justice Black: . . . I don't say this should be adopted. I don't know what should be adopted.

And as if he had mulled it over for a long time during the intervening hours, he pursued it the following day, as the last of the five scheduled confessions cases, *California* v. *Stewart,* was presented to the Court, testing various definitions of compulsion, devising hypothetical situations in which compulsion might or might not be a factor, querying counsel on each matter. But most significantly, in the light of the decision that finally emerged, Black obstinately steered the discussion away from issues of right to counsel and toward issues involving the right not to be compelled to be a witness against oneself.

A few weeks before the Court handed down *Escobedo* in 1964, Justice Stewart had deserted his frequent judicial companions, the dissenters in criminal cases, and had written the majority opinion in *Massiah* v. *United States,* in which the Court had declared that after a defendant was indicted, or formally charged with a federal crime he could not be questioned without his lawyer's being present. The decision had extended the right to counsel from the trial stage to postindictment stage, and this day Stewart had pursued answers to the question of precisely when the actual prosecution of a case, or adversary process, began. In response to John Flynn's suggestion that the police officer's shift from investigation of a crime to accusation of a suspect started the adversary process and required that the suspect be advised of his rights and given legal counsel, Stewart had commented: "[T]hen what you have is the equivalent of a trial . . . and then, I suppose, you have the right to a judge and a jury and everything else that goes with a trial. . . ." Now, as the arguments moved into their final hour, his brother Black fashioned an answer. Reaching into his arsenal of absolutes he responded to William Norris, Roy Stewart's lawyer who had suggested that at some point the Court "must decide what marks the beginning of the criminal prosecution . . ." thus:

> Mr. Justice Black: Why? The Court held a long time ago that what that means is that the Government shall not compel a defendant to give evidence against himself anywhere or under any circumstances. So why do we have to determine when the prosecution actually begins? The words of the Amendment are very simple, and they've been construed as meaning that that means the Government mustn't compel a man to give evidence against himself anywhere, at any time.

Shortly afterward it ended. The arguments in the five confessions cases were completed, and Chief Justice Warren marked the occasion with a brief and unusual observation: "Before calling the next case," he said, "I would like to thank counsel for both sides for having presented the very scholarly arguments in all of these cases. And I would like particularly to express our appreciation to those who took these cases as charity cases or were assigned to them by the courts below." Then he named and thanked each attorney individually.

The justices had it all now: the details of each case; the grim station house facts of life; the philosophical underpinning of the various positions;

the consensus among the states and within segments of the law enforcement community. It remained only for them to sort it out and come to a consensus among themselves.

The questions and comments from the bench had been dominated by the chief justice and Justices Black, Stewart, and Fortas. What little had been said by the others had been insignificant regarding their inclinations in these cases.

Telford Taylor believed the justices had not yet made up their minds. Opposing counsel in Ernest Miranda's case, John Flynn and Gary Nelson, left the courtroom believing the Court had already made its decision.

CHAPTER 3

The confessions cases were not the only ones scheduled for oral argument that week of February 28. As soon as the attorneys for Roy Stewart and the state of California moved out of the front bank of lawyers' tables the afternoon of Wednesday, March 2, the lawyers for the parties to the next scheduled case moved in, and the justices listened to arguments in four more cases during that afternoon and the following day, bringing the total for the week to ten. On Friday they retreated to the conference room to discuss what they had heard.

No one knows except the participants themselves, the justices of the United States Supreme Court, when the decision was made in the case of Ernest Miranda and the four companion cases. The traditional procedure was for the justices to hear oral arguments Monday through Thursday, then adjourn to the conference room on Friday for discussion, voting, and the assignment of opinions while the arguments remained fresh in their minds. That pattern was not always followed precisely, however; some cases required special treatment. Discussion of the public school desegregation cases, their potential for beginning a civil war never far from the justices' consciousness, consumed conference sessions whole or in part for more than two full terms between December 1952, when they were first argued, and May 31, 1955, when the chief justice read the Court's final implementing decision. Because of the controversial and public nature of the confessions cases, it is possible that they were not finally decided that first Friday after argument.

Whether the decision making in the confessions cases was accomplished during one conference or it spanned several sessions, the justices, as tradition required, followed the same procedures as they had the previous November when they decided whether or not to grant cert—that is, discussion followed by voting. The chief justice opened the discussion; each associate justice contributed his views in order of seniority, from the most senior, Hugo Black, to the most junior, Abe Fortas. Conversation ranged from John Harlan's unqualified courtesy to William O. Douglas's scrappiness as he actively promoted disharmony in the belief it would "lead to a better opportunity for compromise." To call it vigorous is understatement. These were strong-minded individuals, the winners of all the races, who had developed over the years strong judicial positions and forceful methods and who generally came to the conference table not, as a later justice commented, in "absolute knife-edged neutrality," but with at least tentative, if not final, views on the cases before them. Some came to convert as much as they did to listen.

Voting procedures following discussion also was faithful to Court tradition: The most junior justice voted first—the rationale being that the more junior the justice, the more susceptible to the influence of his seniors—the senior associate justice next to last, and the chief justice last. However, as Felix Frankfurter once reminded a colleague: "The phrase so often heard around the conference table that 'every vote is tentative' is not an empty utterance. The full scope of its meaning is derived from the fact that no case is decided until . . . the decision is announced from the bench." And he recalled that "at least one important case, since I've been here, was held up for decision as we marched to take our seats on the bench, because shortly before there was a change in the voting." Regardless of judicial denials, decision making necessarily involves public policy making, too. Whether a judge is active or passive, he makes public policy. If the Supreme Court had refrained from intervening in the legal lynching of the Scottsboro boys, if the justices had chosen to overlook the rope burns on the necks of the defendants in *Brown* v. *Mississippi*, would public policy have been affected any the less? In Ernest Miranda's case, whatever the justices should decide, whether they planted the Constitution more firmly in the station house or refused to, they would make public policy.

As they faced the issues in Ernest Miranda's case, they faced also, inevitably, a search of their own souls. There was no simple legal calculus on which to base decision; they required personal answers to what they believed not only in their minds but in their hearts regarding how criminal justice ought to be administered in America one decade from the nation's celebration of its two hundredth birthday.

The justices had divided on the disposition of Danny Escobedo's case along class lines, a not uncommon division among the men on this particular Court. Those justices who had voted to reverse Escobedo's conviction probably would not have been appointed to the United States Supreme Court fifty years before. They had been born to the less advantaged, economically and politically, to people unaccustomed to prosperity and unacquainted with the wielding of power. As justices they represented the fulfillment of America's promise. Yet there remained a coincidence of perspective with those other less advantaged souls whose cases came to the U.S. Supreme Court, a skepticism, if not a distrust, of authority, an understanding of the plight of the poor and ignorant; there remained some intangible but nonetheless real bond between the judges and the judged.

Earl Warren was the recognized leader of these men. When he was born, his father was a $70-a-month repairman for the Southern Pacific Railroad and a member of one of the new unions that were making trouble for owners, demanding safety devices on the machinery the men worked with and decent wages in their pockets. One of the chief justice's earliest memories was of his father's losing the job because he participated in the nationwide railroad strike of 1894. Now Earl Warren's aspirations for a people's Court, one "open to all people and all claims of injustice," were being realized. The tone of his voice and the tenor of his questioning at the recent oral argument of the confessions cases seemed to indicate he was seeking increased safeguarding of the constitutional rights of the accused in the station house.

Hugo Black, the senior associate justice, sitting across the conference table, at the foot, was the youngest of eight children born in rural Harlan, Alabama, to William La Fayette Black—Confederate veteran, farmer until he could no longer make do with the scant rewards of that life, then country storekeeper—and Martha Toland Black. Very early in life Hugo Black had begun to contribute to the family finances, never abundant in the hardscrabble country, by picking cotton and setting type for a weekly newspaper. He never seemed to tire of reminding folks that "it is a long journey from the frontier farm house in the hills of Clay County, Alabama, to the United States Supreme Court." While the chief justice had appeared to be seeking increased protection for the accused during oral argument of the confessions cases, the senior associate justice had appeared to be seeking the constitutional grounds for it.

The senior associate justice had once described the third member of this bloc, William O. Douglas, as having "come into this world with a rush and his first cry must have been a protest against something he saw at a glance was wrong or unjust." Two things largely had fashioned the judicial behavior of William O. Douglas, who had come into this world the son of an impoverished Presbyterian minister on October 16, 1898. The first was a childhood attack of nearly fatal poliomyelitis. His determination to erase entirely the physical and psychological ravages of the disease, which had changed him from a puny child into an enthusiastic outdoorsman capable of strenuous activities, undoubtedly accounted for the development of a certain ideological tenacity and perseverance. The other thing that had shaped him was his poverty, which accounted for the ideology itself.

He long remembered his adolescent years, not so much how hard he had hustled and worked to contribute to the family finances as well as to pay his college and law school tuition, but the people with whom he had worked, picking fruit with the migrant Chicanos, harvesting wheat with the Industrial Workers of the World (the Wobblies), political and social outcasts as they made their way from wheat field to logging camp and mine seeking strength in union. He recalled the forces of law and order firing on unarmed and helpless men, herding them into boxcars and sealing them in, and he had wept: "I thought of all the pompous members of the Establishment of Yakima [Washington, where he grew up] who should have been in those cars." He remembered being hired by a prominent local clergyman as a stool pigeon in Yakima's red-light district, only to discover, in addition to the wells of human suffering there, that his moralistic employer was engaged in some underhanded business dealings elsewhere. This youthful brush with hypocrisy in high places "somehow aligned me emotionally," he later recalled, "with the miserable people who make up the chaff of society."

He was known in the nation's capital, to which he had first come in 1936 as a member of the Securities and Exchange Commission, as an iconoclastic, detached, and occasionally irascible man who, a colleague later recalled, "took a pixie delight sometimes in baiting his critics into even more violent hyperbole." His specialty was the First Amendment's guarantees of freedom of speech, press, and assembly, and his judicial radar homed in on violations with swiftness and certainty. But he was a reliable and alert watchman over individual rights in other areas, including the rights of defendants in criminal cases.

However quiet Douglas had been during the argument of the confessions cases, it was not difficult to guess how he would view them. In 1956 a mental defective, suggestible and subject to intimidation, had been taken into custody by Connecticut State Police on a Saturday afternoon and questioned intermittently by officers until Wednesday night, when, after seeing his wife and ailing daughter and being urged by his wife to tell the truth, he had confessed to participation in a holdup in which two men had been murdered. The suspect had asked for a lawyer during the interrogation, but police had denied the request. He was convicted on the basis of this "confession." In 1961 the U.S. Supreme Court had reversed the conviction. Douglas, in a concurring opinion, had paraphrased some of his old resentments:

> If this accused were the son of a wealthy or prominent person, and demanded a lawyer, can there be any doubt that his request would have been heeded? But petitioner has no social status. He comes from a lowly environment. No class or family is his ally. . . . The system of police interrogation under secret detention falls heaviest on the weak and illiterate—the least articulate segments of our society. . . . The indigent who languishes in jail for want of bail . . . or the member of a minority group without status or power is the one who suffers most when we leave the constitutional right to counsel to the discretion of the police.

William J. Brennan, Jr., fifty-nine, had been a New Jersey Supreme Court justice before he was appointed in 1956 to the United States Supreme Court by President Eisenhower, a prepresidential election ploy calculated to earn some extra Catholic and/or Democratic votes—Brennan was both—for Eisenhower. Brennan was the son of an immigrant from County Roscommon, Ireland, who had begun his new life in America as a coal heaver for the Ballantine brewery in Newark, New Jersey, and had later become a prominent local labor leader. Like Douglas, Brennan had been quiet during the recent arguments of the confessions cases and had given no indication of how he would like to have them decided. He had been since his Court appointment, however, a loyal member of the Warren-Black-Douglas group in criminal cases, and he had stood with the majority in *Escobedo*.

It was fairly clear in the spring of 1966 that these four justices would be more likely to see interrogation room 2 at Phoenix police headquarters from Ernest Miranda's point of view than from Officer Carroll Cooley's.

It was equally clear that four other justices would be inclined to consider the circumstances and conditions of interrogation room 2 from the police officer's perspective, a judicial habit they had formed during the years they had been sitting together on the United States Supreme Court. Their families had been, on the whole, prosperous; some had been influential in public affairs. They had been close to wielders of power, and they were less skeptical of others in the same position.

The antithesis of Douglas, to whom he was next in seniority, Tom Campbell Clark was establishment born and bred. He was the son and grandson of prominent Dallas, Texas, lawyers. He had lived on the best residential street in Dallas, had gone to good southern schools—Virginia Military Institute, the University of Texas—and, in the tradition of the well-to-do, had been installed in the family firm upon graduation from law school in 1922 at the age of twenty-three. For the next decade he had alternated between private practice and public service, at the same time becoming involved in Texas politics, where he had worked closely with the reigning Democrats Tom Connally and Sam Rayburn and from which he had been plucked for the Justice Department in 1937; he had worked his way from the lower echelons of the legal staff to attorney general. As chief law enforcement officer in the nation, he had been one of the principal architects of the Truman administration's program for sniffing out Communists in government. On the U.S. Supreme Court, to which he had been appointed by Truman in 1949, he had tended to align himself with authority, with government, and, in cases involving criminal justice, with the law enforcement officer. His writing in 1961 the Court's opinion that extended the exclusionary rule into the state courts and for the first time imposed the Fourth Amendment on state procedures was something of a departure. More in judicial character was his joining of Justice White's dissent in *Escobedo*, in which White had complained that law enforcement would be "crippled and its task made a great deal more difficult" by that ruling. Clark was unlikely, in the spring of 1966, to vote in a way that he thought would cripple it further.

If America had an aristocracy, John Marshall Harlan would have been a viscount. His great-grandfather had been a lawyer and congressman from Kentucky; his grandfather had been an associate justice of the United States Supreme Court; his father had been a well-to-do Chicago lawyer and civic leader. His education was as aristocratic as his genealogy: Princeton; Oxford, where he was a Rhodes Scholar; and New York Law School. Following graduation he had joined the prestigious Wall Street firm of Root, Clark, Howland, Buckner & Ballantine, and for nearly three decades afterward, he had alternated between the private practice of law and, in the noblesse oblige tradition of his class, public service. When he was appointed to the U.S. Court of Appeals for the Second Circuit by Eisenhower in 1954, he had a wife, a married daughter, a seven-room apartment on the East Side of Manhattan with a view of the river, a nine-room house in Weston, Connecticut, memberships in the Republican party and the Presbyterian church.

"It does sound awfully tame and correct, doesn't it?" he remarked to an interviewer at the time. "If it helps any, we don't have a terribly *good* view of the river—sort of an on-an-angle one—and I don't play golf at all well."

Harlan had been appointed to the U.S. Supreme Court in November 1954, on the death of Robert Jackson, after less than a year on the federal court; he ultimately became the house intellectual. He seemed to see criminal cases from neither the defendant's nor the law enforcement officer's point of view, but more as abstractions, his constant concern the Court's role in the federalist scheme of government. He was Felix Frankfurter's judicial heir and Hugo Black's judicial opposite. Where Black would activate the Court, Harlan would restrain it; where Black would use the Court to right the wrongs society had visited on the unprotected, Harlan would leave social reform to the natural political processes; where Black would apply the Bill of Rights to the states by judicial fiat, Harlan would allow, indeed urge, the states to develop their own fair procedures and practices. The notion in judicial vogue "that all deficiencies in our society which have failed of correction by other means should find a cure in the courts," he had told members of the ABA in August 1963, was a dangerous one. Taking responsibility from a state and giving it to an already too large federal bureaucracy held the potential for unbalancing the delicately balanced federal-state relationships; taking responsibility from a legislator who was beholden to the electorate and giving it to a judge who was beholden to no one held the potential for unbalancing delicately balanced legislative-judicial relationships, all of which contributed to the decline of federalism, a principle of government in which Mr. Justice Harlan devoutly believed. Although he had stood with the majority in *Gideon*, it had not been without misgivings about carrying over "an entire body of federal law"—provisions of the Bill of Rights—and applying it "in full sweep to the States." He had dissented briefly but forcefully in *Escobedo*.

Between the special November 1965 conference and oral argument in the confessions cases, he had distributed to the brethren three opinions in which the U.S. Court of Appeals for the Second Circuit had affirmed criminal convictions through a narrow application of the *Escobedo* ruling.

If Potter Stewart had any social kin on the Court, it would have been John Harlan. Stewart was born in 1915, the oldest son of a well-to-do Cincinnati family; his father had been mayor of Cincinnati for several terms and later an Ohio Supreme Court justice. His education had been elitist: Cincinnati's University School, Hotchkiss, Yale, Cambridge University in England, and Yale Law School. When he joined the navy during World War II, he soon became Lieutenant Stewart; after the war, in which he earned three battle stars serving as a deck officer on oil tankers in the Atlantic and Mediterranean, he had joined a large Cincinnati law firm and, like his brothers Clark and Harlan, developed an interest in public affairs. He had served two terms on the Cincinnati City Council and in 1952 and 1953 as vice-mayor. In 1952, after the Republican National Convention, Stewart had worked southern Ohio for Eisenhower, attempting at the same time to lessen some of the bitterness remaining between the Taft and Eisenhower factions over the outcome of the convention, where Taft, Ohio's favorite son, had lost the presidential nomination. In 1954 Eisenhower had appointed Stewart to the U.S. Court of Appeals for the Sixth Circuit, where he had refrained from philosophizing and stuck to judging, had hewed largely to a centrist position, in which he had insisted on fairness of procedure but had not broadened the application of the Bill of Rights, and had distinguished himself in his closely reasoned and readable opinions in complex tax cases.

On the U.S. Supreme Court, to which Eisenhower had elevated him in 1958, Stewart had remained a pragmatist. He had a reputation for injecting a cooling influence on the fiery passions that frequently flared in the Court's conference room, and like his personal style, his opinions were cool analyses of the issues involved in a case. He wrote no passionate appeals to libertarian abstractions and visualized no ideological utopias but tended to examine the facts and circumstances in each case, then to balance the competing interests. He had dissented with some vigor in *Escobedo*.

Early assessments of his future judicial behavior had placed Byron White, because he had worked on the New Frontier and was known as a close friend of John Kennedy's, in the Warren-Black-Douglas-Brennan bloc in matters of civil liberties. Although he had been on the Court for only three full terms by the spring of 1966, and it was too early to generalize, White was already showing that the New Frontier and an expansionist view of the Bill of Rights were not necessarily interchangeable, and he tended to decide more often than not with the Harlan-Clark-and-occasionally-Stewart bloc. Although he had been poor as a youth in Wellington, Colorado and, like most children there, had begun working in the sugar beet fields at age seven or eight, it had been only the temporary poverty of depression he had known.

His father had been the branch manager of a local lumber supply company, and if the elder White had not enjoyed the affluence or wielded the influence of a Harlan or a Clark, he had, in fact, crossed the line betweeen the less and more advantaged to the middle class in American society. White had, of course, dissented when the U.S. Supreme Court had reversed the conviction of Danny Escobedo.

All this, if the customary division among the justices applied—the first four seeking salvation in the security of the individual, without which neither he nor anyone else could be considered safe, the latter four seeking salvation in society without which they believed equally strongly no one could be considered safe—left the confessions cases at four to four and one unknown.

The ninth justice, the junior one, Abe Fortas, was the crucial vote. He had not been on the Court long enough for the question mark beside his name to be erased. During the first seven months Fortas had sat on the Court, he had written seven opinions, three concurrences, and two dissents. Three had involved issues of criminal justice. In two of these he had indicated he would hold government to the highest standards of conduct in the apprehension of criminals, and in the third he had written: "The right to representation by counsel is not a formality. It is not a grudging gesture to a ritualistic requirement. It is the essence of justice." This last was a juvenile case, to which different procedural standards applied, but it seemed to indicate that his judicial cosmology had survived intact between his argument for Clarence Earl Gideon and his elevation to the highest court in the land. He was also the son of a Jewish cabinetmaker, a member of a poor family, and it was not inconceivable that he shared the perspective of those four justices whose humble origins seemed to define certain aspects of their judicial demeanor. In view of his invocation of Magna Carta at oral argument, he appeared to have some inclination to even the balance of power between the individual and his government. Just how much change he would countenance at this time, however, given his comments to Senator McClellan at his own confirmation hearings the previous August, which indicated he was also keenly aware of the problems law enforcement faced, was in no way evident at this point. At the oral argument in *Gideon* he had chided the justices for their monastic unawareness of the problems of the defendant in the station house, for their concern with federalism rather than with the plight of people; he himself, however, later confessed that he had been personally unfamiliar with the problems Ernest Miranda's case had raised. His vote was by no means sure.

Outside the Court, at the same time the justices were making their decision in the confessions cases, the controversy over them continued unabated, much of it staged explicitly for the benefit of the justices themselves.

On the very day that the U.S. Supreme Court had decided to hear these cases, November 22, 1965, Nathan R. Sobel of the New York Supreme Court had aimed a friendly judicial punch in the *New York Law Journal* at the tendency among law enforcement officers to overrely on confessions in the apprehension of criminals. In a recent survey of 1,000 indictments in criminal cases, the Kings County (Brooklyn) district attorney's office—whose head, William Siegel, had argued for the state in Michael Vignera's case—had discovered that prosecutors in that office had served on the defense a "notice of intention" to use confessions as evidence in only 86, or 8.6 percent, of the cases; no confessions had been involved in the nine murder indictments included in the survey. Admittedly, 1,000 cases were a small sample, and the statistics did not consider additional factors involved in the confessions issue, such as how many times police questioning produced other evidence or demanded the release of the suspect.

However, Sobel declared:

> That confessions are essential to conviction in any substantial number of cases is simply carefully nurtured nonsense.
> What is true is that overzealousness in the use of confessions has resulted in many guilty defendants going free. Those who go free because the prosecutor has blundered may very well exceed the number who go free because the exclusionary rules have deterred police or prosecutors from obtaining confessions. . . . [T]he value of confessions in law enforcement has been grossly exaggerated.

Frank Hogan, district attorney of adjacent New York County, whose office had bungled the George Whitmore case on the basis of a "confession," immediately took issue with Sobel. Speaking at a luncheon given by the Grand Jury Association of New York County, Hogan declared that in countless incidents, it was "the defendant, and only the defendant," whose evidence resulted in conviction. He supported his claim with figures from his own office, which were up from the 50 percent at the time of the Whitmore case a year before; in ninety-one homicide cases pending in New York County now, said Hogan, confessions would be offered as evidence in 62, or 68 percent; his assistants had told him that in twenty-five cases, or 27 percent, indictments could not have been obtained without confessions. "Obviously," he concluded, "the whole purpose of a police investigation is frustrated if a suspect is entitled to have a lawyer during the preliminary questioning, for any lawyer worth his salt will tell him to keep his mouth shut."

If the justices had been interested in the political winds, they had only to read the latest Republican press release. On December 19 the Republican Co-ordinating Committee had issued a policy paper which had been approved by Republican congressional leaders, governors, past presidential candidates, and upper-echelon party officials and which only rephrased the campaign themes of the immediate-past presidential candidate, Barry Goldwater. While the Republicans would not sacrifice "traditional protections for the accused in the courtroom and the police station . . . in the name of law enforcement," they also warned that "procedural rules must not be weighted so heavily on the side of the criminal that the police can no longer protect the law-abiding citizen." They insisted that police "should not be unnecessarily handicapped in their efforts to prevent crime and apprehend criminals."

One major consequence of the U.S. Supreme Court's granting of the writs of certiorari and hearing the oral arguments in Miranda's case was delay of decision in confessions cases in the lower federal and state courts. Better to wait, the reasoning went, in case the Supreme Court made its decision retroactive, and so such decision making came to a virtual standstill now as the judges awaited the highest court's instructions, which, following the arguments, appeared imminent.

The press, scholarly and otherwise, attempted to keep its readers informed of developments. Notes, comments, and leading articles on the issues surrounding confessions were featured in the law journals. The editors of the *Harvard Law Review* put together for their 12,000 readers an uncommonly long and uncommonly comprehensive study of confessions and the legal history involved. The editors of *Time* put Danny Escobedo's picture on the cover of the April 29, 1966, issue, and wove the confessions cases into his personal story inside.

Northwestern University Law School drew 300 leading judges, legal scholars, and police officials to a two-day late April conference which served largely to publicize growing national dismay, even bitterness, as a result of Supreme Court decisions in the field of criminal justice, particularly *Escobedo*. Chicago Police Chief Orlando W. Wilson, whose department had been responsible for Danny Escobedo's case, said what was on a lot of people's minds: *Escobedo* did not "ever make good sense," and it had made law enforcement "infinitely more difficult."

Criminal justice, particularly *Escobedo*, assumed a substantial role in the discussions at the National Association of Attorneys General at their mid-May meeting in Cleveland. On the whole, the chief law enforcement officers of the states, twenty-eight of whom had joined New York State in its brief against expansion of the *Escobedo* ruling, had learned to live with *Escobedo*, and most agreed that even the presence of lawyers in the interrogation room had not particularly hurt the confessions rate. But enthusiasm was still lacking for any extension of *Escobedo*, and the attorneys general were worried by *Dorado*, a California case in which the state supreme court had ruled the suspect must affirmatively waive his constitutional rights if a confession was to be admissible.

The New York assembly passed a bill, 100–31, to provide protection of Fifth and Sixth Amendment rights to criminal suspects in that state. No statement, or confession, the bill stipulated, could be admitted as evidence in court unless the suspect had been informed of the nature of the crime being investigated, of the suspect's right to have a lawyer and to communicate promptly with his lawyer or with relatives or friends, of the suspect's right to remain silent, and of the fact that any statement could be used against him at his trial.

Chapter 3

In the spring of 1966 Senator John L. McClellan, Democrat of Arkansas, chairman of the Senate Judiciary Committee's Subcommittee on Criminal Laws and Procedures, fire-breathing and podium-pounding critic of virtually all U.S. Supreme Court decisions since the Court's desegregation of the public schools, invited to Washington a group of police chiefs and other law enforcement officials from various sections of the nation to testify at hearings before his subcommittee. The ostensible purpose was to plumb their experience for suggestions on improving a packet of anticrime bills, including one modifying the rules on the admissibility of confessions, which McClellan was sponsoring in Congress. The real purpose, however, as the hearings wore on, seemed to be to berate the Supreme Court and to let the justices know the sentiments of grass-roots America on the subject of law enforcement. Warning, perhaps, was too strong a word, but the hearings were not without that element.

The most significant rumblings outside the Court may have been heard following official publication, on March 5, of the long-awaited first draft of the American Law Institute's Model Code of Pre-Arraignment Procedures. At oral argument William Siegel, the Brooklyn prosecutor, had buttressed one of his statements with a reference to the model code, then in preparation, and Hugo Black had interrupted him, typically and not a little contentiously: "What is that Model Code? Is that in the Constitution?" Nevertheless, institute pronouncements carried considerable political, if not constitutional, weight. The membership included nearly all the leading members of the American legal community, and the advisory committee on the Model Code of Pre-Arraignment Procedures project was made up of forty nationally influential law enforcement figures. Federal judges of the stature of J. Edward Lumbard and Henry Friendly, both of whom had already gone on record against any expansion of *Escobedo*; state Judges Walter V. Schaefer of the Illinois Supreme Court and Roger J. Traynor of the California Supreme Court—both of whom before the spring of 1966 was out, were to give major speeches urging the U.S. Supreme Court to proceed slowly in the matter of the confessions cases—police chiefs from the nation's largest cities; scholars from the leading law schools; the Los Angeles public defender; the FBI; the law enforcement arm of the U.S. Treasury Department; the private criminal defense bar—all were represented on the committee. In addition, the ABA Committee on Minimum Standards for Criminal Justice had deferred to the ALI committee on the area of pre-arraignment procedures and contributed ABA people to the project, making the model code, in effect, a joint effort and carrying the political and scholarly weight of virtually the entire American legal establishment.

This model code, like others produced by the institute, was intended as a guide for states to use in modernizing their criminal procedures. It attempted to deal with the procedures from the period of first police contact through to preliminary hearings.

Portions had been redrafted since it had been submitted to the advisory committee the previous summer, when Attorney General Katzenbach and Judge David Bazelon had made their sentiments known in a lively public exchange of letters. It had been submitted again to the advisory committee in November, then redrafted a second time and submitted to the ruling council of the ALI in December and again in March.

Whatever specifics of the draft had been changed—the maximum period a suspect could be detained had been lowered from twenty-four to twenty-two hours, for example—the tenor had not. It included the suspect's right to invoke the Fifth Amendment and to remain silent under questioning, defined the responsibility of police to advise him of that right, and stipulated that written or, preferably, sound recordings be made of the advisement. However, in the matter of the suspect's accessibility to legal counsel, the model code remained essentially at the line drawn in Danny Escobedo's case: A lawyer must be given access to his client at the station house, but the state had no affirmative obligation to provide counsel there, and questioning need not be conditioned on the presence of a lawyer. The underlying assumption was in March what it had been the summer before: Proper questioning by police of suspects who did not have legal advice was constitutionally permissible and socially desirable. Like some elements in Congress and like the bulk of the law enforcement community, the American Law Institute seemed to say that the current trend of U.S. Supreme Court decisions had gone far enough.

Timing of the draft's publication was a critical factor; if the full ALI membership gave its approval at its annual meeting in mid-May, it would put the legal community on record as wanting to hold the line in the rights of suspects at *Escobedo*.

At the ALI annual meeting in the Mayflower Hotel in Washington on May 17, 18, 19, and 20, the model code was the biggest single issue discussed by the membership, consuming the better part of two days. The debate was heated and wide-ranging, as the legal community's most prominent members vied with each other to speak. It was the only occasion on which Warren Burger of the U.S. Court of Appeals for the District of Columbia Circuit was ever "tempted . . . to enter the fray." There were rumors that the Supreme Court opinion had already been written, but Chief Justice Warren, when he appeared to give his annual state of the judiciary address, gave no clue except to say that the Court was up-to-date with its work and expected to hand down decisions in all the cases that had been argued that term in time for the usual June adjournment. Indeed, he sat sphinxlike through part of the discussion of the model code following his address, betraying nothing.

The model code, however, was not brought to a vote at that May meeting. There was little agreement on its provisions, and it was obvious from the discussion that it needed editing, sharpening, clarifying, defining, as well as substantive changes, before a vote could be taken. But the major reason was perhaps the fact that the five confessions cases were being decided at that moment in the United States Supreme Court. Having written the brief in Ernest Miranda's case and having sat at the counsel's table in the Supreme Court while his partner John Flynn argued Miranda's case, John Frank's pleas to the roomful of fellow lawyers had both poignancy and immediacy:

> ... my most earnest plea to my fellow members of the Institute is, as a matter of straight, lawyer-like procedure: Please don't decide our cases here ... please don't here prejudge them by any approval, tentative or otherwise of these positions. ... We have not taken the position that there cannot be voluntary confessions, but we have taken the position that, by God, the poor are entitled to be told of their right to counsel before it's too late, and I believe, having been in the Supreme Court for those arguments, that the United States Supreme Court will shortly adopt that position, and I submit that it would be unlawyer-like in the extreme for us to seek to prejudice that position in any way by any action we take here. ...

"You realize, Mr. Frank, of course," said ALI president Norris Darrell, "that any action that this body may take during this session is tentative and subject to any decision that the Supreme Court may take?"

"I realize, sir, that in all good grace we would bow to authority, but," Frank replied, lightening the moment. "I would rather not tell those fellows what they are supposed to do. I did that already." He did, however, promise James Vorenberg, director of the model code project, that if he was wrong, he would take Vorenberg to lunch the next year and would "eat, with dressing and all, all of those sections, indigestible as they may be."

Frank and the others of his persuasion prevailed, the vote was postponed, and the legal community, shown by the debate to be sharply divided, never did go on record either for or against drawing the lines at *Escobedo*. The U.S. Supreme Court made such a vote unnecessary.*

If the justices of the United States Supreme Court heard the rumblings outside the marble walls, they gave no sign. At some point during that spring of 1966, following the oral arguments, a majority was reached, and since the chief justice was a member of it, it was his task to assign the writing of the opinion. The self-appointed lightning rod on the Court, he had written the majority opinions in the Court's most controversial cases during his chief justiceship. Ernest Miranda's was such a case.†

---

* The decision in the case of Ernest Miranda which would come down the following month required substantial reconsideration and rewriting of sections of the model code. Much modified, it was finally adopted by the ALI membership at its annual meeting in 1975.

† Who speaks for the Supreme Court majority can be a matter of some moment, not without political considerations. Those cases likely to excite public controversy often were writ-

The author of the opinion in Ernest Miranda's case, Chief Justice Earl Warren, appeared oblivious to what was going on outside the Court. He held one of his rare news conferences to celebrate his seventy-fifth birthday on March 19, less than three weeks after the confessions cases had been argued, but he gave no hint, although he did indicate his awareness that decisions of his Court had provoked extensive litigation which, in turn, required more trials and caused dockets to be overcrowded. "We must find a way," he said noncommittally, "to deal with these cases." Otherwise, he gave no inkling that he was absorbed in writing one of the most significant opinions of his chief justiceship. Rather, exuding an exterior calm that sometimes seemed to spill over into blandness, he went about his duties both inside and outside the Court.

The responsibilities of the chief justice were, of course, considerable. Decision making and opinion writing were a substantial part of his work, of course. He had certain procedural duties and prerogatives: He arranged the Court agenda, presided over the Court at open argument and closed conference, and assigned the writing of opinions when he was in the majority. But he was one vote in nine, one among equals, a fact nicely illustrated many years earlier by Justice James C. McReynolds's answer to Chief Justice Hughes when Hughes one day dispatched a messenger for his colleague—it was late, Court was about to open, and the brethren were waiting impatiently in the robing room behind the bench for the absent member. Reported the messenger to Hughes: "Justice McReynolds says to tell you that he doesn't work for you."

But Earl Warren's title was not chief justice of the Supreme Court; it was chief justice of the United States,* a more expansive title. He represented

---

ten by the chief justice himself. It was perhaps not an accident that George Sutherland, economic and social conservative, had written for the Court in the case of the Scottsboro boys. When a justice with a reputation for taking a hard line in criminal cases votes with the majority to reverse a criminal conviction, he may be assigned to write the opinion; Tom Clark, for example, was assigned to write the opinion in *Mapp* v. *Ohio* which put restraints on law enforcement officers by prohibiting the use of illegally obtained evidence in state courts. The other side of that coin is that the so-called law and order justice may vote with the majority *in order to be* assigned the opinion and give it a more conservative tenor.

* The latter title seems, historically, to have been gradually assumed, through usage as much as through official edict. The U.S. Constitution established "one supreme Court" and "such inferior Courts as the Congress may from time to time ordain and establish" (Article 3, section 1), but holds only one reference to the chief justice: "the Chief Justice shall preside" when the president of the United States, having been impeached by the House of Representatives, is tried by the Senate. In the Judiciary Act of 1789, Congress ordered that the "Supreme Court of the United States shall consist of a chief justice and five associate justices" (the number of justices has fluctuated over the past two centuries). From 1789 until 1888 the chief justice's commission designated him "Chief Justice of the Supreme Court of the United States." However, in 1866, Congress for the first time used the title "chief justice of the United States," and the name stuck legislatively and unofficially. Then, in 1888, President Grover Cleveland nominated Melville W. Fuller "to be Chief Justice of the United States," and for the first time the commission was drawn in the same form.

the Court; it had been the Marshall Court, the Taney Court, the Hughes Court and now was the Warren Court. He also spoke for the entire American judiciary, represented the entire American system of justice, and there was a built-in ceremonial aspect to his professional life. Warren had headed the American delegation to the coronation of Pope Paul VI in 1963 and to the funeral of Winston Churchill in 1965. His out-of-court life was filled with formal and official events: groundbreakings, dedications, prayer breakfasts, conferences, swearings-in—he was in great demand in this rank-conscious capital of political ambition for swearings-in—diplomatic receptions, treaty signings, and state dinners. Not all these ceremonial functions were pleasant, and Warren never forgot waiting with other high government officials at Andrews Air Force Base that November day in 1963 for the president's plane to bring back his body from Texas and, when it finally landed, watching Mrs. Kennedy walk down the ramp. "There was that brave girl," Warren said later to his wife, "with her husband's blood still on her, and there was nothing I could do—*nothing.*"

Warren generally avoided the constant rounds of cocktail parties and dinners and opening nights that made up Washington's social life and titillated the readers of the *Washington Post* and *Washington Star.* "I just can't do this kind of work and be out a number of nights a week at social affairs," he said.

A later chief justice would describe the end of the Supreme Court term, particularly May and June, as a time when "tension and pressures are great and patience is in short supply," and Hugo Black had once advised his junior colleague, William J. Brennan, following a "vigorous outburst" by Brennan, to "get out of here and forget it for a few days." The Court, Black had said, "can become like a pressure cooker and it can beat the strongest of men."

This "pressure cooker" atmosphere, however, did not appear to slow Warren's pace that spring of 1966. He was a passionate sports fan—he had had Casey Stengel to lunch at the Court on several occasions, and it was reported that he had the World Series scores delivered to the Court conference room. So it was hardly surprising that he appeared on April 11 at the Washington Senators' opening game in company with Vice President Hubert Humphrey, who threw out the first ball that year, and Postmaster General (and Democratic party functionary) Lawrence F. O'Brien. On April 23 he spoke at the dedication of the School of Law of the University of Maryland in Baltimore, where he offered no clues to the Court's decision in the confessions cases except to invoke Magna Carta and to comment that "we have not yet achieved for the indigent the same equal justice under law which is accorded to those of means."

Hugo Black's eightieth birthday party, a White House judicial reception, the American Jewish Committee's Sixtieth Anniversary banquet, a stag luncheon honoring the president of Nicaragua at the White House, heading the American delegation to the Guyanese Independence Day celebration in late May; his address on the state of the judiciary to the American Law Institute—these were all part of Chief Justice Warren's spring in 1966.

In addition, there was, of course, the daily Court routine. The chief justice received a higher—by $500—salary than the associate justices because his duties included managing the company—the building, the grounds, and the staff. There were more oral arguments, lasting through the end of April, to be heard, conferences on Fridays, agenda to be worked out, and opinions to be written, including the opinion in Ernest Miranda's and the other four confessions cases.

Warren's successor, Chief Justice Burger, once told of an encounter he had had with Warren after the latter's retirement. Warren had retained an office at the Court, customary for retired justices, and Burger had asked the Court gardener to plant a bed of California-colored flowers outside Warren's office window. When he learned of Burger's thoughtfulness, Warren asked his successor where he had found time to think about flowers, and Burger had replied that he walked around the building almost daily for relaxation and relief of frustrations. Laughing, Warren remarked: "You'd better find a bigger place to walk; this place is not large enough to work off the frustrations of a Chief Justice."

In the earliest days of the U.S. Supreme Court, each of the justices wrote a separate opinion in every case. That practice was soon abandoned, however, in part because John Marshall, the fourth chief justice, believed it failed to offer clear, principled guidance to the courts below and in part because the increasing press of business militated against it. Each of the justices remained free, however, to write in concurrence or dissent whenever he was not completely satisfied with the majority's product.

Opinion writing was a demanding and arduous task. At least five strong-willed and knowledgeable judges had to agree on specifics of language as well as general thrust, and every nuance had its attacker and defender. The issues were *always* complex, difficult of resolution, and the consequences for a whole nation, serious; that is why they had come to the Court. The controversial and public nature of the opinion in the confessions cases made the task particularly laborious.

The finished opinion would represent weeks, perhaps months of painstaking research, drafting, and discussion. Earl Warren's style was to "stake out the boundaries" in a first draft, which he either dictated or set down in pencil on yellow lined legal pads. Next he called for suggestions from his law clerks, and together they reviewed the briefs and played back the tapes of the oral arguments. He then assigned his clerks to put together a second draft based on the discussion of the first. The second draft was then revised. Other drafts were written as required until he had what he believed was an unanswerable opinion.

The "unanswerable" opinion then went to the print shop in the building,* where several copies were made for distribution to the other eight justices for suggestions and comments. Dissenters as well as those who had voted in the majority received copies. The dissenters then went to work to reply and to convert if they could.

The chief justice sent around the first draft of the opinion in the confessions cases on May 18—nearly six months since the Court had decided to hear them and about six weeks since they had been argued: a normal gestation period for a controversial decision. He noted in an accompanying memorandum that "there is no mention of retroactivity in this opinion. That issue will be treated in a separate opinion in No. 762—*Johnson* v. *New Jersey*—which I hope to circulate in a few days." To which Justice Harlan responded the following day with a brief memorandum to the brethren: "I am planning to circulate a dissent in these cases in due course." And the contest was on.

It was not uncommon for some members of a working majority to reserve final judgment until the dissent was circulated. Dissents sometimes changed votes, and it had happened that a dissent had become a Court opinion and what had begun as a Court opinion had become a dissent. Sometimes, on the other hand, only minor rewriting or editing of a draft to sharpen the issues was necessary. Other times substantial revisions were called for if the author wanted only to hold a majority. More substantial revisions might be required if the author was trying to achieve unanimity.

The Court functioned as a collegial body—that is, each member passed on all the work; there were no committees or panels. But resemblance to the usual conception of collegial bodies, with their implications of collaboration and cooperation, ended there, and the Court was, a justice said years later, "one of the last citadels of jealously preserved individualism," its functioning closer to that of "nine small, independent law firms."

Comments generally were scribbled on the draft opinions, which were returned to the author for consideration. In addition, memorandums flew between the justices' chambers. The telephone, corridors, the luncheon table in the justices' dining room—all were witnesses to shifts in positions, compromises, concessions, and negotiations until a consensus gradually emerged and the final opinion was written—very much a "symphony."

The chief justice circulated the majority opinion twice more—on June 6 and June 11. Then it went to the basement print shop for the final press run. The following Monday Ernest Miranda, inmate number 27555 at the Arizona State Prison at Florence, would discover, via a television news program, what the United States Supreme Court had made of his case.

---

* Almost all government printing was done in the Government Printing Office on North Capitol Street. Supreme Court printing, however, was done in secrecy in the Court's own print shop in order to prevent leakage to outsiders. Leaks have been rare indeed, almost nonexistent. In 1979 Chief Justice Burger discovered that advance news of Court decisions had been supplied to a television network newsman by a typesetter. The typesetter was promptly transferred out of the print shop, and reporters' freedom in the building was restricted.

CHAPTER 4

The decision in Ernest Miranda's and three of the other confessions cases which had been argued together had been put together in the final decision as one case, under the umbrella of *Miranda v. Arizona*. It was one of seven full opinions handed down on Monday, June 13, 1966. Chief Justice Warren, his voice laden with emotion, read his entire opinion—which consumes sixty pages in the *United States Reports*. The reading required nearly an hour.

Once again the Court had divided along class lines, the justices born to families in humbler circumstances looking at the interrogation room through the eyes of the defendant, those born to families accustomed to privilege and influence looking at it through the eyes of the policeman. The former made up the majority—Warren, Black, Douglas, and Brennan, plus the newest member of the Court, Abe Fortas—and there was something in the opinion for each justice. As another step in mankind's groping "for the proper scope of governmental power of the citizen," the decision rephrased Fortas's comments on the historical perspective at oral arguments. In its description of Ernest Miranda as an "indigent Mexican defendant" and a "seriously disturbed individual" and of Roy Allen Stewart as "an indigent Los Angeles Negro who had dropped out of school in the sixth grade," the decision addressed Mr. Justice Douglas's concern for a tendency of law enforcement to trade on "the weakness of individuals." In its application to "persons in *all* settings in which their freedom of action is curtailed in *any* significant way [italics added]," it attempted to address Mr. Justice Black's previous statement, at oral argument, that the Court need not determine when the prosecu-

166

tion began, that the Fifth Amendment had laid down an absolute rule against compulsory self-incrimination. And for Mr. Justice Brennan, self-appointed gadfly to state courts, the decision reaffirmed the applicability of the Fifth Amendment to practices and procedures there.

No one except the members of the Court knows whether the framework of the opinion was worked out among the members of the majority before the chief justice ever put pen to paper—a system relied on in the past—or whether Warren put the document together himself, his memory refreshed by the oral argument tapes. Remarkably, however, for an opinion that held such a high potential for public controversy, it had changed very little from the first draft circulated a month before. The rewriting of an early ambiguous reference to a lawyer's presence in the interrogation room, the toning down of a derogatory comment on police practices, and some minor editing put the first draft in its final form, its sweep remaining through all the drafts as broad as Anglo-American legal history, its detail as minute as the rules of interrogation procedure. Whatever input the other justices had, the opinion remained, too, a typical Warren opus. There were no apparent legal mysteries to bewilder the uninitiated, no sophisms to ensnare, no scholarly allusions or unfamiliar historical references to clutter. Its lucidity was surpassed only by its high moral tone.

Although the United States Supreme Court had vacillated, hesitated, even sometimes reversed its direction during the three decades since it had for the first time, in *Brown* v. *Mississippi* (1936), reversed a conviction because a confession had been coerced, it had been headed all along toward this moment. Case by tedious case, the standards for the taking of confessions and statements of criminal suspects had been raised by the simple, although inherently subjective, device of reversing convictions when the circumstances of the taking had appeared to violate due process of law. Now, the Court was attempting to remove the element of subjectivity from the judging of cases by grounding the decision on the Fifth Amendment. It was also taking the unprecedented step of imposing stringent rules on law enforcement officers, rules that put restraints on their instincts and restrictions on their zeal. In so doing, the Court was challenging the collective wisdom of police, prosecutors, the attorneys general of more than half of the states, and a number of leading judges.

Warren was not two minutes into the reading of his opinion before the crowd gathered in the courtroom got a good idea of the direction in which the decision was headed.

"We start here," he declared, "as we did in *Escobedo*, with the premise that our holding is not an innovation in our jurisprudence, but is an application of principles long recognized and applied in other settings." The direction was clear; only the distance the Court would travel and the route remained unknown.

Shortly thereafter Warren spelled out the rules—a formula which had been suggested earlier by Victor Earle, Michael Vignera's lawyer, in his brief and at oral argument:

> [T]he prosecution may not use statements, whether exculpatory or inculpatory, stemming from custodial interrogation of the defendant unless it demonstrates the use of procedural safeguards effective to secure the privileges against self-incrimination. By custodial interrogation, we mean questioning initiated by law enforcement officers after a person has been taken into custody or otherwise deprived of his freedom of action in any significant way. . . .

Here it was explained that this was what the Court had meant in *Escobedo* when it spoke of an investigation's being focused on an accused.

> As for the procedural safeguards to be employed, unless other fully effective means are devised to inform accused persons of their rights of silence and to assure a continuous opportunity to exercise it, the following measures are required. Prior to any questioning, the person must be warned that he has a right to remain silent, that any statement he does make may be used as evidence against him, and that he has a right to the presence of an attorney, either retained or appointed. . . .

Thus, the Court resolved the question that had divided the nation's judges following the Court's decision in Danny Escobedo's case.

> The defendant may waive effectuation of these rights, provided the waiver is made voluntarily, knowingly, and intelligently. If, however, he indicates in any manner and at any stage of the process that he wishes to consult with an attorney before speaking there can be no questioning. Likewise, if the individual is alone and indicates in any manner that he does not wish to be interrogated, the police may not question him. The mere fact that he may have answered some questions or volunteered some statements on his own does not deprive him of the right to refrain from answering any further inquiries until he has consulted with an attorney and thereafter consents to be questioned.

The remainder of Warren's opinion relied heavily for its philosophical underpinning on the amicus brief filed in behalf of the ACLU. Here, even the language was identical in parts.

First, Warren in the Court opinion went to some lengths to establish the need for protecting the accused during police interrogation by citing the psychological stratagems for obtaining confessions urged on police not by chiefs in the backwaters of America but by the most modern manual of instruction, whose authors, Fred Inbau and John Reid, were officers of the Chicago Police Scientific Crime Detection Laboratory, had had broad experience in writing for and lecturing to law enforcement authorities over two decades—and had warned, in the 1962 edition of their manual, that the U.S. Supreme Court might very well decide exactly what it was deciding today. Police rarely—although Warren cited an example or two—kicked and beat a suspect anymore. Rather, they isolated him, played on his weaknesses, undermined his will to resist, and, when all else failed, resorted to trickery. Such an atmosphere, Warren declared, carried "its own badge of intimidation" just as "destructive of human dignity" as physical intimidation, and invoking the relevant provision of the Fifth Amendment to the U.S. Constitution, he swelled into his major theme: "The current practice of incommunicado interrogation is at odds with one of our Nation's most cherished principles—that the individual may not be compelled to incriminate himself."

So that there would be no mistake about it, Warren went on to support his earlier statement that today's decision was not an innovation but only a contemporary application of long-recognized principles, not all American in origin. Indeed, he had found in a thirteenth-century commentary on the Book of Judges a biblical grounding for the Fifth Amendment to the U.S. Constitution—". . . the principle that no man is to be declared guilty on his own admission is a divine decree." He described what was generally acknowledged to be the first known public appeal to an accused's right to silence, John Lilburne's eloquent refusal in 1637 to confess in the Court of Star Chamber to political crimes—"another fundamental right I then contended for, was, that no man's conscience ought to be racked by oaths imposed, to answer to questions concerning himself in matters criminal, or pretended to be so," as Lilburne himself had described the proceedings at his trial—after which Parliament had abolished that inquisitorial body. And he traced the American application of the Fifth Amendment through the U.S. Supreme Court's decision in Danny Escobedo's case. Warren concluded: "Today, then, there can be no doubt that the Fifth Amendment privilege is available outside of criminal court proceedings and serves to protect persons in all settings in which their freedom of action is curtailed in any significant way from being compelled to incriminate themselves." Or, as Mr. Justice Black had declared in the last hour of oral argument:

> The Court held a long time ago that what that means is that the Government shall not compel a defendant to give evidence against himself anywhere or under any circumstances. So why do we have to determine when the prosecution actually begins? The words of the Amendment are very simple, and they've been construed as meaning that that means the Government mustn't compel a man to give evidence against himself anywhere, at any time.

To safeguard the Fifth Amendment right, however, Warren then departed from the ACLU brief which had pressed upon the justices the absolute necessity for the presence of a lawyer at all stages. The Court did not go that far. Suspects must be offered counsel, appointed if necessary, but they could also waive their rights and confess.

Perhaps anticipating the uproar that would follow announcement of *Miranda,* Warren acknowledged that "we cannot say that the Constitution necessarily requires adherence to any particular solution for the inherent compulsions of the interrogation process," and invited—indeed encouraged—Congress and the state legislatures to devise whatever methods they pleased to protect the rights of individuals. Unless and until, however, these institutions implemented "procedures which are at least as effective in apprising accused persons of their right of silence and in assuring a continuous opportunity to exercise it," the rules announced today must be followed.

Between the oral arguments and the decision this June day, Solicitor General Marshall, at the request of the Court, had further described in a letter FBI practices regarding criminal suspects about which he had been questioned during the argument: The FBI had for two decades informed criminal suspects of their right to remain silent and to consult with their lawyers; after passage of the Criminal Justice Act of 1964, which provided free counsel for federal defendants unable to pay, the agents were required to inform suspects also of their right to free court-assigned counsel.

The Uniform Code of Military Justice, the English Judges' Rules, and the Evidence Ordinance of Ceylon, Warren declared in his opinion, made similar provisions. India and Scotland had laws on their books protecting criminal defendants at the interrogation stage of proceedings "without marked detrimental effect on criminal law enforcement." So, the implication was, could local American police.

Although this provision of the decision seemed to get lost in the passionate reactions that followed the Court's announcement of its decision, the spontaneous confession—the confession of "a person who enters a police station and states that he wishes to confess to a crime"—was *not* barred by the decision. The decision restricted only those confessions taken from an individual in custody.

Finally, Warren disposed of the cases at hand. In Ernest Miranda's case, the Court reversed the judgment of the Arizona Supreme Court: "[I]t is clear that Miranda was not in any way apprised of his right to consult with an attorney and to have one present during the interrogation, nor was his right not to be compelled to incriminate himself effectively protected in any other manner. Without these warnings the statements were inadmissible." Similarly the convictions of Michael Vignera and Carl Calvin Westover were reversed; in the case of Roy Allen Stewart, the judgment of the California Supreme Court was affirmed, that court having already reversed his conviction on the basis of *Dorado* v. *California.*

The suspense had ended. The Supreme Court of the United States had installed the Fifth Amendment to the Constitution, with the Sixth Amend-

Chapter 4

ment as watchdog, in the station houses of America. In a practical application, it had put police on notice that not only extreme behavior on their part—the beatings, the long detentions, the psychological manipulations—but also their routine behavior was under judicial surveillance. In the legal application, there was no longer any question of whether or not a suspect must retain or request counsel prior to interrogation by police; it was now the government's—state as well as federal—responsibility to offer it, furnish it if necessary, and assume the burden of proof if it was waived. In the social application, there was no longer any need for people with trouble to stand alone in front of the people with uniforms; the people with trouble now possessed the Constitution.

In its historical application, the Court opinion was a tacit acknowledgment of the broadening of judicial perspective from simple disapproval of police brutality three decades before to conferring constitutional rights and the wherewithal and opportunity to use them on all, rich and poor, guilty as well as innocent. It was thus far the highest achievement of civil libertarianism as translated into constitutional terms by the U.S. Supreme Court. Many people looked on the moment as an ending.

But it was only a beginning.

The chief justice had no sooner finished reading when the attacks on the decision began. There was not to be unanimity, a closing of judicial ranks that had given *Gideon* extra momentum toward public acceptance and that can figure more heavily in controversial cases.

The Supreme Court had divided, not surprisingly, in precisely the way it had become accustomed to dividing in these cases. The mild misgivings of Clark and Harlan in *Gideon* had begun it; the dissents of Clark, Harlan, Stewart, and White in *Escobedo* had hardened it and made it a fact of judicial life. Now, once again, Clark, Harlan, Stewart, and White had dissented. Their dissents were later to legitimize the protests of the many people in and out of law enforcement, politics, and academia who believed the Supreme Court had gone too far in the case of Ernest Miranda, who read the history of human liberty differently. The dissents to the decision in Ernest Miranda's case would also provide a judicial skeleton which would be fleshed out by the Court of the 1970s.

As sometimes happened, there was a good deal of acerbity in the dissents from the Court opinion in Ernest Miranda's case, which demonstrated, in addition to some testiness of the authors, that one man's "application of principles long recognized in other settings" was indeed another man's innovation. White's charge that the opinion was "a departure from a long line of precedent" was one of the milder comments. Harlan called the decision "poor constitutional law," as if he were grading a first-year law student's paper. Clark said the "*ipse dixit* [premise] of the majority has no support in our cases."

Although the chief justice in the majority opinion had taken some pains

171

to point out the Court's solicitude for the problems involved in apprehending criminals and clearly stated that "our decision is not intended to hamper the traditional function of police officers in investigating crime," it was, in fact, *Miranda*'s potential for bringing disaster to the delivery of criminal justice that drew the most attention from the dissenters—the very element that would draw the greatest attention outside the Court, lending itself as it did to simplifying, sloganizing, and provoking passionate response.

Tom Clark, known for his affability on and off the bench, followed Warren's reading of the Court opinion, and observers remarked about the "unaccustomed edge in his voice when his turn to dissent came." During the past hour Warren had occasionally and briefly departed from the text of the majority opinion and in one such departure had praised the police "when their services are honorably performed" but had added that when they abandoned fairness, they could "become as great a menace to society as any criminal we have." Clark had long been a supporter of police, and understandably, Warren's words had offended him. He, too, departed from the text of his dissent, challenging the chief justice's assumptions and expressing his own confidence in the law enforcement community, which he believed not only was being unjustifiably maligned that day but was also being deprived of a traditionally effective tool for apprehending criminals. To exclude evidence which had not been obtained in complete conformity with the complex new rules only courted disaster. Wrote the author of the majority opinion in *Mapp* v. *Ohio*, which had required state courts for the first time to exclude evidence obtained as the result of an illegal search or seizure: "Such a strict constitutional specific [as *Miranda* demanded] inserted at the nerve center of crime detection may well kill the patient."

John Marshall Harlan was sixty-seven years old now and nearly blind, able to read only with the aid of a high-powered lens on one eye and the printed page pressed against his face. Still, he insisted on writing his opinions by hand and reciting them on decision days. His dissent in Danny Escobedo's case had been limited to a one-paragraph outburst charging the Court with unjustifiably fettering "perfectly legitimate methods of criminal law enforcement." In Ernest Miranda's case, joined by Stewart and White, he impugned the Court's rationale in installing the Fifth Amendment in the station house; he would have continued to rely on the due process clause of the Fourteenth Amendment, a logic that fitted his scheme of federalism and a principle through which the Court had developed over three decades since *Brown* v. *Mississippi* had been decided "an elaborate, sophisticated, and sensitive approach to admissibility of confessions," one which gave "ample recognition to society's interest in suspect questioning as an instrument of law enforcement." He chastised his brethren for what he considered their impulsiveness, their hasty imposition of new rules while serious efforts at "long-range and lasting reforms" in criminal procedure were still being considered by a committee of the ABA, the American Law Institute, the President's Commission on Law Enforcement and Administration of Justice, and others. But a good deal of Harlan's dissent, like Clark's, addressed the question of *Miranda*'s effect on law enforcement:

> What the Court largely ignores is that its rules impair, if they will not eventually serve wholly to frustrate, an instrument of law enforcement that has long and quite reasonably been thought worth the price paid for it. There can be little doubt that the Court's new code would markedly decrease the number of confessions. . . .
>
> How much harm this decision will inflict on law enforcement cannot fairly be predicted with accuracy. . . . We do know that some crimes cannot be solved without confessions . . . and that the Court is taking a real risk with society's welfare in imposing its new regime on the country. . . .

Byron White's was the last dissent; he was joined in it by Harlan and Stewart. In Danny Escobedo's case, White had criticized the Court for taking another "major step in the direction of the goal which the Court seemingly has in mind—to bar from evidence any admissions obtained from an individual suspected of crime, whether involuntarily or not"; he rejected this step. "The obvious under-pinning of the Court's decision," he said, "is a deep-seated distrust of all confessions," and its ruling would inevitably weaken the capacity of the criminal law to work for the apprehension and conviction of murderers and rapists. Byron White had "no desire whatsoever to share the responsibility for any such impact on the criminal process."

The contentiousness of the various opinions notwithstanding—it was rare that judicial disagreement had any long-term effects on personal relationships; as Hugo Black once put it, the justices "had become professional in our capacity to disagree without being disagreeable"—the justices left the bench in a holiday mood. They were bound for Montrose Park, in the Georgetown section of Washington, and a picnic which their law clerks had arranged for the end of the term.

All except Tom Clark. He returned to his chambers and reread his dissent. The chief justice's characterization of police had deeply offended him, and he decided to answer Warren in print, even though copies of the opinions already had been mailed to *U.S. Law Week* and released that morning to the press. After some minor editing of his brief introduction, the former attorney general added: "The police agencies—all the way from municipal and state forces to the federal bureaus—are responsible for law enforcement and public safety in this country. I am proud of their efforts, which in my view are not fairly characterized by the Court's opinion." Then he left for the picnic in the park.

The day after the Supreme Court's decision in Ernest Miranda's case was announced, on June 14, Justice Fortas greatly increased the complexity of his public life in the future when he caught a plane for Jacksonville, Florida, for a meeting of the Wolfson Family Foundation, to which he had been officially appointed a consultant, the board of the foundation having approved in December 1965 the arrangement he and his friend Louis Wolfson had worked out the previous fall; the foundation had sent him the first check for $20,000, his annual fee, in January 1966. While in Florida, Fortas also visited Wolfson's horse farm at Ocala, where he stayed overnight, then returned to Washington on June 15. The trip coincided with the referral to the Justice Department by the Securities and Exchange Commission of an investigation involving one of Wolfson's companies. Fortas did not, however, he said, participate at that time "in any of Mr. Wolfson's business or legal affairs." A week later Fortas resigned as consultant to the foundation, although he did not return the $20,000 until the following December. This brief interlude in the Court's business, during which the justice attended to personal matters, would return before the decade was out to haunt him, the Court, and the country.

On Monday, June 20, 1966, one week following the Supreme Court's decision in *Miranda* v. *Arizona*, Earl Warren was in California for the funeral of his sister, and Mr. Justice Brennan read the chief justice's opinion in the case of *Johnson* v. *New Jersey*, which had been argued that first week in March with the other confessions cases, addressing the problem of retroactivity, but which had been separated from the others.

The Court's record regarding retroactivity was mixed, dependent upon "the exigencies of the situation." It had declined to make retroactive *Mapp* v. *Ohio* in which evidence obtained through unreasonable search and seizure was excluded from state criminal proceedings—in part because the rule affected evidence "the reliability and relevancy of which is not questioned." On the other hand, the Court did make *Gideon* v. *Wainwright* retroactive: Lacking trial counsel, a defendant's condition was roughly analogous to Gulliver's in the land of the Brobdingnagians, and the potential for a miscarriage of justice was great. *Escobedo* and *Miranda* fell between the two, but closer to *Mapp*: A confession obtained in violation of *Escobedo* and *Miranda* was not so dependable as a bag of heroin obtained through an unreasonable search and seizure, but the potential for conviction of the innocent through violation of *Escobedo* and *Miranda* was considerably less than that which *Gideon* had been intended to avert because over the past three decades the Court had built a strong body of case law that prohibited the use of truly coerced confessions, and that body of law remained available to prisoners, regardless of *Escobedo* and *Miranda*.

Thus, the Court declared, neither *Escobedo* v. *Illinois* nor *Miranda* v. *Arizona* was to be applied retroactively.

There had been some discussion among the justices regarding exactly what the cutoff point ought to be. The chief justice's first draft distributed to the justices a month earlier upheld the New Jersey Supreme Court's decision in *Johnson: Escobedo* did not affect convictions that had become final prior to the date of that decision; likewise, *Miranda*. Now the finished opinion specified that *Escobedo* affected "only those cases in which the *trial began* after June 22, 1964, the date of that decision" (italics added), and *Miranda* applied "only to cases in which the trial began after the date of our decision one week ago." Which reduced the number of eligible cases considerably.

The petitioners in *Johnson*, Sylvester Johnson and Stanley Cassidy, were out of luck, as were a lot of others in the same predicament. Out of luck, too, were the other 100-plus criminal defendants whose petitions, marked "Esco-bedo," had been held pending decision in Ernest Miranda's case. The same day all these, too, were denied writs of certiorari. At that point the only bene-ficiaries of Miranda were Ernest Miranda himself, Michael Vignera, Carl Calvin Westover, and Roy Allen Stewart.

Only Justices Black and Douglas dissented, complaining that "the Court's opinion cuts off many defendants who are now in jail from any hope of relief from unconstitutional convictions."

The decision in *Johnson* did indeed make it abundantly clear that the prisons of America were not going to empty out as a result of *Miranda*, as members of the law enforcement community had feared. Said Chief Justice Warren, who the week before had so severely reprimanded that community: "[R]etroactive application of *Escobedo* and *Miranda* would seriously disrupt the administration of our criminal laws. It would require the retrial or release of numerous prisoners found guilty by trustworthy evidence in conformity with previously announced constitutional standards."

If *Johnson* had been calculated to take some of the sting out of *Miranda*, however, the intent was lost in the hullabaloo that developed following an-nouncement of the decision in Ernest Miranda's case.

It was one thing to get *Miranda* on the books, quite another to have it accepted. No suspect marched to the interrogation room clothed in his new constitutional rights immediately, and in fact, early reactions to the ruling in-dicated it might be some time, if ever, before *Miranda* meant much at all to either the law enforcement officer or the suspect as they confronted each other in the drab and dusty station house.

At the highest level the response was exploratory. FBI Director J. Edgar Hoover, whose agents had been responsible for the case of Carl Calvin West-over's being brought to the Supreme Court and who, understandably con-cerned, had been in frequent contact with the assistant attorney general in charge of the Department of Justice Criminal Division regarding develop-ments in the law of interrogations and confessions, had immediately shot off a memorandum to that official requesting his views on what steps had to be taken to bring federal officers in line with the *Miranda* decision. The attorney general himself, Nicholas Katzenbach, requested that discussion of the decision be added to the agenda of the luncheon meeting of the president's cabinet scheduled for June 16 at the State Department. Reaction elsewhere, however, was less exploratory, more explosive, emotional, and often alarmist. Almost nowhere could there be found the enthusiasm with which *Gideon* had been received. What enthusiasm there was, most of it among defense lawyers like John Flynn and some judges, was obscured by the violence of the attacks.

The dissenters to *Miranda* became judicial heroes, but it was not John Harlan's intellectual discussion of due process of law, the Fourteenth Amendment, and how these fitted into the scheme of federalism that the attackers seized on. It was the dissenters' deeply critical tone—interpreted as a kind of judicial green light—and their fears for the future of law enforcement in America that drew all the attention and provided the platform for assault.

The segment of the law enforcement community most vulnerable to the *Miranda* ruling was, of course, the police, the vehemence of whose response was in proportion to that vulnerability. In every part of the country and in all ranks, police complained bitterly at what they considered this heaviest of reprimands from the Supreme Court so far. In Boston the police commissioner, Edmund L. McNamara, mourned that "criminal trials no longer will be a search for truth, but a search for technical error." In Philadelphia Police Commissioner Edward J. Bell declared that "the present rules and interpretations whether or not so intended—in fact protect the guilty. I do not believe the Constitution was designed as a shield for criminals." In Cleveland, Ohio, Chief of Police Richard Wagner, alluding with some skepticism to the provision in *Miranda* that spontaneous statements and confessions were by no means barred, grumbled that "there is no such thing as a voluntary statement. While the Supreme Court Justices say there is, they have made it impossible to obtain one." An unidentified patrolman in Wisconsin suggested the justices "thought innocent persons were being unduly harassed, forgetting the general public has the right to protest if they felt they were being harassed. Also they are protecting the criminal's rights. There is nothing in the rule about the rights of the innocent public." And William H. Parker, Los Angeles police chief, predicted *Miranda* would effectively end the use of confessions in convicting criminals.

The rhetoric, which was echoed by a number of prosecutors, tended to obscure some of the real problems in *Miranda*, which not even the four dissenters to the decision had foreseen, at least not in their written opinions. One of the first casualties of *Miranda* was police morale. The earliest serious disapproval of police behavior—in the *Brown* and *Chambers* cases as well as others that came to the Court during the 1940s and 1950s—had elicited little response from police, largely because the misconduct cited had been considered atypical. The shift in the Supreme Court's direction from surveillance of the aberrations on the part of law enforcement to surveillance of routine practices and procedures did not sit well with the law enforcement community. Morale had been sliding since the Court in 1961 had banned the use of illegally obtained evidence from state courts via *Mapp* v. *Ohio*, and it had been sliding at an accelerated rate since *Escobedo*.

Partly it had to do with the police officers' image of the justices as well intentioned but misguided, unfamiliar with the facts of everyday living in law enforcement, and overly disposed to fashion rules for dealing with middle-class people, not criminals. Partly it had to do, too, with the officers' professional pride, one manifestation of which was their assumption that training and skill had equipped them to determine guilt and innocence. Police rarely spoke of suspects but described them as "the guilty" or as "criminals." But mostly it had to do with the belief that Miranda was another sign of fundamental distrust undeserved by men whose work demanded a high degree of physical stamina, courage, alertness, common sense, intelligence, and good judgment and in return exacted a high emotional toll, men who every day stood between society and the criminal, putting their lives on the line. As one observer put it, police looked at *Miranda* and felt a "slap at policemen everywhere . . . a personal rebuke."

Another casualty of *Miranda* was a certain procedural orderliness in the station house which almost immediately on publication of the decision gave way to confusion. What, police asked themselves, *could* they do under *Miranda*?

The Phoenix, Arizona, police, whose officers Cooley and Young had been responsible for the crucial interrogation of Ernest Miranda, refused to panic. But the questions Deputy Police Chief Lawrence Wetzel posed on local station KOOL's special program "Has the Supreme Court Handcuffed the Law?" shortly after *Miranda* was announced were the same questions being asked by perplexed police in precincts across America:

> What is meant by depriving freedom in any significant way?
> Does the ruling pertain to the routine interrogation?
> An officer sees a man in an alley under suspicious circumstances—is he required at that time to look to this particular procedure?
> What is meant by intelligently waiving rights?

A survey of police—patrolmen, detectives, and superior officers—in four Wisconsin cities (Madison, Racine, Kenosha, Green Bay) indicated that hardly anyone thoroughly understood even the *Miranda* ruling's basic requirements.

One of the ways police brought some order back to their procedures was to carry what became known as *Miranda* cards: wallet-sized cards on which what became known as the *Miranda* warnings were printed. These were similar from jurisdiction to jurisdiction. The card carried by the Phoenix police stated:

> You have the right to remain silent.
> Anything you say can be used against you in a court of law.

You have the right to the presence of an attorney to assist you prior to questioning and to be with you during questioning if you so desire.

If you cannot afford an attorney you have the right to have an attorney appointed for you prior to questioning.

Do you understand these rights?

Will you voluntarily answer my questions?

These statements, read out by police to suspects, did, of course, inform suspects of their Fifth and Sixth Amendment rights in conformance with the Supreme Court ruling. They did not, however, provide answers to the substantive questions that were plaguing Deputy Chief Wetzel: questions of custody—or when exactly the *Miranda* ruling came into play and when rights must be read—of emergency procedures, of what constituted an intelligent waiver. These questions and others would continue to be asked until they filtered up into the courtrooms of America during the next decade for judges to decide. In the meantime, police in different jurisdictions frequently made different judgments on when custody began precisely or what constituted a valid waiver.

Stories circulated describing extreme adaptations to the *Miranda* ruling: the policeman who looked the other way when a crime was being committed, unsure of his authority now and fearful that if he made a mistake, he, rather than the suspect, would end up on trial. And there were stories that reduced the thrust of the ruling to absurdity: the officer who chased a suspect, ordered him to stop, shot him when he refused, then gave *Miranda* warnings while sponging the bullet wound with a handkerchief.

In an attempt to discover some truths about the chaos in law enforcement said to have been created by *Miranda* and to evaluate the widespread claim that the decision actually got in the way of apprehending criminals, Yale law students made a formal study of a New Haven, Connecticut, police headquarters, its personnel and its procedures, during an eleven-week period in the summer of 1966. They reported that *Miranda*, in fact, had had little immediate impact on police practices, that law enforcement was carrying on business very much as usual. *Miranda* was almost ignored. The study noted that during the two weeks of June following the decision, fewer than half the suspects brought in received warnings that included more than half the elements *Miranda* required, and no suspect had received a full *Miranda* warning.

What compliance there was was only to the letter of the law. Most of the New Haven detectives regarded the requirement to give warnings a useless hindrance to the "natural flow of interrogation," and they were not above hedging a little. Some modified the warning: "Whatever you say may be used *for* or against you in a court of law"; "You don't have to say a word, but you ought to get everything cleared up"; "You don't have to say anything, of course, *but* can you explain how...?"

Chapter 4

According to the Yale study, others made the warnings meaningless by implication that the suspect had better *not* exercise these rights if he knew what was good for him or by giving the warning in a monotonous tone that implied it was a meaningless procedure. Police took care of the rare suspect who asked for a lawyer by not helping locate one. A common device was to hand a suspect a telephone book. Period.

Although *Miranda* required police to stop the interrogation at a suspect's request, few New Haven detectives bothered to inform the suspect of that. As a result, few suspects exercised the right, and those who did could usually be coaxed into talking.

Nor had the various tactics of persuasion urged in the Inbau and Reid textbook which the Court had found so distasteful been removed from interrogations. The New Haven police were found to utilize these as well as a few of their own devising. Threats, promises, displays of sympathy—all these were a standard part of New Haven station house routines. Some outdid even Inbau and Reid.

Detective one to a man suspected of breaking into a liquor store: "That guy should never have left all that liquor in the window to tempt honest guys like you and me."

Detective two to rape suspect: "Say, she's pretty nice. I probably would have done the same thing myself. . . . She probably just let you have your way, and now she's making this charge because she's mad at you. So just tell me how it really happened and I'll see what I can do."

A similar study in Washington, D.C., undertaken by the Institute of Criminal Law and Procedure of the Georgetown University Law School and lasting for a year, indicated that more than two-thirds of the suspects had not been given complete *Miranda* warnings, that half had not been advised of the right to silence, and more than a third were not told of their right to counsel in the station house.

The Neighborhood Legal Services Project, with cooperation from the local bar association and law students, was at the time attempting to provide volunteer attorneys to the station houses of the District around the clock. When a suspect requested counsel, police called a central switchboard manned by project staff twenty-four hours a day. The operator on duty then informed the volunteer attorney on duty of the request, and the attorney sped off to the precinct from which the request had come. However, this post-*Miranda* study indicated that less than a tenth of the total number of suspects even requested counsel. Lawyers complained that police did not stop the questioning of those who did, and as a result, the attorneys often arrived too late to be of assistance.

As for defendants, few of them seemed to understand what it was all about. Some suspects were grateful for the warnings, which they said were "helpful." Others described what may have been early self-consciousness on the part of police: "[T]hey talked like they meant it," and "they wanted it to be known they had about eight people watching as witnesses." Still others believed the police "had some lawyer of their own who was working with them," or "I would have to pay for a lawyer," or "I just have to write for one and wait for him to answer."

The warning of the suspect's right to silence was equally confounding. Several believed it meant they had a right to talk; some believed they had been told they would not be allowed to talk. One suspect said it meant he "should have the right to say something so they can use it in evidence in court," and another said it meant that "if I . . . like try to bribe them, they would use it against me in court."

When the initial shock of the *Miranda* decision wore off, some police departments began compiling their own statistics in an attempt to quantify their losses. To their surprise, the results were not all negative, but no final conclusions could be drawn about the effect of *Miranda* on the apprehension of criminals.

Philadelphia police, compiling statistics between June 19, 1966, and February 25, 1967, found that out of 5,220 arrests in which *Miranda* warnings had been given, 3,695, or 59 percent, of the suspects had refused to make statements. While it was not possible to obtain precise figures on how many cases were lost as a result, "it is definite," said District Attorney Arlen Specter,* an acerbic critic of the recent Supreme Court decisions in criminal cases, "that a substantial number of these prosecutions will result in improper acquittals." New York District Attorney Frank Hogan's findings were more dramatic: During the six-month period prior to the U.S. Supreme Court's decision in *Miranda*, roughly 49 percent of the nonhomicide felony defendants made incriminating statements; from July 1966 through December 1966, the six months immediately following *Miranda*, the rate dropped to 15 percent.

Statistical studies in some other police departments produced quite different results. Los Angeles County at the time had the nation's largest caseload, but because of the California Supreme Court's previous decision in *Dorado*, law enforcement officers had less adjustment to make in procedures. A study there of more than 1,000 felony cases during June and July 1966 revealed that following the Supreme Court's *Miranda* decision, the confessions rate in felony cases had *risen* 10 percent. In Kansas City, Chief of Police Clarence M. Kelley said only 12 percent fewer suspects were giving statements since *Miranda* and that this rate "will probably decline as the case becomes more remote" in the minds of suspects. A study of data in Pittsburgh indicated that following *Miranda*, the number of confessions to police fell off by almost 20 percent, but convictions did not.

In the short run, the effect of the Supreme Court ruling in Ernest

---

* Specter was elected U.S. senator from Pennsylvania in 1980.

Chapter 4

Miranda's case failed to fulfill either the majority's hopes or the dissenters' fears. It was the dissenters' fears, however, that dominated the public interest during the next decade.

Fred Inbau and John Reid did not substantially alter the 1967 edition of their textbook *Criminal Investigations and Confessions*, whose instructions for the obtaining of confessions in some subtly coercive ways had been cited by Chief Justice Warren in *Miranda*. Although this second edition was made necessary by that decision, the authors explained in the Preface, the trade tricks which a majority of the Court had found offensive—the reliance on isolation of the suspect, on psychological stratagems that exploited the weaknesses of the suspect—remained, so far as Inbau and Reid were concerned, justifiable and constitutional techniques. Said the authors in defense of their work:

> [A]ll but a very few of the interrogation tactics and techniques presented in our earlier publication are still valid if used after the recently prescribed warnings have been given to the suspect under interrogation, and after he has waived his self-incrimination privilege and his right to counsel. The Court's critical comments about the procedures we advocated were, we believe, for the purpose of establishing the necessity for the warnings rather than as a condemnation of the procedures themselves. . . . If we are in error with regard to our interpretation of the *Miranda* case, then the Supreme Court has but one more move to make, and that is to outlaw all interrogations of criminal suspects. We say this because of our confidence that effective interrogations can only be conducted by such procedures as the ones we herein describe. In our opinion, the *Miranda* rules that were established by a one-man majority of the Court were unnecessary for the protection of the innocent and they are not soundly derived as constitutional requirements. . . .

Shortly after the *Miranda* decision was announced, Inbau, who was also a professor of law at Northwestern University, organized Americans for Effective Law Enforcement, to combat what he called a trend toward placing individual liberties in criminal cases above the rights of law-abiding citizens to protection from crime and violence. It was to serve as an opposite number, an antidote, to the American Civil Liberties Union, whose amicus brief had supplied the philosophical framework for *Miranda* and whose lawyers had been advancing—successfully, on the whole—the rights of the individual for nearly half a century. Inbau was the first president; James Thompson, who had presented Illinois' case against Danny Escobedo to the U.S. Supreme Court and was now concerned that the "rationale of [*Miranda*] will, perhaps in five or ten years, perhaps a lesser time, be carried further," was vice-president. They intended to put the law enforcement community's point of view, for which the dissenters to *Miranda* had provided encouragement as well as a

181

judicial framework, before the U.S. Supreme Court exactly the way the ACLU had been lobbying for the individual all those years.

Removed from the daily dramas of the police station, their relationships with both the uniformed and the troubled desensitized by the formalities of courtroom procedure, their concern with legalisms and abstractions predominant, judges took a broader, if not necessarily more objective, view of the Supreme Court's ruling in the confessions cases. Here the Court was not entirely without friends, although here, too, there was a good deal of dissension, enough certainly to increase the potential for the politicization of *Miranda* as well as sustain a movement for the ruling's reversal.

A good deal of judicial steam was blown off in the summer of 1966 as the nation's judges gathered at their traditional professional meetings. *Miranda* largely dominated the official programs.

There were those judges who saw the decision through the eyes of the Supreme Court majority. Walter L. Pope of the U.S. Court of Appeals for the Ninth Circuit told the annual judicial conference of that circuit in July 1966: "It seems plain that in *Escobedo* and in *Miranda* the Court majority was again intervening in the governing process to deal with and correct practices which it found, as commonly employed by police, operated to infringe upon the constitutional privilege against self-incrimination through in-custody interrogation." He believed, he said, "we shall be able to live with this decision," then added in a lighter vein, the first sure victims of the decision were not police and not society but "the authors of the quoted police manuals. Poor Mr. Inbau and poor Mr. Reid—they will never be able to sell their books again."

Judge George C. Edwards, Jr., of the U.S. Court of Appeals for the Sixth Circuit had worked summers as a boy in his father's law office and on occasion had accompanied the older man on his rounds of the court and jail. He recalled one visit as he contemplated the meaning of *Miranda* forty years later. While he waited for his father to interview a client through the steel bars, "blows and screams and groans [were] coming from a small room partitioned off in a corner of the lockup where we were. A few moments earlier I had seen several men lead a red-headed prisoner, whose arms were handcuffed behind his back, into that room." He continued:

> Several times in the next few minutes someone went into or out of the small room. And when the door was open, the scene in the room was unforgettable. The red-headed prisoner was spread-eagled over the end of a heavy table. His ankles were shackled to the table legs so that his legs were spread apart. One man stood behind him with a length of rubber hose in his hand. A man on each side of the table had each of his arms twisted so that the prisoner was

bent forward over the table. The prisoner was stripped to the waist and red welts criss-crossed the white skin of his back. . . .

The most macabre memory of all was seeing jail personnel and other prisoners going about their routine jobs without ever looking in the direction of his human anguish.

When Edwards and his father took their story to the grand jury, Edwards was asked whether or not he knew the names of the men in the little room, and when he did not, he was patted on the head and given an apple.

If that story was too old to have relevance in the contemplation of *Miranda*, Edwards had a more recent one, of which he had personal knowledge from his days as police commissioner in the "relatively enlightened city of Detroit, in the relatively civilized state of Michigan in the spring of 1962." In that episode, five Detroit policemen had surrounded a suspect who had been hiding in a coal cellar, then alternately questioned him and punched him in the stomach, and finally threatened him with a baseball bat aimed at his head.

Judge Edwards: "The most significant feature of the *Miranda* decision is that it marks the end of incommunicado interrogation of accused persons." Although he doubted it meant the end of all physical and psychological abuse, its holding that "incommunicado interrogation is inherently coercive" made "the Bill of Rights more meaningful to the individual citizen."

The responses of judges like Pope and Edwards, however, were often obscured by the heavier judicial artillery that was mounted against the ruling.

The Conference of Chief Justices, many of whom had been reversed by the U.S. Supreme Court, had been consistently critical of the Warren Court, and anti-Supreme Court proposals were introduced annually at the August meetings, although these (with the exception of one resolution in 1958 protesting the public school desegregation decisions through the euphemism of protesting federal usurpation of state judicial power) were generally not approved by the entire conference. At the August 1966 meeting, Chief Judge John C. Bell of the Pennsylvania Supreme Court, a frequent critic of U.S. Supreme Court decisions which "shackle the police and virtually tie the hands of district attorneys and trial judges and appellate court judges," proposed that the Conference adopt a resolution that paraphrased Barry Goldwater's 1964 campaign rhetoric; it urged the nation's highest court to "recognize that the scales of justice have been overly weighted in favor of criminals and of persons suspected or accused of crime, and for these reasons reconsider and substantially change or modify the principles, tests, and conditions laid down in *Miranda* v. *Arizona*, and permit the introduction into evidence of confessions which were not coerced but were voluntarily, knowingly and intelligently made. . . ." Bell's resolution was not adopted by the conference. That it articulated some deep-felt judicial resentments, however, became increasingly apparent.

Edward S. Piggins of the Third Judicial Circuit of Michigan found he was sympathetic "with an American public that voices a vigorous protest when it watches confessed rapists and murderers go free to repeat their crimes because their confessions have been barred from evidence for what appears to the lay public, at least, to be an unrelated technicality. . . ."

Chief Judge Lumbard of the U.S. Court of Appeals for the Second Circuit had watched several years of efforts by American Law Institute committee members to devise a model code of pre-arraignment procedures go down the drain in *Miranda*. "These decisions [*Escobedo* as well as *Miranda*]," he told the Conference of Chief Justices at its annual meeting, rephrasing part of Justice Harlan's *Miranda* dissent, "came at a time when much study was being given to working out these procedures through systems or codes to handle them in other ways. One cannot help but wonder whether the accident of the margin of one vote on the Supreme Court is the sensible, statesmanlike and the wise way to bring about drastic and far-reaching changes. . . ."

Whether or not by design—whether the justices of the U.S. Supreme Court were responding to the harshness of the criticism, whether they were responding to the vocal minority within the Court, the dissenters, or whether they were responding to their own fears that the violence that characterized the second half of the 1960s, not only the crime in the streets but the racial violence that had begun in the Watts section of Los Angeles and spread across America, bathing in its own blood, followed by the campus violence that began at Columbia University in 1968 and left a trail of ruin and resentment, might be the beginning of breakdown in America's social order—the Court did, in fact, slow its forward movement in matters of civil libertarianism. *Miranda* v. *Arizona* was long remembered as the high point reached by the United States Supreme Court under Chief Justice Earl Warren.

Over the next two years the justices maintained a low profile. As the debate was joined by the Congress and, ultimately, by the candidates for president, picking up momentum as well as political significance, the justices of the Supreme Court, although they did not back off, no longer plunged forward. Those who supposed *Miranda* was a milestone on the way to requiring the presence of counsel at all interrogations, as the ACLU had urged, were wrong; the Court did not go that extra mile. It did not, as some observers expected, flesh out the basic scheme and require tape recordings or video tapes of interrogations.

When the Supreme Court applied *Miranda* only to those trials begun after June 13, 1966, it automatically diminished the number of cases that would come before it. In those few cases the justices heard over the next two years, they only smoothed out some rough edges on the decision itself. They further defined retroactivity to exclude also *retrials* begun after the operative date. They decided—against the dissents of Warren, Black, Douglas, and Fortas—that the results of otherwise legally authorized blood tests of a suspect, properly administered in a hospital and later used as evidence of the amount of the alcoholic content of a suspect's blood, did not violate the suspect's Fifth and Sixth Amendment rights. Nor, the justices suggested, would the employment of such traditional law enforcement tools of identification as "fingerprinting, photographing, or measurements, to write or speak for identification, to appear in court, to stand, to assume a stance, to walk, or to make a particular gesture" violate constitutional rights, and it was probably no accident that Justice Brennan, having deserted the rest of the *Miranda* majority in this case, was assigned to write the opinion. The Court did extend the *Miranda* ruling to include the early stages of tax fraud investigations conducted by the Internal Revenue Service, and in fact, the IRS later officially revised its procedures for advising taxpayers of their rights to conform to *Miranda* standards.

But the justices stopped there, much the way they had stopped following their decision in *Escobedo*, the way they had often paused following an important and controversial decision. They let the impact be absorbed, listened for the concerns of the administrators of criminal justice, from the beat policeman to the appellate judge, observed how the lower courts dealt with the troublesome questions of what constituted "custody," what standards were required for a suspect's "waiver" of his rights, or how police reacted in emergency situations, all those questions that had plagued Deputy Chief Wetzel of Phoenix. And after the period of waiting and watching was over, they could decide, as they had following *Escobedo*, whether to go on, whether to flesh *Miranda* out. Yale Kamisar of Michigan Law School always thought, he said, that "*Miranda* was the first chapter in a book that was never written."

"Whenever I am told that a landmark decision in a criminal case has settled matters once and for all," federal Judge Irving Kaufman once wrote, "I am reminded of the gentleman of the 1850s who suggested that the Government close the Patent Office because 'there was nothing left to be invented.' " The judicial reality immediately following the *Miranda* decision, far from signifying the resolution of the complicated issues involved in the taking of statements and confessions, only created vexing legal problems. The guidelines that had seemed so specific when Chief Justice Warren had read them from his seat in the center of the bench that June morning—that they were unnecessarily specific was a common complaint among law enforcement officials—had holes large enough for the chief justice and the entire Court to move, nine abreast. The heaviest burden following the Supreme Court's ruling in *Miranda* fell on the lower courts, state and federal.

Defense attorneys had been jubilant when *Miranda* was announced. John Flynn's reaction to his own winning of the case had perhaps been typical of that segment of the legal profession. "Instead of battling as we have for many years to assert . . . that every person has certain constitutional rights," he had said on station KOOL, "the Supreme Court has clearly said that we have those rights." Now he would reap a constitutional harvest.

Lawyers moved to have charges dismissed in cases that had turned on confessions obtained in violation of *Miranda. Time* magazine reported that the ruling had brought about the release of seven Miami, Florida, men charged with rape, a confessed Los Angeles murderer, and a Cincinnati, Ohio, robbery suspect—who promptly went out and found another victim.

There followed, of course, a gush of litigation as the nation's judges, state and federal, attempted to translate the principles of law into workaday rules.

As they had following *Escobedo,* some lower-court judges interpreted *Miranda* broadly and demanded strict adherence by police. Others interpreted it narrowly, allowing police more leeway.

One of the most troublesome of the many troublesome *Miranda* problems that confronted courts was that of custody. *Miranda,* the Supreme Court had said, applied only to "custodial interrogation"—that is, "questioning initiated by law enforcement officers after a person has been taken into custody or otherwise deprived of his freedom of action in any significant way." Lower courts, however, did not always agree: One judge's freedom of movement was another's coercive conditions. The Oregon Supreme Court ruled that a burglary suspect who had come to police headquarters at the request of a state trooper and had been questioned behind closed doors had been questioned in a "coercive environment" and, under *Miranda,* should have been informed of his constitutional rights to remain silent and to consult with a lawyer. The New York Court of Appeals ruled that police had *not* taken a defendant in a murder case into custody although he had been questioned for several hours, part of the time without his shoes, trousers, and undershorts, before being given the warnings required by *Miranda.* This latter ruling was said to allow New York police officers to circumvent *Miranda* by postponing official "custody" until they had obtained the statements they wanted.

Another of the troublesome problems presented by *Miranda* was that of waiver. Not all confessions or statements, the Supreme Court had said, need be excluded as trial evidence; a defendant could if he chose waive his rights to remain silent and to the assistance of counsel, then go ahead and make a statement; such a statement could be used in court. The choice, however, must be made absolutely freely, and the Court placed the burden of proof that it had been squarely on the government. Again, judges could not agree, and what constituted a voluntary, knowing, and intelligent waiver varied from court to court.

Did a woman accused of stealing an unemployment compensation check and fully advised of her rights implicitly waive them when she told a U.S. commissioner her parents would obtain for her an attorney, then decided to confess without one? The U.S. Court of Appeals for the Fifth Circuit said yes and affirmed her conviction. Did a man accused of auto theft implicitly waive his rights when, after being carefully advised of them, he refused to sign a waiver until he had talked with an attorney, then told FBI agents they could, however, continue questioning him until he called one but answered all their questions in the negative? No, said the U.S. Court of Appeals for the Seventh Circuit, he had not waived his rights. He had indicated a desire to remain silent when he refused to sign anything without the advice of a lawyer; at that point, under *Miranda*, all interrogation was supposed to have stopped. Since it did not, and the government had made no effort to prove the defendant had waived his rights, there was no way for the court to know whether his change of position was "the product of intelligence and understanding or of ignorance and confusion."

There were other issues: retroactivity; application to categories of suspects not specified in *Miranda* (military offenders, misdemeanants, juveniles, for example); what to do when incomplete *Miranda* warnings were given. Lawyers found holes for judges to plug for more than a decade.

Where some judges found violations of *Miranda* to be of constitutional dimension, others found them to be harmless errors or "overly technical" applications of the ruling. Some judges seemed to have a natural inclination to exclude suspect evidence; others, to include it.

Some cases turned on narrow, legalistic questions; others, on broader principles. None was simple.

Viven Harris's case was one of the more difficult ones.

The trial of Viven Harris of New Rochelle, New York, on two counts of selling narcotics to an undercover police officer opened in the Westchester County Courthouse, White Plains, on November 30, 1966. Coming just six months after the Supreme Court's *Miranda* ruling, it was one of the many trials in that and the years following in which judges and advocates were still uncertain of all the meanings *Miranda* held. More than others at the time, though, Viven Harris's case had long-range implications for *Miranda*.

Viven Harris was a twenty-three-year-old unemployed gardener who had been nursing a heroin addiction off and on for about five years. At the time of his arrest on January 7, 1966, the governor of New York, Nelson A. Rockefeller, had just declared in his annual message to the state legislature an "all-out attack on a prime cause of crime—narcotics addiction," creating a panic and a scarcity of drugs, and Harris had been keeping his joints from screaming by sipping Robitussin A-C or codeine and terpin hydrate. Two undercover agents, George Bermudez and Richard Parks of the New York City Narcotics Bureau, on loan to the New Rochelle police commissioner, had moved into a cheap rooming house under the names Joe Vegas and Eddie Que, respectively, and infiltrated the small group of pushers and users in the area. They had become friendly with the clientele of the Three-Fours Bar and Grill, including Viven Harris, and when they had become friendly enough, Bermudez, who posed as a snorter although no one remembered ever seeing him snort, had persuaded Harris to procure some small amounts of heroin, for which $12 and a "taste" were the highest price he paid.* It didn't seem much of a case. Neither had Ernest Miranda's at that stage.

New Rochelle police officers took Harris to the Westchester County Courthouse, where he was questioned by Assistant District Attorney Thomas A. Facelle. No record of the original interrogation exists; but Facelle questioned Harris a second time in the presence of other law enforcement officers, and a stenographer took it all down. The transcript indicates Harris confessed. But it also indicates Harris, who was a high school dropout, had some uncertainty regarding what he could or should do to protect himself during the questioning, and although he was not denied legal counsel and nobody laid a hand on him, the prosecutor's persistence in the face of the suspect's obvious confusion and occasional reluctance to talk took the procedure to the very edge of propriety, if not legality.

Afterward Harris commented: "It's like you're white and about eight black men are standing around you and none of them are smiling."

Difficulties over the use at his trial of Harris's statement became apparent immediately. Harris's arrest had taken place six months prior to the Supreme Court's decision in Miranda's case, and Facelle had not told Harris his rights. However, Harris's trial was being held after the Supreme Court's decision in Miranda's case, and the Court had ruled that in all such trials, confessions, statements, or admissions, taken without benefit of *Miranda* warnings, could not be used as evidence against the defendant. It was a serious problem, but Facelle, who was also the prosecutor in this case, devised a way around it. He would use the statement, all right, but in a different way.

Although Harris had admitted the "skag" sales immediately following his arrest, no amount of questioning during his trial elicited answers even remotely similar to those in his confession; in fact, he testified that he had sold the policeman bags of a white powdery substance but that it was not heroin at all because heroin was scarce at the time. It was, rather, baking soda, which under certain conditions gave a sniffer the same sting and which Harris and a coconspirator, after experimenting with such substances as baby's milk formulas, packed in some leftover glassine bags. The substance, turned over to police laboratories, had been analyzed, and the presence of heroin had been detected; but the quantity was never disclosed, and there was always a lingering doubt that maybe Harris had substituted baking soda, as he claimed, and that whatever drug had been found had been, like the glassine bags themselves, leftovers.

* The same night Bermudez and Parks arrested as pushers a total of eleven men, leading the New Rochelle police commissioner to comment: "We've broken the back of the narcotics trade here."

Undeterred, the prosecutor, following the example in a recent New York case, in effect lined up Harris's statement of a year before with his trial testimony. His aim was not to use the previous statement as direct evidence but to make Harris out a liar to the jury or, as it is said in the courts, to impeach the defendant's credibility.

The prosecutor bore down on the defendant. Did the defendant recall being asked these questions and giving these answers:

Question: All right, and he drove you someplace?
Answer: He drove me someplace.
Question: Did you tell him where to go?
Answer: No, he knows where to go. . . .

Viven Harris recalled none of them. The prosecutor continued: Did the defendant perhaps recall other questions asked that night?

Question: He wanted a bag of what?
Answer: Skag.
Question: All right, how much?
Answer: A nickel bag.

Harris vaguely recalled those. Well, then, were they true? Harris wasn't sure. The prosecutor was incredulous.

Harris explained: "Because I—, my joints was down and I needed drugs."

And so, over and over again, the prosecutor persevered, reading Harris's statement of a year before, while Harris recalled only small, unimportant fragments, until the entire statement had been read, entered in the record, heard by the jury. Very little of it coincided with Harris's testimony at his trial.

The jury acquitted Harris on one count of selling narcotics but convicted him on the other. One count was, of course, sufficient and Viven Harris was sent to the state prison at Sing Sing. It was not, however, the end of the case.

At his trial Harris had been represented by a young Legal Aid Society lawyer who had dutifully entered the appropriate objections to the prosecutor's tactics and had been overruled by the judge who was bound by a previous New York State case but who was less than optimistic that he himself would not be overruled. On appeal, the appellate division of the New York State Supreme Court appointed a prominent Westchester County litigator, Joel M. Aurnou, who would in fact take Harris's case to the United States Supreme Court. (Aurnou later defended another Harris—Jean—the woman convicted of murdering Scarsdale diet doctor Herman Tarnower.)

As Aurnou recognized immediately, the basic questions presented by the case of Viven Harris—whether or not a statement illegally obtained from a defendant, otherwise inadmissible in court, could be used to impeach that defendant's credibility—had been given conflicting answers among federal and state courts, and it had been twenty-five years since the U.S. Supreme Court had dealt with it. Like the questions raised regarding the taking of confessions prior to the decision in Ernest Miranda's case, this question was ripe for consideration by the Supreme Court. A decision to allow the admission of tainted evidence held the potential for taking a lot of the spine out of *Miranda*.

CHAPTER 5

Still confined in the Arizona State Prison at Florence, Ernest Miranda had become something of a celebrity among the inmates following the Supreme Court's decision in his case, and in the end, that was about all the decision did do for him. His name had become a symbol, his case a code word among law enforcement people. But outside the state prison the man was all but forgotten.

Initially he had thought the Supreme Court's decision in his case would bring about his release, and his father had bought a bottle of Scotch with which he had planned to celebrate the young man's homecoming. The Supreme Court decision did not, however, free him; it only offered him a new trial, one in which his confession to Officers Cooley and Young could not be used against him as evidence.*

---

* The prison gates did not automatically swing open for any of the other three defendants in the confession cases who had won in the Supreme Court either. In New York City *Michael Vignera* pleaded guilty to a lesser robbery charge and was sentenced to seven and a half to ten years in Sing Sing. Only because he was given credit for time already served was he released.

Carl Calvin Westover was again tried and again convicted. The U.S. Court of Appeals for the Ninth Circuit remanded the case to the federal district court for postconviction hearings on some still unresolved, though not *Escobedo*-related, issues; when these could not be cleared up, the second conviction was set aside, and a third trial ordered. Westover, having been incarcerated all this time, had just about concluded a full ten-year prison term—out of the fifteen originally imposed—and his lawyer plea-bargained to exchange a guilty plea in return for a sentence reduced to that ten-year term. However, Westover still had a California parole violation hanging over his head, and when he was released from federal jurisdiction, the state took him over. Finally, about 1970, he was released, a "burned-out" case.

Roy Allen Stewart's case was taken over by the Los Angeles public defender, Wilbur F.

The second trial of Ernest Miranda for kidnapping and rape in Maricopa County Superior Court was scheduled to open on October 24, 1966, but was postponed by consent of both the prosecution and defense because Lois Ann Jameson, who had married in the meantime, was expecting a baby in November.

When the trial finally opened in mid-February 1967, it was handled with care by court and counsel on both sides. There would be no court-appointed attorney this time: John Flynn took charge of Miranda's defense. There would be no assistant district attorney prosecuting this time; Maricopa County Attorney Robert Corbin, whose reaction to the Supreme Court's ruling in Miranda's case, like that of a lot of other prosecutors, had been that it was a "black day for law enforcement," himself was in charge of the prosecution this time. Lawrence K. Wren of Flagstaff, Arizona, Superior Court, was imported to try the case.

Early on conviction appeared impossible. The prosecution's only evidence, Ernest Miranda's confession to Officers Cooley and Young, had been ruled inadmissible by the United States Supreme Court. Even Judge Wren had thought Miranda would go "bone free."

"Why are you doing this?" Flynn asked Corbin just before the trial began. "You haven't got a case."

At that point Corbin didn't think he had a case either, but, a dedicated crime fighter, he replied, "At least I'll go down fighting."

Then the county attorney "literally stumbled" into the means of conviction. Miranda, who expected to be released from prison following his acquittal at the second trial, had written to welfare authorities questioning the fitness of Twila Hoffman, his common-law wife, to have custody of their daughter because Mrs. Hoffman had had a child by another man while Miranda was in prison. She was angry; she was also scared. If Miranda was freed, she feared, there was no telling what he might do. She brought her story to Robert Corbin.

On March 16, 1963, following Miranda's arrest for the rape of Lois Ann Jameson, Mrs. Hoffman had visited him at the county jail. He asked her if police had told her about his confession. She replied that they had. Miranda then, according to Mrs. Hoffman, confessed to her that he had, in fact, kidnapped and raped Miss Jameson.

Seeing his case begin to take shape, Corbin sent Detective Carroll Cooley to see Mrs. Hoffman, who willingly elaborated on the story of her visit to the jail. Miranda, she said, had told her to get in touch with Lois Ann and give her his promise to marry her if she would agree to drop charges against

---

Littlefield, following *Miranda*. His trials dragged on for three years, beset by defense requests for postponements and continuances—a device Littlefield used to gain time in which his client could establish a record for model prison behavior and, possibly, a reduced sentence as reward. In July 1969 Stewart was again convicted of first-degree murder and robbery. His confession was not used as evidence. His sentence was reduced from death to life imprisonment.

him—he would return to Mrs. Hoffman later, he had said. Mrs. Hoffman was understandably furious. Well, if she wouldn't agree to that, would she agree to show Lois Ann their baby, perhaps appease her, in an attempt to have the charges dropped? Mrs. Hoffman again refused.

County Attorney Corbin's case was made.

Ernest Miranda's retrial opened on Wednesday, February 15, 1967, with the selection of a jury of eight women and four men, a process requiring six hours of questioning. It might have been an omen.

Miranda himself was described as looking "composed and detached, even slightly amused at times" during the early stages. As far as he knew, the prosecution had no case, and he had John Flynn, who battled against the admission of every shred of evidence he legally could. In fact, during the nine days of trial the actual time in which the jury heard testimony totaled one day; the remainder of the time was spent either in the judge's chambers or with the jury out of the courtroom while Flynn and Corbin argued over what evidence could be admitted and what had to be suppressed. "In a way," Flynn later told the judge, "I goofed this case, for I forgot about the jury. I forgot about the question of guilt or innocence and a proper presentation on that point because I became so wrapped up in getting it dismissed on constitutional questions."

The major argument, of course, centered on the admission or suppression of Twila Hoffman's surprise testimony that Miranda had confessed to her at the jail. It was a complex question. It revolved partly around whether or not the testimony of a common-law wife was admissible in the state courts of Arizona. But that was a secondary issue as attorneys and judges all worked night after night until the early hours of the morning, delving "deeply, very deeply," said Judge Wren later, "into what we refer to in Arizona as that vast, dark, and completely mysterious cavern known as the fruit of the poison[ous] tree"—that is, evidence offered by the prosecution which was in any way at all the product of the confession to the police, or "poisonous tree," which the U.S. Supreme Court had ruled inadmissible—and John Flynn argued that Mrs. Hoffman's version of events at the jail was such a product—could not be admitted as evidence against his client.

Persuaded by this lengthy research, however, Judge Wren admitted Twila Hoffman's testimony, and she told her story to the jury. After deliberating for an hour and twenty-three minutes, the jury found Ernest Miranda guilty of kidnapping and rape. On March 1, 1967, exactly one year after the confessions cases had been argued in the U.S. Supreme Court, Ernest Miranda was again sentenced to twenty to thirty years in the Arizona State Prison at Florence, and the bottle of Scotch his father had bought stood unopened on the shelf.

The trial had been, Judge Wren commented later, pointing up an objection widespread in the law enforcement community to the U.S. Supreme Court's decision in *Miranda*, a "nine-day game of constitutional chess" in

which "we had dealt not at all . . . with the basic question of guilt or innocence. Not once had this question even been a part of our thorny legal arguments and motions."

As a judge Warren Burger of the U.S. Court of Appeals for the District
of Columbia Circuit had become more rather than less pugnacious following
the Supreme Court's decision in Ernest Miranda's case, using his written
opinions to warn of judicial Armageddon. Because of the time lag between
the *Miranda* ruling in June 1966 and the arrival of substantive *Miranda* cases
at the lower federal appellate court, Burger's contributions to the growing
body of *Miranda* literature was minor. He had, though, neither changed his
judicial direction nor softened his contentious tone. During the three court
terms 1966, 1967, and 1968, of the ninety-four criminal cases in which he
was involved, he voted to affirm convictions in eighty-two cases, or 87 percent. As he watched convictions which had been based on confessions reversed by his own and other of the nation's courts, he complained with some
bitterness:

> For a generation judicial trends have been to exclude from the jury
> all evidence thought to have been unfairly or improperly secured,
> and more recent holdings place stringent limits on the use of any
> utterance by an accused. In the future trial judges will be evaluating
> only those utterances of an accused which have already passed
> through the screening processes outlined in *McNabb, Mallory,
> Escobedo, Massiah,* and *Miranda.* The prospects now are that trial
> judges, otherwise much overburdened, will not be overworked in
> passing on the voluntariness of the few confessions which will sur-
> vive the application of these cases.

On the lecture circuit, where the facts and circumstances of a particular
case need not constrain his comments, Burger's tone grew even more quarrel-
some. The retrial of Ernest Miranda was exactly the sort of proceeding that
threatened his judicial equanimity. As he saw it, cases like Miranda's, which
had so far consumed four years from the night Lois Ann Jameson had been
driven into the Arizona desert, with no end yet in sight—John Flynn was already planning the appeals—and which turned into games of constitutional
chess rather than trials to determine guilt or innocence, were preventing the
criminal justice system from working. Indeed, what with the Warren Court's
restatement over the past decade of individual rights in cases like *Escobedo*
and *Miranda*—which not only limited the use of evidence but also length-
ened the time required for a case to be tried as well as encouraged lawyers and
defendants to appeal—added to the natural increase in prosecutors' caseloads
and court dockets brought about by the soaring rates of crime, the criminal
justice system did appear headed for disaster. The lines at the courtroom

doors were ever-lengthening, and Judge Burger viewed the situation as not at all the effect the majority on the Warren Court had intended.

In those ways available to a prominent judicial figure, he set about trying to ameliorate conditions that were hindering the fair administration of criminal justice. Shortly after the *Miranda* ruling he participated in a conference on "Legal Manpower Needs of Criminal Law," he spoke to the winter convention of the American College of Trial Lawyers, and he attended a local conference of some 100 lawyers, judges, and others involved in law enforcement that had been called by the president.

In 1968 Burger made an important speech to the Ohio Judicial Conference in which he attacked the U.S. Supreme Court itself. Assigning "responsibility for some of the bitterness in American life today over the administration of criminal justice" to that Court's departure from its constitutional limitations of deciding cases and controversies and its assumption of legislative functions, he criticized its "revising the code of criminal procedure and evidence 'piecemeal' on a case-by-case basis, on inadequate records and incomplete factual data." He recalled that the briefs for the states and the National District Attorneys Association in Ernest Miranda's case had "strongly urged the Supreme Court not to resolve great issues on a narrow record of a few cases." The resolution of great issues, rather, he suggested, deserved the careful attention of expert participants in the field, not Supreme Court justices writing in isolation from events—the broad-based support of the state legislatures.

At another time he challenged the foundations of the adversary system itself. Participating in a discussion at the Center for the Study of Democratic Institutions in Santa Barbara, California, Burger called the adversary system "inefficient" and "wasteful"; it put "all the emphasis on techniques, devices, mechanisms"—mechanisms such as presumption of innocence, reliance on the verdicts of juries, rules of evidence, the right of a defendant to remain silent, the prosecution's responsibility for the burden of proof. Although these "incidents of the adversary system" were planted in Magna Carta by men who had striven to compensate for the imbalance between king and commoner, "are all these devices of the adversary system valid in today's society?" he asked. At the risk of conjuring up "images of the rack and the screw" among his colleagues, Judge Burger said he believed the original reasons against compelling a defendant to answer had been somewhat dissipated in a modern courtroom setting, and "so I am no longer sure," he said, "that the Fifth Amendment concept, in its present form and as presently applied and interpreted, has all the validity attributed to it." At this advanced stage of civilization, when governments wore a veneer of humanity, the necessity for such mechanisms, which he believed had been overdeveloped, was exaggerated; invented to improve the dispensation of justice, these very mechanisms were overloading the system and impairing its efficiency. Or, as he had said on a previous occasion, "It is a truism of political philosophy rooted in history that nations and societies often perish from an excess of their own basic principles."

Burger was no simple naysayer or prophet of doom; where he pointed out problems, he also proposed solutions, and he was brash enough to suggest to the Supreme Court itself a way out of the quagmire it had created. If the justices were not satisfied with the way local courts and police operated, they could, he suggested, sponsor an overhaul of the Federal Rules of Criminal Procedure. Where old-fashioned operating procedures contributed to court-room congestion, he told lower-court judges, modern management methods could be introduced.

In June 1967, a year after Ernest Miranda's case had been decided in the U.S. Supreme Court, the recommendations of the ABA subcommittee of which Burger was chairman, the guidelines for defense and prosecution law-yers, were published, and eight months later they were approved by the ABA House of Delegates at its annual meeting. It was a simple compilation of suggestions for unraveling some of the accumulated knots. The little volume bore the imprint of the chairman: a generally conservative document, advancing the rights of the individual very little and in some cases actually backing off.

The committee urged the extension of the *Gideon* requirement of trial counsel in felony cases to include certain misdemeanor cases and more systematic methods of providing counsel to indigent defendants. Both of these requirements, however, were already being implemented in a number of states.

The committee did not encourage the requiring of counsel at the interrogation stage of the proceedings, although its report was published after the *Miranda* ruling. On the contrary. The U.S. Supreme Court, the committee explained, "has not held that counsel must be provided at this stage but only that statements obtained during such interrogation cannot be admitted at a trial if the accused was not warned of his right to be provided with counsel and actually allowed to have or be provided with counsel if he so requests." There was certainly no advance here, barely a staying even. Counsel, declared the committee, should be "provided to accused as soon as feasible after he is taken into custody, when he appears before a committing magistrate or when he is formally charged . . ."—no more than the pre-*Escobedo* standards suggested as early as 1959 in the study by the Association of the Bar of the City of New York/National Legal Aid and Defender Association.

Burger had developed strong convictions during the decade he had spent as a federal judge; as his positions coincided with increasingly popular ones among his fellow judges and prosecutors, he gained in stature as well as visibility; his opinions were being quoted by other judges, his speeches reprinted in the law reviews. So far, though, his exposure had been largely within the legal community. In May 1967 he ventured out of that group and took a step that was in time to make a significant contribution toward his becoming a national figure.

When, in 1967, Ripon College in Ripon, Wisconsin, was seeking a speaker for its 101st commencement in May, one of the trustees, Robert V. Abendroth, a Milwaukee lawyer who had been Burger's first full-year law clerk a decade before, suggested his former boss. Burger chose for his text "Crime and Punishment," a text he himself admitted was not a conventional commencement subject, but then, as he also said, "these are not ordinary times and people are not being entirely conventional these days." Commencement weather at Ripon was uncommonly cold that year, so cold that speakers at the outdoor exercises could see their breath. Compounding the difficulty for Judge Burger was a residue of discomfort from recent back surgery. But Burger persisted undaunted. As the gods would have it, "Crime and Punishment" was one of the most important speeches, politically speaking, that he ever gave.

He spoke no slogans, he offered no cheap solutions. He translated into lay terms what he had been saying for the past several years in his opinions and lectures: that the administrators of criminal justice, including the courts, reflecting the nation's innate "fear of the power of government and . . . great concern for individual liberty" had brought the system to a point where "it is often very difficult to convict even those who are plainly guilty"; the fair balance between "the needs of society" and the protection of liberty, what Burger called "ordered liberty," had gone askew. He compared American with Scandinavian justice, the latter reflecting less concern for the rights of the individual prior to conviction but extraordinary and humane concern for rehabilitation of the individual after conviction, and he suggested that Americans in positions to do so at least spend some attention on that alternative.

He said little he had not said previously. What was different about this speech was its addressing a general rather than a legal audience and its wider readership: College officials distributed it to the national media, and nearly three months later, on August 7, 1967, it was excerpted in *U.S. News and World Report*, whose pages that year were featuring crime stories.

One who read it was Richard Nixon, who was even then planning his return to presidential politics and whom Burger knew casually—they had met at the 1948 Republican National Convention, where Nixon, a nondelegate, had lobbied for the candidacy of Harold E. Stassen, whose administrative aide Burger was at the time; Republican political matters had thrown them together occasionally in the following years. That summer a mutual friend told Burger that Nixon had been impressed with the District of Columbia judge's approach to the administration of criminal justice.

In July 1967 the Warren Court majority got an unexpected reinforcement when Lyndon Johnson named Solicitor General Thurgood Marshall to the United States Supreme Court, the first black man to be so named. He succeeded Tom Clark, dissenter from the majority ruling in *Miranda*, who had resigned when his son, Ramsey, was named attorney general, in order to head off any questions that might have arisen regarding the propriety of the father's judging government cases initiated by the son.

Marshall's record as a judge of the U.S. Court of Appeals for the Second Circuit from 1961 to 1965 had been more mixed, perhaps, than one might have expected for a former advocate for the NAACP, coauthor of the brief for Izell Chambers those many years before and fighter for constitutional equality for the disadvantaged in America's courtrooms for most of his professional life. He had written some important opinions in which he did, in fact, uphold the rights of the individual. But he had also, in a precursor to *Miranda* subsequently reversed by the United States Supreme Court, voted with the majority to affirm the conviction of a man whose confession to murder, transcribed in a hospital after he had been given a painkiller for a bullet wound, had been used as evidence in court. Of the ninety-one criminal cases in which he had been involved during those years on the federal appellate court, he had voted to affirm convictions in nearly three-quarters. As Solicitor General Marshall he had argued the case against Carl Calvin Westover in the U.S. Supreme Court. And he had more or less successfully sidestepped, as was traditional for nominees, through five days of preconfirmation hearings during which he had been harassed by those senators to whom the color of his skin was important, particularly by Senators McClellan of Arkansas and Eastland of Mississippi, who attempted to elicit his judicial views, especially those regarding the Supreme Court's ruling in *Miranda*. Still, the "liberal" label had stuck, and it was predicted, accurately as it turned out, that Marshall would stand on the Supreme Court for protecting the constitutional rights of the accused. He was one of the last additions to the ranks of those who would do the same.

The year 1968 was crucial for *Miranda*, a turning point, as the frequency of the attacks on it accelerated and the strength of the attackers increased. Actual deeds for the first time accompanied the impassioned rhetoric, and before the year was out, the critics of the Supreme Court succeeded in nullifying *Miranda* legislatively, in preventing a member of the *Miranda* majority from becoming chief justice and in electing one of their own to the presidency.

The legislators led off. Nourished by a growing anti-Court mood in their home districts, they took their text, if not the fine-tuned reasoning, from the *Miranda* dissenters, whom they characterized as judicial heroes and quoted in hearing room and congressional chamber, conferring on them an unaccustomed popularity outside the judiciary and on the majority a nearly villainous role. Chief Justice Warren, in his *Miranda* opinion, had invited "Congress and the States to continue their laudable search for increasingly effective ways of protecting the rights of the individual while promoting efficient enforcement of our criminal laws," and Congress responded, although not, perhaps, in precisely the fashion the chief justice had intended. Led by Senator McClellan of Arkansas, the second-ranking Democrat on the Senate Judiciary Committee and chairman of the Subcommittee on Criminal Laws and Procedures, Congress went on a Court-curbing binge.

The tension among the three branches of government that keeps the powerful from becoming too powerful, from making Caesars of senators, and the body politic operationally healthy have never been so evident as when the Supreme Court and Congress indulge in one of their periodic confrontations. Natural enemies as well as interdependent, the two have endured a love-hate relationship for nearly two centuries, Congress relying on the Court to uphold the laws written there—but jealous of the Court's authority to judge their constitutionality—the Court dependent on the legislature for, ultimately, its members, its money, and certain aspects of its power.

In fits of pique at various times during the first two centuries of the Republic's history, Congress had increased or reduced the number of justices on the Supreme Court seven times—the number was mandated not by the Constitution but by the Judiciary Act of 1789* and therefore has been amenable to legislative manipulation. The legislators had impeached—although the Senate had acquitted him—one Supreme Court justice, Samuel Chase in 1804, and early in the 1970s would attempt to impeach another, William O. Douglas. They had failed to confirm twenty-two appointees, and early in the next decade that number would rise to twenty-six. And on occasion, when final confirmation was not even in serious jeopardy, they went out of their way to make nominees uncomfortable during the confirmation process, hardly subtle reminders to Court and executive alike that Congress held power, too, though it sometimes went unwielded.

Over the past two centuries Congress had flailed away, too, with constitutional amendments, or the threat of them, and by 1965 three of the twenty-four additions to that document† so far had, in fact, been the results of congressional attempts to curb Court power.

---

* The act established the number of justices as six. In 1801 Congress reduced the number to five, in 1802 raised it again to six, in 1807 added a seventh, in 1837 added two to make it nine, and during the Civil War added a tenth. In 1865 Congress reduced the number to seven again, then increased it to its present number, nine, in 1869. In 1937 Franklin Roosevelt, furious at the justices for their unwillingness to uphold New Deal legislation, attempted in his famous Court-packing plan to name additional justices who, he believed, would assure his political philosophy of a Court majority; when Congress and some members of the Court combined to thwart his attempt, the plan failed, and the number remained at nine.

† Amendment 11, ratified in 1795 as a response to the Court's decision in *Chisholm* v. *Georgia*, which upheld the right of citizens of a state to sue another state in federal court, removed from the Supreme Court jurisdiction over cases arising between a state and citizens of another state or foreign country.

Amendment 14, ratified in 1868 and for the past three decades the constitutional rationale for Court intervention in state criminal procedures, was a congressional response to the Supreme Court's decision in the *Dred Scott* case.

Over these two centuries of the Court's existence there had been proposals in Congress to require that either two-thirds or all of the justices agree if
legislative acts were to be found unconstitutional, to limit the justices' terms,
and to limit Court jurisdiction over whichever category of decisions most recently had incurred congressional wrath. The legislators had failed in all but
the last and had succeeded in that only once.*

The easiest and most frequently employed method of punishing the Supreme Court had been to nullify specific unpopular decisions legislatively.
The Omnibus Crime Control and Safe Streets Act of 1968, which was intended to nullify *Miranda* in the federal courts, belonged in this last category.

The preliminaries to its passage, which required two years and a good
deal of congressional hyperventilating, had begun in the summer of 1966, just
after *Miranda* had been handed down.

Congress is not—rarely has been—slow to sense the popular mood. The
temper of the times during the immediate post-*Miranda* months had demanded drastic measures. The land was "full of bloody crimes"; the city was
"full of violence." The FBI reported in 1966 that the crime rate in 1965 had
jumped 6 percent over that of the previous year, for a total of 2,750,000 serious crimes, or an average of 5 per minute, and the U.S. Supreme Court, de-
fying the will of the people, had handed down another decision hamstringing
law enforcement in its efforts to apprehend criminals. Richard Nixon, about
to begin still another campaign for the election of Republican legislators, was
predicting that the issue of crime in the streets was "even more real than it
was in '64." There was a discernible gang busters mentality in the United
States Congress.

Immediately following the Supreme Court's *Miranda* ruling, the crime-
fighting Senator McClellan had thundered, "This 5–4 decision is of such adverse significance to law enforcement that it demands early and thorough examination with a view to ascertaining just what legislation can and should be
enacted to alleviate the obvious damage it will do to society," and he had
promised to "undertake to process expeditiously" a pending measure he was
cosponsoring to make confessions more readily admissible in federal courts.

Democratic Senator Samuel J. Ervin, Jr., of North Carolina, a respected
constitutional scholar who had served on the Burke County Criminal Court
and on the North Carolina Supreme Court before being elected to the Senate, reacted to the U.S. Supreme Court's *Miranda* ruling exactly the way his
colleague from Arkansas had.

Amendment 16 establishing the authority of Congress to enact income tax laws and ratified in 1915 was the result of congressional irritation at the Court's striking down such a law in
1895.

* In 1868 the Radical Republicans in Congress were able to prevent the Court from deciding a case in which the constitutionality of the Reconstruction Acts of 1867 were challenged
by passing a bill removing Court jurisdiction.

Chapter 5

"Enough has been done for those who murder and rape and rob!" he declared. "It is time to do something for those who do not wish to be murdered or raped or robbed." He introduced a constitutional amendment providing that any admission or confession could be used as evidence in court so long as it had been voluntarily given. He would turn the clock back to the 1940s and 1950s.

The Constitutional Amendments Subcommittee of the Senate Judiciary Committee had hastily in midsummer of 1966 held hearings to explore the implications of *Miranda*. One of the witnesses was Truman Capote, author of the best-selling *In Cold Blood*. Capote testified that had the *Miranda* ruling been in effect when the murderers of the Clutter family were captured, the two killers, who were later hanged, would have gone "scot free." Added Alvin A. Dewey of the Kansas Bureau of Investigation, who had taken charge of tracking down the criminals, some Americans were learning their rights increasingly early in life. "In my home town of Garden City, Kansas," he told the subcommittee, "an 11-year-old boy was arrested recently for shoplifting and taken to the police station. He has refused to give his name or the names of his parents, and he told them he wanted an attorney." The subcommittee did not attempt to push an anti-*Miranda* constitutional amendment through Congress that summer. The hearings served, however, as one more vehicle for carrying word of congressional activity in an area of serious concern to voters.

The Supreme Court had few defenders in these times, and little opposition to the tirades surfaced. The justices themselves could hardly argue back. Those few senators and representatives who rose in their chambers in their support were outnumbered, outtalked, and outlasted. The president tried to blunt the effects of the attacks, but ultimately, he, too, failed.

Lyndon Johnson was no less aware of the facts of rising crime and violence, and its potential as a political issue, than were the legislators. Fighting crime became a staple of his domestic program, was given a prominent place in State of the Union and budget messages. He sent a special message to the Congress, wrung his hands at state governors gathered in the White House and at the International Association of Chiefs of Police gathered in Kansas City, called crime conferences, and created commissions to study the causes of crime.

Never, however, did he suggest the Supreme Court was to blame. Never did he suggest the overruling of a Court decision. On the contrary. He consistently refused to link crime rates to Court rulings, and in his charge to his National Crime Commission, called the President's Commission on Law Enforcement and the Administration of Justice, he had directed the members' attention to discovering what steps could be taken "to create greater understanding by those involved in the administration of justice at the state and local level of the efforts of the federal courts to insure protection of individual rights."

Johnson chose other weapons for the fight against crime. He wrote letters to leading members of Congress urging strict gun control legislation. In 1965, prior to the *Miranda* ruling, he had sponsored, and Congress had passed, a Law Enforcement Assistance Act to give federal financial aid to local police departments. Later he sponsored, and Congress enacted, a bill establishing the Federal Judicial Center, where court personnel could be trained in modern administrative methods and research could be done on improving and making more efficient the operations of the nation's courts.

What was bound to bring about a confrontation between the president and the legislators was his opposition to Court curbing and his stubborn insistence, instead, on tying the cure of one social illness to the treatment of another. "We will continue," he told the Conference of State Planning Committees on Criminal Administration in October 1966, an organization whose establishment he himself had urged as a tool in the war against crime, "to accelerate our battle" against crime, but, he added, "for the long-range prospects of this country, I look not to anti-crime laws but to anti-poverty laws."

The conclusions reached by his commissions, when they reported to him, supported the president's position. The President's Commission on Crime in the District of Columbia, having spent $40,000 and seventeen months in studying the problem of crime in the nation's capital, said in its report—which reached Johnson in July 1966, just after the Supreme Court's *Miranda* decision—that court decisions limiting police interrogation had not reduced substantially the number of incriminating statements made by suspects; the local conviction rate was reported at 77 percent when the defendant confessed, 74 percent when he did not; many suspects were reported to have confessed even after consulting lawyers. The experts found that local crime was being committed largely by young blacks who came from broken homes, had dropped out of high school, and were unemployed.

Declared the report: "Radical reduction of crime over the long run will require basic social and economic changes," and reiterated the previously stated goals of Johnson's Great Society: improved education, job training, employment opportunities, and an end to racial segregation.

The Challenge of Crime in a Free Society, the report of the President's Commission on Law Enforcement and the Administration of Justice, which reached the president's desk a few months later, in February 1967, offered precisely the same conclusions. The report contained more than 200 recommendations, most of them aimed in general at making more effective the administration of criminal justice, from police station to penitentiary, by modernizing it through improved technology and humanizing it through increased and higher-quality personnel. The criminal justice system, however, was not "designed to eliminate the conditions in which most crime breeds," the Commission declared. Social and economic measures were also required:

Warring on poverty, inadequate housing and unemployment, is warring on crime. A civil rights law is a law against crime. Money for schools is money against crime. Medical, psychiatric, and family-counseling services are services against crime. . . . A community's most enduring protection against crime is to right the wrongs and cure the illnesses that tempt men to harm their neighbors. . . .

The commission did not, although the president had requested it, take any great pains to create better understanding of the efforts of the federal courts to insure protection of individual rights. Declaring it was too early to "assess the effect of the *Miranda* decision on law enforcement's ability to secure confessions and to solve crimes," the commission acknowledged that "this and other decisions do represent a trend toward findings by the judiciary that previously permitted police practices are unconstitutionally offensive to the dignity and integrity of private citizens." It recommended the creation of new legislative and administrative policies "to guide police through the changing world of permissible activity."

Although the commission had failed to deal squarely with the question of the effects of court decisions on law enforcement, the tone of the report was weighted on the side of upholding the rights of the individual, implying at least that its recommendations for modernizing police work and court systems would accomplish far more than Court-curbing programs. Such implications provoked a vigorous dissent from a group of prominent commission members, including Leon Jaworski of Houston, Texas, a future ABA president, and Lewis F. Powell, Jr., of Richmond, Virginia, a former ABA president—and future Supreme Court justice, who, part of the counterforces to *Miranda* now building, would in later years have considerable influence in determining whether the privilege against compulsory self-incrimination "as recently construed and enlarged [in *Escobedo* and *Miranda*] is justified either by its long and tangled history or by any genuine need in a criminal trial." While the dissenters took pains to declare their agreement with the overall recommendations made by the commission, the road to social and economic change, they argued, was long and hard. What, they asked, was law enforcement to do in the meantime? Could the national anticrime strategy proposed by the commission be implemented, they persisted, "without changes in existing constitutional limitations?" With more gentility of tone but no less determination than some United States senators to dilute the impact of Supreme Court decisions, they urged that "whatever can be done to right the present imbalance through legislation or rule of court should have high priority" and they spelled out these requirements regarding the taking of confessions:

- An adequate opportunity must be provided the police for interrogation at the scene of the crime, during investigations and at the station house, with appropriate safeguards to prevent abuse.

203

• The legitimate place of voluntary confessions in law enforcement must be re-established and their use made dependent upon meeting due process standards of voluntariness.

The split in the commission more or less typified the differences of opinion between Congress, or at least its most outspoken members, and the administration, regarding Chief Justice Warren's charge, in his opinion for the majority in *Miranda*, to nonjudicial branches of the government to seek nonjudicial solutions to the problem of safeguarding the constitutional rights of suspects at the station house. And both the president and Congress, following their different mandates, went off in separate directions.

When in the fall of 1966 Lyndon Johnson had learned the gist of the crime commission report, although he had not yet officially received it, he had his aides meet with representatives from the Justice Department, the Bureau of the Budget, the Department of Housing and Urban Development, and the crime commission itself. Out of this series of meetings emerged a tentative outline for legislation to implement the commission recommendations. As finally drafted by Justice Department lawyers, the legislation proved to be an outgrowth of, updating of, and elaboration on the Law Enforcement Assistance Act of 1965, under which the federal government would seek to channel resources to local law enforcement agencies in order that they might, through research, planning, and improved technology, modernize and so make law enforcement more effective. Intended as the heart of the president's anticrime program, it was submitted to Congress coincident with publication of the crime commission report in February 1967.

But Senator McClellan was ready with a bill of his own. Reminiscent in tone to some of the proposed anti-Court legislation of the late 1950s through which Congress had attempted to nullify Court decisions in loyalty-security cases, McClellan's bill provided, as had Ervin's amendment, that contrary to the Court's ruling in *Miranda* v. *Arizona*, all confessions, so long as they were voluntarily given, were to be admissible as evidence in federal courts; state courts, it was believed, would follow the federal examples, as they often did. The requirement was as vague and ambiguous as "due process of law" and threatened to tax the interpretive powers of the federal judiciary just as heavily. But McClellan's grip on the legislative machinery was strong, and his influence substantial.

The progress of this anticrime legislation through Congress over the next eighteen months, during which the president's and the senator's bills combined and Johnson's chief lobbyist, the attorney general, was in the unenviable position of trying to persuade Congress to finance the former and to dissuade the legislators from passing the latter, focused the issues regarding the strategy to be employed in the war against crime. It also set the scene for the approaching national elections.

The American people's mood of apprehensiveness was apparent when no fewer than twenty-one senators, on their return to Washington in January 1967 following the recent elections for congressional and state offices, rushed to cosponsor the president's anticrime bill. It became increasingly apparent during the spring and summer of 1967 as McClellan, an expert in getting his causes before the public, brought police, prosecutors, judges (including Lawrence Wren of Flagstaff, Arizona, who had presided at Ernest Miranda's second trial), fellow senators, representatives, state legislators, state and county executives before his Subcommittee on Criminal Laws and Procedures, which was studying, in addition to the measures introduced by the administration and the subcommittee chairman himself, a spate of anticrime legislation, most of which also amounted to curbing the power of the United States Supreme Court.

Police in particular contributed to the atmosphere of vengeance upon the judiciary that pervaded the hearings. Although after their early alarmist reactions to *Miranda*, they had more or less come to terms with it and, given a few hours of in-service training, they had been able to alter their practices, to conform to the Court's dictates and still apprehend criminals, they had not come to terms with what they believed was the Court's distrust of them. At the instigation of their "union" organization, the International Association of Chiefs of Police, chiefs nationwide, from small towns and large cities, had inundated Senator McClellan's committee with supportive letters. Most letters praised McClellan's work or let it go at criticizing the Court's decisions. But one chief expressed what may have been the subconscious yearnings of many. "I am so disgusted," he wrote, "with what we have to contend with in law enforcement since the U.S. Supreme Court saw fit to so recklessly interpret the law to benefit lawbreakers, to misinterpret the will of our law makers, that I am resigning my position as chief of police. . . ."

With such an anti-Court focus at the hearings, little attention was paid to other police problems, to the fact that like the courts of America, police in the 1960s were operating with blunderbusses in an atomic age. That, for example, in 1967, 74 percent of the cities with populations of more than 100,-000 did not even have crime laboratories; that in these days of rapid intercontinental transit, intracontinental communications and coordination among police had not advanced much from the days when Earl Warren was a district attorney in California. That there was no systematized educational process for the job of chief, only on-the-job training, and that recruit training was haphazard and superficial at best, familiarizing students with the mechanics of weaponry and law and traffic control but utterly failing to illuminate the complexities of these subjects in relationship to the social and political complexities in which a policeman is involved daily. That departmental administrators generally had no announced and clear-cut policies regarding such day-to-day law enforcement issues as the use of deadly force. That there was widespread corruption in America's police departments. Crime, more or less limited to metropolitan areas for nearly a century, was spreading into suburban and rural areas, where law enforcement officers were ill-prepared to deal with it. Treatment of minorities had advanced very little since Lincoln Steffens had recorded the activities in the office of "Clubber" Williams of the New York City Police Department around the turn of the century. Police departments had added few minority members to their rolls—indeed, former Washington, D.C., Police Chief Jerry Wilson later recalled that until the early 1950s requests for police officers for presidential details actually specified "Send white officers only," and in 1970 a congressman was to warn him that hiring large numbers of blacks for the police force was dangerous because "we won't have anyone to protect us from blacks if there is a revolution."

At sometime near A.D. 800, as England's Anglo-Saxons began to organize themselves in primitive communities, policing of a sort began. It consisted largely then of pursuit by men of the community of criminal suspects, called hue and cry, and the quelling of disturbances and interrogation of strangers caught out at night, called watch and ward. By the nineteenth century, 1,000 years later, policing had advanced only to the point that the city of London had instituted a night watch and special police units to patrol the commercial areas and wharves. As the decade of the 1960s edged toward the seventies, policing as a profession had not yet advanced in proportion to the complexities of contemporary events—or the way contemporary men and women viewed events. But very few of these matters were mentioned at the crime bill hearings.

The new attorney general,* Ramsey Clark, disagreeing with his father's *Miranda* dissent and totally committed to the support of individual liberties as well as to the Johnsonian strategy for waging the war against crime—a position that would have some political significance in the presidential election of 1968—was almost the lone voice for the administration's approach during the subcommittee hearings. Most of the others, particularly those involved in law enforcement at the local level, shared the Arkansas senator's viewpoint, and, McClellan prophesied, "It is quite probable that these hearings and the bills we will be considering will mark the turning point in the struggle against lawlessness in this nation."

Although the administration's proposal for a Law Enforcement Assistance Act passed the House of Representatives, neither that nor McClellan's proposal to admit "voluntary" confessions as evidence in federal courts passed the Senate in 1967. Disputes between the Department of Justice and the subcommittee chairman over how the act should be implemented and over the inclusion of McClellan's confessions measure kept the entire package from reaching the Senate floor, and the legislation died when Congress adjourned in the fall of 1967.

Then, in mid-January 1968, as congressmen again returned to the capi-

---

* Attorney General Katzenbach had been transferred to the State Department as undersecretary.

tal, the Associated Press polled them on what they had found to be the most significant concerns at home. "Overwhelmingly," the newsmen said, "the members reported that anger over riots and crime overshadowed all other domestic issues, and, in many cases, even the war in Vietnam."

At about the same time Richard Nixon, who was increasingly hopeful of winning the Republican presidential nomination the following summer, told the Richmond, Virginia, Chamber of Commerce that the courts must shoulder the burden of responsibility for the nation's crime wave; they had, he said, "gone too far in weakening the peace forces against the forces of crime." And on January 17, President Johnson told Congress in his State of the Union address, "[T]here is no more urgent business before the Congress than to pass the [crime bill] this year. . . ." On February 7 he sent a special message to the legislators reinforcing the comments of the previous speech.

It was plain that crime was going to be an important issue in the approaching national election. That was all the legislators needed to be goaded into action—fast action, for them. The old omnibus crime bill of 1967 was resurrected. Aided by the increasingly serious political emergency, the bill was discussed, areas of disagreement were hammered out, and it was voted out of committee and on to the Senate floor, where it was debated thoroughly. It passed the Senate on May 23, 1968, and the House on June 6, 1968.

The president was far from satisfied with the result. As the bill emerged, his proposal for a Law Enforcement Assistance Act remained the major feature, but the wily Arkansas senator managed to retain his section on the admissibility of confessions and added a section that provided for expanded federal, state, and local government wiretapping of suspected criminals. Following the assassination of Dr. Martin Luther King, Jr., on April 4, a section regulating the interstate sales of handguns was hastily thrown in.

However, Johnson believed the gun control legislation was inadequate, a "halfway step," the wiretapping provision "unwise and potentially dangerous," extending government intrusion on citizens "far beyond the effective and legitimate needs of law enforcement."

Nor did he like the provision for changing the rules of evidence regarding the admissibility of confessions in federal courts. Should federal law enforcement officers follow it, and should a case involving it ultimately come to the Supreme Court, where, given the present make-up of the Court, it might well be declared unconstitutional, there was also the distinct possibility that convictions obtained under it would be thrown out in light of *Miranda.* So the provision, ironically, also held a potential for putting criminals back on the streets rather than taking them off, and Johnson therefore instructed federal law enforcement agencies, in effect, to ignore it. Said he:

The provisions of Title II . . . can, I am advised by the Attorney General, be interpreted in harmony with the Constitution, and

Federal practices in this field will continue to conform to the Constitution.

Under long-standing policies, for example, the Federal Bureau of Investigation and other Federal law enforcement agencies have consistently given suspects full and fair warnings of their constitutional rights. I have asked the Attorney General and the Director of the FBI to assure that these policies will continue. . . .

The order did not endear him to certain senators, particularly the author of Title II, Senator McClellan, and the Arkansas lawmaker would not soon forget it.

The Law Enforcement Assistance Act, however, providing for improved training of police, supplementing police salaries, as well as money for research into developing science and technology for use by local police departments, made it worth accepting the other provisions, distasteful as they seemed, and acting on the basis that there was "more good than bad" in the package, Lyndon Johnson signed into law the Omnibus Crime Control and Safe Streets Act of 1968—as it had come to be called—on July 19, 1968.

Nullifying the effect of *Miranda* was hardly what the majority of the U.S. Supreme Court had had in mind when it had urged Congress to experiment. But it was a campaign year, and although the provisions of the omnibus crime bill applied only to federal jurisdictions where confessions had not been a really serious issue since the FBI had begun giving warnings similar to those required by *Miranda* in the 1940s, the speechmaking sounded good back home. A number of congressmen were rumored to have voted for it, although they privately disapproved of it, because they could not afford to seem soft on crime in an election year, and one senator assuaged his conscience by assuming that "members of the Court, who don't have to worry about being re-elected, will knock down the law as soon as it comes up for a test."

Congress had passed, and the President had signed, the bill just in time for the national party conventions, which were to be held the following month, the Republicans meeting in Miami, the Democrats later in Chicago.

If any of the political picture had become clear by May 1968, it was that Richard Nixon would be the Republican nominee for president that year and that crime would be the number one domestic issue.

Those people who had smugly eliminated the old trouper from the list of presidential candidates following his California defeat and its accompanying legacy of political handicaps had not considered carefully enough the man's resourcefulness and his enormous capacity simply to endure.

In retrospect, Nixon's lack of a political base seems obviously and easily remedied, given his contacts and political imagination. Borrowing a five-passenger plane from his friend millionaire jet manufacturer William Lear, Nixon had taken off in the spring of 1966 to campaign for Republican candidates across the nation. The countryside had rolled by. Seattle, Washington,

Chapter 5

for the traditional Republican Lincoln's Birthday orgy. Montana. Arizona, California. Ohio. Louisiana. Texas. Mississippi. Alaska.

Strom Thurmond's South Carolina, for a $100-a-plate fund raiser attended by 950 newly converted Republicans, and a serious conversation on the way to the Columbia airport with Harry Dent, former aide to Thurmond and in 1966 state Republican chairman. Could he win in 1968? Nixon asked the southern Republican—since 1964, no longer a contradiction in terms—if George Wallace, trying to install his wife Lurleen in the Alabama governorship and claiming the South as his own, translated his current interest in the presidency into a three-legged race?

Answered Dent: Thurmond, not Wallace, was the real power in the South, a leadership forged in 1948, when he had won thirty-nine electoral votes as the Dixiecrat presidential candidate, and tempered in 1964, when he had underwritten Barry Goldwater's presidential candidacy. Thurmond was the man to see.

On to Birmingham, Alabama, and Tulsa, Oklahoma.

And in the fall Nixon did it again: 30,000 miles, five weeks, sixteen grueling hours a day of handshaking and talking about Vietnam, incipient inflation, and, of course, the issue which was not yet number one but was climbing, crime in the streets.

Back in New York, Nixon and his aides took a suite at the Drake Hotel for election night, Tuesday, November 8, 1966, and watched the returns on television. Again the states rolled by. Massachusetts, where Edward Brooke, Republican, had just become the first black elected to the United States Senate since Reconstruction. Maryland, where a former assistant manager of supermarket personnel, Spiro T. Agnew, was elected governor. Tennessee, where Howard Baker, Jr., son-in-law of Senate Republican leader Everett M. Dirksen, was the first popularly elected Republican sent to the U.S. Senate in the state's history. In South Carolina, the voters predictably reelected Strom Thurmond. Republican Claude Kirk won the governorship of Florida. In Michigan it was George Romney for governor, Robert P. Griffin for senator. John G. Tower was re-elected to the Senate from Texas. And in California the new governor was a former movie actor named Ronald Reagan. It was the most dramatic recovery since Franklin Roosevelt's clean Democratic sweep in 1936: 540 additional Republican seats in state legislatures, including 22 in Strom Thurmond's South Carolina; 47 additional seats in the U.S. House of Representatives, 3 additional U.S. Senate seats; and 8 governorships.

As news of their victories flashed across the television screen, Richard Nixon, who had helped so much to make it all possible, was placing calls of congratulation.

Finally, he and a small group of friends set out for one of his favorite New York restaurants, El Morocco, and a "victory dinner" of spaghetti and red wine. If he was disconcerted by George Wallace's promise over national television, as Lurleen Wallace claimed victory in Alabama, that "you can look for us to be in your state all the way from Maine to California," Nixon did not show it.

"There was a lot for me to celebrate," Nixon said. "The first major battle had been met, faced, and surmounted in style." He had, in fact, fashioned a political base that made California and New York look small by comparison, a base made up of the entire nation. If his organization was loose and informal, it was also grateful and dedicated. He had improved his image as a winner and established a new attractiveness to political investors. His handicaps, if they had not completely vanished, were rapidly diminishing.

When he returned to his apartment about 2:30 A.M., he telephoned one of his aides for late returns. As the news continued to be overwhelmingly good, he exulted: "We've beaten hell out of them, and we're going to kill them in '68."

On January 7 and 8, 1967, Nixon had held planning meetings with his top aides at the Waldorf Towers in New York—Suite 31-A of the Waldorf Towers, the home, until his death in 1964, of Herbert Hoover, whom Nixon much admired; Nixon had specifically asked to be assigned to this suite.

"I'm not going to be coy with my oldest friends and closest advisers," he told the group at the outset. "I want you to proceed with plans for winning the Republican presidential nomination next year."

He passed over the issues briefly—the Vietnam War would have ended, he thought, but inflation, race, and crime would survive—and concentrated on strategy planning and delegate counting. A week later, at a delayed fifty-fifth birthday party, he announced his decision to his family. On March 13 he authorized establishment of a national Nixon for President committee with headquarters in Washington.

Nineteen sixty-seven had been a year of quiet consolidation, of courting party leaders in their home states, of strengthening his organization and pinning down convention delegate support. Much of it was concentrated in the South, where not only George Wallace but also now Ronald Reagan constituted serious threats to Nixon's candidacy.

At the same time crime in the streets was becoming the top domestic issue. Ronald Reagan, beginning to be seen on speakers' platforms outside California, thought it might even overtake Vietnam as *the* important issue. George Wallace, who, true to his promise, was taking his campaign into the North, was sure of it.

And in August 1967 the Republican party announced it was forming a task force on crime; its report, called "Crime and Delinquency, a Republican Response," issued eight months later, on April 22, 1968, made street crime an official Republican campaign issue and set out the party position, which was that the Johnson administration had been lax in combating crime and that the public must look to the Republican candidate, whoever he might be,

for "new leadership, new measures, and new directions," including "fundamental revision by Federal and state governments of the rules of criminal
procedure and the laws of appellate review of crime convictions" and new
"legislative guidance . . . to law enforcement and lower courts through a code
of pre-arraignment procedures clearly setting forth the appropriate limits for
police interrogation at the scene of the crime, during investigation and at the
station house."

By May 1968 the candidate, Richard Nixon, and the issue, crime in the
streets, had emerged. Nixon had won primaries in New Hampshire, Wisconsin, Pennsylvania, to be followed shortly by Indiana, Nebraska, Oregon; only
Massachusetts had let him down so far. It was time to issue a position paper.

Relying on an old political formula which had served him well in the
days when he had turned the Communist menace into an election-winning
issue, Nixon had titled the paper "Toward Freedom from Fear" and in about
6,000 words had outlined his views on crime, its causes and cures. He issued
it on May 9, 1968. It served as the basis not only for his political thinking
during the presidential campaign ahead but also for certain acts during his
administration.

Declaring that Lyndon Johnson's War on Poverty was "no substitute for
a war on crime," he blamed the president for the increase in street crime. He
blamed Attorney General Clark, citing the law enforcement officer's opposition to certain provisions of the then-pending omnibus crime bill.

But most of all, he blamed the United States Supreme Court majority,
whose decisions in *Escobedo* and *Miranda* "have had the effect of seriously
hamstringing the peace forces in our society and strengthening the criminal
forces"; taking a cue from the congressmen, he adapted a passage from Mr.
Justice White's *Miranda* dissent for his theme:

> The obvious underpinning of the Court's decision is a deep-seated
> distrust of all confessions . . . the result adds up to a judicial judg-
> ment that evidence from the accused should not be used against
> him in any way, whether compelled or not. This is the not so subtle
> overtone of the opinion—that it is inherently wrong for the police
> to gather evidence from the accused himself.

He concluded:

> From the point of view of the criminal forces, the cumulative im-
> pact of these decisions has been to set free patently guilty individu-
> als on the basis of legal technicalities.
>
> The tragic lesson of guilty men walking free from hundreds of
> courtrooms across the country has not been lost on the criminal
> community.

Nor, by implication, he trusted, would it be lost on the voting public.

Nixon endorsed, of course, all the provisions of the omnibus crime bill except that which would control interstate commerce in handguns. But he especially endorsed Senator McClellan's provision to loosen the requirements for admitting confessions as evidence into federal courts.

As 1968 came into middle age, the forces that would attempt to undo *Miranda* had gained a good deal of strength. Congress had already undercut its effect, at least in federal jurisdictions, and there were those who hoped the states would follow the federal example. The strongest of the Republican candidates for president had indicated his desire to weaken the ruling further. And a federal appeals court judge named Warren Burger, who had indicated some judicial hostility to it, was beginning to be noticed. There remained only opportunity, and that was about to be offered.

The presidential campaign had not been going well for Chief Justice Earl Warren. He had watched as the strongest candidate, Lyndon Johnson, mired in a war he could neither win nor lose, his plans for the Great Society disintegrating as that war consumed all his energies, his popularity disintegrating with them, announced on March 31, 1968, that he would not again seek the Democratic nomination. Then the second strongest Democrat, Robert F. Kennedy, was gunned down in the kitchen of the Ambassador Hotel in Los Angeles in the early-morning hours of June 5 as he was escaping the cheering crowds in the ballroom following his triumph in the California primary the day before. Of the Republicans, Governors George Romney of Michigan and Nelson Rockefeller of New York had already, for all practical purposes, dropped out. Ronald Reagan was still in and was considered a possible candidate, but on the whole, the prospects for winning not only the Republican nomination but also the election in November had improved for Warren's old rival and current critic of the U.S. Supreme Court, Richard Nixon.

Seven days after the assassination of Robert Kennedy, on Wednesday, June 12, 1968, a memorandum from an aide appeared on the president's desk: "Justice Abe Fortas called to say that Chief Justice Warren would like to see the President at the President's convenience. Shall I schedule Chief Justice Warren for an appointment later this week?"

Johnson scrawled a heavy check mark beside the "Yes" column and said he would see the chief justice the following day, June 13.

On Thursday, June 13, at 9:25 A.M., Earl Warren entered the Oval Office in the West Wing of the White House. The room itself, overlooking the Rose Garden and affording troubled presidents a view straight through to the tall statue of Thomas Jefferson across the Tidal Basin, had the look of ultimate power: the American flag, the presidential flag, three television screens and two wire service machines, and the big, impressive-looking desk. Its present occupant did not.

Johnson was seventeen years younger than his visitor, but the worries of the war in Indochina had begun to show in his face and the way he walked. In contrast, Earl Warren's complexion was still ruddy, and his eyes were lively. Although his hair was white, he was the younger looking of the two.

He was seventy-seven years old, Earl Warren told the president, and he wanted to make sure it was Lyndon Johnson who would have the opportunity to appoint his successor. Johnson urged him not to resign, asked him to think it over some more. But for once the president's powers of persuasion failed. Warren's mind was made up.

"Well," Johnson asked, "have you got any candidates?"

"No, Mr. President," the chief justice replied, "that's your problem."

The president thought for a moment. Then he asked: "What do you think about Abe Fortas?"

"I think Abe would be a good chief justice," Warren answered. He left the Oval Office at 9:45, promising to send Johnson his letter of resignation the same day.

Later that day Johnson got in touch with the Senate minority leader, Everett McKinley Dirksen of Illinois. Dirksen was a skilled parliamentary tactician as well as a florid orator. The two men had worked well together as a team on important legislation when Johnson had been majority leader, and the president might well need the Illinois senator's help now. He told Dirksen about Warren's visit.

"Have you any suggestions?" Johnson asked. The two men discussed several possible nominees, including Cyrus Vance, then United States representative to the Paris peace talks.

Finally getting down to business, the president said: "What about Abe Fortas?"

"Well," Dirksen replied, "he was on the Yale Law School faculty. He's a bright, brilliant lawyer, in fact, and now he's been on the Court for three years. I know of nothing," Dirksen declared, "that has come to my attention to impeach his record or to denigrate him in any way."

The two men left it at that for the moment. A week or so later Dirksen promised Johnson he would support Fortas's nomination. The immediate question was why the Senate Republican leader, during a presidential election year in which a Republican's chance of winning was thought at this point to be good, would support a Democratic lame-duck president's choice for such an important post. Dirksen later angrily denied that Johnson had paid for the promise by persuading Illinois Democrats to field a relatively weak candidate for senator against him that year and by reviving the Subversive Activities Control Board in which the senator was particularly interested and the fortunes of which had been languishing. There actually is no record that the two men discussed these subjects at all. But not all debts or payments in Washington are recorded; few, however, are forgotten.

As rumors began to circulate that the chief justice had resigned, suggestions regarding his successor began to inundate the White House. Justice

Douglas almost immediately scribbled a note urging consideration of Fortas for the position. Other candidates included Henry H. Fowler, secretary of the treasury, Attorney General Clark, Texas federal Judges Sarah T. Hughes and Homer Thornberry, and former Senator Thomas Kuchel, whom Warren as governor had appointed to the United States Senate to fill out Richard Nixon's term after the latter was elected vice president in 1952. Evangelist and friend of presidents Billy Graham, appropriately enough, said it was his "prayer" that Johnson give "serious consideration to balancing the Court with a strong conservative as Chief Justice"—Governor John Connally of Texas, for example.

The president discussed the appointment with members of his cabinet and close aides, including the problems associated with a lame-duck president's authority to appoint a chief justice. Attorney General Clark reassured him: There was ample precedent for it, beginning with John Adams's appointment, between his defeat at the polls and his successor's inauguration, of John Marshall. "The President," Clark told Johnson in a memorandum, "is empowered by the Constitution to appoint Justices of the Supreme Court. The President's powers are the same throughout his term." Legally, constitutionally, perhaps. Politically the president's powers are not the same throughout his term, particularly those of a lame-duck president who was at that very moment opposing the popular anti–Supreme Court mood expressed by the Congress in the omnibus crime bill and whose choice for chief justice was a prominent member of the Court's majority. Nevertheless, Johnson pushed on.

He courted the Senate leadership, particularly the southerners, who were not likely to be enthusiastic about the Fortas nomination. Democrat Russell Long of Louisiana had called Fortas "one of the dirty five" who sided with the criminal against the victims of crime. Senator McClellan, author of the anti-*Miranda* provision in the omnibus crime bill which even now the president was doing his best to defeat, had been hard put to conceal his dislike of Fortas back in 1965 during the latter's appearance before the Judiciary Committee as a nominee for associate justice; Fortas's joining with Warren, Black, Douglas, and Brennan in matters of criminal justice including the *Miranda* ruling had not improved his standing with the Arkansas lawmaker. Just recently, riding between the Capitol and the Senate Office Building on the Senate subway, McClellan had told his fellow southerner Senator Eastland of Mississippi he hoped Eastland would not, as chairman of the Judiciary Committee, keep Fortas's nomination from being put to a vote on the Senate floor; he was looking forward to having that "SOB formally submitted to the Senate" so he could fight the nomination there.

On June 25 Johnson summoned Richard Russell of Georgia to the White House. Besides being Johnson's own former mentor, Russell, as chairman of the Armed Services Committee, which he operated more like a fiefdom than an arm of democracy, was one of the most powerful of the southern senators. Russell shared the sentiments of his fellow southerners regarding Abe Fortas, but he was a duck-hunting companion of Homer Thornberry of the U.S. Court of Appeals for the Fifth Circuit, whom Johnson had shrewdly decided to name to Fortas's seat when Fortas became chief justice.

"I will support the nomination of Mr. Fortas for Chief Justice," Russell promised the president, "but I will enthusiastically support Homer Thornberry." Johnson picked up the telephone and called Thornberry while Russell was still in the Oval Office. He told Thornberry what Russell had said, then told Thornberry for the first time that he had decided to nominate him for the Supreme Court. He handed the receiver to Russell, who repeated his assurance of support to the new nominee.

So far, so good. Johnson had the most powerful Republican plus one of the most powerful Democrats—who was also a southerner—enlisted. Then he got his first hint of trouble, which came packaged in the rotund presence of the cherubic-looking and politically canny James Eastland, chairman of the Senate Judiciary Committee. Eastland arrived in Johnson's office on June 26. The president already had the nomination papers "fixed out," Eastland said later. Johnson recounted his conversation with Richard Russell the previous day, hoping the Georgian's promise of support might "moderate Eastland's position." Eastland was aware of Russell's position, he told the president; he did not believe, however, that when everything was said and done, Russell would in fact support Fortas.

"Mr. President," the Mississippian warned, "this appointment is going to be terribly unpopular. He's not going to be confirmed by the Senate and he's going to tear this country up. . . . It will generate a lot of ill feeling in the country."

"Well," the president replied, "I don't want to ask you to do but one thing, and that's not to make a statement."

"I'm not going to make a statement," Eastland said.

"Well, I'm going to ask you something else," the president added. "Will you let him out of the Judiciary Committee?"

"Yes," Eastland promised, but added, "at my own time." What the senator had left unsaid was that "my own time" might well mean after the Republican convention, scheduled for early August. James O. Eastland knew that following the convention, when the Republicans had a ticket and a strong possibility of winning, they would defeat the Fortas nomination. They wanted to name their own chief justice; that, said Eastland, was "just the law of politics."

Later the same day, at his regular press conference, Johnson announced what had become virtually public knowledge, at least in Washington: Chief Justice Earl Warren's resignation. Warren's note was not a simple retirement notice but specified it was to be "effective at your [the president's] pleasure," leaving Johnson and Warren some options. At the same time Johnson announced his choice for Warren's successor: his old friend and adviser, whom he had sent to the Court as associate justice three years before, Abe Fortas of Tennessee. Johnson had already discussed, he said, the appointment with the Senate leadership, Democratic and Republican, as well as with members of the Senate Judiciary Committee, and he anticipated a careful review; but in the end he believed the Senate would confirm the nomination. To succeed Fortas as associate justice, he had named, as a tacit sweetener of southerners, another old friend and fellow Texan, Homer Thornberry.

The reaction—a preview of things to come, although it was not apparent at the time—surprised the president. Senate Republican leader Everett Dirksen had promised his support, and Johnson had expected other Republicans to follow. They did not. Foreseeing a rise in their presidential fortunes come November as well as the specter of a civil libertarian elevated to the highest judicial position in the nation, they followed, instead, Robert P. Griffin of Michigan, who, with Republican Senator George Murphy of California, was circulating a petition opposing any appointment prior to the November elections; by the end of the day it had nineteen signatures, and the Republican senators were threatening to filibuster when the nomination came to the floor for a vote. Senator John G. Tower of Texas added that "with the Court in adjournment and the American people about to pick a new administration which may considerably re-orient the philosophy of our national government, it would be a major mistake to presume to fill such an important role."

Richard Nixon, who had begun to believe he had a good chance of heading that new administration and who was about to launch a campaign a substantial part of which was based on criticism of the United States Supreme Court under Earl Warren, responded indignantly. Abe Fortas, although Nixon did not say it, stood for everything Richard Nixon stood against. While Nixon was chasing so-called subversives out of government during the fifties, Fortas was defending in the courts government employees discharged on security grounds. Now Nixon was chastising the present Supreme Court majority for its oversolicitude for criminal defendants, going so far as to adapt the dissenters' viewpoints to his political campaign; as a lawyer Fortas had fought too, for the rights of criminal defendants in the courts and during his three terms as associate justice, had been a dependable member of the Court majority which was fastidious in protecting those very rights, including those of Ernest Miranda.

Arriving at Lansing, Michigan, in the last month of his pursuit of the Republican presidential nomination, Nixon complained that the timing of the Fortas appointment was all wrong and warned that it could well bring on a "political donnybrook" that would do unforeseeable damage to the Supreme Court's prestige. A "new President with a fresh mandate," he declared, ought by rights to have been allowed to choose the next chief justice. Not a president who was finished.

Chapter 5

The pieces were falling into place. First the legislature had registered its strong dissent to *Miranda*. The presidential candidacy of Richard Nixon held the potential for the executive not only to do likewise but, through future Court appointments, to add the authority of the judiciary. With all three branches of government lining up against *Miranda* its fortunes at this moment in constitutional time, the summer of 1968, looked bleak indeed.

RICHARD NIXON'S BOOK

CHAPTER 1

Convention Hall, Miami Beach, Florida. August 8, 1968.

A lot of southerners would have preferred Ronald Reagan, but the delegates to the Republican National Convention had rejected the California governor. A symbol of the radical right, he could not, they believed as they recalled Barry Goldwater and the presidential election of 1964, win a national election. He had given the winning candidate some panicky moments as he threatened to siphon off southern delegates, but South Carolina's Strom Thurmond, tramping from caucus to caucus, had taken care of it.

A lot of easterners would have preferred Nelson Rockefeller, but the people who made up the core of the Republican party—small-town, middle-class, self-reliant, and self-made—as well as the professionals who brokered the candidacies, had little enthusiasm for the New York governor's social programs and internationalism. He had read his defeat in the primaries and the polls and had withdrawn from the campaign some months earlier. Although he had maintained a staff and a convention headquarters in the Americana Hotel, cheek by jowl with the "spiciest, splashiest, stark-nudest review this side of Paris," the feebleness of his effort to win the presidential nomination at this stage had been surpassed only by its futility.

So there was Richard Nixon again, just as they had predicted in 1964, neither radical conservative nor social adventurer, the "likeliest man to weld together the dissident elements of right and left," the choice of a lukewarm South, a traditionally Republican West and Midwest, and a reluctant Northeast. It was men like Richard Nixon who had made the party of Lincoln a shelter for such discordant elements as William McKinley and Theodore

Roosevelt; the Lodges, senior and junior; Strom Thurmond of South Carolina and Jacob K. Javits of New York. There he was, waggling his fingers in the familiar V sign as the delegates thundered approval and waved their cowboy hats and boaters with the red, white, and blue bands in the air. It was his fourth time to stand before the Republican party as a national candidate, his second time to stand as the party's presidential nominee, to watch the balloons float down from the ceiling, to feel the waves of adulation break over him.

Alone, tramping the beaches of Montauk, Long Island, the week before the convention, returning to his cottage to scribble his thoughts on the now-familiar long yellow legal pads, reading them into a recorder, playing them back, revising, playing back, re-revising, the candidate had honed and polished every line of his speech, practiced every sound and gesture. A few minutes before he strode onstage, he had sat in a mobile trailer outside Convention Hall and made last-minute changes while his make-up was being applied.

Now he looked out over the cheering crowd—predominantly white, Protestant, college-educated businessmen—gathered to hear his acceptance of the nomination to the highest elective office in the nation. The balloons were spent, and the cheering had stopped. The candidate's fingers had stilled their waggling, and the smile had faded from his face. He was troubled, he said, as he looked at America and listened to its sounds. His voice was low and somber.

His was not a complicated message, and he cloaked it in generalities about respect for the flag and interspersed it with euphemisms about forgotten Americans and criminal coddling by the courts. Underneath it all, though, what he had to say was both simple and direct: Invoking the American Revolution and the subsequent amassing of wealth by Americans as "the most successful war on poverty in the history of nations," he would reassure all those middle-class Americans living in fear, the terrible fear of continuing change which had so dramatically and drastically altered the social, economic, and political maps of post–World War II America, the fear of losing what they had, that during a Nixon administration there would be no more change; he would replace its agents, rewrite its precepts, reconstruct its framework, as if such measures could bring back the old America, the one that still lived in their hearts and the paintings of Norman Rockwell.

On the grounds that they had brought the nation only an "ugly harvest of frustration, violence, and failure," he attacked the social and economic programs of the past three decades which threatened the security of white middle-class America—programs to benefit the unemployed, the cities, the poor—and promised to "quit pouring billions of dollars" into them. What had made America great, he declared, was not "what government did for people" but what "people did for themselves over 190 years in this country."

There had been no programs when he, Richard Nixon, had been growing up in Yorba Linda, a small farming community that subsisted on its barley fields and its lemon, orange, and avocado groves about thirty miles from Los Angeles in the heart of Southern California, a country more midwestern than western in its assumptions, peopled as it was largely by immigrants from Ohio, Kansas, and South Dakota. Richard, whose father, Frank Nixon, had come from Columbus, Ohio, his mother from Butlerville, Indiana, had absorbed early in life the dimensions of the American dream, its rigorous requirements having been transplanted to compatible soil under the California sun.

Born on January 9, 1913, Richard was the second of the Nixons' five sons, of whom all but the third, Donald, were named for early English kings (Harold, Richard, Arthur, Edward). He later described his father as a "scrappy, belligerent fighter" from whom the boy had inherited a "respect for learning and hard work, and the will to keep fighting no matter what the odds"; however, despite the elder Nixon's abundant energy, competitiveness, and wide range of skills, he was a luckless man who lacked the ability to master the rudiments of success in any of his various business enterprises, which at one time or another included a lemon grove, a gas station, and a general store. It was always the other fellow who came up with the gold watch, and when in 1922 Frank Nixon, offered the choice between sites in Whittier and Santa Fe Springs two miles away, chose Whittier for his gas station and moved his family there, oil was discovered on the other site the following year.

There had been, though, no whining. The young Nixon had worn hand-me-downs, delivered groceries, picked beans, and pumped gas in his father's station to earn his way during the early years. Later he kept the books in his father's store and managed the vegetable department, worked as a swimming pool janitor one season and as a barker for the wheel of chance at the Slippery Gulch Rodeo in Prescott, Arizona, another—this last while his mother scrubbed floors to support his brother in a tuberculosis sanitorium. The Nixons were poor, never seeming to get ahead of the bills, and had not the young Richard possessed a superior intellect and what became known at Duke University Law School as an "iron butt," the combination of which assured him substantial scholarship help, he might not have been able to go to college at all.

It was the "iron butt" quality of those Americans like himself for whom the dream had come true without government aid that he was describing to the delegates as, wiping tears from his eyes, he compared his own experiences to those of another child who awakens from the sleep of childhood "to a living nightmare of poverty, neglect and despair," who fails in school and ends up on welfare. "For him the American system is one that feeds his stomach and starves his soul," and the Republican candidate declared to the American voters that what the nation needed was not "more millions on welfare rolls but more millions on payrolls." (Cheers and applause.)

As if to heighten the contrast between the people he was speaking to and

Richard Nixon's Book

those he was speaking about, only a few miles to the west, in the sweltering Liberty City ghetto of Miami proper, 600 national guardsmen, equipped with gas masks and armed with flamethrowers, rifles, and sawed-off shotguns, had swept in that day to help local police quell the city's first racial disturbance. It had begun the previous day as a scheduled twelve-hour miniconvention to rally black "vote power." It had quickly turned into an orgy of looting and fire-bombing which, before it spent itself some forty-eight hours later, left three blacks dead and hundreds wounded. It was the most recent in a series of riots since 1965 whose roots lay deep in America's historically discriminatory political, social, and economic soil and which burgeoned at a single incident. The assassination of Dr. Martin Luther King, Jr., the previous spring had set nearly all the nation's black ghettos afire. This latest Miami outburst was believed to have been caused by the failure of Republicans meeting nearby, all isolated by their air conditioning and chicken-wire fences, squads of Florida State Police and blue-and-white uniformed Wackenhut security guards, to hire residents of Liberty City among the many hundreds of local workers engaged to keep the machinery of democracy functioning smoothly during this convention week.

The United States Supreme Court had been the most visible agent of the changes in American life about which the candidate was speaking. The Court had ruled prayer in public schools unconstitutional, destroying an established custom—and who among the delegates this night did not recall the daily opening ceremony of the grammar school, the Pledge of Allegiance and a prayer? At the same time the Court allowed pornography in theaters and on newsstands. Of all the changes the Court had wrought in America, though, that in the relationship between the races was the greatest and most visible. That was the change that most anticipated a redistribution of the American heritage. One did not have to read a Court decision to see its results; one saw it every day in school classrooms, in newly desegregated neighborhoods, in apartment houses, on voting lists. The change was nationwide in varying degrees, but the change had been greatest in the South, Strom Thurmond's home country, where Nixon was doing a good deal of his political banking this year. The public resentment at the nine men who had changed the relationship between the police and their prey was real enough, the fear of crime being second only to the fear of blacks. But the candidate's criticism of the justices this night for their decisions that had "gone too far in weakening of the peace forces as against the criminal forces in this country" meant more than that. He was putting into words a twenty-year accumulation of resentment at the people who were changing life in America and a twenty-year accumulation of fear for the future.

Exploitation of fear was a skill Richard Nixon had mastered over the past two decades. His promises to voters that night that "the wave of crime is not going to be the wave of the future in the United States of America," that the restoration of law and order would be a linchpin of his administration—

promises that elicited louder cheers and longer applause from the delegates in the audience than even his promise to end the war in Vietnam, which had siphoned off the nation's manpower, energies, and resources for more than half of one of those decades—were only superficially different from his promises as congressman, senator, and vice president that he and his fellow Republicans, if elected, would destroy that other threat to the security of American voters, communism.

Richard Nixon had not created the Communist issue then any more than he had created the crime issue—both were real enough—and he had carefully refrained from the excesses indulged in during the same period by his fellow Republican Senator Joseph R. McCarthy of Wisconsin. But he had exploited it during the uncertain days of the postwar period as events in Europe pointed up the dangers in Soviet expansion and Winston Churchill was warning the world's democracies about Moscow's international goals, adding the words *iron curtain* to the vocabularies of the West. As the two great powers seemed to move toward confrontation, Nixon had played on the fears of those who did not perhaps understand the nuances of atomic age politics and saw only the mushroom cloud, who worried about communism, or rather about annihilation, of which the Soviet Union would be the instrument.

Anticommunism had been Nixon's route to high office. Alger Hiss had been the vehicle. Nixon's vow to the convention delegates this night to begin the restoration of law and order in America by appointing a new attorney general to replace Ramsey Clark recalled for many of them his formula for winning political victories: Simplify, sloganize, personalize.

Get Ramsey Clark. Get Alger Hiss.

Much later, two friends of Nixon offered contradictory opinions regarding the significance of the Hiss case in his political career. One friend told him the Hiss case had made him vice president and a candidate for president. The other told him the Hiss case had kept him from being elected president in 1960. Commented Nixon: "Ironically, both of my friends may have been right."

The House of Representatives to which Nixon was elected in 1946, its informal as well as its formal power structure geared to a seniority system that could require twenty years—ten terms—for a member to make his way through the chairs to a minor subcommittee chairmanship, was not a place where a young and ambitious man, however dedicated and hard-working, could get ahead quickly. Unless he wanted to fade into the walls, seldom heard from again, as most of the 435 House members did, he had to find another route, a controversial issue or a popular cause with which to become identified. The coincidence of Richard Nixon's identification with Alger Hiss was perhaps the single most serendipitous event of his entire political career.

Committee work was the lifeblood of the House of Representatives and a congressman's committee assignments shaped his legislative career; a prestigious one—Appropriations, Foreign Relations, Judiciary, for example—was much to be desired. On arrival in Washington in January 1947, the freshman congressman from California's Twelfth District was assigned to the Committee on Education and Labor—not high society, perhaps, but not bad—and the Un-American Activities Committee, whose recent witch-hunting among Hollywood celebrities had robbed it of its former good name. This latter assignment Nixon described at the time, in one of his less prescient moments, as a political "kiss of death."

Nevertheless, he took his duties seriously. He was entirely familiar with the Communist issue itself, having made it the centerpiece of his recent campaign for the House. Now he read all he could on Communist infiltration of American institutions, discussed it with knowledgeable people, and on February 18, 1947, in his maiden speech to the House of Representatives, spoke for the Un-American Activities Committee in asking for a contempt of Congress citation for Gerhart Eisler, the leading Communist agent in America who had refused to testify before the committee. In the early fall of 1947 Nixon had sailed for Europe, a member of a select congressional committee assigned to report on conditions there for use in devising a new foreign aid plan—what became widely known later as the Marshall Plan—and as he observed how local Communist parties were gaining footholds in the European democracies, his opposition to communism was strengthened even more. In the spring of 1948, working with fellow Republican Karl Mundt of South Dakota, Nixon helped prepare, and, as floor manager, shepherded through the House, the Mundt-Nixon bill, which had as its intent the outlawing of the Communist party. Sent to the Senate, it died there in committee; portions were later incorporated into the Internal Security Act of 1950, known as the McCarran Act. Nixon had been in the House for two years with very little to show for it.

Then came the case of Alger Hiss.

In the summer of 1948 the Un-American Activities Committee was winding down a series of hearings during which it had inquired into the subject of foreign espionage in the United States. Suddenly one of the witnesses, Whittaker Chambers, an apostate from communism and in 1948 an editor of *Time*, publicly accused Alger Hiss, former high State Department official, aide to Roosevelt at Yalta, one of the architects of the United Nations, and in 1948 respected head of the Carnegie Endowment for International Peace, of prior membership in the Communist party underground. In a superb performance two days later, his cultured tones, firm voice, and conservative dress contrasting favorably with Chambers's obesity, dishevelment, and faltering testimony—the testimony of an admitted Communist—Hiss appeared before the committee and denied, under oath and categorically, the accusations.

When, that same morning, President Truman, whose administration was being criticized by Republicans for tolerating what they said was subversion in government, called the committee's investigation into espionage a "red herring" whose purpose was to divert the public's attention from the real problems that postwar Americans faced, several committee members wanted to drop the case.

Except for Richard Nixon's stubbornness, the whole Hiss-Chambers affair might have petered out then and there.

However, Nixon's legalistic habit of mind had already caught Hiss's failure, while vehemently and absolutely denying his Communist associations, to deny equally vehemently and absolutely that he had ever known Whittaker Chambers, and his doubts about the veracity of the elegant Harvard Law School–educated Mr. Hiss had begun to surface. Hiss was, Nixon said later, "too suave, too smooth, and too self-confident to be an entirely trustworthy witness." And Nixon, the youngest member of the Un-American Activities Committee, persuaded his senior colleagues that they had nothing to lose and possibly much to gain by pursuing the case further.

There followed—and it was described in detail on page one of nearly every daily newspaper in America—Nixon's relentless pursuit of Hiss, his persevering questioning of the two principals, the televised confrontation between them—the first time a congressional hearing submitted to the klieg lights and cameras of the new medium, a fringe benefit of which was the added national exposure afforded the young California congressman—the melodramatic discovery of Whittaker Chambers's microfilms of State Department documents which appeared to implicate Hiss and which had been hidden in a hollowed-out pumpkin behind Chambers's Maryland farmhouse, the long and tedious trials of Hiss, and finally his conviction for perjury in 1950.*

Volumes have been written about the case of Whittaker Chambers versus Alger Hiss in addition to those written by the two principals. Reporters have ferreted through mounds of transcripts, diaries, letters, memoirs, newspapers, FBI files. Some investigators began as partisans for one or the other of the principals and never wavered in their convictions. Others began as partisans for one of the men and midway transferred their allegiances to the other. Some began as nonpartisan and became partisan. For all the investigations and all the millions of words written on the subject, however, the facts of the relationship among Alger Hiss, Whittaker Chambers, and their country and between themselves remain incomplete.

The facts, however, as they are prone to do, soon fell into disuse, the principals as individuals faded into obscurity. Testimony was cited less and

---

* Hiss served three years and eight months in the federal prison at Lewisburg, Pennsylvania, got time off for good behavior, and was released in November 1954, during the time Nixon was vice president of the United States. He has since lived in New York City, working as a salesman for a printing firm, lecturing on his case, mostly to college student audiences, and trying to clear his name through the courts. His version of events, *In the Court of Public Opinion*, was published in 1957.

Whittaker Chambers left *Time* and retired to his Maryland farm. His autobiography, *Witness*, was published in 1952. He died on July 9, 1961, at the age of sixty.

less; political conviction, more and more. If one was a "liberal," one believed Alger Hiss was the victim of a right-wing conspiracy to discredit the Roosevelt and Truman administrations, Whittaker Chambers a cheap informer, Richard Nixon the devil incarnate, and the Communist conspiracy theory an exaggeration, if not a political hoax. If one was a "conservative," one believed Alger Hiss a traitor, Whittaker Chambers a patriot, Richard Nixon a true-blue American hero, and liberals "soft on communism."

In the short run, the conviction of Alger Hiss reclaimed the good name of the House Un-American Activities Committee whose members had been warning the public for years, without success, that just such questionable characters existed. It offered the junior senator from Wisconsin Joseph McCarthy, in addition to credibility, a premise on which to base his argument that the government, particularly the State Department, was infested with Communists; in fact, on February 9, 1950, two weeks after Hiss had been sentenced to prison, McCarthy, addressing the Republican women of Wheeling, West Virginia, made his first—and best-known—speech on the subject marking the beginning of a witch hunt that named an era and shamed a nation.

In the long run, the Hiss case dramatized the problems posed to the body politic by national tensions, in this case by the growing intensity of the cold war: the potential for divisiveness, the susceptibility to conformity by intimidation, the tendency of people of all persuasions to rely on extreme measures, the inclination to stifle intellectual debate with shibboleths, the desire to blame America's failures on some external force—and the political potential in appeals to fear.

Richard Nixon had made the Hiss case, and the Hiss case made Richard Nixon. Hiss became the symbol of Nixon's anticommunism, a transference that removed some of the complexities surrounding the maintenance of the national security and made the larger issue more comprehensible: a simple political allegory of the struggle between virtue and vice.

The events that ultimately boosted Nixon to the vice presidency of the United States began on a small scale in 1948. Thanks to extensive press coverage of his pursuit of Alger Hiss and the growing popularity of television, Nixon's intense mien had become known outside his California district and, his own reelection to the House assured by his winning of both the local Democratic and Republican primaries the previous June, he was invited to speak across the country in behalf of the Dewey-Warren ticket.

Although in the fall of 1948 the outcome of the Hiss case was uncertain—the pumpkin papers and Hiss's trial were still in the future—and the national candidates were avoiding the issue of domestic communism, Nixon freely discussed his investigation of Hiss, finding considerable interest in it among his audiences. In the fall of 1950, the Hiss case had been resolved in court, Senator McCarthy had become a national figure, domestic communism had become a major political issue, and Nixon was elected to the

Chapter 1

United States Senate following a particularly ugly and now-famous campaign against Helen Gahagan Douglas whom he accused of near-traitorous conduct.

Then, in 1952, it all had paid off when he had come to the notice of another Republican presidential candidate, Dwight Eisenhower, on the basis of his handling of the Hiss case—his doggedness in pursuit of the evidence combined with his "fairness in the investigating process." Eisenhower had introduced him to the Republican National Convention delegates as "a man who has shown statesmanlike qualities in many ways but has a special talent and ability to ferret out any kind of subversive influence wherever it may be found, and the strength and persistence to get rid of it," and instructed Nixon to use the Hiss case, Nixon later recalled, as a "text from which I could preach everywhere in the country," an assignment Nixon carried out with diligence and shrewdness, making Alger Hiss the symbol of the Communist threat and the repository of the nation's fears. He crossed the country, strewing accusations that the Democratic presidential candidate in 1952, Adlai Stevenson, who had given a deposition as a favorable character witness for Hiss, with whom he had worked in the Agricultural Adjustment Administration in 1933 and on United Nations business in the mid-forties, had gone "down the line for the arch traitor of our generation" and asking: "Can such a man as Stevenson be trusted to lead our crusade against Communism?" Two years later, as vice president, Nixon kept the issue alive as he recrossed the country for Republican congressional candidates, reminding his audiences in the thirty-one states where he campaigned that year that Alger Hiss would be out of the penitentiary in a few days and that the previous administration, were it still in power, would probably have given Hiss a federal pension. He would then bring down the house when he declared: "Because of the Eisenhower policies, he will not get a federal pension, and anybody like him will not get a federal pension."*

Communist infiltration of government as a campaign issue had disappeared by 1956, the demise of its political usefulness hastened somewhat by external events which by 1956 seemed to favor the United States. Joseph Stalin had died in March 1953, and the armistice ending the Korean War had been signed the following July; confidence in Western European security had been bolstered by the establishment of the North Atlantic Treaty Organization and in Asian security by the establishment of the Southeast Asia Treaty Organization. Joseph McCarthy was censured by his Senate colleagues. And while the Republican party continued to politic against the seating of Communist China in the United Nations, the emphasis had begun to shift from confrontation toward negotiation, toward summit conferences, disarmament

---

* Alger Hiss was released from prison on November 27, 1954. His government pension was restored to him in March 1972, during Richard Nixon's second term as president, as a result of a court suit. One of the judges on the unanimous three-judge panel, Roger Robb, had been appointed by Nixon.

treaties, and the courting of the emerging third world in order to meet the Communist threat. Alger Hiss was all but forgotten.

But what was not forgotten was Richard Nixon's involvement in Hiss's case and his use of it during subsequent political campaigns. Nixon himself became a symbol of sorts, for the unsavory in political styles—personalizing problems, pugnacity, bitter sarcasm, insinuation, and innuendo—so that when Americans went into the voting booths on November 8, 1960, to choose between Richard Nixon and John Kennedy for president of the United States, the ghost of Alger Hiss returned to make Nixon's character— as Nixon had made the character of others—an issue in the election, and they pulled just enough Democratic levers to elect John Kennedy. It was not the only issue, or even the most important issue that year; but it was a close vote, and there were those who wondered whether Nixon, without the albatross of Alger Hiss, might not have squeaked through to the presidency.

Now in 1968 he had reconditioned the old engine, adapted it to contemporary issues.

Ramsey Clark was a tall, thin, mild-mannered Texan who, like his father, had been taken into the Justice Department as part of a political legacy and worked his way into the attorney general's office. Nixon himself had little fault to find with him, and in mid-campaign, as publicly he criticized Clark, he confided to aides: "Ramsey Clark is really a fine fellow . . . he's done a good job."

As the nation's chief law enforcement officer, Clark had achieved a modest and largely unpublicized success in his attempts to diminish the flow of marijuana and opium through a new Bureau of Narcotics and Dangerous Drugs, for the establishment of which he had been responsible, and to frustrate some operations of organized crime largely through a new program called Strike Forces, which he had also sponsored and which combined federal and local resources in concentrated doses in selected cities. He was committed to the professionalization of law enforcement officers and the betterment of the corrections system. What had been more widely publicized and what Richard Nixon seized on was Clark's putting on record the Justice Department's opposition to what became Title II of the omnibus crime bill as it was making its way through Congress and his determination, after Title II became law, to ignore it and continue to enforce the *Miranda* ruling.

Ramsey Clark had replaced Alger Hiss as villain.

"If you don't have law enforcement officials that back up the police and enforce the law, just forget it," Nixon had told a recent meeting of delegates from seven southern states and the District of Columbia as he went about the business of hustling the votes that would bring him to this moment. The federal government, he had said, had been setting an example of "law softness" instead of law enforcement, and he promised a "new attorney general of the United States who is going to observe the law." He wanted a man who "has had experience in law enforcement. Maybe one of the strong U.S. district attorneys across this country—in a big county."

As the Republican candidate slogged on toward the presidency, the attacks on the attorney general would increase in frequency and volume, his responsibility for crime in the United States heightening.

His acceptance of the Republican nomination for president had been a typical Nixon oration; a tour de force of slogans, *ad hominem* attacks, insinuation, appeals to patriotism, and appeals to fear, the waving arms, modulations of his voice, and the wiping away of tears adding to the emotional climate. The delegates loved it. They applauded when he promised a new foreign policy, but they stomped and cheered when he promised that "the wave of crime is not going to be the wave of the future in the United States of America." And when it was over, it had taken several minutes before they were quiet enough for Dr. Billy Graham, evoking the sacred names of Washington at Valley Forge and Lincoln in the "dark days of the Civil War," to pray for the continued health of America and to give the benediction.

It was not the sort of speech *The New York Times* reporters would think much of, Nixon remarked to William Safire, one of his speech writers, as he unwound over a Scotch and water later that night in his eighteenth-floor penthouse suite at the Hilton Plaza. The candidate shrugged.

CHAPTER 2

The next day, Friday, August 9, 1,000 miles to the west of the "We Want Nixon" chants, the balloons, the red, white, and blue boaters, the telephone rang at the LBJ Ranch, the vacation White House in the central Texas hill country near Austin. Senator James Eastland, for whom the recent events in Miami, particularly the nomination of a man whose preferences in Supreme Court justices coincided with his own, had not been without significance, was calling from San Antonio. Might he drop by the ranch a little later in the day with some Mississippi folks who'd like to "pay their respects" to the president? A surprised but pleased Lyndon Johnson told him to come right on down, and shortly afterward the visitors' plane was seen circling and about to land.

Differences regarding matters of public policy did not necessarily alienate senator from senator, and if Lyndon Johnson and James Eastland had never become intimates, they shared a mutual respect developed during the twelve years they had served together in the United States Senate. Eastland, in fact, despite his obsessions with race and communism, was widely respected among his colleagues, Republican as well as Democrat. He was tough, shrewd, and stubborn, but his word could be depended upon absolutely. If his Gothic politics carried with it a tinge of cynicism, his administration of the Senate Judiciary Committee was fair and democratic, and he was not, said a fellow senator of another political persuasion, "like some of those 'high-minded' ones who beat you by calling a vote when you're in the men's room."

He had earned the chairmanship of the Judiciary Committee through the seniority system: He had been the ranking Democrat when Chairman Harley M. Kilgore of West Virginia died in 1956. The Senate took tradition as well as its prerogatives seriously, from the seniority system to the snuff-boxes on the desks, to the bean soup served in the dining room, where the best tables, along the walls, were traditionally reserved for senior senators. There were a lot of Democrats who would have preferred a less arrogantly racist chairman for this committee, under whose jurisdiction fell nearly all civil rights legislation as well as nominations to the federal judiciary, including the U.S. Supreme Court, of which Eastland had been so critical. But under pressure from the outside to skip over the ranking Democrat, the senators had closed ranks, followed tradition, and elevated the Mississippian. Now he sat in a seat of real power.

It was precisely because of Eastland's position as chairman of the Judiciary Committee, through which the president's nomination of Abe Fortas to be chief justice was proceeding—extraordinarily slowly—that the president was pleased when Eastland invited himself to the ranch for the afternoon, and Johnson greeted his former Senate colleague and the other Mississippians warmly.

So far Eastland's prediction that Fortas would not be confirmed by the Senate could hardly be disputed, although the turn events were taking could not be laid to Johnson's lack of industry. His aides had lunched and breakfasted with recalcitrant or undecided senators, mostly southerners and Republicans from whom the bulk of the opposition was coming. Top-echelon Justice Department officials were in touch with the legislators. Cabinet secretaries had lists of senators to contact. Hawaiian businessmen had been enlisted to lean on Republican Hiram Fong; the California Jewish community, to lean on Republican George Murphy. A local textile manufacturer had promised to get in touch with North Carolina's Sam Ervin. The first Jewish president of the Nebraska bar and former campaign manager for Republican Roman Hruska was in touch with the Nebraska senator, and both business and labor leaders in Michigan "who could be helpful in at least slowing up" Republican Robert Griffin, leader of the opposition to the nomination, had been put to work.

But the outlook was not, in August 1968, encouraging, and the hopes of those who had planned on a Fortas Court to succeed the Warren Court had diminished. Some support had fallen away—Richard Russell of Georgia, on whom Johnson had been counting heavily, had reconsidered his early promise to the president and joined Griffin's movement; some opposition, like that of Senator McClellan, had hardened, following the president's instructions to federal law enforcement to ignore that section of the omnibus crime bill that was intended to nullify *Miranda*.

Supporters of the nomination had hoped the Senate would vote to confirm Fortas before Congress recessed for the national conventions. But they had reckoned without the political sense of the opposition, the advantage in delay, always a formidable weapon, and the added advantage in publicizing the nominee's views, particularly on criminal justice, immediately before the delegates met to choose candidates for an election in which crime as an issue would figure prominently. Instead, in July, the committee had strung out nine days of hearings over nearly three weeks.

It was not politic anymore, even in the South—where despite the persistence of custom in racial relations blacks were beginning to vote in increasing numbers thanks to the Voting Rights Act of 1964—to talk about race, and so the southerners on the Judiciary Committee had paraded out every other reason why this prominent and outspoken member of the majority on that Court should not become chief justice.

Fortas's personal dealings with Louis Wolfson had not been discovered yet, but the senators were not without damaging material. Particularly the southerners on the committee explored in minute detail and with some table thumping the legalistic question of whether or not a vacancy actually existed on the Supreme Court until Earl Warren resigned unequivocally and the ethical questions surrounding Fortas's continued involvement in White House matters long after he had been appointed to the Supreme Court. Authorized by the Constitution only to decide "cases and controversies," the justices of the Supreme Court were supposed to keep their distance from the other branches of government, a matter they had settled early when they had refused to write advisory opinions for President George Washington; however, some presidents had committed political adultery informally, openly as well as clandestinely with certain justices: Woodrow Wilson had had his Louis Brandeis, Harding and Coolidge their William Howard Taft, Hoover his Harlan Fiske Stone, FDR his Felix Frankfurter, Harry Truman his Fred Vinson. Now Lyndon Johnson had his Abe Fortas, a matter the senators did not take lightly.

But the fiercest opposition, eliciting a torrent of senatorial emotion and heightening the hearing room drama, was reserved for the exploration of judicial questions involving the rights of criminal defendants on which Fortas had joined with Warren, Black, Douglas, and Brennan to create the Court majority which the Republican candidate for president was even now accusing of "weakening the peace forces as against the criminal forces in this country." Senator Ervin bore down particularly hard with his questions surrounding the Supreme Court decision in *Miranda v. Arizona,* a ruling which illustrated, he said, "an overweening [*sic*] . . . solicitude for the welfare of those accused of crime, and it overlooks a very significant truth, that society and the victims of crime are just as much entitled to justice as the accused." The *Miranda* ruling, the onetime prosecutor charged, had been "designed to encourage all persons suspected of crime to keep their mouth shut." He added, in an emotional paraphrase of Justice White's dissent to *Miranda:* "It could not have been more efficacious in its design if those who promulgated it and studied the subject had studied for a thousand years to find a rule that will keep anybody from confessing to guilt."

Senator Thurmond had momentarily lost his customary self-possession in recalling a 1957 case in which the rape conviction of Andrew Mallory had been reversed because of an illegally obtained confession. It didn't seem to matter that Fortas had not been on the Supreme Court then; *Mallory* had long rankled; now, like *Miranda*, it had become a code word for the Supreme Court. "Mallory!" Thurmond had thundered. "I want that name to ring in your ears . . . Mallory, a man who raped a woman, admitted his guilt, and the Supreme Court turned him loose on a technicality. . . . Can you as a Justice of the Supreme Court condone such a decision as that? I ask you to answer that question."

Fortas did not, of course, answer it. Outwardly calm and patient, he had sat through four days of questioning in much the same manner he had sat through the same sort of questioning by the same people for the same reasons in 1965: quietly, relying on his sense of humor, ignoring the appeals to emotion, and invoking the judicial prerogative of refusing to answer questions regarding individual cases or regarding issues which might come before the Court.

But the senators had made their point, had shown the public, disinclined to split hairs in matters of judicial behavior, what scoundrels were deciding public policy. The Senate Judiciary Committee, having killed half the summer, had then dropped the whole matter. Congress had recessed for the conventions, and Fortas's nomination remained locked in the committee until the legislators returned after Labor Day.

The requirement in Article II, Section Two of the Constitution that the president's appointments to the Supreme Court be confirmed by the Senate was just one more check in the government system of checks and balances, a way, Alexander Hamilton had argued in *The Federalist*, Number 76, to eliminate a "spirit of favoritism in the president and . . . to prevent the appointment of unfit characters from State prejudice, from family connection, from personal attachment, or from a view to popularity." It was one more method the authors of the document had devised to thwart human temptations. Prior to 1968, the legislature had exercised its veto power in twenty-two out of 128 nominations to the Supreme Court, although of these twenty-two, three had been renominated and subsequently confirmed. Nine of these who were not confirmed had been nominated during a president's last term in office; however, seven appointments made by lame-duck presidents had been confirmed by the Senate. History, then, was not conclusive on that particular question.

Contemporary politics was perhaps more to the point. Lyndon Johnson himself had named eleven persons to the lower federal judiciary since his decision the previous March 31 not to run again, and all eleven had been quietly confirmed by the Senate. Eastland always said that the lame-duck argument against Fortas's confirmation had not been the real reason for the opposition. Fortas's public positions were the real nomination killers, an analysis the July hearings before Eastland's Judiciary Committee, during which the senators had attempted to cook the nominee on a skewer of his positions regarding criminal defendants, including Ernest Miranda, had done nothing to contradict.

Now, the day after the nomination of Richard Nixon, anti-Court candidate, had further strengthened Republican opposition to the Fortas appointment in the Senate, the author of the appointment stood face-to-face with a man who, although he had promised not to block it, was a symbol of southern opposition to it. They took a drive around the ranch.

In Washington, Lyndon Johnson was only the president of the United States; at the ranch, down here on the Pedernales, he was king. In Washington, they snickered at his country manners; here at the ranch, they enjoyed his country hospitality. The president gave the senator the VIP tour.

He patiently tried to sketch for Eastland the Abe Fortas he and Lady Bird knew: the able lawyer, the dear friend, a man of rare quality. But Eastland would not be deterred. Abe Fortas, he told the president, would not be confirmed, and there would be no vacancy for Homer Thornberry.

The two men reminisced about the years they had spent together in the Senate as they inspected the cow barns and herds of Hereford cattle. They railed at each other good-naturedly as they trudged through the auction barn. But the senator remained firm. Abe Fortas would not be confirmed.

Just before dark the Johnsons returned their guests to the plane and waved their good-byes, neither the president nor the senator having yielded. Privately, however, Johnson strongly suspected the Republicans, with whom Eastland was often ideologically allied and with whom he frequently worked closely in the Senate, had promised that come the new administration in January, they would make a considerably more tolerable appointment if the Mississippi senator would just keep Abe Fortas from becoming chief justice of the United States. The nomination of Richard Nixon the night before only reinforced the senator's confidence. And so Johnson realized, following that early August afternoon meeting with Eastland, his noncandidacy having reduced his leverage, his IOUs uncollectible anymore, his dams and his post offices all gone, "we probably could not muster the votes to put the Fortas nomination through. . . ."

Two weeks later Chief Justice Warren told a luncheon meeting of Montana Supreme Court justices that "there seems to be a little maneuvering going on in Washington, and it looks like I'll be back to open the Supreme Court in October."

Back in Washington, Lyndon Johnson, not without some bitterness creeping into his tone, promised that unless Fortas was confirmed, Earl Warren would stay on another five years, no matter *who* won the election.

Chapter 2

* * *

It was hardly evident as George Corley Wallace, spitting periodically into his handkerchief, stepped down the ramp from his ancient propeller-driven DC-4 which had landed minutes earlier at Chicago's Midway Airport, that political prosperity had caught up with him. His eyes were dark-rimmed from exhaustion, his blue suit was shiny, and reporters were complaining about the dry cheese sandwiches and stale coffee aboard the plane. Nevertheless, on this bright, breezy day, the last day of September 1968, the presidential candidate of the American Independent party stood at the peak of his political career. Back in July, pollsters had begun to chart steady evidence of progress as the former Alabama governor's share of the straw votes rose from 13 percent, where it had remained steady for several months, to 21 percent, where it now stood, and Louis Harris was hypothesizing that if voters were to cast their ballots that very day and the two major issues were race and law and order, Wallace's share would "spurt" another five points. Amid defections—five prominent North Carolina Republicans, three of them members of the state executive committee, had recently deserted to join Wallace—the Alabaman was claiming the 170 electoral votes of the entire South and border states, and Richard Nixon's staff was willing to concede as many as 90 or 100. People—not people in bars or at Tupperware parties but people like Republican eminence Gerald Ford—were discussing seriously the possibility of Wallace's keeping either major candidate from getting a majority of the electoral vote on November 5 and dragging the election into the House of Representatives—an eventuality which was conferring on a political upstart a disproportionate measure of power.

The presidential campaign of 1968 was not to be distinguished for its intellectual quality or its thoughtful approach to social problems like crime in the streets. It was already evident that George Wallace, who had told a joint session of the Louisiana legislature on June 22, 1966, only a week following the U.S. Supreme Court's decision in Ernest Miranda's case, that the Court had been "sitting on a continual constitutional convention, changing and altering the law from day to day," and whose anti-Court pronouncements since did not indicate any inclination of his to raise the level of debate, was having a catalytic effect on that campaign.

Chicago. America's second city. Carl Sandburg's "city of the big shoulders." Black slums hidden behind the wall of skyscrapers that lined the lake—the urban secret that could no longer be kept. Cultural beacon for the Midwest. Market for its meat and grain and steel.

Daley's domain, one of the last remnants of 19th-century machine politics. Convention city: scene of the Democratic National Convention the previous month, not only a meeting of the nation's politicians to choose a presidential candidate but an unscheduled meeting of war protesters and police, whose brutal antics, recorded by the television cameras, shocked a nation as

237

well as upstaged the convention proceedings. The emergence of Lyndon Johnson's vice president, Hubert H. Humphrey, as the Democratic candidate and Maine's Senator Edmund S. Muskie as his running mate was anticlimactic. Lake Michigan breezes had cleared away the tear gas, and the men of the sanitation department had picked up the remains of the stink bombs and broken bottles in time for Richard Nixon to open his own campaign for the presidency of the United States here the following week, September 4, and 400,000 Chicagoans had turned out to watch his motorcade as it plowed through the Loop area, heart of the downtown.

Now it was George Wallace's turn to come to Chicago, the first stop on a six-day tour of the North which would take him to thirteen cities in Michigan, Indiana, Ohio, Pennsylvania, New York, and New Jersey. Ethnic signs—in Italian, Polish, Lithuanian—welcomed him as his eight-car motorcade inched along State Street past a noon-hour crowd of 100,000 cheering (and some jeering), confetti-throwing Chicagoans. If the crowd was not as large as the one Nixon had attracted, it was astonishingly large for an invader from Alabama, certainly one of the largest Wallace had attracted north of the Mason-Dixon line during the past four years.

He was a natural campaigner, to which advantage had been added long experience. Hardly anyone in Clayton, Alabama, where Wallace grew up, remembered when he wasn't running for something. Nestled among low, grassy hills in the southeastern corner of the state and ringed by small farms which served to emphasize the contrasts with the rich plantation South, Clayton was the seat of Barbour County, a county which had sent a disproportionate number of governors (seven) plus a lieutenant governor to Montgomery, and politics was catching, offering as it did a way out of the back-country poverty that had afflicted the region for longer than anyone cared to remember. Wherever coffee was served, people gathered to talk not about seed and fertilizer and rain and this year's crop, as people in rural areas do, but about politics. And when the fellow at the next red-plastic-topped table in the local drugstore got elected to office, they talked politics some more, and well, one thing led to another.

His daddy took young George, when he was sixteen, to the State Capitol to run for page, his first campaign, which, after shaking hands with all the state senators and asking for their votes—a fairly sophisticated exercise for a boy—he won. When he graduated from the University of Alabama Law School in 1942, he was already thinking about running for Governor.

He began, however, by running for a lesser office. All one spring after World War II, in which he had served as a flight engineer on a B29, he'd alight from school buses or dusty automobiles in which he'd hitched rides— he didn't own a car—and talk to farmers in their fields. His hair slicked down—then, as decades later, it looked as if he brushed it with shoe polish— his tie askew, he'd stop in drugstores and barbershops. He'd show up at barbecues and church suppers and country sings all over Barbour County. And all of a sudden he was the fellow at the next table in the drugstore who got elected, and he was representing Barbour County in the state assembly up at Montgomery.

Elected an alternate delegate to the Democratic National Convention in 1948, he succeeded the elected delegate when the latter became too sick to attend. When fourteen Alabama delegates and others among the southern delegations, protesting the strong civil rights plank in the national party platform, walked out of the Philadelphia convention and later that summer held their own States' Rights party convention in Birmingham, where they nominated Strom Thurmond of South Carolina for president, George Wallace remained behind with eleven other Alabamans and confined his protest to seconding the nomination of Senator Richard Russell of Georgia for president.

Wallace remained in the state legislature for six years, until 1952. A follower of Alabama's popular populist governor, Big Jim Folsom (whose niece became Wallace's second wife), he came to be regarded back in Barbour County as a "dangerous left-winger" for his legislative offerings in favor of such social programs as new mental hospitals, vocational and trade schools, and even a "free hog-cholera treatment" bill.

When the legislature was not in session, he practiced law in Clayton— the usual fare for a small-town general practice: estates, deeds, wills, and a smattering of criminal law. In view of his subsequent pronouncements regarding the administration of criminal justice, it is worth recounting one of Wallace's own tales of his work as the defense lawyer in the case of a local man accused of murdering his wife by planting sixteen sticks of dynamite under her bed:

> Well, there was never any question who did it. . . . There was right strong community sentiment. They thought it was right ugly of him. So the case came on for trial, and I thought they were going to hang him. But we brought his 14-year-old boy into the courtroom . . . and I sat him down with us at the table. And every time the solicitor would get to working on the jury telling 'em what an awful crime it was, I'd lean over to the boy and say, "Sonny, he's trying to *kill* your daddy." The boy would start cryin' and blubberin' and puttin' his arm around his father. Well, sir, we cried away all afternoon, and when it came my time to sum up, I jus' whispered to the jury: "Please don't kill this boy's daddy." They let him off with life.

In 1952 Wallace was elected to a county judgeship. Then, in 1958, he finally realized his youthful ambition to run for governor. He lost, ran again in 1962, and won. To preserve his political base, since Alabama law prevented him from being reelected, he sponsored his wife's candidacy in 1966, and although she carried out the ceremonial aspects of the governorship and kept a rolling pin on her desk—which was flanked by the American, Georgia, *and* Confederate flags—there was little doubt who the real governor was: He held court in a little office behind the enormous, lushly carpeted, and paneled governor's quarters as if nothing except location had changed. His wife's death from cancer in 1967 slowed him momentarily but did not either distract or divert him from his goals, and having attracted a substantial following when he took his message to the voters of Wisconsin, Indiana, and Maryland in 1964, here he was in 1968 running for president of the United States.

Not as a Democrat, however, although he had grown to political maturity in the Democratic party. There was nowhere for an ambitious southern governor to go in the Democratic party. He was said to have been "within days" of conversion to Republicanism in 1964, as Barry Goldwater stumped his home country on a platform that came close to Wallace's own beliefs; but Strom Thurmond got to the font first, and Wallace apparently did not want his influence at the national level diluted by the powerful senator from South Carolina.

And so he had formed his own American Independent party, a loosely organized coalition of "aginners" with no recognizable roots in the tradition of third parties; certainly it would never achieve the stature of Theodore Roosevelt's Bull Moosers or Robert LaFollette's Progressives. Wallace was the only factor each segment of the American Independent party had in common.

At this moment in his campaign he was working assiduously to get the party on the ballots of the states, and only a few days after he left Chicago, on October 15, fellow Alabaman and alumnus of the University of Alabama, Justice Hugo Black of the U.S. Supreme Court, judicial activist in all the matters Wallace was against, speaking for a majority of the same Supreme Court that was playing the villain's role in Wallace's campaign, declared that "the right to form a party for the advancement of political goals means little if a party can be kept off the election ballot and thus denied an equal opportunity to win votes. So also, the right to vote is heavily burdened if that vote may be cast only for one or two parties at a time when other parties are clamoring for a place on the ballot." Ohio, one of the last states to exclude third-party candidates, was ordered to put George Wallace's name on the ballot in time for the November election.

He held the balance of political power in his hands for this moment in the autumn of 1968. There were several possible consequences. He might, of course, win, although no one really believed that he could. He might force the election into the House of Representatives by winning enough electoral votes in the South and border states to deprive both major candidates of a majority; the result would be electoral chaos, and although it was unlikely that Wallace would be in a position to bargain for southern interests when in the House each state, whose representatives came from the two major parties, had but one vote, no one really knew what would happen, and no one wanted to learn through experience. Or he might push the Republican candidate into increasingly extreme positions.

This last appeared the most likely result. Wallace had sensed in the mood of the white American workingman many of the same fears and frustrations Richard Nixon had sensed in the mood of the white middle-class American, and the only difference between them now was one of style, between redneck and establishment; as the campaign for the presidency wore on, even that difference would diminish.

There were two central facts of George Wallace's existence, both of which made him a hero to the workingmen who lined the streets wherever he went. One was his southern birth. Early in his career, he had told a Sunday-school teacher in Clayton that "we just can't keep the colored folks down like we been doin' around here for years. . . . We got to start treatin' 'em right. They just like everybody else." When in 1958, however, he lost the Alabama gubernatorial election to a diehard segregationist, he had vowed never again to be "outniggahed." On January 14, 1963, he had stood where Jefferson Davis had taken the oath as president of the Confederacy and took the oath as Alabama's new governor, then cried out for all the world to hear: "Segregation now! Segregation tomorrow! Segregation forever!"

In the North his vows translated into slogans about states' rights and federal interference, but they meant the same thing. And because it was the white workingmen whose neighborhoods were being desegregated, whose children were being bused to desegregated schools, whose wives were vulnerable to criminal attack, whose jobs were the first to be threatened by the growing number of black men in the labor market, and who felt powerless to deal with all these threats and frustrations, it was the white workingmen who were also attracted to the combative and at the same time reassuring tone of George Wallace. They stood up and cheered when Wallace berated the justices of the Supreme Court who, they believed, had led this new march of egalitarianism in decisions, in matters of race relations particularly but also in matters of criminal justice; they did not appear to recall that a similar social upheaval, the union movement, had turned steelworkers into homeowners and coal miners into buyers of automobiles, at the expense, it was charged at the time by the establishment, of the economic echelon immediately above.

Wallace had been a populist governor of Alabama, with a special interest in education. During his term he had built fourteen new junior colleges and fifteen trade schools, initiated a free textbook policy, and started a $100 million school construction program so that, as he had promised in his 1962 campaign, "every boy and girl in Alabama could live at home, eat at their daddy's table, go out to the edge of the yard and get on a bus free of charge and go to a two-year trade school or junior college free of charge." But he said little about his populism outside Alabama.

The second significant fact of George Wallace's existence was his poverty. Where Richard Nixon had come from what used to be called shabby genteel—though his poverty was nonetheless real—George Wallace's poverty had been abject, more akin to that of Justice Douglas. Where Richard Nixon had made his way into the Republican establishment, George Wallace, whether by design or not, had remained outside the regular political establishment, independent, iconoclastic. His breath had steamed the window as he watched the Bourbons—the Eastlands, the Thurmonds, the Russells, the Longs—divide up the South, just as the white workingman was watching the economic pie divided, as he believed, inequitably. And Wallace voiced the frustrations, felt the alienation of the American working class.

This candidate, who had been cutting sharply into the major candidates' blue-collar support, had chosen to stage the day's biggest rally in late afternoon on a street corner in suburban Cicero, just west of Chicago proper, where in one of the world's greatest industrial complexes, more than 150 factories were concentrated in less than two square miles. All white, largely working-class, this was Wallace territory. The first of the crowd arrived two hours before the rally was scheduled to begin. They kept coming until 10,000 people were packed into the street, pushing against the ropes that cordoned off the speaker's platform.

Said the Cicero fireman, after ritually cursing the local Republican ruling class: "Wallace is for us, the working class. The other candidates don't give a damn about the working class."

Added an old man standing nearby: "He won't let the niggers walk on him. He won't let nobody walk on him. He'll knock them all down."

"We Want WALLACE!"
"We WANT WALLACE!"
"WE WANT WALLACE!"

And even after the candidate appeared, a diminutive figure flanked by labor leaders from Alabama and Georgia, the chant threatened to drown out his voice. It was less a political rally than a revival meeting.

The crowd loved Wallace, and he loved the crowd back. They shared a visceral passion, given with abandon, not from the mind or even from the heart but from the gut. This was his life, his agony, his ecstasy. It was widely believed among his friends in Alabama that he was only vaguely conscious of any life except campaigning; he rarely knew what he ate, money bored him, and his attention to family, home, and friends, about which ordinary men cared deeply, was cursory at best.

His style was pure redneck, and it had been said that his studying at the University of Alabama had left no visible marks on him. His style, however, was misleading. He possessed wit and urbanity and all the graces for drawing-room success despite some rudeness in his background, and if his tenor twang and back-country accent remained always a part of him, he also knew when to eat sausage with his fingers and when to use a fork, when to say "*elec*toral" and when to say "electo*rial*."

Chapter 2

He happened to be standing on a street corner in Cicero, Illinois. He could have been standing on a flag-draped platform in a Lakeland, Florida, stadium or in a Providence, Rhode Island, ballroom. He had a set speech, although the lack of spontaneity did not appear to diminish either his enthusiasm or his ebullience.

A joke or two. Then he takes on the "pseudo-intellectuals," the "pointy-heads," the "intellectual morons," the "bearded professor who thinks he knows how to settle the Vietnam war when he hasn't got enough sense to park a bicycle straight." (Cheers.) Busing schoolchildren in the name of racial equality comes next. (Raucous cheers.)

"Let's hear it for the local police!!"

George Wallace had recognized the growing alienation of policemen and had capitalized on it in 1964. Now, in 1968, he was making even more determined efforts to win what began to be called the cop vote. And so while Hubert Humphrey, the Democratic candidate for president, was tramping around the nation, urging its citizens to support their local police with higher salaries, better training, more modern equipment, and gun control legislation—all politically bankrupting propositions, underlining as they did the assumption of police inadequacies as well as the high price of crime control— Wallace made do with cheers and scapegoats. Reporters traveling with him began to comment on the large numbers of police who turned out to protect the candidate at airports and hotels and along the routes of his motorcades. They wore gold Wallace tie clasps and Wallace buttons. They crowded around him to grasp his hand or to ask for his autograph, and they generally agreed with a veteran of the Syracuse, New York, police force who said, "Wallace is saying the things in public that we'd like to say and can't. This guy gives us an outlet. . . ."

His fists flail the air; he spits out the words faster and faster as he winds up to Communists and criminals running wild, thanks to the decisions of the United States Supreme Court. He had been promoting this last into the major domestic issue for more than a year, adding for one interviewer that the Supreme Court was a "sorry, lousy, no-account outfit" and for another that he'd sponsor a "mountain-climbing expedition for some of them to draw off some of their excess energy." It's just tragic that murderers and rapists are "just laughin' while the police are crying for help."

But a Wallace administration would change all that, he promises his audience, wildly cheering by now. "If we were president today," he declares, "you wouldn't get stabbed or raped in the shadow of the White House, even if we had to call out 30,000 troops and equip them with two-foot-long bayonets and station them every few feet apart," and he further promises to make the national capital safe "for your children to visit." He adds his now-famous warning: If a criminal "knocks you over the head" on your way home from work, he will be "out of jail before you're out of the hospital and the policeman who arrested him will be on trial." To which he adds, the twang in his voice emphasizing the absurdity of the situation: "But some psychologist says, 'well, he's not to blame, society's to blame. His father didn't take him to see the Pittsburgh Pirates when he was a little boy.' " His tone becomes serious again: "Well, I was raised in a house that didn't even have an indoor toilet. My mama couldn't even buy me a dollar and 15-cent cowboy suit that I saw in the Sears Roebuck window. But I didn't go and bust the window to get it."

The street-corner speech in Cicero ended a long day of campaigning for George Wallace. When it was over, he made his way to the nearby Hyatt House auditorium for a press conference before leaving for Grand Rapids, Michigan, where a raucous crowd of 8,000 would meet him in the high school football stadium the following day, and where the "pointy-heads" and the "bearded professor" and the "lousy no-account" Supreme Court justices would be pressed into service again, like so many marionettes bobbing up and down in the background.

As the nation approached a time which held some of the same potential for damaging judicial institutions as the McCarthy era had held for damaging other American institutions, George Wallace was emerging as the Joseph McCarthy of his day, pushing the Republican presidential candidate into increasingly extreme positions, becoming catalyst to the campaign.

Nixon believed, he later recalled, that the Wallace candidacy would make the race for the presidency "very close," and the Wallace bumper stickers along his motorcade routes and the hecklers in the crowds did nothing to change his mind.

Nixon's position vis-à-vis the Wallace candidacy had been settled early, during that first week after the Republican convention, when the Republican candidate had taken his organization to Mission Beach, California, to plan the fall strategy. It had been decided then that although Nixon would not mention Wallace by name, the Republican would appear as "a more respectable alternative" to the Alabaman, countering his rhetoric "with a velvet-glove version of the mailed fist."

There were a lot of issues in that presidential campaign of 1968. The war in Vietnam dominated, of course, issues of foreign policy. Social Security, welfare, usual fare—inflation and taxes—Lyndon Johnson's War on Poverty were worked into the speeches, Hubert Humphrey, the Democratic candidate, promising to continue his president's government programs, Nixon making it abundantly clear there would be no social adventuring by a Republican administration. But the issue that stood out, its theme in every speech at every airport and on every makeshift stage, the one that was remembered most vividly years later, was the Republican candidate's appeal for "law and order." If he had intended it as a "velvet-glove version of a mailed fist," it had not come out that way in the actual doing. In the end it was no less emotional, no less simplistic, no less grounded in fear than George Wallace's.

In his first major address on "crime in the streets," a half hour talk broadcast over the NBC and CBS radio networks on Sunday, September 29, Nixon did present some skeletal programs against crime which he promised to establish: a cabinet-level National Law Enforcement Council to coordinate federal policies on crime prevention and control, a National Academy of Law Enforcement to help in the modernization and professionalization of local police departments, a National Coordinating Center to coordinate the efforts of independent groups and institutions, and a series of town hall conferences on crime. These promises quickly got lost in the shouting. In most of Nixon's speeches, in fact, it was only the shouting that seemed to be heard at all, and parts became so set that reporters traveling with him could mouth whole paragraphs—ahead of the candidate.

The centerpiece of the law and order campaign engaged in by the Republican candidate for president was the American judiciary and in particular the justices of the United States Supreme Court. A little more than a year previously, in August 1967, Nixon had read in *U.S. News & World Report* excerpts from Warren Burger's commencement speech given at Ripon College in Ripon, Wisconsin. He had been impressed with what Burger said about the administration of American criminal justice. His adaptation of the jurist's ideas to his own speeches for the 1968 presidential campaign held significance, of course, for the immediate future; it was also the beginning of a deeper association between the two men, one that shortly added the voices of the chief executive of the nation and the head of the judiciary to those of the legislative branch against *Miranda.*

Taking the emotional view over Burger's judicial view, as he had during most of his political life, Nixon concentrated on the parts of the speech that cited rising rates of crime and criticized the courts and, by an easy effort of transference, turned the Burger address into a reprimand of courts for their "technicalities" that released "confessed murderers and rapists" and went too far in "weakening the peace forces as against the criminal forces in this country."

If Nixon's law-and-order speeches were more grammatical, if his attacks on the Supreme Court were more tempered than George Wallace's characterization of the Court as a "lousy, no-account outfit," Nixon's appeal was no less emotional; he quoted no arguments, and he cited no constitutional requirements:

Whenever I begin to discuss the Supreme Court, Mr. Humphrey acts like we're in church. . . . I have great respect for the Supreme Court. I respect the men on it. But the Supreme Court is not infallible. It is sometimes wrong. Many of its decisions break down 5–4, and I think that often in recent years, the five man majority has been wrong, and the four man minority has been right.

... And I think that some of the decisions of the Supreme Court have weakened the peace forces as against the criminal forces in this country. I support legislation to restore the balance.

Then, returning to a theme of his acceptance speech, he promised to replace those justices who were soft on crime—the way he believed those many years ago the entire Truman administration was soft on communism—as if they had deliberately defied the commands of the Constitution:

We need more strict constructionists on the highest court of the United States. We need men who have the deepest reverence, not for every decision handed down, but for the Constitution of the United States. In my view, the duty of a Justice of the U.S. Supreme Court is to interpret the law and not to make the law, and the men I appoint will share that view. ...

Unless provoked, as when the Democratic candidate in mid-September had accused him of paying off his debt to South Carolina Republican Senator Strom Thurmond by attacking the courts and helping delay the confirmation of Abe Fortas as chief justice—"He could have Mr. Fortas confirmed in a week if he'd say the word," Humphrey charged, "because it's his troops in the Senate, his supporters, that are blocking the confirmation"—and he had denied any involvement in the maneuvering of the senators, Nixon held his peace on that whole subject. He really didn't need to say anything. His attacks on the Supreme Court majority, of which Fortas was a reliable member in matters of criminal justice, his support of the dissenters made his position plain enough.

Toward the end of every rally, moments before the candidate's arms shot up and his fingers made the double-V sign, he predicted that law and order would return to the nation the moment the incumbent attorney general left the Department of Justice—a prediction for which he was generally rewarded with clapping, stomping, whistling, and shouting. If elected, he would appoint a new secretary of agriculture, too, as all incoming presidents did when they replaced the cabinet—and a new secretary of commerce, secretary of labor, the whole shoot. But he did not make an issue of these other appointments when he talked to farmers in Kansas. Ramsey Clark was the villain of this campaign.

If the dynamics of a Nixon political campaign had changed little during the two decades since he had laid the public's fears of communism on the shoulders of Alger Hiss, its packaging had become more sophisticated. The development was a natural outgrowth of the state of modern communications, which had been adapted successfully—perhaps oversuccessfully—to the advancement of political candidacy and which Richard Nixon in 1968 was carrying to a new level of effectiveness. The ballyhoo, balloons, and bunting all were carefully stage-managed now by a new breed of men who had built a profession out of managing political campaigns. These new election men had backgrounds not in political science or history or law but more often in communications and public relations and even show business, and artistry seemed to supersede the cause itself in importance.

This new breed was distinct from the old political pro, whose loyalties were to a man or a party or a cause and whose career progressed along with his candidate. These younger men had adopted Marshall McLuhan as their guru, and excerpts from his *Understanding Media* had been distributed to Nixon's staff during the primaries. "Image" began to replace "issue" in discussions of strategy. They operated in a lateral—and frequently frictional—relationship with the better known and experienced amateurs like Herbert Brownell, who had managed the political end of Eisenhower's campaigns, and John Mitchell, Nixon's law partner who was managing the political end of his in 1968. They had exploited the new technology, particularly television and the computer, to automate the campaign. They read polls to write speeches. They worried about other such nonpolitical matters as stage sets, camera angles, how to display most advantageously the candidate's sense of humor and personal warmth, and how to hide most effectively his five o'clock shadow. This aspect of the presidential campaign had been reduced to the level of mass merchandising, and the candidate might as well have been a package of cigarettes or a box of cereal.* The candidate and the medium, maturing together, had come a long way since that day in 1948, when the klieg lights were set up in a congressional hearing room for the first time and cameras recorded the questioning of Alger Hiss by a young California congressman.

There was the airport stop, with the candidate seated on a flat-bed truck, flanked by local candidates and mentally rehearsing what he would say about Bismarck, North Dakota, while the local high school band warmed up the audience. There was the major rally where up to 10,000 people, mostly white and middle-class—the Nixon organization had a system for keeping out "undesirables" who might not photograph well—gathered in the biggest auditorium for miles around to be inspired by a 1,000-voice choir singing "The Battle Hymn of the Republic" and the candidate berating Hubert Humphrey, Ramsey Clark, and crime in the streets. There was the television panel show with the candidate issuing freshly made-up from a dressing room—rather than dusty and hot from a Pullman car—to face a panel of hand-picked local interrogators for an hour, expounding on the issues that affected the region in which the show was to be broadcast. (The purpose was to allow Nixon an opportunity to concentrate on local issues, but it also allowed him to fudge certain issues on which there might be regional differences of

---

* See Joe McGinniss's *The Selling of the President 1968* (New York: Trident Press, 1969).

opinion, like the busing of schoolchildren in the name of school desegregation.) And there was the television commercial, during which the law-and-order spiel was delivered against a background of a lonely policeman reaching into a call box or a lone woman walking down a deserted city street on a rainy night, the clack-clack of her heels fading into the darkness. Only the scream was missing.

Once Nixon departed from the new rituals, and that was only to satisfy the voraciousness of the television cameras for new and different material. The place was Ohio, where it had been reported that the Wallace vote was loosening and might be ripe for plucking. And the vehicle chosen was the old-fashioned whistle stop, which had gone out with Harry Truman's presidential race in 1948.

Following one of the biggest rallies of the season the night before—16,000 of the party faithful had turned out in the Cincinnati Garden—during which Nixon had put his political arms around Ohio Attorney General William Saxbe, who was running for the U.S. Senate, promised to "pour it on" for the last two weeks before election, and promised further to "restore again freedom from fear in the United States of America," the Republican candidate gathered together his family, sixty-five Ohio Republicans, fifty members of his staff, fourteen Nixonaires (ex-airline stewardesses for Nixon), nine United Airline stewardesses, and employees of the railroad, and entrained northward. All that day the train clacked up to Cleveland, stopping at factories and farms and small towns, where Nixon, flanked by Secret Service men, told Ohioans about the crime wave that had broken over their quiet land and threatened to drag them under.

"I was looking at some figures that my staff prepared for me on the 45-minute train ride from Lima up here to Deshler," he told the people of Deshler as twilight descended over the grain elevator and the eastern sky began to darken. "In 45 minutes, just 45 minutes . . . here is what happened in America. There was one murder, there were two rapes, there were 41 forcible crimes. . . .

> I was in Philadelphia the other day. I found that a cab driver who had been cruelly murdered and robbed, and the man who murdered and robbed him had confessed the crime, was set free because of a Supreme Court decision. An old woman, who had been brutally robbed and then murdered—the man who confessed the crime was set free because of a Supreme Court decision. . . . And an old man who had been robbed and clubbed to death—and the man who confessed the crime was set free in Las Vegas because of a Supreme Court decision. My friends, when that's happening in thousands of cases all over America, I say this. Some of our courts have gone too far in their decisions weakening the peace forces as against the criminal forces in the United States of America. And we're going to change that. . . . I believe we can have judges on that Court who will respect the Constitution . . ."

Chapter 2

Nixon had edged as close to George Wallace as he dared. His political advisers, including his top aide, John Mitchell, applauded; but his media men were horrified, as were Republican Governor Raymond Shafer of Pennsylvania and John Eisenhower, the former president's son, who were preparing to receive him shortly in Pennsylvania, and at their bidding, he softened his tone some during the last two weeks of the campaign. It was not to be Law and Order Day in Michigan or Pennsylvania or New Jersey or California, states which remained to be wooed, as it had been in Ohio.

In the long run it probably did not make any difference. The campaign was nearing the end. Nixon had had his say. The slogans, spoken over and over again, the fears poked over and over again, the assurances that in a Nixon administration the United States Supreme Court—along with those other social adventurers—would get its comeuppance—these were firmly embedded in the minds of the electorate as well as in political history.

The apparent Olympian detachment and serenity of the justices as the Court opened for business as usual, despite the controversy that swirled beyond the big bronze doors of their building, in no way meant that they were unconcerned about the turn events had taken or that they had no response to the attempt of Congress, succumbing to a seizure of political expediency, to nullify the Court's decision in *Miranda* v. *Arizona* legislatively, and now to Richard Nixon's making the judiciary a major campaign issue, promising that if elected, he would appoint to the Court only "strict constructionists."

"He's talking about you and me," William O. Douglas remarked with good humor to his friend and longtime colleague Hugo Black. Black laughed, of course, but he was alarmed.

Hugo Black had for some time been fretful lest the behavior of the Warren Court provoke an "extreme reaction," a demand by the public for a return to "law and order," and now his fears were being realized as the Republican candidate for president assailed the Supreme Court for what he kept insisting was its heavy responsibility for the nationwide increase in crime. Nixon was making it sound as if Black and Douglas and Bill Brennan and Earl Warren all were out on the streets themselves, egging on the criminals, as if they were not bound by constitutional and statutory limitations but were free to lock up whom they chose, and it was only their insensitivity, the failure to be horrified at the muggings and murders in the streets, that had created crime.

"That fella," Hugo Black commented to his son, Hugo, Jr., "knows nothing about real law and order. He only knows about the kind of law and order it takes to protect and enlarge the property of special privilege. 'Strict construction' to him just means construction for privilege. . . . He and his bunch are bad fellas. I am not sure this country can survive them. . . ."

And so it had happened that in the early fall of 1968 Justice Black, after discussing the propriety of the matter with his brethren William O. Douglas and Earl Warren, yielded to the importunings of CBS correspondent Martin Agronsky, a longtime admirer who had been pleading for just such an opportunity for several years, and agreed to be interviewed on television.

It had not been an easy decision for Black to make. He was a modest and private man, happy that the tradition of the Court discouraged publicity seeking. It was true that some of his brethren had been actively defending the Court outside its walls since that institution had become a public and political issue in the mid-sixties; not only members of the Supreme Court majority—Black himself had recently given the prestigious Carpentier series of lectures at Columbia Law School—but even those who found themselves in the minority a good deal of the time were out stumping the nation's lawyers in defense of the institution. The dissents of this latter group had been pressed into service as philosophical support for the political attacks upon the Court, and it was apparent from the remarks of its members that they were far from comfortable in that role. Potter Stewart in June 1967 had told members of the Florida bar: "It will remain the business of judges to protect the fundamental constitutional rights which will be threatened in ways not possibly envisaged by the Framers." Two months later, in August, Byron White, speaking to the Conference of Chief Justices, had defended the "unavoidable involvement of judges in fundamental procedural and substantive issues" and cited *Miranda* v. *Arizona* as a prime example. "I see," he had declared, although he disagreed with the result reached in that case, "little reason for the judiciary to apologize for doing as best they can the very job which they are bound to do." And Tom Clark, the policeman's justice, had told an audience at the University of Texas in December 1967 that to blame the Supreme Court for the rise in crime was "but a confession and an avoidance—a confession that police techniques of criminal detection are ineffective and an effort to pass the buck on to the Court"; crime was infinitely more complicated than that and did not "yield to easy and permanent solutions."

These were strong words from a group of men who traditionally did not comment, even obliquely, on public affairs. This sort of stumping, however, political as it was in its own way, was limited to audiences of lawyers and judges, the customary channels of judicial politics. To go on national television was another matter. Black had misgivings about his decision to be interviewed right up until the interview was broadcast. Indeed, he nearly changed his mind several times.

Black's wife, Elizabeth Seay Black, has refuted accounts that the justice's decision to submit to the interview had anything to do with the political attacks on the Court at the time. Having resisted Agronsky's gentle pressures for eleven years, Black did, however, agree to it at a time that respect for the Court was at its lowest point in many years, and Black's son, Hugo, Jr., later wrote that the justice had wanted the people of this country to see "in person the man who had been cast as a symbol of the big bad liberal Supreme

Court; the man who was falsely accused of encouraging disorder on the streets and the boldness of rapists. He wanted Americans to see that this man bore a strong resemblance to the ordinary man and shared the same fears and hopes."

So he had gone through with it, despite the doubts. On the morning of September 19 he had watched, not entirely patiently, while television cameramen tramped through the gracious eighteenth-century house in the historic section of Alexandria, Virginia, one of the capital's close-in suburbs, and planted their lights and wove their webs of wiring through the justice's book-lined second-floor study, a warm and intimate place more accustomed to—and suitable for—serious discussions with law clerks, pleasant predinner conversation over a gin or vodka, and late-night opinion-writing sessions.

On the morning of September 20, he had gone up to the study, where a little cake powder having been applied to his face and balding head, then a bit of dark pencil to his eyebrows, he had taken his place behind his big desk and had sat uncomplaining under the hot lights while Agronsky and fellow CBS reporter Eric Sevareid had questioned him about the law, the Constitution, and the Court.

Producer Burton Benjamin had not wanted to interrupt the concentration of the participants as they explored questions that went straight to the heart of the meaning of America, and he had ordered the cameras loaded with hour-long reels in order to keep reloading to a minimum.

When it was all over, and the questions and answers had been frozen on film, the reporters and their crews left as they had come, in a confusion of dollies, microphones, cameras, and wiring, and the study upstairs in the house on South Lee Street was quiet again.

The broadcast originally had been scheduled for a half hour. When producer Benjamin reached National Airport on his way back to New York, he was in a state of high excitement and telephoned Richard Salant, president of CBS.

"This interview is electrifying," he said, "it must be an hour."

While George Wallace and Richard Nixon were taking the case against the United States Supreme Court before the people of the United States, Republican Senator Everett McKinley Dirksen of the flowing white curls, mellifluous tongue, and golden prose was taking it before his colleagues in the United States Senate, and before this day was out, there would be discerned the possibility that those who would change the direction of the Court would have the opportunity.

The fortunes of the Fortas nomination were at low ebb and sinking this first day of October 1968. After Senator Eastland's gloomy prediction in conversation with the President that August afternoon at the LBJ Ranch, the Mississippi Senator, on his return to Washington, had publicly announced his opposition to the nomination. The hearings before the Senate Judiciary Committee, which had ended inconclusively during the summer, had resumed in September, and it had been revealed that Fortas, in what his friends considered a minor indiscretion and his enemies something akin to bribery, had been financed by a group of businessmen in a lectureship at the law school of American University. The issue of cronyism had been revived by the senior senator from Colorado, Republican Gordon Allott, who had called the White House recently regarding provisions of an appropriations bill and been told by one of the president's staff: "Well, the President is away, but Mr. Justice Fortas is here and he's managing this bill for the White House. . . ." When on September 25 the nomination had finally reached the Senate floor for debate, having been approved by the Judiciary Committee, southerners and Republicans had staged a filibuster to keep it from coming to a vote.

Now the preliminary skirmishing among these 100 men had ended, the promises, the threats veiled and not so veiled, the bargains struck, the press conferences, the answering of telephone calls placed by important constituents, the strategy lunches—all were finished as far as this particular issue was concerned. A vote—probably *the* crucial vote, since the opponents of the nomination appeared to be in the ascendancy—was to be taken that day. Now the filibuster that had begun less than a week ago, when Senator Griffin plopped a sixty-page speech down on his highly polished desk and began to read it, was winding down to its final desultory hour. The Senate was about to vote, not on the nomination itself, but only on whether or not to limit debate on it—a euphemism for whether or not to stop the filibuster. It was one of those parliamentary maneuvers behind which a senator could hide if he so desired, although it was rare that a vote for or against cloture, as cutting off the debate or stopping the filibuster was called, did not reveal the true sense of the Senate on the issue before it. For those who would stop the talk, however, it was a more difficult procedure, because a two-thirds rather than a simple majority was required.

The senior senator from Illinois and minority leader, Mr. Dirksen, had promised the president he would strongly support the nomination of Abe Fortas as chief justice of the United States. He had publicly defended the lame-duck executive's right to make the appointment and defended the appointment on its merits against the senators' charges of cronyism. He had said he not only would vote for confirmation but would also vote to stop a filibuster. Three days ago, on September 27, however, he had abruptly changed his mind, and now, only moments before the senators were scheduled to register their votes for and against stopping the filibuster, he rose from the minority leader's desk and urged them not to stop it, not to "gag" themselves, which was the parliamentary way of saying they should defeat the nomination of Abe Fortas.

Dirksen was not unmindful of the fact that it had been his colleague from Michigan rather than himself who had led the opposition to the Fortas nomination, although politically it would seem to have made more sense for the minority leader to oppose a president of the other party. He was not unmindful, either, that his colleague from Michigan had been very successful in amassing the requisite number of votes to defeat cloture, if not the actual nomination, and that twenty-seven of the thirty-six sure ones had come from his own party. And, perhaps most important, he was not unmindful of the fact that his colleague from Michigan had been one of those responsible for ousting Charles Halleck of Indiana from a shaky minority leadership of the House of Representatives in 1965.

He did not mention these matters to his fellow senators as they prepared to cast their votes. Instead, he concentrated his attack on the recent performance of the United States Supreme Court. He spoke in somber tones, and his message was straightforward, his customary effusiveness and florid style abandoned for the moment.

Just this past June, he reminded his colleagues, the justices of the Supreme Court had further expanded the rights of the criminal defendant when they had decided the death sentence could not stand in a case in which all veniremen who had expressed any qualms whatsoever regarding capital punishment had been automatically excluded from the jury. The case had originated in Illinois, and Dirksen had been advised that all twenty-four persons awaiting imposition of the death penalty in his state might have their cases reviewed. The issue had agitated a substantial number of his constituents, who foresaw the opening of the prison gates for twenty-four dangerous men, and he was running for reelection against the state attorney general, William G. Clark, who was campaigning as a crime fighter. The senator, who had helped shape the Republican platform at the recent convention in Miami Beach, including the part that urged a return to "the principle that men are accountable for what they do, that criminals are responsible for their crimes," was moved to protest.

Abe Fortas was not the author of the opinion in *Witherspoon*, as the Illinois case was called—Potter Stewart wrote it—but Fortas had voted in the majority, had helped make that majority. Dirksen said: "If as a result of the Court's decision in the Witherspoon case the 24 convicted murderers are to have their sentences reviewed or set aside, what do I say to the people of Illinois. . . ? What do I say when they allege that I had this one chance to protest and failed to do so?" Then the senator articulated the theme that was becoming increasingly popular among Supreme Court critics: the cause-and-effect condition, as if the Bill of Rights and the social contract, by definition, could not coexist. "Several times," he continued, "the opinions used the expression 'the conscience of the community.' I, too, am thinking of the 'conscience of the community' where the crimes are committed and the conscience of the larger community of the State of Illinois. . . ." He had had enough, he said, of this "abracadabra." He would not help stop the filibuster, and he sat down.

The clerk called the roll to determine the presence of a quorum. Eighty-three Senators answered. Fifty-nine votes would be needed to invoke cloture, only twenty-nine to defeat it—and, in effect, the nomination itself.

The question was read to the Senate: "Is it the sense of the Senate that the debate on the pending motion [to proceed to the consideration of Abe Fortas, of Tennessee, to be chief justice of the United States] shall be brought to a close?" And the clerk called the roll.

"Allott."

"Nay."

"Anderson."

"Yea."

"Baker."

"Nay."

"Bayh."

"Yea."

Bennett and Boggs, nay.

Brooke and Burdick, yea.

And so it went: Goodell and Gore, yea; Griffin and Hansen, nay. Carl Hayden, the senior senator from Arizona and the senior member of the Senate itself, having been a member since 1912, the year Arizona became a state, broke his unbending rule against invoking cloture and voted yea.

But it was no use. Eastland had been right, and although following his warning back in August, the president had increased his arm twisting among the Senators, he had failed to persuade enough of them. The southerners and Republicans were out in force today, and the supporters of cloture commanded only forty-five votes, fourteen short of the required number; the opposition received thirty-three, and cloture was defeated. For the first time in the history of the United States, a filibuster had prevented a Supreme Court nomination from coming to a vote.

The Senate majority leader, Mike Mansfield of Montana, delivered his colleagues a brief lecture. He respected the right of every senator, he said, "to make his views known and to cast his vote as he sees fit." He believed, however, that "we have raised serious questions about the Senate's responsibility to advise and consent." However, he added dispassionately, his voice flat, other urgent legislative matters, including a $71.9 billion defense appropriations bill, awaited action. He routinely returned the Fortas nomination to the calendar of executive appointments and, giving the president time to consider a future course of action, said he would announce his next move within two or three days. His colleagues returned to their own routines of lunching with constituents, speaking engagements, committee work, and attending to other matters of lesser significance and drama than the nomination of the chief justice of the United States.

There was, of course, no necessity for Senator Mansfield to make a next move. The following day, October 2, Abe Fortas wrote the president asking that his nomination be withdrawn, and the president, defeated, agreed. Johnson briefly considered sending up another name, particularly that of former Justice Goldberg, but indications were that another name would fare no better. Senator Eastland, in fact, informed one of the president's aides that "there is a flat Republican policy of opposition" to any new judicial appointments at all. In the end Johnson decided not to risk it.

The United States Supreme Court, as its chief justice had predicted at the beginning of the summer, opened the 1968 term on October 7 with Earl Warren in his customary seat at the center and Abe Fortas, despite Senator Thurmond's strong suggestion that he resign, in his customary seat at the far right end. The Fortas Court, one of the might-have-beens of constitutional history, was ended before it began.

That fall and winter, several senators of mixed political affiliations, invited because they had been helpful to the president, particularly in the matter of Abe Fortas's nomination, appeared at state dinners for visiting potentates. It was about all the leverage Johnson had left now.

November 5, 1968. Election day.

Except in portions of the upper Midwest and Pacific Northwest where it rained, it was "good Democratic weather," the kind that brings out voters: warm, sunny, and clear. Seventy-three million Americans participated that day in the ritual of democracy.

Of the national candidates, Edmund Muskie, Democratic candidate for vice president, was the first to vote. He had flown all night from Los Angeles, where he had participated, with the Democratic presidential candidate, in a final television appeal. After landing at Portland, Maine, Airport, he had gone directly by automobile to Waterville, his hometown, where he had begun his law practice more than two decades previously. He and his wife plus their son and daughter, both of voting age, together entered the South Grammar School, where voting booths had been set up in the kindergarten. After voting, he left for the Fenway-Maine Motor Inn, where he was scheduled to watch the returns that night. After shaving, he went out to play golf with friends.

Spiro Agnew, the Republican candidate for vice president, had breakfast in the governor's mansion at Annapolis, voted shortly afterward, and later also went out to play golf.

George Wallace arrived in his home town of Clayton, Alabama, at noon to vote at the local courthouse. "This movement is highly successful already," he told the hundreds of well-wishers and newsmen who surrounded him on the courthouse steps. "Both parties are talking like we do for one thing. We've shown that a Southerner can be nominated for the Presidency. And the ideas we've been talking about in my judgment are going to be incorporated in the next administration."

Hubert Humphrey and his wife landed in Minneapolis at 7:50 A.M., following a night flight from Los Angeles. An automobile sped them the 40 miles to Marysville, where they voted in the town hall, a small white frame building with bright green ballot boxes and a potbellied stove to keep the poll watchers warm this cold, rainy, typically November day. The Humphreys—he in a blue business suit, she in a fashionable raincoat—stood out among the other voters, most of whom wore the local uniform of peaked cap and checkered wool shirt. He was reported to be "full of good spirits and energy" as he drove off to his lakeside home at Waverly, a mile or so away, for some relaxation before the returns came in.

For the first time since anyone in Johnson City, Texas, could recall, Lyndon Baines Johnson wasn't there on election day at 7:00 A.M. to open the Pedernales Electric Cooperative, Inc., where aluminum ballot boxes had been set up in a model electric kitchen. He himself had been on the ballot for more than thirty years, first as congressman, then senator, then vice president, and then, just four years before, president. Finally, closer to 9:00 than 7:00, the well-known white Lincoln Continental was spotted at the curb, the president in a cowboy suit and boots at the wheel, Mrs. Johnson in a smart red dress and matching coat alongside Yuki, the president's favorite dog. Johnson was quieter now, more somber, the ebullience with which he had led the election-night victory celebrations over those three decades submerged. Sitting at a large table inside the cooperative, he studied the ballot just like any millworker or coal miner, marked it, stopped briefly—much more briefly than usual—to chat outside, then headed back to the ranch, fifteen miles away in the hill country. The last they saw of him that day was the back of his head inside the big Lincoln, inching its way down the main thoroughfare of Johnson City as he tried to avoid the chickens that scurried in front.

Richard Nixon didn't vote that day. He had already voted, absentee, on October 31. Nevertheless, he was up early, at 7:20 A.M. (Pacific time). Following a light breakfast, he made last-minute telephone calls to his brother, his top aides, and Mrs. Dwight Eisenhower, who was sitting with her ailing husband at Walter Reed Hospital in Washington, then gathered up his family and drove to Los Angeles International Airport, where they boarded a plane for New York at 8:45. Someone had pasted an American flag on the plane's body, and there was a sign, "Air Force One," nearby, both of which were used on the presidential plane; but Nixon was not amused on this particular day, and he talked pessimistically about the election outcome as the big jet winged its way east across the plains. At 6:15 P.M., eastern standard time, the candidate landed at Newark Airport. He was bundled quickly into a limousine right at the plane's ramp and driven straight to the Waldorf-Astoria, where he settled into suite 35H to watch the returns.

By the time he arrived in the suite, at 7:05 P.M., and sent his dark blue suit to be pressed, the national networks had been broadcasting returns for an hour, the electronic vote counters gobbling up every tiny smitch of information and trying to make political sense out of the split in the first five votes cast in a remote Vermont hamlet. At that early stage, with 2 percent of the national vote ingested and digested by the computers, Nixon was leading Humphrey, 44 percent to 36 percent, with George Wallace pulling a potentially dangerous 19 percent. Two hours later Nixon's total had shrunk to 41 percent, Humphrey's had risen to 38 percent, and Wallace's, to 20 percent. In another hour Nixon and Humphrey were even. For nearly twelve hours the results seesawed, and the sun had risen over New York City on Wednesday, November 6, before it was finally determined that the blue suit would be needed, that George Wallace had failed to throw the election into the House of Representatives, as had been feared, that Richard Nixon would be the next president of his United States of America.

Hubert Humphrey conceded near noon, when Illinois went Republican. At 12:30 P.M. Nixon appeared publicly for the first time as president-elect in the ballroom of the Waldorf-Astoria to speak the speech of winners: to jump verbally over the net and shake hands with his opponent, to thank those who had worked in the campaign, to pledge a direction for his own administration.

"I saw many signs in this campaign," he told the bleary-eyed workers who had gathered in the ballroom along with the press. ". . . But one that touched me the most was the one that I saw in Deshler, Ohio, at the end of a long day of whistle-stopping. A little town, I suppose five times the population was there in the dusk, almost impossible to see, but a teen-ager held up a sign, 'Bring Us Together.' And that will be the great objective of this administration at the outset, to bring the American people together."

It was a close election in terms of the popular vote: Of the 73 million votes cast, Nixon won by only about 500,000, with Wallace amassing nearly 10 million. Nixon's 43.3 percent was the lowest percentage for a winning candidate since Woodrow Wilson's in 1912—also a three-legged race. The coattails were not long enough to pick up many riders, either, and the Republicans gained only five governorships, five Senate seats—which still gave them only forty-two—and four House seats—which also did not give them a majority—and for the first time in 120 years a president began his first term with both houses of Congress in control of the other party.

In electoral votes, however, Nixon did much better, receiving 301 to Humphrey's 191 and Wallace's 46, totals that confirmed the wisdom of Nixon's original strategy to concentrate on the American heartland and leave the big northeastern industrial states to the Democrats, who usually won them anyway. He did not carry the entire South but divided it with George Wallace. He did, however, manage to pry loose Virginia, Florida, the two

Carolinas, and the border states of Kentucky and Tennessee, perceiving a clear direction for 1972.

George Wallace did not do as well as expected, receiving only 8 percent of the popular vote outside the South. It was one thing to let off steam at a rally, to cheer and applaud the spokesman for one's subconscious, but when it came down to actually voting, the old union members could not bring themselves to abandon the Democrats for George Wallace. But in the South, attracting support from the upcountry as well as the Black Belt, he had done better than Strom Thurmond in 1948, the last of the favorite sons of the Confederacy to field a serious third-party candidacy, and he had proved a dangerous opponent—a change in only 43,000 strategic votes could have denied Nixon his electoral majority—and he might well prove so again.

Where the votes came from also confirmed the wisdom of Nixon's early perceptions of his electorate. The millions of white Protestant, college-educated business and professional people in their fifties who had formed the core of the delegates to the Republican National Convention back in August—the great expanse of the middle class—to whom he had addressed the main messages of his campaign, made up the bulk of his support. Humphrey, in the Democratic tradition, got the youth vote, the minorities, and the blue-collar workers—from the total of those who voted at all, that is; a lot of Americans stayed home that year, and the percentage of eligible men and women who actually voted dropped from 62.1 percent in 1964 to 61 percent in 1968 despite the excitement generated by the issues.

The unending and enervating war in Vietnam counted heavily in the results of the 1968 election, generally interpreted as a massive repudiation of the Johnson administration's policies there, even though no candidate had offered any clear-cut direction toward ending it. But the social issues were no less important. When the votes of Nixon and Wallace, whose common denominator was hostility to social experiment and change, were added together and this total—56.9 percent—was compared with Humphrey's total of 42.7 percent, the rejection of Johnson's domestic antipoverty programs seems even more startling. Johnson summed up his rejection this way:

> ... [T]he Democratic party had pressed too far out in front of the American people. Poll after poll indicated that the average voter thought we had pushed too far and too fast in social reform ... in politics, as in physics, for every action there is a reaction. We had had plenty of action during the five years of my Presidency—in the areas of civil rights, health, education, housing, conservation, poverty, hunger, job training, and consumer protection.... The nation's reaction to these programs helped to decide the 1968 election.
>
> The blue collar worker felt that the Democratic Party had traded his welfare for the welfare of the black man. The middle class suburbanite felt that we were gouging him in order to pay for

the antipoverty programs. The black man, having tasted the fruits of equality, began demanding his rightful share of the American promise faster than most of the nation was willing to let him have it. . . .

The average American was concerned about the rising crime rate and failed to understand that under our Constitution the preservation of law and order is basically the responsibility of local government. Somehow in the minds of most Americans the breakdown of local authority became the fault of the federal government. The votes of all these disenchanted Americans were decisive in the 1968 election. . . .

Richard Nixon's mandate to reconstruct the United States Supreme Court, which during the past decade had been largely responsible for the spirit of social enterprise to which Johnson alluded, and to strengthen the peace forces against the criminal forces could not have been more clearly given.

Law and order was an issue nationwide that year. Both parties used it, in varying degrees and with varying results. Illinois Attorney General William Clark, whose hot breath Republican majority leader Everett Dirksen had felt at his back when he rose in the Senate to speak against the confirmation of Abe Fortas as chief justice of the United States, had run as a crime fighter and lost, although it was improbable that anyone could have defeated the popular senator who had already served three terms in the upper chamber following eight terms in the House. Arizona Republican Barry Goldwater, having popularized the issue in the 1964 presidential campaign, had used it again this year; but he, too, was a veteran senator, and with or without his calling for tougher judges and his hard line toward criminal defendants, he would have been as difficult to oust as the senator from Illinois.

Perhaps no one was more helped by the issue of law and order than one of the participants in the case of Ernest Miranda, young Gary Nelson, who had argued on behalf of the attorney general's office for the state of Arizona in the Supreme Court. The Court's decision in Miranda's case had not been popular in Arizona, and since Nelson had lost, he was one of the "good guys." So when the election of 1968 loomed, who better but ambitious, community-conscious Republican Gary Nelson to run for state attorney general? The Republicans indulged in a little sleight of hand in Nelson's case. The attorney general, Darrell Smith, resigned early, and the Republican governor appointed Nelson to the position on July 1 so he could campaign for the November election as an incumbent. Nelson in turn hired Smith as special legal counsel to the state at a salary of $900 a month. Although Nelson defended his action as a way of insuring a smooth transition between the two administrations, an action, he declared, "that would be perfectly proper in a non-political year," Smith resigned when Democrats protested.

Nelson's campaign generally avoided the excesses of some Arizona candidates—"Let's Cut out the Wrist Slapping and Get Back to the Woodshed," urged a newspaper ad for one candidate for superior court judge in Phoenix—and followed the Nixon line: that America had seen the U.S. Supreme Court expand to "a legislative and policy-making body, as opposed to the judicial forum it was constitutionally designed to be." Locally he urged the defeat of judges who had "weakened respect for the law as we want it to be" and had been "lenient and permissive with habitual criminals and juvenile offenders" along with the election of judges "who promise a different philosophical approach to law and justice."

He later claimed that the coattails of Richard Nixon and Barry Goldwater had been of as much assistance as the campaign he had waged. In any case, though it was a fairly close election, with Nelson receiving a fraction over 50 percent of the vote, he won, and another man had achieved power and prominence because of his stand against Ernest Miranda, one more addition to the forces building against the recent tides of constitutional history.

CHAPTER 3

On Saturday, November 9, four days after the election, Ramsey Clark, whom
Richard Nixon was so anxious to replace as attorney general, received a telephone call at his home at Lake Barcroft, in suburban Virginia, from the U.S.
attorney for the Southern District of New York, Robert Morgenthau. Morgenthau had recently—and successfully—prosecuted financier Louis Wolfson for violation of the securities laws. During its investigation of the case, his
staff had discovered a connection among Wolfson, his family's foundation,
and Associate Justice Abe Fortas of the United States Supreme Court, including knowledge of Fortas's flying visit to Wolfson in Florida in June 1966,
the day after the Supreme Court had handed down the decision in *Miranda*.
Now, Morgenthau reported to his superior, the Internal Revenue Service had
discovered Wolfson's January 1966 payment of $20,000 to Fortas; when au-
ditors checked Fortas's income tax returns, they found he had not reported
the payment; *Life* magazine had gotten hold of the story and intended to
publish it.

Within hours Clark was at the door of Fortas's Georgetown home. Clark
told the justice what Morgenthau had said. Fortas telephoned his secretary,
who brought his tax returns to the house. She worked through the records
while Clark waited.

"Well," said Fortas, "I paid that money back. I decided that I couldn't
do it." Since both transactions had occurred within the same tax year, he had
not paid income tax on the $20,000.

Mentally mopping his brow, Clark assured Fortas that since that was the
case, he could see no reason for further involvement of the Justice Depart-

ment. It seemed to Clark it was "another American University thing . . . just one of these things where he was going to get money for research and lecturing in areas that were very important to him . . . he was very concerned about civil rights, and had worked hard in the area and done a lot of good. . . ." Fortas, Clark advised, might want to inform *Life* of the circumstances, before reputations—both Fortas's and the Court's—were compromised.

Back at the Department of Justice, Clark passed Fortas's explanation on to the Internal Revenue Service and officially closed the case, if case it was at all. He waited for the story to appear in *Life* the following week, and when it did not, he forgot about it. He did not consider it important enough to tell the president.

When the *Life* article failed to materialize, this most recent episode involving the personal affairs of Justice Fortas passed unnoticed in the nation's capital.

CBS News had intended, when the interview with Justice Black had been filmed in September, to televise it as soon after election day as possible, and it was now scheduled for 10:00 P.M. (EST) on December 3. The Blacks joined a few friends at the home of Martin Agronsky, one of the two interviewers, to watch it. It had been titled "Justice Black and the Bill of Rights." It was the first time a sitting justice had been interviewed about the Court and Constitution on television.* Black had insisted on excision of only a few of his comments. One segment involved his membership in the Ku Klux Klan as an ambitious young man, no more politically saintly perhaps than the next fellow; following his appointment to the Supreme Court in 1937, he had addressed the subject in a radio address, then closed it; he would not reopen it now. Other excisions involved the currently controversial subjects of judges advising presidents and the propriety of judges accepting money for making speeches, both of which touched the affairs of his fellow justice Abe Fortas. Judicious editing had turned the rest of the interview into a compact, integrated one-hour show.

The scene in the study was more cozy than formal, almost a discussion among friends, although the visitors showed no lack of deference, the justice no lack of dignity. But sitting at his desk, his fingertips touching in a characteristic pose that those who had watched him in the courtroom would recognize, he also looked relaxed. Occasionally the camera caught him leafing through his well-thumbed copy of the Constitution, which he habitually carried in his right-hand coat pocket, as he searched for the exact words of the authors, so he would get it just right in his answers. All this combined to produce the desired image about which his son later wrote: the "strong resemblance to the ordinary man" with whom he "shared the same fears and hopes."

* Agronsky had interviewed William O. Douglas some years previously for an NBC series called "Look Here," but the Supreme Court had not been the main theme.

In terms schoolboys could understand yet without condescension—pomposity seemed alien to his nature—Black described his own understanding of various clauses in the Bill of Rights and the obligation of judges to construct them strictly. The film was in its last third when, without mentioning the president-elect by name, one of the reporters brought up accusations that the Supreme Court played a role in raising the rates of crime. Black's own opinions for the Court, from *Chambers* in 1940 to *Gideon* in 1962, had helped substantially to establish the historical and constitutional foundations for much of what the Warren Court had done. He as much as any man had cast the Court in its present role.

Black: Well, the Court didn't do it.

Sevareid: The Court didn't do it?

Black: No. The Constitution-makers did it. They were the ones that put in no man should be compelled to convict himself. . . . I don't see how anybody could deny that the Constitution says absolutely and in words that nobody can deny, in the Fifth Amendment, that "no person be compelled in a criminal case, to be a witness against himself." And so, when they say the Court did it, that's just a little wrong. The Constitution did it.

Agronsky: Mr. Justice, do you think that those decisions have made it more difficult for the police to combat crime?

Black: Certainly. Why shouldn't they? What were they written for? Why did they write the Bill of Rights? They practically all relate to the way cases shall be tried. And practically all of them make it more difficult to convict people of crime. . . . They were written to make it more difficult. And what the Court does is try to follow what they wrote, and say you've got to try people in this way. Why did they want a jury? They wanted it so they wouldn't be subjected to one judge who might hang them or convict them for a political crime, or something of that kind. And so they had juries. And they said the same thing about an indictment. That's what they put it in for. They were, every one, intended to make it more difficult before the doors of a prison closed on a man because of his trial.

Agronsky: You're all for that?

Black: Yes, I'm for it. I'm for it. I'm for the Bill of Rights. I'm not saying, now, that I would write every one in the exact language they have written them. But I'll try to enforce them in the exact language they were written. I think when those men in Philadelphia, they had behind them knowledge of a long series of oppressions in Europe. They knew about people getting their tongue torn out, their ears clipped off. Having to fight, fight, fight. I think they wanted to get away from that. . . . [T]his Constitution . . . is, to me, the best document that has ever been written to control a government. . . . It's failed at various times and in various localities. But it's done mighty well, compared with other nations of the world. . . . I think this country has lived because of its Constitution and its laws and its ideals of liberty and equality and freedom. . . .

The words had tumbled out, depth of conviction giving them momentum, spontaneity giving them added animation. Then he read from his 1940 opinion in *Chambers,* and the rhythms gave what he had said a poetical quality and the words, thought out those many years ago and written down first in longhand, gave it added clarity:

> Under our constitutional system, courts stand against any winds that blow as havens of refuge for those who might otherwise suffer because they are helpless, weak, outnumbered, or because they are non-conforming victims of prejudice and public excitement. . . .
>   No higher duty, no more solemn responsibility rests upon this Court, than that of translating into living law, and maintaining this constitutional shield, deliberately planned and inscribed for the benefit of every human being, subject to our Constitution, of whatever race, creed or persuasion.

At the end a CBS announcer offered a free Government Printing Office edition of the Constitution, the kind the justice had illustrated his points with, to anyone who wrote for it.

Except for his statement that in retrospect he might not—he would not say "positively"—have used the controversial phrase "with all deliberate speed" in the second public school desegregation decision in 1955, there was nothing new in Black's answers to his interviewers. Everything he said he had said previously in his Court opinions. But most people don't read Supreme Court opinions, and here he was on national television, talking with characteristic quiet dignity, firmness, boldness, patiently explaining the responsibilities of judges to interpret the Constitution not with prejudice but with interest and explaining what he believed the real meaning of *law and order* was. Intentionally or not, it would stand for a long time as a reasoned rebuttal to Richard Nixon's rhetoric.

The interview was not telecast in Birmingham, Alabama, whose WAPI-TV was beamed into Hugo Black's native Clay County—an old movie, *Tammy Tell Me True,* was shown that night instead. Nationwide a Brigitte Bardot special drew 75 percent of the television audience, to Black's 7 percent. But response to the show was gratifying both to the justice and to CBS News. Black's mail was overwhelmingly congratulatory, dissipating his doubts about the wisdom of the decision to go through with it, and an intense national interest was indicated by the fact that there were no fewer than 125,000 requests for copies of the Constitution offered by CBS—many of which the recipients sent on to the justice, who obligingly autographed each one. Burton Benjamin, the producer, received an Emmy award, as well as the American Bar Association Gavel award.

Chapter 3

And William O. Douglas, always ready with the light touch, warm if sometimes wry, scribbled a quick note the next day:

Dear Hugo,
Cathy and I saw your television show last night and we thought it was excellent. Maybe you will make Cary Grant move over!

As ever,
Bill

The transition period between administrations—the two months or so between the November election and inauguration on January 20—was a peculiarly American celebration, one of the things that made the system function just as surely as the pulling of the levers in the voting booths. Since that first crucial transition following the election of 1800, when for the first time the parties in power changed and a feared Federalist coup did not materialize, transition has been orderly. Over the past century and three-quarters presidents had come and gone with varying degrees of ease, sometimes with good will, sometimes not, but always with the continuity of government given the highest consideration—including on that uncertain afternoon in November 1963, when, in another kind of transition, a nation and a worried world waited in the aftermath of John Kennedy's assassination; if Lyndon Johnson made one thing clear that day as he took the oath of office aboard *Air Force One*, the former president's widow standing beside him in her blood-stained clothes, it was that the United States of America would go on uninterrupted.

The transition between the presidencies of Lyndon Johnson and Richard Nixon went smoothly enough. Both teams were determined to display their good political breeding, and there was a kind of determined good-loser face put on governmental affairs. The president and first lady invited the president-elect and Mrs. Nixon to lunch at the White House on November 11, six days after election, and following the meal the men adjourned to the Cabinet Room for four hours of briefings by the secretaries of state and defense and the various heads of the military and intelligence communities, while the women adjourned to the living quarters, which Mrs. Nixon would soon be adapting for the use of her own family. If there was a deadly seriousness about this encounter, there was also a casual friendliness, as if the Nixons had just bought the house from the Johnsons and the men were off to inspect the plumbing while the women measured the windows for curtains. Senior government officials, who felt as lame as the president, suppressed their feelings of malaise as they prepared, at Johnson's command, transition plans to aid their successors.

There were moments laden with irony, as when Richard Nixon telephoned Earl Warren, whose Court the Republican presidential candidate, now president-elect, had promised the public he would reconstruct, in early December and asked the chief justice, in the interests of "continuity in the

Court," to stay on there "until your successor is appointed"; as when during that same period the president-elect asked the chief justice to administer the oath of office on inauguration day; as when Ramsey Clark, whom the president-elect had vilified in the rhetoric of the campaign, having seen to the security arrangements for the inaugural, insisted on attending the swearing-in of Richard Nixon because, he said, he, too, wanted to demonstrate the continuity of government.

There were poignant moments as when the night of January 19, the last night of Lyndon Johnson's term in office, he wandered alone through the White House offices, empty now, and found on a staff member's desk a note to the man who would occupy it next. "Good luck," was all it said.

Then suddenly it was all over. The Lyndon and Lady Bird silk pillows had disappeared from the local souvenir shops, replaced by Dick and Pat pillows. The man with the little black bag—the "football"—had transferred his loyalties from Lyndon Johnson to Richard Nixon. Vicki Cole, the thirteen-year-old daughter of the Methodist minister from Deshler, Ohio, whose slogan of "Bring Us Together" Nixon had chosen for the theme of his first post-election address and of his first administration generally, had waved her sign from a float parading down Pennsylvania Avenue that cold, gray, and windy inaugural afternoon.

Former President Johnson, wafted home to Texas on *Air Force One* for the last time, courtesy of the new president, was chasing deer around the ranch from his big Lincoln Continental. "It hurts good," he remarked as he looked back on the presidency and ahead at the Pedernales River, hung over with live oaks.

Hubert Humphrey went back to Minnesota, whose senator he had been for many years before becoming Lyndon Johnson's vice president and the Democratic party's presidential nominee in 1968. He worked for a time as a professor of political science at Macalester College in St. Paul, all the time planning for another day.

George Wallace was pretty quiet around inauguration time. But the Wallace for President headquarters in Montgomery was still open, and his people were predicting "more money and a better organization" in 1972.*

Richard Nixon was in the White House.

And John Newton Mitchell, the president's former campaign manager

---

* *Hubert Humphrey* was again elected to the United States Senate from Minnesota in 1970. He tried again for the presidency in 1972 but lost the Democratic nomination to George McGovern, senator from South Dakota. Humphrey died of cancer in January 1978.

Some years before, *George Wallace's* mother had told an interviewer: "Of course, somebody's gonna get George sooner or later. . . . My only consolation is, when it happens, he'll be doing the only thing he's ever cared about doing anyway." On May 15, 1972, campaigning in the Maryland presidential primary at a shopping mall at Laurel, George Wallace was shot by a mentally unstable young man. The shot was not fatal, but Wallace, paralyzed from the waist down, was thereafter confined to a wheelchair. In 1982 he was once again elected governor of Alabama.

and architect of what had come to be called the southern strategy, a former partner at Nixon Mudge, and a skilled municipal bond lawyer—not, as Nixon had promised the delegates in Miami the previous August, a man with wide "experience in law enforcement"—was sitting at the big desk under the domed ceiling of the attorney general's office on the top floor of the main Department of Justice building at Tenth Street and Pennsylvania. He had some distinguished predecessors—Edmund Randolph, the first attorney general; Levi Lincoln; Roger B. Taney; and, in this century, Harlan Fiske Stone, Robert H. Jackson, Francis Biddle. And he had some not-so-distinguished ones: A. Mitchell Palmer, who had hoped to propel himself into the presidency by raising the pitch of anti-Communist hysteria with his "red raids" of 1919 and 1920, and Harry M. Daugherty, who nearly went to jail for his involvement in the Teapot Dome scandal, for example. Like Mitchell, several had been presidential campaign managers—Daugherty had managed Warren G. Harding's campaign; J. Howard McGrath had managed Truman's; Herbert Brownell had managed Eisenhower's; Robert F. Kennedy had managed his brother's. If the office was not so heavily endowed in terms of patronage as the Post Office Department, still, appointment of 94 U.S. attorneys and direct responsibility for some 500 federal judgeships, plus indirect responsibility for the thousands of marshals and other officers of the federal judicial system, was no small currency.

As attorney general Mitchell would direct what had come to be called the largest law office in the world, although among cabinet departments, it ranked with the smaller ones, with only 35,000 employees and a budget of $555 million. His only client was the government of the United States, for whose interests he was directly responsible, from investigation of federal law violations to conduct of federal cases, criminal and civil, in the federal courts, to custody of those convicted of federal crimes. He was to be available when other cabinet members as well as the president asked for legal advice, and he was to supervise the drafting of legislation having to do with federal matters. It was not unlike being on retainer to an especially litigious client.

John Mitchell had been also put in charge of making a profit from the president's biggest political investment: implementing the campaign promises to bring law and order to a crime-ravaged nation. He was, like the president, self-made, having worked his way through the law school at Fordham University during the Depression and then, through sheer persistence and application, having become one of the best bond lawyers in America. It was said that privately he could be a warm and affectionate man, but his public face—cold, aloof, his wry and sometimes devastating comments punctuated by frequent inhalations from the eternal pipe—seemed more the surface expression of an inner toughness and shrewdness. A debate had begun in the capital on whether his coldness, his "unflappability," was a result of hardened nerve ends or whether it only meant he was uninvolved and passionless. As a bond lawyer he had helped set up the legal structure which would allow municipalities to borrow funds to meet the social needs following World War II—the money for housing, for schools, hospitals, freeways—but he was efficient, managerial, a lawyer whose career had been dedicated to advancing his clients' interests but little concerned with the projects on which they spent the sums. The mechanics, which he had raised to a science, interested him, not the human sociology.

The Justice Department's power to affect local crime was limited by the fact that most matters of criminal justice fell under state and local jurisdiction, but there were certain areas in which the federal government was authorized to function. Federal crimes—those involving violations of narcotics laws, for example—came under the jurisdiction of the Department of Justice. The District of Columbia, which had become known, thanks to Richard Nixon, as the "crime capital" of the nation, was a federal enclave. Mitchell would also have something to say about appointments to the federal bench, including the Supreme Court, about which the president had made so much in the recent campaign. It was in connection with this last matter that he would exert the strongest influence.

There were, though, indirect ways in which the federal government affected crime. It set the tone for the states: State courts looked to the federal courts for guidelines; local law enforcement officers looked to the FBI; state legislatures imitated Congress. If the United States Department of Justice took a tough approach, that legitimized it for all.

If anything was clear, in January 1969, as the Nixon men marched on the capital, it was the tone of the new administration and the fact that John Mitchell, who had sat at the right hand of the throne throughout the campaign and would continue to do so, the Abe Fortas of the Nixon administration, would be its symbol. John Mitchell may not have been experienced in the business of law enforcement, but he was not without definite ideas on the subject, and his general philosophy was contained in his frequently stated conviction that his predecessor, Ramsey Clark, had confused the Department of Justice with the Department of Health, Education, and Welfare.

The president had introduced Mitchell on television on December 11, with the rest of his cabinet, as a "devoted" crime fighter. Mitchell had verified the judgment at hearings before the Senate Judiciary Committee, prior to his confirmation, and again at his first press conference on January 21, during which he also announced his top aides, including the new deputy attorney general, Richard Kleindienst, who had first suggested to Barry Goldwater in 1964 the potential of "crime in the streets" as a major campaign theme. The following day, January 22, the president's second day in office, he lunched with his attorney general to discuss—for two full hours, the longest he had spent with any cabinet member—the law; the judges, including the next chief justice of the United States; the climate of fear in the District of Columbia; and wiretapping. The attorney general's assignment could not have been clearer or, given his intimacy with the president—he had a direct line to the White House—more authoritative.

Nixon's plans soon began to take shape. First, there was implementation of legislation already on the books. Whereas Ramsey Clark, under President Johnson's direction, had refused to utilize Title II of the omnibus crime bill of 1968, which allowed the use of confessions obtained "voluntarily" but without benefit of *Miranda* warnings and had, instead, instructed Justice Department personnel to adhere to the *Miranda* ruling as set down by the Supreme Court, John Mitchell's Justice Department people were instructed, on June 11, 1969, in a long memorandum that although it was desirable that the *Miranda* warnings be given prior to talks between federal officials and criminal defendants, a confession prefaced by "less than perfect warnings" or accompanied by a "less than conclusive waiver" might very well be admissible as evidence so long as it was "voluntarily" given. The move by the Justice Department was interpreted as an invitation for further court testing of the *Miranda* decision against the will of Congress.

Next came the writing of new legislation. As the members of the new administration converged on Washington, where they expected to remain for at least four years, preferably eight, they found not one but several cities. There was, of course, the city of tourists, the city of shining monuments, dazzling in the winter sunlight, and old Abe Lincoln, looking down from his marble temple on the Mall could still make a monument-hardened Washingtonian weep. There was the city of diplomats, that two-mile stretch of Massachusetts Avenue between Scott Circle and the Washington Cathedral at Wisconsin Avenue, known as Embassy Row. There was bureaucratic Washington, housed in the drab gray-brown office buildings whose uniform exteriors said much about their inner life. There was political Washington, whose population, much of it transient, walked nevertheless confidently in the corridors of power on Pennsylvania Avenue and Capitol Hill. Then there were the several residential neighborhoods: fashionable Georgetown with its narrow sidewalks of uneven brick, its quaint Federalist row houses, and resident population of Supreme Court justices, cabinet secretaries, senators, media personalities, and psychiatrists—mental stress in this highly competitive world capital of political ambition, it was reported, established the Washington area as the home of more psychiatrists per capita than any other place in the nation—tastefully elegant Wesley Heights built on the rolling hills above Georgetown, home to founding fathers of some of the city's prestigious law firms, to Richard Nixon and Lyndon Johnson when they were vice president, assorted cabinet members, and Nelson Rockefeller when he was in town; Cleveland Park and Chevy Chase, reproductions of America's small towns, with block after block of rambling old houses, hordes of children, Irish setters, and bicycles, and home to junior partners in the city's prestigious law firms, journalists, retired generals, and middle-echelon State Department officials. And there was the hidden city: the various and vast black neighborhoods which covered two of the city's four quadrants as well as parts of the third and fourth, touched all points of the economic and social spectrum, and included the clusters of large and handsome Tudor mansions of the Gold Coast on upper Sixteenth Street in the northwest section of the city; storefront churches with Gospel-singing choirs and pulpit-pounding reverends who could relieve, at least temporarily, the pain of poverty; Fourteenth Street with its crumbling row houses crumbling further from the overstrain of sheltering too many people at once, its neon bars, its prancing women in gaudy fur-fringed pants, its young men with arms swollen by needle jabs—"there is no such thing as an old junkie," they said on Fourteenth Street—leaning against the lamp posts; these neighborhoods included, too, the neat middle- and lower-class houses of Capitol Hill, and the rat-infested slums of Anacostia.

One of the several bonds that united all these cities, the city of the tourist and the city of the diplomat, the city of the cabinet secretary and the city of the black janitress who cleaned his office at night, the city of the lawyer and the city of the junkie was the fear of crime—a fear they all felt, but felt particularly in the cities of the janitress and the junkie because attacks were more frequent there, and the resident populations were more vulnerable.

If Richard Nixon's characterization of Washington as the crime capital of the world was an exaggeration, still the fear of crime was widespread. Guns were kept in bedside tables and under grocery store counters. Office employees refused to work at night because they were afraid to go home in the dark. Bus drivers had stopped making change and demanded "exact change" (30 cents) in return for a ride. Cities around the country were similarly beset. The difference in the District of Columbia was that it was subject to federal laws. And so the Nixon administration chose to make its stand against crime in the streets in the nation's capital itself.

On July 11, the Department of Justice sent to Congress its "crime package," a group of bills aimed at reducing crime in the District of Columbia. At its submission to the legislature, the attorney general called it a "model" program to "point the way for the entire nation at a time when crime and fear of crime are forcing us, a free people, to alter the pattern of our lives." The senior senator from North Carolina, Democrat Sam Ervin, hardly an outspoken supporter of the U.S. Supreme Court's work in the recent past, described the crime package in his typically earthy fashion, "as full of unconstitutional, unjust, and unwise provisions as a mangy house dog is full of fleas . . . a garbage pail of some of the most repressive, nearsighted, intolerant, unfair and vindictive legislation that the Senate has ever been presented . . ."

Interpreting its mandate as permission to wage outright war on crime and criminals whatever the cost in constitutional rights, and having already taken care of *Miranda* and the Fifth Amendment's application to police interrogation through support of Title II of the omnibus crime bill, the Nixon

men proceeded to narrow the application of the Fourth Amendment's prohibition against "unreasonable searches and seizures." Along with a long-
overdue re-organization and streamlining of the District court system—which
may have helped District law enforcement deal with local crime better than
all the repressive measures John Mitchell's Justice Department developed, although it was less eye-catching, less politically profitable—the crime bills authorized law enforcement officers to enter homes without knocking—a controversial provision that became known as no-knock—and to seize any
property if it was believed to have been illegally possessed, stolen, used in a
crime, or if it could be used to identify a crime or criminal. Authority to
wiretap was broadened considerably. The most controversial provision of all,
which went under the enticing euphemism *bail reform*, authorized the pretrial preventive detention of suspects considered dangerous—that is, detention, without bail, of any defendant arrested for a violent crime until trial—
raising serious questions regarding the presumption of innocence on which
much of American criminal procedure is based.

Not all the Nixon administration's measures were repressive. Some were
political. Later in his administration he created a new Office for Drug Abuse
Law Enforcement, the director of which confided that "it was a special elec-
tion-year [1972] effort and that he did not know how long the program would
last after November." Deputy Attorney General Kleindienst often reminded
U.S. attorneys that "it is of utmost importance to keep this Administration in
power and you must do everything you can to insure that result," instructing
them to publicize progress made in restoring law and order as well as to avoid
all controversies that could cost Republican votes.

All of them, however, were small potatoes in terms of potential impact
when compared with the appointment of judges, especially Supreme Court
justices. Every president is acutely aware of the potential for self-perpetuation
by the judiciary. At its most effective, it is like spawning children. And the
risks are about the same: Judges, like children, can demonstrate streaks of independence. The judiciary, however, is the only available legitimate avenue
with any degree of permanence about it, and Richard Nixon, as he had announced during the election campaign, was prepared, even eager, to travel
that route.

He had committed himself during the recent campaign to changing the
ideological complexion of as much of the federal bench as possible, and one
of his first acts following his inauguration was to withdraw the names of five
men nominated by the retiring president to the federal judiciary at the last
minute. It had been another "midnight judges" attempt, a common, if controversial, practice of outgoing presidents since John Adams had named John
Marshall to the chief justiceship in January 1801 following the former's defeat in the election of 1800.* There was precedent for the new president's

* Adams, in fact, in an attempt to fill the new judgeships created by the Judiciary Act of
1801 with loyal Federalists, sent judicial nominations to the Senate for confirmation as late as
March 2, 1801, two days before the new president's inauguration. Jefferson, the incoming presi-

withdrawing and accepting the nominations in modern times: Eisenhower had withdrawn four of Truman's six last-minute judicial appointments, and two were not acted upon; Kennedy had accepted all four nominations Eisenhower had made in January 1961.

Nixon replaced Johnson's five nominees during the next few months with Republicans. Between inauguration in January 1969 and his resignation in August 1974, Nixon appointed 214 judges to the federal bench. It was like an assembly line, with Deputy Attorney General Kleindienst screening the candidates, Attorney General Mitchell pruning the list and suggesting additional names to the president, and the president making the final selections. The fact that 92 percent of them were Republicans was not unusual. Eisenhower's appointments to the federal bench had been 94 percent Republican, Kennedy's 90 percent Democratic, and Johnson's 94 percent Democratic. It only illustrates the common practice of politicizing the judicial appointments. But in Nixon's case, there was an added factor. He had made the federal judiciary, including and especially the U.S. Supreme Court, a major campaign issue, and so for as long as he was president, the federal judiciary, including and especially the Supreme Court, could expect to absorb men who not only were Republicans but would consider it their responsibility to "interpret the law not to make law" and would brake the trend toward "weakening the peace forces as against the criminal forces in the United States of America." Who would remake the federal judiciary in the president's own image.

The U.S. Supreme Court, of course, drew his special attention, and a quick glance at that Court indicated that the new President might have some appointments to make. When Nixon took over in January 1969, Hugo Black was nearly eighty-three, John Harlan was seventy and in failing health, William O. Douglas was seventy-one, Earl Warren was nearly seventy-eight and had already indicated his desire to resign. Warren's replacement would be the first business at hand.

---

dent, instructed his secretary of state, James Madison, not to deliver their commissions; out of the ensuing controversy over whether or not William Marbury was a bona fide appointment as justice of the peace for the District of Columbia, the landmark case of *Marbury* v. *Madison* arose. The U.S. Supreme Court's decision in that case, written by John Marshall, established the authority of the Supreme Court to pass on the constitutionality of acts of Congress and acts of the executive: the principle of judicial review.

CHAPTER 4

Under the terms of Earl Warren's resignation which he had submitted to the former president the previous June, the position was now open. The new president, however, need not act in haste. Under an arrangement worked out between Warren and William P. Rogers, Nixon's secretary of state, to whom he had delegated this particular delicate assignment, the current chief justice had agreed to stay on until the end of the 1968 term—which meant mid- or late June 1969—allowing Nixon some breathing space. Attorney General Mitchell, whom Nixon trusted implicitly—indeed, he excluded all his advisers except Mitchell from deliberations regarding his nominations to the Supreme Court—had been designated a one-man search committee, and it was clear that the David Bazelons of the judicial world need not apply.

Shortly before Nixon's inauguration, Albert Eisele, a reporter in the Washington bureau of the *St. Paul Dispatch* at the time, had been told by an aide to the president-elect that Nixon's first choice for chief justice was Eisele's old Republican acquaintance, St. Paul native Warren Earl Burger of the U.S. Court of Appeals for the District of Columbia Circuit, whose judicial utterances Nixon had adapted to his recent campaign rhetoric. Eisele wrote a story to that effect for his paper, and when it appeared, the major character in it telephoned him.

"What kind of pot have you been smoking?" the jurist asked the reporter.

The conversation continued in a light vein, but beneath the surface banter, the judge appeared to be seriously interested in whether or not he was, in fact, under consideration for the highest judicial post in the country.

Indeed, it was not such a pipe dream as Burger had suggested to Eisele. Burger was not prominent outside the profession, not nearly so well known as John Mitchell or Herbert Brownell or Tom Dewey, all prominent Republicans whom the president was also considering. (Brownell was Nixon's first choice for chief justice, but he had removed himself from consideration when Mitchell informed him that key southern senators would oppose Brownell because of his role, as Eisenhower's attorney general, in sending federal troops to Little Rock, Arkansas, in 1957 to enforce desegregation of the public schools. Dewey removed himself from consideration because of his age— sixty-six. Mitchell did not think it desirable for Nixon to appoint a political friend, following the Fortas debacle, and he also withdrew.) Burger was, however, well known within the legal, particularly the judicial, community. During twelve years on the federal bench his star had risen more or less in proportion to the vigor of his opinions on constitutional, particularly criminal, matters, and he had become something of a spokesman, articulate and respectable, for those judges who believed the Warren Court had overreached itself. Leaders of the organized bar had come to know him through work he had done on the ABA's Committee for Minimum Standards for the Administration of Criminal Justice.

The president had devised five criteria he would use in choosing the new chief justice: The nominee must have "a topflight legal mind"; he had to be "young enough to serve at least ten years"; it would be preferable if he had had experience as both a practicing lawyer and an appeals court judge; of course, having waged a political campaign over judicial philosophy, the president wanted a man who shared his "view that the Court should interpret the Constitution rather than amend it by judicial fiat"; and he must have both the ability and strength to bring the Court together. Burger slipped easily into the first four categories; the fifth was more risky, although Nixon, having known the jurist for twenty years, believed Burger had it. As he studied the list of judges his attorney general had put together for his consideration, Nixon began "looking particularly into the record of Judge Warren E. Burger."

On February 4, 1969, Judge Burger met Nixon for the first time as president of the United States. Coincidentally, only a few days before, Burger had traveled with Chief Justice Warren to Gainesville, Florida, for the dedication of a new law school at the University of Florida—Burger was participating in a panel discussion; Warren was to give the dedication address. During their two-hour plane ride the men had discussed at some length their differing views of the Supreme Court's function, Burger suggesting that "some of the changes in criminal procedure, resulting from opinions of the Court, would perhaps better have been left to the rulemaking process." In the end the judge and the justice had agreed to disagree, but the judge had gained, he said, "a better understanding of the whole problem as it can be seen only from [the Supreme] Court." Now he had been summoned to the White

House to swear in a group of new members of the two-week-old administration by the man who would soon appoint the next chief justice.

Following the brief ceremony in the Fish Room, Nixon ushered Burger into the Oval Office, where they discussed in some detail Burger's much-publicized Ripon College commencement speech. The chief-justiceship was not mentioned, but both men had to have been aware that the moment was pregnant with significance for the future.

Two weeks later Attorney General Mitchell invited Burger, who had built up a broad network of contacts among the nation's federal judges, to assist him in his search for candidates to fill vacancies on the lower courts. Burger responded with the three names that had come immediately to mind and promised, he wrote the attorney general, he would "be able to add others from time to time."

On March 14 the U.S. Court of Appeals for the District of Columbia Circuit handed down a decision in a controversial local criminal case. Instead of affirming the conviction of a confessed and convicted robber, Eugene Frazier, which it probably would have done prior to the *Miranda* decision, the appellate court, unable to determine whether or not the defendant had conclusively waived his *Miranda* rights prior to confessing, returned his case to the local district court to determine the unanswered questions of the voluntariness of the confession. It was exactly the sort of case that drove Burger, whose acerbity was increasing with every decision like this, to judicial distraction. The area of the law was nebulous, made more so by the *Miranda* decision. The distinctions were too fine for Burger's taste. He let the court feel the full force of his judicial impatience:

> The seeming anxiety of judges to protect every accused person from every consequence of his voluntary utterances is giving rise to myriad rules, sub-rules, variations and exceptions which even the most alert and sophisticated lawyers and judges are taxed to follow. Each time judges add nuances to these "rules" we make it less likely that any police officer will be able to follow the guidelines we lay down. We are approaching the predicament of the centipede on the flypaper—each time one leg is placed to give support for relief of a leg already "stuck," another becomes captive and soon all are securely immobilized. Like the hapless centipede on the flypaper, our efforts to extricate ourselves from this self-imposed dilemma will, if we keep it up, soon have all of us immobilized. We are well on our way to forbidding *any* utterance of an accused to be used against him unless it is made in open court. Guilt or innocence becomes irrelevant in the criminal trial as we founder in a morass of artificial rules poorly conceived and often impossible of application.

The timing as well as the language was propitious. The decision was reported in the local press, which was received in quantity at the White House and in which attention was focused not on details of either the case or the decision but on Judge Burger's rousing dissent.*

The end of the Supreme Court term was fast approaching. Still, the president was silent. He decided to bid his old rival—and recent unnamed victim of his campaign rhetoric—Chief Justice Earl Warren, good-bye at a lavish black-tie dinner for 110 on the evening of April 22, and the chandeliers in the State Dining Room of the White House glittered above the vermeil flatware and the tables laden with daisies and carnations. Among those nibbling on the filet mignon Rossini and Caesar salad, along with the entire Warren family and all the justices of the Supreme Court and their wives, were several men who had been mentioned prominently in the media for the chief justiceship: former Republican Governor Dewey of New York, Republican maître d' Herbert Brownell, Attorney General Mitchell, Secretary of State William P. Rogers, Secretary of Defense Melvin Laird, and Charles S. Rhyne, a Duke University classmate of the president's, a former president of the ABA, and, most recently, director of the Citizens for Nixon organization.

The reporters crowded around Dewey, who told them he would not "move to Washington under any circumstances," and Mitchell, who joked, "If the President doesn't tell me soon who it's going to be, I might have to take it myself." But they virtually ignored the presence of white-haired Warren Burger of the U.S. Court of Appeals for the District of Columbia Circuit, who, upon learning that he was the only sitting lower-court judge invited, whispered to his wife "just to be natural if she got the feeling people were looking us over."

One of those who had been the subject of speculation was a dissenter to *Miranda*, Justice Stewart, and the president did, in fact, consider him for promotion. Stewart, however, was not interested, and a week after the party for Chief Justice Warren, he went to the White House and told the president so. It would not be fitting, he said, for a sitting justice to be appointed to a post for which one of his own brethren had failed of confirmation, particularly while the latter remained on the Court. What Stewart could not have known, that afternoon of April 30, as he discussed the chief justiceship with the president in the Oval Office, was that the man who had failed of confirmation was not going to remain on the Court for long.

The events that would force the resignation of Abe Fortas from the United States Supreme Court—and thereby give Richard Nixon the opportunity to appoint a second justice, an opportunity that held the potential to alter the Court majority early in his administration—had been set in motion sometime before Stewart's visit to the president.

* Frazier's case dragged on four more years. His conviction was finally affirmed, with the court sitting *en banc* and David Bazelon dissenting, in 1973. Total time elapsed from arrest in 1966 to final disposition: seven years.

Chapter 4

The former attorney general, Ramsey Clark, had left behind at the Justice Department no record of his discussion the previous November with Abe Fortas regarding the justice's income tax returns for 1966 and the question of the $20,000 he had received from, and returned the same year to his friend, financier Louis Wolfson, and so Will R. Wilson, Nixon's assistant attorney general in charge of the Criminal Division—and a former Texas district attorney and attorney general whose ambitions to higher state office had not been supported by fellow Texas Democrat Lyndon Johnson and who had turned Republican and campaigned for Richard Nixon in 1968—was both surprised and interested when, in early April, William Lambert, a reporter for *Life*, had approached him with the skeleton of a story involving what at best would later be called financial indiscretions in the relationship between Fortas and Wolfson, who had gone to jail on April 25 for violations of the securities laws. Wilson, who had a prosecutor's sense for hanky-panky, immediately mounted his own investigation, enlisting the SEC, the IRS, and the FBI and digging out not only confirmation of *Life*'s proposed story but information implying further Fortas-Wolfson association.

The story, advance proofs of which had been given over the weekend to the Justice Department, where they had been photocopied and delivered to the attorney general and the president, appeared in *Life* on Monday, May 5.* Essentially it described Wolfson's business enterprises, including his complicated adventures in the stock market and the government's case against him, recounted the association of the justice and the financier since 1965 and stated that Fortas had accepted a $20,000 fee from the Wolfson Family Foundation, then returned it eleven months later. Lambert carefully pointed out that there was absolutely no evidence that Fortas had been hired to influence the government's case against Wolfson. However, Wolfson and a codefendant, Lambert charged, had dropped Fortas's name "in strategic places in their efforts to stay out of prison."

Fortas never explained publicly his personal interest in the Wolfson Family Foundation. Years later his former law partner Paul Porter gave this version of it: Fortas, on his return to Washington following a visit to Wolfson in Jacksonville (prior to his appointment to the Supreme Court), told Porter he had been "tremendously impressed." Porter continued:

> "You know, this Lou Wolfson" [Porter quoted Fortas as saying] "is really an unusual person. He has built a wing on the Baptist Hospital there in Jacksonville in memory of his junk-dealer father, and there is a plaque there that [says,] 'This facility is for the healing of the sick and afflicted,' or words to that effect, 'irrespective of race, color, or creed.' Well, to have that prominent in Jacksonville. . . ."
>
> Abe got to talking to Wolfson about his foundation. And he said, "Look, I have got some ideas as to how, if you are going to put

* Under a misleading dating system used by *Life* and other so-called newsmagazines, the issue of *Life* in which the Fortas story appeared was dated May 9.

277

the kind of money in here you say you are, the foundation . . . can effectively do some work in student relations, race relations, etc. Well, there's enough money being spent on medicine and the applied sciences and on research, so I would hope that this foundation takes a bolder, imaginative course." Well, that intrigued Wolfson. Meantime Abe had been slugged up to the Supreme Court by LBJ and Wolfson wrote him a letter of congratulations. . . . Abe wrote him back and said, "Lou, while this will terminate our professional association, I still have great interest and please feel free to discuss your program with me at our mutual convenience." And they had such discussions before Wolfson's indictment.

So Abe prepared some position papers. Then came this thing and Abe got worried about it. Wolfson had sent him a check for the services as a consultant to this foundation. At that point, this poor guy was indicted, his wife was dying of terminal cancer . . . and Wolfson had had a cardiac condition. Abe said, "I can't kick this guy in the teeth under these circumstances. . . ." Then it came tax time, and Abe said, "I'm going to send this damn money back. I probably should not have accepted the check in the first place, but I didn't want to kick him in the teeth."

Fortas responded to the *Life* article with a 300-word statement which he issued from his chambers: Since he had become a member of the Court, he had accepted no fees from Wolfson or his foundation; it was true that he knew Wolfson and had considered undertaking, "consistent with my Court obligations, research functions, studies and writings connected with the work of the foundation," for which the foundation had "tendered a fee to me"; when he realized he couldn't do the work, he had returned the money; the money had not been given with either hope or understanding of Fortas's intervention in Wolfson's behalf, nor had there been any intervention whatsoever.

"At no time," Fortas declared, "have I given Mr. Wolfson or any of his family, associates, foundations or interests any legal advice or services, since becoming a member of the Court. I have not participated as a Justice or otherwise, in any legal or judicial matter affecting any of them."

And while Senator Strom Thurmond repeated his demand of the previous summer that the justice resign, a demand that was seconded by a number of his Senate and House colleagues, Fortas went about his business outwardly as if nothing had happened, appearing in his chambers as usual, working with his clerks on the endless stream of petitions for cert, even giving speeches which had been scheduled prior to the *Life* story's appearance. It looked to a lot of people as if he were trying to ride it out.

In the meantime, however, the IRS, having subpoenaed the files of the Wolfson Family Foundation, had discovered that the question of the returned $20,000 payment was only the shark's fin, part of an agreement the foundation actually had made, in writing, with Fortas, awarding the justice, in return for some vaguely worded responsibilities, $20,000 a year for life, the money to go to his wife following his own death. By Tuesday afternoon, May 6, the day after the *Life* article appeared, Justice Department officials knew all about the agreement, and a copy was on its way from Jacksonville to Will Wilson in Washington.

Late that night, following the attorney general's return from a speaking engagement in New York, Mitchell, Wilson, and one of Wilson's aides met over drinks at Mitchell's apartment in the luxurious new Watergate complex overlooking the Potomac. What had been gossip and innuendo about Fortas suddenly assumed real dimensions. There was an actual document. When Mitchell saw it for the first time, remarked one who accompanied him, he "sucked in his breath." Mitchell decided then and there that only one course of action was appropriate. He would inform the chief justice of the discovery.

The following morning, Wednesday, May 7, Mitchell let the president know of his intention and made an appointment to see Warren at 11:30 A.M.

The meeting, which lasted less than thirty minutes, was apparently cordial, although Warren never discussed it and Mitchell said little except to confirm that it had taken place. Mitchell handed Warren "certain documents," presumably the Fortas-Wolfson Foundation agreement plus some Fortas-Wolfson correspondence which the IRS also had extracted from the foundation files in Jacksonville. The chief justice made no comment. He said he would "take the matter under consideration," but he gave the attorney general no indication of what he would do.

Whether the words *resignation* or *impeachment* ever passed between the two men is neither known nor relevant. In a city where the politically literate read messages in the merest gesture, formal terms need almost never be uttered. It is unlikely that the nation's chief law enforcement officer and the nation's chief judicial officer failed to understand each other: It was, of course, in the Court's best interest to have Justice Fortas resign before information more damaging than ever, already in the hands of the Justice Department, was made public; if Fortas did resign, however, no doubt the federal agencies which were building the case against him could be persuaded to drop it, and the administration was not without influence in the Congress.

What the chief justice did with the information Mitchell had brought him is not known. He had neither constitutional nor statutory authority to discipline a fellow justice; each is an independent operator, fiercely independent. There was some evidence at the time that Warren discussed with Fortas the attorney general's visit and that he may have told the other justices about it. Warren, however, never said a word about the incident publicly.

At the end of the next week Fortas resigned. "The public controversy relating to my association with the Foundation," he told the chief justice in a letter accompanying his resignation and elaborating on his previously stated relationship with the Wolfson Foundation, "is likely to continue and adversely affect the work and position of the Court, absent my resignation. In this circumstance, it seems clear to me that it is not my duty to remain on the Court, but rather to resign in the hope that this will enable the Court to proceed with its vital work free from extraneous stress." He added: "There has been no wrongdoing on my part."

Less than a year before, he had sat on the veranda of his Westport, Connecticut, summer home and had talked of the challenges to the Fortas-Court-to-be, commenting to a *Time* reporter, "It was one thing to have enunciated great principles," as he believed the Warren Court had, "but it is another thing to make them come alive," to carry to its logical conclusion the relationship "between the state, vis-à-vis the individual," about which he had talked during the oral arguments in Ernest Miranda's case, to embark judicially again on "the great human adventure toward some kind of truly civilized order," of which he believed Miranda's case was a part.

Now in May 1969, not only was Fortas not to have this opportunity, but his resignation* would offer the president, sworn to reverse the direction of the Warren Court's "great principles," a second appointment to that Court.

With the emotional climate created by the Fortas affair cooling following the justice's resignation on May 14, the president was freed to reactivate the processing of the appointment of the chief justiceship. He spent the following weekend at the private presidential retreat, Camp David, a luxurious weekend White House with rustic pretensions nestled in the Maryland hills about seventy miles from Washington. Nixon gave a good deal of thought that weekend to the appointment of a new chief justice. In the light of the Fortas matter, he had added another category to his list of requirements: He could not now under any circumstances appoint a friend, like Charles Rhyne. Again, he began to gravitate toward Judge Burger. He telephoned the attorney general to discuss it. He reviewed the situation again.

---

* Following his resignation, Fortas returned to the private practice of law in Washington, not with his old firm but with a smaller firm, on a side street in Georgetown, only a few blocks from his home. He was involved largely in antitrust and securities matters. On March 22, 1982, he returned to the counsel's table at the Court for the first time to argue a case. If the drama of the moment occurred to the participants as Fortas faced three of his former brethren—Justices Brennan, White, and Marshall—as well as the chief justice in whose place he himself might have sat, it was submerged in the formality of the proceedings, and the argument was made without incident, the justices addressing Fortas impersonally as "Counsel" and Fortas addressing his former brethren in the traditional way as "Your Honors." Two weeks later, on April 5, he died suddenly of a ruptured aorta at his home in Georgetown.

Will Wilson, the assistant attorney general who had doggedly pursued the relationship between Fortas and Wolfson, himself resigned about two years later, in October 1971. Accusations of involvement during the mid-sixties, prior to Wilson's joining the Justice Department, with a Houston real estate developer and stock manipulator who pleaded guilty to stock fraud forced his resignation. There had been no wrongdoing on his part, Wilson said, but he would rather leave the administration than embarrass it further. He returned to the private practice of law.

Chapter 4

On Monday morning, May 19, the president again telephoned the attorney general. Begin quietly gathering the necessary clearances for Warren Burger, he instructed Mitchell, the FBI investigation and any other matters that might arise in the course of a Senate hearing. Mitchell got busy.

There were no skeletons in Warren Burger's closet. Two days later, on Wednesday, May 21, Mitchell telephoned Burger at his chambers in the federal courthouse less than half a mile away and asked him to come to the Justice Department within the next few hours.

Burger arrived in Mitchell's office shortly after noon. The president, Mitchell told the judge, had chosen him to be the next chief justice of the United States.

The judge was incredulous—"numb," he told friends later. Why, only last weekend—the very weekend Nixon had spent at Camp David trying to decide on the nominee—Burger had been telling friends in St. Paul, where he was visiting, that he was not in the running, although he might be for the seat of an associate justice at some future date. Like others in Washington, Burger had thought the chief justiceship would go either to Mitchell or Secretary of State Rogers.

Burger said he wanted time to think and to get a physical examination. He was, after all, sixty-one years old.

But Mitchell could not wait. The president planned to announce the appointment that night on television. He had to have an answer.

Burger accepted the appointment.

As if to underline the urgency of the matter, the president telephoned the attorney general. Yes, Mitchell told Nixon, Judge Burger was going to accept the appointment.

A few minutes later Burger left the Justice Department and drove the eight miles to his home in suburban Virginia, where he told his wife the news and that the family was expected at the White House in a few hours.

That afternoon White House staff members got on the phone to key government and party officials. A nominee for the chief justiceship had been selected, they said, but they did not divulge his identity. "You'll like the appointment, I assure you," was all they would say. Many people still believed Associate Justice Potter Stewart was Nixon's choice, and Republican Senator Hugh Scott of Pennsylvania, minority whip, had prepared a statement applauding Stewart's appointment.

At 6:57 that evening, Nixon strode out of the Oval Room upstairs at the White House just as Warren Burger was getting out of the elevator. He walked over to where the judge stood.

"Will you take the job?" the president asked.

Burger hesitated for a moment. "You know," he replied, "I know that question is somewhat facetious, but as I thought about it this afternoon, I had some concern. Sometime," he added, "when we have more time to talk, I want to thank you for this."

Then Nixon apologized for not having invited the Burgers for dinner but asked them to come up for coffee and to meet the cabinet members and their wives following the ceremony that was scheduled to begin momentarily.

"Don't worry about that," Burger reassured the president. "After what I've been through this afternoon, I am just going home to bed."

At 7:00 P.M., speaking from the East Room of the White House, the president introduced his choice for the fifteenth chief justice of the United States over nationwide television. It was all very brief, the barest bones of Burger's biography plus a quick list of his qualifications: "judicial tempera-ment . . . legal philosophy, and above all," the president added in a scarcely veiled allusion to events of recent weeks, "his unquestioned integrity throughout his private and public life."

Burger stepped to the podium, and the nation got its first glimpse of him as a prospective chief justice. Nearly six feet tall, he stood just above eye level with the president, but at 200 pounds, he was somewhat huskier than Nixon. His patrician good looks were accented by abundant white hair combed in a pompadour and bushy white eyebrows. At sixty-one, his skin was hardly wrinkled, and his voice—deep, strong, and clear—bespoke firmness and as-surance.

"At a time like this," he told the television audience, "the best thing to say is very little." He thanked the president and said his appointment was "a tribute to all of the sitting judges of the federal and state systems."

Later that night, after the Burgers had returned to their home, the new nominee for chief justice telephoned Albert Eisele of the *St. Paul Dispatch* Washington bureau, whom he had accused only a few months earlier of hav-ing pipe dreams. He talked to the reporter at some length, then concluded: The appointment was nothing to get very elated about; it was going to be a very sobering task.

There was, of course, immediate criticism of the appointment. Philip Kurland, professor of law at the University of Chicago and a respected stu-dent of and commentator on the Supreme Court, called Burger a "knee-jerk conservative." A colleague on the U.S. Court of Appeals for the District of Columbia Circuit described Burger as a "very emotional guy who somehow tends to make you take the opposite position on issues. To suggest that he can bring the Court together—as hopefully [*sic*] a Chief Justice should—is sim-ply a dream."

But to most people, the appointment of Warren Burger, much less well known outside than inside the judicial community, had been not only a sur-prise but a pleasant surprise. Anthony Amsterdam of the University of Penn-sylvania and the author of the ACLU brief from which the philosophical un-derpinning of the Supreme Court's decision in the case of Ernest Miranda had been derived, described Burger as "the best appointment that could have been expected from the Nixon administration. He is a fine judge and a first-rate legal craftsman. He is a law-and-order man, but he is an enlightened law-and-order man."

The appointment was a particularly pleasant surprise to certain Republican and southern members of Congress.

Republican Everett Dirksen of Illinois, Senate minority leader, the withdrawal of whose support had hastened the doom of Abe Fortas's judicial fortunes: "Number one, he looks like a chief justice. Number two, he acts like a chief justice. Number three, he talks like a chief justice."

Democrat James O. Eastland of Mississippi, chairman of the Senate Judiciary Committee, whose opposition also had done Justice Fortas no good: "I have known Judge Burger personally for many years. He is an outstanding jurist and a very fine man."

Senators John L. McClellan of Arkansas, Sam Ervin of North Carolina, and Strom Thurmond of South Carolina joined in the praise. All were members of the Judiciary Committee, and all had opposed Fortas's nomination. There was little doubt that the Senate would confirm Warren Burger.

At 10:35 on the morning of June 3, thirteen of the eighteen members of the Senate Judiciary Committee gathered in room 2228 of the New Senate Office Building to examine publicly the fitness of Warren Burger to be chief justice of the United States. It would not have been apparent to the casual spectator that the interrogators of Judge Burger at that brief hearing were the same senators who had questioned Fortas in this same room the previous summer. A spirit of cordiality and cooperation pervaded this room where hostility had been evident the previous year. Gentle probing had replaced table-thumping oratory.

Senator Ervin, who a year before had reminded the committee, somewhat testily, that if Abe Fortas had not joined the Supreme Court majority in the case of Ernest Miranda, that decision would have been very different, spoke with warm approval of Judge Burger's previous opinions. Senator Thurmond, who had thundered at Abe Fortas, "Under what authority does the Supreme Court enter that field?" and "Under what authority does the Supreme Court act on that case?" confined himself when Judge Burger sat in the witness's chair to quiet congratulations of the nominee for his "integrity" and "strict construction of the Constitution"—music to Richard Nixon's political ears.

The nominee himself was not unwilling to offer a hint of his future behavior in connection with the Court his predecessor in the witness chair, Abe Fortas, had pronounced an enunciator of "great principles"—and it looked as if some of those "great principles" were going to be put under some strain at least.

Now [Burger declared] procedure is enormously important. Procedure is what protects people. But procedure can carry so much armament that like King Philip's Spanish Armada on the way to

England, the weight made the ships nonmaneuverable and the British were able to sink those that did not sink by their own weight. I think we may—and I am not certain on this—I think we may have approached that point in procedure.

He could not have ingratiated himself more with the members of the Judiciary Committee, whose senior members had been protesting for years the Warren Court's emphasis on procedure as it applied to criminal cases and the rights of defendants.

The entire hearing took an hour and forty minutes. When it was over, the committee went into executive session and voted. The nomination was approved unanimously.

Six days later, on June 9, following a three-hour debate during which the supporters of Abe Fortas sat silent, the full Senate confirmed Burger, 74 to 3 (fellow Minnesotan, Democratic Senator Eugene McCarthy held a seventeen-year-old political and personal grudge against the judge, who had been active in Minnesota politics before coming to Washington in 1953; Democratic Senators Stephen Young of Ohio and Gaylord Nelson of Wisconsin were protesting in their nay votes the haste with which the nomination had been rushed through the confirmation process).

Strom Thurmond articulated the sentiments of many who sat that day in the Senate when he said, "It has been a long time since I have been able to praise a prospective member of the Supreme Court," and prophesied that the appointment of Warren Burger "ushers in a new era of constitutional history."

That new era was ushered in formally two weeks later, on June 23, with unprecedented pomp and ceremony and not a little irony. The attorney general, the solicitor general, the secretary of state, the current president of the American Bar Association, and several former ABA presidents—reflecting Burger's standing in the legal community within which he had practiced his judicial politics—and the president of the United States all were there, seated together at the counsel's tables just below the high bench; three of these men had been considered for the chief justiceship themselves. Scattered about the courtroom were most of the federal judges in the area, retired Supreme Court Justice Stanley Reed, and J. Edgar Hoover of the FBI, as well as the wives of the sitting justices. A few Minnesota friends of the incoming chief justice had come to witness the swearing-in. Mrs. Richard Nixon took a seat next to Mrs. Earl Warren; Mrs. Warren Burger was already sitting nearby. All together 400 guests had been invited.

It was, declared the *New York Times*, a "time of healing," that extraordinary day when the president of the United States, wearing the cutaway coat and striped pants of the government advocate, stood at the lawyers' lectern in

the United States Supreme Court and wished two chief justices, one depart-
ing, the other just arriving, well in the years ahead. As a ritual in the transfer
of power it had few equals.

Richard Nixon was facing as president the men on whose work he had
lavished such scorn and contempt as a presidential candidate, the judges he
had accused of strengthening the criminal forces against the peace forces in
the United States of America. What would he say?

The president was not known for his graciousness, although he could
rise to the occasion when it was demanded of him. Most people remembered
his sulking following his loss of the 1962 California gubernatorial election,
when he had tongue-lashed the press over national television. Few recalled his
generosity and good humor when, as vice president and presiding officer of
the Senate, it had fallen to him to announce formally in the Senate chamber
the results of the electoral college voting in the 1960 presidential election
which he had lost to John Kennedy.

On this June morning in 1969, addressing the justices of the Supreme
Court during the last few minutes of Earl Warren's term, he could not have
been more gracious. He had won, and the extent of his triumph could only be
emphasized by the empty seat at the extreme left, Abe Fortas's, for which
Richard Nixon would shortly have the pleasure of seeking a nominee, and the
secure knowledge that his choice for chief justice, whom he could see sitting
next to the clerk of the Court, was at that very moment robed and waiting to
be sworn in. He had listened expressionless while Justices Marshall and
Stewart had read summaries of the three opinions being handed down that
day, all of which defined certain rights of criminal defendants and authority
of law enforcement officials, to the distinct advantage of the criminal defendants, and overturned several precedents which had been in long service.

Then he had heard the chief justice say, "We are honored today by the
presence of the President of the United States as a member of this Bar.

"Mr. President, may I recognize you at this time."

The president had risen and walked to the lectern. "Mr. Chief Justice,
may it please the Court," he began.

He stood where John Flynn had stood, and Thurgood Marshall and
John Davis, and before them, in other times and other places, Felix Frankfurter and Louis Brandeis and Daniel Webster and Francis Scott Key and
Luther Martin. And he had opened his case with the same words they had
used, and he talked about change and continuity and how the combination
was essential if government as Americans had always known it was to survive.
He said as he began his summation:

> As we look over the history of the Nation we find that what has
> brought us where we are has been continuity with change. No in-
> stitution of the three great institutions of our Government has been
> more responsible for that continuity with change than the Supreme
> Court of the United States.

Over the last 16 years there have been great debates in this country. There have been some disagreements even within this Court. But standing over those debates has been the symbol of the Court as represented by the Chief Justice of the United States: fairness, integrity, dignity.

And he offered his own and the gratitude of the nation for Earl Warren's long dedication to the highest ideals and the public service of his nation. Then, in his concluding remarks, he pressed into one brief paragraph the very essence of change with continuity, describing all the scenes in which the newly elected president had ridden to the Capitol on inauguration day with his predecessor, who was more often than not his political opponent, describing especially the scene all those in the courtroom were about to witness: the retiring chief justice greeting with warmth and administering the oath of office to his successor, although their judicial disagreements ran deep. The words Nixon used were generalities, but it was all there between the lines. Said the president: ". . . this period will be described, not only his but that of his successor, not as the Warren Court, not as the Burger Court, not in personal terms, but in this hallowed moment in this great Chamber, the Supreme Court. It was always that way; may it always be that way. . . ."

Warren responded in kind. If he still nurtured feelings of distrust, even hostility, toward the president, he was prepared, at least publicly, to put them aside, and he thanked Nixon for the "personal, kind words." He concluded his brief remarks with a description of his own vision of the Court, one that also was not without allusions to change and continuity. The Court, he seemed to some of those present to be saying, had survived scandals and calumnies before; it would survive them again.

We do not always agree [Warren said]. . . . It is not likely ever, with human nature as it is, for nine men to agree always on the most important and controversial things of life. If it ever comes to pass, I would say that the Court will have lost its strength and will no longer be a real force in the affairs of our country. But so long as it is manned by men like those who have preceded us and by others like those who sit today, I have no fear of that ever happening. . . .

Following the presentation of the incoming chief justice's commission, the marshal escorted Warren Burger to the center of the bench. Spectators and justices rose. The two chief justices faced each other, men so alike in their climb from poverty to the highest judicial office in the nation, living proof that the American story was not a fiction; so unlike in their judicial ideologies, their differences irreconcilable. The two men were major characters in the American dream. But they had been given different lines to speak, different roles to play. Judge Burger placed his left hand on the Bible and raised his right hand. The chief justice read the oath, clause by clause; Judge Burger repeated it after him:

Chapter 4

You, Warren Earl Burger, do solemnly swear— . . .
I, Warren Earl Burger, do solemnly swear— . . .

The deep baritone voice of the incoming chief justice rang out over the hushed courtroom; no accent betrayed his midwestern origins.

that you will administer justice without respect to persons, and do equal right to the poor and to the rich . . . .
that I will administer justice without respect to persons, and do equal right to the poor and to the rich . . .

The Warren Court had been produced by social and political revolution: the postwar acceleration in man's continuing quest for equality. That Court had in turn produced a social and political revolution, a new and heightened egalitarianism that recognized the victims of racial injustice, the disenfranchised voters, the poor and ignorant among criminal defendants, all the Ernest Mirandas of the world. A People's Court, as its chief for sixteen years had intended.

and that you will support and defend the Constitution of the United States against all enemies . . .
and that I will support and defend the Constitution of the United States against all enemies . . .

The old order was changing. Graciously, peacefully, but changing nonetheless. There would be small changes, immediate changes, obvious changes; there would also be large changes, subtle changes, and slow changes. But changes there would be.

So help you God.
So help me God.

The moment, fragile and precious, had ended. It would be preserved in its entirety only in the memories of the men and women who had watched it.

The 1968 term ended. The justices left the courtroom and made their way to the west conference room, where the retiring chief justice and Mrs. Warren were giving a small reception for the new chief justice and Mrs. Burger.

The man who had criticized *Miranda* had replaced the man who had written it. There was an empty seat at the extreme right, still another opportunity for the president who had campaigned against *Miranda*. Perhaps most important of all, for the first time all three branches of government, the Congress, the president, and finally the judiciary, were now lined up against *Miranda*.

An era as well as a term had ended.

* * *

Change and continuity: Even while the president and the retiring chief justice were addressing the subject, the process had already begun. On June 9, the day the Senate formally approved the appointment of Warren Burger as chief justice of the United States, the nominee had telephoned former Justice Tom Clark, then director of the Federal Judicial Center—a research, development, and training facility for the federal judiciary established in 1968. After he had left the Court in 1967, Clark devoted the remaining decade of his life to improving the quality of justice nationwide. Not only did he serve as first director of the Federal Judicial Center, but he also helped launch the National College of the State Judiciary, where state judges would receive special training. He gave time and attention to organizations working to improve court efficiency, and he himself visited the various circuits, sitting on cases, helping reduce the backlogs. John Frank, writing about the Warren Court, called Clark "the traveling salesman of justice."

Burger had been scheduled to take the oath of office on June 23. Could Clark meet with him and some other experts in court administration for breakfast on June 24? He would like to discuss certain current administrative problems and programs as well as some future projects.

"Why not sooner?" asked the energetic Clark. Burger explained that he was still only a circuit judge, a chief justice designate. He thought it wiser to defer such meetings until he had been formally inducted. Clark agreed.

So it was that on June 24, less than twenty-four hours after the swearing-in ceremony, the new chief justice, the former associate justice, and a varied assortment of lower-court judges and administrators met to discuss the subject Burger considered a dire judicial emergency: the need for court reform. That meeting set the tone for Warren Burger's chief justiceship, his concept of the chief justice not only as decision maker and administrator of the court on which he sat, but as leader of the American legal profession, the prestige of whose high office he would use to improve the administration of justice, not only in the United States Supreme Court and not even limited to the federal judiciary but in the state courts as well and reaching all the way down to the magistrates' courts.

He had complained about court congestion, the delays in the dispensing of justice, the increasing complexities of the administration of the criminal law. Now at last he was in a position to do something about it.

During that early-morning meeting on the day following his installation as chief justice, Warren Burger set out toward a program of judicial reform. It was not a comprehensive plan at that stage. It was, in fact, a small start— added administrative personnel and some new equipment for the federal courts, a touch of modern technology applied to an institution still operating in an age of quill pens. But a start it was.

A week later, on July 1, addressing a meeting of federal judges from the Tenth Circuit (Kansas, Oklahoma, Wyoming, Colorado, New Mexico, Utah), he announced his intention to lead the reform of the administration of justice in this nation. "I intend to take a very active part," he declared. "All the talk of outside activities of judges is totally irrelevant to the administration of justice. Far from withdrawing, I intend to accelerate my activities."

The following month he took his case before a national audience for the first time as chief justice: the American Bar Association meeting in Dallas. If further grounds for believing "the times they were achanging" were needed, they could be discovered here. His predecessor, Earl Warren, had resigned from the organization in anger following its embarrassment of him two decades previously; Burger perceived its 150,000 members as the grass roots of the profession, his constituency, so to speak, and he courted it. For three days that summer of 1969 he glad-handed lawyers and judges, signed autographs, sat in on meetings, and gave five speeches, in all of which he asked the members to join him in his self-assigned mission of reform of the way the American legal profession administered justice. Not just in generalities did he speak—often the case with men in high places—but down-to-earth and practical person that he was, he put forth specific plans: a thorough study of the penal system that was known to encourage crime, changes in legal education, which, he believed, had come to concentrate too much on abstractions, too little on the realities of legal practice; a plan for training a new breed of federal court personnel, managers or administrators, to unclog court calendars.

In time, Burger began to devote an extraordinary amount of his judicial time and energy to such matters, to the detriment, some observers remarked, of his on-the-bench duties. This aspect of the chief justiceship, however, was his way of implementing the soaring promises of his predecessor. He had talked about it before, thrown out suggestions, and, as chairman of an ABA subcommittee, had participated in the formulation of some guidelines. His approach to court reform was consistent with his approach to decision making and writing: straightforward, determined, mechanistic. There wasn't much glory in it; most of the work did not catch the attention of the general public. But Burger believed it was necessary if the overburdened American legal system was to survive. And it was not very long before his efforts were being compared, within the scholarly community at least, with those of William Howard Taft, who as chief justice had remodeled and modernized the entire federal court system.

The 1969 term of the United States Supreme Court, the 180th, opened on October 6. Abe Fortas's empty chair reminded those present that the potential for a change in judicial direction was in the air. As the justices faced the courtroom, they seemed a house divided. On the one side of the ideological spectrum were Justices Black, Douglas, and Brennan, who had voted with the majority in the case of Ernest Miranda, plus Thurgood Marshall. Although as solicitor general he had argued against the imposition on law enforcement of *Miranda* types of rules, his direction since replacing *Miranda* dissenter Tom Clark on the Court in 1967 had pointed toward a renascence of the principles for which Marshall had fought in this very courtroom as a young NAACP lawyer. On the other side of the spectrum were three of the judges who had voted against the majority in the case of Ernest Miranda: Justices John Harlan, Potter Stewart, and Byron White. It was widely believed the new chief justice, appointed by Richard Nixon for just that purpose, would join the latter group. That made it, of course, four and four; who filled Fortas's empty seat would make a majority. Six weeks previously, on August 18, Nixon had nominated Chief Judge Clement F. Haynsworth of the U.S. Court of Appeals for the Fourth Circuit (West Virginia, Virginia, Maryland, North and South Carolina); but the nomination had encountered opposition in the Senate, and as court opened on the traditional first Monday in October, once again the senators and the president were engaged in battle over a Supreme Court nominee.

As the justices had straggled back into the nation's capital following the summer recess, the media had been lavish in their pronouncements upon the future of the Supreme Court under its new chief justice. Observers had been about evenly divided between those who believed the Warren Court would be reversed summarily and those who believed the new Court, as it would be shaped by Richard Nixon over the next few years, would only slow the momentum built up during the Warren stewardship.

One indication that change of some sort was indeed in the air was the presence in the courtroom that morning of Senator Strom Thurmond. Following a thirteen-year self-imposed exile which had grown out of disgust with Warren Court decisions, the South Carolina Republican and southern linchpin of Richard Nixon's presidential candidacy had returned to his former place at the counsel's table from which he had been accustomed to moving the admission of home-state lawyers to the Supreme Court bar.

As was traditional on the first day of a new term, there was little public business. The chief justice admitted ninety-three lawyers to practice before the Court; then the justices left the courtroom and made their way to their private conference room. They would meet there the rest of the week to decide which they would consider of the several hundred petitions for certiorari that had come in over the summer recess as well as the 271 petitions that had been held over from the previous term.

One of the petitions in the pile concerned the case of Ernest Miranda. It had been filed on May 20, 1969, and like so many petitions filed at the end of that term, when the Court was temporarily short two members—Abe Fortas had resigned abruptly; Chief Justice Warren's successor had not yet been sworn in—it had been held over for decision the following term. Miranda's was neither a bellwether nor a landmark case this time around, yet it seems, at least in retrospect, to have been not entirely lacking in symbolic significance.

Following his February 1967 retrial in Maricopa County Superior Court and conviction the second time for rape and kidnapping, Miranda had returned to the Arizona State Prison at Florence, where he had already achieved a certain notoriety and in time would achieve the status of trusty, a high school equivalency diploma, and training in the art of barbering, becoming the warden's personal barber. He seemed, however, not to comprehend entirely the significance of the Supreme Court's decision in his case but viewed it more as a personal achievement—although he deeply regretted the occasion for it—and in his quiet, unassuming way, he kept searching for some way to capitalize on it. He familiarized himself with the fundamentals of the law, particularly the law of evidence, in prison classes, and he considered writing a book about his case. He never did, however, and in the end he was left with little more than the consolation that he had in some way been a dubious hero in the continuing panorama of constitutional history.

Because at his second trial he had been convicted not on the basis of his confession to Officers Cooley and Young that March day in 1963 but on the basis of a second confession to Twila Hoffman when she had visited him at the jail a few days later, an entirely separate constitutional issue had arisen: Was the second confession the result of the first or, as such a result is known in station houses and courtrooms, the "fruit of the poisonous tree"? John Flynn had argued in Maricopa County Superior Court that it was and, as such, it also could not be used as evidence against his client.

When Miranda was convicted the second time, Flynn, with John Frank joining the case for the appellate stages, appealed to the Arizona Supreme Court. When that court again affirmed Miranda's conviction, the lawyers again submitted a petition for certiorari to the United States Supreme Court.

The justices of that Court never give their reasons for either granting or denying certiorari, and so no one knows why this second *Miranda* petition was denied a week after the Court opened, along with 328 others. However, with four votes required for granting cert, it is highly unlikely that they were available. Justice Marshall, whether because he had argued as solicitor general one of the five *Miranda* cases or for other reasons—Supreme Court justices do not reveal their reasons for disqualifying themselves, either—took no part in the consideration of Miranda's second case. It is improbable that the new chief justice would have voted to grant certiorari; this was exactly the sort of case that unnerved him: six years in litigation, the second trial "a game of constitutional chess," which the defense counsel himself, John Flynn, acknowledged had never touched on the issue of guilt or innocence. Justices Harlan, Stewart, and White, dissenters in the first *Miranda* case, would hardly be expected to grant certiorari in one that held potential for expanding it. With the Court functioning with only eight members, those five—one disqualification and four nos—were enough to keep the second *Miranda* case off the Court's 1969 docket.

Six years and seven months after the crime was committed, Ernest Miranda's litigious trail had at last come to an end. Lois Ann Jameson had married and moved from Phoenix; so had Twila Hoffman. And the defendant himself would be eligible for parole within a couple of years. There was a new president of the United States and a new chief justice of the United States.

As constitutional time is reckoned, this second *Miranda* case occupied hardly a moment. As constitutional significance is reckoned, it appeared to have none at all. It did, though, put a period to a long and complex sentence.

The Warren Court, that yeasty mix which could have worked together creatively at perhaps no other time in American history, had gone about as far as it could in proclaiming the supremacy of the individual. A product of its time, the Court had mirrored faithfully the egalitarianism in American society that had grown increasingly impatient following World War II; it had also led, contributing much to the revolution, serving as "the instrument and the motor of time's insistence." To all those who supported equality in the abstract, the Court had declared they must tolerate it in the flesh and had brought the Constitution of the United States within reach of the Ernest Mirandas, fulfilled the bright promises made in the Bill of Rights, and applied its provisions to all, not just a select few. One need not be a baron, a taxpayer, a property owner to claim its protection; one need be only a human being.

Now the old order was changing, and an early-warning signal had come from the Court. It was a small one, dim and not easy to read at the time. But shortly the message would become unmistakable that the work of the Warren Court was done.

CHAPTER 5

January thaw still hovered over Washington; fair and sunny skies, with temperatures reaching into the high forties, had blessed the city all that day, Friday January 30, 1970. Now, as early darkness fell over the city—and the temperature with it—Washingtonians hurrying home from work pushed up their coat collars and thrust their hands in their pockets. Newsmen entering the northwest gate of the White House chatted with police and Secret Service men checking their credentials. Official Washington had become more security conscious since the time when reporters lounged more or less at will outside FDR's office, and even White House regulars were carefully checked before being admitted to the press facilities. The East Room, where the president's press conference was to be held at 6:30 P.M., had been, as usual, closed to the public at noon in preparation.

Inside the mansion itself, the lights, cameras, and wires installed for the occasion by the television cameramen looked out of place beneath the glittering crystal chandeliers of the East Room. Even the simple lectern, decorated only with the presidential seal, ill-suited this elegant salon, originally designed as the "Public Audience Chamber," with its golden draperies and elaborately fluted pilasters and cornices. Guests in flowing gowns and white-tie attire had gathered here to be received by the president prior to state occasions. Weddings and funerals had taken place here, and Pablo Casals had entertained the dinner guests of President and Mrs. Kennedy here in November 1961.

The 300 or so members of the press had taken their seats by 6:15. Some 40 guests and members of the White House staff stood against the back wall.

Precisely at 6:30 the president's press secretary announced, "Ladies and gentlemen, the president of the United States," and Richard Nixon, who had been chatting with reporters, strode to the lectern, which had been placed midway between the portraits of George and Martha Washington—"You always have to make an entrance," he had once told an aide, "you have to walk right in and take charge . . . you sweep in like a leader, and they know you're there."

"Will you be seated, please," the president said, opening this, his ninth press conference since taking office a year ago. The crevices around his eyes seemed slightly deeper, and his hair had turned a shade more silver since inauguration, but he appeared no less calm and confident than he had that day. He was finding it difficult to deliver on his campaign pledges. Inflation had the economy in its grip, and the war in Vietnam seemed no nearer to conclusion than it had before Nixon had taken office. Fear of crime had the streets of the nation's cities in its grip, and upward-spiraling crime rates seemed no nearer to leveling off than they had before Nixon had taken office. He faced a Congress controlled by the Democratic opposition, with which he seemed either unable or unwilling to deal, and his anticrime program, which consisted largely of expanding the Johnson-originated Law Enforcement Assistant Agency (LEAA) and a stern anticrime bill for the District of Columbia, remained bottled up in congressional committees. But he appeared to have adapted the presidency to his own personal rhythms. He looked relaxed as he faced the representatives of the nation's press.

Douglas Cornell of the Associated Press opened the questioning. What were the prospects, he wanted to know, for economic recession? Helen Thomas of United Press International followed Cornell with a question about Vietnam. The Middle East. Two more questions about Vietnam; another on the economy. Finally, the questions on the subject that had been dominating the domestic news for some weeks and that had claimed Nixon's attention since long before he had become the president: the United States Supreme Court and the status of his current choice to replace Justice Fortas, Judge G. Harrold Carswell of Tallahassee, Florida, and the U.S. Court of Appeals for the Fifth Circuit (Texas, Louisiana, Mississippi, Alabama, Georgia, Florida, the Canal Zone*).

Judge Carswell had encountered some unexpected difficulties in the Senate, and there was beginning to be some doubt whether or not that body would confirm him after all. Judge Carswell was the second person and second southerner whom Nixon had named to replace Fortas, recalling scenes in Miami two years before of South Carolina Senator Thurmond winning southern delegations over to Nixon, of Senator Thurmond sitting at the right hand of the Republican nominee when the vice presidential candidate was

* In 1981, having outgrown manageable limits, the Fifth Circuit was divided. Texas, Louisiana, Mississippi, and the Canal Zone remained in the Fifth Circuit. Alabama, Georgia, and Florida were made into a new Eleventh Circuit.

chosen, of Senator Thurmond escorting the Republican nominee to the platform to give his acceptance speech. Judge Clement F. Haynsworth of Greenville, South Carolina, the scholarly chief judge of the U.S. Court of Appeals for the Fourth Circuit had been the first. Civil rights and labor groups, neither of which might have been expected to be enthusiastic about a member of the southern judiciary who had been promoted as a judicial conservative, had delayed his confirmation while questions regarding his professional ethical sensitivities were dug out of his past, and although no evidence of any wrongdoing had been discovered, only a failure to disqualify himself as a judge in a situation regarding which knowledgeable people disagreed, the Senate, more straitlaced than usual following the Fortas scandals, had refused to confirm him.*

If the Senate defeat of the nomination had been a painful rebuff to the president, it had not been a total loss. Southerners in general and followers of George Wallace in particular could not have helped noticing the president's determination to name a southerner to the Supreme Court, and they could sympathize mightily with a loser. Furthermore, Nixon now had the opportunity to name a second person.

Following the Haynsworth defeat, the Senate mood had become somewhat conciliatory, and there was a widespread belief that almost anyone could be confirmed—"anyone who has not been convicted of murder—recently," Republican Senator George Aiken of Vermont had commented wryly.

The president had called in Harry Dent, the young former South Carolina state Republican chairman and administrative assistant to Senator Strom Thurmond, who had been appointed to the president's staff in return for Thurmond's help in the 1968 election and as the president's continuing link with southern voters in the upcoming 1970 congressional and 1972 presidential elections. Judge Haynsworth had been Dent's suggestion.

"Harry," Nixon instructed his aide, "I want you to go out and this time find a good federal judge farther down South and further to the right."

Dent had found George Harrold Carswell, a former federal district judge who had been promoted to the U.S. Court of Appeals for the Fifth Circuit only six months before. It was the deepest South of the Deep South federal

---

* Following the Senate vote on November 21, the judge had issued a statement from his Greenville office. "I must now consider," he said, "whether my usefulness has been so impaired that I should leave the Court of Appeals and return to private life." The president urged him to stay on; so did Hugo Black, who knew him and who, typically, on becoming acquainted, had dug up family correspondence showing that members of his own family in South Carolina and Haynsworths had been friends since "along about Colonial days." Minutes after the Senate vote had been taken, Black had written the rejected judge; he hoped, Black said, "you will accept this as one of the misfortunes of political warfare and continue to serve your country as the good citizen you have been and are." Haynsworth did, in fact, remain a federal judge, distinguishing himself as a mediator and cohesive force among the judges of the Fourth Circuit as well as the author of scholarly and respected opinions with which many disagreed but were persuaded to admire. He resigned as chief judge in April 1981.

circuits. Since in the only case involving *Miranda* issues to which he had been assigned he had written that *"Escobedo* and *Miranda* have made explicit certain specific requirements, thus, hopefully [*sic*] at least, reducing the area where coercion of accused persons is likely to occur," his "strict constructionism" in criminal justice matters did not appear to have been decisive in his nomination. That left his southernness and his demonstrated conservatism on civil rights. As a district judge he had had 60 percent of his civil rights rulings reversed by the court on which he now sat. Soon after his appointment to the Fifth Circuit, he had joined in granting a desegregation delay to five southern states, a delay in which the president himself and the attorney general—who had sent Justice Department lawyers to argue for it—were more than a little interested. On the record, it did not appear likely that Judge Carswell, should the Senate confirm his nomination, would precipitate, or even join in Supreme Court decisions that precipitated, social change. That was what counted.

That and his politics. Formerly a Democrat, Carswell had been persuaded during the Eisenhower presidential campaign of 1952 to take the general's side in a radio debate against a supporter of Adlai Stevenson, against whom Nixon, as the vice presidential candidate, was also campaigning, and Carswell had become known locally as an Eisenhower partisan. Following the election, Eisenhower made Carswell a U.S. attorney, and he became a Republican. In 1958 Eisenhower had promoted him to the federal district court, and in the spring of 1969, having been recommended for promotion by Warren Burger to the attorney general, he was appointed to the Fifth Circuit Court of Appeals. Harry Dent's good friend, William F. Murfin, former Florida Republican state chairman who had been rewarded for *his* efforts in Nixon's presidential campaign with a job in the upper echelons of the Small Business Administration, had suggested Carswell's name to Dent. The judge, after all, Murfin had explained, had already been confirmed by the Senate twice, the last time within the past six months. It had taken the senators just ten minutes to confirm him for the appellate court. It should not be difficult to get him through a third time.

Surprised by the disclosure of Clement Haynsworth's questionable—or at least questioned—judicial ethics as well as by the Senate's willingness to go to the mat for the second time in a year over a presidential appointment, the Justice Department had been meticulous in its investigations of Carswell's financial dealings and holdings. Deputy Attorney General Kleindienst himself had spent two hours with the nominee, asking every conceivable question which might elicit any conceivable embarrassing answer. Carswell had earned high marks.

The Justice Department sleuths, however, had apparently concentrated on Carswell's financial past and had failed to investigate his political past, at least not as thoroughly as had a reporter for a Jacksonville, Florida, television station who discovered the text of a speech Carswell had given in 1948 to an American Legion post in Gordon, Georgia, his home state, when he was running for the Georgia state legislature. Most of the speech was an impassioned denouncement of the black man's postwar drive for racial equality. Echoing the 1948 Dixiecrat slogans of protest against the Democrat's alignment with the black man, he packaged civil rights programs as "Civil-Wrongs" programs, and concluded:

> I am a Southerner by ancestry, birth, training, inclination, belief and practice. I believe that segregation of the races is proper and the only practical and correct way of life in our state. . . . I shall be the last to weaken this firmly established policy of our people. . . . I yield to no man as a fellow candidate, or as a fellow citizen, in the firm, vigorous belief in the principles of white supremacy, and I shall always be so governed. . . .

"God almighty, did I say that? It's horrible!" had been Carswell's immediate reaction when confronted with his words nearly twenty-two years later, in January 1970.

It all had been a long time ago; he supposed he had believed it at the time, but there had been changes, "vast changes, not only in my thinking, but in the country and in the South particularly. . . . This is quite a different day from 1948. . . ." Or, as County Ordinary Wilbur Council, back in Georgia, had remarked, "Ol' Harrold was just playing the game. Back then this county didn't hardly know what an integrationist was."

But it had been too late; the chase was on. Other instances of racial discrimination in Carswell's past were discovered, the most blatant being his role in 1956 in the leasing of a public golf course in Tallahassee to a private club, to which he belonged, for the sole purpose of keeping blacks out. Tales of on-the-bench hostility to black lawyers began to emerge. Analyses of his civil rights decisions, with which the Fifth Circuit docket was top-heavy, indicated a tendency toward slowing the progress of racial equality, reflecting the views of the "plantation crowd," in whose regular routines of banking, business, bridge playing, and bird hunting, the Ernest Mirandas of the world were rarely encountered.

Pressures against the Senate's confirmation of Carswell had begun to build. Although Senators Eastland and Hugh Scott predicted confirmation by a good margin, Carswell's prospects had, in fact, grown bleaker.

The president was prepared when the first question regarding the Carswell nomination was asked about midway in the press conference:

> Q. Mr. President, if you had known about the speech in which he advocated white supremacy, would you have nominated Judge Carswell to the Supreme Court?
>
> The President. Yes, I would. I am not concerned about what Judge

Carswell said 22 years ago when he was a candidate for a State legislature. I am very much concerned about his record of 18 years . . . a record which is impeccable and without a taint of any racism, a record, yes, of strict constructionism as far as the interpretation of the Constitution and the role of the Court, which I think the Court needs, the kind of balance that it needs. . . .

A man was permitted to change his mind, Nixon declared, and in that way he had of turning the tables on his interrogators, he added:

I was reading for example, referring to the press corps here, a very interesting biography of Ralph McGill [outspoken editor and publisher of the *Atlanta Constitution*, who had long argued the cause of racial equality in that paper and who had died in 1969] the other day. In 1940 he wrote a column in which he came out unalterably against integration of education of Southern schools.

He changed his mind later. As you know, he was a very great advocate of integration. That doesn't mean that you question his integrity in his late years because in his early years in the South he took the position that other Southerners were taking. . . .

The Senate, the president predicted, would approve Judge Carswell "overwhelmingly," and he signaled another reporter to ask a question. The newsman changed the subject. But the press had not entirely finished with Judge Carswell's nomination, and a reporter returned to it shortly.

Q. Could you tell us, going back to the Carswell matter, whether or not the two controversial issues raised in the hearings were brought to your attention before you submitted the nomination, during the screening process?

The President. No, they were not. The two controversial issues—I assume you mean the speech that Judge Carswell made when he was a candidate for office and the fact that he had belonged to a restricted golf club—yes. I can only say with regard to the restricted golf club that—I did not know, of course, about the speech—as far as the restricted golf club is concerned, if everybody in Washington in Government service who has belonged or does belong to a restricted golf club were to leave Government service, this would have the highest rate of unemployment of any city in the country.

The questioning of the president continued for the remainder of the half hour, but the Carswell matter was dropped as the reporters once again pursued presidential pronouncements regarding America's involvement in the Vietnam War, the possibilities for success of the peace talks, and the relative strength of American defenses. Then Helen Thomas of United Press International said, as was traditional for the senior wire-service reporter present, "Thank you, Mr. President," and the questioning ended. The reporters rose, and Nixon left, chatting briefly with some he knew as he made his way out of the East Room.

If the president had sidestepped the point when questioned about Carswell's background—which was not that the judge had belonged to a racially segregated golf club but that he had participated in a scheme to evade obeying the law of the land—members of the United States Senate did not.

Judge Carswell's nomination did not proceed so smoothly through the Senate as the early predictions had indicated. It was soon discovered that he had been less than candid with the Judiciary Committee in his explanations of his role in the incorporation of a Tallahassee golf club to avoid its racial desegregation. The rate of reversal of his decisions did not help him, and it was shortly learned that fully one-third of his colleagues on the Fifth Circuit did *not* support his elevation to the Supreme Court. In Carswell's defense, Republican Senator Roman Hruska of Nebraska, a member of the Judiciary Committee and one of the president's men in the Senate, had become an overnight sensation when hurrying from the Senate floor into the path of a radio interviewer, he had thundered: "Even if Carswell were mediocre, there are a lot of mediocre judges and people and lawyers. They are entitled to a little representation, aren't they? [A]nd a little chance? We can't have all Brandeises and Frankfurters and Cardozos and stuff like that there."

As every president knows, a candidate's prospects for confirmation diminish in direct proportion to the increase in time required for confirmation. Lyndon Johnson had sensed this during the struggle over Abe Fortas's nomination and had striven mightily that summer to get him confirmed prior to the Senate's recessing for the national conventions. The supporters of the Carswell nomination realized the truth of that political axiom no less. So, however, did the opponents. At first the opposition consisted of a small band of rather pessimistic senators, whose strategy was to stall for time until enough grass-roots sentiment could be unleashed to force the rejection of Carswell. It worked.

As the proceedings lagged and more and more evidence of Carswell's unfitness for the Supreme Court emerged—there were those who said he was Nixon's revenge on the Senate for its failure to confirm Judge Haynsworth—opposition to his appointment grew. The NAACP was the first to register. Then Judge Elbert P. Tuttle, former chief judge of the Fifth Circuit and one of the most respected men on the federal bench, withdrew his previous endorsement; John Minor Wisdom, an equally respected member of the Fifth Circuit, said he stood with Tuttle. George Meany of the AFL–CIO joined up. Five hundred high-level government workers signed a petition which cited Carswell's "utter lack of qualifications as a jurist"; 350 prominent members of the legal profession took a full-page ad in *The New York Times* and *Washington Post* and other major newspapers; "Judge Carswell does not have the legal or mental qualifications essential for service on the Supreme Court" was the headline; it was sent to every member of the Senate. John

Gardner, former secretary of HEW and at the time director of the Urban Coalition, objected publicly to the nomination. As the opposition across the nation increased, Senate support fell away.

The usual pressures emanated from the White House. Democratic Senator Quentin Burdick of North Dakota, up for reelection this coming fall, was told that if he voted for Carswell's confirmation, his Republican opponent in November would have to make it on his own; if Burdick voted against Carswell, however, he could expect both Nixon and Vice President Spiro Agnew to work North Dakota personally.* Campaign contributors, county chairmen, mayors, state legislators, federal judges, and personal friends of Republican Richard Schweiker of Pennsylvania were urged by administration aides to bring pressure on him to vote for Carswell, although the senator was not up for reelection that year. (Schweiker voted against Carswell.)

The vote on Carswell's nomination in the Senate, when it finally came on April 8, was a proper cliff-hanger. The galleries were packed, and although the vice president, who was presiding in case of a tie, had warned against unseemly outbursts, the ahhhhhs and gasps and occasional applause and cheers could not be hushed as the clerk proceeded through the roll call. When it was all over and the nomination had been defeated, 51–45, the spectators burst into cheers, whistles, and catcalls despite cries for "order" from the Senate floor, and the vice president finally had to demand the galleries be cleared.

When his chief of staff, H. R. Haldeman, brought President Nixon the news, the president limited himself to expressing disappointment. Following a courtesy call to the nominee, during which he urged Carswell to remain on the bench,† Nixon spent the rest of the day closeted with aides in the Executive Office Building, the gray-stone pile next to the White House which at one time had housed the departments of War, Navy, and State and now housed the vice president's staff and the overflow from the president's.

In the early evening, some five hours after the Senate had voted, the president, gathering up his two closest aides, Attorney General Mitchell and Haldeman, boarded the presidential yacht *Sequoia* and set sail down the Potomac for a quiet dinner cruise and some serious talk about his recent nominations to the Supreme Court.

Near noon the following day Mitchell, undeterred by the recent behavior of the Senate, told Senator Eastland that he himself favored naming another southerner to the Court vacancy. The Mississippian offered the attorney general the names of several acceptable southern judges, told Mitchell he didn't care where the nominee was from, so long as he was a "strict constructionist." Nixon was off the hook.

* Burdick voted against Carswell, and Nixon did campaign against him in North Dakota. Burdick was reelected with 62 percent of the vote.

† Less than a week later Carswell announced he had resigned from the U.S. Court of Appeals for the Fifth Circuit in order to run for the Senate. His sponsor was Florida Governor Claude Kirk, an announced white supremacist. Carswell, however, was defeated in the September primary. He retired from public life.

After conferring with Mitchell, the president decided to go outside the South for his next nominee and prepared a statement to that effect. When he issued it at 4:20 P.M., all the accumulated fury which he had controlled at least publicly was unlocked.

He walked to the microphone in the new White House press headquarters, smiled at the reporters gathered there, and hospitably asked them to be seated. His voice was controlled, and his tones were even, but he could no longer suppress the passion in his words:

> ... Judge Carswell, and before him Judge Haynsworth, have been submitted to vicious assaults on their intelligence, on their honesty, and on their character. They have been falsely charged with being racists. But when you strip away all the hypocrisy, the real reason for their rejection was their legal philosophy, a philosophy that I share, of strict construction of the Constitution, and also the accident of their birth, the fact that they were born in the South.

The president had concluded, therefore, that he must find a candidate for the Supreme Court outside the South in order to fulfill his campaign promises, "since the Senate, as it is presently constituted, will not approve a man from the South, who shares my views of strict construction of the Constitution." He had asked Attorney General Mitchell to submit names of judges on state and federal courts; he believed, he said, that a "judge from the North" who shared his views would be confirmed.

Harry Dent, who had had a hand in both nominations and who had watched Nixon's performance with the press, followed the president into the Oval Office afterward to offer his congratulations on the delivery of so stern a rebuke to the Senate. The two men agreed then that Dent should make a tour of the South to explain the president's position and why he could not nominate a third-straight southerner to the Court. To Dent's delight, he discovered that both Nixon and the two rejected judges had become heroes in the South. The nominations and their defeat, he said later, "may have strained some congressional relations and peeved the liberal establishment, but it considerably improved the President's standing with southerners and conservatives. . . ."

In the House of Representatives, the Senate vote on the Carswell nomination also was not without its effect. House Republican leader Gerald R. Ford, following the Haynsworth defeat five months before, had announced he was continuing a study previously begun of possible impeachment action against Justice Douglas, whose behavior on and off the Supreme Court, from his decisions to his divorces, had long irritated segments of American society. Douglas, Ford had charged then, was known to have done work for a charitable organization, the Albert Parvin Foundation, which had Las Vegas gambling connections. He thought sitting justices ought to be held, he had said then, to the same ethical standards as nominees. Now, following the Carswell rejection, Ford announced the start of an actual movement to impeach Douglas.

The president himself urged Ford on by writing a letter to the committee organized to investigate the justice. Citing the obligation of the executive branch "both by precedent and by the necessity of the House of Representatives having all the facts before reaching its decisions" to cooperate, he pledged to "supply relevant information to the legislative branch." The result was that under Nixon's direction and under the authority of this letter, hundreds of documents, including FBI and CIA reports, were turned over to the committee.

The movement, the third of its kind during Douglas's time on the Court, failed like the other two, although the disclosure of his extra-judicial financial dealings with the Parvin Foundation, coming so soon after the disclosure of the suspect dealings of former Justice Abe Fortas with a foundation, served to focus attention on questions of judicial ethics, and some small reforms were achieved. Douglas had, in fact, planned to retire in the spring of 1969, and Chief Justice Warren had reserved a suite of offices for him as a retired justice. But, Douglas said later, "the hound dogs, having got Justice Fortas to resign, had started baying at me. . . . I changed my mind . . . and decided to stay on indefinitely until the last hound dog had stopped snapping at my heels. . . ." On New Year's Day, 1973, longtime baseball fan and former Chief Justice of the United States Earl Warren would make two bets:

> One was that Hank Aaron would break Babe Ruth's home run record [he told dinner guests gathered to honor Douglas] and the other was that Bill Douglas would beat Stephen Field's record for longevity on the Court. Hank Aaron didn't quite make it [that year]; he missed by one home run. That was because so many pitchers walked him he couldn't hit the ball. But they couldn't walk Bill. One of them tried to in the House of Representatives. But the only credit he got was for a wild pitch. So I won one of my bets. . . .

With the nominations to the Supreme Court of Clement Haynsworth and G. Harrold Carswell, Nixon had made his case to the South: kept his promises, paid his political dues. If he had not been able to deliver, he could blame the Senate, a body made up of, he told Dent on the day of Judge Carswell's rejection, a "bunch of bigots."

If Nixon could not have his southerner, however, he would still have his strict constructionist. The one he found was sixty-one-year-old Harry Andrew Blackmun of Rochester, Minnesota, and the U.S. Court of Appeals for the Eighth Circuit (North and South Dakota, Nebraska, Minnesota, Iowa, Missouri, and Arkansas).

He did not consult Harry Dent this time. The president consulted no one except John Mitchell—not the American Bar Association, which had been rating nominees since Eisenhower's presidency; not important members of the Senate, which had to confirm all such nominations. If he recalled his own days in the Senate and the jealousy of that body toward the exercise of its prerogatives, he did not demonstrate it, and unlike his predecessor, who generally sounded out Senate leaders before making candidates public, Nixon kept the name of his nominee a secret between himself and the attorney general, until the last possible minute.

The FBI had conducted a substantially more thorough background investigation to make sure that this time there would be no surprises or damaging revelations like those that had defeated the two most recent nominees. On April 10 the judge had come to Washington, where he had been looked over by Attorney General Mitchell at the Justice Department, then handed up to the White House, where he had spent forty-five minutes chatting with the president himself. Shortly before the nomination was made public by the president's press secretary, Deputy Attorney General Kleindienst had met a group of key Republican senators in a private Capitol hideaway behind the stacks of the Senate document room—an area reserved for just such clandestine meetings—and announced the nomination as a *fait accompli*.

It was widely reported that Chief Justice Burger had suggested Blackmun's name to the president, and under the circumstances, that was not an untoward assumption. The two men had grown up together in the same tough, poor neighborhood of St. Paul and gone to kindergarten and elementary school together. They had separated during college years. Burger had gone to local institutions; Blackmun had gone east to Harvard College on a scholarship, then worked his way through Harvard Law School. But he had returned to practice law in Minneapolis, and the friendship of the two men had endured and continued through two decades of legal practice in and around the Twin Cities. Burger had been best man at Blackmun's wedding.

In 1950, Blackmun had been appointed general counsel for the Mayo Clinic and had moved to Rochester. In 1959 Eisenhower had appointed him to the federal circuit court; the president was said to have done so on the recommendation also of Warren Burger, then a federal judge himself. Warren Burger and Harry Blackmun never had worked together either on cases or in court, but they had remained close friends, continuing to use each other as "a sounding board" at times of personal crisis in their lives.

They were, however, different sorts of people. Burger was tall, solidly built, handsome as a youth and as a middle-aged man, a commanding presence. Blackmun was of medium height and build, the sort of man who tended to melt into the crowd at the symphony. Some years later pickets marching on the Supreme Court to protest the Court's decision legalizing abortion never noticed Blackmun, its author, walking past them during the lunch hour.

Burger's manner was hearty. Blackmun was a quiet man, a collector of stamps and a reader of books. Burger was an inveterate lecturer and prolific writer, an advocate of causes. Blackmun rarely did any of these things.

Where Burger's opinions on the U.S. Court of Appeals for the District of Columbia Circuit had often displayed passion, Blackmun's opinions for the Eighth Circuit were more often unemotional and matter-of-fact, though meticulous, explorations of all the arguments in a case, thorough analyses of both sides, and balanced expositions of the decisions, all of which made for a certain long-windedness on occasion. But like the man, they were modest, cautious, and unassuming in tone.

Whether or not he would have emerged from the long list of able federal judges without the political support of his old friend is, of course, unknown. President Nixon had been "highly impressed with Judge Blackmun's personal qualities," the president's press secretary said in announcing the nomination to the Supreme Court, and believed the judge to be "a man of outstanding abilities . . . legal skills and judicial temperament." In addition—and most important now that homage to the South had been paid—the president believed Blackmun to be a strict constructionist.

Blackmun himself once said he had been, legally speaking, "brought up in the Felix Frankfurter tradition," whose student he had been at Harvard Law School, and his opinions for the federal circuit court demonstrated that the two men shared a perspective on the nature of federalism—a reluctance to involve the judiciary in what both men considered nonjusticiable matters, an inclination to involve the other coordinate branches of government in the formation of public policy. Judicial restraint this approach was called.

But there was an important difference in the nature of this restraint as the two men interpreted their judicial roles. In Blackmun's hands, restraint was passive and passionless. In his former teacher's, it was active, virile, fiery, possessing a vitality of its own.

Felix Frankfurter had no delusions regarding the roles government had played down through the ages. His experience with its arbitrariness had been personal—a boyhood spent in Vienna, where the law was subject to the whim of whoever was in power, an adulthood spent trying to mitigate the effects of persecution on colleagues, family, and friends abroad, including an uncle, an eighty-two-year-old Viennese scholar tossed into jail by Nazi ruffians in 1938 not because he had committed a crime but because he was a Jew. Frankfurter understood just how easy it was to abuse power, how government processes can combine to crush the Solomon Frankfurters, the Izell Chamberses, the Ernest Mirandas. His judicial debates with his brother Black over the merits of the Fourteenth Amendment's due process of law clause versus application of the Bill of Rights to the states seldom failed to involve Magna Carta, the framers of the Constitution, the heroes of American civil libertarianism, James Otis, John Adams, and, yes, even George Sutherland of the Darwinian social and economic views, whose judicial stature had increased enormously in Frankfurter's eyes through his writing the Supreme Court's decision in the case of the Scottsboro boys. Frankfurter's opinions often were lectures on the meaning of academic or political freedom. And at a time when it was common to equate judicial restraint with abdication of judicial responsibility, his writings were more often urgings, even demands, that Congress or the president or some state governor act in matters where he believed his own hands had been judicially tied, and, failing that, the people act at the polls. His trust lay in a lively political system; his confidence lay in the people to make it work.

Harry Blackmun, who had been nominated to the same Court on which Frankfurter had sat for twenty-three years, displayed no such inner judicial dynamics. If Blackmun had been materially poor as a boy, he had been politically rich. The uncertainty of a small Viennese boy, the pain and frustration of an uncle's imprisonment—these lay outside the realm of his experience. And he seemed not only to lack Frankfurter's intensity and passion but to have a certain judicial complacency not unlike that of his old friend the chief justice. Blackmun, like Burger, seemed to start from the premise that if government was not always right, it was at least benevolent, certainly virtuous, its only purpose the well-being of the people, and so both men demonstrated a high degree of tolerence for error in the behavior of the agents of government, including police officers, even for some minimum suppression of liberty, in order that government might remain intact and secure, the better to serve the people. His was not a perspective that encouraged the expansion of individual rights, and Blackmun's, like Burger's, inclination in criminal matters seemed to be to hew closely to the letter of the law where the defendant was concerned and to allow the state a little—not much, just a little—more leeway. As a federal judge Blackmun had participated in only a few cases involving *Miranda* issues and had written nothing with intimations of the future in these, but his basic trust in the integrity of law enforcement had resulted in his deciding with the government and against the defendant in 81 percent of the criminal cases in which he had been involved over the past five years. In a time and place, particularly a place, far removed from Star Chamber proceedings and Nazi persecutions and all the other instruments governments had employed over the centuries in their unending quest for self-perpetuation, it was a judicial approach given widespread credence. But it boded ill for the Ernest Mirandas.

Blackmun breezed through the brief Senate Judiciary Committee hearings, held on April 24 in room 2228 of the New Senate Office Building, the same chamber in which Abe Fortas and Clement Haynsworth and Harrold Carswell and Blackmun himself, prior to his confirmation as a circuit judge eleven years earlier, had been questioned. He had provided the committee with complete information, from his judicial opinions to his income tax returns, and he had taken the precaution of meeting with committee members before the hearing. Consequently, the senators displayed their sweetest sides when they questioned him in public—"A man of your caliber makes the battles worthwhile," commented Senator Birch Bayh, who had led the opposition to Judges Haynsworth and Carswell—and the nominee was all candor, so that it was hardly a surprise when the committee met two weeks later and voted, 17–0, to send the nomination to the Senate floor with the recommendation that it be confirmed. Nor was it a surprise on May 11, following less than an hour's debate, during which the only rancorous contribution was made by southern senators protesting the application of a double standard to Supreme Court nominations, when the Senate confirmed the appointment of Harry Blackmun to the United States Supreme Court, 94–0.

He took the oath on June 9, 1970. It was administered by his old friend and new colleague Chief Justice Burger. He was the ninety-eighth man appointed to the Court. Following the Court session, the chief justice and the new associate justice went to the White House, where they had coffee with the president. By early afternoon the new associate justice was at work in his chambers, the same chambers vacated thirteen months earlier by Abe Fortas.

Despite the defeats of his two southern nominees to the Supreme Court, the president, politically speaking, was still ahead. He had made his pitch to the South, and only eighteen months after taking office, he had been able to appoint men he considered two solid advocates of judicial strict constructionism to the United States Supreme Court, just the way he had promised in his campaign. These appointments, although politically motivated, were bound to have their effect on judicial matters, including, especially perhaps, certain Warren Court decisions. Like *Miranda.*

Scheduled during prime campaign time, September 27 to October 5, to make his second trip to Europe as president, Richard Nixon had intended originally to stay out of the 1970 congressional elections and to leave the campaign oratory, as Eisenhower had done with *his* vice president, to Vice President Agnew, whose talent for it was considerable. A good deal of the groundwork, of course, had been laid before the president left the country.

The South, on which he was building his plans for reelection in 1972, already had been softened by his two unsuccessful nominations to the U.S. Supreme Court and administration support for delay in the desegregation of the public schools.

Two strict constructionists had been appointed to the Supreme Court in the hopes they would counteract the trend to weaken "the peace forces as against the criminal forces."

Legislatively the president, who had sent thirteen anticrime bills to Congress during the past year, had given Republicans some useful talking points. The D.C. crime bill, complete with its controversial provision for preventive detention of potentially dangerous offenders as well as its long-overdue provisions for reorganization of the local court systems, had survived a year of hearings, heated congressional debates, and determined attempts to amend some of its repressive provisions and had finally passed both houses of Congress—"We've got a war on our hands, a war against crime," Senator McClellan had shouted on the Senate floor, "are we going to soften up?" It was signed by the president on July 29, 1970, the only one of the anticrime bills to have become law. The attorney general called it a model anticrime package; the senior senator from North Carolina, Sam Ervin, a hard-nosed legislator, especially in matters concerning crime and criminals, called it a blueprint for a police state. But it had its political uses, as did all those other bills submitted by the administration and ignored by Congress. As the president himself had put it in remarks to reporters in late summer, setting the tone for another election campaign which, like that of 1968, was not destined to raise the quality of politics in America: "Now, if we don't get a better batting average than one out of 13, we are going to have to get some new batters at the plate. . . ."

Prior to his departure, Nixon had privately called in a number of Republican congressmen, potential senatorial candidates, and persuaded them to make their moves this year. A number of Democratic incumbents appeared politically vulnerable; others—a few Republicans as well as Democrats—he wanted to dislodge in revenge for their having voted against his recent nominations to the Supreme Court.

When the president left the country, he had felt confident that his party would gain a number of House and Senate seats, despite the fact that it was an off year, a traditionally frustrating time for the party of an incumbent president. On his return, however, he had discovered the Republican campaigns in total disarray and Republican candidates in "serious trouble in every single race," and so the old warrior had dusted off his armor, sharpened his sword, and prepared once again to lead the attack.

When he left for Europe, the Republicans had successfully preempted and were in control of what was known that year as the "Social Issue," advanced as the deciding issue of the 1970 elections by authors Richard Scammon, former director of the Census Bureau, and Ben Wattenberg, a former speech writer, whose new book on political demography, *The Real Majority*, was being highly praised. It was not a new issue, only a more precisely defined and articulated version of an old one: official scholarly recognition of what George Wallace and Richard Nixon had been saying in their respective styles all along. It concerned the bewilderment, discontent, the fear generated by the social upheavals of the 1960s, and how these upheavals—the civil rights revolution, the turmoil on the campuses, the crime and violence in the streets—had affected the average American voter, whom they described as the forty-seven-year-old wife of a machinist living in a suburb of Dayton, Ohio: one of the "forgotten Americans" to whom Richard Nixon had directed the brunt of his speech accepting the Republican nomination for president two years before.

This woman was afraid to walk the streets alone at night, afraid of blacks moving into her neighborhood, and afraid for her son, who was sharing his college campus with a drug subculture. Fear was again the key to the "Social Issue." Fear of crime; fear of blacks; fear of change; fear of acknowledging the rights of the less fortunate—a forty-seven-year-old housewife's haunting fear of losing all she had.

When he returned from Europe, the president had found the Democrats were outbidding their opponents for political sponsorship of the social issue. The effect on voters of the Democratic candidate for senator in California, John V. Tunney, a protégé of Senator Edward Kennedy of Massachusetts, being seen on television commercials riding around in a police car, or Democratic incumbent Philip A. Hart of Michigan, long an outspoken advocate of curbing crime by attacking poverty and social injustice, also being seen in the company of a uniformed policeman in television advertisements, largely blunted Republican charges that Democrats were "soft on crime." When the Democrats added to the "Social Issue" the vagaries of the economy—"If you had $100 on January 20, 1969," Hubert Humphrey told audiences during his campaign in Minnesota for reelection to the Senate following his 1968 defeat for the presidency, "you have $87.50 now"—the effect looked unpromising for Republicans.

The president "set out to capture the vote of the 47-year-old housewife" upon his return from abroad. Pursued again, as in 1968, by the specter of George Wallace, who had needed no social science textbook to tell him what he understood intuitively, who was running again for governor of Alabama and threatening to run again for the presidency of the United States in 1972, Nixon, too, perhaps was not entirely without the haunting fear of losing all he had. And if anything, the climate of fear was exploited even more than in 1968.

Standing on the steps of the Buncombe County, North Carolina, Courthouse, or on the stage of the Highland High School in Albuquerque, New Mexico, at an improvised speaker's platform at Teterboro Airport in New Jersey, in the Mormon Tabernacle at Salt Lake City, or on the roof of his limousine in San Jose, California, where he was egged and stoned toward the end of the campaign, his arms flailing, voice crescendoing, he had identical messages for the voters, an echo reverberating all the way from the same airports and podiums on which he had stood two years before: ". . . We believe that it is time to stop the attitude of condoning and, by condoning it, encouraging the permissive attitude toward crime and criminal elements in this country. . . ." He needed, he told his fellow Americans, new men in the Senate and House, "new batters at the plate," who would sense the urgency of the crime threat, who would see that the laws written to curb those criminal elements were passed without all the delay his own recent legislative submissions had encountered in Congress. In Phoenix, Arizona, the last stop of the campaign, the city where *Miranda* had begun, the tone of his speeches had become so rancorous that John Mitchell himself had said he sounded as if he were running for "District Attorney of Phoenix, rather than the President of the United States addressing the American people at the end of an important national campaign."

When his fellow Americans went to the polls on November 3, overall the results of the president's stumping were not encouraging. He had campaigned in twenty-one states for thirty-six candidates, and two-thirds of them had lost. There had been some important victories. Democratic Senator Albert Gore of Tennessee, a rare southerner who had voted for a number of civil rights bills during his thirty-two years in Congress and who had voted against the confirmation of G. Harrold Carswell to the Supreme Court as well as against important administration programs, had been a special target of both Nixon and the vice president, and he was defeated by Republican William E. Brock III. Democrat Joseph Tydings of Maryland had voted against the Carswell appointment but had supported the administration-backed preventive detention provision in the D.C. crime bill; Vice President Agnew, however, had put him on the list of "radiclibs," and the Maryland Senator had lost to Republican J. Glenn Beall, Jr. In New York, Republican Charles Goodell, appointed to Robert Kennedy's Senate seat in 1968, having opposed the president's Supreme Court nominations as well as the conduct of the war in Vietnam and having become one of the administration's special interests in the 1970 election, lost to Conservative party candidate James Buckley, who was strongly supported by the Nixon administration.

Other than these, however, the president had little to show for his efforts. Representative George P. Bush of Texas, who had been persuaded to run for the Senate by the President and who had gotten massive help from the White House, lost to Democrat Lloyd M. Bentsen, Jr. Representative William C. Cramer of Florida, who also had been persuaded to run for the Senate by the president and had received strong presidential support, lost to Democrat Lawton Chiles. Seven of the ten congressmen Nixon had persuaded to run for the Senate lost. Democratic Senator Harrison A. Williams of Delaware made his opposition to the president an issue in his campaign and defeated Republican Nelson Gross, for whom the president himself had stumped. And so it went.

The Democrats lost two Senate seats altogether, but the loss reduced their majority only from twelve to ten. They gained nine House seats, giving them a majority of seventy-five. They were still very much in control.

The Democrats also gained eleven governorships. One they retained was Georgia, where an obscure peanut farmer, Jimmy Carter, won over his Republican opponent, Hal Suit, for whom both the president and vice president had campaigned. Ronald Reagan was reelected in California, although the margin of his victory was less than it had been previously. George Wallace was an easy winner in Alabama, with a spectacular 76 percent of the vote.

The geography of adversity was as damaging to the president as the arithmetic. The South, Nixon's hope for 1972, was especially hard hit, with only Tennessee's voters electing any Republicans to the Senate or governor's mansion at all. In South Carolina, Republican segregationist Congressman Albert Watson, backed by Senator Strom Thurmond, lost the governorship to a Democratic moderate on civil rights issues. Democrats also made inroads in the Midwest and West, other areas on which the president planned to rely in 1972. All this provoked the Democrats, for whom victory in 1972 had seemed far out of reach, to revive hope, to begin making plans. Richard Nixon had not been reelected yet, by any means.

To minimize the effect of the 1970 election results, the president, too, began immediately to focus on 1972, meeting with aides, dictating plans and instructions, setting up an organization. He believed that although consolidating a "constituency on the Social Issue had met with only mixed success . . . the basic strategy was right." But its use would probably take another form, and when Herbert G. Klein, his communications director, was asked in a postelection interview whether the administration would continue to use law and order as an issue against Democrats, he replied, "I don't think so."

If Nixon was to be reelected in 1972, some other way must be found. And so the president embarked on a course of action, the escalation of which in later years would have consequences for the nation and persuade a lot of people to question whether he had ever been dedicated to the concept of law and order. It began in a small way, as a simple, even naïve, exercise in political preservation; it differed not in principle but only in degree from the methods employed by other heads of state in other places at other times.

> Sometimes I ordered a tail [he later wrote] on a front-running Democrat; sometimes I urged that department and agency files be checked for any indications of suspicious or illegal activities involving prominent Democrats. I told my staff that we should come up with the kind of imaginative dirty tricks that our Democratic opponents used against us and others so effectively in previous campaigns. . . .

It would end in national disaster.

CHAPTER 6

Every now and then since assuming the office of chief justice of the United States in June 1969, according to Justice Douglas, Warren Burger would remind his brethren gathered around the conference table that certain precedents set by the Warren Court should be overruled. *Reynolds* v. *Sims*, which had been written by his predecessor and which required both houses of state legislatures to be apportioned on the basis of population, was one. *Gideon* v. *Wainwright*, which required that indigent defendants in felony cases be provided with legal assistance at their trials, was another. *Miranda* v. *Arizona* was a third.

Opportunity at least to take some of the backbone out of *Miranda* had not been long in presenting itself. Three days after the Senate Judiciary Committee hearings on the nomination of Clement Haynsworth to the U.S. Supreme Court had ended, on September 27, 1969, Joel Martin Aurnou, well-known Westchester County, New York, lawyer, had filed with the Court a petition for certiorari in the case of Viven Harris, convicted of selling heroin in a New Rochelle, New York, bar to an undercover police officer. The case, having to do with the exclusion of evidence in a criminal trial, must have had special appeal to the chief justice, who during his years as a circuit judge had labored mightily, both on and off the U.S. Court of Appeals for the District of Columbia Circuit, for the dismemberment of the exclusionary rule, or the Suppression Doctrine, as he called it.

Aurnou argued in the petition for cert that Viven Harris's statement, given in the district attorney's office without benefit of *Miranda* warnings, should not have been used at his trial to impeach his credibility. Said Aurnou, quoting the lone dissent to the New York State Court of Appeals' affirmance of Harris's conviction:

> [T]o allow the use of an illegally obtained confession or statement even for impeachment purposes was violative of a court's responsibility to preserve and maintain basic constitutional rights. Not alone a need to deter official misconduct but a regard for "the imperative of judicial integrity" . . . mandates that a confession which was unlawfully taken from a defendant should not be used for any purpose.

Viven Harris's case was important both for its timeliness—the first *Miranda* case of any dimension to come before the Court under Chief Justice Burger—and for the questions it raised. The legal issue was this: A confession was obtained illegally, under conditions prohibited by the *Miranda* ruling—a confession which could not be used by the prosecutor as evidence on which to *build* his case against the defendant. Could it be used, however, to impeach the defendant's credibility—that is, to make him out a liar in front of the jury? The legalistic nature of this question tended to obscure some of the larger questions:

• Once illegally obtained evidence could be used for any purpose at all, could these purposes be expanded and the courtrooms of America be opened to other sorts of illegally obtained evidence? It was as direct an attack on the exclusionary rule as had been mounted during Chief Justice Burger's brief time in office.

• What would be the effect of putting an illegally gotten confession before a jury? Every criminal lawyer knows that a judge's instructions to a venireman to consider evidence not for its substantive value but only for indications of a defendant's credibility are futile, that evidence once heard can hardly be forgotten.

• Would the possibility of being made to look untruthful effectively deter defendants from taking the witness stand at their trials, thus denying them a linchpin of defense? Was a defendant damned if he did and damned if he didn't?

• Or was *Miranda* providing a hiding place for perjurers?

• Would allowing an illegally obtained confession into the courtroom, even though only for impeachment purposes, encourage police to obfuscate, if not in time completely to ignore, the requirement to give suspects full *Miranda* warnings?

• Perhaps most important of all, was the integrity of the judicial process and the government itself impugned in its attempt to convict a lawbreaker on the basis of evidence obtained by unlawful means?

Although the confusions and contradictions surrounding the impeachment issue did not nearly approach the proportions of confusions and contradictions regarding confessions during the immediate pre-*Miranda* months, state and federal courts were at this point having to decide this issue with some regularity, and they were not always in agreement. In his brief for Viven Harris, Aurnou supported his arguments with citations from sixteen separate jurisdictions which had, in the light of *Miranda*, refused to admit confessions like Viven Harris's for impeachment purposes—including one from Burger's old bench, the U.S. Court of Appeals for the District of Columbia Circuit, written by Judge J. Skelly Wright, a member of that group of judges who tended to follow Judge Burger's professional opponent, David Bazelon, in criminal matters. In response, James J. Duggan, the representative of the Westchester County district attorney's office who would argue the case in the Supreme Court, supported *his* arguments with citations from eight jurisdictions which had admitted for impeachment purposes statements and confessions obtained illegally under the *Miranda* ruling.

In September 1969, when Aurnou filed the petition for his client, the U.S. Supreme Court had been operating at less than full strength as a result of the resignation of Abe Fortas the previous spring, and a decision whether or not to grant the Westchester County lawyer's request to be heard had not been made immediately. Because of its significance, however, Viven Harris's case may have been one of those channeled into a "Hold for Haynsworth" file which the justices had established when it looked as if that judge would be confirmed, then transferred to a "Hold for Justice X" file following his rejection in November. Not until June 1, 1970, after the Senate's rejection of Judge Carswell and the subsequent confirmation of Harry Blackmun, was certiorari finally granted.

Just over six months later, on the afternoon of December 17, 1970, Joel Aurnou stood where John Flynn had stood four years earlier to argue the case of Ernest Miranda. Aurnou was thirty-six years old, a short, round-faced, bespectacled man given to a dramatic courtroom manner as well as the dogged pursuit and compilation of evidence.

The Court he faced was quite different from that John Flynn had faced. In the center chair sat not Earl Warren, author of the majority opinion in Ernest Miranda's case, but Warren Burger who hoped to overrule it. Richard Nixon's first appointment to the Supreme Court, Burger was still rather new at his job. He had not, however, been at all reluctant to use the power that accompanied the office. Following his suggestion to the ABA in the summer of 1969 that a program for training court managers be established, he had immediately drawn up a rough blueprint for it during his September vacation, and within less than a year, having received support, expertise, and momentum from the ABA and other professional organizations, the Institute for Court Management had opened at the University of Denver. He had been responsible that same summer for persuading the ABA to undertake a serious and thorough examination of the American corrections system; he himself had spent a good deal of time visiting local prisons to learn about conditions firsthand, and he had delivered a major speech on prison reform just last winter. This past August he had begun a tradition of giving a state of the judiciary talk at the ABA's annual meeting in which he generally offered suggestions for unsnarling some phase of judicial operations. It was the sort of work that seemed to agree with his utilitarian nature. He made few suggestions that were new, but he had a talent for bringing together and articulating ideas that had been abroad in the legal world for years. He himself had discussed them as a circuit court judge. But people seemed more inclined to listen when it was the chief justice of the United States who was speaking. He seemed, in fact, to enjoy that phase of his office somewhat more than decision making, and he was devoting ever-larger amounts of time to it.

However, this December afternoon he was composed and businesslike as he took up the case of Viven Harris. If he was unsmiling, he was unfailingly courteous, his firm baritone kindly and inviting, belying the ordeal the lawyer before him was about to endure in his first appearance before the justices of the United States Supreme Court. Aurnou began to recite the basic facts of Viven Harris's case.

Flanking the chief justice were the two senior justices, Hugo Black, eighty-four, on his right, William O. Douglas, seventy-two, on his left. Age was beginning to show on their faces. This would, in fact, be Black's last term. He had had a slight stroke on the tennis court recently but had seemed "fit" when the term opened; nevertheless, toward the end of it, he would give his wife a signed but undated letter of retirement to be used in the event he should at some future time be unable to function. Of the original *Miranda* majority, William J. Brennan, sixty-four, also remained, and Thurgood Marshall, heavier, jowlier, his straight black hair grayer now than when he had stood where Aurnou was standing and addressed the justices in behalf of Carl Calvin Westover, had joined this group more often than not when decisions were made in criminal cases.

Of the dissenters in *Miranda*, there were John Harlan, seventy-one—it would be *his* last term, too—plus Potter Stewart and Byron White, both in their mid-fifties, at the peak of their powers. At the far right end of the bench, as Aurnou faced it, sat the Court's newest member, Harry Blackmun. Sworn in just the previous June, he had taken his seat in the courtroom for the first time when the term opened on October 5. His judicial inclinations during the eleven years he had sat on the circuit court combined with his long personal friendship with the chief justice had provoked the media to connect him with his old friend and lump them together as the "Minnesota Twins."

There was no invocation of Magna Carta or even the Fifth and Sixth Amendments to the Constitution during Aurnou's presentation of Viven Harris's case to the justices, as there had been at the arguments in Ernest Miranda's case. There was no impassioned "But is it *fair?*" from the center of the bench, not even a "Where does it say *that* in the Constitution?" from the senior associate justice; Mr. Justice Black was quiet this afternoon, content to rock gently back and forth as he listened.

There was little opportunity for Aurnou's customary courtroom theatrics. The talk here was all of a legalistic nature as the participants slugged out the meaning of *Miranda*. The justices asked tough questions, and the hour sped by as they explored how the trial judge had handled the issues raised by Aurnou regarding the prosecutor's use of the inadmissible confession, what precedents existed for using illegally obtained evidence and how the standards had been determined, whether the inadmissible statement had actually been coerced and what constituted coercion. The question of the government's lawlessness in obtaining the confession and its integrity in using it, like the perspective of history, never entered the discussion.

Finding himself in the majority at the conference following the argument, Chief Justice Burger assigned to himself the writing of the opinion in Viven Harris's case. As a federal appellate judge, having become adept at allowing the inclusion of evidence at trials that some other judges might have found less tolerable, now as chief justice he was able to threaten seriously one application of the exclusionary rule.

The exclusionary rule was a peculiarly American invention for which there was no equivalent in Roman law or English common law, the traditional sources of American practices and procedures—a lack which opponents of the rule rarely failed to cite as evidence of its questionable worth.

The Constitution of the United States said nothing about an exclusionary rule either. It was a judge-made device given constitutional dimension through judicial decision. It surfaced for the first time in 1886, when the U.S. Supreme Court, supported by quotations from the writings of James Otis and John Adams, declared a man's private papers inadmissible as evidence in court because they had been seized illegally, in violation of the Fourth Amendment to the Constitution. Over the next couple of decades its fortunes declined; then it reappeared in 1914, when the U.S. Supreme Court reversed the conviction of a Kansas City, Missouri, express company employee accused of illegal use of the mails. He had been arrested without a warrant, his house had been ransacked, also without a warrant, and police had made off with various of his papers, which were later introduced as evidence at his trial. This decision is usually cited as the modern origin of the exclusionary rule. It applied, however, only in federal courts; it was not until 1961 that the Supreme Court ruled it must apply in state courts, too.

The original purpose of the rule had involved matters of principle, lofty restatements of constitutional underpinnings. Said Justice William R. Day for the Court in 1914: "The efforts of the courts and their officials to bring the guilty to punishment, praiseworthy as they are, are not to be aided by the sacrifice of those great principles established by years of endeavor and suffering which have resulted in their embodiment in the fundamental law of the land . . . ."

Said Justice Tom Clark in 1961, agreeing, despite a predisposition to decide cases in favor of law enforcement:

> There are those who say, as did Justice (then Judge) Cardozo, that under our constitutional exclusionary rule, "[t]he criminal is to go free because the constable has blundered." . . . In some cases this will undoubtedly be the result. . . . [However, if] the criminal goes free . . . it is the law that sets him free. Nothing can destroy a government more quickly than its failure to observe its own laws.

Despite these statements of principled purpose, the exclusionary rule had come to be over the half century of its existence little more than a simple tool for enforcing the Constitution, a restraint on police misbehavior, and discussion of it generally centered not on its applicability to issues of government integrity but on whether or not it worked as a deterrent to official lawlessness. Workability was Warren Burger's measuring stick.

There were judges and scholars and lawyers, even some prosecutors—although not many policemen—who believed the exclusionary rule was the most reliable way to deter lawlessness among law enforcement officers. And there were judges and scholars and lawyers and prosecutors who believed the exclusionary rule the most *un*reliable way to deter lawlessness among law enforcement officers.

There were also those who opposed the use of the exclusionary rule under certain conditions and not under others. People who opposed its application to violations of the Fourth Amendment's prohibition of unreasonable searches and seizures—to which it has most often been applied—opposed it on the grounds that ten bags of heroin are, after all, ten bags of heroin, whether the policeman entered a man's house legally with a search warrant or whether he broke down the door. The evidence was dependable and, it was believed, established guilt accurately. The same people might, on the other hand, approve use of the exclusionary rule in connection with violations of the Fifth Amendment's guarantee against compulsory self-incrimination on the grounds that a forced confession was highly *un*dependable evidence and did not necessarily establish guilt. Warren Burger did not always differentiate between them. Certainly not in Viven Harris's case.

The chief justice's announcement of the Court's decision in *Harris v. New York* on February 24, 1971, was casual, more casual than a decision that would have repercussions over the next decade at least deserved. If, understandably, he felt some relish at overruling his old colleagues—and judicial rivals—on the U.S. Court of Appeals for the District of Columbia Circuit, it did not show in his voice. He passed off *Harris* as "of interest mostly to members of the bar" and "not worth describing from the bench." It was also brief: just eleven paragraphs, seven of which were devoted to describing the facts of the case itself and its progress through the New York State Courts.

He took his logic, as he had as a circuit judge in similar cases, from a

Chapter 6

1954 Supreme Court decision, *Walder* v. *United States*, in which Felix Frankfurter had written for the majority:

> It is one thing to say that the Government cannot make an affirmative use of evidence unlawfully obtained. It is quite another to say that the defendant can turn the illegal method by which evidence in the Government's possession was obtained to his own advantage, and provide himself with a shield against contradiction of his untruths. . . . [T]here is hardly justification for letting the defendant affirmatively resort to perjurious testimony in reliance on the Government's disability to challenge his credibility. . . .

Burger had come to the same conclusion as Frankfurter had sixteen years before: Otherwise inadmissible statements, if trustworthy, might be used to attack the credibility of a defendant's trial testimony. The chief justice had no intention, he declared, of overruling *Miranda.* However, he said, "The shield provided by *Miranda* cannot be perverted into a license to use perjury by way of a defense, free from the risk of confrontation with prior inconsistent utterances. . . ." Viven Harris, in effect, had been shown to be a liar by the Westchester County prosecutor, and his conviction was affirmed.

At conference, William Brennan, a pillar of the former Warren Court majority, had voted with the chief justice; he had to, he said, unless *Walder* was to be overruled. On reflection, however, he decided *Walder* did not control the case, and he dissented with some vehemence. Douglas, who had dissented in *Walder*, joined him, as did Marshall; Black dissented alone and without explanation, though he told the brethren privately that having reread his dissent in *Walder*, he did not think he could join the majority in *Harris*.

Brennan insisted in his dissent that *Miranda* protected the "individual from being compelled to incriminate himself in *any* manner" and that the *Harris* majority was attacking the integrity of the adversary system itself. Although he noted with encouragement that no fewer than six federal courts of appeals and the appellate courts of no fewer than fourteen states had refused to distinguish between the methods of introducing confessions and had decided "[a]n incriminating statement is as incriminating when used to impeach credibility as it is when used as direct proof of guilt and no constitutional distinction can legitimately be drawn" and that only three state appellate courts would have agreed with the U.S. Supreme Court majority, he was not sanguine regarding the future with *Harris*.

> [T]o the extent that *Miranda* was aimed at deterring police practices in disregard of the Constitution [Brennan concluded], I fear that today's holding will seriously undermine the achievement of that objective. The Court today tells the police that they may freely interrogate an accused incommunicado and without counsel and know that although any statement they obtain in violation of Miranda cannot be used on the State's direct case, it may be introduced if the defendant has the temerity to testify in his own de-

317

fense. This goes far toward undoing much of the progress made in conforming police methods to the Constitution.

The brevity of the majority opinion and the casualness with which the chief justice delivered it belied its importance. For Burger himself, finally in a position to influence the administration of criminal justice about which he had been writing and lecturing as long as he had been a judge, particularly the exclusionary rule, it was a personal triumph.

Harris did not, of course, directly overrule *Miranda.* The Supreme Court almost never directly overrules a precedent so soon after establishing it; the Court may chop at it or fail to take it to its logical conclusion, but a much longer time is required for overruling; between *Betts* and *Gideon* lay twenty years. The point about *Harris*, however, was that the lid was off *Miranda.* As soon as evidence could be included rather than suppressed or excluded in a trial for any reason, there was no telling where the justices would stop.

As it had been in the decision in the case of Ernest Miranda, the Supreme Court had divided in *Harris*, 5–4; the three dissenters in *Miranda* joined with the two Nixon appointees to make a majority. It was a slim majority, but much of the work of the Warren Court had been accomplished with a majority just that slim. And it was a natural majority, the alignment of the *Miranda* dissenters with the Nixon appointees, a bellwether, indicating the emergence of a new ruling class on the Court and, potentially, the whittling away of much the Warren Court had fashioned, not only by the highest court in the land but by lower courts, state and federal, which tended to adopt the letter as well as the tone of the law. Indeed, the chief justice's conclusion that *Miranda*'s "shield . . . cannot be perverted into a license to use perjury" became one of the most quoted judicial statements in America in the months following his announcement of the *Harris* decision. Whether such a group would hold together ultimately to overrule *Miranda*, however, could not yet be certain. The map to the justices' minds could not be read in one opinion.

Hugo Black did not return to his seat on the Supreme Court for the 1971 term. His health had been declining for some time, and on August 28 he was taken to the Naval Medical Center in suburban Bethesda. Recognizing the seriousness of his condition, he sent his resignation to the president on September 17. Following a series of strokes, he died on September 26. He was eighty-five years old. He had sat on the Supreme Court of the United States for thirty-four years. His service had spanned the administrations of six presidents.

Carrying out his request, his family chose a plain pine coffin. They stuffed the pocket of his suit coat not with sweetmeats as if he were an ancient Egyptian pharoah but with several copies of the Government Printing Office edition of the United States Constitution, which he had kept close at hand for many years. The coffin, knotty and streaked, stood out in the splendiferous setting of Washington National Cathedral, where his funeral was held. A thousand people came, including President Nixon, who sat expressionless while a minister read from the justice's concurring opinion in the *Pentagon Papers* case of the previous term, in which he had upheld the absolute First Amendment right of press freedom against the contentions of that same president. The minister also read from the late justice's own library: Aeschylus, Cicero, Virgil, Diogenes, and Thomas Jefferson, all Black favorites. His brethren served as honorary pallbearers, and he was buried later that day in Arlington National Cemetery among senators and presidents and the plain soldiers who had fought for their country.

If any justice in the Court's history, now approaching 200 years, had the effect of a constitutional amendment, Hugo Black had had that effect. He was bold and creative in his thinking, truly one of the poets, and when the others outvoted him, leaving him alone with his adventurousness, he showed that poets could be tenacious, too, and he held fast to his ideas, losing friends and gaining them over the years, but mostly gaining, until his own judicial star was in the ascendancy and what had been poetry became law, too. Legislative apportionment—"they thought I was crazy," he said later about his brethren when they read his 1946 dissent arguing that the Constitution required equality of representation and that it was enforceable in the courts. The outrageous notion that the Bill of Rights applied to the states as well as the federal government. Most memorable of all, perhaps, that "no man shall be deprived of counsel merely because of his poverty," which only blew in the wind in 1942, became the law of the land in 1963 in the case of Clarence Earl Gideon. Hugo Black, more than any other one man perhaps, had made *Miranda* possible.

John Harlan did not return to his seat on the Supreme Court for the 1971 term either. When Black was taken to the naval hospital at Bethesda, his next-door neighbor in the VIP tower had been his longtime colleague, who was at the time suffering from back pains. The pains were later diagnosed as cancer of the spine. On September 24, the day before Black's death, Harlan sent his resignation to the president. He died three months later, on December 29, 1971, in George Washington University Hospital, in Northwest Washington.

A few people used to joke about John Harlan; they would mention him as a presidential possibility—on the Whig ticket. But Abe Fortas had been much nearer the mark with his description of Harlan as one who had helped keep "exactly the right mix in the carburetor" of the Court. And when Harlan had wanted to resign, believing his near-blindness was slowing the work of the Court, Chief Justice Warren had persuaded him to stay on. "No, John," Warren had said, "your contribution from the opposite point of view is too valuable," and unknown to Harlan, Warren had hired an extra secretary for him out of Warren's own pocket. Where Black was lyrical, Harlan was analytical; where Black soared, Harlan plodded. But his intellect was no less stalwart than Black's. The great dissenter of the Warren Court, Harlan did not see his dissents become the law of the land, as Hugo Black did. But his contribution, though less well known outside the legal community, was no less substantial than Black's, and one commentator on the Supreme Court, upon the passing of the two justices in the fall of 1971, mourned not the loss of an activist and a restrainer, a liberal and a conservative but the loss of "the quality of quality."

When the United States Supreme Court opened the 1971 term on October 4, William O. Douglas had moved into the seat of the senior associate justice which his friend and colleague the late Hugo Black had occupied since 1945, and the other justices had moved up two seats in seniority, leaving both end seats empty. Again, the Court was operating without its full complement, and again, decisions and arguments in important cases had been postponed pending the seating of the two new justices.

Less than three weeks later, on October 21, the president announced on national television—which was becoming an arm of the presidency—his choices for the two end seats: Lewis Powell, sixty-four, of Richmond, Virginia, a prominent practicing lawyer and former president of the American Bar Association; and William Hubbs Rehnquist, forty-seven, formerly of Phoenix, Arizona, and currently head of the Justice Department's Office of Legal Counsel, a position described by Nixon as "the President's lawyer's lawyer." He had used three criteria in making the selections: He had wanted strict constructionists; he still wanted to appoint a southerner; and, above all, he wanted them to be confirmed. He had, he said, made a "serious and intense" search for a woman to fill one of the seats but found that "in general the women judges and lawyers qualified to be nominated for the Supreme Court were too liberal to meet the strict constructionist criterion I had established." Said the president when he presented his nominees to the American people, still echoing the rhetoric of his campaign three years previous:

> As a judicial conservative, I believe some Court decisions have gone too far in the past in weakening the peace forces as against the criminal forces in our society. In maintaining, as it must be maintained, the delicate balance between the rights of society and defendants accused of crimes, I believe the peace forces must not be denied the legal tools they need to protect the innocent from criminal elements. And I believe we can strengthen the hand of the peace forces without compromising our precious principle that the rights of individuals accused of crimes must always be protected.
>
> It is with these criteria in mind that I have selected the two men whose names I will send to the Senate tomorrow. . . .

In the history of the U.S. Supreme Court, only three justices had been older than Lewis Powell at the time of their appointments: Horace H. Lurton, who was sixty-five; Charles Evans Hughes, who was sixty-seven when he was appointed the second time in 1930; and Harlan Fiske Stone, who was sixty-eight when he was elevated to the chief justiceship in 1941. Indeed, Powell had cited age as a factor in declining the appointment when he had been considered previously by the Nixon administration for the seat vacated by Abe Fortas. But the president had persevered. "Ten years of Powell," he had said, "is worth 30 years of anyone else."

Tall and slim, with a gentle and courtly manner that hid a basic shyness, Lewis Powell was the prototype of the southern gentleman, establishment born and bred. The first Powell to land in Virginia was an original Jamestown colonist. The nominee himself had had a private-school secondary education and four years as an undergraduate at Washington and Lee, where Virginia gentlemen are sent and where he was president of the student body as well as Phi Beta Kappa. He continued at Washington and Lee Law School, from which he was graduated first in his class in 1931, then took a postgraduate year at Harvard Law School, where he, like Blackmun, was a student of then professor Felix Frankfurter. Except for thirty-three months spent as an air force intelligence officer in North Africa during World War II, he had spent the rest of his professional life in the private practice of law in Richmond, becoming an expert in corporate law as well as a director of several major corporations, including Philip Morris, Squibb, Ethyl, and Chesapeake and Potomac Telephone. His acquaintance with the Ernest Mirandas of the world had been more in the abstract than the real, limited in the noblesse oblige tradition to membership on bar committees, public service projects, and presidential commissions.

Lewis Powell was a southerner, with southern roots and southern traditions, but he was not a segregationist. He belonged, he acknowledged at the time of his nomination to the Supreme Court, to two clubs which discriminated on the basis of race and to two clubs which did not. His law firm, at the time of his appointment one of the oldest, largest (with upwards of 100 lawyers), and most prestigious in the state, had never employed a black lawyer. But as chairman of the Richmond School Board from 1952 to 1961 he had been influential in keeping the local public schools open and in their eventual peaceful desegregation, despite the demands of politicians for "massive resistance" to the U.S. Supreme Court's decision in *Brown* v. *Board of Education*. Then, just the last year, he had written, at the request of Virginia's governor, an amicus curiae brief to buttress the state's case against busing in the U.S. Supreme Court. One commentator characterized him as neither segregationist nor integrationist, but as a legalist.

Politically he had supported, along with a number of Virginia bankers and businessmen, the reelection to the Senate in 1970 of Democrat and political conservative Harry F. Byrd, Jr., as had the president, who had made it clear to Virginia Republicans that he did not want them to nominate a strong opponent.

In matters of criminal justice, Powell, at the outset of his presidency of the ABA in 1964, had made the launching and financing of the ABA's project on formulating minimum standards for the administration of criminal justice a top priority (his new chief-to-be, Warren Burger, had been chairman of a subcommittee). Over the years Powell had articulated some concerns about the lengths to which the U.S. Supreme Court had gone in protecting the rights of criminal defendants and "correspondingly limited the powers of law enforcement," and regarding the *Miranda* ruling in particular, he had joined, as a member of the president's crime commission, the dissenters to the 1967 report and urged, in effect, a return to the voluntariness standard for admitting confessions in court. The need, he had said just the previous August, writing in the *Richmond Times-Dispatch*, was for "greater protection—not of criminals but of law-abiding citizens." He was questioned closely during hearings before the Senate Judiciary Committee prior to his confirmation regarding his criticism of the Supreme Court's approach to confessions as evidenced by its decisions in *Miranda* and *Escobedo*. He refused, in the time-honored tradition of nominees, to say whether he would still like to see these decisions overruled, but it was apparent in his testimony, taken as a whole, that he would. Which would add another justice to the Burger-Stewart-White-Blackmun axis—a majority.

Shortly before President Nixon announced William Rehnquist as his selection for the last vacant seat on the U.S. Supreme Court, Department of Justice gossip to that effect filtered into Rehnquist's office. He, of course, denied that he was even being considered.

"I'm not from the South," he argued, smiling, "I'm not a woman, and I'm not mediocre."

On all points he was correct. First in his class at Stanford Law School, from which he was graduated in 1952, he was admired as a gifted scholar by faculty and students alike. He won a coveted Supreme Court clerkship following graduation and came East to clerk for Justice Robert Jackson. When it was over, he decided to settle in the Southwest—he had grown up in Milwaukee—and tossed a coin: heads for Phoenix; tails, Albuquerque. The coin came up heads.

He settled in Phoenix, where again he built a reputation for professional brilliance in his law practice. Like Lewis Powell's, William Rehnquist's clients were largely businessmen, and although by 1965, when Robert Corcoran of the local ACLU was looking for a lawyer to represent Ernest Miranda in the United States Supreme Court, William Rehnquist's name was a prominent one among Phoenix attorneys, he was not the sort of lawyer ACLU officials normally looked to. The Ernest Mirandas were strangers to William Rehnquist, not only because his clientele was largely corporate but because he would not have been particularly sympathetic to the goals of the ACLU in the case.

Privately Rehnquist was known as a quiet and gentle man with a fine sense of humor and a pleasant manner; publicly he was known as a brilliant, outspoken, and uncompromising conservative. He had been labeled the "school conservative" at Stanford. Memorandums he wrote as a clerk to Jackson, one urging the justice to vote against the Court's hearing the last appeal of Ethel and Julius Rosenberg, convicted atomic spies; another lamenting the possibility that the Court might decide to outlaw segregation in the public schools, assured the label's sticking—publication of the latter while his nomination to the Supreme Court was pending threatened his confirmation, although whether the memo articulated his own or Jackson's views never was entirely clear. Soon after moving to Phoenix, he had joined the extreme right wing of the Republican party then winning control in Arizona. In 1957, in his first political speech—to the Maricopa County Young Republicans—he denounced the "left wing" of the Supreme Court, Earl Warren, William O. Douglas, and Hugo Black, who, he charged, were "making the Constitution say what they wanted it to say." A few months later, in December 1957, he wrote for *U.S. News & World Report* an article on the Supreme Court which was widely publicized because of his authoritative viewpoint as an ex-clerk and in which he accused the majority of his fellow clerks, who, he said, stood politically to the " 'left' of either the nation or the Court" of allowing "unconscious bias" to creep into their work; he implied that the justices might be influenced by the clerk's politics. In 1964 he had been active in Barry Goldwater's campaign under the direction of Richard Kleindienst, the originator of the law-and-order issue in that and the following presidential campaign. In 1968, when the Republicans won the presidency and Richard Kleindienst was appointed deputy attorney general, he brought Rehnquist to Washington with him, the latter being appointed head of the Justice Department's Office of Legal Counsel, an equivalent in rank to assistant attorney general. In the Justice Department, Rehnquist had been the administration's chief advocate for the D.C. crime bill, particularly its provision for preventive detention, which had passed in 1970.

Although his long sideburns and bright shirts and ties belied his inner conservatism, William Rehnquist, the president expected, would fit nicely into a strict constructionist judicial pattern. Both he and Powell were confirmed by the Senate in early December and sworn in by the chief justice on January 7, 1972.

Richard Nixon had done exactly what he had promised that hot August night in Miami three and one half years before, when he had so expertly stroked the resentment and fear of change his audience harbored regarding the United States Supreme Court. He had in effect packed the Court with conservatives, men who were less inclined to hear the complaints of injustice from the poor, the ignored, the abused, who seemed less inclined to continue in the redistribution of the social and political resources of the nation.

Together they added up to one short of a majority. They had only to align themselves with the two remaining dissenters to *Miranda*, Stewart and White, and they would be in a position to complete what had begun in *Harris* and bring about counterrevolution. Even before the appointments of Powell and Rehnquist, some civil libertarians had detected a slight shift. Aryah Neier, executive director of the ACLU, complained that the organization generally had won 80 percent of its cases during the Warren years, but under this new Court—people were already divided on whether to call it the Nixon Court or the Burger Court—the rate had dropped to 50 percent during the past year, and he anticipated further decline.

At this critical moment *Miranda*, like some other Warren Court rulings, appeared doomed. What had been only vague questions three and one half years before had become reality, and the wherewithal to effect another judicial revolution was actually in place. Richard Nixon was still sitting behind the big desk in the Oval Office, and John Mitchell was still sitting in the attorney general's office a half mile farther along Pennsylvania Avenue.

Another half mile to the east, on Capitol Hill, lived the Congress, which had already made inroads in *Miranda* via the omnibus crime bill of 1968, and like the public it represented and to whose vagaries of mood it reacted, it, too, did not appear to be seeking a respite in the war on crime.

Across the street sat the Supreme Court.

It appeared that the opponents of *Miranda* had wrested almost complete control of public policy and were poised to undo all that had been done during the past three decades.

Or so it was thought at the time.

WARREN BURGER'S BOOK

CHAPTER 1

April 19, 1955. The United States Supreme Court, Washington, D.C.

Mr. Justice Frankfurter was being unusually waspish even for him this afternoon, buzzing about the attorneys facing him from the lectern just below the bench. It was certainly not apparent that he and Thurman Arnold of Arnold, Fortas & Porter, a former federal judge and in today's case the attorney for the petitioner, were old friends. The attorney for the government, Assistant Attorney General Warren Burger, was, like his opponent, doing his lawyer's best to fend off the attacks. But the little justice with the pince-nez and peppery manner persisted, swooping in, interrupting, questioning, qualifying, correcting, cornering.

The case involved a challenge to the government's employee loyalty-security program. The Hiss case had officially ended; Alger Hiss had been convicted of perjury, had served time in federal prison, and had been released the previous year. But the legacy of conspiracy—the public's fears of espionage, even revolution, which had been fanned for political gain and to which this loyalty-security program for removing suspect employees from government service was supposed to have been one answer—still polluted the air of America. The justices, including John Marshall Harlan, who had been sworn in only three weeks previously, were questioning the attorneys closely.

In the courtroom prominent members of the local bar mingled with security officers for several of the government agencies which had a substantial stake in the outcome of this case. Former Secretary of State Dean Acheson, not without some experience in these matters and Vice President Nixon's candidate for archvillain in the recent congressional elections, was also there.

327

The petitioner himself, Dr. John Punnett Peters, internationally respected authority on nutrition and metabolism, professor at Yale University Medical School, and, until he was fired on June 12, 1953, following an investigation of his political associations, a consultant to the Department of Health, Education, and Welfare, was there, too, flanked by his daughter and son and looking dapper in an Ivy League sort of way. Not far away sat Dorothy Bailey, whose dismissal from the Department of Labor under similar circumstances had been challenged unsuccessfully in this same Supreme Court two years earlier.

The case was officially known as *John P. Peters* versus *Oveta Culp Hobby, Secretary of Health, Education and Welfare.* At the time the impact of the case had been measured narrowly: How would it affect the government's procedures for dealing with what was perceived as in-house Communist subversion, and how would it fit into the historical context of constitutional interpretation? In that context, it was neither the most nor the least important in the series of communism-related cases the Supreme Court decided during that decade.

In retrospect, however, its ironies outstripped the significance of the case in judicial or constitutional terms. For one thing, the events of the *Peters* case provided an arena for Warren Burger's debut in the forum of judicial politics, an opportunity for an early, indicative display of considerable political as well as legal ability.

For another thing, this *Peters* case marked the first critical confrontation between Earl Warren and Warren Burger over the question that was to preoccupy and divide the two men and the people of their country for the next quarter century: What price security? In 1955 the question—highly controversial and highly emotional, as that question nearly always was—revolved around the threat of the Communist conspiracy. On this particular day it revolved specifically around whether a government employee, accused of disloyalty, had a right to the protection of the Constitution's due process of law, which included the right to confront one's accusers, or whether considerations of national security nullified that right. Some years later, in the debates leading up to and following the Supreme Court's decision in *Miranda* v. *Arizona,* the question revolved around the threat of crime in the streets and whether an accused, during a different sort of national crisis, continued to hold the constitutional protections guaranteed in the Bill of Rights or whether again security considerations could remove them.

Finally, this *Peters* case was an instance in which Warren Burger confronted in a legalistic manner and at a judicial level the same problems of national security that Richard Nixon had been confronting in an emotional manner on a political level for nearly the past decade, since his first campaign for the U.S. House of Representatives in 1946. It was a preview of the relationship which would develop between the two men twenty-odd years later, when they confronted the problems of crime and the affinity of their ideas would bring them together again.

The *Peters* case was a baffling one. John Peters, when he became a special consultant to the United States Public Health Service of the Federal Security Agency* in 1948, was an eminent member of the American medical profession. He had achieved that eminence through his research, his writings, and his work as an educator at Yale.

But he also had the stuff of the reformer in him. He was idealistic, nonconforming, iconoclastic, stubborn in controversy, impatient with lesser creatures, and hard-driving. He worked assiduously for such measures as government support for medical research, medical education, and adequate care for the "medically indigent," all radical measures in the 1930s and 1940s, and he found himself in frequent conflict with the American Medical Association, which in those days had a tendency to equate social measures with communism. His idealism and humanitarianism had not been limited to medicine, but had carried him into political movements, and his name had appeared on the letterheads of organizations which had been listed as Communist fronts: organizations like the American Friends of Spanish Democracy and the Medical Aid Division of the Spanish Refugee Relief Campaign in the late 1930s, the National Council of American-Soviet Friendship and the Independent Citizens Committee of the Arts, Sciences and Professions in the 1940s. He was typical of many Americans at the time, particularly scientists who in their enthusiasm for humanistic causes and naïveté toward political consequences had been brought into association with groups which the attorney general of the United States had officially labeled subversive.

Peters's work for the Public Health Service required his presence in Washington only irregularly—fewer than ten times a year. It was neither confidential nor sensitive. He simply helped screen proposals for federal assistance to medical research institutions. He did not need, and he did not have, access to classified material.

Twice—in 1949 and in 1951, when cold war tensions were often at the snapping point and Americans were discovering spies, or at least subversives, among their neighbors and co-workers following the dramatic events of the Hiss case—Peters's loyalty to his country had been questioned by a federal board of inquiry, both times on the basis of evidence supplied by unidentified informants, and twice he had been cleared. However, in April 1953 Peters was notified by the Loyalty Review Board of the Civil Service Commission— a central board which supervised the security programs of the various federal agencies and reviewed their findings—that it was about to reopen his case, and a hearing was scheduled. Again he was faced with the unsubstantiated

* The functions of the Federal Security Agency were transferred to the Department of Health, Education, and Welfare, headed by Secretary Hobby, in 1953.

charges, the faceless and nameless accusers, and again he attempted to convince the government of his loyalty. He denied membership in the Communist party, answered all questions put to him, and freely discussed his political beliefs and his motivations for engaging in the suspect activities and associations. He brought along several character witnesses, including a former president of Yale, a former dean of the Yale Medical School, and a federal circuit judge, all of whom testified to their belief in Peters's loyalty to his country.

On the one side, the board had the record of two previous clearances plus the favorable evidence given by the doctor and his highly respected friends—all of it given under oath. On the other side, it had secret statements given by unsworn, anonymous informants—unidentified even to the members of the board itself.

Despite what appeared to be an overwhelmingly persuasive case in the doctor's favor and an overwhelmingly questionable collection of evidence against him, this time he was not cleared. The Loyalty Review Board determined that "on all the evidence, there is a reasonable doubt" as to Dr. Peters's loyalty to the Government of the United States. In late May he was informed that he had been barred from the federal service for three years and his consultantship was canceled. His request for a rehearing was denied.

Having nowhere to appeal the decision within the government civil service, Peters took his case to court. It was, he said, "a matter of principle."

Another factor which would be significant in later years was the emergence of Abe Fortas, who was on the Peters brief with Arnold, and his law firm as fighters in the courts for the constitutional rights of the accused, be they politically or criminally accused. While Richard Nixon was touring the country in his various political capacities attacking the previous administration's "coddling" of Communists, and while Warren Burger was defending the government's right to remove suspect employees in the name of the national security, Fortas and his law partners were defending the rights of the discharged employees through all the available legal channels; two decades later he was defending the rights of the criminally accused first as an advocate, then as a justice of the U.S. Supreme Court at the same time Nixon and Burger, each in their separate ways, were bemoaning the national judicial oversolicitude for those very rights.

By the mid-fifties the law firm of Arnold, Fortas & Porter had established a reputation for challenging precisely the sort of government employee security regulations that had resulted in the dismissal of Dr. Peters. The partners had become involved in the field more or less by accident—a friend of another member of the firm had been fired as a suspected security risk, unjustly as the lawyers saw it—and Fortas, who later said he had "felt passionately" about these Communist cases, had taken it to the Supreme Court.

Fortas had lost the case, but panic-stricken government workers, many of whom found their cases shunned by other lawyers, saw the firm as their only hope and turned to it. The three partners agreed to take all the loyalty cases they could manage. The attorneys accepted no fees for this part of their work, and at the time there was more vilification than congratulation when they won a case; indeed, some of their paying clients protested the men's commitment to these particular cases. But when a partner questioned if the firm could afford to take so many, time-consuming as they were, Fortas was said to have replied: "We have to. If we don't do it, nobody else will."

In Dr. Peters's case, there was the added factor of the Yale connection—Thurman Arnold and Abe Fortas both had taught at Yale Law School—and on February 18, 1954, Arnold, Fortas & Porter filed a complaint for Peters against the secretary of health, education, and welfare in the local federal district court. The attorneys charged the government with firing Peters and with damaging his professional reputation without due process of administrative law. Peters, they declared, should be reinstated, and the derogatory records in his case destroyed.

Five days later, on February 23, Assistant Attorney General Warren Burger notified Attorney General Herbert Brownell that the action had been initiated, adding that the legal issues were similar to those that had been raised in the *Bailey* case, which the government had won in the courts, including the United States Supreme Court.* The *Peters* case, he added, was also similar to two cases being handled by Burger's Civil Division, one the case of a Foreign Service officer who had been discharged and another attacking the merchant seaman's security program which the Coast Guard operated.

The United States District Court for the District of Columbia had decided Dr. Peters's case in favor of the government, whose position was, Burger explained in a memorandum to the attorney general, that "from the beginning of our Constitutional history, appointment to and removal from federal office has always been regarded as a matter of Executive discretion limited and subject to limitation only by express acts of Congress." Peters's complaint, in other words, did not belong in the courts; it was strictly an executive branch matter, and if amenable to remedy at all, it would have to be at the hands of the president or Congress.

Peters's lawyers then took the case to the U.S. Court of Appeals for the District of Columbia Circuit, which affirmed the district court judgment in an unsigned opinion on August 5, 1954. On September 29, Thurman Arnold of Arnold, Fortas & Porter filed a petition for certiorari in the U.S. Supreme Court, declaring that the constitutional issue had not been decided in the *Bailey* case. He did not say in the petition that the

---

* The issues in the *Bailey* case had not been decided by the U.S. Supreme Court. Justice Tom Clark, former attorney general and author of an executive order under whose authority Bailey had been fired, had disqualified himself, and an equally divided Court, 4–4, without opinion, had only let stand the decision of the U.S. Court of Appeals for the District of Columbia Circuit, which had gone against Dorothy Bailey and upheld the government.

Court itself had changed since the *Bailey* case had been before it in 1951, that a new chief justice, Earl Warren, had been appointed, and that the Court seemed increasingly inclined to uphold the rights of the individual during the past two years.

A copy of the petition for cert was received in the Department of Justice the following day, and Solicitor General Simon E. Sobeloff directed Burger to have the donkey work done on the government's reply within two weeks.

The government reply did not significantly differ from Burger's memorandum to Brownell: Courts could not interfere in the hiring and firing of nonjudicial government personnel. Certiorari should be denied.

Six weeks after the petition was filed, on November 15, 1954, the Supreme Court agreed to hear the case. The maneuvering within the Justice Department that followed could have had no little effect on the professional future of the assistant attorney general in charge of the Civil Division.

The Justice Department was divided on the *Peters* case. Attorney General Brownell, a former Wall Street lawyer who had been masterminding national campaigns for the Republican party for a decade, including Eisenhower's in 1952, was a believer in the Communist conspiracy, whose plotters "resort to secret meeting places, secret schools, even secret symbols or numbers in place of names" as they proceed on their mission of world enslavement. Brownell believed that Communists had infiltrated the 2.3 million federal employees, and although the president's Employment Security Program and the Subversive Activities Control Board had accomplished much good, "we cannot lower our guard." Allowing people like Peters to confront their accusers—that is, giving names and faces to secret informants—would, of course, end their usefulness as well as dry up these and other sources, which translated into lowering our guard. In this time of crisis the national security could not afford it.

Solicitor General Simon Ernest Sobeloff, the son of Russian immigrants, who had worked his way through law school and into prominence among Maryland Republicans and local legal and government circles, was no less dedicated than the attorney general to destruction of the Communist menace, and like the attorney general, he believed in its conspiratorial character. But he was not convinced that the strategy the government was mapping in the *Peters* case was either correct or effective. He had noted the direction of the wind from the Supreme Court in recent years, and recalling the government's arguments in the *Bailey* case which were similar to the arguments being advanced in the *Peters* case four years later, he suggested in a January 1955 memorandum to the attorney general that their persuasiveness that day was doubtful; indeed, recollecting the character of the Court's decision in the *Bailey* case, which was really a nondecision, he was not certain the arguments had been acceptable even then.

Sobeloff agreed that federal employment was an executive matter, that no one had a right to a federal job, "any more than he has a right to a radio station license or an air route certificate," he told the attorney general. But, he added, "it does not, as the Court had said, follow that he has no right to due process. An administrative agency cannot act arbitrarily in denying an application for a license without a fair hearing . . . not because the applicant has a right to a license, but rather because he has a right to fair treatment at the hands of the government." There were, he said, unmistakable indications in recent Court opinions that "the same obligation is owing to Government employees." Soboloff suggested, so as "to avert a possibly disastrous defeat for the entire security program," a radical departure from prior Justice Department policy in the *Peters* case: "We [should] make a partial confession of error."

Soboloff recognized a threat to national security in disclosing sources to the suspect employee himself, but he did not believe that factor would weigh very heavily with the Supreme Court as presently constituted. "The notion that a person can be punished for crime on the basis of testimony the nature of which he does not know, given by unidentified persons who are not subjected to any examination whatsoever, is, of course, inconsistent with basic Anglo-American concepts of justice"; he doubted the Court would buy it.

He reminded the attorney general of the president's pledge in his recent State of the Union message: "We shall continue to ferret out and to destroy communist subversion. We shall, in the process, carefully preserve our traditions and the basic rights of every American citizen." And, Soboloff concluded, "Now is the time, and this case is the appropriate occasion, I believe, for showing the country that the Administration is as firmly pledged to the second sentence as to the first."

There was, in fact, some discussion in the solicitor general's office of confessing error and thereby avoiding an opinion by the Supreme Court. Warren Burger, however, objected strongly; to prolong the uncertainty would only "postpone for a little while," he argued, "the date of final reckoning."

The Soboloff view did not prevail; Brownell's did. So the solicitor general went to the attorney general and told him that the position the department was planning to take was "so at loggerheads with his own personal view that he couldn't argue it conscientiously." There was precedent for such a move. Thomas Thacher, Herbert Hoover's solicitor general, had frequently noted his dissent to the government position. But there was not much. However, as Soboloff* told his friend David Bazelon of the U.S. Court of Appeals

* It was said at the time that Soboloff's refusal to argue for the government in the *Peters* case cost him a Supreme Court appointment, and Eisenhower did, in fact, make three more appointments to the Court following that case: William J. Brennan, Jr., Charles Whittaker, and Potter Stewart. However, Brownell called the allegation gossip and maintained that he and the solicitor general remained close friends for many years afterward, the attorney general being a frequent guest at Passover Seders in the Soboloff home. Soboloff was, in fact, appointed to the U.S. Court of Appeals for the Fourth Circuit in 1956, and the attorney general's representative

for the District of Columbia, he did it "because I have to be able to live with myself." The brief which the government submitted to the Supreme Court was signed only by Brownell, Warren Burger, two other assistant attorneys general, and two lower-echelon Justice Department lawyers. Its most notable feature was its answer in no uncertain terms to the question "What price security?"

In times of crisis, when the society was threatened, whether by Communists or rapists, government could ill afford fastidiousness in connection with the constitutional promises to the individual, the brief writers declared, and went on to give general directions for the balancing act it would be asked to do now in connection with Communists, later in connection with rapists:

> In essence, the problem is one of balancing the conflicting individual and national interests involved. . . . Jealous concern for the protection of individual rights is, at all times, a central factor in every aspect of American life. . . . [T]he security of this country . . . requires not merely protection of its borders from external force but also protection within from subversive activities . . .
>
> The attainment of these two goals, to protect the individual while at the same time achieving effective implementation of a national security program, was the constant purpose of the loyalty program and the procedure utilized in that program. . . .

Imperfect though it was, the system of using information supplied by anonymous undercover informers had proved useful and efficient in keeping sabotage and espionage to a minimum. It could not and should not be abandoned. The rights of the individual were the price of the national security.

When the solicitor general dropped out of the *Peters* case, there arose the question of who should replace him at oral argument in the Supreme Court. Time was flying. Strategy had to be planned; arguments, prepared.

In due course Assistant Attorney General Warren Burger volunteered to argue the *Peters* case, and Attorney General Brownell accepted the younger man's services with enthusiasm. Politically it was a wise move on the part of the assistant attorney general, and in retrospect it marks an important step in a professional journey that culminated fifteen years later in his appointment as chief justice of the United States.

Warren Burger was not an illogical choice. He was, after two years as an assistant attorney general, a veteran advocate for the government in the U.S. Supreme Court. Although he had built his reputation during these years in the Justice Department around admiralty claims cases primarily, he was entirely familiar with the issues raised by the *Peters* case. Indeed, in addition to

---

at the confirmation hearings, when questioned about the *Peters* case, read from a speech Brownell had given in November 1955. It began: "The administration of Government would surely be impaired if composed solely of 'yes' men. . . . Unless we want responsible officials in Government to abdicate their function we must expect that they will have reasonable disagreements and exercise independent judgment . . . it should be welcomed. . . ."

having written the government's response to Peters's petition for cert and worked on the government's brief over the past five months, he had cut his political teeth on these issues back in St. Paul, Minnesota, when in the fall of 1952 he had debated them publicly, standing in one night for the local Republican candidate for Congress and arguing forcefully against the Democratic candidate, Eugene J. McCarthy, for improved security controls on government employees (it was generally conceded that Burger had the best of the debate; McCarthy won the election). And if he did not indulge in the excesses of others regarding the threat of Communist subversion, he was not without strong conviction on that issue, being described some years later as a fundamentalist on the matter, an "old-fashioned working-class patriot" in whom "the significance of America as the fulfillment of the German peasant's dream is very strong."

The Court Burger faced this day in April 1955 was a transitional Court. The last gasps of the Vinson Court had not yet been heard; the Warren Court had not yet achieved maturity, the chief justice having arrived less than two years before. Arranged along each side of the center chair, the justices were almost evenly divided between judicial time past and judicial time present, the former represented by Stanley Reed, Sherman Minton, and Harold H. Burton, who were approaching the end of their Court years; the latter represented by—in addition to the chief justice—Senior Associate Justice Hugo Black and William O. Douglas, who were fashioning the core of the majority of the future, plus Tom Clark and John Harlan, prominent members-to-be of the Warren Court but more often in dissent. Felix Frankfurter straddled both times ideologically and chronologically, although he did not survive all the Warren years.

To date, challenges to the constitutionality of federal statutes and executive orders devised to discourage the growth of internal subversion had not fared particularly well in the United States Supreme Court, whose mood seemed to coincide with that of the public and whose majority—usually Chief Justice Vinson prior to his death in 1953 and Justices Reed, Minton, Burton, and Clark with frequent support from Frankfurter—had managed to uphold their application without confronting directly the constitutional issues.

The *Peters* case, in which it was widely believed the constitutional issues might finally be confronted, was being argued in an emotional climate unusual, although not unprecedented, for Supreme Court cases. Lawyers for neither party had limited their arguments to the courtrooms. Attorney General Brownell had spoken out publicly on the issues, advancing the government's case. Assistant Attorney General Burger had lunched with newsmen, answered unfavorable editorials that came to his attention, and, prior to oral argument in the Supreme Court, dispatched copies of the government's brief to the chief legal officers of forty-seven government departments and agencies. On the Peters side, as one observer put it, "Messrs. Arnold, Fortas and

Porter eat regularly and have many friends who are also reporters," and he concluded that "every reporter who followed the story knew that few lawyers for either side passed the salad course on any day during the critical weeks without imparting a few careful phrases about the case to a scribbling friend."

Following the prescribed procedure, Thurman Arnold, the attorney for Dr. Peters, had begun the oral argument. His heavy sarcasm, as he had described the doctor's work for the government—"It was apparent that Dr. Peters had the ability to fool the eminent people he had known all his life," Arnold had said, "and without this secret informant, he might still be pouring Soviet theory on metabolism and nutrition into the attentive and gullible ear of the Surgeon General of the United States"—had done nothing to lower the emotional temperature, to bring the issues into the sphere of rational discussion. Justice Frankfurter, who was frequently able to hide his natural ebullience behind a thorny exterior, had responded in kind. "It is important," he had observed acidly following Arnold's lumping some issues of a previous case with issues in the *Peters* case, "not to make things that are a little different the same."

After the first few minutes the discussion had assumed a calmer, if not necessarily more orderly, tone, as each justice, typically, pursued his own line of thought. The justices, particularly Reed, Minton, Burton, and Frankfurter, had questioned Arnold sharply regarding the narrow aspects of the case: how a consultant like Dr. Peters fitted into the scheme of government employment; the terms under which a government employee could be dismissed; whether disloyalty was comparable to criminal behavior; whether hearings were required; the authority of the various boards that had ruled in Dr. Peters's case; the procedures involved; the intended scope and the actual scope of the executive orders under which the doctor's case had been undertaken; whether the government had conformed to its own regulations. These were the areas the justices concentrated on, leading some spectators to believe they were looking for a way to decide the case on some issue short of a constitutional one, a belief that was strengthened when, Thurman Arnold having stated to the justices that he hoped the case would be decided not on narrow but on constitutional grounds, Justice Frankfurter retorted: "The question is not what you would like to whittle it down to, or not. The problem before this Court is to decide all legal questions that arise on this record and to reach Constitutional questions last, not first."

Arnold answered each justice in turn, less acidly now, although his thinking processes were being pushed rapidly from subject to subject and his ability to bring the discussion back to his point was being sorely tested. But he persisted. He was shooting the moon. "We say," he declared, "that the Government cannot, by a formal hearing before what is alleged to be an independent Board, try and condemn a citizen for disloyalty to his country, an offense involving infamy, and ruin, without due process of law. . . ." The hearings at which Peters had had to defend his behavior, lacking the presence of his accusers, had been rendered meaningless, "the form but not the substance" of a trial. The government could not have it both ways. Nor could it, in its dealings with the public, as Simon Sobeloff had pointed out in his memorandum to the Attorney General, act arbitrarily; the public was entitled not to jobs but to "fair treatment."

Arnold had concluded in less than his allotted hour, in spite of the justices' close questioning, and had reserved fifteen minutes for his partner, Paul Porter, for rebuttal at the end of the government's presentation of its case.

Then it was Warren Burger's turn. His movements as he faced the justices, graceful and soft, suggested a smaller man. His smooth face and blond hair, combed back in a low pompadour in the style of the time and just beginning to gray, suggested a man younger than forty-eight. He was poised, properly deferential to the justices but firm in his speech, like the veteran advocate he was, his deep baritone carrying to the farthest reaches of the courtroom, and he was vigorous in his advocacy of the government's position.

He looked at ease standing at the lawyer's lectern, clad in the traditional morning coat and striped pants, the uniform of the government advocate. Directly opposite sat the chief justice in his black robe; he was tall, like Burger, but at sixty-four, his blond hair was a little thinner and a good deal grayer.

The chief justice was less vocal today than he would be during the arguments of some future cases. Was he recalling, perhaps, as the government advocate put forward the case for the national security, his own first criminal case? On his first day as assistant district attorney, back in Alameda County in 1920, he had been assigned to sit with one of the older prosecutors who was trying a man under the Criminal Syndicalism Act of 1919, a repressive statute passed by the California legislature in response to the post–World War I public fears of the militant trade unionism of the IWW. The fellow on trial was an ideological radical; but Warren was never convinced he was a terrorist, and the principal witnesses against him were "some repulsive informers" about whom Warren felt "squeamish." Said Warren about the case some years later: "It is easy for some people to be carried away by an ideological approval of violence without their having any intention of inciting or participating in such action. When conviction rests upon the testimony of paid informers, injustice is likely to follow."

The justices were no gentler with Burger than they had been with Peters's attorney. The justices identified with the old Vinson Court, their questions seemingly directed toward eliciting narrow definitions, specific metes and bounds for specific government actions, were less active now. The arguments in behalf of the government now provoked Warren Court justices into action, their questions seemingly directed more toward eliciting principles involved in the case, leading some spectators to the conclusion that the Court was split and that at least some of the justices were inclined to decide the case on constitutional grounds, as the attorney for Dr. Peters had hoped.

337

Burger stood firm. In Justice Department discussions of the case he had "emphatically" dissented from the view that a "Federal employee cannot be dismissed without a proceeding which meets the Constitutional standards of due process guaranteed to a person accused of a crime . . . [That] is not the law now and, although it may become so, it should be over our most vigorous opposition." He had not changed his mind, and he patiently reviewed for the Court the legislation since 1912 that regulated government employment and its termination, explaining at length that a government employee could, in fact, be dismissed administratively, describing the procedural safeguards contained in the legislation, reiterating that constitutional provisions did not apply. An administrative hearing was not, after all, a trial, however persistently Mr. Justice Black tried to draw the analogy. Under existing dismissal procedures, John Peters had not been denied due process of law. The freedom of the individual, the rights, the protections promised by the Constitution— these did not enter the discussion. They rarely would, then or later, in a Burger discussion of a case.

At one point the chief justice, Hugo Black, and Felix Frankfurter together attacked the assistant attorney general when he disclosed that not only Dr. Peters but the justices of the U.S. Supreme Court themselves, as well as members of the various loyalty boards and even cabinet members, would not be allowed access to *all* sources of information used against the Yale professor. No one except the FBI itself, it seemed, was to be trusted.

But mostly the government advocate was called upon to unravel complicated legalistic problems of administrative law. Like his opposite number, he answered with self-assurance, displaying a broad knowledge of precedent. He was not given much time to discuss the government's philosophy of security, but in the little time he had he made his position plain. There were occasions, he reminded the justices, on which judges freely used confidential information as aids to decision making: in setting probation and determining sentences, for example; he cited a case in which Black himself had written for the Court that a state judge, on the basis of a presentence report made by a probation officer or, as the defendant's lawyers had claimed, unknown informants, could decide between sentencing a man to life imprisonment or sending him to the electric chair. And although Mr. Justice Black waggled his finger at the assistant attorney general in his best prosecutorial fashion and pursued the argument vigorously, his face reddening, Burger later recalled, Burger refused to back down. When these occasions were compared with the situations involving national security, it was plain what the priorities were; his next sentences would be paraphrased and elaborated on years later in his lectures, his writings, and his opinions from both benches on which he sat.

> We submit [he told the justices in 1955] that the needs of the Government with respect to the security program vastly outweigh the need of the Court and the Government in . . . [the less sensitive areas], and that weighing these two needs against the right, and

reconciling them that should be resolved in favor of the Government, and that the Government's decision to do it in this way, the best they [sic] know how, should be sustained.

The national security came first then and later.

The arguments in the case of *Peters* v. *Hobby* ran overtime, consuming the entire afternoon—such was the judicial interest in it. Following Paul Porter's rebuttal, for which his partner had reserved the time, the justices again swooped down on Burger to clear up some matters further, and it was not until 4:40 P.M. that the chief justice concluded the session. Justice Burton noted in his diary that night that the government lawyer had been "very good." Burton's opinion was a widespread one, even among people who were not in agreement with the assistant attorney general's arguments.

The vote in conference on the first Saturday following the arguments, April 23, was six (Warren, Black, Frankfurter, Douglas, Harlan, Clark) to three (Reed, Burton, Minton) in favor of reversing the judgment of the lower courts—a victory for Dr. Peters. Justice Burton later changed his mind and joined the majority, making it seven to two.

Several weeks later, on Monday, June 6, 1955, the decision of the U.S. Supreme Court in the case of *Peters* v. *Hobby* was announced. Chief Justice Warren had written the opinion. The decision went against the young government attorney and marked the beginning of a judicial movement toward the support of individual rights over repressive government programs to maintain the national security.

Following the public build-up of the case, however, it was an anticlimax. The Court was not at this time prepared, Warren declared, to confront the constitutional issues that Peters's counsel had argued. "These issues, if reached by the Court," Warren explained, "would obviously present serious and far-reaching problems in reconciling fundamental constitutional guarantees with the procedures used to determine the loyalty of government personnel." The Court could, however, decide for Dr. Peters* on the grounds that the Loyalty Review Board's conduct of his case had under principles of administrative law exceeded its authority; it declared his dismissal from government service invalid and ordered all derogatory records in his file erased. This was indeed early Warren. It would, in fact, require two more years before he would be able to assemble a majority willing to face directly the constitutional questions involved in this and other internal security cases.

There were indications that he himself might have been willing. He had made an offhand remark shortly before the *Peters* case had come before the Supreme Court: "To the extent that anyone indiscriminately charges individuals or groups of individuals with dishonesty or subversion or whatever it

---

* Peters died later in the year at the age of sixty-nine.

might be that would destroy reputation, that is, in my opinion, not in the American tradition and should not be encouraged." But it was rumored at the time that Justices Frankfurter, who had indicated at oral argument his reluctance to decide the case on constitutional grounds, and Black, who wrote in a concurrence that it should have been decided on constitutional grounds, were engaged in a battle for the chief justice's judicial soul, and the opinion in this case showed a strong Frankfurter influence. Indeed, much of the underpinning—that the Loyalty Review Board had acted in violation of the executive order under which it had been created—bore a remarkable resemblance to the reasoning advanced in a memorandum written by Justice Frankfurter shortly after the case had been argued, as well as a Frankfurterian reluctance to adjudicate constitutional issues when they could be avoided.

Or it may simply have been that Warren, who had hardly lost his awareness of the political facts of life when he put on the chief justice's robes, recognized the danger in deciding the case on the basis of constitutional due process of law—the danger of losing at least Frankfurter, Burton, Harlan, and Clark and being left with Black and Douglas, making a minority of three.

As far as the White House was concerned, it mattered little whether the Supreme Court interfered with executive matters or security matters on constitutional or technical grounds. The effect was the same. The president and his men were not pleased with the opinion.

Earl Warren had begun the process of estrangement from his sponsor the previous spring, when he had written the opinion for a unanimous Supreme Court in the public school desegregation cases, and the Court over which he presided had begun to move in the direction of increased concern for the rights of the individual, a direction which came frequently into conflict with established social policy and which would in succeeding terms be heavily underlined by its decisions in a plethora of internal security cases of which the *Peters* case was an early direction finder. In the end Eisenhower would express his regret to the chief justice himself, as the two traveled on *Air Force One* to Sir Winston Churchill's funeral in London some years later, would inform Warren how disappointed he had been in the chief justice's performance in "those Communist cases."

In contrast, Warren Burger's participation in this particular "Communist case" was more likely to advance his own future in the politics of his profession. He had volunteered to argue it, controversial as it was, presenting a point of view that coincided neatly with the administration's and identifying himself with the so-called judicial hard-liners. He had acquitted himself well.

Whether or not the president was personally aware of the past record and recent performance of his assistant attorney general in charge of the Civil Division of the Justice Department is not known. If he was, he was probably not disappointed, as he had been in his choice for the chief justiceship. Attorney General Brownell, however, was keenly aware of the performance as well as of the solid record Burger had made during his two-year stewardship of the Civil Division, and he did not forget it.

The chief justice and the assistant attorney general had faced each other in the courtroom. It was not obvious then, but one's star was in its acme; the other's, in its ascendancy. The one represented the present; the other represented the future.

Warren Earl Burger had exhibited early on the qualities of character that had brought him to this juncture in his life. He had been born in 1907 to Swiss-German parents living in Dayton Bluffs, a craft-union AFL neighborhood of St. Paul, Minnesota, the effeteness of whose Yankee ruling class was being immortalized during his youth and early adulthood by fellow townsman F. Scott Fitzgerald. As a newsboy slogging through the snow, delivering his papers by toboggan, even on skis, pushing against a wind that frequently dropped the city's temperatures to thirty degrees below zero—prick a St. Paulite, and he will nearly always credit the sub-zero weather with whatever worldly success the sons of Minnesota have achieved—but always delivering, Burger had proved he had the determination and ingenuity to fulfill the ambitious side of his nature. He had gone to the University of Minnesota night school for his undergraduate degree, but he had not entirely fulfilled the intellectual side of his nature, and he recalled much later in his life that as an assistant attorney general he had been "aware of great gaps" in his education. Having made the acquaintance of Hugo Black through a mutual friend, he had secured from the justice a reading list of classics, history, and philosophy.

When James Otis, senior partner in the firm Burger joined following graduation from St. Paul Law School (later renamed William Mitchell College of Law) more or less "adopted" the young lawyer professionally, made Burger his protégé, encouraged him, nurtured his talent, and imparted legal tradition to the son of the traveling salesman and sometime railroad cargo inspector, Burger had shown he had intelligence and considerable amiability—indeed, a nascent political savoir-faire—all of which had served to help him reach the upper echelons of St. Paul's legal and civic establishment.

His political fortunes had risen similarly. As a young man he had tied his future to Harold Stassen, had worked closely as an adviser to Stassen since 1938, when the latter was elected governor of Minnesota, and had gone to the 1952 Republican National Convention as Stassen's closest aide. There, however, he had not only, in his first known split with Stassen, persuaded the Minnesota delegation to shift its support to Eisenhower, but, as Minnesota's representative to the convention's Credentials Committee, scene of a struggle between rival Eisenhower and Taft factions over convention seating, had been instrumental in getting the Eisenhower delegates seated. When the new administration was looking for dependable high-level appointees, Warren Burger seemed an obvious choice.

Like that of a character from the Horatio Alger books he had consumed as a child, his life in St. Paul had been American rags to riches, and when he left for Washington in 1953, at age forty-six, the newly appointed assistant attorney general lived in a house on Summit Avenue, Fitzgerald's "Crest Avenue" where the home of railroad baron James J. Hill still stood and where the drawing rooms of the old-line bankers and lawyers were not always open to the brewers and other commercial and industrial newcomers or to the Germans, Swiss, Scandinavians, and Irish who made up the bulk of St. Paul's population.

He had intended originally to return to his law practice in St. Paul after a few years in the Justice Department; but doctors had advised his wife, who was in failing health at the time, that the harshness of the northern climate could only aggravate her condition, and he had changed his plans. Discussing his professional situation with Attorney General Brownell one day, Burger had remarked that he didn't know what he was going to do. Brownell suggested a federal judgeship. But these appointments were usually made on the basis of geopolitical considerations, and although it had been reported that Minnesota's senior senator, Republican Edward J. Thye, had put Warren Burger's name at the top of his list for a judgeship, Burger would have had to return to Minnesota and sit on the bench there. Then Chief Judge Harold M. Stephens of the U.S. Court of Appeals for the District of Columbia Circuit died in May 1955. On June 21, two weeks after the Supreme Court had announced its decision in the *Peters* case, the man who had so ably argued the government's position, Warren Burger, was nominated by President Eisenhower to the seat left vacant by the death of Judge Stephens.

When the idea of the federal judgeship had first arisen, some time before, Burger had not been at all sure that this was the direction he wanted his career to take, that he was ready to give up the private practice of law, and he had gone to New York to visit John Harlan, who was still then on the U.S. Court of Appeals for the Second Circuit and whose career in the law, Burger thought, somewhat paralleled his own—Burger had been in private practice twenty-one years, Harlan thirty years before he became a judge. As the two men talked in Harlan's chambers at the U.S. Courthouse in Foley Square, exploring the conditions of private practice and government work, comparing, contrasting, it became clear to the judge that the assistant attorney general was headed for the bench. Burger still hesitated; he was not yet sure.

How, he asked, did Harlan like the life of a circuit judge after spending so many years as an advocate?

Harlan smiled. "It's not nearly as much fun as law practice," he replied, "but after 20 or 30 years at it I think possibly there is a greater opportunity to grow on the bench than in the daily grind of a big firm practice."

Burger was still uncertain, even after the judgeship had become a real offer. A naturally methodical man, he "sat down and figured it out like an actuarial table—what he would need for retirement," an old friend commented later. "He put it all down on paper. He took out a pencil and weighed every blasted thing."

And he had decided to become a judge.

His confirmation was delayed for several months when three former Justice Department employees testified before the Senate Judiciary Committee that they had been fired by the incoming Republican appointee for political reasons. On the contrary, Burger said, they had been fired for incompetence and on the recommendation of his Democratic predecessors in the department. He was finally confirmed on March 28, 1956, and took his oath on April 13, 1956. He described himself at the time as a "moderate liberal."

Because the U.S. Court of Appeals for the District of Columbia Circuit was a national court, deciding cases with national dimensions, the president's men in the Justice Department—the traditional source of names for appointment to the federal judiciary—tended to seek out top quality. No federal court appointment was made wholly without political considerations, and Griffin B. Bell, President Jimmy Carter's first attorney general, was fond of describing how he had become a federal judge in 1961: "I had three friends—a President and two Senators." Appointments to the court for the District of Columbia Circuit, however, tended to be somewhat less political than those to the other ten circuits.

These appointments were also unbound by the geographical factors that limited those to the other circuits, and there was the entire nation from which to choose. The eight judges Warren Burger joined in 1956 had been appointed from the District of Columbia (three, although only one had been born there), Kentucky, Illinois, New Mexico, New York, and Connecticut. Burger was the first ever on that court from Minnesota. Such geographical variety tended to give the court an uncommonly national perspective.

The U.S. Court of Appeals for the District of Columbia Circuit, like the federal judiciary nationwide—and historically—did, however, reflect the general make-up of the American ruling class. When Burger took his seat, no blacks had ever been appointed to it—the first one, Spottswood W. Robinson III, would not be appointed until 1966. David Bazelon, appointed in 1950, was its first Jewish judge. No woman had ever been appointed; Patricia M. Wald would be the first, in 1979.

After a brief period of judicial shyness as a "freshman" judge, Warren Burger had made his reputation in the role of articulate spokesman for the court's bloc of conservative judges both on and off the bench, the bloc that would, during the Warren Court's heyday, reflect the dissenters to it—John Harlan, Potter Stewart, Byron White, Tom Clark—particularly in matters involving questions of criminal justice.

Warren Burger was not, of course, the only judge who stood against the tide of the Warren Court. But he was more outspoken than most, particularly as the decisions of the court on which he was sitting increasingly mirrored the majority on the higher court, positions from which he dissented vigorously.

At the same time he was articulate, constructive in his criticism, amiable in his person, and the combination marked him for particular attention. A genteel aggressiveness always seemed to have marked his passages, propelling him from the working-class neighborhood where he had been born in St. Paul to Summit Avenue, from relative obscurity as an assistant attorney general to a judgeship on the nation's second most important court, from the professional patronage of James Otis and Harold Stassen to Herbert Brownell and Richard Nixon. There was a discernible political side to his nature, despite his apparent lack of interest in elective office for himself. In his own way and in his own field, he was as political a being as his predecessor in the chief justiceship and the president who would elevate him to it.

In *The Brethren*, authors Bob Woodward and Scott Armstrong, writing with some awe at Chief Justice Warren's prescience, described a scene in which Warren, in November 1968—five months before President Nixon named the new chief justice and a time when speculation regarding who ,would fill the position was a frequent subject of Washington conversations— accurately predicted the name of his successor. Actually, given Warren's familiarity with the federal judiciary generally and the local appellate court specifically,* with Nixon's cast of mind and the facts of Warren Burger's career, it would have been more surprising if Warren had *not* predicted the name of his successor accurately.

* Traditionally, each of the eleven circuits is supervised by a U.S. Supreme Court Justice. At the time Earl Warren was in charge of the District of Columbia Circuit.

344

CHAPTER 2

Some things about the United States Supreme Court appear never to change. The pomp and ceremony of the proceedings, the majesty of the setting that accompany the deciding of great public issues inspire an appropriate awe that knots the intestines of young lawyers arguing their first cases and clogs the throats of spectators sitting in the pewlike seats. Chief Justice Warren Burger himself could still recall many years later his own sense of awe at the proceedings when he visited the Court for the first time, a young lawyer on his honeymoon, a sense so overwhelming that he could not bring himself to utilize a letter of introduction to fellow St. Paulite Pierce Butler given him by his mentor, James Otis, and he had returned to St. Paul without meeting the justice.*

Another unchanging face of Supreme Court institutional life is the regularity of the attacks on it. While the Court's standing in the national esteem fluctuates, it can usually be counted on to draw a serious burst of fire at least once a decade, give or take a couple of years. Sure enough, as the eighties opened, reacting to the Court's continuing concern with social problems, particularly to its 1973 decision that state laws prohibiting abortion were unconstitutional, and discerning a growing public support, the 1980 Republican platform promised "the appointment of judges . . . who respect traditional family values and the sanctity of innocent human life," and by the following

---

* Some years later Butler was a guest at a St. Paul Bar Association dinner of which Warren Burger was chairman. The justice scribbled a brief message on the local lawyer's place card: "Next time, come in."

spring the new Congress, largely Republican-powered, had before it no fewer than twenty bills to undermine federal judicial authority.

Other things do change. Some change suddenly and dramatically; some change slowly and subtly but nonetheless profoundly.

The changes in the physical appearance of the Court building itself during the 1970s fell somewhere between the two categories. During the first few years of his chief justiceship, Warren Burger made the thirty-five-year-old edifice, beneficiary of only spasmodic attempts at upkeep, look like what it was: the nation's highest judicial institution. Walls and ceilings were repainted; the justices' chambers, enlarged. The old straight bench, an acoustical disaster which hindered rather than encouraged communication among the justices as they sat facing the courtroom so that their voices were lost to each other, was replaced by a shallow U-shaped bench, and finally Justice Rehnquist at one end could hear his brother Powell's questions and comments from the other. The plain water glasses used by the justices during the Court's public sessions were replaced by silver tumblers, a gift of the chief justice. New guidelines for lawyers preparing to argue before the Court specified for the first time "conservative business dress" and implied that flashy sport coats and bright ties on men, sweaters and pantsuits on women were judicially déclassé. The chief justice borrowed paintings from the National Portrait Gallery and had them hung in the justices' private conference room. He furnished their private dining room with fine antiques, some lent by himself and his wife from their personal collection, others donated—a 1790 Chippendale table and chairs were given by the widow of Thurman Arnold of Arnold, Fortas & Porter, who had for many years distinguished himself as an advocate before the Court. The huge empty corridors on the ground floor, beneath the courtroom, were decorated with portraits of the justices who had sat on the Court since the beginning and other Court memorabilia, all set out by the Supreme Court Historical Society, which Burger established. The first female page in the Court's history was appointed in 1972. Also in line with events of the 1970s, a strict security system, similar to that used in airports for the past several years, was set up in the marble hall immediately outside the courtroom.

Substantive changes—in the men who occupied the bench and the judicial direction of the Court—fell into the latter category of slow, subtle, but nonetheless profound changes.

The potential for change in the fortunes of *Miranda* were discerned early in the seventies. Fred Inbau, author of the police manual whose instructions regarding interrogation of criminal suspects had so offended the *Miranda* majority that it had been held up to judicial ridicule, now was optimistic about the future, declaring in the 1972 edition of his textbook that the overruling of *Miranda* was "a not unreasonable expectation in view of the changes occurring in the composition of the Court." And William J. Brennan, a member of the *Miranda* majority, was grumbling in 1973 that the

346

Court had distorted *Miranda*'s constitutional principles and, he supposed, would ultimately overrule it. The world had turned upside down.

Beginning with the resignation of Chief Justice Warren and the appointment of Chief Justice Burger in 1969, the center of gravity on the Supreme Court had, in fact, shifted. The law-and-order justices had gradually taken control. The senior justices among them were the remaining two dissenters to *Miranda*, Potter Stewart and Byron White, who, Richard Nixon had assured the American people, were the ones who had decided correctly in that case. Neither man had ever recanted from his original *Miranda* dissent.

The junior justices among them were the four strict constructionists whom Nixon himself had appointed:

Chief Justice Warren Burger. The passage of years since he had argued the government's case against John Peters and the good life in Washington had affected his appearance. His hair was white silk now, and his waistline had thickened some, so that he came close to conforming to Felix Frankfurter's picture of the ideal Supreme Court justice: "tall and broad with a little bit of a bay window." The inner dynamics of the man during these years, however, had been little affected. He had cited the national security as the operative factor in the case against Peters, and in 1968, in an opinion for the U.S. Court of Appeals for the District of Columbia Circuit, he had written regarding a clash between the First Amendment's guarantee of freedom of speech and what he had conceived as a threat to the national security: "When the interests to be protected are evaluated in the light of First Amendment safeguards, the consequences here sought to be prevented afford a valued basis for reasonable limitation on speech. . . ."* Regarding the *Miranda* ruling, it seemed probable the chief justice would look at cases from Officer Cooley's side of the interrogation table, the criminal justice system from Gary Nelson's perspective in the state attorney general's office. During the hearings held prior to his confirmation as chief justice, Burger had compared the American system of criminal justice and its concern with procedure to King Philip's Armada, which had sunk under its own weight, and in the only case involving *Miranda* issues to come before the Court since he had been appointed to it, Viven Harris's case, he had written the Court opinion in which the admission of evidence obtained in violation of *Miranda* had been allowed. As the seventies got under way, the direction of the chief justice appeared predictable.

Harry Blackmun, corporation lawyer before he became a federal judge, who had already become the chief justice's frequent judicial ally.

Lewis Powell, Virginia gentleman, his acquaintance with the realities of station house life largely secondhand.

* In a per curiam decision seven months later, a month before Burger's appointment to the Supreme Court, the United States Supreme Court had overruled him. Said Douglas in a separate concurrence: "Suppression of speech as an effective police measure is an old, old device, outlawed by our Constitution."

William Rehnquist, who had indicated where his judicial sympathies would lie generally as a Goldwater lieutenant in the 1964 presidential campaign and as an officer in Richard Nixon's Justice Department. Both Powell and Rehnquist had announced their disagreement with *Miranda* specifically prior to their Court appointments, the former in his dissent to the report of the president's crime commission in 1967, the latter in political speeches back in Arizona.

Of the old *Miranda* majority, only William O. Douglas, in addition to Brennan, remained. With Hugo Black gone, he was the senior associate justice now. He sat to the immediate left of the chief justice as one faced the bench, and in 1973 he would set a record for longevity on the United States Supreme Court: thirty-four years, 196 days. But the fire was going out of him as he pushed toward his mid-seventies, and the ashes of irascibility were almost all that remained. These two justices, plus Thurgood Marshall, whose interest in the plight of the criminal defendant appeared to have revived since he had argued the federal government's case against what ultimately became the *Miranda* ruling and who, once on the Supreme Court, consistently dissented against any narrowing of *Miranda*, made up a fairly solid minority as the 1970s began. But a futile minority it was.

Although a majority on the Court was ill-disposed to the precedent of *Miranda* and despite opportunities during the decade following the full flowering in 1971 of Richard Nixon's campaign promises in connection with the Supreme Court to overrule it, such a precipitous course of action raises too many questions within the legal community regarding judicial stability, even judicial integrity, and the Court rarely takes it. What the justices did, however, may have been more effective and in the end longer-lasting. They reversed the logic of it. The logic of *Brown* v. *Mississippi*, of *Chambers* and *Gideon* and *Escobedo* and all those in between which had put a premium on the exclusion of illegally obtained evidence and the integrity of the government role in the dispensing of justice, on the role of proper procedure in the administration of criminal affairs, which had put new force in the Bill of Rights and applied it to state matters, which had prevailed for three decades and for which *Miranda* had supplied what seemed to be at the time a capstone, was replaced by the logic of *Harris* v. *New York*. As Hugo Black's and Earl Warren's had been the gradually emerging judicial logic of the forties, fifties, and sixties, now the federalism of John Harlan, Tom Clark's concern for the handcuffing of police, Byron White's and Potter Stewart's interest in balancing the rights of the individual and the society—the concerns of the dissenters to *Miranda*—were emerging as the judicial logic of the seventies.

As a practical matter, *Harris* proved a mixed blessing. It had not, as the dissenters to it had feared it would, particularly encouraged law enforcement officers to dispense with the ritual of giving criminal suspects the warnings required by *Miranda*. It did, however, on occasion make defense lawyers, who generally find it advantageous to show the defendant as a person to the jury, think twice about having him testify in court if there was any possibility at all he might contradict a previous statement to police. At the same time it put a powerful weapon in the hands of the prosecutor, and convictions under certain circumstances became easier to obtain.

As the opening wedge of judicial attempts to pry *Miranda* loose from the legal structure, *Harris* proved more valuable, opening the courtrooms of America to illegally obtained evidence, the admission of which, like murder and revolution, is easier to rationalize the second time. The judicial utility of ill-gotten confessions, having gradually diminished between *Brown* and *Miranda*, now began to increase.

In 1974, three years after the Court had decided *Harris*, it took another significant step in connection with *Miranda*. The case, *Michigan* v. *Tucker*, involved a conviction for rape on the basis of information obtained during an interrogation which had not been preceded by complete *Miranda* warnings—Tucker had been told he had a right to remain silent and had been asked if he wanted a lawyer, but he had not been told that as an indigent he would be provided with one. His own statements had, in fact, been excluded at his trial, but the statements of a witness who had been identified only through the legally faulty interrogation session had been admitted. A federal court reversed the conviction. The Oakland County prosecutor, in whose jurisdiction the case had originated, decided to test it in the Supreme Court. "I said to myself," he later recalled, " 'If there ever was a Court that was willing to listen to a prosecutor's problem, it's the Burger Court.' And I was right."

Tucker looked like a typical "fruit of the poisonous tree" case, asking whether or not in this instance evidence obtained as the fruit of ill-gotten evidence must also be excluded in court along with the ill-gotten evidence itself. The Supreme Court, however, fooled everybody. It did not even address that issue. Instead, it redefined the *Miranda* ruling itself.

Although the *Miranda* majority had stated that criminal suspects must be advised of their constitutional rights prior to any interrogation, the justices had gone on to qualify these instructions. "[W]e cannot say," Warren had written, "that the Constitution necessarily requires adherence to any particular solution for the inherent compulsion of the interrogation process. . . ." The Court did not intend to "create a constitutional straitjacket." Seizing on this passage now in his opinion for the Court in *Tucker*, the youngest and newest member, Mr. Justice Rehnquist, declared that while the ruling did indeed protect a person's Fifth and Sixth Amendment rights, the ruling itself had less than constitutional stature, it was only a "prophylactic," and therefore the warnings that were coming to be a part of the station house scenery were not, as many people had presumed they were, constitutionally required; they were, in fact, often unnecessary. Explained Justice Rehnquist:

349

The privilege against compulsory self-incrimination was developed by painful opposition to a course of ecclesiastical inquisitions and Star Chamber proceedings occurring several centuries ago. . . . Certainly no one could contend that the interrogation faced by [Tucker] bore any resemblance to the historical practices at which the right against compulsory self-incrimination was aimed. . . . [H]is statements could hardly be termed involuntary as that term has been defined in the decisions of this Court. . . .

The question for decision was not whether the *Miranda* requirements had been disregarded; they had, although inadvertently. The question the Court had to decide was "how sweeping the judicially imposed consequences of this disregard shall be." Police having acted in good faith in this case and thereby nullifying the deterrent purpose of the exclusionary rule, the Court decided there would be no consequences; Tucker's conviction would be affirmed. Declared Justice Rehnquist, enunciating what was to become the dominating logic of the Supreme Court of the seventies: ". . . [T]he law does not require that a defendant receive a perfect trial, only a fair one."

The tone had indeed changed. The point the Warren Court had tried to make in rulings like *Escobedo* and *Miranda* was that it was adherence to procedural requirements that made a trial fair. But the point was lost on the Court of the seventies. As standards for the behavior of law enforcement officers lowered and procedural requirements disappeared, skepticism of police turned to trust. No longer did the finger of accusation point at authority and demand that "No person . . . shall be compelled in any criminal case to be a witness against himself" or that "In all criminal prosecutions, the accused shall enjoy the right . . . to have the Assistance of Counsel for his defence." These strictures stayed on the books, but the devices created to implement them were fast being chipped away, and a doctrine of fairness, with all its vagueness, was replacing them. "Fair" trial, "fair" procedures—these were only a coat of paint away from the old due process of law concept on the basis of which cases had been decided those many years prior to *Gideon*—to the judicial dismay of Hugo Black. One man's "fair" trial was another man's lynching. It was not that the justices of the seventies would have tolerated the conditions under which the Scottsboro boys had stood trial, nor would they have tolerated the appearance in court of defendants with rope burns on their necks. But this revived standard of fairness opened the courts to judicial arbitrariness once again.

Following their decisions in *Harris* v. *New York* and *Michigan* v. *Tucker*, the justices, evaluating specific situations and rarely alluding to *Miranda*'s principles, became adept at including evidence their predecessors probably would have excluded—indeed, Justice Brennan, one of the last remaining members of the *Miranda* majority, consistently undergirded his frequent and vigorous dissents with quotations from *Miranda*'s constitutional precepts and procedural requirements as well as the reasoning behind them.

In one case, Internal Revenue Service officers visited a private home to question a man whose tax returns were under investigation. They not only questioned him but also inspected his tax records, all without informing him that he need not answer their questions and that he had a right to consult a lawyer. The chief justice, who had been bucking the Warren Court since his days in the Justice Department and who was now often finding himself in the unaccustomed but enviable position of spokesman for the Court majority, had no difficulty at all allowing the use of this man's statements as evidence.

"Although," he wrote for the Court, "the 'focus' of an investigation may indeed have been on [defendant] at the time of the interview in the sense that it was his tax liability which was under scrutiny, he hardly found himself in the custodial situation described by the *Miranda* court as the basis for its holding."

To which Justice Brennan, who tended to translate specific situations into broad principles and who was finding himself in the unaccustomed and unenviable position of dissenter, replied:

[T]he warnings are also mandated when the taxpayer is, as here, interrogated by the Intelligence Division agents of the Internal Revenue Service in surroundings where, as in the case of the subject in "custody," the practical compulsion to respond to questions about his tax returns is comparable to the psychological pressures described in *Miranda.* Interrogation under conditions that have the practical consequence of compelling the taxpayer to make disclosures, and interrogation in "custody" having the same consequence, are in my views peas from the same pod.

Beginning with *Harris* in 1971, through October Term 1975, ten cases were decided on the basis of *Miranda* issues. In seven, or 70 percent, the evidence in question was declared admissible against the defendant. No physical brutality was involved in these cases; there were no cases of confessions through starvation or protracted questioning or weeklong detention, the sort of thing Izell Chambers had endured three decades before under the authority of the Pompano, Florida, police. Although there were exceptions, law enforcement had become somewhat more civilized since the 1930s. Which was precisely the point the new majority was making: Ernest Miranda's own case had been wrongly decided, clearly an instance of judicial overreaction.

Coinciding with the changes in the plot of judicial drama were changes in the cast. Heroes had become villains and vice versa; not only had dissenters become the majority, but James Thompson, who had argued *Escobedo* for the state in the Supreme Court and lost, was elected governor of Illinois in 1976 and, as the decade of the eighties began, was appointed cochairman of the U.S. attorney general's Task Force on Violent Crime. The organization of which he had been a cofounder in the aftermath of *Miranda*, Americans for Effective Law Enforcement, was in the courts arguing constitutional issues from the law enforcement officer's point of view.

In the mid-sixties, when Ernest Miranda's case was making its way through the courts, the high point of the Supreme Court's civil libertarianism, more than 90 percent of the Court's criminal docket was made up of cases brought by defendants who had lost in the lower courts, less than 10 percent brought by prosecutors, and at least one assistant in the office of Solicitor General Marshall that year "viewed it as either futile or foolhardy" to pursue to the Supreme Court a case which the government had lost in a lower court; it would have little chance there.

By the mid-seventies, however, the proportion of cases brought by criminal defendants which the Court agreed to hear had dropped below 25 percent, the prosecutor's share had risen above 75 percent, and prosecutors, thus emboldened, were filing three times as many criminal appeals, while lawyers for criminal defendants had to look elsewhere for relief. Regarding cases involving specific *Miranda* issues, the Court granted certiorari in less than 3 percent of the *Miranda* cases filed by criminal defendants and to more than half of those filed by the government. Now it was not *Escobedo* v. *Illinois* or *Miranda* v. *Arizona,* but *Michigan* v. *Tucker* and *Oregon* v. *Hass,* and *North Carolina* v. *Butler.* As the Oakland County, Michigan, prosecutor preparing to take the case for the state of Michigan against Tommy Tucker to the Supreme Court had correctly characterized it, the United States Supreme Court was a prosecutor's court now.

Judicial concern had shifted from procedures to results, from constitutionality to product reliability. Due process of law, constitutional guarantees to the individual, the soaring invocations of the framers of the Constitution—these words were rarely used. The integrity of the state seemed to be beneath discussion.

Before his first term had ended, Richard Nixon had had the satisfaction of seeing the justices he had appointed to the Supreme Court vote together in 82 percent of the cases during the first six months they had sat together—frequently joined by Justice White, they already had begun to form a majority. Nixon's campaign literature, as he prepared to run for reelection in 1972, had confidently capitalized on his fulfillment of the promises he had made in 1968, predicting that these first four appointments could be "expected to give a strict interpretation of the Constitution, and protect the interests of the average, law-abiding American."

One of those four appointments, Justice Powell, speaking at an ABA luncheon in 1976, explained in general terms that the Court had indeed changed direction:

> Few would deny that the Warren Court . . . vastly expanded the role of the judiciary by construing the Constitution in dramatically bold and unprecedented ways. Much of the expansion was a reaction to the sluggishness of the legislative branch in addressing urgent needs for reform.
>
> It was perhaps inevitable . . . that a period of consolidation

and leveling off would follow. Changes in personnel did bring, as they have in the past, fresh and different assumptions and perceptions as to the role of the Court and certain constitutional issues. . . . [I]n recent years the Court has decided a number of criminal cases differently from what might have been expected during the decade of the 60s. But it is alarmist to suggest any significant weakening of the basic rights of persons accused of crime. A more traditional, and, in my view, a sounder balance is evolving between the rights of accused persons and the right of a civilized society to have a criminal justice system that is effective as well as fair. . . .

Earlier the same year, in a rare public response to criticism of the Court and its rulings, the chief justice had declared the record of the so-called Burger Court on protecting individual rights at least as good as the record of any earlier court. He saw, he said, no change at all in the United States Supreme Court's treatment of the previous Court's decision in the case of Ernest Miranda. He was not, however, above a little gallows humor on the subject. As Justice Douglas reported in his *Memoirs*, Burger told members of the press assembled at their annual Gridiron Dinner in 1971 that he did not mind dissents on his Court at all. "As a matter of fact," he joked, "if I have four votes with me on an opinion, let the defendant have four votes."

The pages of the American Bar Association's monthly *Journal* were considerably enlivened during the spring and summer of 1973 by a spirited argument regarding what ought to be done about the continuing heavy increase in the work load of the U.S. Supreme Court. The swollen caseload from the lower courts having reached the apex of the judicial pyramid, the number of cases filed there had tripled during the past two decades, and there was some question whether or not the justices could continue to deal with their own docket. Several prominent members of the legal profession participated in the debate. But the main contestants were the retired chief justice, Earl Warren, and the sitting chief justice, Warren Burger, whose very positions guaranteed weight would be given their words. What these two men said served to underscore the differences between them, between the Warren Court, which had encouraged Ernest Miranda's and the other confessions cases, and the Burger Court, which discouraged such cases, between the past and the present.

They were men of different times, Earl Warren and Warren Burger were, the former born into the twilight of the individualistic nineteenth century, the latter born into the early days of the twentieth century inevitably less individualistic, its symbols the data bank and the Xerox machine, its social concerns submissive to the computer. In maturity, the former sought salvation in the condition of man, the latter sought it in the condition of men.

The two men had confronted each other frequently since Earl Warren had decided against the government advocate in the case of John Peters nearly two decades before. Cases in which Burger had participated during his thirteen years as a judge of the U.S. Court of Appeals for the District of Columbia Circuit had made their way to the U.S. Supreme Court, and Earl Warren had participated in the overruling of three-quarters of them. Now they faced each other, their judicial maxims unsheathed, for the last time. Only superficially did the issues have to do with the number of cases before the Court. These were not indeed simple mathematical problems; they were political and social, even philosophical. They reopened the question of who could be heard in the United States Supreme Court, who could not, and who was to distinguish between the two. They touched the heart of the American judicial process.

The judicial outlooks of the two chief justices epitomized the arguments. Warren Burger had announced his position early in that very *Peters* case: Aside from the questions of national security it had presented, the case itself did not, he believed, belong in the courts at all; remedy should be sought with the president or Congress. As he had argued in *Peters*, there were a lot of problems, he believed, which courts were not authorized to decide. Thirteen years later, in 1968, in the dramatic case of *Powell* v. *McCormack*, in which the House of Representatives had excluded from membership the congressman from New York's Eighteenth Congressional District, Adam Clayton Powell, Jr., because of his questionable use of public funds and the congressman had taken his case against the House to the federal courts, Judge Burger, for the U.S. Court of Appeals for the District of Columbia Circuit, had invoked the name of federalism and its requirement of equality between the branches of government to declare that the judiciary was not empowered to interfere in such internal matters of the legislature. Consider, he urged, "the blow to representative government were judges either so rash or so sure of their infallibility as to think they should command an elected co-equal branch in these circumstances." Like John Peters's, Adam Clayton Powell's case did not belong in the courts.

Just over three months later, on June 16, 1969, one week before Burger took the oath as chief justice of the United States, the sitting chief justice, Earl Warren, writing one of his last opinions for the U.S. Supreme Court, had overruled his successor, advancing his own interpretation of federalism: "Our system of government requires that federal courts on occasion interpret the Constitution in a manner at variance with the construction given by another branch." Since Adam Clayton Powell had been "duly elected by the voters of the 18th Congressional District of New York and was not ineligible to serve under any provision of the Constitution, the House was without power to exclude him from its membership."

Underlying the two men's opinions was their difference in judicial values. It was Earl Warren's People's Court against Warren Burger's cost accounting.

Under Warren the Supreme Court, through its willingness to apply judicial solutions to social problems when other avenues had been barricaded, had positively encouraged the poor, the disadvantaged, the accused, the victimized to bring the causes of their discontent to the courts. As a result, all the courts, including—perhaps especially—the United States Supreme Court, were congested beyond previous judicial credulity and contemporary ability to deal with it. When John Marshall was appointed chief justice in 1801, the position had been believed to be no more than a sinecure. Only 10 cases came before the Court during that entire term; over the next five years only 120 cases were brought. From that time on, however, the number had increased gradually until by the 1926 term the Court had 667 cases on its docket, and by the October term of 1965, the year Ernest Miranda's case was argued and decided, no fewer than 3,284 cases, including 484 brought over from the previous term, crowded the docket. By the 1972 term the figure had risen to 4,640.

Chief Justice Burger was determined to do something about it. Far from encouraging people to take their claims for redress, whether against public or private misconduct, to the courts, Burger positively *dis*couraged it, and the Court over which he presided, through a series of technical rulings over the dissents of Douglas, Brennan, and Marshall, set up procedural barriers and other limits on the accessibility of the federal courts, making cases more expensive and difficult to initiate. The effect was to lock the doors of the federal courthouse to a lot of Americans, most of them poor: the inmates of prisons, indigent women in need of abortion, illegitimate children, victims of zoning ordinances that discriminated against the poor, and other of the nation's discriminated-against and underprivileged. In 1976 the Society of American Law Teachers accused the Burger Court of cutting back on the rights of the individual less through its decisions, as had been anticipated when the Nixon appointees all came together, than by taking away the judicial forum in which Americans traditionally had fought for these rights.

This diminishing accessibility of the federal courts, however, was not an entirely surprising development, and there were those who recalled the chief justice's warning of July 1971, two years after his appointment: Those young people who had entered law school in order to achieve social change through the courts might well face some disappointments in the future: it was not, he had declared, "the route by which basic changes in the [sic] country like ours should be made."

As criticism of the Court mounted, joined by the ACLU, consumer groups, environmentalists, and other public interest groups, the chief justice defended its rulings with equanimity. He was not one, he told the House of Representatives in 1977, to underestimate the "indispensable role of the federal judicial system in righting ancient wrongs to large segments of our population, in reapportionment and in human rights." But, he added, "the need to rely on federal courts as primary sources of justice . . . has passed." In view of the intolerable increase in cases initiated—federal appellate filings had increased 43.9 percent and district court filings 25.7 percent between 1971 and 1976, without the addition of a single judgeship, delaying, if not denying, justice to a lot of Americans—"the opportunity to litigate is not in itself an assurance of effective justice. We must remain concerned that we do not bestow access to the federal courts so casually and unwisely that access to justice becomes illusory," he declared.

The reformer in him did not let him stop there. Reform of the judicial system had become the chief justice's specialty, and he divided his responsibilities between it and deciding cases. It was hardly a glamorous calling. It lacked drama and heroism and often tangible results. But it seemed to suit him. He had a penchant for methodology, a talent for efficiency, an appreciation of management techniques. He was not a charismatic figure. His talks lacked the inspirational style of a Black or a Frankfurter—largely because they were appeals to pragmatism rather than political philosophy. Workability was a prime consideration for Burger. "Will it work? How will it work?" he seemed to ask himself frequently as he wrote. The effect on society underlay every paragraph, and the imagery he employed to make his points served the added purpose of putting stress on that approach. Medicine was a favorite metaphor, but he used the image of the medical craftsman, the solid professional, not the researcher; the factory was another, but the image was of the worker or manager, not the designer or inventor. A Burger engineer "checks the pressure gauges on his boilers"; he probably would not invent a new heating system. But the chief justice was indefatigable, and although he was in his late sixties, he mustered the energy to pack up and go to the judicial conferences, where he tirelessly goaded the heathen to reform, although he frequently faced apathy, skepticism, and resistance.

By 1973, his failures and success were about equal. His frequent calls for reform of the corrections system, which was failing to correct and whose graduates were providing more than half of the criminal defendants in court cases, went largely unanswered, as such calls traditionally had. A Judiciary Committee hearing regarding the fitness of a nominee to serve on the Supreme Court often drew crowds of spectators, press, and television. A hearing regarding policies in the federal prisons more often went largely unattended, even by the senators themselves.

Burger's proposal for creation of a Federal Judicial Council to advise Congress on the effects of pending legislation on the courts, another source of substantial amounts of litigation, was not acted upon. Nor was his proposal for a new National Institute of Justice to conduct research into the problems of the courts, much the way the National Institutes of Health conducted research into medical matters. A new federal rules of evidence code, drafted by a committee appointed by the chief justice and containing several controversial provisions, was shelved by Congress.

On the other side, the chief justice had successfully sponsored a program to train court administrators in the ways of modern management, worked for the establishment of state-federal judicial councils in several states for coordinating activities on the two levels, and inspired the establishment of the National Center for State Courts at Williamsburg, Virginia, a service and research agency intended to do for the state courts what the Federal Judicial Center had been doing for the federal courts since its organization in 1967.

Burger's attempts at reform were not universally received with enthusiasm. Philip Kurland, professor of law at the University of Chicago, who had also been a frequent critic of the Warren Court, accused him of overstepping the bounds of his office and taking on too political a coloration:

> The Chief Justice and his brethren have a big enough task before them without becoming a self-centered law reform commission. . . . The Chief Justice of the United States is not particularly well equipped, either in his person or [in] his office, to supervise substantive or procedural law reform throughout the nation. Such behavior at worst gives the impression that he is attempting to circumvent the Court's own decisions by judicial and legislative politicking, probably because he cannot command for that purpose a majority of the tribunal over which he was appointed to preside. At best such activities suggest that the job of a Supreme Court justice is only a part-time task. Better that he teach lower court judges their jobs by example than precept.

Warren Burger's old rival on the U.S. Court of Appeals for the District of Columbia, David Bazelon, without mentioning either the chief justice or his specific programs by name, declared that the nation was being oversold on judicial efficiency. Better, he said in the annual James Madison Lecture on Constitutional Law at New York University Law School in April 1971, to "repair the institutions that provide uninhabitable housing, insufficient food, medieval medical care and inadequate educations to the people who commit crimes."

Another former colleague on the court of appeals, Edward A. Tamm, contradicted these assessments. Citing Burger's own statement at his confirmation hearings that the chief justice "has a very large responsibility to see that the judicial system functions more efficiently," Judge Tamm (joined by Paul C. Reardon, retired justice of the Supreme Judicial Court of Massachusetts) wrote that "it was not until Warren E. Burger was appointed Chief Justice of the United States that sustained progress in the administration of justice began to be made on a national scale."

One area of reform still to be explored was the potential for bringing the operations of the United States Supreme Court under control. The increase in the number of cases filed had rankled the chief justice ever since his assumption of the office, and in 1971 he had appointed an eight-member committee of prominent lawyers and legal scholars, headed by Paul A. Freund of Harvard Law School, to study the caseload of the Court under the auspices of the Federal Judicial Center.

The committee had analyzed the Supreme Court's caseload statistically and had judged it unacceptable. "The task of decision," it had declared, "must clearly be a process, not an event, a process at the opposite pole from the 'processing' of cases in a high-speed, high-volume enterprise," which, as the study group perceived it, the Supreme Court was in imminent danger of becoming as a result of the enormous—and multiplying—number of cases being filed there each year. The committee recommended, in order to keep the Court from drowning in its own docket, the creation of an entirely new court, a Washington-based national court of appeals made up of a rotating panel of federal circuit judges, to act as a buffer between those thousands of petitioners and the nine Supreme Court justices. This new court would screen all petitions for Supreme Court review. It would screen *out* all those considered insignificant. It would hear arguments and adjudicate certain cases. From more than 4,000 cases pouring into the Supreme Court each year, the number would drop to an estimated—and, the logic went, more manageable—400.

The decisions of the newly created court would be final. There would be no appeal to the Supreme Court, not from rejection of a petition or from a ruling in a case. The situation so created would not be unlike putting someone in the front office to receive callers and to handle so far as possible their affairs. His main responsibility would be, however, to keep people away from the boss.

Following the ABA's publication of excerpts from the committee's report in the February 1973 issue of its *Journal*, its chairman, Paul Freund, himself had argued in behalf of establishing the proposed national court of appeals in the March issue, and Eugene Gressman, a prominent Washington lawyer, had dissented. The following month Justice Rehnquist had, without actually conferring his imprimatur, written that given the burdens on the contemporary Court, the recommendation of the Freund committee ought at least to be considered.

Then, in the July issue, the two chief justices, the one retired, the one sitting, at the peak of his powers, faced each other across the pages of the ABA *Journal*.

His brethren had not expected Earl Warren to slow his pace when he left the Court, and they had been right. He had maintained chambers there, had written a small book—a simple statement of some of his judicial and political views called *A Republic If You Can Keep It*—and had intended to write others. But such a sedentary life ill suited a man who had been an activist for half a century, and soon he began to accept the invitations to speak that were coming to him from all over the country. On his retirement, the justices had given him a specially made Winchester shotgun, and he sometimes combined these speaking engagements with one of his favorite recreations, duck hunting.

He had been lecturing on college and university campuses for several months, engaging in informal discussions with students, meeting with faculty, playing the role of some kindly judicial grandfather as he explained his concepts of the Court and Constitution, when in December 1972 the Freund committee published its report. The genial grandfather image vanished immediately, and the Viking emerged in its place.

Earl Warren had reached his limit. As chief justice he had quietly, even with good humor—although it was reported that inwardly he had raged—endured the insults of his profession, his people, and his president. But in 1973 he was no longer the chief justice, and with the loosening of the ties of office, there also had come a certain loosening of the judicial tongue.

The retired chief justice, whose arguments had been reprinted in the ABA *Journal* from a speech he had given on Law Day, May 1, viewed the scheme for a national court of appeals less as a way of lightening the burdens of the justices than as a cynical and formidable device to keep the United States Supreme Court from actively enforcing constitutional rights, a device to prevent the justices from considering cases from previously unheard petitioners who might disturb the status quo.

The statistics on which the Freund committee had based its assessment of the Court's workload, Earl Warren argued, said next to nothing. They ignored, first of all, the fact that most—probably 90 percent—of the cases filed in the Supreme Court were frivolous, and although the number was large, this group of cases consumed very little of a justice's time. Justice Brennan demonstrated dramatically in a later issue of the *Journal* (where he also registered his dissent to the committee report partly on the ground that the justices were not overworked) just how frivolous they could be when he described a few of the questions presented in one week's batch of petitions for cert: "Are Negroes in fact Indians and therefore entitled to Indians' exemptions from federal income taxes?" "Are the federal income tax laws unconstitutional insofar as they do not provide a deduction for depletion of the human body?" "Does a ban on drivers' turning right on a red light constitute an unreasonable burden on interstate commerce?"

The conclusions of the Freund committee were, declared Warren, based on "a facile and unevaluated use of numbers reminiscent of the McCarthy days" and left the American public with a "false impression as to the workload of the Court and the ability of the Justices to manage" it. The fact was, the former chief justice said, drawing on his own long experience, that in spite of the expanding caseload, "for more than 40 years the Court has never had a backlog," and he himself, in the sixteen years he had headed the Court, had never had a complaint from the justices "that the necessary screening process was becoming so intolerable that their capacity to do the necessary research and opinion writing was beginning to suffer."

Justice Douglas, who claimed he need work only a four-day week to keep pace with Court business, had actually complained that the Court sat too infrequently, heard and decided too few cases. The previous term he had wanted to add 105 cases to the calendar, and in a typical Douglas gesture of defiance, he customarily finished his work each term about two weeks before the other justices and left for his summer place in Goose Prairie.

Justice Marshall saw no need for the added encumbrance of a new tribunal. "Unless this situation changes substantially . . . ," he declared, "I think we can continue to handle our docket without outside help."*

The Freund committee's figures also ignored—and this was far more important to a man whose responsibility it was to interpret the Constitution—the positive value of the large flow of cases through the Court which served "to inform the justices of what is happening in the system of justice" and enabled them, in the "highly personalized and necessarily discretionary" selection and denial of cases, to "establish our national priorities in constitutional and legal matters," an important function of the Court which could not be delegated to a rotating panel of lower-court judges.

"Dealing effectively with any part of the Supreme Court's workload requires a broad overlook and an innovative approach to the law and the Constitution, an overlook and approach that are acquired only by those who serve on the Supreme Court," Warren said.

In other words, the figures ignored the mystique of the United States Supreme Court. Stanching the flow of those thousands of cases through the Court, however frivolous some of them seemed, would deprive the Court of its soul. It was an activist view of Court and Constitution, but Earl Warren had never yet been accused of passivity. Underlying Warren's words was always this unspoken question: Would a panel of lower-court judges, "honorable and dedicated" but limited by the "conservative bounds of their own judicial experience . . . trained to follow precedent" and understandably sympathetic with their "fellow judges whose rulings are under attack," pass on to the Supreme Court for consideration the rough, ungrammatical penciled petition for cert of a Clarence Earl Gideon? Following the Supreme Court decision in Danny Escobedo's case, would these lower-court judges have collected 180-odd confessions cases, all of them contributing to the big picture of the problems involved in police interrogation, from which to

---

* In the late summer of 1982, Justices White, Powell, and John P. Stevens (who replaced Douglas in 1975) complained in speeches at the ABA meetings, and Justice Brennan complained in one to the Third Circuit Judicial Conference that the Supreme Court docket had become so overloaded that the quality of justice would suffer. The previous term the Court had intended to schedule conferences to discuss ways of lightening the load. However, sighed Stevens, as the justices wrestled with the issues in the large number of difficult cases that had come in, no such conference was ever scheduled; "we were too busy to decide whether there was anything we could do about the problem of being too busy."

choose final appropriate combination of cases for granting cert?

Would the final triumph of the forces that had built against *Miranda*—the political attacks, the legal attacks, the legislative overruling—culminate in a simple system to keep the Ernest Mirandas out of the Court altogether?

Had it all been for nothing, the long and unsteady movement from the nineteenth-century Court's worship of liberty of contract to the mid-twentieth-century Court's recognition of liberty of the person, the emergence, finally, of Earl Warren's People's Court? Warren concluded:

> The Supreme Court must remain open to all people and to all claims of injustice. The public faith in the Court and the esteem in which it is held rest in large part upon the knowledge that the Court is always here to right the major wrongs that do occur within our legal system and to advance and protect our precious constitutional liberties and privileges. And part of that public faith and esteem depends on the certainty that, when all other judicial remedies have been exhausted, the Supreme Court will at least consider and listen to the citizen's final plea.

Chief Justice Burger's answer, which he had given in a speech to the American Law Institute on May 15 and which was reprinted cheek by jowl with the former chief justice's charges in the July issue of the ABA *Journal*, was a defense of his committee, of its members—Warren had criticized it as having no judges or justices, those most immediately concerned with the problems being studied; Burger had countered with "War is too important to be left to generals"—and of its work, which, he declared, was "beyond challenge." His answer to the substantive charges made by his predecessor consisted largely of a long and entirely dispassionate analysis of Supreme Court caseloads and their rapid growth. Having erected barriers in front of the Court's entrance, he had now reduced the Gideons and Mirandas to statistics. He did not comment on Warren's plea for them. It was as if there were no institutional history, no institutional character, no institutional mystique. Efficiency was what mattered.

At the end of the 1970 term, on July 4, 1971, in an interview with a *New York Times* reporter, Chief Justice Burger had said that "the primary role of the Court is to decide cases," and he had gone on to make it clear that there ought to be a lot fewer of them. Then, toward the end, the reporter had asked: "What do you see as the greatest challenge to the Supreme Court in the next few years?" The Chief Justice had replied: "I would say the greatest challenge is to try to keep up with the volume of work and maintain the kind of quality that ought to come from this Court." His perspective had not changed between that interview and publication of the Freund committee's report, and he concluded his remarks in the ABA *Journal* this way:

> It would be comforting, should I come to have grandchildren, for them to read that grandfather and his eight colleagues disposed of

three, four, or five times as many cases as the Justices of 1935 or 1943, and did it with consistently high quality. But to be entirely candid, I do not regard myself as an advocate who could carry that burden of proof.

In three years the nation would celebrate its 200th birthday; eleven years later, in 1987, the Constitution itself would be similarly honored. Would people then still be talking about promoting "the general Welfare" or securing "the Blessings of Liberty to ourselves and our Posterity"? Or would these be reduced to some sophisticated system of cost accounting?

Chief Justice Burger did not give the national court of appeals his seal of approval. He would defer his conclusion, he said, until all the arguments and alternatives had been fully explored and recorded. But he would accept no criticism of his committee's methods or its analysis of the problem.*

It was clear, though, from his argument that if a national court of appeals was not the appropriate solution to the impossible logistics of the United States Supreme Court, something similar was. The Court could not go on as it had during the past several years.

The national court of appeals did not come to fruition. The debate continued within the legal profession, and the idea was revived from time to time over the next decade. But no ground swell developed for it. By 1973 the American public had become so engrossed in other events whose kinship with constitutional issues could not be reduced to statistics and which did indeed go to the heart of the mystique of the democratic process. Lumped together, they became known as Watergate.

* Speaking at the ABA meeting in February 1983 and predicting either "a breakdown of the system—or some of the Justices"—under the ever increasing number of Supreme Court cases, Burger asked Congress to create immediately a Temporary Emergency Court of Appeals with the limited function of deciding conflicts among the federal circuits. This interim and temporary (he suggested a life of five years) panel, the Chief Justice suggested, would reduce drastically the number of cases coming to the Supreme Court and at the same time would provide a "concrete example of the utility ... [of] an intermediate reviewing court such as the Freund Committee had recommended."

CHAPTER 3

The assemblage—senators and representatives of the Ninety-third Congress, justices of the Supreme Court, members of the cabinet, the vice president—rose as the president, smiling and looking confident, entered the packed House chamber of the Capitol the night of January 30, 1974, and strode down the aisle to the rostrum from which he would deliver the 186th State of the Union message. There were some in that particular assemblage, however, who had gotten to their feet only reluctantly, and who were careful afterward to attribute the gesture to respect for the office, and not for the man.

The American Constitution, which commanded that the president "shall from time to time give to the Congress information of the state of the Union," was the source of the tradition of this speech, and the American Constitution, for quite different reasons, was uppermost in the minds of a lot of people that night. The assembled representatives were empowered under the Constitution to impeach the president, and the question of whether they could or should had been a major subject of conversation for some weeks as the unfolding of events continued to reveal the depths of political corruption in which he and his men were involved. The assembled senators, should the members of the House decide to proceed with impeachment, were empowered by the Constitution to try the case. The chief justice of the United States was commanded to preside over the trial. If it came to that. There were many who prayed that it wouldn't.

"It was five years ago on the steps of this Capitol that I took the oath of office as your President," Richard Nixon said in introducing the traditional message of past accomplishment and future task.

His voice was calm; his hands were relaxed on the rostrum. There was color in his face, all of which contradicted the local rumors that his isolation of the past month in the White House, at Camp David, over the recent holidays at San Clemente, his California retreat, had indicated failing emotional health. Tonight he looked fit and cheerful, as if the state of the Union were the only matter the assemblage had come to hear. As if the smoke detectors had not gone off, as if there had been no Watergate.

"In those five years, because of the initiatives undertaken by this Administration, the world has changed. America has changed. . . ."

Was it only five years? It seemed longer. So much had happened, not all of it because of the initiatives taken by Richard Nixon's administration. Eighteen-year-olds had gotten the vote by constitutional amendment. Feminism, playing its perpetual game of follow the leader, was showing another spurt of energy as it clung to the tail of the black revolution—again. Terrorism had become an arm of diplomacy; gas lines, temporarily a way of life. Jogging was about to replace streaking as the national sport. Cuisinarts and cocaine were amusing the middle classes. Fast-food parlors were beginning to dominate the popular architecture as well as the popular palate, and, in the idiom of the day, the hamburger had begun to look as well as taste as if it had been cooked by computer. Americans were living longer, but their problems were more complex and took longer to solve, and people wondered if there was an overall gain. The problems of governing had become more complex, too, and questions regarding the adequacy of the American system as constituted, the executive power lodged in one man, were cropping up more and more frequently.

The national agony of Vietnam had ended. The young men had come home—except for the 58,655 who had died there—and the agony had begun anew as Americans tried to soothe and cool the places where their souls had been seared, as if the napalm had burned the living, too.

The president, bundled in his fur-collared coat, smiling confidently, had stood at the Great Wall, and with his opening of the door to mainland China, the alignments between East and West had begun to shift.

Unlike 1968, Liberty City had huddled quietly in the shadow of Miami Beach during the Republican National Convention proceedings in 1972, and President Nixon's acceptance of the nomination was delivered in an atmosphere of apparent calm.

Despite Nixon's early promises that he would countenance no social adventuring during his administration, the momentum which had previously built up could not be stopped altogether. Maynard Jackson, a black man, was mayor in Atlanta, and Walter Washington, another black man, was mayor in the nation's capital. Within the decade, Richard Arrington, also black, would be mayor in George Wallace's Birmingham. White collars were stretching around black necks. Black women took tennis lessons on suburban courts. Black children went to private schools.

But the ghetto streets could be only partially hidden. The storefronts boarded up following the riots that had marked the assassination of Dr. Martin Luther King, Jr., in April 1968 were still boarded up, the passage of time noted only by the peeling of paint. Black men, big, husky black men, stocking caps stretched over their ears to keep out the cold, waited on street corners or at ramshackle neighborhood employment centers for a diminishing number of daily jobs, and when the jobs did not materialize, the men drowned themselves in wine and whiskey. Murder and cirrhosis of the liver were leading causes of death in black men. Little black children sold heroin, and other little black children went to schools that had leaking toilets and learned their lessons out of ravaged textbooks, and if they survived the neglect and if they survived the violence in the corridors and the schoolyards, they might learn to read and write and count. But many did not.

"Five years ago, crime was increasing at a rate that struck fear across the nation. . . ."

Now in 1974, the president declared:

"The 17-year-rise in crime has been stopped. We can confidently say today that we are finally beginning to win the war on crime. . . ."

The rate of increase, in fact, had slowed slightly, and in 1972, for the first time since 1964, crime had not been a major issue in a national election. The president had pointed out his accomplishments rapidly enough, his satisfaction with the falling crime figures and his pride in his appointments to the U.S. Supreme Court, but crime had not had nearly the prominence in 1972 as it had had in 1968 or 1964 or some of the off-year congressional elections. The president had virtually ignored the subject in his inaugural address, although the inauguration itself, the swearings-in by Chief Justice Warren Burger, had reminded all Americans that promises made at the previous inauguration had been faithfully kept.

He had promised that steamy night in Miami in 1968, though, as he responded to the cheers following his nomination as the Republican presidential candidate, that "The crime wave is not going to be the wave of the future in the United States of America," and to that end he had appointed four "strict constructionists" to the Supreme Court and sent a packet of anticrime bills to Congress. But he had not fulfilled his promise. If, as he said, the rate of rise in crime was slipping, the rise itself was not. The street crime which he had exploited to win the position he held that night—the stabbings in dark streets, the burglaries of suburban homes, rapes in the laundry rooms of apartment houses, muggings, auto thefts—had not decreased at all. We had not even begun to fight the war on crime, much less begun to win it, as the president was suggesting. This year there would be an overall rise of 18 percent over 1973, with murder increasing 6 percent, forcible rape 8 percent, aggravated assault 8 percent, robbery 15 percent, larceny-theft 21 percent, burglary 8 percent, and auto theft 5 percent.

The FBI statistics did not include white-collar crime. If they did, one of the statistics might have been the vice president of the United States himself, Spiro T. Agnew. Agnew had taken a hard line toward criminal defendants during the two national campaigns in which he had participated as the vice presidential candidate. Then, in October 1973, he had chosen not to contest a charge of income tax evasion and had resigned rather than face prosecution for extortion and bribery during the time he had been a Maryland county executive and governor of the state. He was fined $10,000 and placed on unsupervised probation. Nixon had appointed Republican Representative Gerald R. Ford of Michigan, Justice Douglas's old congressional antagonist, to succeed Agnew as vice president.

The president spoke for about forty minutes. He did not allude to Watergate but talked confidently of the remaining three years of his administration.

Then he closed the manila folder containing the text of his speech and began to speak extemporaneously. He spoke to the assembled government of the United States and to the uncounted millions watching the television screens in their living rooms, and he spoke now with feeling, his voice not always steady.

"I would like to add a personal word with regard to an issue that has been of great concern to all Americans over the past year. I refer, of course, to the investigations of the so-called Watergate affair."

It had begun on a smaller scale: the ordering of a "tail" on a "front-running Democrat," a command that aides devise some "imaginative dirty tricks" to be played on political opponents, just a little insurance against defeat at the polls, a head of state exercising his prerogative of self-perpetuation—the American version of techniques that had been developed and refined elsewhere over many centuries.

The president had been vacationing in Florida on the night of June 16–17, 1972, just over a year and a half before. That night, five men had been arrested for breaking into and trying to bug the Democratic National Committee headquarters at the Watergate, the apartment and office complex in Northwest Washington overlooking the Potomac River—the same complex where the former attorney general, John Mitchell, lived and where he had received the news from his aides one spring night in 1969 that they did indeed have the goods on Associate Justice of the Supreme Court Abe Fortas. Nixon had dismissed the break-in at the time as a prank. Two days later his closest White House adviser, H. R. Haldeman, informed him that "the break-in of the Democratic National Committee involved someone who is on the payroll of the Committee to Re-elect the President." It was reported that the president in his anger not at the illegality of the escapade but at its stupidity had thrown an ashtray across a room in his Key Biscayne home. But it had been done and could not be undone. The frantic—and increasingly unsuccessful—attempts to cover it up, the lies, the subterfuges, the evasions by the lowliest and the mightiest of his White House staff and on the part of the president himself had led him to this time and place, where Watergate could no longer be ignored.

As he spoke to the American government assembled in the House chamber that wintry night in January 1974, the president was living a lie. Six days after the break-in, according to tapes on which his White House conversations had been recorded secretly, he had been told that the break-in had been part of a larger plan of political espionage approved by his friend and adviser, the nation's former chief law enforcement officer, John Mitchell, who had resigned to direct the president's reelection campaign, and that it had been financed by campaign funds. And the president of the United States, the crime fighter, the man who was going to strengthen the peace forces against the criminal forces in this country, who had appointed no-nonsense strict constructionists to the Supreme Court, had reacted like a mugger trapped by police in an alley: He had tried to run away. He had been so desperate that he had been willing to pervert the purposes of the nation's leading law enforcement agency, and he had instructed the Central Intelligence Agency, in the name of national security, to call off the FBI. And then he had lied to the nation about it: He had not, he had said, intended to impede the FBI investigations.

Now several participants in the break-ins had been indicted in a federal court; five had pleaded guilty; two had been tried and convicted. Three men in the highest White House echelons, including H. R. Haldeman, had resigned, the president's standing in the Gallup poll—27 percent approval of his behavior—was at an all-time low.

> I have provided to the Special Prosecutor voluntarily a great deal of material [Nixon said]. I believe that I have provided all the material that he needs to conclude his investigations and to proceed to prosecute the guilty and to clear the innocent.

Leon Jaworski of Houston, Texas, a prosecutor at the Nuremberg war crimes trials and a former president of the American Bar Association was the second special prosecutor appointed to investigate the case. The president had fired the first one, Archibald Cox, for displaying a little too much independence.

> I believe the time has come to bring that investigation and the other investigations of this matter to an end [the president continued]. One year of Watergate is enough.

Republicans cheered and applauded. Nixon went on:

> I recognize that the House Judiciary Committee has a special re-
> sponsibility in this area, and I want to indicate on this occasion that
> I will cooperate with the Judiciary Committee in its investigation.

Did he recall perhaps his pledge, indeed the executive branch's obliga-
tion, as he himself had put it only four years ago, when members of the
House of Representatives were preparing a similar action against Justice
Douglas, "to supply relevant information to the legislative branch" and his
subsequent instructions to appropriate government officials, including the
FBI and CIA, to turn over the appropriate documents and reports?

Peter W. Rodino, Jr., the Democratic representative from New Jersey
who was chairman of that House Judiciary Committee, which was considering the impeachment of the President, sat quietly, his face expressionless,
his arms folded. Nearly 100 members of the House of Representatives had already indicated their willingness to vote for impeachment.

Sam Ervin, chairman of the Senate Select Committee on Presidential
Campaign Activities, which had been organized to investigate the events that
had become connected and labeled "Watergate" and which itself had become known as the Watergate Committee, also sat quietly and solemnly
through the president's speech. He was seventy-seven years old. He had
served two decades in the Senate. He had already announced he would not
run for reelection. Politics could not touch him in his pursuit of the President. Senator Ervin's select committee had subpoenaed certain White House
tape recordings of presidential conversations following the president's refusal
to surrender them.

Applause was sustained as the president ended his talk, but not so enthusiastic as that accorded several of his predecessors on similar occasions. Republicans in the audience may have recalled the president's telling them only
a week before: "There is a time to be timid. There is a time to be conciliatory.
There is a time, even, to fly and there is a time to fight. And I'm going to
fight like hell."

The assemblage rose as the president left the rostrum. It included Peter
Rodino and Sam Ervin, but the latter, like many in the chamber, did not applaud.

Earl Warren was not applauding the performance of his old political
rival, the president, either. His criticism of the Freund committee's proposal
for a national court of appeals had been one of his most strident public outbursts. Although he was in failing health, it was not to be his last.

Following treatment in January 1974 at a hospital in California for what
was said at the time to be a minor heart episode suffered during a visit with
his daughter and son-in-law in Beverly Hills—he had a history of coronary ar-

tery disease and severe angina pectoris—the retired chief justice, who was be-having like anyone except a senior citizen, had resumed his rigorous speaking schedule, against his doctor's advice.

The previous fall he had refused, when approached, to join the discus-sions of a group that was mapping out a scheme for the president's impeach-ment, and he had refused to add his voice to those who were shouting for it. But he had not hesitated to speak out publicly about his fears for the nation, and he continued into the spring of 1974.

If he felt personal bitterness toward the president who had made the Court over which Warren had presided for sixteen years a political issue, not only substantially debasing the quality of American politics for a time but in effect impugning by innuendo the integrity of the justices, Warren sup-pressed it, at least publicly, and he directed his remarks to the effects of the Watergate scandals on the national well-being. He named no names; he did not deal in personalities. He listed the offices and how they had been cor-rupted during the administration of the man who had promised to strengthen the peace forces against the criminal forces. He counted them off:

  • [T]he resignation of the Vice-President and his acknowl-edgement of guilt. . . .
  • [T]he recent Attorney General of the United States is under indictment. . . .
  • [T]he former official counsel to the President has pled [*sic*] guilty. . . .
  • The Chairman of the fund-raising activities in the campaign for the re-election of the President, himself a recent member of the Cabinet, is under indictment. . . .
  • The personal lawyer of the President and many others are under criminal investigation. . . .
  • Our President, himself a lawyer, is beleaguered in all of these White House revelations, compendiously known as Water-gate.

Such behavior was anathema to Earl Warren. Official lawlessness was not to be countenanced in any form, and some people recalled a scene at the Court nearly a decade and a half before, during the special August 1958 term, when the then chief justice expressed in no uncertain terms his contempt for it—along with his astonishment that such brazenness existed. The Court was sitting for the Little Rock, Arkansas, school case involving the local school board's request that the Court suspend its public school desegregation orders in the face of the resistance of the people of Little Rock; indeed, the governor of Arkansas had encouraged them, telling them that Supreme Court deci-sions were not the law of the land.

"Mr. Chief Justice, you've been the Governor of a great state," one of the lawyers began. The chief justice interrupted; as governor of California, he had, he declared, "abided by the decisions of the courts." The lawyer persisted. Warren again interrupted: "I have never heard such an argument made in a court of justice before, and I have tried many a case through many a year. I never heard a lawyer say that the statement of a Governor as to what was legal or illegal should control the action of any court."

Eight years later, in June 1966, he had told police, not without similar contempt for their methods of investigating crime, that they, too, must obey the law and take appropriate steps to insure that a suspect in a criminal case was not compelled to incriminate himself in violation of the Fifth Amendment to the Constitution, that the law did not allow them to take advantage of weaknesses, of the Ernest Mirandas.

Now Warren was telling the president of the United States that he, too, must obey the law, that his position, however exalted, did not elevate him above the legal necessities.

Warren did not fear, he said over and over, that one man could destroy a system of government that had survived 200 years of attacks and emerged the stronger each time. He did fear, however, "the feeling of cynicism about our underlying institutions" that already had begun to develop among young people, the nation's investment in its own future, and he feared they might turn away. He also feared that in the frustrations of national crisis, the panic, the fright, people would succumb to the instant security offered by the numerous ad hoc remedies and short-term solutions being aired, fragile and temporary though these were. It would not be the first time.

Warren himself had been invited to participate in such a movement, one to abolish the vice presidency and leave the succession to the presidency to the speaker of the House, the president pro tempore of the Senate, or some member of the cabinet. As if the lust for power lay in the office, not the man. Others had suggested the Department of Justice be removed from the executive branch of government and set up in an independent agency subject to the supervision of Congress. Similar suggestions had been made regarding the FBI. Constitutional amendments to redefine the power of the president were being circulated. Warren warned against all these, explaining again and again that the American system, with its built-in checks and balances, the Congress, the president, the judges, the people, each authorized in its own way to check on the other, would repel this latest attack. And he had asked:

> Wouldn't it be reassuring then if we come out of Watergate with a
> new commitment to the rights of man through a modern Magna
> Charta for governmental conduct supplementing that which grew
> out of the abuses of King John more than 750 years ago?

He spoke his message tirelessly, largely on college campuses, where he appealed to the reason of young people, particularly law students, often coupling his appeals with attacks on movements to undercut the authority of the United States Supreme Court. Eventually, however, he could no longer endure the physical toll.

On May 11 he spoke at the commencement exercises of the University of Santa Clara Law School. On May 17 he had to cancel his appearance at the NAACP's dinner to celebrate the twentieth anniversary of the Supreme Court's decision in *Brown* v. *Board of Education*. He recovered in time to make a scheduled speech on May 21 at Morehouse College in Atlanta, where the gymnasium was filled to overflowing.

Then, on May 23, he was back in the hospital, and a week later he wrote the chancellor of the University of California at Santa Cruz that he had to cancel his address to the graduating class, which had been scheduled for the following month, urging the chancellor to pass on to the students his plea that they learn well the lesson of Watergate:

> I have never known anything bad happening to our Nation through adherence to the Constitution as it now stands. We are only in great national trouble when people violate or circumvent the Constitution. . . . I believe . . . we do not tear down good buildings merely because they have been occupied by bad tenants. Our country will survive this tragedy and will do so if an enlightened citizenry will give its attention to the affairs of government on all its levels. . . .

Had Warren been a sitting member of the Supreme Court, he could have been treated at Bethesda Naval Hospital, which would have been his preference. But because he was retired, presidential approval was required for his admission, and the president refused to sign the order. Later the president changed his mind, but then Warren refused the offer, and he was treated at Georgetown University Hospital.

He was discharged on June 2 to complete his recovery at home, which had been, for two decades, a spacious apartment in the comfortable Sheraton-Park Hotel, off upper Connecticut Avenue in Northwest Washington. His secretary came each day, and he worked on his memoirs for as long as his diminishing powers of concentration would allow, writing in longhand on yellow legal pads. But there were no more speaking engagements.

On July 2 he returned to Georgetown University Hospital. This time it was coronary insufficiency and congestive heart failure. At the outset he was reported to be in fair condition.

Six days later, on July 8, the United States Supreme Court heard arguments in the case of *United States* v. *Nixon*. Leon Jaworski, the special prosecutor appointed to investigate Watergate, was not soft on crime or criminals; as a member of the president's National Crime Commission in the mid-sixties, he had dissented from its 1967 report and supported the overruling of *Miranda* and *Escobedo*, which had, he believed—and he never changed his mind, he said later—tied the hands of law enforcement officers. Having acted extremely independently in his investigation of Watergate and having probed very deeply, and having discerned analogies between what had happened in Germany forty years before and what was happening here in America in the mid-1970s, he told the packed courtroom—some spectators had waited two days to get in—that the president had no right to withhold the tape recordings of his White House conversations with his aides which had been subpoenaed by the federal district court as evidence in the prosecution of those aides. He, Leon Jaworski, an independent prosecutor, was unwilling that "the evidence from the White House be confined to what a single person, highly interested in the outcome, is willing to make available." Executive privilege was not absolute, although the attorney for the president was claiming it was. It was now up to the United States Supreme Court to apply the checks and adjust the balances in the American system.

But Earl Warren, as restless in his hospital bed during Jaworski's arguments as Richard Nixon was reported to be 3,000 miles away, isolated in his California retreat as he awaited the Court's decision, was never to know the outcome of this case, perhaps the most passionately felt of all.

The next evening, July 9, following a late-afternoon visit from two of his former brethren, Justices Douglas and Brennan, during which he had refused to discuss his health but had appeared weak and exhausted—though completely lucid and interested in the "big case"—his condition worsened. At 8:10 P.M. he died of cardiac arrest. He was eighty-three years old. Fifty of those eighty-three years he had spent in public service.

At the instigation of Chief Justice Burger, a man described by Justice Douglas as having "a keen sense of the proprieties," Earl Warren's flag-draped coffin was carried up the front steps of the Supreme Court by nine Court policemen and set down in the foyer of the Great Hall, where it lay in state. His chair, draped in black, stood behind. He was the first justice to be so honored.

Following a brief ceremony, military guards and former law clerks stood vigil for thirty-six hours while 10,000 people filed past. On Friday, July 12, with nine active justices and four former justices serving as honorary pallbearers, his coffin was taken to Washington National Cathedral, where 1,000 people, including the president, attended funeral services, and from there to Arlington National Cemetery, where he was buried on a grassy hill among the tens of thousands of other soldiers who had fought for their country.

Nearly two weeks later, on July 24, the flag over the Supreme Court still flew at half-mast when Chief Justice Burger, leaning forward in his chair at the center of the bench, briefly eulogized his predecessor, then proceeded with the announcement the crowd had come to hear: the decision of the United States Supreme Court in the case of *United States* v. *Nixon.* The chief justice droned on, his voice expressing little, his face expressing less, reason begetting reason, only to beget more reasons, until finally the dimensions of what the Court had done became clear.

It had decided unanimously—except for Justice Rehnquist, a former high-level officer in the Nixon administration, who disqualified himself—and was now telling the president of the United States, who had appointed four of its members to give a strict construction to the Constitution, that his privilege was not, in fact, absolute, that he was not above the law, that he must obey it. The Constitution commanded the policeman to obey the law, it commanded the judge to obey the law, and it commanded the president of the United States to obey the law. John Marshall had established that nearly 175 years before, when he had spoken to Thomas Jefferson in strikingly similar terms. The principle was holding firm.

It could not have been easy for these men to make the decision they made. Certainly not for Powell who early in the discussions had suggested raising the standards of evidence for the president, making it easier for him. Not even for Douglas, for all his announced pleasure in besting his old antagonist.

It must have been particularly difficult for the chief justice. As a judge he had been reluctant over the years to tell another branch of government what to do and had shrunk from bringing to bear the full power of his office. In *The Brethren*, Bob Woodward and Scott Armstrong reported that Burger had hesitated and vacillated in this case. Nevertheless, at the first conference of the justices following oral arguments, he had volunteered to write the opinion, and now he brought the full force of the judiciary down on the president, the man responsible for his sitting where he now sat. The tapes must be surrendered to the government. The United States Supreme Court said so. Perhaps at no other time in these men's lives did the oath they had taken to uphold the Constitution hold so much meaning. But in the end their loyalty, like that of Alvin Moore and John Flynn and the dissenters to *Miranda* who afterward had publicly defended the Court as an institution, was to the law.

And in the end it was not John Marshall or Earl Warren or Warren Burger who held the nation together. It was the Constitution in its broadest terms and application, that remarkable little document that allowed Ernest Miranda, a poor, mentally disturbed laborer, to win his case in this highest of courts and the president of the United States to lose *his*. It was vindication enough.

On July 27, 1974, the House Judiciary Committee recommended, by a vote of 27 to 11, three articles of impeachment against the president.

On August 5 the president surrendered the subpoenaed tape recordings. They were used to convict some of Nixon's top aides, including John Mitchell, the former attorney general, of conspiracy and obstruction of justice for their attempts to impede a grand jury investigation of the 1972 break-in at the Democratic national headquarters in the Watergate.* They also established the fact that Nixon had known about the Watergate break-in all along, that

---

* On appeal, Mitchell tried to utilize the logic of *Miranda*, arguing that the use at his trial of his testimony before the House Judiciary Committee, which he charged had been compelled, had violated the Fifth Amendment. But the U.S. Court of Appeals for the District of Columbia Circuit had reviewed the meaning of *Miranda* to date and concluded his constitutional rights had not been violated; his conviction was affirmed. The United States Supreme

he had tried to cover it up. The man who had campaigned on promises to enforce the law had in fact circumvented it.

If anyone still doubted the premise that underlay the Constitution, that the greed and ambitions that had motivated George III would never be wholly alien to humanity, that presidents forever required restraint, Richard Nixon had provided the answer.

On August 9, six years and one day after the president, in accepting the Republican nomination, had brought down the convention hall in Miami with his promises to "restore order and respect for law in this country," following tearful good-byes on the south lawn of the White House to Vice President and Mrs. Ford, President Nixon and his family boarded a helicopter which took them to nearby Andrews Air Force Base. There they boarded the president's plane, the *Spirit of '76*, which took them to California. The president's resignation took effect at twelve o'clock noon, when he was halfway across the country.

The president had appointed nearly a majority of justices to the United States Supreme Court, all of them supposed to have been strict constructionists, in order to strengthen the peace forces against the criminal forces. If they had not overruled *Miranda*, they had at least reversed its logic, and evidence which otherwise might never have seen the light of day was admitted to courtrooms and used in the conviction of the criminally accused. In a related development the justices of the Supreme Court had also narrowed the meaning of the exclusionary rule as it was applied to the Fourth Amendment's prohibition against unreasonable searches and seizures, and another source of evidence of crime was legitimized.

Congress had tried to emasculate *Miranda* through the omnibus crime bill of 1968, and the president in his term and a half had sponsored reams of anticrime legislation, some of which was passed—in particular, the reform of the bail laws in the District of Columbia to allow judges to incarcerate defendants considered dangerous prior to their trials.

It was as if muscular law enforcement required bullying, as if official vigilantism would return the nation to some idyllic time past when the system had worked, when criminals had been apprehended efficiently, prosecuted speedily, and imprisoned with dispatch, although, as Charles Silberman, a contemporary commentator on crime and punishment, pointed out in *Criminal Violence, Criminal Justice*, the last recorded instance of that happening was when Cain slew Abel and he was "caught and punished by a Higher Judge."

Court denied certiorari. Mitchell served nineteen months of a two-and-a-half- to eight-year sentence and was paroled in January 1979. In 1981 he was a partner in Global Research, a Washington firm selling armored cars and security devices abroad.

Chapter 3

All this tough legal talk had had no impact whatsoever on the incidence of crime which had continued to increase—in 1981, 30 percent of the nation's households were touched by a crime of some sort; 10 percent, by violent crime: rape, robbery, assault—and there was not a shred of evidence that it ever would. The evidence, in fact, was to the contrary.

When pickpocketing was a capital crime, Leonard Levy wrote in *Against the Law*, "pickpockets fleeced the crowds that turned out to watch other pickpockets being hanged."

In America, law enforcement had held the upper hand for a century and a half before the rights of criminal defendants had even begun to be noticed in the 1930s. The reports of the Wickersham Commission in 1931 had demonstrated just how easy it was for zeal to turn a cop into a bully. But stomping on civil and constitutional rights had not stopped crime and violence.

Florida in recent years reinstated the death penalty, then with the influx of refugees and drugs from the Caribbean, underwent one of the worst crime waves in its history—the death penalty, after all, while it sounded good in a political speech, had, of course, no effect at all on the sentences given drug dealers, burglars, robbers, auto thieves, muggers, what street crime was all about. The California legislature approved heavier penalties for rape; then lawyers realized that the increased penalties also increased the danger for women, that if a rapist were to be given the same sentence as a murderer, he might just as well murder, too.

On the other hand, there had been compiled some empirical evidence—and none to the contrary—that the conviction of criminals was only very rarely hindered by law enforcement's failure to resort to intimidation, although persuading the public to think otherwise had not lost its political utility with the demise of Richard Nixon.

The principal arguments for the pretrial preventive detention of criminal defendants—that release lessened the likelihood they would appear in court and left them free to commit more crimes—were challenged in a 1981 report by the Lazar Institute of Washington, D.C. The investigation, commissioned by the Department of Justice, covered eight big-city jurisdictions from across the country.

The final analysis indicated that the overwhelming majority of defendants—87.4 percent—released either on bail or without financial conditions imposed appeared for all required court dates, that many of those who did not appear were not trying to evade justice but had forgotten or become ill or, in a few cases, had been jailed on another charge. The "fugitive" rate was only 2 percent of all released defendants. The investigators also found that the overwhelming majority of defendants released were *not* rearrested: 84 percent. Although the study had been commissioned by the Justice Department, the final report was made public not by that department but by the Lazar Institute.

The popular belief that the exclusionary rule frees criminals has also

375

been challenged statistically. An analysis of 260 arrests for robbery in California showed that no evidence was excluded on *Miranda* grounds. An analysis of criminal court dockets in an Illinois county showed that of 114 defendants who had confessed their crimes to police, only 7 challenged the admissibility of the confession, and only 1 of these successfully.

The most authoritative analysis of the effect of the exclusionary rule was one done by the General Accounting Office and issued in 1979 by the comptroller general of the United States. The GAO investigators had studied the criminal dockets in thirty-eight United States attorneys' offices, a total of 2,804 cases. They found that defendants were, in fact, less likely to be convicted when evidence was excluded. However, they found that evidence was rarely excluded. Only a minute number of defendants (4.4 percent) even filed motions to exclude confessions, and 10.5 percent filed motions to exclude evidence on the basis of Fourth Amendment (search and seizure) violations, the largest category and the principal subject of investigation by the GAO. In only 1.3 percent of the total cases was evidence actually suppressed as a result of filing a Fourth Amendment motion, and in the largest offices, those where the seized evidence was the most susceptible to challenge, more than half the defendants were convicted anyway.

Two years later, in 1981, the Americans for Effective Law Enforcement submitted a position paper to the attorney general's Task Force on Violent Crime recommending abolition of the exclusionary rule. The comptroller general's report was neither referred to nor cited. In fact, the paper cited no empirical evidence that the rule had an adverse effect on the conviction of criminals.

Nevertheless, the task force, two of whose members, James Thompson, and Frank Carrington, were cofounders of Americans for Effective Law Enforcement, recommended redefining the exclusionary rule to "limit its application to circumstances in which an officer did not act either reasonably, or in good faith, or both." The report was an ideological document and cited not a line of empirical evidence to support its recommendations or its statements. It declared as fact that the present application of the exclusionary rule "depresses police morale and allows criminals to go free when constables unwittingly blunder" as well as "diminishes public respect for the courts and our judicial process."

The Department of Justice made the report public as soon as it rolled off the press and distributed it with dispatch. It spoke to those people who had been seduced into believing, through their elected officials, that the exclusionary rule was useless in that it did not deter police misconduct and that it was dangerous because it set criminals free on a "technicality." The report did not even address the matter of government integrity. It did not consider the possibility that illegally gotten evidence had to be excluded to avoid the taint of collusion between lawless law enforcement officers and the judiciary, which ultimately would be the agency responsible for deciding whether a policeman had acted in "good faith" or deliberately—out of such beginnings great tyrannies have grown. The possibility that the government's role as lawbreaker might also breed contempt for the law, might "diminish public respect for the courts," was not mentioned.

That there is a large gap between the number of crimes committed and the number of convictions obtained, even between the number of arrests and convictions, is not disputed. That it is due to the Warren Court's "coddling" of criminals, to lower-court leniency, or even to the clogging of court dockets and overuse of plea bargaining are no longer fashionable arguments to advance, except among ideologues and office-seekers.

A more commonly advanced explanation is that prosecutors drop cases. They drop them because witnesses refuse to cooperate. They drop them because victims refuse to press charges. And they drop them because the evidence police bring them is inadequate. There is beginning to be an interest in discovering the qualities necessary for good police work; in a study of 2,418 Washington, D.C., police over one year, for example, it was found that 15 percent of the officers made half of all arrests that led to conviction. But these are complex matters and do not lend themselves to slogans and simplistic solutions. They are subjects for social scientists. It has not appeared politically popular to suggest that police work might be inadequate.

Studies in New York City by the Vera Institute of Justice and in Washington, D.C., by the Institute for Law and Social Research—in which it was also demonstrated that exclusionary rules had a negligible effect on the outcome of cases—gave statistical support to an explanation for what appeared to be unacceptable rates of criminal convictions that had been around for a long time: that in most criminal cases, both the victim and the offender knew each other and that these cases were often handled differently from those called stranger cases, with prosecutors and judges meting out a somewhat sterner justice in the latter and, in fact, compiling a fairly solid, although hardly perfect, record for punishing the guilty.

Still, the crime figures spiraled upward at the same time the degree of violence seemed to increase: nuns raped; buildings burned; joggers murdered; students pushed onto subway tracks; hostages taken. And a new generation was coming along if the graffiti in school washrooms and slogans scrawled across the tops of theme papers were any indication.

Although studies indicated that strict enforcement of a strict gun control law held some potential for a decrease in the number of gun-related assaults, robberies, and homicides, there had been virtually no support at a high national level for passage of effective gun control legislation. Guns were cheap and readily available. They were sold at roadside stands as casually as fried

377

chicken in Virginia and North Carolina, and in a 1981 television documentary a reporter was offered "any gun you want in an hour and a half" by Los Angeles youths.

Drugs were not cheap; but they were available clandestinely, and the drug traffic continued unabated, leaving behind a lengthening line of destroyed bodies and broken lives, not only those of the addicts but those of the victims from whom they stole the wherewithal to purchase their highs.

Virtually nothing had been done about the nation's prisons except to overcrowd them more until they were unsafe for inmates and guards alike, although these pits of human misery were acknowledged by nearly everyone in law enforcement and the social sciences to be the most fertile of all breeding grounds for crime. Like the courts, the prisons had been a particular interest of Chief Justice Burger in his crusade for reform of the administration of criminal justice; perhaps he had hoped the prestige of his office would command some attention. But men and women still emerged from prison unable to read and write, unskilled in any marketable craft, stigmatized by their past, their psyches and their characters ruined almost beyond repair by the prison experience which bred its own special kind of savagery and violence.

There had been some support for President Johnson's War on Poverty as at least a partial solution to the problem of crime, but like the war itself, it had been short-lived, its days numbered by the deepening involvement of the president—and America's resources—in the war in Indochina.

There had been little exploration of the psychology of poverty, of increased credence given to the idea that the poor stole less in order to acquire things they were without than to improve their self-image, which had been damaged more by their poverty than had their economic status. Guns, violence—these were instant equalizers; the frustration of watching a four-lane highway being laid beside your home because you were poor and politically insignificant and unable to stop it could be alleviated somewhat by the possession of a gun (as one travels across the country, a noticeable fact of urban life is the great number of times first the railroad tracks, then the turnpikes and beltways to convey the affluent commuter to and from the suburbs cut through the neighborhoods of the poor).

There was a lot of talk about and some studies done to measure the impact of television's violence on crime. There was very little talk, though, about an even more prevalent and possibly influential picture on the television screen: the creature comforts of middle-class America. The homes of ghetto people did not serve as backgrounds for toothpaste or soap ads, the bathrooms and kitchens of the middle class did; they were heated in winter and air-conditioned in summer and needed only a quick application of the right detergent; kitchens had hot and cold running water, dishwashers, electric stoves, automatic washing machines; and the people who lived there, even while cleaning up the greasiest floors, never had a wrinkle in their shirts. Their children didn't carry knives or guns or even bottle openers. They were smiling kids. They brushed their teeth and ate their cereal. In the end this aspect of the ever-present medium and its stimulation of the greed and envy glands may have had a good deal more to do with crime in the streets than all the violence Telly Savalas would have to deal with. A gun, after all, was a powerful leveler. A lot faster than a Square Deal or a New Deal, a civil rights bill, a vote.

There had been no notice taken of a related phenomenon: the oppressiveness of 200 years of racial discrimination and the psychology of rebellion. In 1980 black smoke from Liberty City, only a salt breeze away from the pleasure craft plying Biscayne Bay off Miami Beach, again splotched the blue southern sky as blacks fire-bombed whole blocks. In the same fashion they had protested the failure of the Republicans meeting nearby in 1968 to hire them; this time they were protesting white Florida's administration of criminal justice. The rioting had broken out less than three hours after an all-white jury in Tampa had acquitted four white Miami police officers charged with the fatal beating of a black insurance executive, the fifth in a series of incidents in which black men had reportedly been manhandled by white officers of the law. While this protest had focused on racial discrimination by law enforcement, its causes went deeper, into racial discrimination in employment and housing and education and all the other areas where frustrations breed. Crime is only another symptom of underlying rage. As George Jackson, writing from Soledad, put it, "being born a slave in a captive society and never experiencing any objective basis for expectation had the effect of preparing me for the progressively traumatic misfortunes that lead so many black men to the prison gate. . . ."

By encouraging people who had been discriminated against in the public schools, at the polls, in police stations, to bring their grievances to the courts, the United States Supreme Court may have helped avert political revolution in this country during the 1960s. But the Fourteenth Amendment's promise of "equal protection of the laws" could not be applied to the subtler social and economic discrimination minorities encountered, to which criminal violence, another symptom of revolution, was one response. But there was little exploration on an official level of this second revolution.

There was little official interest in understanding the behavior of adolescents and young adults who made up the bulk of the prison population in America. You never heard a discussion among elected officials of the role models for young criminals: the drug pushers rolling around in gaudy Cadillacs; the white-collar criminals; the income tax evaders and expense account padders; the land fraud salesmen who stole with fountain pens as surely as young Americans stole with guns; Congressmen who took bribes. A vice president of the United States who had had to resign to avoid prosecution. A president of the United States who had had to resign to avoid impeachment.

There was not much discussion of the relationship of family disintegration or social upheaval and urban alienation to the rising crime rates. When people talked about gun control, for example, they contrasted the low number of deaths by gunshot per year in England, West Germany, Israel, Japan, the Scandinavian countries—all countries with strict gun control laws—with the number per year in the United States, where gun control was minimal: The former rarely reaches out of the two-figure range; the latter reaches out beyond 10,000. But in addition to the decreased availability of weapons, there are other factors at work against high rates of death by gunshot in these countries. Contrast the social unity of England or Japan, say, with the social diversity of the United States, the strong role tradition plays in conditioning, in social pressures, in conformity in West Germany or Scandinavia, with the lack of tradition in the United States.

Rare to nonexistent was the probing in officialdom of the complexities of the American character, of whose darker side crime and violence may have been one expression. Violence had long been a way of life in America: The West had been won by violence, its winning a significant part of the popular culture; labor peace had been bought with guns and clubs. The frontier mentality, the courage and adventurousness that had tamed a continent—could these have been perverted in their glorification of the gun and brute force to produce criminals so that by the middle of the nineteenth century there was no such thing as a "safe" city? It had been only during a few past decades, in fact, when the national energies had been consumed first by the Great Depression, then by World War II, that the domestic scene had been relatively tranquil, a development that made the rising crime rates of the 1960s and 1970s seem even more startling to those who had grown up in the 1930s and 1940s, the middle class of the 1960s. The American ideals of equality and upward mobility which required aggressiveness and courage, as well as social heterogeneity—could these, too, have been perverted? Could the best in a society, unrestrained, be also its own worst characteristic, ambition out of control its cardinal sin?

These concerns and others did not fall strictly under law enforcement, of course, but there was no attempt to synthesize the phenomena of which crime was but one expression, to bring together law enforcement and sociology and the behavioral sciences, to get at the roots, to understand the causes. There seemed to be little communication between the various segments of the law enforcement community, let alone between law enforcement and other agencies involved in the search for solutions to the problem of crime. Drift substituted for direction, repression for reason.

One can always find a political market for repression, for encroachment on constitutional rights, particularly if they are the constitutional rights of the poor or the black or the mentally ill. A quick fix, a temporary high—and the pusher is out of office before it wears off. But then the joints begin to ache again.

* * *

Chapter 3

Things had not been going well for Ernest Miranda in the summer of 1974. Having served one-third of his sentence and become eligible for parole in February 1970, he had been refused four times, and even when it had been granted in December 1972, the decision of the three-man parole board had not been unanimous. Dissenter Walter Michael of Phoenix had explained his negative vote this way: "This man has been convicted of the worst felonies a man can be convicted of. He said today that he has sought psychiatric help for ten years but had never received any. I want him to get that help before I'll release him. . . ."

The help had not been forthcoming, he had been released from the Arizona State Prison just before Christmas 1972, and he had returned to the home of his stepmother and two brothers in Mesa. His father had been killed in an automobile accident the previous October, less than two months before Ernest was paroled. He had never been able to share with his son the bottle of Scotch he had bought as a homecoming present some years before.

From prison Miranda had written to a friend in 1970: "You must know how bad I want to obtain my release. But not just a release. I want to make something of myself, to obtain an education and elevate myself in society. I know that this will be hard for me but, only at first. . . ." He had, in fact, earned a high school equivalency degree in prison, but it did not do him much good when he got out. Employment for a convicted felon was not easily found in Phoenix—or anywhere else.

In addition to the community prejudices that made an ex-convict's reentry into the job market difficult, state licensing laws—society's *official* prejudice against the fellow who theoretically had done his time, paid his dues—made it virtually impossible. If it was a devastating comment on society's self-confidence in its own attempts at reform and rehabilitation, it was nonetheless real and widespread. In most states, including Arizona, occupations from physician to salesman of cemetery plots required some sort of licensing, and it was generally not available to ex-convicts. Miranda had become an expert barber in prison and had regularly cut the hair of the warden and guards as well as inmates in return for packages of cigarettes. But Arizona law prohibited ex-felons from obtaining a barber's license at the time, and he was again reduced to the menial jobs he had had when he left for prison in 1963: warehouseman, produceman, delivery-truck driver, the $1.50- to $2-an-hour jobs.

In February 1970, a year and a half before Miranda was paroled, the chief justice of the United States, Warren Burger, who had been visiting prisons in the Washington, D.C., area to gain firsthand knowledge of what went on behind the walls, had told the Association of the Bar of the City of New York:

> . . . When a sheriff or marshal takes a man from the courthouse in a prison van and transports him to confinement for two or three or ten years, *this is our act. We* have tolled the bell for him. And . . .

we have made him our collective responsibility. We are free to do something about him; he is not. . . .

To have any hope of correcting, reforming, rehabilitating or changing these people calls for a wide variety of programs including diagnosis, counselling, education and vocational training and often intensive psychiatric therapy. . . . Few prisons today have even a minimal education or vocational training program to condition the prisoner for his return to society as a useful self-supporting human being.

The training programs in most state institutions are limited to a few skills, and there is almost no effort to correlate training programs with the demand for particular skills. It is no help to prisoners to learn to be pants pressers if pants pressers are a glut in the labor market or bricklayers or plumbers if they will not be admitted into a union. . . .

And he concluded: "We take on a burden when we put a man behind walls *and that burden is to give him a chance to change.*

"If we deny him that, we deny his status as a human being, and to deny that is to diminish our own humanity and plant the seeds of future anguish for ourselves."

Ernest Miranda spoke out of personal anguish when he wrote:

I would venture to add that the greatest barrier to rehabilitation of man is caused by society itself, in its attitudes toward the offender. Society will put a man in prison, lock him up and forget about him. . . .

The basic purpose of a prison is to keep an offender incapacitated and under control, with little or no regard for his human needs. The most important thing to any man is to have the freedom and respect of being a human being. A man going to prison . . . loses all sense of responsibility and self-respect.

Is it not enough that this man has been treated like an animal. . . ? Society does not think so, the general public will not even accept him as a normal member of society once he is released. The ex-offender remains an offender, no matter how much he has adjusted and is a useful and law abiding citizen of the community.

During the years since the Supreme Court decision bearing his name had been handed down, Ernest Miranda had felt a vague sense of having been cheated. The decision had not carried with it the freedom he had expected: There had been no limousine at the prison gate to carry him away, and he had gotten only a new trial, in which he had been convicted the second time. The decision had become a staple of the criminal and constitutional lawbooks, and he did not understand why he did not share in the royalties.

And in some sort of dimly defined, perhaps compensatory, perhaps defiant gesture, he had had printed a pack of *Miranda* cards, like those police had become accustomed to carrying, and was selling them, autographed, for $1.50 apiece, on the steps of the Maricopa County Courthouse.

Ernest Miranda had, however, achieved a fame of a sort. He was easily recognized by local police, and since his driving skills left a good deal to be desired, he was ticketed often. Eventually he had lost his license and was reduced to riding a ten-speed bicycle. Although not exclusively.

On Sunday, July 13, 1974, Officer Michael Breedlove had stopped Miranda for driving a car on the wrong side of the road in downtown Tempe, like Mesa, a suburb of Phoenix. The officer had asked for identification; but Miranda had none with him, except for an old newspaper clipping about his case, and he had proudly informed the policeman that he was *the* Miranda. But he had no driver's license. It had been suspended.

A search of his pockets had produced three amphetamines, and a search of the automobile had produced a loaded .38-caliber revolver from under the driver's seat. Miranda was booked into the county jail, charged with illegal possession of a firearm and of dangerous drugs.

His lawyer, Henry J. Florence, well known locally for his defense of narcotics cases, was ultimately able to convince a court prior to trial that there had been no provocation for Officer Breedlove to search the car Miranda had been driving—which was not his but belonged to a friend. The judge declared the search unconstitutional and ruled that its fruits must be suppressed. The charges were dropped.

The ruling in a court of law, however, could not keep Miranda free. A parolee, which he still was, had no constitutional rights, and possession of guns and amphetamines violated the conditions of his parole. On January 16, 1975, he was once more packed off to the Arizona State Prison at Florence.

At age thirty-three, when he was sent back to prison, he had spent a sizable chunk of life in public custody. He had spent part of his adolescence in the custody of the state, first at the Arizona State Industrial School, then the Los Angeles County Detention Home and the California Youth Authority. He had done hard labor for six months in the post stockade at Fort Campbell, Kentucky, and a year in federal prisons at Chillicothe, Ohio, and Fort Lompoc, California, all before his twentieth birthday. He had spent nine of the years between the ages of twenty and thirty-three at the Arizona State Prison at Florence, to which he was now returning.

He had ached for help. He had sent out all the signals of a troubled man, and they had been ignored. He had sent out the signals of a man trying desperately to help himself, and they, too, had been ignored. And he had written his own epitaph: "Incarceration no doubt protects society; this we do not deny, but only for a period of time. Yes, while a man is incarcerated he will not commit any more crimes against society, but will he be deterred from committing any new crimes once he is released? In reality, incarceration serves no purpose without the proper rehabilitation."

The lives of the principal characters in Ernest Miranda's story took various turns during the decade of the 1970s.

Robert Corbin, prosecutor at Miranda's second trial, was elected attorney general of Arizona in 1978.

Robert Corcoran, in 1965 the local ACLU attorney who had recommended Ernest Miranda's case to John Flynn, was appointed later to the Maricopa County Superior Court then to the Arizona Court of Appeals.

Yale McFate, Maricopa County Superior Court judge at Miranda's trial, retired in 1979. Frequently recalled to both the trial and appellate benches, he temporarily filled the position of Court of Appeals Justice Sandra Day O'Connor when she was appointed to the U.S. Supreme Court in 1981.

Lawrence T. Wren, presiding judge at Miranda's second trial, died suddenly in 1982 at the age of fifty-six.

Ernest McFarland, author of the Arizona Supreme Court opinion in Miranda's case, retired in 1971.

Gary Nelson, who had argued for Arizona in the U.S. Supreme Court, was appointed in 1974, following six years as state attorney general, to the state court of appeals. In 1978 the Maricopa County Bar Association, charging that his performance "fell below the carefully drawn standards agreed on by the Maricopa County Bar Association," opposed his retention, as did the Pima County Bar Association (Tucson), and he was voted out of office in the November general election. Judge Sandra Day O'Connor, then of the Maricopa County Superior Court, was appointed to succeed him.

John Frank remained a nationally prominent appellate lawyer and commentator on legal and constitutional issues and events. His book *American Law: The Case for Radical Reform*, a thirty-eight-point comprehensive "Marshall Plan" for reconstruction of the legal system emphasizing civil problems and procedures, appeared in 1969, to widespread acclaim within the legal community.

Since arguing Miranda's case in the Supreme Court, John Flynn had acquired a national prominence and had been invited to participate in seminars, meetings, and bar committee discussions involving the administration of criminal justice. He had left Lewis & Roca and in the latter part of the decade was a partner in a small firm. One wall of his office was decorated with *Miranda* memorabilia: a reproduction of a *New York Times* article on Ernest Miranda's case and a quill pen which his partner at the time, John Frank, had spirited from the Supreme Court for him.

In January 1980, while taking his first skiing lesson, the latest adventure of an adventurous man, Flynn died of a heart attack. He left no will and no life insurance, only a pile of debts. His former partner and cocounsel in Ernest Miranda's case, John Frank, delivered the eulogy at his funeral, where prominent judges, lawyers, and others of the city's prosperous and important mingled with men in their work clothes whose cases Flynn had fought in the courts. Said Frank:

Chapter 3

Taking cases for nothing was one of John's specialties. As a money loser, he was a kind of Typhoid Mary of the legal profession, carrying his ever-mounting deficits from firm to firm. John gave away more legal work in a year than most lawyers live on. Partly, this was because he was a deplorable businessman; partly, it was because he couldn't say No. He spent his splendid abilities on the poor, and occasionally, the evil; he was a magnificent sucker for a good cause, Justice meant something to him, even if he had to pay for it.

In 1981, David Miranda, twenty-three, the son of Ernest Miranda's brother Reuben, graduated from the police academy and became an officer on the Phoenix police force.

CHAPTER 4

Because of the intense pain in his side, the senior associate justice, William O. Douglas, had already had to leave the courtroom three times during the first hour of oral argument in a complicated tax case the morning of Wednesday, November 12, 1975. Finally, at about 11:00 A.M., he leaned toward the chief justice, who was sitting to his immediate left, and whispered that he would like to have a private word with him prior to lunch, which that day was to have been a celebration in the justices' private dining room in honor of Harry Blackmun's sixty-seventh birthday. Then Douglas, the spitfire of the bench for thirty-six and a half years, his energy drained now, haggardness where rugged good looks had been, a wheelchair replacing the sturdy legs that he had spent a good deal of his youth strengthening, left the courtroom for the last time as a sitting justice.

Vacationing in the Bahamas the previous December, he had suffered a stroke on New Year's Eve, and his left side had been partially paralyzed. Gerald Ford, the former Michigan representative who had led the attempt to impeach Douglas in 1970 and who had succeeded to the presidency on the resignation of Richard Nixon in August 1974, had sent a jet to Nassau to bring the justice home, a gesture that reportedly provoked the ailing Douglas to comment, "My God, you know they'll drop us in Havana."

He had spent several weeks in Walter Reed Hospital and had returned to the Court on March 19. But it was not the same Douglas who had left for Nassau three months before, wearing his jaunty new tweed hat. His voice was high pitched, and some of his words were slurred, giving his speech an uncertainty that had never been there before. If the fires had not been entirely quenched, it was clear that they would not regain the color and strength of their former blaze.

For the rest of the year, Douglas's attendance at the Court had been sporadic. He had been in and out of physical therapy, but his improvement had not been remarkable. He had been in and out of Court, whose backlog was steadily piling up as the most important cases were held over pending his return, which he kept promising. His annual vacation at Goose Prairie did little to improve his condition this time.

He had returned for the opening of the 1975 term on October 6, determined to continue on the bench, but it was evident that his powers had diminished. He was sometimes seen dozing on the bench, and he had to be wheeled out of conference before the justices adjourned.

He decided to resign.

The chief justice and the other brethren left the bench just after noon. A few minutes later Douglas handed his letter of retirement to the chief justice and asked him to forward it to President Ford, as was the custom. The two justices then went to the second-floor dining room, where the chief justice announced the news to the assembled brethren. It was reported that there was not a dry eye in the place.*

Of the *Miranda* majority, only William Brennan remained now.

There was talk in Washington that Ford would name a woman to replace Douglas if he named anyone at all. There was also talk that Democrats on the Senate Judiciary Committee might try to block any appointment made by the nation's only unelected president in history—who happened also to be a Republican. But just over two weeks after Douglas's retirement the president nominated, on the recommendation of Attorney General Edward Levi, who had known the nominee well in Chicago, John Paul Stevens of the U.S. Court of Appeals for the Seventh Circuit. He was readily confirmed by the Senate, despite the predicted opposition from Democrats, and sworn in on December 19, 1975, in the presence of both the president and Douglas, who had come to the courtroom in his wheelchair.

Stevens's appointment brought the number of former judges on the Supreme Court to six (Burger, Brennan, Stewart, Marshall, Blackmun, and Stevens himself) and former federal judges to five (Brennan was a former state judge). Five of those six (all except Marshall) had been appointed by Republican presidents, who tended to view the Supreme Court strictly as a legal forum whose continuance depended upon judicial experience, in contrast

---

* Following his retirement, Douglas continued to maintain chambers at the Court, as other retired justices had done, and he came in more or less regularly to work on his memoirs. *Go East, Young Man,* the story of his early life was published in 1974; *The Court Years* was published posthumously in late 1980. Court watchers said he had difficulty adjusting to retirement, that at first he considered himself a kind of tenth member of the Court and went so far as to circulate to the justices memorandums regarding current cases for a time. He died on January 19, 1980.

with Democrats, who seemed to see it as a policy maker and tended toward appointments of public, often political prominence.

Stevens was not a Douglas. He was a quiet, mild-mannered middle-sized man of fifty-five with gray hair and blue eyes who was often described as shy, although people who knew him talked about his quiet sense of humor. As rich as Douglas had been poor in his youth, Stevens came from a prosperous Chicago family that had made its money in the insurance business and had once owned the fashionable Stevens and LaSalle hotels.

Like Douglas and others of the justices, Stevens had demonstrated above-average academic abilities: Phi Beta Kappa as an undergraduate and first place in his class at Northwestern University Law School, after which he had been a clerk to Supreme Court Justice Wiley Rutledge.

But unlike Douglas, he had spent most of his professional life in the private practice of law, largely antitrust and corporate law. The most flamboyant thing about him, following his appointment to the Seventh Circuit five years before by Richard Nixon, had been not his opinions but his bright bow ties. Again, unlike Douglas's, Stevens's opinions were workmanlike, solid, even scholarly. Law school professors called him a "judge's judge."

If there were inner fires, they did not at first illuminate his opinions. If, like Douglas, he had developed a judicial creed in which he believed passionately, that was not evident either. He strove mightily to keep his mind open to the claims of all the parties to a case and to administer even-handed justice so far as was lawfully possible. But no strong philosophic currents had so far emerged.

Regarding the eleven cases involving *Miranda* issues which he had decided during his five years on the federal appellate court, he had voted to allow the admission of the confession or statement in question as evidence in nine. But in three court opinions and two dissents he had written in these cases, he had simply laid the case at issue beside the *Miranda* opinion and squared one with the other. He had offered no dicta, no hint of his judicial inclinations in *Miranda* matters.

And so when he appeared in Washington, it was widely debated whether he would join the four Nixon appointees, led by Rehnquist and the chief justice and frequently enough allied with Justices Stewart and White to make a fairly solid working majority, particularly in matters involving the administration of criminal justice, or whether he would join the dissenters, their ranks further depleted by the loss of Douglas, leaving only Brennan and Marshall.

In fact, as the weeks blended into months and the months into years, if he was not as predictable as his predecessor on the Court—one justice described him as the "wild card" among the nine—in those cases involving *Miranda* issues, he did more often than not step into Douglas's shoes or at least into one shoe. He lacked Douglas's fire, and he rarely invoked constitutional themes in his opinions; his lower-court manner of deciding cases on narrow legalistic grounds did not loosen much, one result of which was to make him less predictable than his predecessor. If he did not look at law and order from the inside of a boxcar crowded with Wobblies, as Douglas had, he did seem at least to consider the defendant's point of view, and he appeared not at all sure that law enforcement officers were all so blameless as the Court majority made them out. In ten of the eleven cases involving *Miranda* issues in which he participated during his first six terms on the Supreme Court, he reversed his own lower-court record and voted to *exclude* confessions or statements. If there seemed no cause yet for rejoicing among those who would keep *Miranda* intact, there was some cautious optimism that Stevens might establish a judicial rapport with Justices Brennan and Marshall.

Miranda was not dead yet.

Not by a long shot. And for those who thought so, the U.S. Supreme Court had a surprise or two.

Decisions like those in *Harris* and *Tucker* and others of the early to middle seventies were giving prosecutors heart, much the way *Brown* and *Chambers* and *Gideon* and *Escobedo* had given defense lawyers heart at other times. Between the appointment of Warren Burger to the chief justiceship in 1969 through the end of the 1974 term, the Court had decided for the defendant in only one case on the basis of *Miranda* issues, and the question in that case had been not whether the requirements of *Miranda* had been violated by police—they had not—but whether giving *Miranda* warnings could compensate for breaking into and searching a suspect's apartment without a warrant—whether honoring the Fifth Amendment could make up for violating the Fourth. The Supreme Court said no. Six months later, on December 15, 1975, the Court granted certiorari in the case of *Brewer* v. *Williams* in which the attorney general of Iowa was asking it specifically to overrule *Miranda* v. *Arizona*. Police manual author Fred Inbau, who had speculated on that very possibility in the latest edition of his book in 1972, filed an amicus curiae brief in behalf of Americans for Effective Law Enforcement. It was joined by attorneys general from twenty-one states; the Louisiana attorney general filed a separate brief. It, too, urged the reversal of *Miranda*.

At the time *Brewer* v. *Williams* appeared to be exactly the vehicle to obliterate *Miranda*: it was a gruesome case; had it occurred thirty years before, the defendant, a black man, would have been lynched. On the other hand, "A shocking case," Felix Frankfurter once commented, "puts law to its severest test."

The facts of the case were unchallenged by either defense or prosecution: On December 24, 1968, the Powers family attended a wrestling tournament at the Des Moines, Iowa, YMCA. When ten-year-old Pamela Powers failed to return from a trip to the rest room, a search was begun. Police were called after she could not be located in the building.

Robert Williams, an escaped mental patient, who had a room on the seventh floor of the YMCA building, was seen in the lobby coming from the elevator, carrying some clothing and a large bundle wrapped in a blanket. He spoke to several people on the way out, explaining to one that he was carrying a mannequin. He asked a fourteen-year-old boy to open first the street door and then the door of his Buick parked at the curb. As Williams put the bundle in the passenger's seat, the boy "saw two legs in it and they were skinny and white." The following day Williams' car was found by police in Davenport, Iowa, 160 miles away. A warrant was issued for his arrest.

On the morning of December 26 Williams telephoned a Des Moines lawyer, who advised the fugitive to surrender to Davenport police, and Williams did so. He was given *Miranda* warnings three times. He was in touch with lawyers in Davenport and Des Moines, both of whom told him not to discuss the crime with the police who had come from Des Moines for him and who were to drive him back there. He was properly arraigned before a judge in Davenport. And Des Moines police agreed not to question him before he reached his lawyer back in Des Moines. Everything seemed to be in order.

The crucial points about the case revolved around the automobile trip of several hours between Davenport and Des Moines. Williams had promised that when he got to Des Moines and had seen his lawyer, "I am going to tell you the whole story." Police, however, did not have to wait that long. One of the officers, Captain Cleatus M. Leaming, chief of Des Moines detectives, knew not only that Williams was a former mental patient but that he was interested in religion. It was not long before the subject of religion came up in what had been a wide-ranging conversation. Addressing Williams as Reverend, the detective made what became famous afterward as the "Christian burial speech":

> I want to give you something to think about while we're traveling down the road. . . . [I]t's raining, it's sleeting, it's freezing, driving is very treacherous, visibility is poor, it's going to be dark early this evening. They are predicting several inches of snow for tonight, and I feel that you yourself are the only person that knows where this little girl's body is, that you yourself have only been there once, and if you get a snow on top of it you yourself may be unable to find it. And, since we will be going right past the area on the way into Des Moines, I feel that we could stop and locate the body, that the parents of this little girl should be entitled to a Christian burial for the little girl who was snatched away from them on Christmas [E]ve and murdered. And I feel we should stop and locate it on the way in rather than waiting [sic] until morning and trying to come back out after a snow storm and possibly not being able to find it at all. . . . I do not want you to answer me. I don't want to discuss it any further. Just think about it as we're riding down the road.

And, as they rode down the highway, Williams did, in fact, direct the police-men to the body of Pamela Powers as well as make incriminating statements regarding the child's shoes and a blanket. Williams was found guilty of mur-der.

However disapproving one might be of the detective's manipulation of Williams into confessing, it was difficult to fault his motives and zeal in his pursuit of the perpetrator of such a heinous crime. Some years later Leaming explained:

> I didn't even know what ... ["psychological coercion"] meant, until I looked them up in the dictionary after I was accused of using it. . . . Shucks, I was just being a good old-fashioned cop. . . . I have never seen a prisoner physically abused, though I heard about those things in the early days. . . .
>
> That type of questioning just doesn't work. They'll just resist harder.
>
> You have to butter 'em up, sweet talk 'em, use that—what's the word?—"psychological coercion."

In his brief for the state the Iowa attorney general, Richard C. Turner, reviewed with obvious nostalgia the days when a man committed a murder one day, was captured the next day, tried on the third day, and hanged on the fourth. At oral argument, on October 4, 1976, he declared, "We in the heartland ask this Court to reassess the situation and give a little less em-phasis to rights and a little more to duty," and he asked the Court to "over-turn its decision in the *Miranda* case."

When Williams's lawyer who had been appointed by the Court, Robert D. Bartels of the University of Iowa Law School faculty, counted up the jus-tices on the Court, he had discovered that the original *Miranda* majority was nearly extinct but that two dissenters remained and enough people who had expressed dissatisfaction with *Miranda* had joined the Court to make an easy majority for overruling. He decided he did not want Williams's case to turn on the survival of *Miranda,* and he argued, instead, that it was a strict Sixth Amendment case, that Williams's right to counsel on the trip between Dav-enport and Des Moines had been violated.

Three months after the oral arguments, on January 25, 1977, and before the decision in *Brewer* was announced, the Court gave additional encourage-ment to those who believed *Miranda* might be overruled shortly when it de-cided a case in which many details were reminiscent of those in Ernest Miranda's in precisely the opposite way.

Carl Mathiason, a parolee, was suspected of burglarizing a home near Pendleton, Oregon. On going voluntarily to the state patrol headquarters at the request of a state policeman investigating the crime, Mathiason, like Miranda, was ushered into an office and the door closed. He was told that he was not under arrest but that police believed he had commited the burglary, his fingerprints had been found at the scene—not true—and his "truthfulness would possibly be considered by the district attorney or judge." Mathiason sat for a few minutes, then admitted the theft. Only at that point did the officer advise him of his constitutional rights and give him the warnings required by *Miranda,* following which a confession was taped. Like Ernest Miranda's own interrogation, the whole proceeding had been routine, civilized as interrogations go. Whether subtle pressures had been at work depend upon perspective.

Mathiason was convicted. On appeal, the Supreme Court of Oregon declared he had been questioned in a "coercive environment" and reversed the conviction. In a per curiam opinion—to which Justice Marshall dissented, declaring there were here "mischiefs equivalent to," although "different from, custodial interrogation"—the justices of the U.S. Supreme Court said that since Mathiason had not been in true custody, since he had not been under arrest and had been free to leave, *Miranda* did not apply:

> Any interview of one suspected of a crime by a police officer will have coercive aspects to it, simply by virtue of the fact that the police officer is part of a law enforcement system which may ultimately cause the suspect to be charged with a crime. But police officers are not required to administer *Miranda* warnings to everyone whom they question. Nor is the requirement of warnings to be imposed simply because the questioning takes place in the station house, or because the questioned person is one whom the police suspect. *Miranda* warnings are required only where there has been such a restriction on a person's freedom as to render him "in custody." It was *that* sort of coercive environment to which *Miranda* by its terms was made applicable, and to which it is limited.

The confession in question was declared admissible evidence in court. The definition of *custody* was narrowed. Another brace had been taken out of *Miranda.*

Two months later, on March 23, 1977, the Supreme Court announced its decision in *Brewer* v. *Williams* and surprised a lot of people. The Court had not, as expected, overruled *Miranda;* it had not even decided the case on *Miranda* grounds. Like Williams's lawyer, it had taken the Sixth Amendment route to decision. Potter Stewart, *Miranda* dissenter and generally sensitive to the felt necessities of the social order, wrote the Court opinion, in which he was joined by Justices Brennan, Marshall, Powell, and the newest justice, Stevens—judicial homogeneity was no more a staple of the Burger Court than it had been of the Warren Court and 5–4 decisions, like this one, were common.

However hideous the crime and however highly motivated the agent of the law, Stewart declared, behavior like Captain Leaming's in this case could not be tolerated:

There can be no serious doubt . . . that Detective Leaming deliberately and designedly set out to elicit information from Williams just as surely as—and perhaps more effectively than—if he had formally interrogated him. . . . [H]e purposely sought during Williams' isolation from his lawyers to obtain as much incriminating information as possible. . . .

The crime of which Williams was convicted was senseless and brutal, calling for swift and energetic action by the police to apprehend the perpetrator and gather evidence with which he could be convicted. No mission of law enforcement officials is more important. Yet, "[d]isinterested zeal for the public good does not assure either wisdom or right in the methods it pursues" . . . [S]o clear a violation of the Sixth and Fourteenth Amendments as occurred here cannot be condoned. The pressures on state executive and judicial officers charged with the administration of the criminal law are great, especially when the crime is murder and the victim a small child. But it is precisely the predictability of those pressures that makes imperative a resolute loyalty to the guarantees that the Constitution extends to us all.

Underlying Stewart's words seems to be a deep regret that the loyalty of police to the law had not matched his and that the overzealousness of the Des Moines detective was now forcing the Court to suppress Williams's confession. Nevertheless, the Court declared, Williams's statements, made in the isolation of the police car racing a winter storm to Des Moines, should not have been admitted at his trial. He must have a new trial.*

Normally Chief Justice Burger asked the justices to announce decisions briefly. On the day the Court's decision in *Brewer* v. *Williams* was announced, he himself read passionately from his dissent—which had been joined by Justices Blackmun and Rehnquist (Blackmun also wrote a separate dissent which was joined by White and Rehnquist).

The result in this case [Burger declared] ought to be intolerable in any society which purports to call itself an organized society. It continues the Court—by the narrowest margin—on the much criticized course of punishing the public for the mistakes and misdeeds of law enforcement officers instead of punishing the officer directly, if in fact he is guilty of wrongdoing. It mechanically and blindly keeps reliable evidence from juries whether the claimed constitutional violation involves gross police misconduct or honest human error.

Once again, the despised exclusionary rule had been carried to the point of absurdity with obvious disregard of the consequences. As a judge of the U.S.

---

* Justice Marshall, in a concurrence, wrote that he doubted "very much that there is any chance a dangerous criminal will be loosed on the streets, the bloodcurdling cries of the dissents notwithstanding." Williams was, in fact, retried, reconvicted, and resentenced to life imprisonment.

Court of Appeals for the District of Columbia Circuit, Burger had talked and written against application of the rule, at the same time offering a scheme for establishing local independent commissions to oversee police behavior and punish malefactors appropriately instead of excluding evidence from courtrooms; the idea had not caught on, and he had had little more to say about it. In 1971, in a dissent to a case in which the Supreme Court had ruled inadmissible evidence obtained in violation of Fourth Amendment standards, he had raged about the "high price [the exclusionary rule] extracts from society—the release of countless guilty criminals" and had suggested Congress adopt "an administrative or quasi-judicial remedy against the government itself to afford compensation and restitution for persons whose Fourth Amendment rights have been violated." Congress had not acted. But Burger himself turned down at least one way that might have held potential for ameliorating the effects of the exclusionary rule: When in 1976, in the case of *Rizzo* v. *Goode,* in which intervention of the federal courts was asked to curb excesses of the Philadelphia Police Department, the chief justice had looked the other way and had helped create a majority that refused to intervene.

In his dissent to *Brewer* v. *Williams,* he did not offer any more specific suggestions regarding the exclusionary rule. He only explained, not very patiently, how the Court in the years since he had become chief justice had begun to move away from automatic application of it:

> Today's holding interrupts what has been a more rational perception of the constitutional and social utility of excluding reliable evidence from the truthseeking process.... [In its recent holdings the Court has] repeatedly emphasized that deterrence of unconstitutional or otherwise unlawful police conduct is the only valid justification for excluding reliable and probative evidence from the criminal factfinding process.... Accordingly, unlawfully obtained evidence is not automatically excluded from the factfinding process in all circumstances. In a variety of contexts we inquire whether application of the rule will promote its objectives sufficiently to justify the enormous cost it imposes on society....

He made no mention of the rule's original purpose: to insure the integrity of the state. Once again the Constitution was submitted to cost-accounting. And he made it plain that in the context of *Brewer* v. *Williams,* he did not believe society could afford it.

Two decades before, in this very courtroom, Assistant Attorney General Burger had argued in behalf of the United States government against Dr. John Peters that attacks on the internal security system were too expensive for society to bear in a time of crisis; then the crisis had been the threat of Communist subversion; today, criminals roving the streets. If you had asked Warren Burger in 1977, "What price security?" the answer would not have changed over two decades.

Following his reading of his dissent, Burger added to what he had written, displaying the full depth of his displeasure in what the majority had done: "With the decision by the narrowest margin, only one convert is needed to bring back rationality" to the Court.

Brewer v. *Williams* marked the high point of the efforts to overrule *Miranda* outright, and they had failed. The Court did not even appear inclined to, although it remained generally a prosecutor's court. By 1981, Americans for Effective Law Enforcement had submitted amicus curiae briefs in thirty-six U.S. Supreme Court cases, twenty-four, or two-thirds, of which that Court decided for law enforcement against the criminal defendant, and the Court's standards for finding a *Miranda* violation remained difficult to meet. In a California case decided at the end of the 1980 term, a juvenile had been convicted of murder on the basis of a confession given to a police sergeant following the officer's rambling, ambiguous, and obfuscating explanation of the young man's rights under *Miranda*. A California appellate court had found the recitation inadequate for giving the boy the crucial information that he could have a lawyer, free of charge, present for the impending interrogation. What the California court viewed as ambiguity and obfuscation, however, the U.S. Supreme Court viewed as flexibility. In a per curiam opinion—to which Brennan, Marshall, and Stevens dissented—it declared the boy's confession admissible evidence: "This Court has never indicated that the 'rigidity' of *Miranda* extends to the precise formulation of the warnings given a criminal defendant. . . . Quite the contrary, *Miranda* itself indicated that no talismanic incantation was required to satisfy its strictures."

What the Court in 1978 did find violated *Miranda* was the behavior of Tucson, Arizona, police who had continued, after giving *Miranda* warnings, to question Rufus Mincey in his hospital bed, barely conscious and encumbered by tubes, needles, and a breathing apparatus, although Mincey repeatedly had asked them to stop. "It is hard to imagine," wrote *Miranda* dissenter Stewart for the majority, "a situation less conducive to the exercise of 'a rational intellect and a free will' than Mincey's." In 1980, in a per curiam opinion, the justices found substandard the behavior of a Louisiana police officer who had testified that he had read a defendant the rights required by *Miranda* prior to interrogation but could not recall what the rights were or whether the defendant had waived them or even understood them. In 1981 they found substandard the behavior of Arizona police who gave *Miranda* warnings but continued questioning a suspect although the suspect had said he did not want to talk to them and did, in fact, want a lawyer. *Miranda* dissenter White wrote the opinion; Chief Justice Burger concurred, but only in the judgment, not the reasoning, which followed the reasoning of *Miranda*. Said Burger, coming close to the old due process of law rationale as the basis for his concurrence, when the defendant told an officer he did not want to speak to anyone and the " 'officer told him *that he had to . . .*' [t]his is enough for me."

In a companion decision handed down the same day, the justices declared that a court-ordered pretrial psychiatric examination of a defendant bore some analogies to the custodial interrogation dealt with those many years ago in *Miranda;* the testimony obtained as a result of that examination—prior to which the defendant had not been told of his right to remain silent and at which his court-appointed lawyer was not present—should have been excluded from the sentencing phase of his trial. Chief Justice Burger wrote the opinion. It was carefully constructed, applying only to this case and these conditions, and its grounding was in the Fifth and Sixth Amendments, using *Miranda* only as the "prophylactic" the Court had labeled it seven years earlier in *Tucker.* Burger did, however, write extensively of *Miranda's* "purpose" and "considerations." As he himself had said in a concurrence to a 1980 opinion in which *Miranda* issues were operative: "The meaning of *Miranda* has become reasonably clear and law enforcement practices have adjusted to its strictures: I would neither overrule *Miranda,* disparage it, nor extend it at this late date. . . ."

Even the justices of the Arizona Supreme Court who were still being overruled on *Miranda* matters by the U.S. Supreme Court fifteen years after they had been overruled in the original case, agreed that *Miranda* was "here to stay."

During the last five terms of the decade, 1976 through 1980, the U.S. Supreme Court decided ten cases involving *Miranda* issues: Half the decisions went against the state; half, against the defendant. The chief justice voted against the defendant in seven. In all twenty *Miranda* cases which the Court decided between Burger's appointment as chief justice and the end of the 1980 term, the chief justice voted against the defendant and for the state in fourteen, or 70 percent. The four Nixon appointees sat together in nineteen cases involving *Miranda* issues (all except *Harris*) and voted as a bloc in fourteen, their votes going against the criminal defendant in nine of the fourteen. They had done their share to strengthen the peace forces against the criminal forces.

Although it was clear that the Burger Court would add no new links to the chain of precedents that had begun with the case of the Scottsboro boys, it was equally clear that the last link, *Miranda,* was not going to be removed, although it might collect some rust.

As it turned out, all the steam and muscle Congress had lavished on passage of the omnibus crime bill in 1968 with its provision intended to nullify *Miranda* had been wasted. If the legislators had made some political mileage out of it at home, that was about all they made; it may have been all they really wanted. But a decade after its passage there were U.S. attorneys, whose prosecution of cases the legislation had been meant to facilitate, who were unaware of its existence, fewer than two dozen cases based on the provision that challenged *Miranda* had made their way into federal appellate courts, and its constitutionality had not been tested in the United States Supreme Court. Congress had not been able to erase *Miranda*; it was rarely even discussed there anymore, and when Sandra Day O'Connor was appointed to the Supreme Court to succeed *Miranda* dissenter Potter Stewart after he had resigned in the summer of 1981, the Senate Judiciary Committee under Senator Strom Thurmond of South Carolina, who had succeeded to the chairmanship the same year, had explored her views on the *Miranda* ruling briefly and without the customary oratory.

For all of Richard Nixon's talk about manning the federal bench with strict constructionists who would not exclude evidence from the courtrooms of America on the basis of "technicalities"—like violations of the *Miranda* ruling—the fact is that Nixon's appointees to the federal courts were only slightly less disposed to exclude confessions than those appointed by either his predecessors or his successors. In a survey of nearly 600 cases in which *Miranda* issues figured that came to the federal circuit courts during the period from 1970 to 1980, it was found that very few confessions or statements were excluded as evidence no matter which judges heard them: Roosevelt-appointed judges decided in favor of *in*cluding confessions or statements in 82.9 percent of the cases; Truman-appointed judges, 73.3 percent; Eisenhower-appointed judges, 85.1 percent; Kennedy-appointed judges, 83.7 percent; Johnson-appointed judges, 76.3 percent; Nixon-appointed judges, 86.9 percent; Ford-appointed judges, 79.5 percent; and Carter-appointed judges, 66.6 percent. Most convictions were affirmed not because this or that judge was a hard-liner, but because many of the questions raised were frivolous or irrelevant or because *Miranda* could not in good conscience be stretched to fit every situation. Where violations of *Miranda* were plain, even judges appointed by Nixon were willing to suppress the ill-gotten gain. Their loyalty was to the law; they were not, perhaps, so malleable as men in high political positions might have hoped.

The strongest support for *Miranda*, in the 1970s, however, came from the most unexpected quarter of all, the men and women who had been criticized by, overruled by, and alienated from the United States Supreme Court for nearly all the Warren years, the state court judges. As the U.S. Supreme Court for three decades following its decision in the case of the Scottsboro boys had compensated for state neglect of the rights of criminal defendants, now the state courts were compensating for the U.S. Supreme Court's new negligence of them. The highest federal court had become involved because state courts had defaulted; now their roles were reversed.

If the movement had a leader at all, it was Mr. Justice Brennan of the United States Supreme Court, the senior associate justice following Douglas's resignation and the only sitting justice to have been a state court judge. Felix Frankfurter was said to have remarked about Brennan, who had been one of Frankfurter's students at Harvard Law School: "I always wanted my students to think for themselves, but Brennan goes too far." The statement was the more ironic when in 1962, in the first of the Warren Court's reapportionment decisions—*Baker* v. *Carr*, the one that held that federal courts did, in fact, have jurisdiction over the apportionment of state legislatures, allowed city and suburban voters to challenge the constitutionality of legislative districts apportioned to favor rural areas, and reversed the 1946 Frankfurter decision in which he had warned the courts to stay out of this particular "political thicket"—Frankfurter's erstwhile student wrote the Court opinion, his most important opinion thus far, perhaps ever; the eighty-year-old justice and former teacher filed his last and one of his most passionate dissents.*

Justice Brennan had considered the Court's decision in that case liberating, as conferring a new freedom on the citizens of a state to experiment with their economic and social and political programs which had not been to that time meaningful because "the political processes [had been] controlled by only some of the people." Chief Justice Warren had always insisted *Baker* v. *Carr* and its progeny were expressions of states' rights, establishing for the states "the power to govern themselves," although they had not always been considered such at the time, had provoked a harshly critical reaction, particularly in states where the traditionally powerful did not relinquish power with ease, and had generated a rash of proposals to gag the federal judiciary. Now, in the 1970s, "the power to govern themselves" was taking on new meaning.

William J. Brennan was not in the habit of limiting his public utterances to his formal opinions for the U.S. Supreme Court. For the two decades during which he had been a member of it, he had been accustomed to speaking his mind to his fellow judges. Sometimes he used the academic dais as his forum. At other times he used the judicial conference. He could on occasion be prevailed upon to attend a state bar association meeting, particularly in his home state of New Jersey. Whether he called his talk "The Bill of Rights and the States" or "The Role of the Court—the Challenge of the Future" or "Some Aspects of Federalism" or "Guardians of Our Liberties—State Courts No Less Than Federal," it made little difference. His sermon did not change.

He took his text from a Supreme Court case of 1886, *Boyd* v. *United States*, which had been written by fellow New Jerseyite Joseph P. Bradley—an added source of pride, he always said: ". . . [C]onstitutional provisions for the security of the person and property should be liberally construed. It is the duty of courts to be watchful for the constitutional rights of the citizen, and against any stealthy encroachment thereon." "Courts" he had said; not federal courts alone, but all courts, including state courts. In abbreviated form, that about summed up the judicial credo of Justice Brennan, and during his years on the bench he had lost few opportunities to impart it, urging it especially on state courts, in whose functioning he took a proprietary interest not

---

* On April 5, 1962, Frankfurter suffered a stroke which forced him to retire from the Court the following summer. He died on February 22, 1965.

only because he had served on the New Jersey courts but because they were the basic nutrients in the metabolism of the body politic, their interaction, with the national government as well as with each other, creating the tensions so necessary to maintain the healthy complexion of federalism.

He knew something about constitutional history and how the earliest of the states had written their own constitutions long before the federal Constitution had been put together. These earliest of the immigrants to America knew what tortures could be inflicted in the name of conformity, what punishments could be meted out for crimes of conscience as well as what methods could be devised for discovering the guilty. They recognized the criminal law as it existed then was the tyrant's tool, and they knew their safety depended ultimately on well-defined, built-in procedures. Their experience had taught them that government was arbitrary, ruthless, tyrannical, and greedy, its only mission self-preservation. And they meant to protect themselves from it.

By the time of the American Revolution each of the thirteen colonies had hammered out a constitution. Each had approached its task rather haphazardly, seeming to make random provisions and overbroad generalizations. New Jersey's constitution of 1776, for example, guaranteed "the same privileges of witnesses and counsel, as their prosecutors are or shall be entitled to," but did not specify what these were. Some constitutions included bills of rights; others did not. The authors copied principles and phrases from each other but often left out significant provisions. Although all the infant polities recognized the necessity to enumerate some individual rights, no two states enumerated all the same rights, and the only right common to all thirteen was trial by jury. By 1783, when New Hampshire's constitution was completed, eight states guaranteed the right of an accused to counsel (New Jersey, Pennsylvania, Delaware, Maryland, New York, Vermont, Massachusetts, and New Hampshire); eight states guaranteed the right against compulsory self-incrimination (Virginia, Pennsylvania, Delaware, Maryland, North Carolina, Vermont, Massachusetts, and New Hampshire); three states (Connecticut, Georgia, and South Carolina) guaranteed neither.

These rights, which fell under the general heading of criminal procedure, were meant largely to protect men accused of religious and political crimes, not common thieves, and in 1968 federal circuit Judge Henry J. Friendly had wondered publicly whether the right not to be compelled to incriminate oneself "would ever have come into existence if its proponents had been murderers and rapists rather than John Lilburne in London and William Bradford in Philadelphia. . . ."

Brennan recognized that the states had been the original source of federal authority, that it was representatives of the states who had written the federal Constitution, virtually lifting out sections from the state constitutions and inserting them in the federal. He knew that the federal government had survived only because the states, in ratifying the Constitution, had surren-

399

dered authority. He understood their aspirations to equality, even on occasion to supremacy.

In his early days on the U.S. Supreme Court, Brennan had not been entirely satisfied, however, with the performance of the state courts. As he had watched cases come to the Supreme Court from all parts of the nation, he had seen too many abuses of state power, and he had observed in 1961, five years after his appointment, "Far too many cases come from the states to the Supreme Court presenting dismal pictures of official lawlessness, of illegal searches and seizures, illegal detentions attended by prolonged interrogation and coerced admissions of guilt, of the denial of counsel and, downright brutality."

And he had joined the bloc of justices, led by Chief Justice Warren, who were actively attempting to provide protection against just such abuses and were quite willing to impose the federal Bill of Rights on recalcitrant states to accomplish their purpose. Reasoned Brennan, in another contradiction of Frankfurter: "Judicial self-restraint which defers too much to the sovereign powers of the states and reserves judicial intervention for only the most revolting cases will not serve to enhance Madison's priceless gift of 'the great rights of mankind secured under this Constitution.' "

He would have preferred that the states themselves raise their standards, and at the height of state fury against the meddling of the United States Supreme Court, in the mid-sixties, he had frankly urged them to, telling the Conference of Chief Justices: "If the states shoulder this burden and undertake to make the responsibility for the vindication of our most cherished rights their own in this difficult area of criminal justice, the frictions and irritants that presently exist in some measure between the state and Federal courts will rapidly disappear."

Although it was little noted at the time, the states were responding. Slowly, to be sure; not in every court and not in every case or even in a majority of courts and cases. Indeed, in Ernest Miranda's case, twenty-nine states had argued *against* the U.S. Supreme Court's expanding the constitutional rights of criminal defendants in the station house, and John Flynn, arguing for Miranda, had described his own state of Arizona's sluggishness and the Arizona Supreme Court's reluctance to protect the rights of criminal suspects, begging the highest federal court to step in and resolve the issues in Miranda's case precisely because, he explained, if they were left to the state courts and legislature, "it would be another 46 years before the Fifth Amendment right in the scope it was intended . . . by this Court in *Escobedo* will reach the state of Arizona."

Nevertheless, in retrospect, a movement in the several states to guard against the encroachment on the constitutional rights of criminal defendants was gaining momentum. When, in 1961, the U.S. Supreme Court had ruled that illegally obtained evidence was not admissible in state courts, twenty-six states already had exclusionary rules. In 1963, when the Court decided *Gid-*

eon, all but five states made some provision for counsel in felony cases. In 1971, when the Court extended the *Gideon* ruling to poor defendants accused of certain misdemeanors—those which carried penalties of imprisonment for six months, a $1,000 fine, or both—thirty-one states already had similar rules in place.

And so, in the 1970s, when the four justices of the U.S. Supreme Court appointed by Richard Nixon merged with the dissenters to *Miranda* to form a majority which was a little less fastidious than its predecessor in its guardianship of the rights of the individual citizen, especially the individual citizen accused of a crime, and Justice Brennan found himself in the unaccustomed role of dissenter, the conditions that governed the judicial weather in the United States produced another climactic phenomenon that became known as state court activism. On the state benches the traditional time lag between judicial generations was ending, and the spirit of the Warren Court was being absorbed posthumously. A new breed of judges had begun to emerge. The older generation was retiring, and a new generation was replacing it. Its character had been shaped in its youth, when it had been acclimatized to the post–World War II acceleration of egalitarianism that had attached constitutional rights to the Gideons and Mirandas. It had been thrust into professional maturity amid the innovations of the Warren Court. Indeed, this generation had known little of judicial life prior to the Warren years, and few of its members so much as blinked at what had been done then. The rules were firmly in place. *Gideon, Escobedo, Miranda*—they were landmarks, staples in the judicial vocabulary, the very substance of operating procedures in the various criminal justice systems.

As it had in the 1960s, the movement was developing slowly, unevenly, and unspectacularly. But Brennan had detected it, and as he watched his brethren in the Supreme Court majority pull back from the previous majority's aggressive application of the Bill of Rights, he not only concurred in the increasing aggressiveness of state criminal justice along these lines but launched a campaign to further it.

He had watched, he explained in 1975, the U.S. Supreme Court's erosion of *Miranda* rights since the 1971 decision in the case of Viven Harris had made available to prosecutors for impeachment purposes statements of an accused obtained in violation of *Miranda*'s requirements; he himself had dissented in *Harris*, remarking at the time that not only six federal courts of appeals but also the appellate courts of fourteen states had agreed with his reasoning. He supposed, he added now, the U.S. Supreme Court had embarked on a course that would end only in the "ultimate overruling of *Miranda*'s enforcement of the privilege against incrimination."

However, he noted, striking a note that would become more familiar in his dissents and lectures over the next several years, "understandably, state courts and legislatures are, as matters of state law, increasingly according protections once provided as federal rights but now increasingly depreciated by decisions of this Court." Hawaii's highest court had totally rejected *Harris* as a matter of state constitutional law. Pennsylvania's supreme court followed shortly, as did California's, the latter particularly defiant; it declared:

> *Harris* is not persuasive authority in any state prosecution in California. . . . We pause . . . to reaffirm the independent nature of the California Constitution and our responsibility to separately define and protect the rights of California citizens despite conflicting decisions of the United States Supreme Court interpreting the federal Constitution.

The Texas Court of Criminal Appeals rejected *Harris* on the basis of state statute. And the supreme court of Brennan's home state of New Jersey, whose constitution provided no privilege against compulsory self-incrimination, rejected it as a matter of public policy.

The Wisconsin Supreme Court cited state procedural requirements in criminal cases as the basis for tightening the rules for obtaining a waiver of a suspect's *Miranda* rights. The New York Court of Appeals was basing decisions in cases involving illegal questioning on the state constitution. Other states were rejecting U.S. Supreme Court decisions on similar grounds.

These develoments were not, of course, uniform in fifty states, and what high courts in New Jersey and Wisconsin and California did had no impact on what high courts in Arizona or New Hampshire or Louisiana would do. Developments were, in fact, so uneven that one student of the state courts compared them to a "shell game."

Brennan, however, was not so pessimistic, and in 1979, when his fellow justices put what he considered unreasonable limits on its decision to require states to provide counsel for defendants in misdemeanor cases—the Court had refused to extend the requirement to defendants accused of crime for which no imprisonment was actually imposed—he was able to point out that at least thirty-three states had set more liberal standards for the appointment of counsel—New York, for example, provided counsel in all misdemeanor cases except traffic violations—and the defendant in the very case before the Court that day would have been entitled to appointed counsel. Moreover, he added, these standards had not wreaked havoc on state court dockets, as his brethren had argued they would.

What seemed particularly encouraging to Brennan in these troubling times was that the states which had defied the rulings of the U.S. Supreme Court had done it in such a way as put them out of reach of that Court: It could neither overturn these state decisions nor even review them, so long as they were based on state constitutional requirements or statutes that were at least as protective of individual rights as the federal constitutional requirements. And he frequently reminded state judges, his tone exhortatory, that "no State is precluded by the [Court's] decision[s] from adhering to *higher* standards under state law. Each State has the power to impose *higher* standards governing police practices under state law than is required by the Federal Constitution [italics added]." Indeed, he added, buttressing his argument, the U.S. Supreme Court had declared it so.

And then he would tell the story of a Pennsylvania case that had come to the Court. The supreme court of that state, on the basis of state law, had adopted an aspect of *Miranda* beyond what the U.S. Supreme Court had specifically allowed, and the latter had agreed to review the case. Then, a month later, the order granting certiorari had been rescinded. The Court itself had erred; "the judgment" of the Pennsylvania court, the justices declared, "rests upon an adequate state ground."

Since most crimes are violations of state laws and most criminal defendants are tried in state courts, the activism developing among state-court judges made *Miranda* look healthy indeed.

More than a decade before, in March 1963, Ernest Miranda had "confessed" to the kidnapping and rape of Lois Ann Jameson, and the United States Supreme Court had redeemed the promises of the Bill of Rights. Now the responsibility for guarding the rights of the Ernest Mirandas was shifting to the states, which were redeeming the promises of their own constitutions and the scheme of federalism. Together, they made implicit promises to the future. Mr. Justice Brennan was encouraged as well as encouraging, and he thought, he said, musing on the vicissitudes of liberty over the centuries, that Mr. Madison, author of the Bill of Rights himself, would have approved, his own conviction being that the courts, all courts, "will be naturally led to resist every encroachment upon rights expressly stipulated for . . ."*

Police stations still smelled of Lysol a decade and a half following the United States Supreme Court's decision in Ernest Miranda's case. The same people who had roamed the corridors with the peeling paint the night Danny Escobedo was questioned still roamed there: those with uniforms, those with briefcases, and those with trouble. The trouble was the same, too: homicide, rape, prostitution, burglary, marital problems, narcotics—all the devices men had discovered to destroy themselves and each other.

There was one change, though. *Miranda* had come to the station house. Reading a suspect his constitutional rights was as familiar a procedure to a police officer as strapping on his gun. Settled policy. Particularly among younger officers, who, like the state court judges who had come to the bench with *Gideon, Escobedo,* and *Miranda* already in place, had grown up with them professionally, they were accepted, if not always with enthusiasm, at least with compliance. Despite the increase in freedom to dispense with the

* When in the winter of 1982 there were thirty bills before Congress to strip the federal courts, including the Supreme Court, of jurisdiction in social matters—prayer in public schools, abortion, school desegregation—it was the Conference of Chief Justices, who for a quarter century had asserted their independence in their periodic outbursts at the rulings of the Supreme Court, which unanimously and vigorously condemned the movement, viewing the proposed legislation as a "hazardous experiment with the vulnerable fabric of the nation's judiciary systems."

reading conferred by the omnibus crime bill of 1968, FBI policy regarding *Miranda* continued to be based on court decisions. The *FBI Legal Handbook for Special Agents* explicitly instructed members of the department to warn all suspects of their constitutional rights. Agents still carried advise-of-rights forms in their attaché cases, read them prior to interrogation, had the accused read them, made sure they were understood, and got any waivers signed; they were not about to lose cases on *Miranda* violations. The word *Miranda* had become a staple of the law enforcement community's vocabulary, and prosecutors and judges alike referred to the station house ritual of giving *Miranda* warnings as "mirandizing." The Hill Street blues read them over national television, and in a nationally syndicated comic strip, Peppermint Patty, on her first assignment as a school safety patrol, read them to a kindergartener who had crossed the street improperly. *Miranda* had become part of the popular culture.

The early years under *Miranda* had not been easy for police. According to a 1971 survey of fifty-one chiefs by a Harvard Law School student, they believed *Miranda* was losing confessions for them, that other evidence was difficult to get unless suspects could be interrogated, that without interrogations detection resources were being diverted into the solving of petty crimes, leaving less time for the investigation of felonies. In other studies, older officers were found to adjust to the limitations of the ruling with more difficulty than younger ones, small-town departments with more difficulty than metropolitan units. Not all officers adjusted immediately, and in 1970, Tom Clark, whose hurt had been so deep at Chief Justice Warren's characterization of the law enforcement community in the reading of the *Miranda* opinion that he had rewritten a section of his dissent, read some warnings of his own to that community.

> Although *Miranda* ... has been on the books of the Supreme Court since 1966 [he wrote in an opinion for the U.S. Court of Appeals of the Seventh Circuit on which he was sitting temporarily] and has been publicized more widely than any opinion of the Court since *Brown* v. *Board of Education* ... the mandate of the case is followed in the breach. The police just will not give the warnings required and the prosecutors continue to present the resulting illicit evidence to juries ... it is suggested that the prosecutors enforce *Miranda* to the letter and that police obey it with like diligence; otherwise the courts may have to act to correct a presently alarming situation.

The confusion regarding what police could and could not do under *Miranda* was largely dissipated—and with it, some of the resistance—by training sessions. In Syracuse, New York, law professors from the local university worked with the city police department, which in turn ran seminars for area sheriffs and town and village police. In Philadelphia the local bar association set up a police education program, during which 3,000 officers at a rate of 100 a week for thirty weeks took a daylong seminar given by a prosecutor, a defense attorney, and a judge. The FBI gave training sessions in towns and cities across the country. Some of these lectures were criticized for their failure to urge local police to reform their ways and for their legalistic approach to *Miranda*, which was interpreted on occasion as emphasizing the legal ways to avoid situations requiring *Miranda*; nevertheless, the practical applications of the ruling were explained in the kind of detail needed by an officer chasing a suspect down an alley.

The early resentment never died entirely, and Cleatus Leaming, the Des Moines, Iowa, detective whose Christian burial speech had persuaded Robert Williams to confess and who retired as assistant chief in 1975, complained in 1977: "You know, during my career as police officer, I really wanted to some day be a professional interrogator, but *Miranda* and all those other Court decisions changed that." Much of the anger subsided, however, as police gradually adapted their procedures to the Supreme Court's requirements, and it turned out that *Miranda* had inhibited the apprehension of criminals by police somewhat less than had been feared. Although empirical studies of the decision's impact on the administration of criminal justice were scarce following the first flurry of interest immediately after *Miranda* had been handed down in 1966, few in law enforcement circles were prepared to say in the late 1970s that the dire predictions of the dissenters to the decision had materialized. There was some feeling that in the early days a few criminals might have walked free because of *Miranda*, but it was only a few. And there were a few diehards; Carroll Cooley, whose interrogation of Miranda himself had not passed Court inspection, remained convinced ten years later that the decision in that case had hampered police considerably and allowed a lot of guilty people to evade the questioning which would have led to their conviction. Others, police and prosecutors both, seemed to feel that *Miranda* had had little to do with the number of confessions given or statements made, that suspects who were going to confess, particularly those who needed the release confession offered or who thought they could gain some favor from it, would confess regardless of their knowledge of their constitutional rights, and those who would not did not. And Tom Clark, dissenter to *Miranda* and the law enforcement community's representative on the U.S. Supreme Court prior to his retirement in 1967, had publicly confessed his "error" in his "appraisal of its effects upon the successful detection and prosecution of crime."

A lot of people felt that the effects of the *Miranda* ruling on police had been, in fact, salutary. If it had not been solely responsible for the improvement in police effectiveness, if technological developments, larger and better deployed manpower, better-educated police—advanced degrees in sociology and criminology were becoming more common among chiefs, and by 1982 perhaps half the police officers in the country had earned at least some college credits—better police-community relations and a host of other improvements in the station house were helping law enforcement in its constantly uphill battle against crime. *Miranda* had contributed something to the professionalization of the patrolman who could no longer rely on the quick and easy confession but now had to dig for evidence in his crime solving, a development to which the increased workloads of the crime laboratories testified. If *Miranda* had not changed the police officer's perspective, if it had not persuaded him to shift entirely his priorities from clearance rates to some broader vision of the rule of law, it had had an impact on the chiefs, who had read in the ruling a judicial warning that the behavior of their officers was not above review or reproach and that they had better formulate department policies with an eye to controlling the unfettered discretion of these men and women that had been tolerated in the past, a development to which the increased use of tape recorders, even videotapes, during interrogations testified.

Perfection had not, of course, been achieved. The ritual of the *Miranda* warning was not always carried out in the spirit the justices of the Supreme Court had perhaps intended. A defense lawyer put it this way: "I know police officers whom I would trust with anything in my life. I know if they were giving *Miranda* warnings, they would do so with all the attention as if it were their own brother or sister who was the recipient of the warning. And I know others who would lie fifteen times under oath that they had given *Miranda* warnings. Not only had they not mumbled them, they couldn't even recite them."

How much *Miranda* protected the rights of the criminal defendant was not certain and was probably at best mixed. One judge reported that complaints about the physical abuse of prisoners during interrogation had declined markedly. Another judge reported that from his observation of trial witnesses, *Miranda* and *Escobedo* and others had been responsible for a vast improvement in the caliber of testimony given by police officers, that a new respect for the liberty of the person, a new concept of justice, seemed to have developed.

On the other hand, long after the *Miranda* ruling had been handed down, there were police officers who would say, "Give me an hour alone with a defendant, and I'll get him to confess to anything." There were officers who deliberately postponed the moment of actually placing a suspect in custody in order to avoid reading the *Miranda* warnings and, they hoped, get a confession. The reading of *Miranda* warnings did not guarantee a suspect's comprehension of them, particularly if they were mumbled incoherently or read perfunctorily like so much unnecessary razzmatazz.

Miranda warnings did not protect the constitutional rights of a young, mentally deficient District of Columbia man whom Secret Service agents arrested in 1972 for trying to spend a $1 bill on which the $1 sign had been covered with a "10" from a $10 bill. The federal officers arrested him, carefully advised him of his constitutional rights, then forced him to strip and stand naked while they questioned him.

Miranda warnings had not protected the rights of Robert Williams, whom Des Moines, Iowa, police had manipulated into confession to the murder of ten-year-old Pamela Powers with what became known as the "Christian burial speech."

Miranda did not protect from police brutality Evasio Hernandez, whom Coral Gables, Florida, police arrested one midnight in June 1976 for violation of narcotics laws. The officers advised Hernandez of his rights, and when he invoked his right to remain silent, they locked him, with two cosuspects, into the back of the patrol wagon, where they held him incommunicado and in close confinement for five hours. Until he confessed.

Miranda gave no protection from police overbearing to Peter Reilly of New Canaan, Connecticut, accused of murdering his mother. Police carefully advised him of his rights, and eighteen-year-old Peter, unacquainted with the ways of law enforcement, turned down the offer of a lawyer and asked instead for a lie detector test, after which police viciously and deliberately manipulated him into confessing. Peter Reilly was convicted on the basis of his confession, but public interest in the case, including that of playwright Arthur Miller, inspired further investigation. Ultimately the charges were dropped when new evidence placed Reilly miles from the scene of the crime at the time it had occurred.

The *Miranda* ruling itself held inherent weaknesses; the major one was that it allowed a suspect to waive his rights without the advice of a lawyer. A lawyer would never have allowed what happened to Peter Reilly.

If anyone still doubted government's potential for malevolence against which the Constitution was intended to protect the citizen, if anyone still doubted the need for restraints on police as well as presidents, these men had provided answers.

It was perhaps as a symbol that *Miranda* had the most salutary impact, less tangible than the others but nonetheless real. Placing this ritual, however incoherently mumbled, however perfunctorily read, however abused, between a policeman and a suspect served, it was generally acknowledged, a civilizing purpose, reminding the officer of the law that however miserable the one who stood before him, however savage the crime of which he was accused, he was still a man, possessed of all the attributes, including the constitutional rights, of other men.

In a historical context *Miranda* was a statement of aspiration. It had been 700 years in the writing, counting only from Magna Carta. John Lilburne was a minor character in it; the ghostly figures of Izell Chambers and Clarence Earl Gideon and Danny Escobedo marched between the lines. Abe Fortas, who had suggested at oral argument that the cases of these convicted rapists and murderers and holdup men were not just isolated cases but held some meaning for political history, said some years later about *Miranda*: "[S]omeday, in a better world, it may be a predicate for a ruling that confessions obtained by police or prosecutor, from a person in custody, are inadmissible if taken in the absence of counsel." More than looking toward only some more civilized rule of evidence, however, the decision by the United States Supreme Court in the case of Ernest Miranda looked toward some higher degree of civilization itself.

Miranda had endured attacks from every segment of the public. It had been maligned by candidates for high political office and by those already holding high political office. It had been buffeted by judges, by prosecutors, and by police. Scholars had kicked it around academe. More than a decade later even the man in the street still held definite opinions about that ruling. Some of the attacks had been intellectual, reasoned, and well intentioned; others had been emotional and unreasoned, their only purpose the advancement of a candidacy or an avenging assault on the United States Supreme Court. *Miranda* had also been defended and been enforced, not always perfectly by any means and not in every case by every prosecutor and every police officer and every judge. But enough. And there had been judges and police officers and district attorneys who had not believed in either its legality or its morality, but they had obeyed it. Their loyalty was to the law, and *Miranda* had survived.

Miranda the man was less fortunate.

Phoenix, Arizona. January 31, 1976.

Flanked by $1-a-night flophouses, La Amapola, a dusty bar in the Deuce section of Phoenix, Arizona, was living room to the local street people. Its red and green neon sign dulled by the years' accumulation of dead moths, it had seen, as well as better days, a fair amount of violence, and the fistfight this Saturday night was not unusual. A poker game. A little cheating. An alcohol-fueled quarrel over a handful of small change lying on the bar. For thirty-four-year-old Ernesto Miranda, a Phoenix appliance store deliveryman, ex-convict, and suspected drug dealer—although so far he had been too cagey for police—and for the two illegal Mexican immigrants with whom he had been playing cards, it was hardly an uncommon sequence of events.

After the fight Miranda went to the men's room to wash the blood from his hands. While he was gone, one of the Mexicans drew a knife—an ugly six-inch hooked blade, the kind used to cut lettuce.

"Finish it with this," he told his companion, handing over the knife.

Miranda returned, tried to take the knife away. The Mexican stabbed him, once in the stomach and once in the upper left chest. He was dead on arrival at Good Samaritan Hospital. He had been paid that day, but no money was found on his body.

The killer fled, disappearing down an alley. His accomplice was caught. Before taking him to police headquarters, two Phoenix police officers read— one in English, one in Spanish—to him from a card:

> You have the right to remain silent.
> Anything you say can be used against you in a court of law.

Chapter 4

You have the right to the presence of an attorney to assist you prior to questioning and to be with you during questioning if you so desire.

If you cannot afford an attorney you have the right to have an attorney appointed for you prior to questioning.

Do you understand these rights?

Will you voluntarily answer my questions?

BIBLIOGRAPHY AND SOURCE NOTES

LIST OF ABBREVIATIONS

ABA: American Bar Association
ACLU: American Civil Liberties Union
ADS: Arizona Daily Star
AELE: Americans for Effective Law Enforcement
ALI: American Law Institute
AR: Arizona Republic
ASA: Arizona State Archives, Phoenix
CCJ: Conference of Chief Justices
CQ: Congressional Quarterly
CR: Congressional Record
DNC-NA: Democratic National Committee, National Archives
DOJ-Civil: Department of Justice, Civil Division
DOJ-Criminal: Department of Justice, Criminal Division
EM-mss: Ernest Miranda manuscript collection, ASA, Phoenix
Escobedo: Escobedo v. Illinois, 378 U.S. 478 (1964)
FBI: Federal Bureau of Investigation
F.R.D.: *Federal Rules Decisions*
Gideon: Gideon v. Wainwright, 372 U.S. 335 (1963)
Harris: Harris v. New York, 401 U.S. 222 (1971)
HLS: Harvard Law School
IACP: International Association of Chiefs of Police
JFK: John F. Kennedy Library, Boston, Mass.
LBJ: Lyndon B. Johnson Library, Austin, Texas
LC: Library of Congress, Washington, D.C.
LJ: Law Journal
LQ: Law Quarterly
LR: Law Review
LW: U.S. Law Week
Miranda: Miranda v. Arizona, 384 U.S. 436 (1966)

411

Bibliography and Source Notes

NA: National Archives, Washington, D.C.
NAACP: National Association for the Advancement of Colored People
NAAG: National Association of Attorneys General
NCLOE: National Commission on Law Observance and Enforcement
NYT: *The New York Times*
Peters: Peters v. Hobby, 349 U.S. 331 (1955)
PPP: *The Public Papers of the Presidents*
R and B: U.S. Supreme Court records and briefs
RNC: Republican National Committee
RNC-NA: Republican National Committee, National Archives
SEP: *Saturday Evening Post*
Tr-MC: Transcript of proceedings, Maricopa County Superior Court, June 20, 1963/*Arizona v. Miranda*
Tr-SC: Transcript of proceedings, U.S. Supreme Court
UCR: *Uniform Crime Reports*
UC-OHP: University of California at Berkeley, Earl Warren Oral History Project
U.S. News: *U.S. News & World Report*
Williams: Brewer v. Williams, 430 U.S. 387 (1977)
WP: *Washington Post*
WS: *Washington Star*

SOURCES

1. Interviews

Each name is followed by a brief description of the person. This is intended to indicate his or her significance in the narrative, *not* his or her present position. A few interviews had more than one purpose.

Those entries followed by an (L) were conducted by letter. Those entries followed by a (T) were conducted by telephone. Those followed by an (M) were conducted at meetings between the author and interviewee.

Robert V. Abendroth, Warren Burger's first full-year law clerk, 1956–57. (T) June 29, 1982.
Martin Agronsky, CBS reporter with Eric Sevareid for "Justice Black and the Bill of Rights." (T) Sept. 16, 1980.
Anthony G. Amsterdam, author, ACLU amicus curiae brief for *Miranda*. (L) May 2, 1980.
Joel Martin Aurnou, counsel for Viven Harris. (L) Aug. 15, 1979, July 2, 1982.
Sidney Baker, president, Western Pennsylvania Trial Lawyers Association. (M) April 14, 1979, Pittsburgh, Pa.
Robert Bartels, counsel for Robert Williams; professor of law, University of Iowa. (T) March 27, 1979.
David L. Bazelon, chief judge, U.S. Court of Appeals for the District of Columbia Circuit. (M) Feb. 15, 1979, Washington, D.C.
Burton Benjamin, producer, "Justice Black and the Bill of Rights." (L) Sept. 8, 1980.
Frederick L. Brown, judge, Massachusetts Court of Appeals. (M) Aug. 5, 1981, Boston.
Herbert Brownell, U.S. Attorney General, 1953–57. (M) March 22, 1978, New York, N.Y.
Levin H. Campbell, judge, U.S. Court of Appeals for the First Circuit. (M) Aug. 5, 1981, Boston.
Gerald Caplan, professor of law, George Washington University. (M) May 14, 1980, Washington, D.C.
Frank Carrington, founder, AELE. (T) Oct. 22, 1979, Oct. 14, 1981.
Leslie V. Chalmers, special prosecutor, argued the state's case in *North Carolina v. Butler*. (T) May 1, 1979.
Irving Clark, cocounsel, with Warren Burger, *State v. Peery*; director, St. Paul Council on Human Relations. (L) Sept. 23, 1980.
Ronald K. L. Collins, Supreme Court fellow, 1981–82. (M) Sept. 21, 1981, Washington, D.C.

Bibliography and Source Notes

Robert K. Corbin, Maricopa County Attorney, prosecutor at Miranda's second trial. (M) Aug. 7, 1978, Phoenix.
Robert J. Corcoran, Phoenix ACLU attorney, 1965. (L) July 12, 1979.
Bernard D. Crooke, Montgomery County, Md., chief of police. (M) Sept. 26, 1976, Rockville, Md.
Verne Countryman, professor of law, Harvard. (L) Nov. 5, 1980.
Victor M. Earle III, counsel for Michael Vignera. (L) July 9, 1980.
George C. Edwards, Jr., chief judge, U.S. Court of Appeals for the Sixth Circuit. (L) Sept. 9, 1980.
Albert Eisele, reporter, *St. Paul*, Minn., *Dispatch*. (M) Feb. 14, 1979, Washington, D.C.
Thomas A. Facelle, prosecutor in Viven Harris's case. (L) July 29, 1982.
F. Conger Fawcett, counsel for Carl Calvin Westover. (L) April 25, 1979.
Newman Flanagan, Suffolk County, Mass., district attorney. (M) July 29, 1981, Boston.
Henry J. Florence, counsel for Ernest Miranda, 1974. (M) Aug. 7, 1978, Phoenix.
John J. Flynn, counsel for Miranda, *Miranda* v. *Arizona*. (M) Aug. 8, 1978, Phoenix, and (T) Aug. 10, 1979.
Abe Fortas, counsel for Clarence Earl Gideon, associate justice of the Supreme Court. (M) Sept. 18, 1979, Washington, D.C.
John P. Frank, counsel for Miranda, *Miranda* v. *Arizona*. (M) Aug. 10, 1978, Phoenix; (L) Feb. 20, 1980, April 29, 1980.
John Graecen, associate director, National Center for State Courts. (T) Feb. 4, 1980.
Jack Greenberg, director, NAACP Legal Defense Fund. (M) March 11, 1980, New York, N.Y.
M. Gene Haeberle, counsel for Sylvester Johnson and Stanley Cassidy. (T) Jan. 9, 1981.
James T. Hale, law clerk to Chief Justice Warren. (T) Sept. 12, 1979.
Garry Hayes, executive director, Police Executive Research Forum. (M) March 6, 1980.
Leon Jaworski, member, President's Commission on Law Enforcement and the Administration of Criminal Justice. (L) June 18, 1979.
Yale Kamisar, professor of law, University of Michigan. (T) Jan. 14, 1982.
Nicholas deB. Katzenbach, U.S. attorney general, 1965–67. (L) July 14, 1980, Oct. 8, 1980.
Roger G. Kennedy, friend of Warren Burger. (M) March 26, 1980, Washington, D.C.
Richard G. Kleindienst, deputy U.S. attorney general, 1969–72. (M) Feb. 1, 1979, Alexandria, Va.
Barry L. Kroll, counsel for Danny Escobedo. (T) May 1, 1979. (L) May 13, 1980, Oct. 1, 1981.
Peter Kuh, criminal defense lawyer. (M) April 13, 1980, Washington, D.C.
Rex E. Lee, law clerk to Byron R. White; Phoenix, Ariz., attorney, 1964–72. (T) Oct. 27, 1978.
Daniel P. Levitt, law clerk to Abe Fortas. (M) Dec. 27, 1979, New York, N.Y.
Nathan Lewin, law clerk to John M. Harlan; Washington, D.C., attorney. (M) July 3, 1979, Washington.
Wilbur T. Littlefield, Los Angeles public defender, counsel for Roy Stewart following *Miranda*. (T) June 20, 1980.
J. Edward Lumbard, senior judge, U.S. Court of Appeals for the Second Circuit; chairman, ABA Special Committee on Minimum Standards for the Administration of Criminal Justice. (M) Oct. 15, 1980, New York, N.Y.
Jonathan Marks, criminal defense attorney. (M) March 12, 1980, New York, N.Y.
Ervin Matthews, Miranda's last parole officer. (M) Aug. 9, 1978, Phoenix.
Ernest W. McFarland, author, State v. Miranda, 98 Ariz. 18 (1965). (L) May 11, 1979.
Yale McFate, Maricopa County Superior Court judge in Miranda's case. (T) Dec. 19, 1978. (L) June 1, 1982.
Monroe G. McKay, member of Lewis & Roca during preparation of Miranda's case; judge, U.S. Court of Appeals for the Tenth Circuit. (L) Jan. 16, 1980.
Carey McWilliams, author, editor, longtime observer of California politics. (M) March 11, 1980, New York, N.Y.
Daniel J. Meador, assistant U.S. attorney general for Improvements in the Administration of Justice. (M) July 18, 1979, Washington, D.C.
David A. Mills, criminal defense attorney. (M) July 22, 1981, Boston.
Alvin Moore, trial counsel for Miranda. (L) Sept. 16, 1978; May 18, 1979, Nov. 26, 1979.
H. Carl Moultrie, chief judge, D.C. Superior Court. (M) July 18, 1979, Washington.
George Napper, chief of police, Atlanta, Ga. (M) July 25, 1978, Atlanta.

Bibliography and Source Notes

Arnette Nelson, director of public relations, Ripon College, Ripon, Wis. (L) June 17, 1982.
Gary K. Nelson, argued *Miranda* for the state of Arizona. (T) Sept. 11, 1978.
James C. Otis, former law partner of Warren Burger; justice, Minnesota Supreme Court. (T) June 5, 1980.
Gordon C. Rhea, executive assistant U.S. attorney. (M) Dec. 3, 1981. Washington, D.C.
William E. Rodriguez, El Paso, Texas, chief of police. (M) Aug. 4, 1978, El Paso.
H. David Rosenbloom, law clerk to Abe Fortas. (M) March 14, 1979, Washington, D.C.
Thomas J. Sardino, Syracuse, N.Y., chief of police. (M) June 14, 1979, Syracuse.
Frederick F. Schauer, associate professor, Marshall-Wythe School of Law, College of William and Mary. (M) Nov. 13, 1979, Williamsburg, Va.
Bobby Shirley, Austin, Texas, police lieutenant. (M) Aug. 1, 1978, Austin.
Stanford Schmuckler, counsel for Sylvester Johnson and Stanley Cassidy. (T) Sept. 4, 1980, March 4, 1982.
Barry Silverman, friend of Miranda. (M) Aug. 8, 1978, Phoenix. (L) May 16, 1979.
Barbara A.H. Smith, chief, criminal appellate division, Massachusetts Dept. of Justice. (M) July 7, 1981, Boston.
Brownlow Speer, Massachusetts Defenders' Committee attorney. (M) July 31, 1981, Boston.
Richard G. Stearns, Norfolk County, Mass., special prosecutor. (M) July 23, 1981, Dedham, Mass.
Eugene F. Sullivan, Jr., Oswego County, N.Y., former district attorney and county judge. (M) June 16, 1979, Fulton, N.Y.
Edward A. Tamm, judge, U.S. Court of Appeals for the District of Columbia Circuit. (M) March 15, 1979, Washington.
Telford Taylor, author, amicus curiae brief for N.Y. in *Miranda*. (M) March 11, 1980, New York, N.Y.
James Vorenberg, principal draftsman, ALI Model Code of Pre-Arraignment Procedure; staff director, President's Commission on Law Enforcement and the Administration of Justice; professor, Harvard Law School. (T) Sept. 4, 1979.
George C. Wallace, candidate for president, 1968. (M) July 26, 1978, Montgomery, Ala.
Jack Wallace, judge, Alabama Third Circuit; George C. Wallace's brother. (M) July 27, 1978, Clayton, Ala.
Will R. Wilson, assistant U.S. attorney general, Criminal Division, 1969–71. (M) July 31, 1978, Austin, Texas.
Melvin L. Wulf, ACLU legal director during preparation of ACLU brief in *Miranda*. (T) May 15, 1980.

2. Manuscript sources

Arizona State Archives (ASA), Phoenix
Federal Bureau of Investigation (FBI), Washington, D.C.
Harvard Law School (HLS), Cambridge, Mass.
Lyndon B. Johnson Library (LBJ), Austin, Texas
John F. Kennedy Library (JFK), Boston, Mass.
Library of Congress, (LC), Washington, D.C.
Seeley G. Mudd Manuscript Library, Princeton University, Princeton, N.J.
National Archives (NA), Washington, D.C.
University of California at Berkeley, Bancroft Library (Earl Warren oral history project; copies at Marshall-Wythe School of Law, College of William and Mary, Williamsburg, Va.) (UC-OHP)
U.S. Department of Justice (DOJ), Washington, D.C.

3. Oral history projects (OHP)

Ramsey Clark, LBJ
Tom C. Clark, LBJ
Everett M. Dirksen, LBJ
William O. Douglas, JFK
James O. Eastland, LBJ
Abe Fortas, LBJ
Hubert H. Humphrey, LBJ

Bibliography and Source Notes

Nicholas deB. Katzenbach, LBJ
Robert F. Kennedy (vols. 5, 6, 7), JFK
Anthony Lewis, JFK
Thurgood Marshall, JFK, LBJ
Thruston B. Morton, LBJ
Patrick V. Murphy, LBJ
Paul A. Porter, LBJ
Joseph L. Rauh, Jr., LBJ
Earl Warren, LBJ
Earl Warren, UC-OHP
   "Conversations with Earl Warren"
   "Perspectives on the Alameda County District Attorney's Office"
   "Robert B. Powers: Law Enforcement Race Relations 1930–1960"
   "Merrell F. Small: The Office of the Governor under Earl Warren"
   "Earl Warren: The Chief Justiceship"
   "Earl Warren: The Governor's Family"
   "Helen R. MacGregor. A Career in Public Service with Earl Warren"
   "The Warrens: Four Personal Views"
   "Earl Warren's Campaigns"
   "Japanese-American Relocation Reviewed"
Will Wilson, LBJ

4. Documents: hearings, proceedings, reports, and other records

American Bar Association (ABA). *Annual Report.* Issues as cited.
―――. Advisory Committee on the Prosecution and Defense Functions. *Standards Relating to Providing Defense Services.* 1967.
American Law Institute (ALI). *Proceedings.* Issues as cited.
Americans for Effective Law Enforcement (AELE). *Amicus Curiae Briefs in Decided Cases.* AELE Ref. No. 2666.
―――. *The Exclusionary Rule.* Position Paper No. 8, June 2, 1981.
Attorney General's Committee on Poverty and the Administration of Federal Criminal Justice. *Report.* Washington, D.C., Feb. 25, 1963.
Attorney General's Task Force on Violent Crime. *Final Report.* Washington, D.C., Aug. 17, 1981.
Clerk of the Senate. *Civilian Nominations.* Washington, D.C. Issues as cited.
Columbia University. *Constitutions of the United States National and State,* vols. 1–6, 1978.
Comptroller General of the United States. *Impact of the Exclusionary Rule on Federal Criminal Prosecutions.* Washington, D.C., April 19, 1979.
Conference of Chief Justices (CCJ). *Proceedings.* Issues as cited.
―――. *Resolutions.* Adopted at the Fifth Midyear Meeting Conference of Chief Justices, Williamsburg, Va., Jan. 30, 1982.
Federal Bureau of Investigation (FBI). *Uniform Crime Reports (UCR).* Issues as cited.
―――. *Legal Handbook for Special Agents.* 1980.
Forst, Brian, Judith Lucianovic, and Sarah J. Cox. *What Happens After Arrest?* Institute for Law and Social Research, Washington, D.C., May 1978.
Gallup, George H. *The Gallup Poll. Public Opinion,* 1935–71, vols. 1–3. New York, 1972.
Highlights of Interim Findings and Implications. Institute for Law and Social Research, Washington, D.C., 1977.
International Association of Chiefs of Police (IACP). *The Police Yearbook.* Issues as cited.
Kurland, Philip B., and Gerhard Casper, eds. *Landmark Briefs and Arguments of the Supreme Court of the United States: Constitutional Law.* Arlington, Va., 1975.
Lazar Institute. *Pretrial Release: An Evaluation of Defendant Outcomes and Program Impacts* (Summary and policy analysis). Washington, D.C., 1981.
National Association of Attorneys General (NAAG). *Conference Proceedings.* Issues as cited.
National Commission on Law Observance and Enforcement (NCLOE). *Report on Criminal Procedure* (Number 8). Washington, D.C., 1931.
―――. *Report on Lawlessness in Law Enforcement* (Number 11). Washington, D.C., 1931.
―――. *Report on Police* (Number 14). Washington, D.C., 1931.

Bibliography and Source Notes

National League of Cities, United States Conference of Mayors. *Rape*. Washington, D.C., 1974.

Pierce, Glenn L., and William J. Bowers. *The Impact of the Bartley-Foxx Gun Law on Crime in Massachusetts*. Boston, 1979.

The President's Commission on Crime in the District of Columbia. *Report*. Washington, D.C., 1966.

The President's Commission on Law Enforcement and the Administration of Criminal Justice. *The Challenge of Crime in a Free Society*. New York, 1968.

Republican National Committee (RNC). *Official Report of the Proceedings*. Issues as cited.

Transcript of Proceedings, Maricopa County Superior Court, June 20, 1963. *Arizona v. Miranda* (Tr-Mc).

Transcript of Proceedings in the U.S. Supreme Court. Cases as cited (Tr-SC).

U.S. Attorney General. *Annual Report*. Washington, D.C. Issues as cited.

U.S. Commission on Civil Rights. *Police Practices and the Preservation of Civil Rights*. Consultation. Washington, D.C., Dec. 12–13, 1978.

————. *The State of Civil Rights*. Washington, D.C., Feb. 1978.

U.S. Congress. House. Committee on the Judiciary. Special Subcommittee. *Associate Justice William O. Douglas: Final Report*, Sept. 17, 1970.

————. *Associate Justice William O. Douglas: First Report*, June 20, 1970.

U.S. Congress. House. Committee on the Judiciary. Subcommittee on Courts, Civil Liberties and the Administration of Justice. *State of the Judiciary and Access to Justice: Hearings*, June and July 1977.

U.S. Congress. House. Select Committee on Crime. *Street Crime in America: Hearings*, April–May 1973.

U.S. Congress. Senate. Committee on the District of Columbia. *Crime in the National Capital: Hearings*, March 1969–Oct. 1970.

U.S. Congress. Senate. Committee on the Judiciary. *Harry A. Blackmun: Hearing*, April 19, 1970.

————. *John N. Mitchell, Attorney General Designate: Hearing*, Jan. 14, 1969.

————. *Legislative History of the United States Circuit Courts of Appeal and the Judges Who Served During the Period 1801 Through March 1958*. 1958.

————. *Nomination of Abe Fortas: Hearing*, Aug. 5, 1965.

————. *Nomination of John Paul Stevens: Hearings*, Dec. 8–10, 1975.

————. *Nomination of Sandra Day O'Connor: Hearings*, Sept. 9–11, 1981.

————. *Nomination of Simon E. Sobeloff to Be United States Circuit Judge: Hearings*, May–June 1956.

————. *Nomination of Thurgood Marshall to Be Associate Justice of the Supreme Court: Hearings*, July 13–14, 1967.

————. *Nomination of Warren E. Burger to Be Chief Justice of the United States: Hearing*, June 3, 1969.

————. *Nominations of Abe Fortas of Tennessee, to Be Chief Justice of the United States and Homer Thornberry of Texas, to Be Associate Justice of the Supreme Court of the United States: Hearings*, July 11–Sept. 16, 1968 (vols. 1, 2).

————. *Nominations of Richard G. Kleindienst to Be Deputy Attorney General, William H. Rehnquist to Be Assistant Attorney General, Legal Counsel; Will Wilson to Be Assistant Attorney General, Criminal Division . . . : Hearing*, Jan. 29, 1969.

————. *Nominations of William H. Rehnquist and Lewis F. Powell, Jr.: Hearings*, Nov. 3–10, 1971.

————. *Omnibus Crime Control and Safe Streets Act of 1967: Report*, 1968.

————. *The Supreme Court of the United States: Hearings and Reports on . . . Nominations of Supreme Court Justices by the Senate Judiciary Committee, 1916–1972* (compiled by Roy M. Mersky and J. Myron Jacobstein). Vols. 5 (Earl Warren), 10 (Clement F. Haynsworth), 11 (G. Harrold Carswell).

U.S. Congress. Senate. Committee on the Judiciary. Subcommittee on Constitutional Rights. *Preventive Detention: Hearings*, May, June 1970.

U.S. Congress. Senate. Committee on the Judiciary. Subcommittee on Criminal Laws and Procedures. *Controlling Crime Through More Effective Law Enforcement: Hearings*, March–July 1967.

Bibliography and Source Notes

————. *Criminal Laws and Procedures: Hearings*, March, May 1966.

U.S. Department of Justice, National Institute of Law Enforcement and Criminal Justice. *Prosecution of Adult Felony Defendants in Los Angeles County: A Policy Perspective*. Washington, D.C., 1973.

U.S. Department of Justice, National Minority Advisory Council on Criminal Justice. *The Inequality of Justice: A Report on Crime and the Administration of Justice in the Minority Community*. Washington, D.C., Jan. 1982.

U.S. Presidents. *Public Papers of the Presidents of the United States* (PPP). Washington, D.C., volumes as cited.

U.S. Supreme Court. *Records and Briefs* (R and B). Cases as cited.

Vera Institute of Justice. *Felony Arrests: Their Prosecution and Disposition in New York City's Courts*. New York, 1981.

5. Unpublished material

a. Records

U.S. Supreme Court. *Records of the Supreme Court of the United States*. Case records (trial transcripts, lower court judgments, petitions for certiorari, correspondence, tape recordings of oral arguments in the U.S. Supreme Court; the original transcripts of the oral arguments are error-ridden; the tape recordings provide the only accurate accounts), RG 267, National Archives (NA).

b. Radio, television transcripts

"A Conversation with Earl Warren." Brandeis Television Recollections, WGBH-TV, Boston, distributor, 1972.

"A Conversation with Earl Warren." McClatchey Broadcasting, June 25, 1969.

"Has the Supreme Court Handcuffed the Law?" Station KOOL, Phoenix, Ariz., June 21, 1966.

"Justice Black and the Bill of Rights." CBS News Special, Dec. 3, 1969.

"The Warren Years." NET Journal, June 30, 1969.

c. Texts of speeches

Bazelon, David L. "Crime: Towards a Constructive Debate." Feb. 28, 1981.

Burger, Warren E. "Agenda for 2000 A.D.—Need for Systematic Anticipation." April 7, 1976.

————. "Annual Report on the State of the Judiciary." Feb. 15, 1976; Feb. 11, 1979; Feb. 3, 1980.

————. "For Whom the Bell Tolls." Feb. 17, 1970.

————. "Prison Reform." May 9, 1979.

————. "Remarks." May 21, 1967; May 17, 1977; May 27, 1977.

————. "Report on the Federal Judicial Branch." Aug. 6, 1973.

————. "Report to the American Bar Association." Feb. 13, 1977.

————. "State of the Federal Judiciary." Aug. 10, 1970; July 5, 1971.

————. "Year-end Reports." 1977–80.

Frank, John P. "In Cheerful Retrospect." Jan. 30, 1980.

Powell, Lewis F., Jr. "Report on the Court." Aug. 11, 1976.

d. Personal collections

Robert J. Corcoran. Correspondence, Ernest Miranda's case.

Daniel P. Levitt. Ernest Miranda files.

Barry Silverman. Ernest Miranda files.

e. Miscellaneous

Morris, Jeffrey Brandon. "The Secondmost Important Court. The United States Court of Appeals for the District of Columbia Circuit." Unpublished Ph.D. thesis, Columbia University, 1972.

Bibliography and Source Notes

Society of American Law Teachers. "Supreme Court Denial of Citizens Access to Federal Courts to Challenge Unconstitutional or Other Unlawful Actions: The Record of the Burger Court." Statement, Oct. 1976.

6. Published material: books, articles

Abraham, Henry J. *Justices and Presidents*. New York, 1974.

Ahern, James F. *Police in Trouble*. New York, 1972.

Amsterdam, Anthony G. "The Rights of Suspects." *The Rights of Americans*. Ed. Norman Dorsen. New York, 1970–71.

Arnold, William A. *Back When It All Began: The Early Nixon Years*. New York, 1975.

Association of the Bar of the City of New York. *Equal Justice for the Accused*. Garden City, N.Y., 1959.

Aubrey, Arthur S., Jr., and Rudolph R. Caputo. *Criminal Interrogation*. Springfield, Ill., 1972.

Bakken, Gordon M. "The Arizona Constitutional Convention of 1910." 1978 *Arizona State LJ*, 1.

Barnard, William D. *Dixiecrats and Democrats*. University, Ala., 1974.

Bassett, James. " 'Unpartisan' Chief Justice of the U.S." *NYT*, Oct. 11, 1953, vi, 10.

Bazelon, David L. "The Concept of Responsibility." 53 *Georgetown LJ* 6 (1964).

———. "The Defective Assistance of Counsel." 42 *University of Cincinnati LR* 1 (1973).

———. "The Imperative to Punish." *Atlantic Monthly*, July 1960, 41.

———. "New Gods for Old: 'Efficient' Courts in a Democratic Society." 46 *New York University LR* 653 (1971).

———. "Tribute to Simon E. Sobeloff." 34 *Maryland LR* 486 (1974).

Bell, John C., Jr. "Crime and Criminals." *FBI Law Enforcement Bulletin*, Jan. 1969, 2.

Black, Elizabeth Seay. "Hugo Black: A Memorial Portrait." *Supreme Court Historical Society Yearbook*, 1982, 72.

Black, Hugo L. *A Constitutional Faith*. New York, 1968.

Black, Hugo L., Jr. *Hugo Black: My Father*. New York, 1975.

Boyd, James. "I Gave Thurmond 100% Loyalty and Now I Give Mr. Nixon 100%." *NYT*, Feb. 1, 1970, vi, 12.

Brennan, William J., Jr. *An Affair with Freedom*. Ed. Stephen J. Friedman. New York, 1963.

———. "Chief Justice Warren." 89 *Harvard LR* 1 (1974).

———. "Extension of the Bill of Rights to the States." 44 *Journal of Urban Law* 11 (1966).

———. "Guardians of Our Liberties—State Courts No Less Than Federal." 15 *The Judges' Journal* 82 (1976).

———. "Justice Brennan Calls National Court of Appeals Proposal 'Fundamentally Unnecessary and Ill Advised.' " 59 *ABA Journal* 835 (1973).

———. "Some Aspects of Federalism." CCJ, *Proceedings*, 1964, 57.

———. "State Constitutions and the Protection of Individual Rights." (A slightly edited version of "Guardians of Our Liberties," above) 90 *Harvard LR* 489 (1977).

———. "State Court Decisions and the Supreme Court." 31 *Pennsylvania Bar Association Quarterly* 393 (1960).

———. "State Supreme Court Judge Versus United States Supreme Court Justice: A Change in Perspective." 19 *University of Florida LR* 225 (1966).

Brown, Frederick L. "Future Judicial Oversight of the Conduct of Custodial Interrogations: A Growing Massachusetts Responsibility." 62 *Massachusetts LQ* 143 (1977).

Brownlee, E. Gardner. "A Judge's Views on Law Enforcement Education and Training." *FBI Law Enforcement Bulletin*, Sept. 1973, 8.

Burger, Warren E. "Address of Chief Justice Warren E. Burger Before the Fifth Circuit Judicial Conference." 21 *Journal of Public Law* 271 (1972).

———. "Counsel for the Prosecution and Defense—Their Roles Under the Minimum Standards." 8 *The American Criminal LQ* 2 (1969).

———. "Court Reform. Priority to Methods and Machinery." *Vital Speeches*, vol. 37, 386.

———. "The Courts on Trial." 22 F.R.D. 71 (1957).

———. "The Deferred Maintenance of Judicial Machinery." 54 *Judicature* 410 (1971).

———. "External Checks—Views of a Jurist." *The Police Yearbook*, 1965, 126.

———. "The Fragility of Freedom." *Vital Speeches*, vol. 39, 514.

———. "Has the Time Come?" 55 F.R.D. 119 (1972).

Bibliography and Source Notes

————. "How Can We Cope? The Constitution After 200 Years." 65 ABA *Journal* 201 (1979).

————. "Report on the Federal Judicial Branch—1974." 60 ABA *Journal* 1193 (1974).

————. "State of the Federal Judiciary." 58 ABA *Journal* 1049 (1972).

————. "The State of the Judiciary—1975." 61 ABA *Journal* 439 (1975).

————. "Tribute to Simon E. Soberoff." 34 *Maryland LR* 483 (1974).

————. "Who Will Watch the Watchmen?" 14 *American University LR* 1 (1964).

Byrnes, James F. *All in One Lifetime*. New York, 1958.

————. "The Supreme Court Must Be Curbed." *U.S. News*, May 18, 1956, 50.

Caplan, Gerald. "Reflections on the Nationalization of Crime, 1964–1968." 3 *Arizona State University LJ* 583 (1973).

Capote, Truman. *In Cold Blood*. New York, 1965.

Caspar, Jonathan D. *Lawyers Before the Supreme Court*. Urbana, Ill., 1972.

Chase, Harold W. *Federal Judges. The Appointing Process*. Minneapolis, 1972.

Chester, Lewis, Godfrey Hodgson, and Bruce Page. *An American Melodrama. The Presidential Campaign of 1968*. London, 1969.

Clark, Ramsey. *Crime in America*. New York, 1970.

Clark, Tom C. "Bill Douglas—A Portrait." 28 *Baylor LR* 215 (1976).

————. "Criminal Justice in America." 46 *Texas LR* 742 (1968).

————. "Dedication to Chief Justice Earl Warren." 48 *Nebraska LR* 6 (1968).

————. "Gideon Revisited." 15 *Arizona LR* 343 (1973).

————. "The Office of the Attorney General." 19 *Tennessee LR* 150 (1946).

————. "The Supreme Court Conference." 37 *Texas LR* 273 (1959).

Collins, Ronald K. L. "Away from a Reactionary Approach for Reliance on State Constitutions." 9 *Hastings Constitutional LQ* 201 (1981).

————, and Robert Welsh. "*Miranda*'s Fate in the Burger Court." *The Center Magazine*, Sept./Oct. 1980, 43.

————. "Taking State Constitutions Seriously." *The Center Magazine*, Sept/Oct. 1981, 6.

Congressional Quarterly. *Guide to the U.S. Supreme Court*. Washington, D.C., 1979.

Conrat, Maisie and Richart. *Executive Order 9066*. California Historical Society, 1972.

Cox, Archibald. *The Warren Court*. Cambridge, Mass., 1968.

Cray, Ed. *The Big Blue Line*. New York, 1967.

"Creation of New National Court of Appeals Is Proposed by Blue-Ribbon Study Group." 59 ABA *Journal* 139 (1973).

Daughtray, Martha Craig. "State Court Activism and Other Symptoms of the New Federalism." 45 *Tennessee LR* 731 (1978).

Davenport, John. "The U.S., the Law, and Chief Justice Burger." *Fortune*, Sept. 1970, 146.

Dent, Harry S. *The Prodigal South Returns to Power*. New York, 1978.

Dershowitz, Alan M. and John Hart Ely. "*Harris v. New York*: Some Anxious Observations on the Candor and Logic of the Emerging Nixon Majority." 80 *Yale LJ* 1198 (1971).

De Toledano, Ralph. *One Man Alone: Richard Nixon*. New York, 1969.

"Developments in the Law—Confessions." 79 *Harvard LR* 935 (1966).

Donovan, Robert J. "Over-Nominated and Under-Elected, Still a Promising Candidate." *NYT*, April 25, 1965, vi, 14.

Douglas, Charles G., III. "State Judicial Activism—the New Role for State Bills of Rights." 12 *Suffolk University LR* 1123 (1978).

Douglas, William O. *The Court Years 1939–1975*. New York, 1980.

————. *Go East, Young Man*. New York, 1974.

————. "Tribute to Simon E. Soberoff." 34 *Maryland LR* 484 (1974).

————. "World of Earl Warren: as Chief Justice." 60 ABA *Journal* 1232 (1974).

Drew, Elizabeth. *Washington Journal*. New York, 1975.

Dunne, Gerald T. *Hugo Black and the Judicial Revolution*. New York, 1977.

Duscha, Julius. "Chief Justice Burger Asks: 'If It Doesn't Make Good Sense, How Can It Make Good Law?'" *NYT*, Oct. 5, 1969, vi, 30.

Edwards, George C., Jr. "Interrogation of Criminal Defendants." 35 *Fordham LR* 186 (1966).

Eisele, Albert. *Almost to the Presidency*. Blue Earth, Minn., 1972.

Eisenhower, Dwight D. *Mandate for Change*. Garden City, N.Y., 1963.

Ely, John Hart. "The Chief." 88 *Harvard LR* 11 (1974).

Bibliography and Source Notes

Ennis, Bruce J. "A.C.L.U.: 60 Years of Volunteer Lawyering." 66 ABA *Journal* 1080 (1980).

Fellman, David. *The Defendant's Rights Today.* Madison, Wis., 1976.

Foote, Joseph. "Mr. Justice Brennan, a Profile." 18 *HLS Bulletin* 4 (1966).

Fortas, Abe. "Chief Justice Warren: The Enigma of Leadership." 88 *Yale LJ* 405 (1975).

————. "Dangers to the Rule of Law." 54 ABA *Journal* 957 (1968).

Frady, Marshall. *Wallace.* New York, 1968.

Frank, John P. "Affirmative Opinion on Justice Warren." NYT, Oct. 3, 1954, vi, 17.

————. *Cases and Materials on Constitutional Law.* Chicago, 1952.

————. *Cases on the Constitution.* New York, 1951.

————. "Hugo L. Black." *New Republic,* Oct. 9, 1971, 15.

————. *Mr. Justice Black: The Man and His Opinions.* New York, 1949.

————. *My Son's Story.* New York, 1951.

————. *The Warren Court.* New York, 1964.

Frankfurter, Felix. *Mr. Justice Holmes and the Supreme Court.* New York, 1965.

Freund, Paul A. "To Amend—or Not to Amend—the Constitution." NYT, Dec. 13, 1965, vi, 117.

————. "Why We Need the National Court of Appeals." 59 ABA *Journal* 247 (1973).

Friedman, Leon. *The Justices of the United States Supreme Court 1969–1978* (vol. 5 of Friedman and Israel, below), New York, 1978.

————, and Fred L. Israel. *The Justices of the United States Supreme Court 1789–1969,* vols. 3 and 4. New York, 1969.

Friendly, Henry J. "The Bill of Rights as a Code of Criminal Procedure." 53 *California LR* 929 (1965).

————. "The Fifth Amendment Tomorrow: The Case of Constitutional Change." 37 *University of Cincinnati LR* 671 (1968).

Furstenburg, Frank F., Jr. "Public Reaction to Crime in the Streets." 40 *The American Scholar* 601 (1971).

Galie, Peter J. "State Constitutional Guarantees and Protection of Defendants' Rights: The Case of New York, 1960–1978." 28 *Buffalo LR* 157 (1979).

Gilbert, Brian. "The Irony of the Peters Case." *New Republic,* June 13, 1955, 11.

Glueck, Sheldon. *Crime and Justice.* Cambridge, Mass., 1945.

Goldberg, Arthur J. "Equal Justice for the Poor, Too." NYT, March 15, 1964, vi, 24.

Goldwater, Barry. *The Conscience of a Conservative.* New York, 1960.

————. *With No Apologies.* New York, 1979.

Goodman, Walter. *The Committee.* New York, 1968.

Goulden, Joseph C. *The Benchwarmers.* New York, 1974.

————. *The Super Lawyers.* New York, 1971.

Graham, Fred P. "Low-Key and Liberal." NYT, April 2, 1967, vi, 30.

————. "The Many-Sided Justice Fortas." NYT, June 4, 1967, vi, 26.

————. *The Self-Inflicted Wound.* New York, 1970.

Greenberg, Jack. *Race Relations and American Law.* New York, 1959.

Gressman, Eugene. "The National Court of Appeals: A Dissent." 59 ABA *Journal* 253 (1973).

Gunther, John. *Inside USA.* New York, 1951.

Hand, Learned. *The Bill of Rights.* Cambridge, Mass., 1958.

Harlan, John M. "Thoughts at a Dedication: Keeping the Judicial Function in Balance." 49 ABA *Journal* 194 (1963).

Harris, Richard. "Crime in New York." *New Yorker,* Sept. 26, 1977, 56.

————. *The Fear of Crime.* New York, 1969.

————. *Freedom Spent.* New York, 1976.

————. *Justice.* London, 1960.

————. "Reflections: The New Justice." *New Yorker,* March 25, 1972, 44.

Howard, A. E. Dick. "Mr. Justice Powell and the Emerging Nixon Majority." 70 *Michigan LR* 445 (1972).

————. *The Road from Runnymede.* Charlottesville, Va., 1968.

————. "State Courts and Constitutional Rights in the Day of the Burger Court." 62 *Virginia LR* 873 (1976).

Hughes, Charles Evans. *The Supreme Court of the United States.* New York, 1966.

Bibliography and Source Notes

Hugo Black and the Bill of Rights. Proceedings of the Hugo Black Symposium on "The Bill of Rights and American Democracy." Ed. Virginia van der Veer Hamilton. University, Ala., 1978.

Huston, Luther. *The Department of Justice.* New York, 1967.

Inbau, Fred E., Marvin E. Aspen, and Frank Carrington. *Evidence Law for the Police.* Philadelphia, 1972.

Inbau, Fred E., and John E. Reid. *Criminal Interrogation and Confessions.* Baltimore, 1962.

———. *Criminal Interrogation and Confessions.* Baltimore, 1967.

"Interrogations in New Haven: The Impact of *Miranda.*" 76 *Yale LJ* 1519 (1967).

Jackson, George. *Soledad Brother.* New York, 1970.

Jenkins, Herbert. *Keeping the Peace.* New York, 1970.

Jenkins, Ray. "George Wallace Figures to Win Even If He Loses." *NYT,* April 7, 1968, vi, 26.

———. "The Queen of Alabama and the Prince Consort." *NYT,* May 21, 1967, vi, 26.

Johnson, Claudia T. *A White House Diary.* New York, 1970.

Johnson, Lyndon Baines. *The Vantage Point.* New York, 1971.

Kamisar, Yale. *Basic Criminal Procedure.* St. Paul, Minn., 1980.

———. *Criminal Procedure.* St. Paul, Minn., 1981.

———. *Police Interrogations and Confessions.* Ann Arbor, Mich., 1980.

———. "When the Cops Were Not 'Handcuffed.' " *NYT,* Nov. 7, 1965, vi, 34.

Katcher, Leo. *Earl Warren: A Political Biography.* New York, 1967.

Katzenbach, Nicholas deB. "Law and Order. Has the Supreme Court Gone Too Far?" *Look,* Oct. 29, 1968, 27.

Kaufman, Irving R. "*Miranda* and the Police. The Confessions Debate Continues." *NYT,* Oct. 2, 1966, vi, 37.

———. "The Supreme Court and Its Critics." *Atlantic Monthly,* Dec. 1963, 47.

———. "The Uncertain Criminal Law: Rights, Wrongs, and Doubts." *Atlantic Monthly,* Jan. 1965, 61.

Kilpatrick, James J. "What Makes Wallace Run?" *National Review,* April 18, 1967, 400.

Kluger, Richard. *Simple Justice.* New York, 1975.

Knebel, Fletcher. "A Visit with Justice Brennan." *Look,* Dec. 18, 1962, 127.

Kurland, Philip B. *Politics, the Constitution and the Warren Court.* Chicago, 1970.

———. "The Court Should Decide Less and Explain More." *NYT,* June 9, 1968, vi, 34.

———. "Enter the Burger Court: The Constitutional Business of the Supreme Court, O.T. 1969." *Supreme Court Review,* 1970, 1.

———. "The Lord Chancellor of the United States." *Trial Magazine,* Nov./Dec. 1971, 11.

———. "1970 Term: Notes on the Emergence of the Burger Court." *Supreme Court Review,* 1971, 265.

———. "1971 Term: The Year of the Stewart-White Court." *Supreme Court Review,* 1972, 181.

Lachicotte, Alberta M. *Rebel Senator. Strom Thurmond of South Carolina.* New York, 1966.

Lambert, William. "The Justice . . . and the Stock Manipulator." *Life,* May 9, 1969, 32.

Levy, Leonard W. *Against the Law.* New York, 1974.

———. *Origins of the Fifth Amendment.* New York, 1968.

Lewin, Nathan. "Avoiding the Supreme Court." *NYT,* Oct. 17, 1976, vi, 31.

———. "Justice Harlan: 'The Full Measure of the Man.' " 58 *ABA Journal* 579 (1972).

———. "A Peculiar Sense of Justice." *Saturday Review,* May 28, 1977, 15.

Lewis, Anthony. *Gideon's Trumpet.* New York, 1966.

———. "Historic Changes in the Supreme Court." *NYT,* June 17, 1962, vi, 7.

———. "Justice Black at 75: Still the Dissenter." *NYT,* Feb. 26, 1961, vi, 13.

———. "A Man Born to Act, Not to Muse." *NYT,* June 30, 1968, vi, 9.

———. "New Look at the Chief Justice." *NYT,* Jan. 19, 1964, vi, 9.

———. "Nine Very Human Men." *NYT,* Jan. 17, 1965, vi, 18.

———. "Our Extraordinary Solicitor General." *The Reporter,* May 5, 1955, 27.

———. "A Talk with Warren on Crime, the Court, the Country." *NYT,* Oct. 19, 1969, vi, 34.

Liebman, Lance. "Swing Man on the Supreme Court." *NYT,* Oct. 8, 1972, vi, 16.

Linde, Hans A. "First Things First: Rediscovering the States' Bill of Rights." 9 *University of Baltimore LR* 379 (1980).

Bibliography and Source Notes

Lipset, Seymour Martin. "Why Cops Hate Liberals—and Vice Versa." *Atlantic Monthly*, March 1969, 76.

Lumbard, J. Edward. "John Harlan: in Public Service 1925–1971." 85 *Harvard LR* 372 (1971).

Mason, Alpheus Thomas. "The Supreme Court Under Fire Again." *The Reporter*, Sept. 24, 1964, 45.

———. "The Warren Court and the Bill of Rights." *Yale Review*, winter 1967, 197.

———. "Understanding the Warren Court: Judicial Restraint and Judicial Duty." *Political Science Quarterly*, Dec. 1966, 523.

McDonald, Donald. "A Center Report/Criminal Justice." *The Center Magazine*, Nov. 1968, 69.

McGinniss, Joe. *The Selling of the President 1968*. New York, 1969.

McWilliams, Carey. *California: The Great Exception*. Santa Barbara, 1976.

———. "The Education of Earl Warren." *Nation*, Oct. 12, 1974, 325.

Meador, Daniel J. *Mr. Justice Black and His Books*. Charlottesville, Va., 1974.

———. *Preludes to Gideon*. Charlottesville, Va., 1967.

Medalie, Richard J. *From Escobedo to Miranda*. Washington, D.C., 1966.

———, Leonard Zeitz, and Paul Alexander. "Custodial Police Interrogation in Our Nation's Capital: The Attempt to Implement *Miranda*." 66 *Michigan LR* 1347 (1968).

Miller, Arthur S. "Lord Chancellor Warren Earl Burger." *Society*, March/April 1973, 18.

Milner, Neal. *The Court and Local Law Enforcement*. Beverly Hills, Cal., 1971.

Miranda, Ernest. "A Client Speaks Out." Undated, unnotated, but obviously published article from Miranda's last parole officer's files.

Mitchell, John N. "Bail Reform and the Constitutionality of Pretrial Detention." 55 *Virginia LR* 1223 (1969).

Morrison, Donald M. "Apostle of Justice." *The Pennsylvania Gazette*, Oct. 1977, 17.

Murphy, Patrick V. *Commissioner*. New York, 1977.

Murphy, Walter F. *Congress and the Court*. Chicago, 1962.

——— and C. Herman Pritchett. *Courts, Judges, and Politics*. New York, 1974.

Navasky, Victor S. *Kennedy Justice*. New York, 1971.

"The New Federalism: Toward a Principled Interpretation of the State Constitution." 29 *Stanford LR* 297 (1977).

Nixon, Richard M. *The Memoirs of Richard Nixon*. New York, 1978.

———. *Six Crises*. Garden City, N.Y., 1962.

———. "What Has Happened to America?" *Reader's Digest*, Oct. 1967, 49.

Oberdorfer, Don. "Ex-Democrat, Ex-Dixiecrat, Today's Nixiecrat." *NYT*, Oct. 6, 1968, vi, 36.

"The One Hundred and First Justice: An Analysis of the Opinions of Justice John Paul Stevens Sitting as Judge on the Seventh Circuit Court of Appeals." 29 *Vanderbilt LR* 125 (1976).

Paul, John Rodman, and Cyril Norman Hugh Long. *John Punnett Peters*. New York, 1958.

Phillips, Kevin P. *The Emerging Republican Majority*. Garden City, N.Y., 1970.

Pollack, Jack Harrison. *Earl Warren*. Englewood Cliffs, N.J., 1979.

Pope, Walter L. "*Escobedo*, Then *Miranda*, and Now *Johnson v. United States*." 40 F.R.D. 351 (1966).

Porter, Mary Cornelia. "State Supreme Courts and the Legacy of the Warren Court." 8 *Publius* 55 (1978).

Pound, Roscoe. *Criminal Justice in America*. New York, 1972.

Powell, Lewis F., Jr. "Impressions of a New Justice." Virginia Bar Association *Proceedings*, 1972, 217.

———. "Respect for Law and Due Process—the Foundation of a Free Society." 18 *University of Florida LR* 1 (1965).

———. "What the Justices Are Saying." 62 *ABA Journal* 1454 (1976).

———. "What Really Goes On at the Supreme Court." 66 *ABA Journal* 721 (1980).

"Protecting Fundamental Rights in State Courts: Fitting a State Peg to a Federal Hole." 12 *Harvard Civil Rights Civil Liberties LR* 63 (1977).

Rehnquist, William H. "The Bar Admission Cases: A Strange Judicial Aberration." 44 *ABA Journal* 229 (1958).

———. "Chief Justices I Never Knew." 3 *Hastings Constitutional LQ* 637 (1976).

———. "The Making of a Supreme Court Justice." *Harvard Law Record*, Oct. 8, 1959, 7.

———. "The Supreme Court: Past and Present." 59 *ABA Journal* 361 (1973).

Bibliography and Source Notes

————. "Who Writes the Decisions of the Supreme Court?" *U.S. News*, Dec. 13, 1957, 74.

Reichley, A. James. "The Texas Banker Who Bought Politicians." *Fortune*, Dec. 1971, 94.

Reiss, Albert J., Jr. and Donald J. Black. "Interrogation and the Criminal Process." American Academy of Political and Social Science, *Annals*, Nov. 1967, 47.

"Retired Chief Justice Warren Attacks, Chief Justice Burger Defends Freund Study Group's Composition and Proposal." 59 ABA *Journal* 721, (1973).

Reynolds, Quentin. *Courtroom*. New York, 1957.

Richardson, William A. "Chief Justice of the United States or Chief Justice of the Supreme Court of the United States." *New England Historical and Genealogical Register*, vol. 49 (1895), 275.

Ripon Society. *Ripon's Republican Who's Who at Convention '68*. Cambridge, Mass., 1968.

Ritz, Wilfred. "State Criminal Confession Cases: Subsequent Developments in Cases Reversed by the U.S. Supreme Court and Some Current Problems." 19 *Washington and Lee LR* 202 (1962).

————. "Twenty-five Years of State Criminal Cases in the U.S. Supreme Court." 19 *Washington and Lee LR* 35 (1962).

Rodell, Fred. "The Complexities of Mr. Justice Fortas." *NYT*, July 28, 1968, vi, 12.

————. "It Is the Earl Warren Court." *NYT*, March 13, 1966, vi, 30.

Rosenbloom, David Lee. *The Election Men*. New York, 1973.

Roth, Jeffrey A., and Paul B. Wice. *Pretrial Release and Misconduct in the District of Columbia*. Washington, D.C., 1978.

Rovere, Richard. *The Goldwater Caper*. New York, 1965.

Safire, William. *Before the Fall*. Garden City, N.Y., 1975.

Scammon, Richard M., and Ben J. Wattenberg. *The Real Majority*. New York, 1970.

Schaefer, Roger C. "Patrolman Perspectives on *Miranda*." 1971 *Law and the Social Order*, 81.

Schaefer, Walter V. "Is the Adversary System Working in Optimal Fashion?" 70 F.R.D. 79, 159 (1976).

————. *The Suspect and Society*. Evanston, Ill., 1967.

Schiller, Andrew. "People in Trouble." *Harper's*, April 1964, 145.

Schlesinger, Arthur M., Jr. *Robert Kennedy and His Times*. New York, 1978.

————, and Fred L. Israel, eds. *History of American Presidential Elections, 1789–1968*, vol. 4. New York, 1971.

Schrock, Thomas S., Robert C. Welsh, and Ronald K. L. Collins. "Interrogational Rights: Reflections on *Miranda* v. *Arizona*." 52 *Southern California LR* 1 (1978).

Scott, George M. "The Career Prosecutor Looks at Crime and the Court." CCJ, *Proceedings*, 1968, 27.

Seeburger, Richard H., and R. Stanton Wettrick, Jr. "*Miranda* in Pittsburgh—A Statistical Study." 29 *University of Pittsburgh LR* 1 (1967).

Seymour, Whitney North, Jr. *United States Attorney*. New York, 1975.

Shapiro, David L. "Mr. Justice Rehnquist: A Preliminary View." 90 *Harvard LR* 293 (1976).

Sherrill, Robert. *Gothic Politics in the Deep South*. New York, 1968.

Shogan, Robert. *A Question of Judgment*. Indianapolis, 1972.

Silberman, Charles E. *Criminal Violence, Criminal Justice*. New York, 1980.

Silverman, Barry. "Ernesto Miranda: A Friend's Remembrance of His Life and Hard Times." *The Devil's Advocate*, March 1976, 1.

Silverstein, Lee. *Defense of the Poor in Criminal Cases in American State Courts*, vols. 1–3. Chicago, 1965.

Simon, James F. *In His Own Image*. New York, 1973.

————. *Independent Journey*. New York, 1980.

Sobel, Nathan R. "The Exclusionary Rule in the Law of Confessions." *New York LJ*, Nov, 22, 1965, 1.

Steele, John L. "Haynsworth v. the U.S. Senate (1969)." *Fortune*, March 1970, 90.

Steinberg, Harris B. "The Defense Counsel Looks at Crime and the Courts." CCJ, *Proceedings*, 1968, 34.

Stewart, Potter. "The Nine of Us: Guardians of the Constitution." 41 *Florida Bar Journal* 1090 (1967).

Stone, Geoffrey R. "The *Miranda* Doctrine in the Burger Court." *Supreme Court Review*, 1977, 99.

Bibliography and Source Notes

Swindler, William F. "The Chief Justice and Law Reform, 1921–1971." *Supreme Court Review,* 1971, 241.

———. *Court and Constitution in the 20th Century,* vols. 1 and 2. New York, 1970, 1974.

———. "The Court, the Constitution, and Chief Justice Burger." 27 *Vanderbilt LR* 443 (1974).

Tamm, Edward A., and Paul C. Reardon. "Warren E. Burger and the Administration of Justice." 1981 *Brigham Young LR,* 447.

Taylor, Telford. *Two Studies in Constitutional Interpretation.* Columbus, Ohio, 1969.

Thompson, James R. "Detention After Arrest and In-Custody Investigation: Some Exclusionary Principles." 1966 *University of Illinois Law Forum,* 390.

Thurmond, J. Strom. *The Faith We Have Not Kept.* San Diego, 1968.

Totenberg, Nina. "Behind the Marble, Beneath the Robes." *NYT,* March 16, 1975, vi, 15.

Traynor, Roger J. "The Devils of Due Process in Criminal Detection, Detention, and Trial." 33 *University of Chicago LR* 657 (1966).

United States Court of Appeals for the District of Columbia Circuit. *History of the United States Court of Appeals for the District of Columbia Circuit in the Country's Bicentennial Year.* Washington, D.C., 1977.

Valentine, Lewis J. *Night Stick.* New York, 1947.

Van Allen, Edward J. *Our Handcuffed Police.* Mineola, N.Y., 1968.

Viorst, Milton. "Attorney General Mitchell's Philosophy Is 'The Justice Department Is an Institution for Law Enforcement, Not Social Improvement.'" *NYT,* Aug. 10, 1969, vi, 10.

Vorenberg, James. "A.L.I. Approves Model Code of Pre-Arraignment Procedure." 61 *ABA Journal* 1213 (1975).

———, and James Q. Wilson. "Is the Court Handcuffing the Cops?" *NYT,* May 11, 1969, vi, 32.

Warren, Earl. "Address." 14 *Santa Clara Lawyer* 740 (1974).

———. "Administration of Justice." CCJ, *Proceedings,* 1968, 1.

———. "The Advocate and the Administration of Justice in an Urban Society." 47 *Texas LR* 615 (1969).

———. "Cooperation Between Police and District Attorneys." 15 *The Police Journal,* May 1928, 14.

———. "Dedication of the John Sherman Myers Building, American University." 14 *American University LR* 117 (1965).

———. "The Law and the Future." *Fortune,* Nov. 1955, 106.

———. "Law, Lawyers, and Ethics." 23 *DePaul LR* 633 (1974).

———. "Let's Not Weaken the Supreme Court." 60 *ABA Journal* 677 (1974).

———. *The Memoirs of Chief Justice Earl Warren.* Garden City, N.Y., 1977.

———. "Notre Dame Law School Civil Rights Lectures." 48 *Notre Dame Lawyer* 14 (1972).

———. "Organizing the Community to Combat Crime." *Proceedings of the Attorney General's Conference on Crime,* 321.

———. "The Place of the County in the Administration of Criminal Law." 2 *Federal Bar Association Journal* 195 (1935).

———. *A Republic If You Can Keep It.* New York, 1972.

———. "A Response to Recent Proposals to Dilute the Jurisdiction of the Supreme Court." 20 *Loyola LR* 222 (1974).

———. "Responsibilities of the Legal Profession." 26 *Maryland LR* 103 (1966).

———. "A State Department of Justice." 21 *ABA Journal* 311 (1935).

———. "What's Wrong with Law Enforcement?" 12 *Tax Digest* 370 (1934).

Watson, Nelson A., and James W. Sterling. *Police and Their Opinions.* Washington, D.C., 1969.

Weaver, John D. *Warren: The Man, the Court, the Era.* Boston, 1967.

Weaver, Warren, Jr. "Mr. Justice Rehnquist, Dissenting." *NYT,* Oct. 13, 1974, vi, 36.

Weinstein, Allen. *Perjury.* New York, 1978.

White, G. Edward. *Earl Warren: A Public Life.* New York, 1982.

White, Theodore F. *Breach of Faith.* New York, 1975.

———. *The Making of the President 1964.* New York, 1965.

———. *The Making of the President 1968.* New York, 1969.

———. *The Making of the President 1972.* New York, 1973.

Bibliography and Source Notes

White, William S. *Citadel.* New York, 1956.
Wilkes, Donald E., Jr. "More on the New Federalism in Criminal Procedure." 63 *Kentucky LJ* 873 (1975).
———. "The New Federalism in Criminal Procedure: State Court Evasion of the Burger Court." 62 *Kentucky LJ* 421 (1974).
Wilkinson, J. Harvie, III. *Serving Justice.* New York, 1974.
Wilson, Jerry. *Police Report.* Boston, 1975.
Wishman, Seymour. *Confessions of a Criminal Lawyer.* New York, 1981.
Witcover, Jules. "The Availability of Richard Nixon." *The Reporter,* Aug. 11, 1966, 27.
———. "George Wallace Isn't Kidding." *The Reporter,* Feb. 23, 1967, 23.
———. *The Resurrection of Richard Nixon.* New York, 1970.
Wolfstone, Gary L. "*Miranda*—a Survey of Its Impact." 7 *The Prosecutor* 26 (1971).
Woodward, Bob, and Scott Armstrong. *The Brethren.* New York, 1979.
Wooten, James. *Dasher.* New York, 1978.
Wren, Lawrence T. "*Miranda* Years: Another Decade?" *Trial Magazine,* July 1977, 45.
Wright, Alfred. "A Modest All-American Who Sits on the Highest Bench." *Sports Illustrated,* Dec. 10, 1962, 85.
Wright, J. Skelly. "The Courts Have Failed the Poor." *NYT,* March 9, 1969, vi, 26.
———. "Crime in the Streets and the New McCarthyism." *New Republic,* Oct. 9, 1965, 10.
———. "The New Role of Defense Counsel under *Escobedo* and *Miranda.*" 52 *ABA Journal* 1117 (1966).
Younger, Evelle J. "Interrogation of Criminal Defendants—Some Views on *Miranda.*" 35 *Fordham LR* 255 (1966).
———. "Prosecution Problems." 53 *ABA Journal* 695 (1967).
Zeisel, Hans. "Crime and Law-and-Order." 40 *The American Scholar,* 1971, 624.
Ziegler, Donald E. "Constitutional Rights of the Accused—Developing Dichotomy Between Federal and State Law." 48 *Pennsylvania Bar Association Quarterly* 241 (1977).
Zion, Sidney. "A Decade of Constitutional Revision." *NYT,* Nov. 11, 1979, vi, 26.
———. "The Suspect Confesses—But Who Believes HIM?" *NYT,* May 16, 1965, vi, 20.
———. "Thurgood Marshall Takes a New 'Tush-Tush' Job." *NYT,* Aug. 22, 1965, vi, 11.

SOURCE NOTES

Book 1/Ernest Miranda's Book

Chapter 1

page
3   *The Longest Day:* AR, March 2, 1963, 41
3–5   The account of events from 11:15 P.M. March 2 through the arrival of a Phoenix police officer at Lois Ann Jameson's home at 2:08 A.M. March 3 was assembled from the reports of Phoenix police for March 3, 1963, in EM-mss, ASA; the trial testimony of the victim, her sister, Police Officers Cooley and Young, Tr-MC; and Silverman, "Ernesto," 1.
5   Statistics of rape: FBI, *UCR* 1963, 80; 1962, 71; 1958, 41; 1964, 81; 1970, 92.
5–8   The account of the police investigation was assembled from the reports of Phoenix police for March 3, March 7, March 14, March 16, 1963, in EM-mss, ASA; Arizona v. Miranda, 104 Ariz. 174, 177 (1969); Silverman, "Ernesto," 3.
8   Although the shame . . . difficult to convince: See National League of Cities, *Rape,* 10; Vera Institute of Justice, *Felony Arrests,* 42–52; Silberman, *Criminal Violence,* 23.
8–9   The account of the investigation which led police to Miranda was assembled from police reports of March 14, 1963, EM-mss, ASA; Arizona v. Miranda, 104 Ariz. 174, 177 (1969); Silverman, "Ernesto," 3.
9–12   Ernest Miranda's background: Except for the events in Nashville, Tennessee, on pp. 10–11, which were related to the author in a letter of January 24, 1980, by Miranda's court-appointed lawyer, who preferred to remain anonymous, the events of

Miranda's past were culled from the reports of psychiatrists Leo Rubinow (June 4, 1963) and James M. Kilgore (May 28, 1963), EM-mss, ASA; Silverman, "Ernesto," 2–3; AR, Nov. 1, 1972, C 10.

12   Miranda's apprehension: AR, Feb. 2, 1976, 1; ADS, Feb. 23, 1973, 16.

12   "There are three kinds of people here . . .": Schiller, "People," 145.

12   The line-up: photograph in Barry Silverman's files; John J. Flynn to author; police reports of March 14, 1963, EM-mss, ASA.

12   Constitutional protections of the courtroom: See U.S. Constitution, Amendments 5 and 6; Arizona constitution, Article 2, Sections 10 and 24.

12n.   FBI practice: letter, FBI spokesman to author, May 3, 1979.

12   "mansion . . .": Kamisar, Police Interrogation, 31–32.

12–13   "Do you intend . . . to array . . .": Bakken, "The Arizona Constitutional," 7.

13   "the better and safer course": Wagner v. Arizona, 43 Ariz. 560, 562 (1934).

13   Miranda's interrogation: Miranda v. Arizona petition for certiorari, May 20, 1969, 3 (denied, 396 U.S. 868, 1969), U.S. Supreme Court, Records, NA; Tr-MC, 37–40; AR, Feb. 2, 1976, 4; ADS, Feb. 23, 1973, 16.

14   Miranda's confession: Witness/suspect statement, EM-mss, ASA.

15   General direction of state legislation: Association of the Bar of the City of New York, Equal Justice, 98–111.

15   Provision for counsel at trial stage: Betts v. Brady, 316 U.S. 455, 477 ff. (appendix) (1942).

15   Gideon v. Wainwright, 372 U.S. 335 (1963).

15   Roundup of state provisions for counsel: Association of the Bar of the City of New York, Equal Justice, 98–111.

15   "upon request of the defendant . . .": West's Annotated California Codes, Government Code, Section 2706.

15   "If the rights of the defendant . . .": Association of the Bar of the City of New York, Equal Justice, 60.

15–16   Allen Committee: Attorney General's Committee on Poverty, Report, Feb. 25, 1963, 44–45; NYT, March 7, 1963, 5 (western edition), March 9, 1963, 1, 4; Harris, Justice, 60.

16   Ford Foundation grant to ALI: NYT, April 22, 1963, 30.

16   "of greatest tension . . .": ALI, Proceedings, 1963, 53.

17   "it is problematical . . .": Inbau and Reid, Criminal Interrogation, 1962, 164–65.

17   The further interrogations, booking, and arraignment of Miranda: Miranda v. Arizona, petition for certiorari, May 20, 1969, 3–4 (denied, 396 U.S. 868, 1969), in U.S. Supreme Court, Records, NA; reports of Phoenix police, March 21, 1963, and undated, EM-mss, ASA; Arizona v. Miranda, 98 Ariz. 11, 14 (1965); AR, March 14, 1963, 2; ADS, Feb. 23, 1973, 1 B.

17–18   Alvin Moore's background: Moore to author.

18   The quality of the criminal defense bar: Bazelon, "Defective," 7–14.

18   Moore's fees for Miranda's defense: Moore to author.

18   What fees criminal lawyers got . . . ill-prepared: Bazelon, "Defective," 10–16.

19   Columbia University Law School curriculum: Columbia University Law School Announcement, 1963–68.

19   "[I]t is hard to see how students . . .": Frank, Warren Court, 114.

19   "I did not desire . . ."; "Someone has to do it . . .": Capote, In Cold Blood, 257.

19–20   Alvin Moore's background: Moore to author.

20   "as an attorney, and as a father . . .": Tr-MC, 55.

20   Alvin Moore's background: Moore to author.

20–21   The insanity plea in Miranda's case: Moore to author; records and reports in EM-mss, ASA.

21–24   Miranda's trial: Tr-MC, 10–70; AR, June 21, 1963, 9; Moore to author.

24n.   Establishment of Arizona State Court of Appeals: 96 Arizona vii; 97 Arizona xxiv.

24–25   "Was this statement made voluntarily . . .": brief for Ernest Miranda, microfilm number Cr 1394, EM-mss, ASA.

Bibliography and Source Notes

Chapter 2

26   "least dangerous"; Alexander Hamilton, *The Federalist*, No. 78.

27   The final day of the 1963 term: *NYT*, June 23, 1964, 1.

27   For some of the most criticized Warren Court decisions, see Brown v. Board of Education of Topeka, Kansas, 347 U.S. 483 (1954); Baker v. Carr, 369 U.S. 186 (1962); Watkins v. United States, 354 U.S. 178 (1957); Yates v. United States, 356 U.S. 363 (1958); Sweezy v. New Hampshire, 354 U.S. 234 (1957); Pennsylvania v. Nelson, 350 U.S. 497 (1956); Mallory v. United States, 354 U.S. 449 (1957); Mapp v. Ohio, 367 U.S. 643 (1961).

27   Congressional retaliation: *CR* 109, 8755–56; *CR* 110, 9509–10; *Newsweek*, May 4, 1964, 19; *CQ, Guide*, 663.

27   Judge Learned Hand: Hand, *Bill of Rights*, particularly 73.

27   Conference of Chief Justices: *CR* 104, A7782–88.

27   American Bar Association: Warren, *Memoirs*, 322–25.

27   National Association of Attorneys General: NAAG, *Conference Proceedings*, 1957, 153–54.

27   International Association of Chiefs of Police, the American Legion: Walker F. Murphy, *Congress and the Courts*, 119–20.

27   Omaha Women's Club: *CR* 106, A2319.

28   1963 term: Reynolds v. Sims, 377 U.S. 533 (1964); Baggett v. Bullitt, 377 U.S. 360 (1964); Griffin v. School Board of Prince Edward County, 377 U.S. 218 (1964).

28   Decisions of June 22, 1964: Griffin v. Maryland, 378 U.S. 130; Fallen v. United States, 378 U.S. 139; Bouie v. City of Columbia, 378 U.S. 347; Bell v. Maryland, 378 U.S. 226; Aptheker v. Secretary of State, 378 U.S. 500; Jacobellis v. Ohio, 378 U.S. 184; see *Jacobellis* at 197 for Stewart's "But I know it. . . ."

28–30   The details of the crime and interrogation have been assembled from *Escobedo*; Kurland, *Landmark*, v. 59, 589–90; description of Chicago police headquarters from Schiller, "People," 145.

30–31   Barry Kroll's background and involvement in *Escobedo*: Kroll to author.

31   Lawyers who argued before the Supreme Court: Caspar, *Lawyers Before*; "casuals," 107.

31   Briefing *Escobedo*: Kroll to author; Escobedo v. Illinois, 375 U.S. 902 (1963); Kurland, *Landmark*, v. 59, 588–95.

31–32   Oral argument of *Escobedo*: Kurland, *Landmark*, v. 59, 744, 777.

33   Goldberg's Supreme Court record: See Cleary v. Bolger, 371 U.S. 392 (1963); Townsend v. Sain, 372 U.S. 293 (1963); Draper v. Washington, 372 U.S. 487 (1963); Haynes v. Washington, 373 U.S. 503 (1963); Ker v. California, 374 U.S. 23 (1963); Malloy v. Hogan, 378 U.S. 1 (1964).

33   Goldberg's opinion: *Escobedo*, 488–91.

34   Criminal cases criticized by law enforcement: See, for example, Mallory v. United States, 354 U.S. 449 (1957); Mapp v. Ohio, 367 U.S. 643 (1961); Massiah v. United States, 377 U.S. 201 (1964); Malloy v. Hogan, 378 U.S. 1 (1964).

34   "fight by Marquis of Queensberry rules . . .": *NYT*, May 14, 1965, 39.

34   "Some day, I guess, the Court . . .": *NYT*, March 21, 1965, 61.

35   "is an appeal to the brooding spirit": Hughes, *The Supreme Court*, 68.

35   "ill-conceived . . .": *Escobedo*, 493.

35   Records of the dissenters: The full *Escobedo* Court had been together for two terms, 1962 and 1963 (vols. 370–78 of *United States Reports*). It had decided ten cases involving confessions, all in favor of criminal defendants, Gallegos v. Colorado, 370 U.S. 49 (1962); Cleary v. Bolger, 371 U.S. 392 (1963); Wong Sun v. United States, 371 U.S. 471 (1963); Townsend v. Sain, 372 U.S. 293 (1963); Fay v. Noia, 372 U.S. 391 (1963); Lynum v. Illinois, 372 U.S. 528 (1963); Haynes v. Washington, 373 U.S. 503 (1963); Massiah v. United States, 377 U.S. 201 (1964); Malloy v. Hogan, 378 U.S. 1 (1964); Jackson v. Denno, 378 U.S. 368 (1964); Justices Harlan, Stewart, and Clark dissented in eight of these cases.

35   "converts a routine police investigation . . .": *Escobedo*, 494

35   "naive" . . . to think "the new constitutional right . . .": *Escobedo*, 495.

Bibliography and Source Notes

Chapter 3

37   Nixon by the fire: Nixon, *Memoirs*, 265; Theodore H. White, *Making . . . 1968*, 43–44.
38   New York City lawyer: Theodore H. White, *Making . . . 1968*, 43–44; Donovan, "Over-Nominated, 14; *NYT*, Dec. 19, 1963, 1, 18; Witcover, "Availability," 28–29.
38   "there was no other life . . .": Nixon, *Memoirs*, 265.
39   Crime rates: FBI, *UCR*, 1962, 1; 1963, 6; 1964, 1.
40   "Let us not be guilty . . .": RNC, *Official Report*, 1964, 186.
40   "do all I can . . .": *NYT*, July 17, 1964, 11.
40   "Security from domestic violence . . .": RNC, *Official Report*, 1964, 414.
40   Kleindienst's suggestion: U.S. Congress, Committee on the Judiciary, "Nominations of Richard Kleindienst . . .", Jan. 29, 1969, 2.
40   September 3 . . .: *NYT*, Sept. 4, 1964, 12.
40   September 11 . . . : *WP*, Sept. 12, 1964, A6.
40–41   September 15 . . . : "Campaign Speech at Al Lang Field," DNC-NA.
41   September 16 . . . : *NYT*, Sept. 17, 1964, 28.
41   September 29 . . . : *NYT*, Sept. 30, 1964, 28.
41   Johnson's campaign: OHPs, Hubert H. Humphrey, Interview II, and Joseph Rauh, LBJ; Murphy, *Congress and the Courts*, 260–61; president's public statements on crime—see especially his "Special Message to the Congress on the Needs of the Nation's Capital," Feb. 15, 1965, *PPP*, 1965, 1888–90; "Special Message to Congress on Law Enforcement . . .", March 8, 1965, *PPP*, 1965, 263–71; Lyndon B. Johnson, *Vantage*, 334–36.
41   "ultimatum diplomacy": Rovere, *Goldwater*, 179.
41–42   Johnson's campaign and win: Theodore H. White, *Making . . . 1964*, 384; Schlesinger and Israel, *History*, v. 4, 3588–90; *Newsweek*, Nov. 9, 1964, 25–39; *Time*, Nov. 4, 1964, 3–14.
42   "People react to fear . . .": Safire, *Before*, 8.
43   J. Strom Thurmond: Dent, *Prodigal*, 64–66; Lachicotte, *Strom*, 229–44; Chester, Hodgson, Page, *American*, 477; Witcover, *Resurrection*, 309; *WP*, March 6, 1982, A2.
43–44   Nixon's disinclination to run in 1964: Nixon, *Memoirs*, 259–63; Theodore H. White, *Making . . . 1968*, 48–49; Witcover, *Resurrection*, 95–96; Schlesinger and Israel, *History*, v. 4, 3711.
44   "extreme state of disarray"; "a significant advantage . . .": Nixon, *Memoirs*, 264.
45   "I started not only to think seriously . . .": Nixon, *Memoirs*, 265.
45   "Dick . . . I will never forget it . . .": Nixon, *Memoirs*, 266.
45   Spring and summer 1965: Nixon, *Memoirs*, 263–66; Witcover, *Resurrection*, 99–102 and 113–14.

Chapter 4

46   "shocked if the Supreme Court . . .": CCJ, *Proceedings*, 36.
47–48   Bazelon versus Katzenbach: *WS*, Aug. 4, 1965, A 1, A 4.
48   The Whitmore case: Zion, "The Suspect," 30; Gray, *Blue Line*, 77–80; *NYT*, Sept. 10, 1965, 38, and Dec. 2, 1965, 1; *Newsweek*, Feb. 8, 1965, 30–31.
49–50   Miranda's conviction affirmed: Arizona v. Miranda, 98 Ariz. 18, 32–37 (1965).
50n.   Robbery charge: Arizona v. Miranda, 98 Ariz. 11 (1965).
50   "What is the purpose of the right to counsel? . . .": Arizona v. Miranda, 98 Ariz. 18, 35–36 (1965).
50   Reaction of Arizona prosecutors: *AR*, April 23, 1965, 17, 20.
50   Courts which interpreted *Escobedo* narrowly: See United States *ex rel*. Townsend v. Ogilvie, 334 F.2d 837 (7th Cir. 1964); Sturgis v. Maryland, 201 A.2d 681 (1964); Illinois v. Hartgraves, 202 N.E.2d 33 (1964); Wamsley v. (Commonwealth) Virginia, 137 S.E.2d 865 (1964); McQueen v. Maxwell, 201 N.E.2d 701 (1964); Brown v. State, 131 N.W.2d 169 (Wis. 1964).
50   Courts which interpreted *Escobedo* broadly: See United States v. Guerra, 334 F.2d 138 (2d Cir. 1964); People v. Dorado, 398 P.2d 361 (Cal. 1965); Oregon v. Neely,

428

	395 P.2d 557 (Ore. 1964); Commonwealth v. McCarthy, 200 N.E.2d 264 (Mass. 1964); Campbell v. Tennessee, 384 S.W.2d 4 (Tenn. 1964).
50–51	Hoover-Vinson exchange: interagency correspondence, J. Edgar Hoover and F. M. Vinson, Jr., June 14, July 29, Sept. 1, Sept. 10, Oct. 11, Oct. 14, 1965; FBI files.
51	Courts in New Jersey . . . : State v. Smith, 202 A.2d 669 (N.J. 1964).
51	Courts in Pennsylvania . . . : Commonwealth v. Negri, 419 Pa. 117 (1965).
51	U.S. Court of Appeals for the Third Circuit: United States *ex rel.* Russo v. New Jersey, 351 F.2d 429 (1965).
51	Instruction of the New Jersey Supreme Court chief justice: *NYT*, June 9, 1965, 1, 32.
51	"creates a serious problem . . .": Commonwealth v. Negri, 419 Pa. 117, 121 (1965).
51	Washington, D.C., crime statistics: *WP*, June 27, 1965, A 1.
51	Three episodes of crimes: *WP*, July 23, A 3; July 30, A 3; July 31, 1965, A 1.
52	The two ideologically opposed blocs: Goulden, *Benchwarmers*, 253; Morris, *Secondmost*, 199, 294; *NYT*, May 22, 1969, 36.
53	Burger's 1964–65 record: See vols. 118–122, U.S. App. D.C.
53	The eleven *Escobedo* cases: See Jones v. United States, 342 F.2d 863 (1964); Jackson v. United States, 337 F.2d 136 (1964); Greenwell v. United States, 336 F.2d 962 (1964); Johnson v. United States, 344 F.2d 163 (1964); Long v. United States, 338 F.2d 549 (1964); Kennedy v. United States, 353 F.2d 462 (1965); Naples v. United States, 344 F.2d 508 (1964); Williams v. United States, 345 F.2d 733 (1965); Hutcherson v. United States, 351 F.2d 748 (1965); Cephus v. United States, 352 F.2d 663 (1965); Pennewell v. United States, 353 F.2d 870 (1965).
53	"the competing interests . . .": Arizona v. Miranda, 98 Ariz. 18, 35 (1965).
53–54	Warren Burger's background: James C. Otis, Roger G. Kennedy, and Irving Clark to author; State v. Peery, 28 N.W.2d 851 (1947).
54	"rash of sweeping claims . . .": Kennedy v. United States, 353 F.2d 462, 467, 464 (1965).
54	Case of Monte Durham: Durham v. United States, 214 F.2d 862 (1954).
55	"Whether a free choice to do wrong . . .": *NYT*, May 21, 1979, A 20.
55	"welfare criminology": *NYT*, May 21, 1979, A 20.
55–56	"not to be read as rendering inadmissible . . .": Cephus v. United States, 352 F.2d 663, 665 (1965).
56	Most difficult part of the transition: Robert Abendroth to author.
56–57	"We are beginning to realize . . .": Bazelon, "The Concept," 6.
57	Origin of exclusionary rule: Weeks v. United States, 232 U.S. 383 (1914).
57	"That the rule of exclusion . . .": Tate v. United States, 283 F.2d 377, 380, n. 4 (1960).
57	"we can deter Peter . . .": Burger, "External Checks," 128.
57	Burger's lecture: Burger, "Who Will Watch," 14–19, 23.
58	Bazelon/ABA: ABA, *Annual Report*, 1962, 111; 1963, 77; 1964, 96; 1965, 84.
58	Lumbard/*Escobedo*: United States v. Robinson, 354 F.2d 109 (1965); United States v. Cone, 354 F.2d 119 (1965).
58	Burger/ABA: See ABA, *Annual Report*, 1931–65.
58	Search for a chairman: J. Edward Lumbard to author.

Chapter 5

60	Miranda's sense of injustice: John J. Flynn to author.
60	70 percent of petitions dismissed: Brennan, "Justice Brennan Calls," 837.
60–61	Miranda's first petition for cert: Letter, John F. Davis, clerk, to Ernest Miranda, June 18, 1965; U.S. Supreme Court, *Records*, NA.
61	ACLU background: Ennis, "A.C.L.U.," 1080–83.
61	Corcoran's attention to Miranda's case: Robert J. Corcoran to author.
62	Corcoran-Moore correspondence: Robert J. Corcoran to Alvin Moore, June 15, 1965; Robert J. Corcoran to Ernest Miranda, June 24, 1965; Robert J. Corcoran correspondence, Ernest Miranda's case; Alvin Moore to author.
62	Rex Lee's involvement in Miranda's case: Rex E. Lee and Robert J. Corcoran to author.

Bibliography and Source Notes

62–63 Recruitment of John Flynn: Robert J. Corcoran to author.
62–63 Lewis & Roca as a law firm: Monroe G. McKay to author.
63 Costs of Miranda's case: Robert J. Corcoran and John J. Flynn to author.
63 "Your letter . . . has made me very happy . . .": Ernest Miranda to Robert J. Corcoran, July 5, 1965; Robert J. Corcoran correspondence, Ernest Miranda's case.
63 Flynn's courtroom prowess: *AR*, Jan. 31, 1980, 1.
63 AWOL: Frank, "In Cheerful," 1.
63–64 Stumbling into criminal law: John J. Flynn to author.
64 As deputy county attorney: Frank, "In Cheerful," 1.
64 "Muhammed Ali of Arizona . . .": *People*, Sept. 18, 1978, 28.
64 Flynn's stamina, "when he went in for a fight . . .": Frank, "In Cheerful," 4.
64 "It gets to you" . . . "I fought it . . .": John J. Flynn to author.
65 Frank's heroes: Frank, *My Son's Story*, 11–12; Frank, "Hugo Black," 15.
65 Frank's public service: Kluger, *Simple*, 275–76, 535.
65 Frank's interest in appellate work: John P. Frank to author.
65 "This is a damned Fascist outrage": Frank, "Hugo," 15.
66 "To this day I don't know . . .": ALI, *Proceedings*, 1969, 73–74.
67 Failures of state criminal justice systems: NCLOE, *Report on Lawlessness* (No. 11), 55–83.
67–68 "[I]n a capital case . . .": Powell v. Alabama, 287 U.S. 45, 71 (1932).
68n. 1935 Scottsboro case: Norris v. Alabama, 294 U.S. 587 (1935).
68n. Where are they now?: Reynolds, *Courtroom*, 240–303; *NYT*, Oct. 26, 1976, 1, 20; *WP*, July 8, 1977, A 14.
68n. Resolution of *Brown*: Ritz, "State Criminal," 209.
68 "The State is free . . .": Brown v. Mississippi, 297 U.S. 278, 285–86 (1936).
69 "shoot the works clause": Hugo Black, Jr., *Hugo Black*, 259.
69 Black's definitive statements on his judicial philosophy can be found in his dissent to Adamson v. California, 332 U.S. 46, 70 ff. (1947), and *A Constitutional Faith*.
70 "a construction which gives due process . . ."; "they offend . . .": Malinsky v. New York, 324 U.S. 401, 415, 417 (1945).
71 Black's footnoting: See, for example, Chambers v. Florida, 309 U.S. 227, 235–36, n. 8 (1940).
71 "I have never been able . . .": Hugo Black, *A Constitutional*, 36.
71 "I dissented every time . . .": Hugo Black, OHP for LBJ; it was not, however, given to LBJ and survives only in the Black papers, LC.
72 Flynn and Frank disagree: John J. Flynn to author.
72 "sharp factual dispute": Frank, *Cases and Materials*, 767.
72 NAACP interest in cases, shoestring financing: Jack Greenberg to author; letter, S. D. McGill to NAACP publicity dept., Feb. 15, 1940, NAACP papers, LC.
72 Marshall's involvement: See, for example, Lyons v. Oklahoma, 322 U.S. 596 (1944); Taylor v. Alabama, 335 U.S. 252 (1948); telegram, Thurgood Marshall to Leon A. Ransom, Jan. 3, 1939 [*sic*], an obvious error in date, NAACP papers, LC.
73 "We find that a uniform practice . . .": *Birmingham Age-Herald*, Sept. 18, 1915, 5.
73 Results of Black investigation: Frank, *Mr. Justice*, 28–29.
74 Editorial on Black's resignation: *Birmingham Ledger*, Aug. 3, 1917.
74 Between 1940 . . . thirty-six cases: Chambers v. Florida, 309 U.S. 227 (1940); White v. Texas, 310 U.S. 530 (1940); Lisenba v. California, 314 U.S. 219 (1941); Ward v. Texas, 316 U.S. 547 (1942); Lyons v. Oklahoma, 322 U.S. 596 (1944); Malinsky v. New York, 324 U.S. 401 (1945); Haley v. Ohio, 332 U.S. 596 (1948); Lee v. Mississippi, 332 U.S. 742 (1948); Taylor v. Alabama, 335 U.S. 252 (1948); Watts v. Indiana, 338 U.S. 49 (1949); Turner v. Pennsylvania, 338 U.S. 62 (1949); Harris v. South Carolina, 338 U.S. 68 (1949); Gallegos v. Nebraska, 342 U.S. 55 (1951); Stein v. New York, 346 U.S. 156 (1953); Brown v. Allen, 344 U.S. 443 (1953); Stroble v. California, 343 U.S. 181 (1952); Leyra v. Denno, 347 U.S. 556 (1954); Herman v. Claudy, 350 U.S. 116 (1956); Fikes v. Alabama, 352 U.S. 191 (1957); Thomas v. Arizona, 356 U.S. 390 (1958); Payne v. Arkansas, 356 U.S. 560 (1958); Crooker v. California, 357 U.S. 433 (1958); Ashdown v. Utah, 357 U.S. 426 (1958); Spano v. New York, 360 U.S. 315 (1959); Ashcraft v. Tennessee, 322 U.S. 143 (1944); Blackburn v. Alabama, 361 U.S. 199 (1960); Rogers v. Richmond, 365

Bibliography and Source Notes

U.S. 534 (1961); Reck v. Pate, 367 U.S. 433 (1961); Culombe v. Connecticut, 367 U.S. 568 (1961); Gallegos v. Colorado, 370 U.S. 49 (1962); Fay v. Noia, 372 U.S. 391 (1963); Townsend v. Sain, 372 U.S. 293 (1963); Lynum v. Illinois, 372 U.S. 528 (1963); Haynes v. Washington, 373 U.S. 503 (1963); Malloy v. Hogan, 378 U.S. 1 (1964); Jackson v. Denno, 378 U.S. 368 (1964).

74   In 26 . . . in one: Black wrote *Chambers, White, Leyra, Herman, Ashcraft;* he concurred in *Watts, Turner, Harris, Spano, Culombe;* he dissented in *Lisenba, Lyons, Gallegos* (v. *Nebraska*), *Brown, Stein, Stroble, Thomas, Crooker, Ashdown;* he took no part in *Taylor;* he voted with the majority in favor of the criminal defendant in the other twenty-six cases cited above.

74n.   Resolution of Chambers: Ritz, "State Criminal," 210.

74   "there has been a current of opinion . . ."; "the determination to preserve . . ."; "by the argument that law enforcement methods . . ."; Chambers v. Florida, 309 U.S. 227, 235–36 (n. 8), 236, 237, 240–41 (1940).

75   Black's estimate of his *Chambers* opinion: Elizabeth Black, "Hugo Black," 77.

75   Editorial comment and Black's mail re *Chambers:* clippings and correspondence in the papers of Hugo Black, LC.

75   Congressional notice of *Chambers:* CR 86, 730.

75–76   Contemporary methods of arm twisting: confidential sources.

76   Black right to counsel opinions: Johnson v. Zerbst, 304 U.S. 458 (1938); Betts v. Brady, 316 U.S. 455, 474 (1942); Gideon v. Wainwright, 372 U.S. 335 (1963).

76   Black law clerk involvement in right to counsel cases: Hudson v. North Carolina, 363 U.S. 697 (1960); William Joslin; McNeal v. Culver, 365 U.S. 109 (1961), C. Sam Daniels; Chewning v. Cunningham, 368 U.S. 443 (1962), Daniel J. Meador; Carnley v. Cochran, 369 U.S. 506 (1962), Harold A. Ward III; Meador, "Justice Black," 63.

77   Black's 1938 opinion: Johnson v. Zerbst, 304 U.S. 458 (1938).

77   "only one duty . . .": Butler v. United States, 297 U.S. 1, 62 (1936).

77   "while want of counsel" . . . ; "Denial to the poor . . .": Betts v. Brady, 316 U.S. 455, 473, 476 (1942).

78   "an expanding rather than contracting . . .": NYT, Aug. 2, 1942, iv, 6.

78–79   Statistics in state right to counsel cases, 1940–1962: convictions affirmed, 1940–53—Avery v. Alabama, 308 U.S. 444 (1940); Betts v. Brady, 316 U.S. 455 (1942); Canizio v. New York, 327 U.S. 82 (1946); Foster v. Illinois, 332 U.S. 134 (1947); Bute v. Illinois, 333 U.S. 640 (1948); Gryger v. Burke, 334 U.S. 728 (1948); Quicksall v. Michigan, 339 U.S. 660 (1950); convictions reversed, 1940–53—Smith v. O'Grady, 312 U.S. 329 (1941); Williams v. Kaiser, 323 U.S. 471 (1945); Tomkins v. Missouri, 323 U.S. 485 (1945); Rice v. Olson, 324 U.S. 786 (1945); *In re* Oliver, 333 U.S. 257 (1948); Townsend v. Burke, 334 U.S. 736 (1948); Wade v. Mayo, 334 U.S. 672 (1948); Uveges v. Pennsylvania, 335 U.S. 437 (1948); Gibbs v. Burke, 337 U.S. 773 (1949); Palmer v. Ashe, 342 U.S. 134 (1951); Keenan v. Burke, 342 U.S. 881 (1951); Hawk v. Olson, 326 U.S. 271 (1945); convictions affirmed, 1954–62—*In re* Groban, 352 U.S. 330 (1957); Crooker v. California, 357 U.S. 433 (1958); convictions reversed, 1954–62—Chandler v. Warden, 348 U.S. 3 (1954); Massey v. Moore, 348 U.S. 105 (1954); Herman v. Claudy, 350 U.S. 116 (1956); Reece v. Georgia, 350 U.S. 85 (1955); Moore v. Michigan, 355 U.S. 155 (1957); Cash v. Culver, 358 U.S. 633 (1959); Wilde v. Wyoming, 362 U.S. 607 (1960); Hudson v. North Carolina, 363 U.S. 697 (1960); McNeal v. Culver, 365 U.S. 109 (1961); Reynolds v. Cochran, 365 U.S. 525 (1961); Hamilton v. Alabama, 368 U.S. 52 (1961); Chewning v. Cunningham, 368 U.S. 443 (1962); Carnley v. Cochran, 369 U.S. 506 (1962).

79–81   Gideon's case: The details of Gideon have been assembled from Lewis, *Gideon's Trumpet;* Friedman and Israel, *The Justices,* v. 4, 3016–17; 42 F.R.D. 437, 523; Kurland and Caspar, *Landmark,* v. 57, 612 ff.

81   Fortas's hope for unanimity: Abe Fortas to author.

81   "[A] provision of the Bill of Rights . . .": *Gideon,* 342.

81n.   Gideon's later life: NYT, Feb. 12, 1972, 29.

81   Opening prison gates: Fellman, *Defendant's Rights,* 217.

82   All but five of the fifty: *Gideon,* brief for petitioner, 8, R and B.

82   NYT survey: NYT, June 13, 1963, 39.

Bibliography and Source Notes

82   "what happens to these poor . . ."; "there is a right to counsel . . .": Kurland and Caspar, *Landmark*, v. 57, 617, 623–24.

82   "Miranda problem was certainly . . .": Abe Fortas to author.

83   "It seems to me . . .": John P. Frank to author.

83   Flynn/Frank continued disagreement: John J. Flynn to author.

83–85 Petition for certiorari and state's response: Miranda v. Arizona, No. 759, OT 1965, U.S. Supreme Court, *Records*, NA.

Chapter 6

86   "the law is in a state . . .": Commonwealth v. Negri, 419 Pa. 117, 121 (1965).

87   Watching lower-court responses: See Mapp v. Ohio, 367 U.S. 643, 654 (1961).

87   "worming in . . .": John P. Frank to author.

87   *Escobedo* cases to the Court: petitions for certiorari, OT 1965, U.S. Supreme Court, *Records*, NA; Daniel P. Levitt to author.

88   Third Judicial Circuit conference: See 39 F.R.D. 375, 423 ff.

88   "It was a good discussion . . .": "I have an idea . . .": 39 F.R.D. 375, 453, 473, 477.

88–89 "unproductive . . ."; "there is a growing body . . .": *NYT*, Jan. 30, 1965, 1, 24.

89   "Paris just before the Maginot Line . . .": *NYT*, March 21, 1965, 61.

89   Congressional summer of 1965: *NYT*, Aug. 5, 1965, 1, 11; *WP*, Aug. 6, 1965, 1, 8.

90   Fortas's background: See Lewis, *Gideon's*, 48–52; Shogan, *A Question*, 67–71; William O. Douglas, *Go East*, 174.

90–91 Fortas/Johnson 1948 episode: Abe Fortas OHP, 2–4, 6–8, LBJ; Paul Porter OHP, 12–16, LBJ; letter, Hugo Black to Mrs. Carl Hill, Sept. 4, 1968, Hugo Black papers, LC; *NYT*, Sept. 25, 1948, 7, and Sept. 29, 1948, 22; *Time*, June 28, 1948, 14; Shogan, *A Question*, 83–86; White, *Citadel*, 102–05.

91   U.S. Supreme Court decision: Johnson v. Stevenson, 336 U.S. 904 (1948).

91*n.* "That is not really the reason . . .": Paul Porter OHP, 15–16, LBJ.

92   "God almighty . . ."; "Look, you don't suppose . . ."; "Oh, I think . . .": Paul Porter OHP, 29–31, LBJ.

92   "I told him . . .": Lyndon Johnson, *Vantage*, 545.

92   Fortas never said yes: Abe Fortas OHP, 25, LBJ.

92   Special pockets in Eastland's pants: Sherrill, *Gothic*, 210.

92   "Jim Eastland could be standing . . .": Schlesinger, *Robert Kennedy*, 252.

92–94 Questioning of Fortas: U.S. Congress, Senate, Committee on the Judiciary, *Nomination of Abe Fortas*, Aug. 5, 1965, 41–45.

95   Thurmond's speech: *CR* 111, 20054–55.

95–96 Nixon's summer of 1965: *NYT*, Aug. 17, 1965, 52; *WP*, Aug. 1, 1965, A 2; *Newsweek*, Sept. 27, 1965, 27–28; Donovan, "Over-Nominated," 92.

Chapter 7

97   "I'm still not convinced . . .": letter, Abe Fortas to Hugo Black, Feb. 27, 1966; Hugo Black papers, LC.

98   126 cases: petitions for certiorari, OT 1965, U.S. Supreme Court *Records*, NA.

98   Douglas's party: *WP*, Oct. 23, 1965, B 4.

98   Fortas/Wolfson involvement: *NYT*, May 16, 1969, 20; Shogan, *A Question*, 193–96.

98   "love of secrecy . . .": Felix Frankfurter, "Mr. Justice Roberts," in *Of Law and Men* (Hamden, Conn., 1956), 207.

98–103 The general outline of the conference: The most authoritative accounts of the conference and the rules for granting of certiorari are found in Brennan, "State Court Decisions," 393 ff.; Byrnes, *All in One*, 137; Tom C. Clark, "The Supreme Court Conference," 273 ff.

99   "De Lawd Hisself": Leonard Baker, *Back to Back* (New York, 1967), 30.

99   John Marshall Harlan: 409 U.S. xxvii (1972).

99   William J. Brennan: Morrison, "Apostle," 21.

99   "an unusually likeable fellow . . .": letter, John Frank to Hugo Black, Aug. 15, 1946, in Hugo Black papers, LC.

100–101 Some cases more equal than others: Daniel P. Levitt to author.

101   "no two seemed to have . . .": U.S. Congress, Senate, Committee on the Judiciary, *Nomination of Simon E. Sobeloff*, 90.

Bibliography and Source Notes

101   "more a matter of 'feel' . . .": "Retired Chief Justice Warren," 728.

101   Court awareness of criticism: Daniel P. Levitt to author.

101–102 ALI's awaited model code/Vorenberg: Graham, *Self-Inflicted*, 155, 169–70.

101   "It would be disheartening . . .": Friendly, "The Bill of Rights," 929, 954.

102   Chief Justice Warren's late October memo: memorandum to the conference, Oct. 27, 1965, John M. Harlan papers, Seeley G. Mudd Manuscript Library.

102   Postponement of discussion: memorandum to the conference from the chief justice, Nov. 3, 1965, John M. Harlan papers, Seeley G. Mudd Manuscript Library.

102–103 "When an arrest is validly made . . .": United States v. Robinson, 354, F.2d 109, 114, 115 (1965).

103   101 cases: conference list, Monday, Nov. 22, 1965, in John M. Harlan papers, Seeley G. Mudd Manuscript Library.

103   150 "Escobedo" cases: petitions for certiorari, OT 1965, U.S. Supreme Court, *Records*, NA.

103   "part of my idea . . .": *NYT*, July 11, 1974, 35.

103   Hugo Black's expansionist interpretation, Tom Clark's narrow one: John M. Harlan's conference notes, Nov. 22, 1965, in John M. Harlan papers, Seeley G. Mudd Manuscript Library.

103   Fortas's instructions to law clerk: "Memorandum for Dan" from A.F., Daniel P. Levitt's *Miranda* files.

103   "make haste slowly": John M. Harlan's conference notes, Nov. 22, 1965, in John M. Harlan papers, Seeley G. Mudd Manuscript Library.

103   "salient features"; "full and effective warning . . .": *Miranda*, 445.

103   "thrust into an unfamiliar . . ."; "potentiality for compulsion . . ."; "seriously disturbed . . .": *Miranda*, 456–57.

104   "despite the presence . . ."; need for confessions exaggerated: *Miranda*, 481.

104   Carl Calvin Westover's case: Westover v. United States, petition for certiorari, No. 761, OT 1965, U.S. Supreme Court *Records*, NA.

104–105 Michael Vignera's case: Vignera v. New York, petition for certiorari, No. 760, OT 1965, U.S. Supreme Court, *Records*, NA.

105   Sylvester Johnson's and Stanley Cassidy's case: Johnson et al. v. New Jersey, petition for certiorari, No. 762, OT 1965, U.S. Supreme Court *Records*, NA.

105   Roy Allen Stewart's case: note, William O. Douglas to the chief justice, Oct. 6, 1965, and "Memorandum of Mr. Justice Douglas," Nov. 29, 1965, in John M. Harlan papers, Seeley G. Mudd Manuscript Library; California v. Stewart, 400 P.2d 97, 103 (Cal. 1965); petition for certiorari, No. 584, OT 1965, U.S. Supreme Court, *Records*, NA.

105   Convicted burglar with swollen hands and face: petition for certiorari (French v. Illinois), No. 1328, 15, OT 1965, U.S. Supreme Court *Records*, NA.

105–106 Two brutal cases passed over: respondent's brief (Bean v. Nevada), No. 303, 10–12, OT 1965, U.S. Supreme Court, *Records*, NA; Clemons v. State, 398 S.W.2d 563 (1965); Daniel P. Levitt to author.

106   Law firm of Lewis & Roca: Monroe G. McKay to author.

106–110 Briefs for Miranda, Arizona, ACLU, National District Attorneys Association, and the attorney general of New York: in *Miranda*, R and B.

108–109 Louis Lefkowitz's interview: *NYT*, Dec. 5, 1965, 1, 33.

109   "not simply go whole hog . . ."; "go slow . . ."; "vestigial": Telford Taylor to author.

109–110 Three states: see People v. Dorado, 398 P.2d 361 (Cal. 1965); State v. Neely, 395 P.2d 557 (Ore. 1964); State v. Dufour, 206 A.2d 82 (R.I. 1965); brief for attorney general of New York, *Miranda*, U.S. Supreme Court, R and B.

110   John Frank's extra copies: letter, John Frank to Ed Cullinan, Jan. 10, 1966, No. 759, OT 1965, U.S. Supreme Court, *Records*, NA.

Book 2/Earl Warren's Book

Chapter 1

113   Methias Warren's murder: *San Francisco Chronicle*, May 15, 1938, 1, 4; May 16, 1938, 1, 4.

114 "the judgment of a member . . .": Warren, *Memoirs*, 125.

114 "some itinerant came . . .": Warren, *Memoirs*, 126.

114 Parade of suspects: *San Francisco Chronicle*, May 17, 1938, 1, 4; May 18, 1938, 1, 6; May 19, 1938, 5; May 21, 1938, 11; May 22, 1938, 11; May 23, 1938, 5; Oct. 22, 1938, 3; Oct. 25, 1938, 10.

114 "the boss told us all . . .": Katcher, *Earl Warren*, 102.

114–115 The question of an informer in the cell: Robert B. Powers OHP, 19, UC-OHP.

115 "When I got there . . .": Katcher, *Earl Warren*, 102.

115–130 Bare biographical material—but not commentary—on Warren comes from Friedman and Israel, *The Justices*, v. 4, 2721; Katcher, *Earl Warren*; Pollack, *Earl Warren*; John D. Weaver, *Warren*; G. Edward White, *Earl Warren*.

116 "both vigorous and fair": John D. Weaver, *Warren*, 42.

116–117 Warren's conduct of the district attorney's office: Lloyd G. Jester OHP, 4, 30–31; Frank Coakley OHP, 54–55; Willard Shea OHP 25–26, UC-OHP.

117 "in those days . . .": "Conversations with Earl Warren," 77, UC-OHP.

117–118 Robbery of Columbia Steel Works payrolls: Warren, *Memoirs*, 110 n.

118 "is facing today . . .": Warren, "What's Wrong," 730.

118–119 Warren's campaign for streamlining state criminal justice: *San Francisco Chronicle*, Nov. 5, 1934, 2; Richard H. Chamberlain OHP, 12–16, UC-OHP; Warren, *Memoirs*, 109–111; "Organizing," 321 ff.; "A State Department of Justice, 311 ff.; "What's Wrong," 370; Griffin v. California, 380 U.S. 609, 614 (1965).

118–119 Later Court decisions: Carter v. Kentucky, 450 U.S. 288 (1981); Bruno v. United States, 308 U.S. 287 (1939).

120 Old-timers' recollections; "cultivating"; "[E]very law officer . . ."; Robert B. Powers OHP, 8–11, UC-OHP.

120–121n. This note was assembled from Korematsu v. United States, 323 U.S. 214 (1941); Kluger, *Simple*, 661; Shogan, *A Question*, 51–54; Warren, *Memoirs*, 148–50; Conrat, *Executive*, 110–11; NYT, Nov. 26, 1971, 76.

121 "the biggest damn . . .": Warren, *Memoirs*, 5.

122 "[T]here would then be available . . .": Eisenhower, *Mandate*, 230.

122 "been the equivalent . . .": U.S. Congress, Senate, Committee on the Judiciary, Subcommittee on Separation of Powers, *Advice and Consent*, 2.

123 Warren/Nixon feud: Arnold, *Back When*, 30–31; William O. Douglas, *Court Years*, 227.

123 "Earl Warren might as well be sitting . . .": Arnold, *Back When*, 36.

124 Warren/Nixon feud irrelevant: Eisenhower, *Mandate*, 46.

124 "the usual Potomac fever gossip"; president promises Warren first Supreme Court vacancy: Brownell, OHP 1, 60–61, UC-OHP.

124 "dream": Brownell to author.

124 "thereafter made his plans. . .": Brownell OHP, 3, UC-OHP.

124 Solicitor general offer and acceptance: Warren, *Memoirs*, 267–68.

124 Warren announces no fourth term: NYT, Sept. 4, 1953, 1, 8.

124 Warren reads about John Marshall: Kluger, *Simple*, 666.

124 Chief justiceship offered and accepted: Brownell OHP, 8–9, UC-OHP; Eisenhower, *Mandate*, 226–29.

124 "I certainly wanted . . .": PPP, 1953, 619.

124–125 Warren's statistics: *New Yorker*, Oct. 10, 1953, 29–30; NYT, Oct. 1, 1953, 1.

125 "Earl Warren is honest . . .": Gunther, *Inside*, 18.

125 Bland manager of a team of all-stars: Katcher, *Earl Warren*, 6.

125 "Don't worry about that . . .": "Retired Chief Justice Warren," 728.

126 "Our cases evidence the fact . . .": Irvine v. California, 347 U.S. 128, 135–36 (1954).

126 "We are confident . . .": Burns v. Ohio, 360 U.S. 252 (1959).

126 "where the Supreme Court of a state . . .": CR 109, 19849.

126–127 Warren/Supreme Court cases 1953 ff.: See, for example, Leyra v. Denno, 347 U.S. 556 (1954); Rogers v. Richmond, 365 U.S. 534 (1961); Culombe v. Connecticut, 367 U.S. 568 (1961); Gallegos v. Colorado, 370 U.S. 49 (1962); Gideon; Escobedo.

127 Warren joins dissents: See Thomas v. Arizona, 356 U.S. 390 (1958); Crooker v. California, 357 U.S. 433 (1958).

Bibliography and Source Notes

127 Mapp v. Ohio, 367 U.S. 643 (1961).
127 "Many California counties . . .": *CR* 110, 15860.
127 Baker v. Carr: 369 U.S. 186 (1962).
127 ". . . it would seem reasonable . . .": Reynolds v. Sims, 377 U.S. 533, 565 (1964).
128 "It is always easier . . .": *NYT*, July 11, 1974, 35.
129 U.S. and state laws struck down by the U.S. Supreme Court: See Swindler, *Court and Constitution*, v. 1, 344–45.
129n. Judicial backgrounds: See Friedman and Israel, *The Justices*, v. 1–4, and Friedman, *The Justices*, v. 5; *NYT*, Sept. 3, 1981, B 12.

Chapter 2

131 Warren's prayer: Simon, *Image*, 58.
132 "scared to death"; "I think" . . . "that what the Court . . ."; Fifth Amendment case. . . : John J. Flynn to author.
132 Practicing for the Supreme Court; "outrageous social policy": Monroe G. McKay to author.
132 Flynn's early arrival: *ADS*, Feb. 23, 1973, 16.
133 "with a mouth like a mastiff . . .": Stephen Vincent Benét, "The Devil and Daniel Webster" (*Pocket Book of Short Stories*, New York, 1941), 12.
133 "First came the one . . .": 349 U.S. xliv (1954).
133 "Number 759 . . ."; "Mr. Flynn . . .": Tr-SC, *Miranda*, 1.
134 "vigorous, restive . . .": *WP*, Feb. 27, 1966, E 2.
134 Douglas's behavior at oral argument: Clark, "Bill Douglas," 219.
134 Harlan's behavior at oral argument: Lewin, "Justice Harlan," 579.
135 Fawcett's background: F. Conger Fawcett to author.
136 Miranda was heard first: note, Alexander Stevas, clerk of the U.S. Supreme Court, to author, July 1982.
137 "You said that Miranda . . ."; "That is correct": Tr-SC, *Miranda*, 5.
137 "What do you think . . ."; "I think that the man . . .": Tr-SC, *Miranda*, 12, 15–16.
138 "You have said several times . . .": Tr-SC, *Miranda*, 17; Kurland and Casper, *Landmark*, 852.
138 "I would say that it certainly . . .": Tr-SC, *Miranda*, 18.
138 "has to have a gun . . .": Tr-SC, *Miranda*, 20, 21.
138 "[T]he Constitution of the State . . .": Tr-SC, *Miranda*, 23–24.
139 "I think if the extreme position . . .": Tr-SC, *Miranda*, 35–36.
139 Telford Taylor's switch in time: Telford Taylor to author.
140 Taylor's arguments: Tr-SC, *Miranda*, 43–54.
141 "The Chief Justice: May I ask you . . .": Tr-SC, *Miranda*, 63–66.
142 "As a prosecutor . . .": Tr-SC, *Miranda*, 69.
142 "When the proceeding has become accusatory . . .": brief for petitioner, Vignera v. New York, 384 U.S. 436, 38–39, R and B.
142 "The Chief of Police in the District of Columbia . . .": Tr-SC, *Miranda*, 78.
143 "highest type of evidence"; "want to be deprived . . .": Tr-SC, *Miranda*, 95.
143 "Mr. Justice Fortas: Mr. Siegel, I suppose . . .": Tr-SC, *Miranda*, 96–97.
145 "Mr. Justice Fortas . . . In other words . . .": Tr-SC, *Miranda*, 98–99.
145 "We just *can't equalize* . . .": Tr-SC, *Miranda*, 138.
145 "The Chief Justice: What would you do . . .": Tr-SC, *Miranda*, 145.
145–146 "Equal protection and due process . . .": brief for petitioner, Chambers v. Florida, 309 U.S. 227, 32, R and B.
146 "Mr. Marshall: I have always . . .": Tr-SC, *Miranda*, 145–47.
146 "Mr. Justice Black: Would it be . . .": Tr-SC, *Miranda*, 180.
147 Massiah v. United States, 337 U.S. 201 (1964).
147 "Then what you have . . .": Tr-SC, *Miranda*, 13.
147 "Must decide what marks . . ."; "Mr. Justice Black: Why? . . .": Kurland and Caspar, *Landmark*, v. 63, 953.
147 "Before calling . . .": Kurland and Caspar, *Landmark*, v. 63, 970.

Bibliography and Source Notes

Chapter 3

150　John Harlan's unqualified courtesy: 409 U.S. xxviii (1972).
150　Douglas' scrappiness; "lead to a . . .": Clark, "Bill Douglas," 219.
150　"absolute knife-edged . . .": Rehnquist, "Chief Justices," 647.
150　"The phrase so often heard . . .": Felix Frankfurter to Charles Whittaker, Oct. 24, 1957, Frankfurter papers, LC.
151–156　General biographical material comes from Friedman and Israel, *The Justices*, vols. 3 and 4.
151　"open to all . . .": Warren, "Retired Chief Justice," 730.
151　"it is a long journey . . .": *Hugo Black and the Bill of Rights*, xiii.
151　"come into this world . . .": *NYT*, Jan. 20, 1980, 28.
151–152　Douglas's early years: Douglas, *Go East*.
152　"I thought of all . . .": "somehow aligned me . . .": Douglas, *Go East*, 85, 62.
152　"took a pixie delight . . .": 449 U.S. xxxii (1980).
152　"If this accused . . .": Culombe v. Connecticut, 367 U.S. 568, 640–41 (1961).
153　Brennan a loyal member of the Warren-Black-Douglas axis: In eleven confessions cases during the three terms preceding this one, 1962, 1963, 1964, Brennan joined that bloc 100 percent. See Cleary v. Bolger, 371 U.S. 392 (1963); Wong Sun v. United States, 371 U.S. 471 (1963); Townsend v. Sain, 372 U.S. 293 (1963); Fay v. Noia, 372 U.S. 391 (1963); Lynum v. Illinois, 372 U.S. 528 (1963); Haynes v. Washington, 373 U.S. 503 (1963); Massiah v. United States, 377 U.S. 201 (1964); Malloy v. Hogan, 378 U.S. 1 (1964); Jackson v. Denno, 378 U.S. 368 (1964); Escobedo; Douglas v. Alabama, 380 U.S. 415 (1965).
153–154　"Crippled and its task made . . .": *Escobedo*, 499.
154　"It does sound awfully tame . . .": *New Yorker*, Dec. 4, 1954, 41.
154　"that all deficiencies . . .": Harlan, "Thoughts at a Dedication," 943.
154　"an entire body . . .": *Gideon*, 352.
155　Between the special November 1965 conference . . . : memorandums, John M. Harlan to the brethren, Nov. 30, 1965 and Dec. 13, 1965, John M. Harlan papers, Seeley G. Mudd Manuscript Library.
156　Fortas's three opinions in criminal cases: United States v. Romano, 382 U.S. 136 (1965); Giaccio v. Pennsylvania, 382 U.S. 399 (1965); Kent v. United States, 383 U.S. 541 (1966).
156　"The right to representation . . .": Kent v. United States, 383 U.S. 541, 561 (1966).
157　"That confessions are essential . . .": Sobel, "The Exclusionary," 4–5.
157　"the defendant, and only . . ."; "Obviously the whole purpose . . .": *NYT*, Dec. 2, 1965, 1, 52.
157–158　"traditional protections . . .": *NYT*, Dec. 20, 1965, 23.
158　Press interest in confessions cases: See 70 *Harvard LR* 935 (1966); Traynor, "The Devils," 657–80; Schaefer, "The Suspect," 78–81; *Time*, April 29, 1966, 25.
158　"ever make good sense . . .": *NYT*, April 30, 1966, 13, May 1, 1966, 73.
158　Concern of NAAG: NAAG, *Conference Proceedings*, 1966, 9, 31–32, 39–43, 45–47, 125–32; *NYT*, May 18, 1966, 27.
158　New York assembly: *NYT*, May 24, 1966, 35.
159　Congressional interest in confessions cases: U.S. Congress, Senate, Committee on the Judiciary, Subcommittee on Criminal Laws and Procedures, *Criminal Laws*, March, May 1966.
159　"What is that Model Code . . .": Tr-SC, *Miranda*, 104.
159–161　Account of ALI meeting assembled from ALI, *Proceedings*, 1966, 52–59, 557–58; *NYT*, March 6, 70, March 7, 26, May 17, 24, May 19, 29, May 22, 1966, iv, 9; Graham, *Self-Inflicted*, 172–75; Vorenberg, "A.L.I. Approves," 1214–15.
160　"tempted . . . to enter the fray": ALI, *Proceedings*, 1970, 24.
160　Warren sat sphinxlike . . . : James Vorenberg to author.
160–161　No vote taken: *NYT*, May 22, 1966, iv, 9; ALI, *Proceedings*, 1969, 41.
161　"my most earnest plea . . .": ALI, *Proceedings*, 1966, 242–43.
161*n*.　The decision . . . : Vorenberg, "A.L.I. Approves," 1212–15.
162　"We must find . . .": *NYT*, March 19, 1966, 17.
162　"Justice McReynolds . . .": Rehnquist, "The Supreme," p. 362.

Bibliography and Source Notes

162n. The latter title . . . : William Richardson, "Chief Justice," 275–79.
163 "There was that brave . . .": Pollack, *Earl*, 222.
163 "I just can't do . . .": CR 928, 4267; Warren, *Memoirs*, 343.
163 "tension and pressure . . .": 405 U.S. lvii.
163 This "pressure cooker" atmosphere . . . "those of means": Douglas, *Go East*, 435: *Newsweek*, May 11, 1964, 25; WP, April 12, 1966, 49; Warren, "Responsibilities," 26 *Maryland LR*, 103, 109.
164 "You'd better find . . .": 421 U.S. xxxiv–xxxv.
164 Warren's working habits: Frank, "Affirmative," 17; Frank, *The Warren Court*, 34; *Time*, Dec. 21, 1953, 17.
165n. The 1979 leak: NYT, April 25, 1979, A 14; May 29, 1979, 19.
165 First draft of *Miranda*, May 18: John M. Harlan papers, Seeley G. Mudd Manuscript Library.
165 "there is no mention . . .": memorandum, "E.W." to the conference, May 18, 1966, John M. Harlan papers, Seeley G. Mudd Manuscript Library.
165 "I am planning to circulate . . .": memorandum, "J.M.H." to the conference, May 19, 1966, John M. Harlan papers, Seeley G. Mudd Manuscript Library.
165 The forging of opinions: see Stewart, "Inside," A 17; Powell, "Report," 1–4.
165 Two more drafts: John M. Harlan papers, Seeley G. Mudd Manuscript Library.
165 Miranda's hearing the news: Barry Silverman to author.

Chapter 4

166 Reading of *Miranda*: NYT, June 14, 1966, 25; Graham, *Self-Inflicted*, 192.
166 "for the proper . . .": *Miranda*, 460.
166 "indigent Mexican . . .": *Miranda*, 457.
166 "the weakness of individuals": *Miranda*, 455.
166 "persons in all . . .": *Miranda*, 467.
167 Changes in *Miranda*, May 18–June 13: compare May 18 draft (7, 12, 23, 27, 29, 31, 33, 40, 41), John M. Harlan papers, Seeley G. Mudd Manuscript Library, with the final *Miranda*.
167 "We start here . . .": *Miranda*, 442.
168 "[T]he prosecution may not use . . .": *Miranda*, 444–45.
168–169 Police interrogation practices: *Miranda*, 448–58.
169 "its own badge . . ."; "destructive . . ."; "The current practice . . .": *Miranda*, 457–58.
169 ". . . the principle that no man . . .": *Miranda*, 458, n. 27.
169 "another fundamental right . . .": *Miranda*, 459.
169 "Today, then, there can be no doubt . . .": *Miranda*, 467.
169 "The Court held a long time ago . . .": Kurland and Caspar, *Landmark*, v. 63, 953.
169–170 ACLU had urged presence of counsel: ACLU brief at 3, in 384 U.S. 436, R and B.
170 "we cannot say . . ."; "procedures which are at least . . .": *Miranda*, 467.
170 FBI and foreign practices: *Miranda*, 483–89.
170 "a person who enters a police station . . .": *Miranda*, 478.
170 "[I]t is clear . . .": *Miranda*, 492.
170 Disposition of the cases: *Miranda*, 493–99.
171 "application of principles . . .": *Miranda*, 442.
171 "a departure . . .": *Miranda*, 531.
171 "poor constitutional law": *Miranda*, 504.
171 "*ipse dixit* . . .": *Miranda*, 500.
172 "our decision is not intended . . .": *Miranda*, 477.
172 "unaccustomed edge . . .": Graham, *Self-Inflicted*, 192.
172 "when their services . . .": NYT, June 14, 1966, 25.
172 "Such a strict constitutional . . .": *Miranda*, 500.
172 "perfectly legitimate methods . . .": *Escobedo*, 493.
172 "an elaborate, sophisticated . . .": *Miranda*, 508–09.
172 "long-range and lasting . . .": *Miranda*, 524.
173 "What the Court largely ignores . . .": *Miranda*, 516–17.
173 "major step in the direction . . .": *Escobedo*, 495.
173 "The obvious under-pinning . . .": *Miranda*, 537.

Bibliography and Source Notes

173 "no desire . . ." *Miranda*, 542.

173 "had become professional . . .": *Hugo Black and the Bill of Rights*, 5.

173 Tom Clark's rewrite: Daniel P. Levitt to author; compare 34 *LW* 4540 with *Miranda*, 500; Graham, *Self-Inflicted*, 193.

173–174 Abe Fortas's Florida trip: Shogan, *A Question*, 210–12.

174 "in any of Mr. Wolfson's . . .": *WP*, Jan. 23, 1977, A 12.

174 Brennan's reading of *Johnson* v. *New Jersey*: *NYT*, June 21, 1966, 1.

174 "the exigencies of the situation"; "the reliability and relevancy . . .": Johnson v. New Jersey, 384 U.S. 719, 727 (1966).

175 Chief justice's first draft: in John M. Harlan papers, Seeley G. Mudd Manuscript Library (see p. 1).

175 "only those cases . . .": "only to cases . . .": Johnson v. New Jersey, 384 U.S. 719, 721.

175 "the Court's opinion cuts off . . .": Linkletter v. Walker, 381 U.S. 618, 652 (1965).

175 "[R]etroactive application of *Escobedo* . . .": Johnson v. New Jersey, 384 U.S. 719, 731.

175 Hoover memorandum: Interagency correspondence, J. E. Hoover to F. M. Vinson, Jr., June 15, 1966, FBI files.

175–176 Katzenbach's request for cabinet discussion: memorandum, Robert E. Kintner to the president, June 15, 1966, 9:30 A.M.; the agenda for that meeting lists this item: "Introduction to the Attorney General. As you all know, the Supreme Court on Monday handed down a far-reaching decision designed to protect the legal rights of criminal speeches. This Supreme Court decision has wide-spread ramifications on the practices of police departments, offices of Federal and District Attorneys, and on all law enforcement agencies—Federal, State, and local. . . . I thought it would be helpful if the Attorney General analyzes the decision in relation to federal law enforcement. . . ." These documents are from the Lyndon B. Johnson Library; Mr. Katzenbach, however, queried in 1980, wrote the author (July 14, Oct. 8, 1980) that he was unable to recall the meeting.

176 "criminal trials no longer . . .": *NYT*, June 20, 1966, 15.

176 "the present rules . . .": *U.S. News*, June 27, 1966, 32.

176 "there is no such thing . . .": *NYT*, June 20, 1966, 15.

176 "thought innocent persons . . .": Milner, *The Court*, 191.

176 Parker's prediction: *U.S. News*, June 27, 1966, 33.

177 Police perceptions of Miranda: "Interrogations in New Haven," 1610–12; Milner, *The Court*, 190–99; Jenkins, *Keeping*, 136.

177 "What is meant by . . .": "Has the Supreme Court . . .," station KOOL, Phoenix, Arizona, June 21, 1966.

177 Survey of Wisconsin police: Milner, *The Court*, 42–43.

178 Tales of police behavior: U.S. Congress, Senate, Committee on the Judiciary, Subcommittee on Criminal Laws and Procedures, *Controlling Crime*, 549, 544.

178 New Haven police behavior: "Interrogations in New Haven," 1521, 1539–45, 1550, 1552–53, 1613.

179 Washington, D.C., study: Medalie, Zeitz, Alexander, "Custodial Police," 1348–50, 1374–75; *NYT*, May 14, 1968, 60.

180 Philadelphia police statistics: U.S. Congress, Senate, Committee on the Judiciary, Subcommittee on Criminal Laws and Procedures, *Controlling Crime*, 200–01.

180 Hogan's findings: *NYT*, July 13, 1967, 1.

180 Los Angeles statistics: Younger, "Interrogation," 260.

180 Kansas City figures: *Wall Street Journal*, Dec. 15, 1966, 16.

180 Pittsburgh data: Seeburger and Wettrick, "Miranda in Pittsburgh," 23.

181 Inbau and Reid texts: Compare 1962 and 1967 editions of *Criminal Interrogation*; the emphasis on isolation criticized by the Court (*Miranda*, 449–50) is still on page 1; the stratagems of kindness and rationalization criticized by the Court (*Miranda*, 451–52) are on p. 44 (p. 40 of the 1962 edition); the Mutt and Jeff routine criticized by the Court (*Miranda*, 452) are on 62 (58, 1962 edition); see also the preface, 1967 edition, vii, and General Introduction, 1.

181–182 Founding of AELE: Frank Carrington to author; *NYT*, July 12, 1967, 47.

181   "rationale of [*Miranda*] will . . .": Thompson, "Detention," 421.
182   "It seems plain . . .": 40 F.R.D. 351, 352, 353, 357.
182–183 "blows and screams . . ."; "Several times . . ."; "The most macabre memory of all . . ."; "relatively enlightened . . ."; "The most significant . . .": Edwards, "Interrogation," 184–88.
183   "shackle the police . . .": Bell, "Crime and Criminals," 4.
183   "recognize that the scales . . .": CCJ, *Proceedings*, 1966, 103; NYT, Aug. 9, 1964, 66.
184   "with an American public . . .": U.S. Congress, Senate, Committee on the Judiciary, Subcommittee on Criminal Laws and Procedures, *Controlling Crime*, 886.
184   "These decisions . . .": CCJ, *Proceedings*, 1966, 60.
184   Retroactivity further defined: Jenkins v. Delaware, 395 U.S. 213 (1969).
185   "fingerprinting, photographing . . .": Schmerber v. California, 384 U.S. 757, 763 (1966).
185   IRS case: Mathis v. United States, 391 U.S. 1 (1968).
185   IRS revision of procedures: IRS News Release No. IR-949.
185   "Miranda was the first chapter . . .": Yale Kamisar to author.
185   "Whenever I am told . . .": Kaufman, "The Supreme Court," 66.
186   *Time*'s report on *Miranda*: *Time*, Aug. 5, 1966, 39.
186   Oregon Supreme Court's interpretation: Mathiason v. Oregon, 549 P.2d 673 (Ore. 1976).
186   New York Supreme Court interpretation: People v. Yukl, 25 N.Y.2d 585 (1969); Jonathan Marks to author.
186–187 Fifth Circuit on waiver: Narro v. United States, 370 F.2d 329 (1966).
187   Seventh Circuit on waiver: United States v. Neilsen, 392 F.2d 849, 853 (1968).
187–190 Viven Harris's case was compiled from Harris v. New York, statement of petitioner, trial transcript in Westchester County Court (July 21, 1966), petition for certiorari, and brief for petitioner, No. 206, OT 1970, U.S. Supreme Court, *Records*, NA; NYT, Jan. 6, 1966, 16, Jan. 9, 1966, 34, Feb. 24, 1966, 1, 24; *New Rochelle* (N.Y.) *Standard-Star*, March 4, 1971.
189–190 Aurnou's involvement: Aurnou to author.

Chapter 5

191   Miranda stays in prison: Silverman, "Ernesto," 3, 4.
191–192n.Fate of Vignera, Westover, Stewart: Victor M. Earle III, F.
192   Conger Fawcett, Wilbur T. Littlefield to author.
192   Miranda's second trial scheduled: NYT, Oct. 24, 1966, 4.
192   "black day . . .": AR, June 16, 1966, 19.
192   "bone free": U.S. Congress, Senate, Committee on the Judiciary, Subcommittee on Criminal Laws and Procedures, *Controlling Crime*, 527.
192   "Why are you doing . . ."; Twila Hoffman's interest: Robert K. Corbin to author.
193   "composed and detached . . .": AR, Feb. 16, 1967, 17.
193   "In a way, I goofed . . ."; "deeply, very deeply . . ."; "nine-day game . . .": U.S. Congress, Senate, Committee on the Judiciary, Subcommittee on Criminal Laws and Procedures, *Controlling Crime*, 527–30; Nardone v. United States, 308 U.S. 338, 341 (1939); John Flynn to author; AR, Feb. 17, 1967, 23, Feb. 22, 1967, 23, Feb. 24, 1967, 1, 4, 15; ADS, March 2, 1967.
194   1966–68 court terms: See 123–132 U.S. App. D.C.
194   "For a generation judicial trends . . .": Clifton v. United States, 371 F.2d 354, 360 (1966).
195   "responsibility for some . . ."; "revising the code of criminal procedure . . ."; "strongly urged . . .": U.S. Congress, Senate, Committee on the Judiciary, *Nomination of Warren E. Burger*, 39–44.
195   "inefficient . . ."; "all the emphasis . . ."; "incidents of the adversary system"; "are all these devices . . ."; "images of the rack . . ."; "so I am no longer . . .": McDonald, "A Center Report," 69–72.
196   "It is a truism . . .": Burger, "Remarks," May 21, 1967, 4.
196   Overhaul the rules; introduce modern management techniques: U.S. Congress, Sen-

Bibliography and Source Notes

ate, Committee on the Judiciary, *Nomination of Warren E. Burger*, 40–41; Burger, "The Courts," 71 ff.

196   Burger's subcommittee report: ABA, Advisory Committee on the Prosecution and Defense Functions, *Standards Relating*, especially 37–40, 43–45.

197   Ripon College commencement address: Arnette Nelson and Robert V. Abendroth to author; Burger, "Remarks," May 21, 1967.

197   *U.S. News* story: *U.S. News*, Aug. 7, 1967, 70; *U.S. News*, index, 1967, 20, 21, 48, 50, 51, 52.

197   Nixon impressed: Duscha, "The Chief Justice Says," 30.

197–198   Marshall's record and appointment: see vols. 293–347, F.2d (2d Cir.), 1961–65; United States *ex rel.* Jackson v. Denno, 309 F.2d 573 (1962); U.S. Congress, Senate, Committee on the Judiciary, *Nomination of Thurgood Marshall to Be Associate Justice of the Supreme Court*, 1967.

198–199   "Congress and the States . . .": *Miranda*, 490.

200   "full of bloody . . .": Ezekiel 9:9.

200   FBI figures: *NYT*, July 28, 1966, 30.

200   "even more real . . .": *NYT*, Sept. 4, 1966, iv, 5.

200   "This 5–4 decision . . ." *WS*, June 14, 1966, A 4.

201   "Enough has been done . . .": *NYT*, July 23, 1966, 54.

201   Hearings of the Constitutional Amendments Subcommittee: *NYT*, July 22, 22; *WP*, July 22, A 2; *Newsweek*, Aug. 1, 1966, 27–28; the hearings transcripts were never published.

201   "to create greater understanding . . .": *PPP*, 1965, 269.

202   "We will continue . . .": *NYT*, Oct. 16, 1966, 64.

202   "Radical reduction . . .": President's Commission on Crime in the District of Columbia, *Report*, 854.

202   Conclusions reached: *NYT*, Jan. 1, 1967, 42; Harris, *Fear*, 15–17.

203   "Warring on poverty . . ."; "assess the effect . . ."; "this and other decisions . . ."; "to guide police . . ."; "as recently construed and enlarged . . ."; "without changes . . ."; "whatever can be done . . ."; An adequate opportunity . . . : President's Commission on Law Enforcement, *The Challenge*, 69, 245, 676, 679, 680.

204   Johnson's anticrime bill: DOJ, administrative history, "Omnibus Crime Control and Safe Streets," 1–2, 8–9, LBJ.

204–205   American mood, congressional sensitivity to it: Harris, *Fear*, 19–20.

205   McClellan's hearings: U.S. Congress, Senate, Committee on the Judiciary, Subcommittee on Criminal Laws and Procedures, *Controlling Crime*.

205–206   On nonjudicial problems encountered by police, see Ahern, *Police*, 87–90; Asch, *Police*, 22; Murphy, *Commissioner*, 27–28, 56; Lincoln Steffens, *The Autobiography of Lincoln Steffens* (New York, 1931), 206–09; Wilson, *Police*, 61–63, 228–29; *NYT*, June 14, 1968, 36; *U.S. News*, Jan. 29, 1973, 76.

206   For Ramsey Clark's views on criminal justice, see his *Crime in America*.

206   "It is quite probable . . .": U.S. Congress, Senate, Committee on the Judiciary, Subcommittee on Criminal Law and Procedures, *Controlling Crime*, 31.

207   "Overwhelmingly the members . . ."; "gone too far . . .": Harris, *Fear*, 67.

207   "[T]here is no more urgent . . .": *PPP*, 1968 (v. 1), 30.

207–208   Johnson on omnibus bill: *PPP*, 1968, 725–27.

208   Campaign year: Ramsey Clark, OHP, 10–11, LBJ.

208   "members of the Court . . .": Harris, "Reflections," 58.

208–209   Nixon sets out: Witcover, "Availability," 27–28; *NYT*, Feb. 10, 1966, 24.

209   Nixon in South Carolina: Dent, *Prodigal*, 76–77.

209–210   1966 congressional campaign: Nixon, *Memoirs*, 271–77; Chester, Hodgson, Page, *American*, 185–86; Harris, *Fear*, 67–68; White, *Making . . . 1968*, 51–52; Witcover, "Availability," 27; *Resurrection*, 154–57, 169–70; *NYT*, Nov. 1, 1966, 20; *Time*, Nov. 18, 1966, 23–30.

210–211   Nixon prepares for 1968: Nixon, *Memoirs*, 279, 293–94; Safire, *Before*, 42–43; White, *Making . . . 1968*, 52–53; *NYT*, March 14, 1, 1967, 26; May 28, 1967, iv, 13; Aug. 2, 1967, 25; Sept. 29, 1967, 31.

212   "Justice Abe Fortas called . . .": memorandum, James R. Jones to Lyndon Johnson, June 12, 1968, LBJ.

Bibliography and Source Notes

212–213 Warren/Johnson meeting: memorandum, James R. Jones to Lyndon Johnson, June 13, 1968, LBJ.
213 Johnson urged him to think it over: *PPP*, 1968–69, 863.
213 "Well," Johnson asked. . . : Earl Warren, OHP, 31, LBJ.
213 Johnson/Dirksen meeting: Everett M. Dirksen, OHP, 9–14, LBJ; Shogan, *A Question*, 150–52.
213–214 Douglas urged Fortas: William O. Douglas to Lyndon Johnson, June 18, 1968, LBJ.
214 Other suggestions: Pollack, *Earl*, 276–77.
214 "The President is empowered . . .": memorandum, Ramsey Clark to Lyndon Johnson, June 24, 1968, LBJ.
214 "one of the dirty five": McClellan's efforts; "SOB formally submitted . . .": memorandum, Mike Manatos to Lyndon Johnson, June 25, 1968, LBJ.
214–215 Johnson/Russell meeting: Lyndon B. Johnson, *Vantage*, 545–46; Shogan, *A Question*, 150.
215 Eastland/Johnson meeting: Lyndon B. Johnson, *Vantage*, 546–47; James O. Eastland, OHP, 17–19, LBJ.
216 Reaction to Fortas's nomination: *NYT*, June 22, 1968, 1, 16; June 23, 1968, 1, 30; June 27, 1968, 1, 30; Shogan, *A Question*, 154–57.
216 Nixon's reaction: *NYT*, June 27, 1968, 21.

Book 3/Richard Nixon's Book

Chapter 1

221–222 There was Richard Nixon again: see Chester, Hodgson, Page, *American*, 434–40, 456–60; Dent, *Prodigal*, 81; Theodore H. White, *Making . . . 1968*, 224–242.
222 Preparing the speech: *NYT*, Aug. 3, 1968, 10; Theodore H. White, *Making . . . 1968*, 253–54; Witcover, *Resurrection*, 327, Safire, *Before*, 53.
222 white, Protestant . . .: See Ripon Society, *Ripon's Republican*.
222 "the most successful war . . ."; "ugly harvest . . ."; "quit pouring . . ."; "what government did . . ."; "people did . . .": RNC, *Proceedings*, 1968, 448.
222–223 Nixon's background: see Nixon, *Memoirs*, 1–13.
222 Wiping tears from his eyes . . . : *WP*, Aug. 9, 1968, 1.
223 "to a living nightmare . . ."; "For him the American system . . .";
223 "more millions on welfare . . .": RNC, *Proceedings*, 1968, 451, 448.
223–224 Liberty City riots: *Miami Herald*, Aug. 8, A 25; Aug. 9, A 1–2; Aug. 10, 1968, 1, 22, 6 A; White, *Making . . . 1968*, 30.
224 "gone too far . . ."; "the wave of crime . . ."; RNC, *Proceedings*, 1968, 447.
225 Nixon's vow to replace Ramsey Clark: RNC, *Proceedings*, 1968, 447.
225 Nixon's two friends: Nixon, *Six Crises*, 1.
226 "kiss of death": De Toledano, *One Man Alone*, 64.
226 Nixon's maiden speech: Nixon, *Memoirs*, 45.
226 Nixon's anti-Communist activities: Nixon, *Memoirs*, 46–52.
226–227 Details of the Hiss/Nixon matter are taken from Nixon, *Memoirs*, 52–50; *Six Crises*, 1–71; Weinstein, *Perjury*, 7–59.
227n. Hiss's later life: *WP*, Nov. 9, 1980, L1, L5.
228 Nixon's role in 1948 campaign: Nixon, *Six Crises* 45–46.
229 "fairness in the investigating process": Eisenhower, *Mandate*, 46.
229 "a man who has shown . . .": RNC, *Proceedings*, 1952, 432.
229 "text from which . . .": Nixon, *Memoirs*, 88.
229 "down the line . . .": Weinstein, *Perjury*, 511.
229 "Can such a man as Stevenson . . .": Schlesinger and Israel, *History*, v. 4, 3246.
229 "Because of the Eisenhower policies . . .": *NYT*, Oct. 11, 1954, 28.
229n. Hiss's release and government pension: *NYT*, March 4, 1972, 25.
230 "Ramsey Clark is really . . .": Harris, *Justice*, 15.
230 Clark's accomplishments at DOJ: Harris, *Justice*, 29–30, 35, 40–41.
230 "If you don't have law enforcement officials . . .": *Miami Herald*, Aug. 7, 1968, 22.
231 "dark days of the Civil War": RNC, *Proceedings*, 1968, 453.
231 Nixon's unwinding: Safire, *Before*, 56.

Bibliography and Source Notes

Chapter 2

232   Eastland visits LBJ: Claudia T. Johnson, *A White House*, 701; Lyndon B. Johnson, *Vantage*, 547.

232   "like some of those 'high-minded' . . .": NYT, March 27, 1978, A 24.

232–233   Eastland's rise to power: White, *Citadel*, 192–94.

233   Johnson's efforts for Fortas: memorandums, Mike Manatos to Lyndon Johnson, June 26, June 28, July 2, July 9, July 10, 1968, LBJ.

233   Justice Dept. officials for Fortas: memorandums, William T. Finley, Jr., to Mike Manatos, June 28, June 29, 1968, LBJ.

233   Cabinet secretaries for Fortas: memorandum, Barefoot Sanders to Lyndon Johnson, June 28, LBJ.

233   Hawaiian businessmen for Fortas: memorandum, Jim Gaither to Joe Califano, July 1, 1968, LBJ.

233   California Jewish community: memorandum, Irv Sprague to Barefoot Sanders, June 28, 1968, LBJ.

233   First Jewish president, Nebraska bar: memorandum, Harry C. McPherson, Jr., to Lyndon Johnson, July 10, 1968, LBJ.

233   "who could be helpful . . .": letter, Walter Reuther to Joe Califano, July 10, 1968, LBJ: NYT, July 3, 1968, 14.

234   Fortas hearings, July 1968: U.S. Congress, Senate, Committee on the Judiciary, *Nominations of Abe Fortas and Homer Thornberry*, July 1968 (v. 1); see especially 134, 136, 191.

235–236   Eleven Johnson judgeships confirmed: news release, Senator Wayne Morse, July 1, 1968, 3, LBJ.

236   Eastland denies lame-duck factor: James O. Eastland, OHP, 19, LBJ.

236   Johnson/Eastland meeting, Johnson's recognition of defeat: Claudia T. Johnson, *A White House*, 702; Lyndon B. Johnson, *Vantage*, 547.

236   "there seems to be a little maneuvering . . .": NYT, Aug. 24, 1968, 12.

236   Johnson back in Washington: Pollack, *Earl*, 281.

237   Wallace lands in Chicago: Chester, Hodgson, Page, *American*, 652; White, *Making . . . 1968*, 348.

237   Wallace's growing popularity as shown in polls: White, *Making . . . 1968*, 347: NYT, Oct. 1, 1968, 34.

237   Republican defections, predictions for Wallace vote: Chester, Hodgson, Page, *American*, 668–69, 654–56: NYT, Sept. 4, 1968, 32.

237   "sitting as a continual . . .": NYT, June 23, 1966, 5.

238   Wallace in Chicago: See for Oct. 1, 1968, *Chicago Daily News*, 4; *Chicago Tribune*, 1, 2: NYT, 68; WP, 1, 2.

238–239   Wallace biographical material: See Frady, *Wallace*; Chester, Hodgson, Page, *American*.

238   Gubernatorial aspirations: Wooten, *Dasher*.

239   "Well, there was never any question . . .": Kilpatrick, "What Makes," 404–05.

240   "the right to form a party . . .": Williams v. Rhodes, 393 U.S. 23, 31 (1968).

241   "we just can't keep . . .": Frady, *Wallace*, 141.

241   "outniggahed": Frady, *Wallace*, quoted in White, *Making . . . 1968*, 344.

241   "Segregation now! . . .": Chester, Hodgson, Page, *American*, 267.

241   "every boy and girl . . .": Jack Wallace to author.

242   Wallace in Cicero: See for Oct. 1, 1968, *Chicago Daily News*, 3; *Chicago Tribune*, 1, 2; NYT, 32; WP, 1, 2.

243–244   The Wallace set speech: Ray Jenkins, "George Wallace Figures," 26, 66, 69: Kilpatrick, "What Makes," 402; Lipset, "Why Cops," 76; NYT, July 30, 1968, 27; Sept. 8, 1968, 28; Sept. 12, 1968, 36; Sept. 17, 1968, 39; Nov. 3, 1968, 78.

244   Day's end: See for Oct. 2, 1968, *Chicago Daily News*, 3; WP, A 2.

244   "very close": Nixon, *Memoirs*, 316.

244   "a more respectable . . .": Witcover, *Resurrection*, 364–65.

245   Nixon and Burger's Ripon College speech: Nixon, *Memoirs*, 420.

245–246   "Whenever I begin to discuss . . .": speech, London, Ohio, Oct. 22, 1968, DNC-NA.

246   "He could have Mr. Fortas confirmed . . .": NYT, Sept. 14, 1968, 1.

246 Replacing the attorney general: Harris, *Justice*, 13.
246–248 The packaging of Nixon: Chester, Hodgson, Page, *American*, 614, 679–83; McGinniss, *Selling*, 67–72; Rosenbloom, *The Election*, 2–4, 10–11; Schlesinger and Israel, *History*, v. 4, 3739–40; Witcover, *Resurrection*, 385.
248 Nixon in Ohio: texts of speeches for release Oct. 21, Cincinnati, Oct. 22, 23, London, Ohio, DNC-NA; *NYT*, Oct. 23, 1968, 28: Safire, *Before*, 82–83; White, *Making . . . 1968*, 373–75; Witcover, *Resurrection*, 423–26.
249 Party officials' reaction: Witcover, *Resurrection*, 425–26.
249 "He's talking about . . .": Dunne, *Hugo Black*, 409.
249 "extreme reaction"; "That fella . . .": Hugo Black, Jr., *Hugo Black*, 242–45.
249–250 Black's decision to speak out: Martin Agronsky to author.
250 "It will remain the business . . .": Stewart, "The Nine," 1097.
250 "unavoidable involvement . . .": CCJ, *Proceedings*, 1967, 42, 43.
250 "but a confession . . .": Tom C. Clark, "Criminal," 742–43.
250 Elizabeth Black's refutation: Elizabeth S. Black, "Hugo Black," 84 and note 67, on 93.
250–251 "in person the man . . .": Hugo Black, Jr., *Hugo Black*, 44.
251 Filming the interview: Martin Agronsky to author; Elizabeth S. Black, "Hugo Black," 74–75; Meador, *Mr. Justice*, 6; *WP*, July 5, 1970, E3.
251 Burton Benjamin's involvement, reaction: Burton Benjamin to author.
252 "Well, the President is away . . .": Thruston Morton OHP, 22, LBJ.
252 Dirksen for and against Fortas: *WP*, Sept. 28, 1968, 1, 6; *NYT*, Sept. 28, 1968, 41.
252–254 Dirksen's Senate speech: *CR* 114, 28932–34; see also Witherspoon v. Illinois, 391 U.S. 510 (1968).
255 Johnson considered Goldberg: memorandum, Barefoot Sanders to Lyndon Johnson, Dec. 9, 1968, LBJ; *PPP*, 1968–69, 1342; *NYT*, Oct. 11, 1968, 1, 20.
255 "there is a flat Republican policy . . .": memorandum, Mike Manatos to Lyndon Johnson, Oct. 10, 1968, LBJ.
255 White House invitations: memorandums, Mike Manatos to Bess Abell, Sept. 16, and to Carol Carlyle, Nov. 1, 1968, LBJ.
255–258 Election day, 1968: See *NYT*, Nov. 6, 1968, 20, 22, 25; *WP*, Nov. 6, 1968, A 9; Nixon, *Memoirs*, 330–35; Chester, Hodgson, Page, *American*, 786–89; Phillips, *The Emerging*, 25–26, 33, 35, 36–69, 206, 449; White, *Making . . . 1968*, 388–96, 330–31; Witcover, *Resurrection*, 449–53.
258–259 "[T]he Democratic party had pressed . . .": Lyndon B. Johnson, *Vantage*, 549.
259–261 Gary Nelson's victory: Gary Nelson to author; *AR*, July 23, Oct. 11, Oct 23, Nov. 4, 1968; *ADS*, July 2, July 23, 1968.

Chapter 3

261–262 Fortas/Clark meeting: Ramsey Clark OHP, 19–21, LBJ; Shogan, *A Question*, 215–19.
262 CBS News had intended . . . Court and Constitution on television: Dunne, *Hugo Black*, 412–16; letter, Hugo Black to Sidney Davis, Dec. 7, 1969, Black papers, LC; *NYT*, Dec. 4, 1968, 1.
262n. Douglas interview: Martin Agronsky to author.
262 Black's excisions: letter, Hugo Black to Burton Benjamin, Sept. 30, 1968, Black papers, LC.
262 Black: Well, the Court didn't do it . . . : transcript, "Justice Black," 11–14.
264 "Under our constitutional system . . .": Chambers v. Florida, 309 U.S. 227, 241 (1940); transcript, "Justice Black," 13.
264 "positively"; "with all . . .": transcript, "Justice Black," 14.
264 Alabama television, national rating: letters, Hugo Black to William G. Symmens, Dec. 10, 1968, and Francis Lamb to Salli Adler, April 9, 1969, Black papers, LC; *Anniston (Ala.) Star*, Dec. 5, 1968.
265 "Dear Hugo, Cathy and I . . .": note, William O. Douglas to Hugo Black, Dec. 4, 1968, Black papers, LC.
265 Johnson/Nixon transition: Lyndon B. Johnson, *Vantage*, 555–57; Nixon, *Memoirs*, 336–37; *NYT*, Nov. 12, 1968, 1, 46.

Bibliography and Source Notes

265–266 "continuity . . .": Earl Warren, OHP, 33, LBJ.
  266 Ramsey Clark to inauguration: Harris, *Justice*, 146.
  266 "Good luck": Lyndon B. Johnson, *Vantage*, 560.
  266 Johnson/Humphrey/Wallace go home: Chester, Hodgson, Page, *American*, 780–82.
  266n. "Of course, somebody's gonna get George . . .": Frady, *Wallace*, 63.
  267 Mitchell's background, estimates of his character: Viorst, "Attorney General Mitchell's," 68, 70, 74; *Newsweek*, Sept. 8, 1969, 29; Elizabeth Drew, "Report," *Atlantic Monthly*, May 1969, 8; *Current Biography*, 1969, 291–93.
  268 "devoted" crime fighter: NYT, Dec. 12, 1968, 37.
  269 Mitchell's Justice Department instructed on *Miranda*: memorandum, Will Wilson to United States attorneys, June 11, 1969, DOJ-Criminal.
270–271 Preventive detention legislation: *CQ Almanac*, 1970, 208–10.
  271 "it was a special election year . . ."; "it is of utmost importance . . .": Seymour, *United States Attorney*, 132, 226.
271–272 Precedent for withdrawal of nominations: clerk of the Senate, *Civilian*, 1953; *PPP*, 1969, 20–21; Harris, *Justice*, 157.
  272 Judicial appointments: *CQ Almanac*, 1974, 954.

Chapter 4

  273 Nixon's arrangement for breathing space: Nixon, *Memoirs*, 419.
  273 "What kind of pot . . .": Albert Eisele to author.
  274 Brownell, Dewey, and Mitchell ineligible: Nixon, *Memoirs*, 418; *PPP*, 1969, 394; Friedman and Israel, *The Justices*, v. 4, 311 ff.
  274 Five criteria; interest in Burger: Nixon, *Memoirs*, 419–20.
274–275 Burger/Nixon meeting: Duscha, "The Chief Justice Says," 30; *PPP*, 1969, 56; Woodward and Armstrong, *The Brethren*, 11–13.
  274 Warren and Burger trip to Florida: 421 U.S. xxxii–iii.
  275 Mitchell/Burger in search of judges: WP, June 13, 1974, A 22.
  275 "The seeming anxiety of judges . . .": Frazier v. United States, 419 F.2d. 1161, 1176 (dissent), (1969).
275–276 Press reporting of the case: WP, 1, WS, 2, March 15, 1969.
  276n. Frazier v. United States, 476 F.2d 891 (1973).
  276 White House party for Warren: See for April 24, 1969, NYT, 51: WP, H 1, H 2; WS, C 1, C 3; Duscha, "The Chief Justice Says," 30.
  276 Consideration of Stewart: Nixon, *Memoirs*, 419; NYT, May 28, 1969, 36.
276–279 Events that forced Fortas's resignation: *Life*, May 9, 1969; Shogan, *A Question*, 226 ff.
277–278 "You know, this Lou Wolfson . . .": Paul Porter OHP, 38–40, LBJ.
  278 Fortas's statement: NYT, May 5, 1969, 23.
  279 Fortas's resignation: Shogan, *A Question*, 235–61.
279–280 Fortas's statement: NYT, May 16, 1969, 20.
  280 "It was one thing to have enunciated . . .": *Time*, July 5, 1968, 13.
  280n. Fortas after resignation: WP, Dec. 16, 1979, B 1; oral argument, March 22, 1982, Rivera-Rodriguez v. Popular Democratic Party; WP, April 7, 1982, 1.
  280n. Will Wilson's departure: NYT, Aug. 27, 1971, 31; Aug. 28, 1971, 14; Aug. 29, 1971, iv, 10; Oct. 16, 1971, 1; Oct. 17, 1971, 14; Reichley, "The Texas Banker," 94 ff.
  280 Camp David weekend: *PPP*, 1969, 391–95.
  281 Burger/Mitchell meeting: Duscha, "The Chief Justice Says," 30: *St. Paul Dispatch*, May 22, 1969, 1, 2.
  281 White House staff work: Dent, *Prodigal*, 207.
  281 Stewart still in the running: *National Observer*, May 26, 1969, 1.
281–282 Burger/Nixon meeting, television presentation: *PPP*, 1969, 395, 398; NYT, May 22, 1969, 36.
282–283 Thoughts on the appointment: Albert Eisele to author.
  282 "knee-jerk conservative": *Time*, May 30, 1969, 16.
  282 "very emotional guy . . .": NYT, May 22, 1969, 36.
282–283 "the best appointment . . .": *Time*, May 30, 1969, 16.
  283 "Number one . . .": NYT, May 22, 1969, 36–37.

Bibliography and Source Notes

283   Southern senators join in praise: *NYT*, May 22, 1969, 37.
283–284 Judiciary Committee hearings: U.S. Congress, Senate, Committee on the Judiciary, *Nomination of Warren E. Burger*, especially 21; *NYT*, June 4, 1, 16, 20; *WP*, June 4, 1969, A 9.
284   Senate confirmation: *CR* 115, 15174–95; *NYT*, June 10, 1969, 1, 26.
284–287 Account assembled from *PPP*, 1969, 480–82; 395 U.S. vii–xi (1969); *CR* 107, 290–91; memorandum, Chief Justice Warren to Hugo Black, Black papers, LC; *NYT*, June 24, 1969, 1, 24; *WP*, June 24, 1969, 1, 12; Friedman and Israel, *The Justices*, v. 4, 3136–41; Simon, *Image*, 2.
288   June 24 meeting: 434 U.S. xxviii (1978); 21 *Journal of Public Law* (1972), 276; Frank, *The Warren Court*, 77.
289   "I intend to take a very active part . . .": *NYT*, July 2, 1969, 2, 15.
289   ABA meeting: *U.S. News*, Dec. 14, 1970, 42; *Time*, Aug. 22, 1969, 58; Simon, *Image*, 94–96.
289   Comparison with Taft: See Swindler, "The Chief Justice and Law Reform," 247 ff.
290   Thurmond's return: *NYT*, Oct. 7, 1969, 32.
291   Miranda in prison: Robert Corbin, Erwin Matthews, Barry Silverman to author; Silverman, "Ernesto," 3; *NYT*, Sept. 7, 1975, 31.
291   Miranda's petition for certiorari; denial: Miranda v. Arizona, No. 314, OT 1968, U.S. Supreme Court, *Records*, NA; Arizona v. Miranda, 450 P.2d 364 (Ariz. 1969); 396 U.S. 868 ff. (1969).
291   Marriages of Lois Ann Jameson, Twila Hoffman: Barry Silverman to author.
292   "the instrument . . .": Fortas, "Chief Justice," 411.

Chapter 5

293   Press conference: *PPP*, 1970, 44; *WP*, Jan. 31, 1970, A 1, A 11, B 5.
294   "You always have to make an entrance . . .": Safire, *Before*, 53.
294   Early questions: *PPP*, 1970, 36–39.
295n. Haynsworth later: letters, Hugo Black to John Frank, Sept. 8, Hugo Black to Clement F. Haynsworth, Nov. 21 and Dec. 11, 1969, Black papers, LC; *Newsweek*, Dec. 1, 1969, 21; *WP*, April 9, 1979, A 1, A 4, and Jan. 27, 1981, A 2.
295   "anyone who has not been convicted . . .": Shogan, *A Question*, 271.
295   Nixon/Dent project: Dent, *Prodigal*, 210.
296   "*Escobedo* and *Miranda* have made explicit . . .": Boulden v. Holman, 384 F.2d 102, 106 (1967).
295–296 Carswell's record: *Time*, Feb. 2, 1970, 8–9.
296   Burger's recommendation of Carswell: *WP*, June 13, 1974, A 22.
296   Murfin's recommendation of Carswell: Dent, *Prodigal*, 210.
297   "I am a southerner . . .": U.S. Congress, Senate, Committee on the Judiciary, *The Supreme*, v. 11, 22–23; *NYT*, Jan. 23, 1970, 1, 16.
297   "God almighty . . .": *Time*, Feb. 2, 1970, 8.
297   "Ol' Harrold was just . . .": *NYT*, Jan. 23, 1970, 16.
297–298 Press conference questions on Carswell: *PPP*, 1970, 39–40.
299–300 Carswell's defeat: See U.S. Congress, Senate, Committee on the Judiciary, *The Supreme*, v. 11; Harris, *Decision*.
299   "even if Carswell were mediocre . . .": Harris, *Decision*, 110.
299   "Judge Carswell does not have . . ." *WP*, March 16, 1970, B 4.
300   Pressures on Burdick: Harris, *Decision*, 191.
300   Vote on Carswell: Harris, *Decision*, 200; *NYT*, April 9, 1970, 1, 13, 32: *Newsweek*, April 20, 1970, 39; *Time*, April 20, 1970, 12–13.
300–301 Nixon's reaction: *NYT*, April 12, 1970, iv, 1; *Time*, April 20, 1970, 8–9; *WP*, April 19, 1970, A 20.
301   "Judge Carswell, and before him Judge Haynsworth . . .": *PPP*, 1970, 345–46.
301   Dent sent South: Dent, *Prodigal*, 211–12.
301–302 Douglas impeachment attempt: U.S. Congress, House Committee on the Judiciary, Special Subcommittee, "Associate Justice," *First Report*, 28–42, 12–14, 20–25; *PPP*, 1975, 184–85; *NYT*, April 14, 1970, 1.

302 "the hound dogs . . .": Douglas, *Court Years*, 376–77.
302 "One was that Hank Aaron . . .": Pollack, *Earl*, 299.
302 "bunch of bigots": Dent, *Prodigal*, 212.
303 Burger/Blackmun relationship: *NYT*, April 15, 1970, 34; April 20, 1970, 16.
304 "highly impressed . . .": *NYT*, April 15, 1970, 34.
304 "brought up in the Felix . . .": Friedman, *The Justices*, v. 5, 4.
304–305 His judicial debates . . . : See, for example, Malinsky v. New York, 324 U.S. 401, 413–415 (1945); Rochin v. California, 342 U.S. 165 (1952); see also Frankfurter, *Mr. Justice Holmes and the Supreme Court*.
305 Frankfurter's opinions . . . : See, for example, Sweezy v. New Hampshire, 354 U.S. 234, 255 (1957); West Virginia State Board of Education v. Barnette, 319 U.S. 624, 646 (1943); Baker v. Carr, 369 U.S. 186, 266 (1962).
305 Blackmun's perspective: See, for example, Jarrett v. United States, 423 F.2d 966 (1970); Patterson v. United States, 385 F.2d 728 (1967); Ashe v. Swenson, 399 F.2d 40 (1968); United States v. Bonds, 422 F.2d 660, 666 (1970).
305 81 percent: see v. 356–423 F.2d; of the 101 criminal cases in which Blackmun was involved between 1966 and his appointment (see U.S. Congress, Senate, Committee on the Judiciary, *Harry A. Blackmun*, 110–32), he voted against the criminal defendant in all but 19.
305–306 Blackmun confirmation: U.S. Congress, Senate, Committee on the Judiciary, *Harry A. Blackmun*; *NYT*, April 30, 1970, 1; May 6, 1970, 1; May 10, 1970, iv, 11; May 13, 1970, 1, 25; June 10, 1970, 1, 20.
306 1970 elections: Nixon, *Memoirs*, 491–96.
306–307 Nixon's legislative record: PPP, 1970, 626.
307 "We've got a war . . .": *NYT*, Jan. 23, 1970, 21.
307 Mitchell and Ervin on preventive detention: *CQ, Nixon, the Second Year of His Presidency*, 64.
307 "Now, if we don't get a better . . .": PPP, 1970, 641.
307 Recruiting new batters: *NYT*, Sept. 28, 1969, 1, 37; April 26, 1970, 80; Oct. 1, 1970, 22; Oct. 21, 1970, 54.
307 "serious trouble . . .": Nixon, *Memoirs*, 491.
308 Tunney, Kennedy, Hart: Nixon, *Memoirs*, 491–92; *NYT*, Oct. 12, 1970, 22; *Newsweek*, Oct. 19, 1970, 32–33.
308 "If you had $100 . . .": *Newsweek*, Nov. 16, 1970, 32.
308 "set out to capture . . .": Nixon, *Memoirs*, 491.
308 ". . . We believe that it is time . . .": PPP, 1970, 913.
309 "District Attorney of Phoenix . . .": Nixon, *Memoirs*, 494.
310 "constituency on the Social Issue . . .": Nixon, *Memoirs*, 494–96.
310 "I don't think so": *NYT*, Nov. 9, 1970, 1.
310 Sometimes I ordered a tail . . . : Nixon, *Memoirs*, 496.

Chapter 6

311 Burger's targets: Douglas, *Court Years*, 231.
312 "[T]o allow the use of an illegally . . .": petition for certiorari, Harris v. New York, No. 206, OT 1970, U.S. Supreme Court, *Records*, NA.
313 Harris brief: brief for petitioner, 12–13, *Harris*, R and B.
313 Opinion from Burger's old bench: Procter v. United States, 404 F.2d 819 (1968).
313 New York's brief: brief for respondent, 14, in *Harris*, R and B.
313 Certiorari granted: 398 U.S. 937 (1970).
313 Aurnou's style: *NYT*, Jan. 12, 1981, B 2.
314 Black's undated retirement letter: Douglas, *Go East*, 452; Dunne, *Hugo Black*, 434.
314–315 Oral argument: Tr-SC, 401 U.S. 222 (1971).
315 Burger's skill at including evidence: see Gordon v. United States, 383 F.2d 936 (1967); Lockley v. United States, 270 F.2d 915, 918–21 (dissent) (1959).
315 First instance of exclusionary rule: Boyd v. United States, 116 U.S. 616 (1886).
315 1914 reappearance: Weeks v. United States, 232 U.S. 383.
315 1961 application to state courts: Mapp v. Ohio, 367 U.S. 643.

Bibliography and Source Notes

315   "The efforts of the courts . . .": Weeks v. United States, 232 U.S. 383, 393.

316   "There are those who say . . .": Mapp v. Ohio, 367 U.S. 643, 659.

316   "of interest mostly . . .": Dershowitz and Ely, "*Harris*," 1198.

317   "It is one thing to say . . .": Walder v. United States, 347 U.S. 62, 65 (1954).

317   "The shield provided . . .": *Harris*, 226.

317   Brennan at conference: note, William J. Brennan to the chief justice, Jan. 6, 1971, John M. Harlan papers, Seeley G. Mudd Manuscript Library.

317   Black's private opinion of *Harris:* note, Hugo Black to the chief justice, Jan. 5, 1971, John M. Harlan Papers, Seeley G. Mudd Manuscript Library.

317–318   Brennan dissent: *Harris*, 232.

318   Black's death: *NYT*, Sept. 26, 1971, 76.

318–319   Black's funeral: Hugo Black, Jr., *Hugo Black*, 266; Frank, "Hugo Black" (*Arizona State University LJ*, Oct. 1971), 2; *NYT*, Sept. 29, 1971, 37.

319   "they thought I was crazy": *NYT*, Sept. 26, 1971, 76.

319   Harlan's death: Hugo Black, Jr., *Hugo Black*, 257; *NYT*, Sept. 24, 1971, 1; Dec. 30, 1971, 1.

319   "exactly the right mix . . .": Rodell, "The Complexities," 68.

319   "No, John . . .": "Earl Warren: The Governor's Family," James Warren OHP, 11–12, UC-OHP.

320   "the quality of quality": Kurland, "1970 Term," 265.

320   Powell and Rehnquist appointments: Nixon, *Memoirs*, 423; PPP, 1971, 1053–55.

321   "Ten years of Powell . . .": Nixon, *Memoirs*, 423–24.

322   Details of Powell's background compiled from Friedman, *The Justices*, v. 5, 64–65; Wilkenson, *Serving*, 81; *Time*, Nov. 1, 1971, 18; 50 ABA *Journal* (1964), 891, 924; 51 ABA *Journal* (1965), 101; *Richmond Times-Dispatch*, Aug. 1, 1971, in *NYT*, Nov. 3, 1971, 47.

322   "I'm not from the South . . .": Simon, *Image*, 237–38.

322   Details of Rehnquist's background compiled from Friedman, *The Justices*, v. 5, 109 ff.; Rehnquist, "Who Writes," 74–75; *Time*, Nov. 1, 1971, 19; *NYT*, Oct. 28, 1971, 26; Warren Weaver, Jr., "Mr. Justice Rehnquist," 36, 94, 96, 98: Simon, *Image*, 233.

323   "school conservative": Kluger, *Simple*, 608 n.

323   Rehnquist's memorandums: Simon, *Independent*, 302–03; Kluger, *Simple*, 605–09.

324   Aryah Neier on the Court: *Time*, Nov. 1, 1971, 17.

Book 4/Warren Burger's Book

Chapter 1

327–328   Oral argument scene: *NYT*, 16; *WS*, A 2, A 20, April 20, 1955.

329   Peters's background: Paul and Long, *John Punnett Peters*, 349–51, 357–59.

329   Peters's name on letterheads: *U.S. News*, May 13, 1955, 56–57.

329–330   Peters/Loyalty Review Board: petition for certiorari, *Peters* R and B; memorandum, Warren E. Burger to attorney general, March 31, 1955, *Peters*, DOJ-Civil.

330   "a matter of principle": *Time*, May 2, 1955, 21.

330–331   Arnold, Fortas & Porter law firm: Shogan, *A Question*, 57–60; Douglas, *Go East*, 313; Fortas to author.

331   Complaint: *Peters*, DOJ-Civil.

331   Burger notifies Brownell: memorandum, Warren E. Burger to Herbert Brownell, Feb. 23, 1954, *Peters*, DOJ-Civil.

331n.   The *Bailey* case: Bailey v. Richardson, 341 U.S. 918 (1951).

331   "from the beginning . . .": memorandum, Warren E. Burger to attorney general, March 31, 1955, *Peters*, DOJ-Civil.

331   U.S. Court of Appeals for the District of Columbia Circuit, *Peters*, DOJ-Civil.

332   Soberoff instructions to Burger: memorandum, solicitor general to Warren E. Burger, Sept. 30, 1954, *Peters*, DOJ-Civil.

332   Government reply: memorandum for respondents in opposition, Oct. 1954, *Peters*, DOJ-Civil.

332   Cert granted: 348 U.S. 882 (1954).

332 "resort to secret meeting places . . .": *U.S. News,* April 1, 1955, 68; April 29, 1955, 54–56.

332 Soboloff memorandum: memorandum, solicitor general to attorney general, Jan. 14, 1955, *Peters,* DOJ-Civil.

333 "postpone for a little . . .": memorandum, Warren E. Burger to J. Lee Rankin, Jan. 25, 1955, *Peters,* DOJ-Civil.

333 "so at loggerheads . . .": Herbert Brownell to author.

333–334n.Soboloff/Brownell relationship; "The administration of Government . . .": Herbert Brownell to author; U.S. Congress, Senate, Committee on the Judiciary, *Nomination of Simon E. Soboloff,* 74–75.

334 "because I have to be able . . .": Bazelon, "Tribute," 488.

334 "In essence, the problem is one of balancing . . .": brief for respondent, 24, 101, *Peters,* R and B.

334 Burger volunteered: Brownell to author.

334–335 Burger's background: *NYT,* Jan. 15, 1956, v, 10; Eisele, *Almost,* 115–16; Roger G. Kennedy to author.

335 Challenges to date: See, for example, Dennis v. United States, 341 U.S. 494 (1951); Bailey v. Richardson, 341 U.S. 918 (1951).

335 Brownell speaks out: See *U.S. News,* April 1, 1955, 68.

335 Burger's lunching with newsmen: *St. Paul Dispatch,* April 9, 1955, 3.

335 Burger answers editorials: letters, Warren E. Burger to *Detroit Free Press,* May 12, May 24, 1955, *Peters,* DOJ-Civil.

335 Burger sends copies of the government brief . . . : letters, Warren E. Burger, March 17, 1955, to Bernard M. Shanley (secretary to the president), Gerald D. Morgan (special counsel to the president), Maxwell M. Rabb (secretary to the cabinet), and Robert Cutler (special assistant to the president for national security affairs); to the counsel to the Department of the Army, legal adviser to the State Department, solicitors for the Agriculture, Interior, Labor, and Post Office departments; to the general counsel for the Air Force, Commerce, Defense, HEW, Navy, and Treasury departments, plus the Atomic Energy Commission, Civil Aeronautics Board, Civil Service Commission, Defense Transport Administration, Farm Credit Administration, Federal Civil Defense Administration, Federal Communications Commission, Federal Deposit Insurance Corporation, Federal Mediation and Conciliation Service, Federal Power Commission, Federal Reserve board of governors, Foreign Claims Settlement Commission, Foreign Operations Administration, General Services Administration, National Advisory Committee for Aeronautics (also to the security officer), National Labor Relations Board (also one to the chairman), National Science Foundation, Office of Defense Mobilization, Railroad Retirement Board, Securities and Exchange Commission, Selective Service System, Small Business Administration, Tariff Commission, Tennessee Valley Authority, United States Information Agency, Veterans Administration; to the Interstate Commerce Commission chief counsel, Federal Trade Commission legal adviser, Housing and Home Finance Agency law division director, *Peters,* DOJ-Civil.

335–336 "Messrs. Arnold, Fortas and Porter eat . . .": Gilbert, "Irony," 12.

336 "It was apparent . . ." Tr-SC, *Peters,* 5, 9, 16.

336 "We say," he declared . . . : Tr-SC, *Peters,* 17.

337 Warren's first day on the job: Warren, *Memoirs,* 62.

338 "emphatically"; "Federal employee cannot . . .": memorandum, Warren E. Burger to J. Lee Rankin, Jan. 25, 1955, *Peters,* DOJ-Civil.

338–339 Burger at oral argument: Tr-SC, *Peters,* 30–84, especially 81–82.

338 Burger/Black exchange: Tr-SC, *Peters,* 77–81; *Hugo Black and the Bill of Rights,* 3–4.

339 "very good": Harold H. Burton, diary entry for April 19, 1955, Burton papers, LC.

339 Conference voting: Burton, OT 1954 docket book, Burton papers LC.

339 "These issues, if reached . . .": *Peters,* 338.

339–340 "To the extent that anyone . . .": Frank, "Affirmative," 5.

340 Underpinning: memorandum, Felix Frankfurter to the Court, April 1955, Frankfurter papers, LC.

340 Plethora of internal security cases: See, for example, Pennsylvania v. Nelson, 350

U.S. 497 (1956); Jencks v. United States, 353 U.S. 657 (1957); Watkins v. United States, 354 U.S. 178 (1957); Sweezy v. New Hampshire, 354 U.S. 234 (1957); Yates v. United States, 356 U.S. 363 (1958); Kent v. Dulles, 357 U.S. 116 (1958).

340   "those Communist cases": Warren, *Memoirs*, 5.
341   Newsboy resourcefulness: *St. Paul Pioneer Press*, Oct. 2, 1956.
341   "aware of great gaps": *Hugo Black and the Bill of Rights*, 5.
341   Protégé to James Otis: James C. Otis (son) to author.
342   Judgeship suggestion: Herbert Brownell to author.
342   Burger on Thye's list: *St. Paul Pioneer Press*, June 9, 1955.
342   Nomination: NYT, June 22, 1955, 59.
342   Burger/Harlan meeting: 409 U.S. xxix (1972).
342–343   "sat down and figured it out . . .": NYT, May 25, 1969, 55.
343   Confirmation delay, confirmation, oath: NYT, May 25, 1969, 55; *St. Paul Pioneer Press*, Aug. 2, 1955; NYT, March 29, 1956, 27; April 14, 1956, 10.
343   "I had three friends . . .": NYT, Feb. 18, 1978, 22.
343   Appointments to U.S. Court of Appeals for the District of Columbia Circuit: Morris, *Secondmost*, 1–3, 11–13, 155–57; Chase, *Federal Judges*, 46: U.S. Congress, Senate, Committee on the Judiciary, *Legislative History*, 28.
343   "freshman": Morris, *Secondmost*, 186–89.
344   Warren predicts his successor: Woodward and Armstrong, *Brethren*, 9–11.

Chapter 2

345   Burger's honeymoon: ALI, *Proceedings*, 1972, 475.
345n.   "Next time, come in": NYT, July 25, 1975, 21.
345   "the appointment of judges . . .": NYT, July 13, 1980, 14.
346   bills to undercut the Court: NYT, May 30, 1981, 8.
346   Physical changes: Lewin, "A Peculiar Sense," 15; Simon, *Image*, 133: NYT, March 11, 1974, 19; Sept. 19, 1971, 78; Sept. 20, 1972, 43; July 24, 1975, 14; *St. Paul Dispatch*, July 24, 1975; *Time*, Dec. 10, 1973, 83.
346   "a not unreasonable expectation": Inbau and Reid, *Evidence Law*, 54.
346–347   Brennan re *Miranda*: Michigan v. Mosley, 423 U.S. 96, 112 (1975).
347   "tall and broad . . .": WS, June 10, 1962.
347   "When the interests to be protected . . .": Watts v. United States 402 F.2d 676, 683 (1968).
347n.   "Suppression of speech . . ."; Watts v. United States, 394 U.S. 705, 712 (1969).
348   Marshall's record on *Miranda:* Of twenty cases involving evidence obtained in violation of *Miranda* (see notes for pp. 351, 396), Marshall voted to exclude it in sixteen, or four-fifths.
348–349   *Harris* effects: Newman Flanagan, John J. Flynn, Peter Kuh, H. Carl Moultrie, Gordon Rhea, Thomas J. Sardino, Brownlow Speer, Eugene F. Sullivan, Jr., to author; see also Wishman, *Confessions*, 216.
349   "I said to myself . . .": *Newsweek*, Jan. 7, 1974, 46.
349   "[W]e cannot say . . .": *Miranda*, 467; Michigan v. Tucker, 417 U.S. 433, 444 (1974).
350   "The privilege against . . ."; ". . . only a fair one": Michigan v. Tucker, 417 U.S. 433, 440, 446.
350–351   Court skill at including evidence: See Oregon v. Hass, 420 U.S. 714 (1975); Michigan v. Mosley, 423 U.S. 96 (1975); Beckwith v. United States, 425 U.S. 341 (1976); Oregon v. Mathiason, 429 U.S. 492 (1977); North Carolina v. Butler, 441 U.S. 369 (1979); Fare v. Michael C, 442 U.S. 707 (1979); Rhode Island v. Innis, 446 U.S. 291 (1980); California v. Prysock, 453 U.S. 355 (1981); Brennan dissented in all these.
351   "Although the 'focus' . . .": Beckwith v. United States, 425 U.S. 341, 347, 349–50 (1976).
351   Ten *Miranda* cases, 1971–OT 1975: Harris v. New York, 401 U.S. 222 (1971); Michigan v. Tucker, 417 U.S. 433 (1974); Oregon v. Hass, 420 U.S. 714 (1975); United States v. Hale, 422 U.S. 171 (1975); Brown v. Illinois, 422 U.S. 590 (1975); Michigan v. Mosley, 423 U.S. 96 (1975); Baxter v. Palmigiano, 425 U.S. 308 (1976); Beckwith v. United States, 425 U.S. 341 (1976); United States v. Mandujano, 425

U.S. 564 (1976); Doyle v. Ohio, 426 U.S. 610 (1976); evidence was included in *Harris, Tucker, Hass, Mosley, Baxter, Beckwith, Mandujano.*

352   Shift from defendant's to prosecutor's court: Lewin, "Avoiding," 31, 90.

352   82 percent: *NYT*, July 2, 1972, iv, 1.

352   "expected to give a strict . . .": *NYT*, May 24, 1972, 28.

352   Few would deny . . . : Powell, "What the Justices," 1455.

353   Burger's perception of the Court: *NYT*, April 9, 1976, 1, 51.

353   "As a matter of fact . . .": Douglas, *Court Years*, 231.

354   Warren reverses Burger: During Burger's time on the U.S. Court of Appeals for the District of Columbia Circuit (1956–69) he voted with the majority in thirty-four cases that were reviewed by the U.S. Supreme Court (see vols. 352–395, U.S. Reports; vols. 96–131, U.S. App.D.C.); of these thirty-four, Earl Warren voted to reverse that majority in twenty-three and to reverse in part three others.

354   "the blow to representative government . . .": Powell v. McCormack, 395 F.2d 577, 605 (1968).

354   "Our system of government . . .": "duly elected . . .": Powell v. McCormack, 395 U.S. 486, 549, 550 (1969).

355   Limiting access to the Supreme Court: See, for example, Snyder v. Harris, 394 U.S. 332 (1969); Younger v. Harris, 401 U.S. 37 (1971); Warth v. Seldin, 422 U.S. 490 (1975); Stone v. Powell, 428 U.S. 465 (1976); United States v. Frady, 102 S.Ct. 1584 (1982) (Brennan dissent); U.S. Congress, Senate, Committee on the Judiciary, Subcommittee on Constitutional Rights, *Causes of Popular Dissatisfaction*, 2–4, 49–50, 60–62.

355   Criticism of limitation: Society of American Law Teachers, "Supreme Court Denial," 1–25.

355   "the route by which basic changes . . .": *NYT*, July 4, 1977, 20.

355–356   "indispensable role . . .": U.S. Congress, House, Committee on the Judiciary, Subcommittee on Courts, Civil Liberties, and the Administration of Justice, *State of the Judiciary*, 6–10.

356   Burger's metaphors: See, for example, Burger, "Who Will Watch," 13–16; Burger, "Remarks," May 21, 1967, 5.

356–357   His failures and successes: *NYT*, Dec. 30, 1973, 24.

357   "The Chief Justice and his brethren . . .": Kurland, "The Lord Chancellor," 28. oversold on judicial efficiency; "repair the institutions . . .": Bazelon, "New Gods," 654 ff.

357   "has a very large responsibility . . ."; "it was not until . . .": Tamm and Reardon, "Warren E. Burger," 448–49.

358   Freund report: 59 *ABA Journal* (Feb. 1973), 139 ff.

358   Expectations of Warren retirement: Brennan, "Chief Justice Warren," 4.

359   Cynical; formidable; statistical interpretation: "Retired Chief Justice," 726–27.

359   "Are Negroes in fact . . .": Brennan, "Justice Brennan Calls," 835 ff.

359–360   Warren's criticisms: "Retired Chief Justice," 725 ff.

360   Douglas/Marshall on workload: *NYT*, Nov. 3, 1972, 34; Nov. 13, 1975, 60; May 2, 1975, 8.

360*n.*   "We were too busy . . .": Stevens to American Judicature Society, August 6, 1982, 4.

360   "honorable and dedicated . . .": "The Supreme Court must remain open": "Retired Chief Justice," 728, 730.

361   Burger's answer: "Retired Chief Justice," 721 ff.

Chapter 3

363   Setting for State of the Union: *WP*, Jan. 31, 1974, A 9.

363–368   State of the Union message: *PPP*, 1974, 47 ff.

366   1974 crime statistics: FBI, *UCR*, 1974, 10.

366–368   Watergate details: Nixon, *Memoirs*; Drew. *Washington Journal*; Theodore H. White, *Breach of Faith*.

368   Congressional reaction: *NYT*, 21; *WP*, A 9, for Jan. 31, 1974.

Bibliography and Source Notes

368   "There is a time . . .": *NYT*, Jan. 17, 1974, iv, 1.

368–372   Earl Warren's final months are recounted in Pollack, *Earl*, 314–27.

369   "[T]he resignation . . .": Warren, "Law, Lawyers," 636.

369–370   Warren/Little Rock desegregation case: *NYT*, July 11, 1974, 31.

370   "the feeling of cynicism . . .": Warren, "A Response," 222.

370   Warren invited to participate; remedies: Warren, "Address," 744.

370   "Wouldn't it be reassuring . . .": Warren, "Law, Lawyers," 640.

371   "I have never known anything bad . . .": Pollack, *Earl*, 323.

371   He never changed his mind: Leon Jaworski to author.

371–372   Oral arguments, *United States* v. *Nixon*: Drew, *Washington Journal*, 305, 306–08.

372   Brennan/Douglas visit to Warren: Brennan, "Chief Justice Warren," 4; Douglas, *Court Years*, 238–39.

372   Warren's funeral: Pollack, *Earl*, 329–30; Douglas, *Court Years*, 239; *NYT*, July 11, 1974, 34; *PPP*, 1974, 583.

372–373   Decision in Nixon's case: United States v. Nixon, 418 U.S. 683 (1974).

373   Deliberations in Nixon's case: Woodward and Armstrong, *Brethren*, 287–347.

373–374n.Mitchell and Miranda; Court denies certiorari: United States v. Haldeman, 559 F. 2d 31 (1976); Mitchell v. United States, 431 U.S. 933 (1977).

374   "caught and punished . . .": Silberman, *Criminal Violence*, 230.

375   Thirty percent . . . : *NYT*, Sept. 20, 1982, B 13.

375   "pickpockets fleeced . . .": Levy, *Against*, 4–5.

375   Florida's crime wave; California/rape: *NYT*, Dec. 13, 1981, iv, 28; Jan. 2, 1982, 16.

375   Challenge to effectiveness of preventive detention: Lazar Institute, *Pretrial Release*, see especially v–x.

376   Robbery arrests/California; Illinois criminal dockets: Silberman, *Criminal Violence*, 353–56.

376   Comptroller General's report: Comptroller General of the United States, "Impact." AELE/exclusionary rule: AELE, "The Exclusionary."

376   Task force report: Attorney General's Task Force on Violent Crime, *Final Report*, 55–56.

377   Crime/conviction relationships: Forst, Lucianovic, Cox, *What Happens*, 47–57, 89–90; Vera Institute of Justice, *Felony Arrests*, xi, xii–iii; Silberman, *Criminal Violence*, 343–45; Wishman, *Confessions*, 111–12; *NYT*, Feb. 12, 1982, 1, Feb. 25, 1982, B 6.

377–380   For a thoughtful and reasoned contemporary discussion of crime as a social phenomenon, see Silberman, *Criminal Violence*.

377–378   Effectiveness of gun control: Pierce and Bowers, *The Impact*, 87–93; *NYT*, June 18, 1979, D 14; May 31, 1981, iv, 6 E; Oct. 7, 1981, 26.

379   Liberty City, 1980: *NYT*, May 18, 1980, A 1, B 10; May 19, 1980, B 10; May 20, 1980, A 1, B 11.

379   "being born a slave . . .": Jackson, *Soledad*, 9.

381   Miranda, prison/parole: ADS, June (undated, from the *Star* files) 1972 and Dec. 12, 1972.

381   "You must know how bad . . .": letter, Ernest Miranda to Barry Silverman, Aug. 1970; Barry Silverman's files.

381–382   ". . . When a sheriff or marshal . . .": Burger, "For Whom the Bell Tolls," 5, 8, 9, 17.

382   "I would venture to add . . .": Miranda, "A Client Speaks."

382   Miranda's disappointment: John J. Flynn to author; Silverman, "Ernesto," 3–4.

383   Selling autographed cards: *NYT*, Feb. 2, 1976, 14.

383   Miranda's rearrest: Henry J. Florence to author; *AR*, July 16, 1974, B 1; Aug. 27, 1974, B 1, B 4.

383   "Incarceration no doubt protects . . .": Miranda, "A Client."

384   Robert Corbin: *AR*, Nov. 9, 1978, 1, 12.

384   Robert Corcoran: *AR*, Dec. 20, 1976, B 1.

384   Yale McFate: Yale McFate to author.

384   Laurence Wren: *Arizona Weekly Gazette*, Sept. 7, 1982.

Bibliography and Source Notes

384   Ernest McFarland: *ADS*, Jan. 1, 1971.
384   Gary Nelson: *AR*, May 31, 1974, 1, 4; Dec. 19, 1976, A 12; Sept. 9, 1978, A 1, A 5; Sept. 10, 1978, A 1, A 4; Nov. 9, 1978, A 13.
384   John J. Flynn: *AR*, Jan. 27, 1980, 1, 3; Jan. 31, 1980, 1; Dec. 14, 1980, B 4.
385   "Taking cases for nothing . . .": Frank, "In Cheerful," 3.
385   David Miranda: *Arizona Business Gazette*, April 21, 1981, B 1.

Chapter 4

386   Douglas's last Court session: *NYT*, Nov. 13, 1975, 1, 60; Nov. 14, 1975, 15; *WS*, Nov. 13, 1975, A 7.
386   "My God, you know . . .": Woodward and Armstrong, *Brethren*, 357.
386–387   Douglas's illness, resignation: See for 1975, *NYT*, Jan. 31, 34; March 21, 31, March 25, 5, and March 26, 24; April 11, 44; July 8, 17, and July 13, iv, 2; Sept. 30, 28; Oct. 7, 16, and Oct. 30, 41; Nov. 13, 60, and Nov. 14, 15; Woodward and Armstrong, *Brethren*, 394.
387n.   Douglas's retirement: Woodward and Armstrong, *Brethren*, 396–400.
387–388   Stevens, biographical details: *Current Biography*, May 1976, 31; Friedman, *The Justices*, v. 5, 149–62.
388   Eleven *Miranda* cases: United States v. Davis, 437 F.2d 928 (1971); United States v. Reid, 437 F.2d 1166 (1971); United States v. Matos, 444 F.2d 1071 (1971); United States v. Comiskey, 460 F.2d 1293 (1972); United States v. Springer, 460 F.2d 1344 (1972); United States v. Sicilia, 475 F.2d 308 (1973); United States v. Fowler, 476 F.2d 1091 (1973); United States v. Tweed, 503 F.2d 1127 (1974); United States v. Oliver, 505 F.2d 301 (1974); United States v. Jeffers, 520 F.2d 1256 (1975); United States *ex rel.* Hudson v. Cannon, 529 F.2d 890 (1976).
388   "wild card": *NYT*, Feb. 6, 1977, 24.
389   Ten of eleven *Miranda* cases: Stevens voted to include evidence in Doyle v. Ohio, 426 U.S. 610 (1976), to exclude it in Oregon v. Mathiason, 429 U.S. 492 (1977); Mincey v. Arizona, 437 U.S. 385 (1978); North Carolina v. Butler, 441 U.S. 369 (1979); Fare v. Michael C., 442 U.S. 707 (1979); Dunaway v. New York, 442 U.S. 200 (1979); Tague v. Louisiana, 444 U.S. 469 (1980); Rhode Island v. Innis, 446 U.S. 291 (1980); Estelle v. Smith, 451 U.S. 454 (1981); Edwards v. Arizona, 451 U.S. 477 (1981); California v. Prysock, 453 U.S. 355 (1981).
389   The one decision for the defendant: Brown v. Illinois, 422 U.S. 590 (1975).
389   Certiorari granted: 423 U.S. 1031 (1975).
389   AELE urges reversal: AELE, amicus curiae brief, 3, *Williams*, R and B.
389   "A shocking case . . .": Fisher v. United States, 328 U.S. 463, 477 (dissent) (1946).
390   "saw two legs in it . . .": *Williams*, 390.
390   "I am going to tell you . . .": *Williams*, 392.
390   "I want to give you . . .": *Williams*, 392–93.
391   "I didn't even know what . . .": Kamisar, *Police Interrogations*, 139.
391   The days when a man committed a murder . . . : brief for petitioner, 72, *Williams*, R and B.
391   "We in the heartland . . .": *NYT*, Oct. 4, 1976, 15.
391   Bartels's reasoning: Robert Bartels to author.
391–392   Oregon v. Mathiason, 429 U.S. 492 (1977).
393   "There can be no serious doubt . . .": *Williams*, 399–406.
393   "doubted very much . . ."; Williams's sentence to life imprisonment: *Williams*, 408–09; Kamisar, *Police Interrogation*, 113.
393   Burger's request for brevity: *WS*, March 23, 1977, 1.
393   "The result in this case . . .": *Williams*, 415, 421–22.
394   "high price . . .": Bivens v. 6 Unknown Named Federal Bureau of Narcotics Agents, 403 U.S. 388, 416 (1971).
394   Rizzo v. Goode, 423 U.S. 362 (1976).
394   "Today's holding interrupts . . .": *Williams*, 421–22.
395   "With the decision . . .": *WS*, March 23, 1977, 1.
395   AELE record in the Court: AELE, "Amicus Curiae," 1–6.
395   "This Court has never indicated . . .": California v. Prysock, 453 U.S. 355, 359 (1981).

Bibliography and Source Notes

395 "It is hard to imagine . . .": Mincey v. Arizona, 437 U.S. 385, 398 (1978).
395 Louisiana case: Tague v. Louisiana, 444 U.S. 469 (1980).
395 " 'officer told him that. . . .' ": Edwards v. Arizona, 451 U.S. 477, 488 (1981).
396 "purpose"; "considerations": Estelle v. Smith, 451 U.S. 454, 466–67 (1982).
396 "here to stay": *Arizona Business Gazette*, June 23, 1981, B 1.
396 "The meaning of Miranda . . .": Rhode Island v. Innis, 446 U.S. 291 (1980).
396 1976–1980 Miranda cases: Oregon v. Mathiason, 429 U.S. 492 (1977); Mincey v. Arizona, 437 U.S. 385 (1978); North Carolina v. Butler, 441 U.S. 369 (1979); Fare v. Michael C., 442 U.S. 707 (1979); Dunaway v. New York, 442 U.S. 200 (1979); Tague v. Louisiana, 444 U.S. 469 (1980); Rhode Island v. Innis, 446 U.S. 291 (1980); Estelle v. Smith, 451 U.S. 454 (1981); Edwards v. Arizona, 451 U.S. 477 (1981); California v. Prysock, 453 U.S. 355 (1981); Burger voted against the defendant in *Mathiason, Butler, Michael C., Dunaway, Tague, Innis, Prysock.* (In the 10 *Miranda* cases decided prior to OT 1976, see note for p. 351, Burger voted against the defendant in *Harris, Tucker, Hass, Mosley, Palmagiano, Beckwith, Mandujano.*)
396 The Nixon justices voted together in *Tucker, Hass, Brown, Mosley, Palmagiano, Beckwith, Mandujano, Mincey, Mathiason, Hale, Innis, Smith, Edwards, Prysock;* against the defendant in all but *Brown, Mincey, Hale, Smith, Edwards.*
396 U.S. attorneys unaware: Gordon C. Rhea to author.
396 Fewer than two dozen cases: *U.S. Code Annotated*, 1981 supplement, 251.
397 O'Connor hearings: U.S. Congress, Senate, Committee on the Judiciary, *Nomination of Sandra Day O'Connor*, 146.
397 Survey of nearly 600 cases: see v. 420–636, *Federal Reporter*, Second Series (excluding cases involving issues of retroactivity).
397 "I always wanted my students . . .": Brennan, *Affair*, 6–7.
398 Baker v. Carr, 396 U.S. 186 (1962).
398 "political thicket": Colegrove v. Green, 328 U.S. 549, 556 (1946).
398 "the political processes . . .": Brennan, "Some Aspects," 65.
398 "the power to govern themselves": "A Conversation" (McClatchey Broadcasting), 10.
398 ". . . [C]onstitutional provisions for the security . . .": Boyd v. United States, 116 U.S. 616 (1886).
398–399 Brennan's constitutional history: Brennan, "Guardians," 102.
399 State constitutions' provisions: Columbia University, *Constitutions*, under the appropriate states.
399 "would ever have come into existence . . .": Friendly, "The Fifth Amendment Tomorrow," 678–79.
400 "Far too many cases . . ."; "Judicial self-restraint . . .": Brennan, *Affair*, 32.
400 "If the states shoulder . . .": Brennan, "Some Aspects," 68.
400 "it would be another 46 years . . .": Tr-SC, *Miranda*, 24.
401 Extension of *Gideon* to misdemeanors: Argersinger v. Hamlin, 407 U.S. 25 (1971).
401 New generation of judges: Vern Countryman and Brownlow Speer to author.
401 Brennan dissents: Michigan v. Mosley, 423 U.S. 96, 112 ff. (1975); *Harris*, 231.
402 Hawaii's highest court: State v. Santiago, 492 P.2d 657 (1971).
402 Pennsylvania's supreme court: Commonwealth v. Triplett, 341 A.2d 62 (1975).
402 "*Harris* is not persuasive . . .": People v. Disbrow, 545 P.2d 272, 280 (1976).
402 Texas Court of Criminal Appeals: Butler v. State, 493 S.W.2d 190 (1973).
402 New Jersey Supreme Court: State v. Miller, 337 A.2d 36, 45 n. 1 (1975).
402 Wisconsin Supreme Court: Micale v. State, 251 N.W.2d 458 (1977).
402 New York Court of Appeals: Galie, "State Constitutional," 157 ff.
402 Other states: See Linde, "First Things," 379 ff.; Brown, Gross, Ryan, "Future Judicial," 143 ff.; Charles Douglas, "State Judicial Activism," 1123 ff.; Wilkes, "More on the New Federalism," 873 ff.; Wilkes, "The New Federalism," 421 ff.; Daughtray, "State Court Activism," 731 ff.
402 "shell game": Collins, "Away from a Reactionary," 218.
402 Brennan/1979 case: Scott v. Illinois, 440 U.S. 367, 384–89 (1979).
402–403 Encouragement to Brennan: Brennan, "Guardians," 102; Oregon v. Hass, 420 U.S. 714, 719 (1975).
402 "no State is precluded . . .": Michigan v. Mosely, 423 U.S. 96, 121 (1975).

453

Bibliography and Source Notes

403 Then he would tell the story: Michigan v. Mosley, 423 U.S. 96, 120–21 (1975).

403 "the judgment . . .": Commonwealth v. Ware, 406 U.S. 910 (1972).

403 "will be naturally led . . .": Brennan, "Guardians," 103.

403n. "hazardous experiment . . .": CCJ, "Resolutions" adopted, Jan. 30, 1982.

403–404 Miranda had come to the station house: Henry J. Florence, Bernard D. Crooke, John Gracen, Gary Hayes, Gordon C. Rhea, Richard G. Stearns to author.

403–404 FBI policy/practices: FBI spokesman to author (March 2, 1982); FBI, Legal Handbook for Special Agents, 80–81; Jonathan Marks to author.

404 Survey of fifty-one chiefs: Wolfstone, "Miranda," 26–27.

404 Older/younger officers, small/large departments: See Milner, The Court, 208–20.

404 "Although Miranda . . . has been on the books . . .": United States v. Jackson, 429 F.2d 1368, 1372, 1373 (1970).

404 Syracuse training: Thomas J. Sardino to author.

404–405 Philadelphia training: Stanford Schmuckler to author.

405 FBI training: FBI spokesman to author (May 3, 1979).

405 Criticism of FBI: Milner, The Court, 65–66.

405 "You know, during my career . . .": Des Moines Register, April 7, 1977, 1B.

405–406 Miranda's effect on apprehension of criminals: Leslie V. Chalmers, Robert K. Corbin, Bernard D. Crooke, Gary Hayes, William E. Rodriguez, Richard G. Stearns to author.

405 Carroll Cooley: AR, Feb. 2, 1976, A 4.

405 More on Miranda's effect on apprehension of criminals: Wilbur Littlefield, Stanford Schmuckler, Brownlow Speer, Richard G. Stearns, Will Wilson to author; Jenkins, Keeping, 126; Schaefer, "Is the Adversary," 167.

405 "error"; "appraisal of its effects": Tom C. Clark, "Criminal Justice," 845.

405 Advanced degrees among police chiefs: Parade, March 21, 1982, 4.

406 Miranda/professionalization of police: George Napper, William E. Rodriguez, Thomas Sardino, Brownlow Speer to author; Ramsey Clark, Crime, 325.

406 Impact on chiefs: Gary Hayes to author; "Interrogations in New Haven," 1616.

406 "I know police officers . . .": David A. Mills to author.

406 One judge reported: George C. Edwards, Jr., to author.

406 Another judge reported: "Brownlee, "A Judge's Views," 9.

406 "Give me an hour alone . . .": Stanford Schmuckler to author.

406 Postponing custody: Jonathan Marks to author.

406 Young, mentally deficient District of Columbia man: United States v. Blocker, 354 F. Supp. 1195 (1973).

406–407 Robert Williams: Williams.

407 Evasio Hernandez: United States v. Hernandez, 574 F.2d 1362 (1978).

407 Peter Reilly: Bartels, A Death; NYT, Nov. 25, 1976, 1, 26.

407 Miranda weaknesses: Kamisar, Police Interrogations, 223.

407 "[S]omeday, in a better world . . .": Fortas, "Chief Justice Warren," 411.

408 Miranda's death: account compiled from author's interviews with Erwin Matthews and Barry Silverman; reports of Phoenix police for Jan. 31, 1976, in Barry Silverman's files; NYT, Feb. 2, 1976, 14; WP, Feb. 15, 1976, K 3.

INDEX

════════════════

Index

Index

Index

Index

Index

Index

Liva Baker was born in Plymouth, Pennsylvania and educated at Smith College and the Columbia University Graduate School of Journalism. She is the author of a biography of Felix Frankfurter and a critique of women's education, *I'm Radcliffe! Fly Me!*, and has written for such magazines as *American Heritage* and *Smithsonian*. She is married to writer Leonard Baker and is the mother of two grown children.